ARCHITECTURE AND THE CANADIAN FABRIC

Edited by Rhodri Windsor Liscombe

ARCHITECTURE AND THE CANADIAN FABRIC

20 19 18 17 16 15 14 13 12 11   5 4 3 2 1

Printed in Canada on paper that is processed chlorine- and acid-free, with vegetable-based inks.

Library and Archives Canada Cataloguing in Publication

Architecture and the Canadian fabric / edited by Rhodri Windsor Liscombe.

Includes bibliographical references and index.
ISBN 978-0-7748-1939-8

1. Architecture and society – Canada. 2. Architecture – Political aspects – Canada. 3. Architecture – Canada – History. I. Liscombe, Rhodri Windsor, 1946-

NA740.A744 2011   720.1'030971   C2011-903648-7

Canadä

UBC Press gratefully acknowledges the financial support for our publishing program of the Government of Canada (through the Canada Book Fund), the Canada Council for the Arts, and the British Columbia Arts Council.

This book has been published with the help of a grant from the Canadian Federation for the Humanities and Social Sciences, through the Aid to Scholarly Publications Program, using funds provided by the Social Sciences and Humanities Research Council of Canada, and with the help of the K.D. Srivastava Fund.

UBC Press
The University of British Columbia
2029 West Mall
Vancouver, BC V6T 1Z2
www.ubcpress.ca

TO ARCHIVISTS AND LIBRARIANS

for their commitment to preserving the very fabric of history

Contents

Figures

Acknowledgments

This anthology represents the scholarship and patience of its contributors and of those who enabled and assisted their research. The manuscript was prepared with the expert assistance of Deana Holmes and then received the unstinting support and astute counsel of our editor at UBC Press, Melissa Pitts, and latterly of Ann Macklem and Robert Lewis, who undertook the final editing process. We authors owe individual debts of gratitude to colleagues and family who helped to forward this reconsideration of the work of architecture in the formation of modern Canadian society. The dedication page speaks to the many institutions and collections in Canada and abroad that made archival and bibliographic material available to the authors. Lastly, we should acknowledge the financial assistance for research and publication received from in particular the Social Sciences and Humanities Research Council of Canada and the Aid to Scholarly Publications Program of the Canadian Federation for the Humanities and Social Sciences. In a larger purview, it is incumbent upon us to acknowledge the ongoing significance of the design professions to the development of Canada.

ARCHITECTURE AND THE CANADIAN FABRIC

Introduction
Writing into Canadian Architectural History

RHODRI WINDSOR LISCOMBE

Canada is among the oldest of modern states and earliest of postcolonial nations. Its emergence as a nation-state from French colonialism, British imperialism, and United States hegemony involved processes at work in supposedly more established nations.[1] Even before the Confederation of Canada in 1867, architectural design and planning had played a potent role in the formation of Canada's colonial and provincial regimes – including the diverse use of functional and ornamental building by the indigenous inhabitants of its current territory. The Confederation was quite literally *built* from a collection of entities and contesting forces, including those of class, ethnicity, and association, built as much to appropriate its geography from indigenous stewardship as it was to exploit the resources it contained; perhaps appropriately, it was for a considerable period after Confederation – into the 1950s – named the Dominion of Canada.[2] Set against its very physical extent – sublime in scale and topography – was, until recently at least, the relatively small size of its population, infrastructures, urban development, and built environment. Yet it is this same contrast between relative physical, chronological, and socio-economic dimensions that makes Canada a unique subject of study in terms of political, cultural, and architectural constitution.

A cohering concept for these interrelated developments is fabrication. The term captures the plurality of design mentality and activity, a combination well appreciated by architects. But it has a broader compass of meaning especially relevant to the postcontact and post-Confederation eras. We speak of the fabric of a piece of clothing, of a building, or of a component of society, often in either a literary or political vein. The verb "to fabricate" and the noun "fabrication" variously describe positive and negative, inclusionary and exclusionary, authentic and artificial methods of creation, constitution, and conduct. Fabric(ation) thus encompasses matters of technical organization, ideological agenda, economic system, and social culture. This confluence of policy, structure, and value was articulated in a speech to the Vancouver Canadian Club by Dr. Henry Tory in August 1907: "The whole fabric of our democratic civilization rests upon our schools, and through them directly upon our universities."[3] In this instance, schools would seem to be only the metaphorical extension of what is taught and learned in them – the fabric of civilization – but schools and universities were (and are) edifices of material structure, buildings that have specified inclusion and, more often than not, exclusion. Their physical presence, almost always imposing and incorporating visual elements iconic of contemporary authority systems, gives clear meaning to what types of philosophy and what types of proponent were allowed to inhabit the "building" of democracy.

The term "fabrication" also emphasizes the constitutive power of modes of continuity and commonality, typified by architecture and technology, while acknowledging contrary phenomena of resistance and rupture. Such reconfigurative and even oppositional power nicely articulates the abstract yet practical components of architectural (and national) articulation. Buildings and plans, across a breadth of design interest, exert considerable influence in their spatial-social situations that reach well beyond the period of their construction – often embracing the transient registers of stylistic fashion. Building and town planning generate considerable economic activity as well as accommodate or promote political and corporate interest, communal institution, or personal lifestyle. Building and planning not only articulate the current specifications of culture but also mark the changing cultural values within their very fabric and fabrication. Moreover, architecural building – the main subject of this anthology – proceeds from a two-dimensional scheme to a multidimensional signification of patron's requirement and architect's capability, the latter further modified by user and spectator. And although the facades might express paramount effect, the interiors alike exert substantive affect.[4] Each aspect of building interweaves a variable mix of utility, technique, and aesthetic – linked to larger understandings of local, national, and international function.

Architecture, in company with nation, is in these senses fabricated.[5] It is built up from theoretical and technological data through communicative media of text and image.[6] An example is the part-utopic, part-strategic scheme for an Arctic town – combining aspects of Modern Movement planning with technologies that seemed capable of enabling Canadian development and sovereignty in the region – published in the 6 January 1962 issue of the *Illustrated London News* (Figure 0.1). The scheme exemplifies how architectural design adapts the imagined to the instrumental in the representation, and re-presentation, of interest within community. Most critically, architecture derives from some form of privilege and some level of authority, a respective capacity that is subject to alteration far beyond the temporal and cultural parameters it usually claims to stabilize. As both container and incubator of meaning, architecture manifests presumptions of society and, during the modern era, of nation, while also registering their respective reiteration and redefinition. From before transoceanic immigration into the territory now constituted as Canada, architectural construction – consciously designed building – has served to fabricate identities of kinship and of social and legalistic (national) identity. This anthology relates how architecture is fabricated within place and how it, in turn, has fabricated nation – from mixed sources and with equally mixed objectives and outcomes.

Architecture, both building and planning, across the Canadas counters David Cannadine's assertion that Canada has lacked internally generated monuments, myths, heroes, and traditions.[7] In fact, quite the reverse is true. The record of drawn plans and built environments – often a rebuilding of past ideals and iconographies once appropriated by other regimes – reveals an extensive, if contested and incomplete, series of national projects. Their variety in part explains the decision to publish this anthology on the socio-political, and thereby economic and cultural, work of architecture. The range and significance of architecture and town planning in the Canadian Confederation bear comparison with the much more extensive and extensively studied United States, and even, to a lesser degree, with the built fabric of Canada's chief colonial homelands, Britain and France.

The clash of competing colonizing systems on the outskirts of Quebec City, the capital of New France, was valorized during the Dominion era in popular books like Dr. W.H. Fitchett's *Deeds That Won the Empire* (which by 1909 had gone through twenty-eight reprints distributed around the British world).[8] Despite its ethnocentricity – Fitchett was an Australian educator of British descent – the book both responded to and formed public opinion in a manner akin to the discursive impress of architecture in the social arena.[9] Buildings, especially those in the burgeoning settlements of the Canadas, acted along the lines Fitchett attributed to the deeds of "historic fortitude." They constructed "the elements of robust citizenship" through their attempted formal

Figure 0.1 Scheme for an Arctic town by the Department of Northern Affairs. | Published in *Illustrated London News*, 6 January 1962.

and iconographic signification of the bonding of political association and personal alliance.[10] Such actions and associations required emblematic and material expression to be signified culturally and realized politically, enlisting architecture's capacity to both mark place and transcend time. However, this same capacity often curtails deeper contradictions between iconographic and geographic considerations. Frequently in Canada, this has been made manifest through the appetite for importing design practitioners and thereby taste (or more truly fashion), usually only partially capable of modification to the remarkably varied "real estate" of Canada.

One example from the early history of permanent British control in erstwhile New France is the commissioning in late 1811 and early 1812 of designs for a British American legislature at Quebec City just prior to conflict with the United States.[11] The British governor-in-chief clearly regarded its construction as a component of the strategic defence of colonial authority. In this respect, the commission paralleled Fitchett's location, once conventional, of the generation of national identity in singular events and specific places – each sharing the promise of durability so often ascribed to both nationalism and architecture. In never having been implemented, the designs for this legislature underscore these disjunctions as well as the ideational fabric directed to the fabrication of future national structures. Three drawings for the main facade of two buildings drawn by two architects remain, one for a New Senate House and the other for a Government House. They were submitted from England by Joseph Gandy, Sir John Soane's amanuensis, and Jeffry Wyatt, later Sir Jeffry Wyattville (Figure 0.2). And their commissioning and dispatch of plans, elevations, and sections demonstrated the compression of space and time enabled by both colonial and architectural practice.

Fitchett's valorization of "historic fortitude" and its relationship to "robust citizenship" are now highly contested – the latter for its inclination to write and rewrite variations of the same hegemonic narrative, and the former for its idealization of fortitude as the mark of the conqueror, not the survival of the conquered. The built fabric of Canada, as amplified in its writing-up by historians and critics, provides a built chronology of the tensions in the type and tone of discourse over hundreds of years. The material form of the nation's buildings, whether still present or barely discernible in a fading archival photograph, recount a history that reveals, if not fortitude in a monolithic sense, then resilience through diversity.

So the anthology does not purport to be a comprehensive analysis or to pursue a singular critical approach. Neither is the purpose to explore the writing of the history of Canada, nor of nationalism, nor yet of architecture. Instead,

Figure 0.2 Designs for the entrance front of the Senate and of the Government House, Quebec City, respectively in the neo-Classical and neo-Gothic modes, by Joseph Gandy and Jeffry Wyatt, dated 1812. | Library and Archives Canada, 2358/e002418507 *(upper)*, 2361/e002418504 *(lower)*.

this volume offers a sequence of investigations of architectural form-making and architectural formations of Canadian society through the material and symbolic disposition of structure and space. Underlying each investigation is the contention that architecture concentrates, moulds, and mediates current societal values, while also serving as a more prominent marker of collective experience, memory, and identity. Furthermore, as both a social process and an individual pursuit set in time, architecture additionally integrates different interests and intentions reflective of broader cultural discourse and activity.[12]

The richness of the Canadian structural tradition is admirably recounted – or rather recovered from the varied patterns of settlement, ethnicity, and building typology – by Harold Kalman in *A History of Canadian Architecture* (1994).[13] It was published at the junction between diverging approaches to writing, and reading, architectural history. Kalman's focus on major practitioners or monuments, and on formal (typological) or aesthetic (stylistic) issues, has since given way to closer analysis, or postmodern deconstruction, of the economic and political factors determining both architectural culture and critical discourse. This change is particularly evident in the questioning of essentialist narratives of cultural production as well as in attention to the peripheral, supposedly marginal, spaces of practice and recognition of the place of hegemonic systems in social and critical operations. The study of the history of architecture has also been influenced by the theoretical strategies of the Frankfurt and Paris Schools, exemplified respectively by Theodor Adorno, Walter Benjamin, or Martin Heidegger, and Pierre Bourdieu, Henri Lefebvre, or Michel Foucault; their publications have stimulated a remarkable legacy of critical thinking, including about the making of space and place in association with the gamut of architectural production represented by, among others, Marc Augé, Edward Casey, and Doreen Massey.[14] These strategies, which illuminate the architectural dimensions (built typology and environment) of epistemology, stimulated an analysis of the everyday scene that was as deeply serious as prior inquiries into the architecturally inscribed cultural sphere.[15] Such unpacking of component factors has an unintentional prior figuring in the diverse composition of standard prefabricated units in the Habitat housing Moshe Safdie designed for the Centennial Exposition at Montreal in 1967 (Figure 0.3).

In company with all academic discourse, architectural history has become a much more multidisciplinary and even interdisciplinary enterprise. In response, this anthology seeks to further the innovative literature on Canadian social and cultural formation exemplified by *Painting the Maple* (1998), edited by Veronica Strong-Boag, Sherrill Grace, Avigail Eisenberg, and Joan Anderson; *Tropes and Territories* (2007), edited by Marta Dvořák and William New; *A Great Duty* (2003), by Leonard B. Kuffert; and *Beyond Wilderness* (2007), edited by John O'Brian and Peter White.[16] All four books bring out the challenges and contestations, inclusions and exclusions, associated with nationalist projects such as Canada. Each also gives voice to those often overlooked in the promulgation of a comprehensive nationalist fabric of governance and culture by dominant groups: most notably women, Aboriginals, and those from formerly marginalized ethnicities. Similarly, the essays therein foreground new and often cross-disciplinary investigation particularly associated with historiographical, literary and visual-cultural, feminist, and postcolonial studies. They also draw upon a much more diverse range of documentary materials that give greater prominence to experiential and anecdotal evidence. Lastly, they demonstrate how Canadian social development and cultural production afford a rich vein

Figure 0.3 Habitat housing complex, Expo '67, Montreal, designed by Moshe Safdie. | Reproduced by permission of *Canadian Architect*.

for critical analysis – and how creative practice therefore both denotes dominant values and connotes collective attitudes.

The denotative and connotative aspects of architectural design have been the subject of sophisticated analysis by Umberto Eco. A major instance is his 1973 essay "Function and Sign: Semiotics of Architecture," which Neil Leach selected for *Rethinking Architecture* (1996), an anthology of innovative theoretical and historiographical approaches to redefining the role of architecture in later-modern society.[17] In this essay, Eco also provides a discerning description of "architectural objects" operating in the realm of "mass communication." Eco asserts that the "discourse" of architecture is aimed "at mass appeal" and is "psychologically persuasive." It is "experienced inattentively," it "can never be interpreted in an aberrant way" but "fluctuates between being rather coercive ... and rather indifferent," and it belongs to "the realm of everyday life" and is "a business." Eco captures the range of the interpretation of architectural effect and affect in buildings commanding national or local urban space argued by contributors to this anthology.

Similarly inclusive definitions of "nation" and "nationalism" are accepted in this anthology. Such scope is marked out by the writings of Benedict Anderson, Eric Hobsbawm, and more broadly David Harvey, Fredric Jameson, and Giorgio Agamben on the legislated and invented, imagined and virtual, exploitative and exclusionary, but it is not limited by any one construction.[18] Consequently, nation and state are considered as having been constituted through such processes as the consolidation or projection of geo-ethnic power through the acquisition of material resources (of wealth, territory, and population), as well as through adherence to shared myth, ritual, convention, and allegiance. The main thrust is held to be the so-called logic emanating from the systems of capital investment, colonial expansion, commercial activity, and technological capability (typified in Canada by the industrial development of the Pre-Cambrian Shield). These systems led to the consolidation of the European – and American – regimes, and it was the competition between these regimes through which Canada began an initial path toward nationhood. This path, as this anthology indicates, comprised many kinds and overlapping scales of collectivized community and allied identity formation – noting that in Canada the term "nation" is further complicated by its use to describe indigenous as well as immigrant socio-political groupings. Thus the operative definition of "nation" here parallels the plural definition of public and private space argued by Ali Madaupour.[19]

To register this range of effect and affect with respect to the formation of the Canadian state, the anthology has seven parts. These follow an overall chronological order modified by a thematic analytic, intended to encompass the many levels of architectural agency. The chronological order comprises, first, "Architectural Culture in French Canada and Before"; second, "Upper Canadian Architecture"; third, "Building the Confederation"; fourth, "Reconstructing Canada"; fifth, "Styling Modern Nationhood"; sixth, "Fabricating Canadian Spaces in the Late/Postmodern Era"; and seventh, "Identities of Canadian Architecture." Building on Kalman's comprehensive account of Canadian architectural development and typology, the volume seeks to disclose the architectural representation of the ideological impetuses and material conditions at work in building the Canadian Confederation. Attention to impetuses and conditions further reveal the patterns of colonization and alienation, while also setting individual or corporate initiative against larger groupings of economy and culture. In addition, the chapters variously demonstrate the extent to which buildings, and the built environment, operate as a regulatory factor and a discursive presence in daily life – and that they perform at the conscious and subconscious levels of multiple and singular social activity.[20]

Consequently, the series of chapters – briefly contextualized in the introductions to each part – begins with initial encounters between Aboriginal peoples and early settlers. Bringing out the significance of wording and imaging preliminary to design execution, Judi Loach considers the fabric of linguistic and phenomenological definitions developed by the Jesuit missionaries to comprehend the indigenous territory and society. This includes indications of how such definitions framed the thinking of those who helped to establish New France. The anthology then continues through a sequence of focused studies of place and space-making that both represents and interrogates the larger constitution of national and architectural culture in Canada. These studies begin with Marc Grignon's reading of a celebrated late-seventeenth-century view of Quebec City to disclose the intense competition to impose sectional hierarchy on the imaginary and real space of New France's capital. The subsequent imposition of British colonial authority contributed to new patterns of settlement and regime in the Maritimes and St. Lawrence Basin that included the renaming of New France as Lower Canada. The different cultural orientation encompassed a switch in architectural idiom from Continental Baroque to Anglo-Palladian norms enhanced by the migration northward of Loyalists during the American War of Independence.

This phase of postcontact world-making reinforced the building-up of such strategic British centres as Halifax in Nova Scotia. It also sustained development in Upper Canada, from 1841 until Confederation defined as Canada West in the United Province of Canada, much of which territory is now contained in the province of Ontario. The most thriving city was York, later renamed Toronto. Its early development depended on the construction of both utilitarian and emblematic buildings that demonstrate the commercial underpinnings of architecture and its diverse agency in establishing civic and national identity. The impact of functional infrastructure, no less than elevated building types like churches, is recounted in chapters by Barry Magrill and Sharon Vattay, respectively on St. James Cathedral and Toronto's urban markets.

Their close analysis of the built form and its social presence is succeeded by three chapters that variously indicate the very significant shifts in scale and ambition, architectonically and politically, associated with Confederation. Like architectural construction itself, Confederation was constructed over time and space to assume an increasing general coherence that yet retained distinct components; additionally, as can occur in architecture and more so in planning, its construction would reveal incompletely considered problems or anomalous conditions. The bold idea of a continental nation spanning diverse existing colonial entities and as yet unsurveyed territories (being a multivalent response to American Manifest Destiny and a reflection of continued British imperial expansion) was embedded in the architectural magnificence and sophisticated planning of the Parliament Buildings at Ottawa. Christopher Thomas reconsiders what might be termed the architectural and thereby cultural politics of the legislature of Confederation. The narrative of power and place is taken up in the new western terminus of Confederation Canada – Vancouver, British Columbia – by Geoffrey Carr. He deconstructs contesting personal, commercial, and racial motives framing the construction of a high-rise office building for a local newspaper. With comparable attention to design analysis but also to the theorization of cultural practice, Michael Windover places real estate development in the emergence of another media, radio, which, together with the sport of ice hockey, helped to articulate national consciousness.

There follow two chapters examining aspects of the post–Second World War "Reconstruction" of Canada when government policy enacted independent nationhood and engendered compounding popular conviction in a distinct national culture, notwithstanding increasing demographic, regional, and economic change. An important motivator of changed, proto-postcolonial ideology as well as of design practice was the Modern Movement in architecture and planning. Blending architectural with popular cultural inquiry, Lucie Morisset walks readers around and through the immediate, physical, and contingent spaces of the Quebec bungalow. By contrast with this process of adaptation, Alan Marcus charts the less benign impact of utopic modernization onto the federal project of Arctic sovereignty with particular respect to a scheme for redeveloping Resolute Bay, now Qausuittuq, on Cornwallis Island. A different indication of international practice with a national objective is traced in the next part, which also contains a pair of chapters. These reflect the determined official statement of unique Canadian nationhood during the 1970s and 1980s, when architecture was accorded notable prominence. Réjean Legault chooses the rapid designation of the Brutalist-styled Fathers of Confederation Building at Charlottetown, Prince Edward Island, to excavate the intersecting architectural and historiographical structure of this later Modernist design idiom. The articulation of mature national status, including recognition of its Aboriginal constituent, is recounted by Laura Hourston Hanks in her study of the National Museum of Civilization at Ottawa. The corresponding external impact of Canadian culture – from high theory to populist quotidian and professional design practice – is demonstrated in three chapters on the contemporary late-, or post-, modern era. Richard Cavell elucidates the formulation by the Canadian theorist Marshall McLuhan of a prescient but generally misinterpreted ideation of the urban conurbations that seem set to supersede nation. The disruption of the older polity by the globalized economy, but also the fabrication of new coalescing identities through everyday commerce, informs Justin McGrail's critique of big-box stores. In my chapter, I take up the monetarist reconfiguration of community in considering contemporary conditions of design practice in Canada. I focus on the marketing of condominium property at Vancouver – a model of sorts for international urban redevelopment at least prior to the financial collapse of October 2008.

The final suite of chapters returns, first, to the supposedly outdated yet still potent concept of identity and, second, to the related problems of history – appropriately with reference to the relatively recent recovery of the Aboriginal foundations of the modern fabric of Canada. Nicholas Olsberg and Michael McMordie – each incidentally important figures in the study and promotion of Canadian architectural culture – respectively ponder the repute of Arthur Erickson, arguably the first Canadian architect to attain international celebrity, and the meaning of identity for Canadian architectural practice at the Millennium. The final chapter, by Daniel Millette, both measures historical Aboriginal architectural production and introduces its contemporary manifestation into the discourse of Canadian architecture.

These studies of architectural articulation of the engines and institutions of nationhood are obviously selective. But they have been selected on the basis of the confluence of types of architectural and national design, with a relatively greater emphasis on post-1945 development since Canadian citizenship existed only beginning in 1947. Consequently, the geographical sites, architectural issues, and historiographical perspectives are multifarious – a paralleling of the by now conventional description of contemporary Canadian national identity as multicultural. The several perspectives of the contributing scholars also enhance the variety of critical inquiry, which deliberately includes aesthetic, typological, sociological, historical and historiographical, as well as theoretical interpretation of policy and practice in national and architectural fabrication. The anthology is thus about the uses and even misuses of architecture in the modern and late/postmodern project – about, too, the way architecture, from the monumental to the everyday, impacts the individual and social enactment of national consciousness.

Those focused studies of architecture's role in building community and nation merit a broader contextualization of historical events and design idiom. The history of Canada can be described as a fashioning of limited spheres of agency often managed by distant authority in search of new resources, as the

Canadian scholar Harold Innis has demonstrated in his innovative work *Empire and Communications* (1950).[21] Most notable have been those economic and political institutions successively situated in France, Britain, the United States, and the Pacific Rim. Consequently, Canadian politicians, technicians, and writers have tended to describe the nation in terms of geography, transportation, and resource development (the dynamics and discourses of modernity). Ironically, perhaps, the power of political economy was rather subsumed in traditional architectural history by a concentration on biography, chronology, typology, and taste or style. The emphasis on formal appearance, structural innovation, and monumental building echoed the architectural culture both before and after the signing of the British North America (BNA) Act, which established the Canadian Confederation and the Dominion of Canada in 1867.

The BNA Act built on imperial and regional colonial legislative accommodations predating Lord Durham's report of 1839. The Durham Report modelled the governmental narration – through policy *and* building – of British imperial expansion as a framework of orders and fabrics that came to be known as Indirect Rule. Like the many written and delineated documents of empire, this report refashioned the natural geography and artificial topography constituting Canada.[22] Its chief formal characteristics were a series of instrumental hierarchies – covering those financial no less than ideological constitutions of culture – that can be compared with the Classical Orders of architecture.[23] Most obvious were the increasing subjugation (latterly through assimilation) of the indigenous peoples, the separating-off of French Canadian culture (churlishly decried by Lord Durham), and the general privileging of British attitudes and systems whatever the actual demographic of the flows of immigrants and capital that enabled the settlement of territory deemed Canadian.

British power was manifested in, arguably, the initial defining moments of transcontinental national consciousness: the suppression of the Métis freedom movement in 1885 (usually named the North West or Riel Rebellion) and the opening of the Canadian Pacific Railway line to Vancouver on the Pacific Coast in 1888. The accommodations of growing Canadian nationalism culminated in the 1918 Functional Principle – resulting in Canadian representation separate from Britain at the League of Nations – and in the 1926 Balfour Declaration. As capital or capstone of distinct Canadian national structure, the Balfour Declaration acknowledged Canada's autonomy in the British Commonwealth of Nations. It undergirded the 1931 Statute of Westminster, which granted full governmental independence to Canada, except, at its own request, in matters of constitutional change. The apotheosis in the architecture of nationhood was topped out by the final signing-away of any residual imperial authority by Queen

Elizabeth II in April 1982, conducted, with obvious conscious symbolism, in front of the Parliament Buildings (although the current building had replaced the original architectonic signifier of Confederation after its destruction by fire in 1916).[24]

Significantly, however, the final staging of nationhood occurred midway between resurgent contestations of Confederation. These were the secessionist movements focused in the province of Quebec, which were echoed in western Canadian alienation and in Aboriginal nationalism, including the political recovery of Métis identity. These movements gathered momentum in the wake of the Centennial, celebrated in the spectacular, if transient, architectural display of Expo '67.

It was held at Montreal, then still the capital city of the nation's economy and of its culture of Two Solitudes.[25] The organization of Expo '67 revealed the scale and increasing multiplicity of the natural, financial, and social resources of the country. But it also disclosed the very different agendas at play – typified by Moshe Safdie's socialist, standardized Habitat housing complex, as against Buckminster Fuller's capitalist, technocratic United States pavilion. The apparent stitching together through architecture and spectacle of a now more inclusionary and independent confederated nation, from the 49th parallel to the Arctic archipelago and from the Atlantic seaboard to the Pacific shore, masked changes in the economic as much as cultural structure of contemporary Canada. Financial and even popular cultural hegemony had shifted fully to the United States but was beginning to be influenced by the emergence of the Asian economies as well as by the radical alteration in the racial and ethnic demography of immigration.

Nonetheless, the 1967 Centennial marked a high point in federal interventionist policy in the cultural arena, a policy that started with the 1951 Massey-Lévesque Commission on the Arts in Canada. One beneficiary had been the Canadian architectural profession, through the Massey Medals for Design awarded annually across the provinces and territories forming the nation; these were subsequently replaced by the Governor General's Medals in Architecture. These awards exhibit the continuing value ascribed to architecture in defining the local, regional, and national culture. The successive criteria for such awards reflect the evolving politics of national identity. The political shifts were exemplified by the 1986 North American Free Trade Agreement with the United States (subsequently extended to include Mexico) and by the 1992 referendum on the Charlottetown Accord, which aimed unsuccessfully to finally resolve the constitutional place of Quebec/French Canada.[26]

These conflicted events echoed the contestation underlying the constitution of nations. In Canada this heritage, especially the foundational idea of Two Founding Nations, is manifest in the phrasing of the two "national" anthems. Throughout the era of Anglo-Canadian predominance, this anthem, including in French Canada (i.e., Quebec and to a smaller extent New Brunswick), was "The Maple Leaf Forever." The anthem was played across Canada on 2 November 1936 by bands at the main broadcasting centres to inaugurate the Canadian Broadcasting Corporation as the latest of the infrastructures, or in this instance, virtual systems or fabrics, uniting the dispersed population and territory of Canada (its television service began in 1952). This anthem recited the transposition onto "Canada's fair domain" of British paradigms after General James Wolfe's conquest of New France in 1759. Since well before the repatriation of the Constitution in 1982, the official anthem had become "O Canada," with its bilingual wording of nation as the "true north strong and free" in spite of the increasingly diverse demographic and ethnicity of its population.

Yet the imaginary nation of each anthem was nonetheless founded on erasure, exclusion, and discrimination, evincing the French political theorist Ernest Renan's observation, made in 1882, that an ability to forget is one requisite of national development.[27] These more melancholy pillars of Canadian nationalism – and indeed of most nationalisms – are depicted with brilliant clarity and ongoing irony in Ken Lum's 2001 sculptural group *Four Boats Stranded: Red and Yellow, Black and White,* which sits atop the rotunda of Francis Rattenbury's third Vancouver Courthouse (1906-11, remodelled as the Vancouver Art Gallery by Arthur Erickson and Associates, 1979-81).[28] In precise form, yet spectral presence, the models of vessels signifying Aboriginal community, imperial discovery, racial discrimination (the infamous *Komagata Maru*), or globalized labour migration surmount the erstwhile architectural housing of one engine of property acquisition and trading that continues to determine much of the nation's material and mental fabric. The compounding appetite for resources and profit as well as newer concepts of national purpose and citizen rights have, nevertheless, brought fuller recognition of the indigenous contribution to the structuration of Canada.

A major feature of this structuration is the construction of history.[29] By this is meant the definition not merely of chronologies but also of topics, issues, and analytics. In Canada the writing of history is still predominantly a framing of knowing founded in Eurocentric fabrics of thought and action. Even in 1991 the British Columbia Supreme Court could, in the Delgamuukw case, determine that the absence of written history and of documented economic and technical systems excluded First Nations peoples from modern society and full political recognition.[30] This judgment articulated a cornerstone – or, in more recent thinking, a weak foundation – of everyday Canadian practice even into the twenty-first century; the deeds to the first house I purchased in 1988 on the University Endowment Lands in Vancouver forbade my selling the property to anyone of Asian origin despite the increasingly Pacific-Asian structure of the local and regional economy. The Eurocentric framework of Canada had been proudly stated in the history published in 1941 by the celebrated Canadian humorist and political economist Stephen Leacock. The "silent growth of a nation," he wrote in the "Foreword" to *Canada: The Foundations of Its Future,* was a consequence of the "very lack of history" in North America, if yet simultaneously the "foundation of history itself."[31] Indeed, Leacock entitled his first chapter "The Empty Continent." This phrase recalls the importance of natural or artificial transportation systems intended to speed transit across the land mass that became Canada, as exemplified by the quest for the North West Passage. The phrase also houses an implicit epistemological fabric of explicit exclusion. Consequently, it is a highly revealing statement of the desire for evident signifiers of legitimacy – of the array of fabricated tradition, technology, taste, and testament built into architecture.

Architecture, apart from erecting visible infrastructure that stakes claims to possession and authority, has traditionally asserted cultural instrumentality, spanning the past, present, and future – compare Leacock's Canadian *tabula rasa* awaiting symbolic signification and functional ordering: "Our country waited [for European settlement], its mighty rivers moved, silent and mysterious, from the heart of an unknown continent."[32] Nation for Leacock required the self-conscious assertion of material and mental forms of meaning and technique that he considered absent from the kinship societies of First Nations. A similar chasm of understanding and action attached to the respective significance for indigenes and immigrants of "nature" – a word justifiably identified as the most complex in the English language by the cultural historian and theorist Raymond Williams.[33] Generally, the natural environment for the former enshrined every aspect of their existence, whereas for most of the latter it presented both problem and opportunity: a phenomenon to be controlled and commodified. The hold of nature is manifest in the prominence of natural features or conditions in the symbolic and literary statement of national identity – from the Maple Leaf flag to the mythologies of Canadian consciousness.[34] The natural order has regained its pre-eminence in both political debate and professional practice through recognition of environmental fragility. Among progressive design practitioners, nature has become less a phenomenon to be surmounted than a priority to be sustained through architectural and urban development.

The contrast had been articulated during the era of negotiating Confederation by an anonymous botanist in a review printed in the 1858 *Canadian Nationalist and Geologist.* "Physically considered," the reviewer commented, "British America is noble territory, grand in its natural features, rich in its varied resources. Politically, it is a loosely united aggregate of petty states, separated by banners of race, local interest, distance and insufficient means of communication."[35] Architecture, and its ascending professional associate, engineering, appeared to most contemporaries capable of resolving this abundance of opportunity but insufficiency of capacity. Architecture could supply artefacts of, as well as for, unified national purpose and organization worthy of "its natural features as fixing its future destiny." And the role assigned to architecture in consensus and country building was indicated by one of those active in fabricating the political architecture of Confederation and a national citizenry, Thomas D'Arcy McGee. In his article "A Further Plea for British American Nationality," written for the October 1863 issue of the *British American Magazine,* McGee averred that the idea of Confederation "begats a whole progeny, kindred to itself – such as ideas of extension, construction, permanence, grandeur and historical renown."[36]

The long and conflicted history of the territories and peoples grouped under the geo-political structure of Canada produced a diverse built fabric and related array of architectural or planning projects. These represent the processes, powers, and peoples involved in its evolving (re)fabrication. As argued above, the terms "fabric" and "fabrication" capture the artifice underlying national policy no less than architectural, cultural, or commercial enterprise. They also allude to the scripting and imaging preceding the aesthetic, ideological, and technical enactment of collective – including architectural – development.

As noted, back in 1811 Sir George Prévost, the governor-in-chief of Lower Canada, confronted United States aggression leading to the War of 1812. He clearly regarded the construction of government buildings for Lower Canada (only designs for the Government House and the New Senate House apparently survive) as the emblematic, yet also real, statement of strategic purpose (see Figure 0.2). These would visualize and organize the military and governmental infrastructures required to defend the geographical colonial construct of Quebec, the former New France contiguous with Upper Canada (later consolidated as the province of Ontario). The architects Joseph Gandy and Jeffry Wyatt understood their role, or rather the role to be performed by the imagined facility of governance. It was to represent the origins, as well as the assertion, of British colonial *puissance*. So they appropriated historical architectural iconography favoured in contemporary British privileged society. Even if the Classical Orders – and the Medieval Gothic also presciently proposed by Wyatt in advance of the neo-Gothic Houses of Parliament at London (1837-65) – could be modified to the United Kingdom, their formal language and structural logic were alien to British North American conditions. However, architecture has always served the causes of cultural transfer and/or power projection through surmounting as much as appropriating the natural domain and local conditions. That no set of designs for the Lower Canada Parliament was implemented and no building begun does not diminish the signification of architecture's work in the fashioning of collective identity and in the formation of society. The drive for what became the United Province of Canada was accompanied by the appropriation of Classic Revival edifices in urban centres such as Kingston and in Montreal for its legislature; and the creation of the Dominion of Canada in 1867 had been preceded by legislation commissioning a new federal administrative complex of impressive buildings at Ottawa.

Comparable interplays between imported architectural convention and adapted architectural idiom grew alongside immigration. The rapid diversification of the Canadian demographic occurred against the backdrop of sheer territorial size, stimulating the ambition for uniform national *and* distinctive regional architectural idioms. This divergence is evident in one major component of the confederated regime. The construction of the transcontinental railway and telegraph system became architecturally, and even culturally, objectified in the series of hotels built successively by the Canadian Pacific, Canadian Northern, and Grand Trunk Pacific Railways. Hotels, alongside rail tracks and telegraph lines, enabled the consumption of geographical resources. This in turn opened up new spaces of commercial and social enterprise, which were central to modernity; to its chief modality, commodification; and to its main construct, the nation. In moving goods and, more so, people and capital across territory and time, the railway and the telegraph created new, and reinforced older, economies of land that stimulated the development of other building types. Most visible among these were tourist facilities ranging from grand hotels to therapeutic facilities and mountain lodges (Figure 0.4).[37]

Their function was compound, serving not only as commercial platforms but also as corporate symbols *and* national icons. The intermixture of financial with ideological imperatives typified the imbrication of economy with nation during the later-modern era. Similarly, the Canadian railway hotels – castles, for one insightful historian of architecture aware of their regulatory and mythic

Figure 0.4 Aerial view of the Château Frontenac Hotel, Quebec City, drawn by the architect Bruce Price in 1886. | Reproduced by permission of the Maxwell Archive, John Bland Canadian Architecture Collection, McGill University Library.

operation – interwove current stylistic fashion in hotel design with local or localizing precedent.[38] Generally, the commissions derived from a comparable confluence of complex motive or heritage. For instance, the Château Frontenac, built in 1892-93 on a commanding eminence above and alongside the historic capital of New France, was commissioned by the Canadian Pacific Railway's Yankee chief executive, William Van Horne (who took British [Canadian] citizenship to receive his knighthood) and designed by his Yankee architect, Bruce Price. It was purportedly modelled on the nearby Château St. Louis in Quebec City but primarily derived from the Scots Baronial conventions of British and US urban and tourist railway hotels. These Baronial hotels had aped the town houses and country mansions that the Scottish nobility could afford to build partly as a consequence of the second wave of industrial expansion in Britain. Whereas they had reinvented the French Renaissance–inspired tradition of their architectural patrimony, the railway entrepreneurs in Canada endeavoured to create an instant patrimony of national enterprise.

Figure 0.5 Exterior of the Supreme Court of Canada, from *The Supreme Court of Canada and Its Justices.* | Photograph by Philippe Landreville. Reproduced with the permission of the Minister of Public Works and Government Services, and courtesy of Health Canada, 2010.

The hotels aestheticized the harsher appropriation of place being enacted by resource and agricultural development alongside the rail and telegraph lines. Simultaneously, they accommodated the mobile middle and leisured classes plus the agents of external and internal empire; their basements usually included larger rooms for travelling salesmen to display merchandise to local merchants.

Thus these apparently benign monuments of economic growth and civic pride indirectly proliferated the tensions of national fabrication, particularly via the process of immigrant settlement and further alienation of Aboriginal traditional lands. Nonetheless, the touristic consumption of topography enabled by the railway hostelries conveyed the simulacra of national identity founded on external economic and governmental forces.[39] Eventually, the architectural mode assumed a nationalist marque by virtue of longevity in Canada. This nationalism was exemplified by the Château-Baronial visage of the Confederation Building (Department of Public Works, 1928-31) and of the Supreme Court of Canada (Ernest Cormier, 1938-46), each built west of Parliament in Ottawa (Figure 0.5). Other nationalist cultural manifestations, exemplified by the officially endorsed Group of Seven painters, depended on imported techniques of a privileged consumption of landscape that thereby assumed complementary and complimentary characteristics of identity.[40]

These mechanisms of nation-state have continued into late/postmodern conditions and are evident in architecture's integration into our present fame economy/culture, as encapsulated in the epithet "starchitecture." This has accompanied the re-emergence of the city-state and urban region in the physical manifestation of nationhood (exemplified by patriotism engendered by the 2010 Winter Olympics held at Vancouver). Metropolitan and national status requires the centring of real cultural mass on signature architectural edifices as part of acceptance onto the global stage of international political economy. With respect to Canada, the narrative began in the post–Second World War decades, signalled by the flurry of international press coverage on the design of the Kitimat townsite for Alcan in northern British Columbia (1952-53) (Figure 0.6).[41] Appropriately for Canadian socio-economic history, its original conception melded company town with utopian community, blending architectural modernity with architectural Modernism. A comparable admixture of universalist and regionalist civic nationalism occurred in the redevelopment of Canada's major urban sites: Montreal, Toronto, and Vancouver. Schemes for large-scale commercial and, latterly, market housing accommodated local and national ambition through the attraction of offshore capital and high-profile architects. Examples in Montreal are the Place Ville Marie office complex (1958-62) and Stock Exchange (Victoria) Tower (1962-66), respectively designed by the (Chinese) American architect I.M. Pei and Italian architect-engineer P.L. Nervi (Figure 0.7).

The necessity of international sanction is equally evident in Toronto. There, Viljo Revell's competition-winning 1958 scheme for the new City Hall elevated the architecturally undistinguished town into the realm of transoceanic celebrity

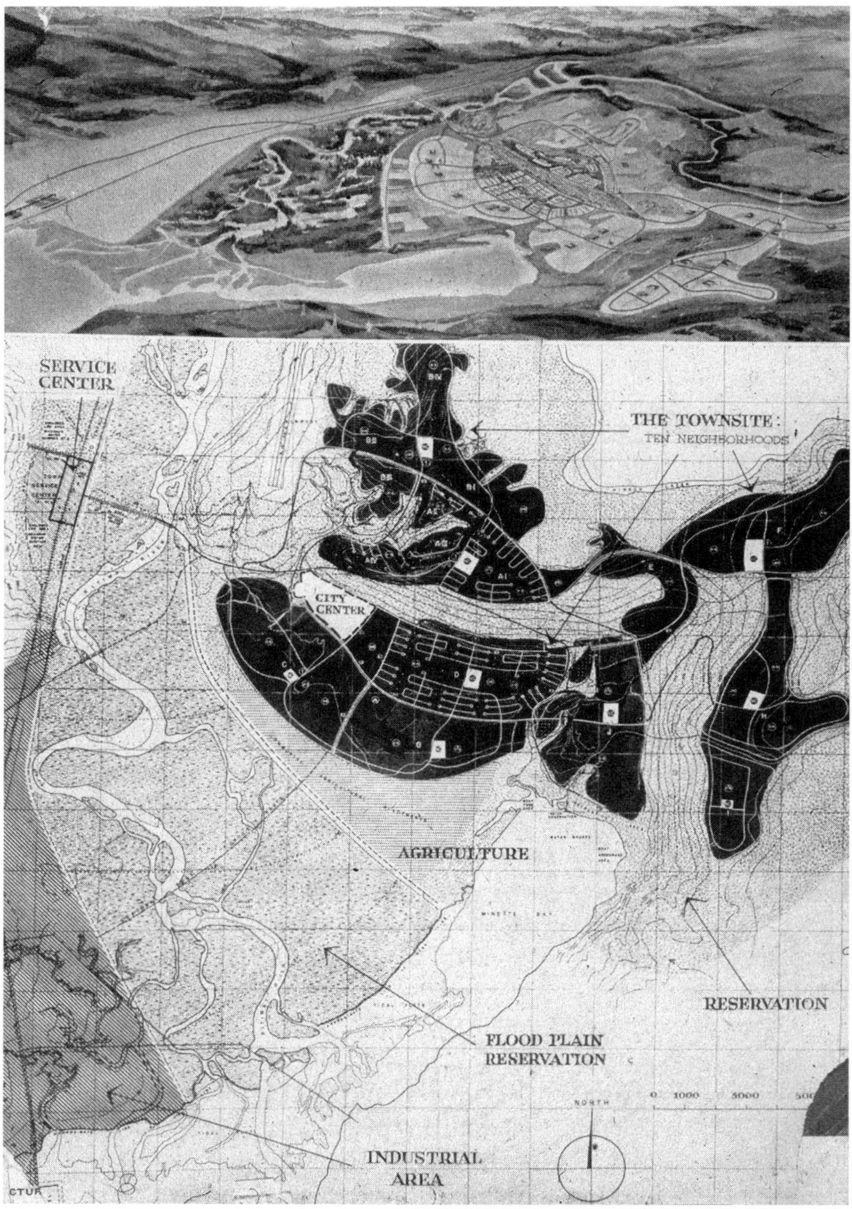

Figure 0.6 Planning map and scheme for the Kitimat townsite in northern British Columbia. | Published in *Architectural Forum*, July 1954.

Figure 0.7 Aerial view of Montreal showing the Canadian Imperial Bank of Commerce (lower right), architects Peter Dickinson with Ross, Fish, Duchenes and Barrett, 1958-63; and Place Ville Marie office complex (centre), architect I.M. Pei, 1958-62. | Reproduced by permission of the Visual Resources Centre, University of British Columbia.

upon completion in 1965 (in collaboration with the local firm of J.B. Parkin Associates) (Figure 0.8).[42] Revell's twin elliptical office stacks sheltering the visibly accessible domed civic debating chamber heralded an ongoing series of instant concoctions of civic/national identity through signature, chiefly commercial, architectural commissions. These superseded the prestige briefly accruing to the series of public-housing schemes managed by the federal Canada Mortgage and Housing Corporation (Figure 0.9). Typical of the iconic commercial complexes were the elegantly functionalist dark glazed towers of the Toronto Dominion Centre (1963-69), designed by the German-born American architect Mies van der Rohe.

Figure 0.8 Toronto City Hall, architects Viljo Revell with J.B. Parkin Associates, 1962-65. | Reproduced by permission of the Visual Resources Centre, University of British Columbia.

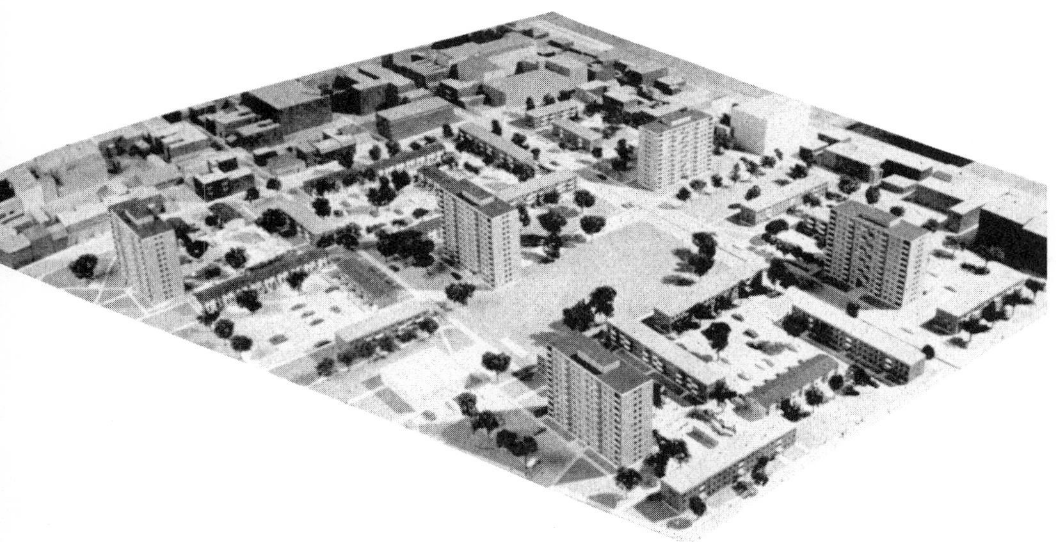

Figure 0.9 Model of the Jeanne Mance Housing Project, Montreal, 1958, designed by Canada Mortgage and Housing Corporation in conjunction with Greenspoon, Friedlander and Dunn, and Jacques Morin. | Courtesy of *Canadian Architect*.

The sanction of international prestige has continued in three more recent commissions in which overseas architects have collaborated with local firms: the British architect Will Alsop with Robbie, Young and Wright on the Sharp Centre for Design at the Ontario College of Art and Design (2001-04) (Figure 0.10); the American Daniel Libeskind with Bregman and Hamann on the Michael Lee-Chin "Crystal" at the Royal Ontario Museum (2007-09); and the Canadian-born American Frank Gehry, who returned to his native city when designing the major refurbishment of the Art Gallery of Ontario (2004-08). An opposite flow is typified by the Uruguayan-born Canadian Carlos Ott, whose international renown began after he won the competition for the Bastille Opera at Paris in 1983.

The story continues in the furious redevelopment of downtown Vancouver as a high-density, high-rise residential precinct affording safe haven to the capital and persons of the global elite in Canada's western domain. One episode in what has come to be termed "Vancouverism" is the hiring of the world-renowned UK firm created by Norman Foster to design Jameson Tower.[43] Although slowed by the 2008-09 financial collapse, the tower's financial and aesthetic remit is its status as a skyscraping lynchpin of development intended to transform a section

Figure 0.10 The Sharp Centre for Design, Ontario College of Art and Design, Toronto. | Photograph by Richard Johnson, www.interiorimages.ca.

of the city into Rodeo Drive North (a financial extension of Vancouver's repute as Canada's less clement northern outpost of the American movie industry, popularized as "Brollywood") (Figure 0.11). Foster's name, almost more than his architectural creativity, is deployed to assure developer and prospective purchaser that they have invested wisely in this civic site of national participation in the grounding of world capital flow. The concrete architectural but also populist cultural dimension of capitalism is typified in one accoutrement – beyond the plethora of high-end appliances – supplied for the denizens of a hotel–cum–residential condominium constructed several city blocks to the northwest of the Jameson. This condominium, the Shangri-La (designed in 2004 by James Cheng, a successful Vancouver neo-Modernist, and opened in 2009), was planned to include an outpost of the Vancouver Art Gallery. A kiosk for works from its collection, this facility recalls the longstanding social cachet of the fine arts, one that corresponds with architecture's continuing heritage of transforming wealth into gentility and power into civilization.

Figure 0.11 Advertisement for Jameson House Condominium, Vancouver, architects Norman Foster and Partners. | Published in the *Vancouver Sun*, 2 November 2006.

Figure 0.12 Courtyard and upper terrace of the Canadian Chancery, Washington, DC, architect Arthur Erickson, 1983-86. | Photograph by Ricardo L. Castro.

Cultural institutions have performed a comparable function of national political validation. In the context of Canada, Prime Minister Pierre Elliott Trudeau sought to validate full Canadian independence as much through the fast-tracked commissions for the National Gallery of Canada and Museum of Civilization (originally of Man) in Ottawa as through repatriation of the Constitution or the erection of Arthur Erickson's Canadian Chancery in Washington, DC.[44] The chancery's architectural reconfiguration of the neo-imperialist Classicism of the adjacent Republican bureaux is matched by the parodic alignment of its facades with the focal point of the US Capitol (Figure 0.12). Erickson's inventive response to detailed specification and overwhelming context was matched by Safdie's modernization of Gothic and Château-Baronial iconography in the National Gallery. The historical referencing manifested the intersection of mutually validating international and national visual culture on display in its galleries.

The problem of art collecting and cultural property is more apparent in the ethnographic displays within the Museum of Civilization. It was designed by Douglas Cardinal, whose ancestry interweaves that of indigene and immigrant. He conceived a building that purportedly synthesized the great compositional themes of northern American landscape as the proper formal expression of postcolonial multicultural nationhood.[45] Howsoever inspired by his own reverence for nature, Cardinal's design concept depends upon the range of technical and visual formulas that constitute the communicative force of architecture. The museum and gallery operate as conveyors of meaning that replicate the cultural politics of collective economy in company with most legislative, institutional, and corporate architecture. Their material presence corresponds, indeed, with the nation-building mythic power Fitchett invested in military deeds such as the Battle of the Heights of Abraham.

In some respects, Fitchett's interpretation of the constitutive power of events can be compared with the societal impact of architecture. The power of architecture in imposing the claims of regime, objectifying collective values, and asserting belief or status or identity has been central to its theorization. Vitruvius, Alberti, Palladio, Chambers, Ledoux, Semper, Le Corbusier, and Rossi represent those more readily recognizable writers on the socio-cultural performance of architecture.[46] The potent and pervasive conveyance, or visual/spatial coalescing, of meaning for publics and individuals was, for another example, aphorized by the celebrated Arts and Crafts architect and architectural theorist William Lethaby in a phrase from his 1891 book *An Introduction to the History and Theory of the Art of Building*: "Architecture is the matrix of civilization."[47] Part of architecture's power derives from its multidisciplinary practice and enterprise, together with its close connection with the dynamics of social operation and individual subjectivity. The panoply of architectural design fabricates identity in constructing the built environment of community, including nation and state.

NOTES

1 These processes are examined in Colin Coates, ed., *Imperial Canada, 1867-1917* (Edinburgh: Centre of Canadian Studies, 1997). See also J.L. Granatstein and Norman Hilmer, *For Better or for Worse: Canada and the United States to the 1990s* (Toronto: Copp Clark, Pitman, 1991).

2 J.M. Bumsted, *The Peoples of Canada: A Pre-Confederation History* (Don Mills, ON: Oxford University Press, 2009); J.M. Bumsted, *The Peoples of Canada: A Post-Confederation History* (Don Mills, ON: Oxford University Press, 2008). See also Kenneth McNaught, *The Pelican History of Canada* (Harmondsworth, UK: Penguin, 1982).

3 Tory, a faculty member at McGill University, was recommending the establishment of a provincial university for British Columbia, and his speech was repeated in the *Vancouver Daily News Advertiser,* 28 August 1907; see newspaper cutting, University of British Columbia Archives, President's Office Fonds, box 8, file 4. A more recent example is the advertisement for the AON Corporation on the 2007 in-flight entertainment aboard Air Canada airliners, which claims that the insurance and investment business has made AON "Part of the Fabric of Canada." The journal of the Society of Architectural Historians of Australia and New Zealand is entitled *Fabrications,* and Joseph Rosa, curator of the San Francisco Museum of Modern Art exhibition *Glamour: Fashion + Industrial Design + Architecture,* entitled his introduction to the accompanying publication "Fabricating Affluence"; see Joseph Rosa, "Fabricating Affluence," in *Glamour: Fashion + Industrial Design + Architecture,* ed. Joseph Rosa, 16-23 (New Haven, CT: Yale University Press, 2004). In a similar vein, Ada Louise Huxtable has published *The Unreal America: Architecture and Illusion* (New York: New Press, 1997).

4 The literature on affect, and on the nature of affect in the everyday environment, is examined by Nigel Thrift, "Intensities of Feeling: Toward a Spatial Politics of Affect," *Geografiska Annaler, Series B,* 86, 1 (2004): 57-78. A related aspect of ordinary experience crossing into the architectural domain is lifestyle; see David Chaney, *Lifestyles* (London: Routledge, 1996), and David Bell and Joanne Hollows, *Historicizing Lifestyle: Mediating Taste, Consumption and Identity from the 1900s to the 1970s* (Aldershort, UK: Ashgate, 2006). Two other critical perspectives are offered by Witold Rybczynski, *Looking Around: A Journey through Architecture* (Toronto: HarperCollins, 1992), and Stewart Brand, *How Buildings Learn: What Happens after They're Built* (New York: Viking, 1994).

5 The complex processes outlined here receive more detailed analysis in a series of articles edited by Carmen Popescu for *National Identities* 8, 3 (2006). Also of particular relevance are Carmen Popescu, "Space, Time: Identity," *National Identities* 8, 3 (2006): 189-206; and Peter Scriver, "Placing In-between: Thinking through Architecture in the Construction of Colonial-Modern Identities," *National Identities* 8, 3 (2006): 207-23.

6 The visual aspects of architectural representation are dismissed in Kester Rattenbury, ed., *This Is Not Architecture: Media Constructions* (London: Routledge, 2002), most notably by Alberto Perez-Gomez, "The Revelation of Order: Perspective and Architectural Representation," 3-25.

7 David Cannadine, "Imperial Canada: Old History, New Problems," in *Imperial Canada, 1867-1917,* ed. Colin Coates, 1-19 (Edinburgh: Centre of Canadian Studies, 1995). An interesting study of the creation of distinctive social mythology in the Canadas is Gillian Poulter, *Becoming Native in a Foreign Land: Sport, Visual Culture and Public Spectacle in the Construction of National Identity in Montreal, 1840-85* (Vancouver: UBC Press, 2008).

8 W.H. Fitchett, *Deeds That Won the Empire* (London: Smith Elder, 1897).

9 The discursive impress of institutional architecture in settler communities in western Canada is examined by Rhodri Windsor Liscombe, "Fabricating Legalities of State in the Imperial West: The Social Work of the Courthouse in Late Victorian and Edwardian British Columbia," *Law Text Culture* 8 (2005): 57-82.

10 Fitchett, *Deeds,* vi.

11 These plans are discussed briefly and illustrated in Harold Kalman, *A History of Canadian Architecture* (Don Mills, ON: Oxford University Press, 1994), vol. 1, 257-59.

12 Among a growing literature are Thomas Markus, *Buildings and Power: Freedom and Control in the Origin of Modern Building Types* (London: Routledge, 1993); Greig Crysler, *Writing Spaces: Discourses of Architecture, Urbanism, and the Built Environment, 1960-2000* (London: Routledge, 2003); and Dana Arnold and Andrew Ballantyne, eds., *Architecture as Experience: Radical Change in Spatial Practice* (London: Routledge, 2004). The literature on time, including its relation to social and historical organization, is extensive, ranging from Stephen Kern, *The Culture of Time and Space* (Cambridge, MA: Harvard University Press, 1983); to Peter McInerney, *Time and Experience* (Philadelphia: Temple University Press, 1991); John Brough and Lester Embree, eds., *The Many Faces of Time* (Dordrecht: Kluwer, 2000); and Penelope Corfield, *Time and the Shape of History* (New Haven, CT: Yale University Press, 2007).

13 Kalman's *A History of Canadian Architecture* was reissued in a single volume as *A Concise History of Canadian Architecture* (Toronto: Oxford University Press, 2000). An invaluable resource for historical data on Canadian architects and buildings is the online dictionary compiled by Robert Hill at http://www.dictionaryofarchitectsincanada.org.

14 The rich range of theoretical reconsideration of architecture is well summarized in Neil Leach, ed., *Rethinking Architecture: A Reader in Cultural Theory* (London: Routledge, 1997); works by the later theorists include Marc Auge, *Non-Places: Introduction to the Anthropology of Supermodernity* (London: Verso, 1995), Edward Casey, *Fate of Place: A Philosophical History* (Berkeley: University of California Press, 1997), and Doreen Massey, *For Space* (Londan: Sage, 2005). Among examples of innovative reassessment of architectural design practice is Barbara Arciszewska and Elizabeth McKellar, eds., *Articulating British Classicism: New Approaches to Eighteenth-Century Architecture* (London: Ashgate, 2004).

15 One interesting example centred in contemporary Vancouver is Thomas Hutton, "Spatiality, Built Form, and Creative Industry Development in the Inner City," *Environment and Planning* 38 (2006): 1819-41. The larger perspective of place-making in relation to wider political and cultural interests is examined by Kim Dovey, *Framing Places: Mediating Power in Built Form* (London: Routledge, 1999).

16 Veronica Strong-Boag, Sherrill Grace, Avigail Eisenberg, and Joan Anderson, eds., *Painting the Maple: Essays on Race, Gender, and the Construction of Canada* (Vancouver: UBC Press, 1998); Marta Dvořák and W.H. New, eds., *Tropes and Territories: Short Fiction, Postcolonial Readings, Canadian Writing in Context* (Montreal and Kingston: McGill-Queen's University Press, 2007); Leonard B. Kuffert, *A Great Duty: Canadian Responses to Modern Life and Mass Culture, 1939-1967* (Montreal and Kingston: McGill-Queen's University Press, 2003); John O'Brian and Peter White, eds., *Beyond Wilderness: The Group of Seven, Canadian Identity, and Contemporary Art* (Montreal and Kingston: McGill-Queen's University Press, 2007).

17 Umberto Eco, "Function and Sign: Semiotics of Architecture," in *Rethinking Architecture: A Reader in Cultural Theory,* ed. Neil Leach, 192-202 (London: Routledge, 1997).

18 Their writings include Benedict Anderson, *Imagined Communities: Reflections on the Origin and Spread of Nationalism,* rev. ed. (London: Verso, 2002); Eric Hobsbawm, *The Invention of Tradition* (Cambridge, UK: Cambridge University Press, 1992); Eric Hobsbawm and Terence Ranger, *Nations and Nationalism since 1780: Programme, Myth, Reality* (Cambridge, UK: Cambridge University Press, 1992); David Harvey, *Spaces of Hope* (Berkeley: University of California Press, 2000); Fredric Jameson, *Postmodernism, or The Cultural Logic of Capitalism* (Durham, NC: Duke University Press, 1991); and Giorgio

Agamben, *Coming Community*, trans. M. Hardt (Minneapolis: University of Minnesota Press, 1998). See also Hugh Seton-Watson, *Nations and States: An Enquiry into the Origins of Nations and the Politics of Nationalism* (London: Methuen, 1997); and with particular reference to Canada, Paul Bennett and Cornelius Jaenen, eds., *Emerging Identities: Selected Problems and Interpretations in Canadian History* (Scarborough, ON: Prentice-Hall, 1986). With respect to the Canadian discourse, see Philip Resnick, *Thinking English Canada* (Toronto: Stoddart, 1994); and Will Kymlicka, *Finding Our Way: Rethinking Ethnocultural Relations in Canada* (Toronto: Oxford University Press, 1998).

19 Ali Madaupour, *Public and Private Spaces of the City* (London: Routledge, 2003).

20 The literature is again extensive and includes Derek Gregory and John Urry, eds., *Social Relations and Spatial Structure* (New York: St. Martin's Press, 1985); and more generally David Lloyd and Paul Thomas, *Culture and the State* (London: Routledge, 1998). A broader perspective centred on twentieth-century transatlantic design appears in Panayotis Tournikiotis, *The Historiography of Modern Architecture* (Cambridge, MA: MIT Press, 1999).

21 Harold Innis, *Empire and Communications* (Toronto: University of Toronto Press, 1950).

22 Ged Martin, *The Durham Report and British Policy: A Critical Essay* (Cambridge, UK: Cambridge University Press, 1972); Ged Martin, *Britain and the Origins of Canadian Confederation, 1837-67* (Vancouver: UBC Press, 1995); Allan Greer and Ian Radforth, eds., *Colonial Leviathan: State Formation in Mid-Nineteenth-Century Canada* (Toronto: University of Toronto Press, 1992). The importance of geography and resources is indicated in R. Douglas Francis, Richard Jones, and Donald Smith, *Destinies: Canadian History since Confederation* (Toronto: Harcourt Canada, 2000).

23 Joseph Rykwert, *The Dancing Column: On Order in Architecture* (Cambridge, MA: MIT Press, 1996).

24 Carolyn Young, *The Glory of Ottawa* (Montreal and Kingston: McGill-Queen's University Press, 1995).

25 The term originates in Hugh McLennan's novel *Two Solitudes* (New York: Duell, Sloan and Pearce, 1945). On the anthems and their historical contexts, see Jeffrey Kashen and Suzanne Morton, *Documents in Post-Confederation Canadian History* (Don Mills, ON: Addison-Wesley, 1998), esp. 118-19.

26 These developments are reviewed in Kenneth Norrie, Douglas Owram, and J.C. Herbert Emery, *A History of the Canadian Economy* (Scarborough, ON: Nelson, 2002).

27 Cited in Resnick, *Thinking English Canada*, 93. Resnick, among his other studies of Canadian political culture, has published *The European Roots of Canadian Identity* (Peterborough, ON: Broadview, 2005).

28 Lum's practice is examined by Michael Turner in the catalogue to an exhibition at the Vancouver Contemporary Art Gallery, *Ken Lum* (Vancouver: Contemporary Art Gallery, 2001).

29 The idea and practice of history are analyzed by Eric Hobsbawm, *On History* (London: Weidenfeld, Nicolson, 1997); and by Harry Harootunian, *History's Disquiet: Modernity, Cultural Practice and the Question of Everyday Life* (New York: Columbia University Press, 2000).

30 This episode is examined in Robin Fisher, "Judging History: Reflections on the Reasons for Judgment in *Delgamuukw v. B.C.*," *BC Studies* 95 (1992): 43-54; and in Richard Daly, *Our Box Was Full: An Ethnography for the Delgamuukw Plaintiffs* (Vancouver: UBC Press, 2005). The process of land alienation is related in Cole Harris, *Making Native Space: Colonialism, Resistance, and Reserves in British Columbia* (Vancouver: UBC Press, 2002).

31 Stephen Leacock, *Canada: The Foundations of Its Future* (Montreal: privately printed, 1941), xxvii, xxviii; the book was financed by and dedicated to Samuel Bronfman, creator of the Seagram Corporation.

32 Ibid., 27.

33 Raymond Williams, *Keywords: A Vocabulary of Culture and Society* (New York: Oxford University Press, 1983).

34 The naturalistic figure of Canadian identity was sanctioned by Northrop Frye in *Bush Garden: Essays on the Canadian Imagination* (Toronto: Anansi, 1971).

35 Quoted in Suzanne Zeller, *Inventing Canada: Early Victorian Science and the Idea of a Transcontinental Nation* (Toronto: University of Toronto Press, 1987), 7.

36 Quoted in ibid., 7.

37 A Canadian regional perspective is provided by Patricia Jason, *Wild Things: Nature, Culture and Tourism in Ontario, 1790-1914* (Toronto: University of Toronto Press, 1995). See also Pierre Du Prey, *Ah Wilderness: Resort Architecture in the Thousand Islands* (Kingston: Agnes Etherington Art Centre, 2004); and Thomas Strickland, "Medicinal Vacations: Private Hospitals, Hotels and Consumers, 1890-1935" (MA thesis, McGill University, 2006).

38 Rhodri Windsor Liscombe, "Nationalism or Cultural Imperialism? The Château Style in Canada," *Architectural History* 36 (1993): 127-44; the allusion to castles was made by Abraham Rogatnick, "Canadian Castles: Phenomenon of the Railway Hotel," *Architectural Review* 141, 843 (May 1967): 364-72.

39 The literature on tourism as economic power is extensive and includes Philip Scranton and Janet Davidson, eds., *The Business of Tourism: Place, Faith and History* (Philadelphia: University of Pennsylvania Press, 2007); and Andrew Church and Tim Coles, *Tourism, Power and Space* (London: Routledge, 2007).

40 Leslie Dawn, *National Visions, National Blindness: Canadian Art and Identities in the 1920s* (Vancouver: UBC Press, 2006). See also James Vilora, "The Politics of the 'We' in the Construction of Collective Identities in the Histories of Architecture in Canada," *Journal of the Society for the Study of Architecture in Canada* 24, 4 (1999): 10-17.

41 The *Architectural Forum* devoted the bulk of three issues to the project in July, August, and October 1954; see also Rhodri Windsor Liscombe, *The New Spirit: Modern Architecture in Vancouver, 1938-1963* (Montreal: Canadian Centre for Architecture, 1997), 66-67.

42 As one example of international coverage of Toronto City Hall, this author vividly recalls viewing a television program on its design by the British Broadcasting Corporation. The competition was supervised by the architect and educator Eric Arthur and discussed in his book *Toronto: No Mean City*, 3rd rev. ed. (Toronto: University of Toronto Press, 1986). See also Robert Fulford, *Accidental City: The Transformation of Toronto* (Toronto: MacFarlane Walter and Ross, 1995).

43 This neologism appeared in the early 1990s with the particular reference to this version of New Urbanism promoted by the Vancouver city planner Larry Beasley. See Trevor Boddy, "Vancouverism vs. Lower Manhattanism: Shaping the High Density City," *Vancouver Sun*, 20 September 2005; Douglas Coupland, *City of Glass* (Vancouver: Douglas and McIntyre, 2001); and Lance Berelowitz, *Dream City: Vancouver and the Global Imagination* (Vancouver: Douglas and McIntyre, 2005).

44 Trudeau recounted his political and cultural concepts and policies in the arts in *Memoirs* (Toronto: McClelland and Stewart, 1993).

45 Cardinal's career is studied in Trevor Boddy, *The Architecture of Douglas Cardinal* (Edmonton: NeWest, 1988).

46 The literature on architectural theory, architectural books, and pattern books includes Eileen Harris, *British Architectural Books and Writers, 1556-1785* (Cambridge, UK: Cambridge University Press, 1990); Anthony Vidler, *Claude-Nicolas Ledoux: Architecture and Social Reform at the End of the Ancien Regime* (Cambridge, MA: MIT Press, 1990); and Linda Smeins, *Building an American Identity: Pattern Book Houses and Communities* (Walnut Creek, CA: Alta Mira, 1999). The importance of books in architectural practice, especially during the Victorian era in Canada, is demonstrated in Geoffrey Simmins, *Fred Cumberland: Building the Victorian Dream* (Toronto: University of Toronto Press, 1997).

47 William Lethaby, *An Introduction to the History and Theory of the Art of Building* (1891; Home University Library in Modern Knowledge ed., London: Williams and Norgate, 1912), 7. In *Architecture, Mysticism and Myth*, Lethaby stressed the symbolic aspect, stating in the "Introduction" that it "enshrined ideas." See William Lethaby, *Architecture, Mysticism and Myth* (1891; reprint, New York: George Braziller, 1975), 6.

PART 1
ARCHITECTURAL CULTURE IN FRENCH CANADA AND BEFORE

The organization of this anthology corresponds with the main temporal and geographical phases of foreign intervention in Canada during the modern era. European settlement of Canada was stimulated by secular political and commercial but also religious objectives. Its beginnings on the eastern shoreline and along the St. Laurent/Lawrence River are examined in chapters by Judi Loach and Marc Grignon. In "First Impressions: How French Jesuits Framed Canada," Loach analyzes the written record of encounter with the remarkable topography and indigenous peoples compiled as the *Relations* by French Jesuit missionaries from 1632 to 1672. Her careful reading of the Jesuit response to the very different natural and social conditions found in Canada reveals a framing (in the constitutive and ironic senses) that informs and structures subsequent French colonial policy and action. She discloses the importance both of redemptive intentionality and of transposed assumption in the formation of the French project in the New World. The Jesuits represented Acadia as a new Eden capable of a higher destiny than the more materialist enterprise of merchant adventurers such as Samuel de Champlain. Grignon studies a later stage in the establishment of a permanent colonial regime at Quebec City in "Visibility, Symbolic Landscape, and Power: Jean-Baptiste-Louis Franquelin's View of Quebec City in 1688." He concentrates on Franquelin's carefully oriented and organized vista of the capital of New France. The admixture of sight, site, and insight, or imaginary representation, is another aspect of the symbolic dimension of culture inscribed through objects of cultural production. Franquelin's view is shown to have delineated the contesting individual and institutional assertion of authority locally as well as between sovereign and colonial regime. The hierarchy of power relations was reflected in the placement and prominence of the skyline, of buildings. The Jesuits' mental-cum-literary description of this potential new resource of French religious endeavour is as significant to understanding subsequent Canadian architectural culture as the visual-cum-cartographic definition of governance by Franquelin. His view projected court society onto the vastly different local geography in the same manner that the architecture he drew visibly transferred cultural as well as political conventions into a new social world, the contours of which he did not know.

The Jesuit *Relations* and depictions such as Franquelin's view of Quebec illustrate the importance of symbolic representation to the self-legitimation of colonial projects – a corresponding appropriation of religious and rational value to justify alienation of Aboriginal patrimony and imposition of an alien economic and social order. The paraphernalia of colonization included some level of orderly construction and/or architectural pretension alongside naval/military and survey/resource expedition. The cultural significance of architecture and built form increased as competition for transoceanic resource acquisition and related commerce pushed colonial expansion along the river systems of the continent.

1

First Impressions
How French Jesuits Framed Canada

JUDI LOACH

First impressions play a disproportionate role in structuring our long-term perception of places and subsequently our creative reconfiguration of them – our construction of supposedly new places. In the case of that part of "New France" the French knew as "Canada," the first impressions gained by the French back in France were predominantly formed through the *Relations* (literally "accounts") published in Paris by Jesuit missionaries, recounting what they had observed of this new land with their own eyes.[1] These eyes, however, were profoundly conditioned by their minds, which interpreted such visual sensory data through mental structures framed by Thomist theology and further reinforced by their practice of Ignatian devotional exercises. It is therefore important to explore these Jesuits' perceptions and conceptions of Canada (while bearing in mind their particular presentation of them, specifically for purposes of advancing Christian mission). In this way, we can better understand their fundamental contribution to an initial construction of this place in the minds of their fellow citizens back in France and in turn better equip ourselves for appraising the subsequent contribution made by France to "constructing a Canadian fabric."

Such an endeavour might hardly seem worth the effort involved, given the paucity of material – notably architecture and settlement patterns – that survives from what has been called the "Heroic Age" of New France, the years between its foundation and the 1660s. My argument, however, is that the initial perceptions and interpretations largely determined subsequent ones and that knowledge of these initial perceptions and conceptions is thus crucial to uncovering such intentions as continue into later periods and in turn underlie material remains extant from these periods. This chapter, therefore, focuses on rediscovering the most initial perceptions and conceptions of Canada promulgated by the very first Jesuit missionaries there (1611-13).

This chapter aims to stimulate a rereading of material and documentary evidence already known in light of the intentions of those responsible for originating it. Evidently, this chapter has been researched from literary sources, rather than visual ones or material remains, since the latter no longer survive for the particular place and period with which I am concerned here: a certain part of today's eastern Canada – Acadia – in the very early years of the seventeenth century.[2] The contemporary documents available to us present evidence of material no longer extant and therefore inaccessible to our own eyes. They force us to reconstruct within our own minds the material realities that they describe, by simultaneously exercising our imaginations and drawing on memories of what we have already seen elsewhere. In reading these documents today, we are thus drawn, unconsciously, to mimic the experience of the original readers, for whom the material realities described were equally unavailable to the visual sense, sitting as they were on the far side of a vast, and then far more rarely crossed, ocean. In their case, however, the realities described were hitherto wholly unknown, often to the extent of being almost unimaginable, as the writers – contemporaries and compatriots of the intended readers – were well aware. These writers, therefore, depended upon metaphor and simile, deploying everyday language developed to represent French actualities so as to bring their foreign experience into the mind's eye of their distant readers. We are disadvantaged, most immediately in that we are unable to recover the sense of strangeness, and therefore exoticism, with which these reports were imbued for their original readers. More profoundly, however, we are less familiar than were the Jesuits' pious readers, trained in Ignatian spiritual exercises, with the mental practices expected of readers here: the active engagement of memory and imagination so as to translate verbal imagery into mental pictures, with indeed an expectation of being drawn, through them, into a certain course of action.

THE FIRST FRENCH ACCOUNTS OF CANADA

The Jesuits' *Relations* of the life of their Canadian Mission, published annually from 1632 to 1673, have long been recognized by historians as having exerted disproportionately great influence on the French public when its image of New France was being formed, in the early to mid-seventeenth century. Although Europeans had been fishing the Grand Banks – around Newfoundland and the Maritimes – from the mid-fifteenth century onward, and Jacques Cartier had taken possession of the country in the name of François I in 1534, no accounts of these lands were published in France until the end of the sixteenth century, when, from 1599 onward, Samuel de Champlain published accounts of his *Voyages*. In 1609 the Parisian lawyer and businessman Marc Lescarbot had, on returning from his visit to Acadia, fulfilled a request from friends to write a history of the place he had visited, resulting in a three-volume *Histoire de la Nouvelle France* (translated as *Story of New France*). In 1632 the Récollet friar Gabriel Sagard published his *Grand voyage aux pays des Hurons* (usually translated as *Long Journey into the Country of the Hurons*), both narrating his courageous journey made almost a decade earlier (in 1623) and describing the Natives he had observed during his stay in Huronia; he followed this, in 1636, with his own *Histoire du Canada (History of Canada)*. Finally, Pierre Boucher's *Histoire véritable et naturelle (True and Natural History)*, published in 1662, constituted a longer-term reflection than the others cited, since Boucher, having emigrated to Canada with his family in 1634 as a twelve-year-old child, had spent nearly thirty years there before writing his book. Having acquired a fluent knowledge of the Huron language from Jesuit missionaries, he became the governor's interpreter in Quebec and eventually governor himself; as such, he returned to France in 1661 to ask for the nascent colony's royal protection against the Iroquois, a request that in turn elicited another from the king, that he write this book on the colony and its future.

Given that the Jesuit *Relations* were not the only, nor indeed the earliest, accounts, one needs to ask why they were so influential. The main reason offered at the time for the greater impact of the Jesuit *Relations* in comparison with the other sources cited was that they were held to be the most accurate, and therefore most authoritative, source of knowledge about the new land. In fact, not only do historians concur with this judgment today,[3] but anthropologists also continue to use them as reliable sources of evidence, albeit more critically than did most scholars of earlier generations.[4] Written up by Jesuit missionaries from their personal diaries and letters, the *Relations* (the French word meaning "account," "story," or "narration" and often referring to a travel journal) were the result of firsthand accounts by individual eyewitnesses. The first Jesuits to reach Canada – unlike mariners or traders such as Cartier, Champlain, or Lescarbot – almost certainly lacked any prior contact with those Europeans familiar with the land: largely illiterate fishermen, fur trappers, and loggers, who were predominately Huguenot and therefore hostile to Catholics, let alone Jesuits. Consequently, this "New France" generated a greater sense of shock in these missionaries than in their near contemporary compatriots working there, and this is evident from the remarkably animated and original character of the earliest Jesuit accounts.

Yet equally, as the Society of Jesus became the dominant religious order there, its members progressively accumulated a uniquely profound knowledge of the land and its indigenous people – through living among them over a long period and across a relatively large area – which in turn was reflected in their *Relations*. In addition, these writings benefited from being grounded in, and continually supported by, the Jesuits' substantial scholarship that informed their understanding of what they observed.

Such a combination was unparalleled in the rival works. Although Champlain and Boucher each had experience of long years of journeying around Canada, both lacked the Jesuits' advantage of higher education. The other non-Jesuit publications available at this time, although based on firsthand observations, suffered from the relative brevity of their authors' stays in Canada – Lescarbot and Sagard each spending less than a year there – which consequently limited their experience of the place. Other reasons why the Jesuit *Relations* would have made an unrivalled impression upon contemporary readers remain apparent to readers today. First, the Jesuits' sensation of strangeness on their arrival in Canada led them to write in precisely the way most appreciated by fashionable, salon society of the day, fascinated as it was by all that was exotic.[5]

Second, the *Relations* were written by men who were highly trained and experienced in writing and who therefore best understood how to use the medium of publication most effectively. The education followed by all Jesuits began with a five-year rhetoric cycle, devised to assure structured thinking and clear verbal expression alike; they subsequently followed a two- to three-year cycle in philosophy, including the study of logic, and a four-year theology cycle. This formal education was interpolated by periods of teaching the rhetoric cycle and of practical training, notably in preaching and thus in practising the communication skills acquired through formal tuition. As schoolmasters, scholars, orators, and festival organizers, Jesuits gained experience in writing for publication and became adept in exploiting the written word as a medium of persuasion directed toward a mass public. Indeed, most of the Jesuit writers of these *Relations* also authored other explicitly Catholic publications.[6]

None of the other authors writing on Canada had received such an intense education in formal writing and logical argument. Lescarbot, as barrister, obviously had acquired certain skills in oratory but not necessarily in rhetorical prose-writing; furthermore, he probably lacked the philosophical, and therefore scientific, foundations that enabled the Jesuits to appreciate the significance of the flora and fauna, let alone the Native peoples, which they found in this new land. In fact, Sagard alone had enjoyed anything approaching the Jesuits' standard of education, but even his was considerably inferior to theirs.

A further reason why the Jesuit *Relations* made the most impact in forming the French image of Canada is that they, uniquely, were issued annually, through four decades. Their regularity, and reiteration, contributed to making the deepest impression on the nation's psyche because these characteristics endowed them with a sense of constancy and thus reliability. Yet, conversely, their annual appearance also ensured that their contents were always up-to-date and immediate; their topicality, like that of newspapers, contributed to their popularity in salon society, and, as with newspapers, their sense of novelty and exoticism served to enhance their inherent value. In fact, they were bestsellers of their day, eagerly read by a wide range of society (from the royal court through the rising middle classes) and of ages (from professors to schoolboys).[7]

THE CONTEXT OF THE JESUIT *RELATIONS'* ORIGIN AND DEVELOPMENT

The *Relations* began life principally as the annual reports required by the Jesuits' General (in Rome) from each of the order's Provinces – and their respective Missions – every year. Because the reports were sent from the mission field to the Provincial for editing along with other reports from across the Province, with the author changing each few years, the series forms a multi-authored work.[8] The reports took the form of letters (literally called *Litterae Annuae,* or Annual Letters) and, destined for Rome, were composed in Latin. The Canadian Mission's letters, like those from other foreign – and notably exotic – Missions, were then redrafted, in French, to reach a wider public;[9] the primary aim was to impress potential supporters, involve them in raising funds necessary for the Mission's continuation, and demonstrate the results achieved by their donations,[10] but secondarily they might also attract men to join this foreign Mission. In the process, editing ensured that the published works were edifying by suppressing certain material, but this was not done as much to protect the reputation of the Catholic Church as one might suspect, or even to safeguard the privacy of certain individuals mentioned. Rather, such editing removed material irrelevant to, or even distracting from, the goal of edification so that the product fulfilled the Horatian nostrum "docere et delectare" (to teach and to delight), which the Jesuits followed, believing instruction to be effective only when enjoyable.[11]

That the period of the *Relations'* publication – from the 1630s to 1660s – coincides with that of major French colonization can hardly be accidental, given how the Jesuits consciously exploited the medium of print for political and more broadly propagandist ends. In 1625 the English had returned Canada to the French, and shortly thereafter the Jesuits had re-entered the land, this time following the Récollets to the St. Lawrence River, instead of installing themselves in Acadia as before. Given their commitment to thorough teaching of the faith prior to baptism of neophytes, the Jesuits had acquired a conviction that they must help the Natives to leave their hunter-gatherer lifestyle for that of agricultural settlements. Colonization was therefore a matter of spiritual import, endowed with a sense of urgency not because of the race to claim lands for the French Crown against English and Dutch competition but rather to secure the souls of Natives by bringing them into the Catholic Church instead of losing them to Protestants or unbelievers. Hence one of the Jesuits' first initiatives, as early as 1626, was to establish a college in Quebec.

Yet another expulsion of the French from Canada, in 1629 – the moment when Quebec first fell into the hands of the English – served to increase the Jesuits' sense of urgency. Although the French returned just a few years later, throughout the 1630s the French Crown showed no interest in funding the colonization of Canada directly, depending instead upon the efforts made by societies such as the Jesuits. It was within this context that the *Relations* were conceived as a means to persuade wealthy Catholics back in France of the immediate need to finance the Jesuit Mission in Canada and to convince politically influential Catholics at court of the longer-term need to change official policy so as to finance Catholic colonization.

Following the return of the French in 1632, the next few years saw the most significant attempt at colonization so far, this time around the St. Lawrence River instead of in Acadia, with around seventy settlers arriving there and a couple of new settlements being inaugurated; the one at Trois Rivières was to prove to be of some importance as a trading centre, as the main advance fortification for what would become Montreal, and as a more productive base than Quebec for agriculture, fishing, and hunting. Nevertheless, stagnation then ensued, soon exacerbated by the dilution of already meager resources through the establishment of a colony at Ville Marie, today's Montreal.[12]

At the French return to Canada in 1632, the Jesuits also relocated to the St. Lawrence River, instead of Acadia, since Louis XIII decreed that the latter should become the exclusive preserve of Capuchin activity;[13] in addition, it would fall under the English again from 1655.[14] As numerous historians have already noted, from 1632 to 1659 the history of Roman Catholicism in Canada effectively became that of the Jesuits since they became the sole religious authority there, at least outside Acadia, and thus throughout the region of greatest development. Sagard's *Long Journey,* published significantly in 1632, claimed that his own order, the Récollets, which had been the first established along the St. Lawrence, had been ousted by the Jesuits; and this in turn may have provoked the Jesuits to begin publishing their own *Relations* that very year.

The unity of purpose due to consolidating all mission activity within a single order facilitated progress. In 1632 the Jesuits founded a "seminary" *(seminaire),* or college, for Indian boys at Notre-Dame des Anges, just outside Quebec, and another for French colonists in Quebec itself.[15] In the late 1630s they arranged for a French order of nuns to set up a hospital, the Hôtel-Dieu at Quebec (initially located at Sillery). Meanwhile, they convinced another order, the Ursulines, to set up a school for girls in Quebec, catering to French and Natives together. At the same time, they realized their longstanding dream of founding a settlement for Indians – at Sillery, near Quebec – where physical cultivation and spiritual conversion would advance hand-in-hand.[16] Finally, in 1634, they established a Mission in Huronia (around Lake Huron, now Georgian Bay), a six-week journey, by canoe and porterage, from Quebec; from 1639 this was consolidated at Sainte-Marie, and by the time of its destruction by the Iroquois a decade later, the Mission employed no fewer than eighteen Jesuits and twenty-four lay assistants.[17] Moreover, from 1647 to 1659 the Jesuit Superior enjoyed equal authority with the two secular governors on the council ruling all Canada.[18]

THE RANGE OF JESUIT PUBLICATIONS

The *Relations,* however, do not cover all of the early-seventeenth-century Jesuit publications on Canada. In fact, there were three distinct types of official publication, of which the well-known series of *Relations* running from 1632 to 1672 constituted the central one.[19] After a while, the Society of Jesus felt that the Mission's activities should be recorded for posterity and that the Annual Letters had too ephemeral a quality for this purpose. The Parisian Jesuit François du Creux was therefore commissioned to write a multivolume history, *Historia Canadensis* (published in 1664).[20] In retelling this tale of French discovery and early colonization of Canada in Latin, the universal language of Western antiquity, and in the form of Classical Roman narrative, he transformed these recent frontier tales of derring-do into a timeless heroic epic. For just as its Roman precedents had recounted the conquest of exotic nations beyond the eastern borders of the Roman Empire, this work now told a new, but nevertheless comparable, tale of claiming lands lying outside the civilized world of Europe, pushing back its effective Western frontier farther than ever before. In their strangeness, the wild and unknown places described here paralleled those being encountered by Jesuits at the other extremities of the globe, most evidently in the Far East but equally on the Russian steppes, in the deserts of the Levant, or in the jungles of South America. Just as the epics of Roman antiquity had memorialized the advance of European – meaning Roman – civilization, so Counter-Reformation accounts, notably the Jesuits' *Historia Canadensis,* celebrated and commemorated the current conquest by European – meaning Roman Catholic – religion. This latter aspect was dramatized by the detailed description of the capture and torture of Jesuit missionaries by the Iroquois and of their subsequent martyrdom.

The *Relations* themselves, dating from the period of the Jesuits' installation in Canada (i.e., from 1625 onward), had in fact been preceded by a single *Relation,* published in 1616,[21] covering the Jesuits' first, but unsuccessful, attempt at establishing a Mission there in 1611. This had thus been written in the wake of a Protestant – and essentially English – expulsion of the French, and therefore of Roman Catholics, from Acadia in 1613. In the face of this seeming failure to establish a Mission in Canada, the Jesuits needed to convince their putative patrons of the Catholic duty to improve the lives of these Natives through Christianization, which, the Jesuits believed, depended upon colonization. That the Récollets had succeeded in inaugurating a Mission on the St. Lawrence lent credibility to the Jesuits' claims that Canada's Native peoples could indeed be converted.

Detailed examination of the text of this 1616 *Relation,* written by Pierre Biard, one of the two Jesuits who undertook the expedition it describes, shows that it is of greater importance than has hitherto been appreciated. For this book would become the single work that most determined the mould for the works that followed, thus more than any other creating the French "first impressions," and hence longer-term image, of Canada. Scholars in general, however, and historians in particular, have focused almost exclusively on the later series of *Relations* and secondarily on du Creux's *Historia Canadensis.* Just as the perceptions and interpretations of the first French-language Jesuit writing about Canada in the seventeenth century established the optic through which Biard's compatriots subsequently viewed it, so too the perspective established by the first major study of Jesuit activity in North America, by a French scholar and published at the end of the nineteenth century, seems to have set the mould for successive historians; for here this Jesuit author relegated his account of the "Mission des Jésuites en Acadie" to a "Chapitre préliminaire," separated from the numbered chapters (derived from the *Relations*) covering all subsequent Jesuit activity in Canada.[22] Such relative disregard of the first widely promoted description of Canada by a Frenchman has been largely due to two causes: first, it constitutes an account of a "vain attempt" to establish a French colony and has therefore subsequently been disregarded as lacking any historic significance; second, as twentieth-century historians have demonstrated, the account it provides is a far from objective one,[23] being written to persuade the reader of the Jesuits' point of view. Yet precisely because of this original intention (with its inherent bias), it became the account that influenced Catholic contemporaries back in France – including the court – more than did any other of the first accounts, namely those by Champlain, Lescarbot, or Sagard. It is for this reason that this source is taken here as the basis for the examination of the initial French (Jesuit) perception of Canada.

THE EPHEMERALITY OF THE MATERIAL EVIDENCE AND THE JESUITS' MINIMAL RECORDING OF IT

Although Biard obviously wanted to describe as many *curiosités* as possible in order to incite his readers' interest, he does not offer much detail concerning architecture or settlement patterns. This can be frustrating since the tribes he met were essentially nomadic and their physical structures therefore temporary ones, which have not survived to our own times. At one level – the Jesuits' concerns being for the Christianization of the Native peoples – Biard's examination of them focuses on their natural and moral condition, thus mentioning their clothing and dwelling only in passing. At another level, his comparative lack of interest in their buildings might imply that they did not seem sufficiently different from those already familiar in France to be worth mentioning to his readers there. Nevertheless, these observations recorded by the first Jesuit writer on Canada are particularly valuable because he had rapidly acquired more extensive and intensive knowledge of the Native peoples' living conditions than had his compatriots, for whom contact with a few Native intermediaries (e.g., bringing furs from the hinterland) at the water's edge sufficed; instead, his missionary objectives forced him to move inland, to meet entire communities, and to do so "on their own ground."

Biard observes how the first thing the Natives did whenever they set up camp was to light a fire and then, within an hour or two (but sometimes as little as half an hour), "make themselves huts" *(se cabaner)*. This building type, alone, seems to Biard different enough from French forms of construction to justify relatively detailed description (together with the observation that women were responsible for its erection). Poles were collected from the nearby woods and then arranged in a ring around the fire so as to lean together at the top, just leaving a small hole through which smoke from the fire could leave. This structure was then covered over with skins, or waterproof sheets of woven reeds, or bark. In other words, Biard describes the kind of building generally known as a wigwam. He then explains how the Natives laid bags at the feet of the poles, spread a layer of pine needles over the rest of the ground, and then covered this in turn with sheets of woven reeds or with sealskins ("as fine as velvet"). At night they lay with their heads on the bags with their feet toward the fire, thus ensuring that they kept warm regardless of how cold it was outside. Biard notes, however, that this conical form – which proved comparatively easy to heat – was used only in winter and that in the summer months the structure took a different form, wider and longer in plan, so as to facilitate air movement through it – in other words, a typical longhouse.[24] He gives no details whatsoever as to patterns of settlement layout, simply saying that the Natives only ever built by "good water" and "with a pleasant view,"[25] thus suggesting that such layout seemed unimportant to the Natives.

As for the Jesuits' own housing, Biard offers no description whatsoever. He states clearly that when his Jesuit companion Ennemond Massé spent time living among the Indians, and therefore sharing their very primitive living conditions, he had "for roof, a dreadful hut: for resting place, the earth";[26] the context suggests that this "hut" was a wigwam. Jesuits would sometimes live in the Indians' own homes with them when travelling on missions in rural areas, and they perhaps even lived in huts built for them by Indians or in similar huts that they built themselves when they lived apart in such areas; certainly, Biard uses the same term *(cabane)* throughout, regardless of whether he is referring to their own homes or to those of the Natives.[27] The Jesuits were, however, unlikely to share the Indians' homes whenever they were working in settlements, where their work was as much with the French traders or settlers as with the Canadian Natives. Biard's omission of detail here might be due to the Jesuits' simple repetition of French vernacular practices (as in building the kind of hut used by alpine shepherds when staying with their flocks in summer pastures), which may have been considered of no interest to readers already familiar with these.

Despite its lack of detail concerning architecture or settlement layout, Biard's account is crucial for gaining an understanding of how the French formed any idea of Canada as a place since it moulded the subsequent French perception and conception of New France: (divine) nature outdoes human artefact. Faced with landscapes as extraordinary – for a seventeenth-century European – as the wild places of Canada, Pierre Biard, the first French Jesuit to write about them for a French audience, could describe them only in terms of the experience he had in common with his readers, that of the Old World. This is epitomized by his reaction to his first encounter with an iceberg, for him – and his readers alike – a hitherto unknown and even unimaginable phenomenon; he therefore depicts it to them as being as if "the Church of Notre-Dame in Paris, together with part of its island, houses and palaces, went floating off on water."[28]

Biard's striking simile illustrates a less immediately evident, but more pervasive, assumption underlying all his writing: that New France could be described in terms of France, specifically because objective facts implied that the two places should be directly comparable. For him, Canada was this "twin land with our own"[29] because it was situated on the same parallel of latitude. It was therefore subject to the same constellations, together with their predictable celestial influences, and thus could be expected to enjoy the same climate.[30] In this spirit, Biard compares the new settlement of St.-Sauveur with Bordeaux.[31]

This approach determines Biard's ordering of the first part of his *Relation*, which gives a general, thematic account of New France, comparing it throughout with France itself. His first chapter deals with the extent of the land of New France (and of its discovery by the French). The next chapter concerns the climate there, and the third treats the qualities of the land itself in terms of its agricultural use and of the peoples found on it. In the fourth chapter, he describes these Native peoples, including their manner of dressing, shelter, and lifestyle.

Biard adopts a rational – yet empirical, pre-Cartesian – approach, one typical of early-modern science, beginning with observation before moving on to predict the natural conditions prevailing in New France;[32] he then pursues this further in seeking an explanation for the unexpected discrepancy between these conditions and the reality that he encountered there.[33] In fact, his setting-out of the parallel between the physical location of these two "Frances" is on each occasion directly followed by his admission of the actual differences between them: "Nevertheless, despite what astrologers say, one has to admit that the land [*païs*] there ... is colder than our France, and that there is greater variety [there] concerning weather and seasons."[34] On the one hand, he remarks that, in Canada, in summer, "the heat is as intolerable, or more so, than in France."[35] On the other hand, he observes that at Port-Royal,[36] in Acadia, the snow lay on the ground from late November through to the end of February, at least in the woods, unless (as often happened) there was a lot of rain or a wind from the South.[37] Furthermore, "when the North West wind [called the Galerne] gets into one of its frenzies, the cold there is intolerable."[38]

Consequently, the crops that were cultivated there were more limited than in France, consisting mainly of peas and beans, and even these grew less well than they did back home. This, Biard notes, was despite the earth being "as good as in France," as was evident from its "black colour" and the vegetation growing on it: "tall, strong and powerful trees" and "grass and hay often as high as a man."[39] He reiterates this observation later, saying that, "the land there, would be worth as much as that here, if it were to be cultivated."[40] On setting up the short-lived Mission at St.-Sauveur, the Jesuits carried out a series of agricultural experiments, sowing seeds for a series of different crops – including peas, beans, and "all sorts of garden plants" – and then noting the results three months later, in early autumn. The wheat had not even appeared above ground, but this was considered normal as it had been sown out of season; the barley had produced ears, but these had not yet ripened; the peas and beans *(faisoles)*[41] were perfectly good but still green; and other beans were only in flower. But "all the rest had come along admirably, even the onions and chives, the seeds [*pepins*] had sprouted [*ietté*], some a complete foot, the smallest half as much."[42]

The striking difference in climate, and consequently in agricultural production, provoked Biard to inquire as to the cause of the "wintry weather" *(frimas)* and "greater cold" experienced in Canada.[43] This surprised him, not least because it was more severe than in higher mountainous zones with which he was acquainted in France, namely the Alps and the Massif Central.[44] Applying rational analysis, Biard proceeded to deduce that the reasons for this difference must have been due to the earth *(terre)* rather than to the heavens *(ciel),* since he assumed the latter to act consistently on both sides of the Atlantic.[45] In the same, rational spirit he turned to objective observation, noting that, outside the woods, the snow hardly remained on the ground any longer than it did in France.[46] No doubt, his own exploration of the land, by boat – along sea coasts and up rivers – influenced the first conclusion he drew from his observations, that the climatic difference between the two countries must have been due to Canada having a "more watery" *(plus aquatique)* landscape: "This region much cut up [*fort entrecoupée*] by maritime inlets [*seins*] and bays, and its lands, indented with water, is besides soaked by rivers and lakes."[47]

More significantly, in his opinion, the difference between the two places was due to the fact of the land being left uncultivated *(inculte)* in Canada or, indeed, not cleared at all. The severe cold encountered there, he surmises, was above all due to the "wildness and fallow condition of the land [*la sauvagine et friche du pays*]."[48] As he then explains in greater detail, this land being "no more than an infinite forest," the "ground [*sol*] is not warmed by the sun for long."[49] This ubiquity – and endlessness – of the forest is a recurring theme in Biard's *Relation*, with him claiming that "the entire land is nothing but a perpetual forest" and that "there is nothing open [except] the edges of the seas, lakes and rivers."[50] Indeed, this theme is repeated in all the early French accounts, showing that it evidently struck all the first French explorers. Biard continues, "This effect [of intense cold] is accentuated by the crust on the earth, resulting from it not being worked, and by the trees, keeping the earth in perpetual shade";[51] consequently, the snow or rainwater stood on the ground for longer. Moreover, on these lands, "cold, gloomy and relentless vapors" were generated whenever winds blew, mists arose whenever the air was still, and a "biting ice" appeared whenever the winds "[rose] up in anger." Biard believed that, as the land was cleared and worked, the sun would be able to have greater effect on it, and therefore the cold and fogs would disappear. He cited as evidence for this hypothesis his own experience, in the small part where "we [Jesuits] have worked" in Acadia, "since here the snow melts more than elsewhere, and the mists lift first."[52]

It was as a direct result of this rational deduction, derived from objective observations, combined with a contemporary belief in humankind's inexorable progress, that Biard concluded that colonization offered the best solution for the improvement of both this land and the lives of all living there: "If the land was inhabited, and cultivated, in addition breaths of hot dry smoke would rise from the inhabited dwellings."[53] It is worth noting that the word he uses here to describe negatively the uncultivated state of the land is "*inculte,*" literally meaning unkempt. This word, however, could equally be applied to people, as indeed it is, albeit implicitly, in this passage; in this latter case, it denotes people who are uneducated or uncivilized.

It should be emphasized that the idea of promoting colonization does not derive here from any avaricious exploitation of the land (or its peoples) so much as from a sense of intelligent and responsible stewardship (which will bring about longer-term returns). This is reflected in the insistence that one cannot expect to find all resources everywhere,[54] and also in a warning against the (abusive) illusion that all natural resources will be found everywhere in abundance.[55]

Biard's comparison of old and new France, specifically in terms of climate and agricultural production, and above all his interpretation of their differences demonstrate the kind of early-modern scientific approach we might well expect from one who had benefited from the complete three cycles of Jesuit education;[56] but his preoccupation with weather and his practical knowledge of cultivating crops evidenced here suggest that he also possessed firsthand experience of farming, specifically of that common to peasants used to cultivating mountainous terrain. Such a hypothesis is reinforced by his horticultural experiments at St.-Sauveur, in which he contrasted starkly with his compatriots brought to New France from towns across the motherland by secular would-be colonizers (the Sieurs de Monts or de Poutrincourt), men who proved so lacking in experience of farming or fishing that they were forced to rely on imported supplies. In other words, Biard read into the new land that he found in Canada possibilities deduced from his personal experience of Alpine peasant life.

In this respect, that the French Jesuits' first – and therefore highly determining – account was written by Biard (c. 1567-1622) turns out to be significant, for although he had been appointed to teach the highest-level courses (those in theology) at prestigious colleges in France,[57] and was widely recognized for his learning even by opponents of the order,[58] he may well have come from a family engaged in agriculture at quite a modest level. Nothing is known of his family background, but the prevalent assumption (probably deriving from distant anti-Jesuit propaganda) that the Jesuits recruited from a social elite is far from the actuality of seventeenth-century practice.[59] Instead, it is now clear that although the Jesuits indeed created an elite, it was meritocratic, rather than aristocratic, in nature, formed from individuals regardless of their social origin but who were both endowed with natural intelligence and committed to working hard toward its development.

Likewise, the younger father who accompanied Biard to Canada, Ennemond Massé (1574-1646), displayed a considerable degree of proficiency in do-it-yourself skills, suggesting that he too may have come from a similarly modest social background – in his case, that of an artisan family.[60] In his *Relation,* Biard seems quite astounded by Massé's abilities of this type, particularly admiring Massé's capacity in sawing large planks and in plugging the cracks in old doors or around old windows so as to prevent draughts entering their simple home (a crucial skill in freezing Canada); in fact, Biard goes as far as to call Massé a "good architect."[61] Born in Lyons, Massé was most likely to have absorbed these practical skills within an artisan, rather than a peasant, milieu. Such a relatively modest social background, however, did not preclude advancement within the order. In Massé's case, his superiors recognized and acknowledged his managerial and administrative abilities by appointing him as *ministre* and *procureur* at Lyons, then as assistant *(socius)* to Pierre Coton, the king's confessor, at Paris, and later as Rector to the prestigious college at La Flèche, the French Jesuits' first royal foundation.[62] In other words, although Biard's and Massé's careers prove that they were intelligent and well educated, both seem to have grown up in relatively modest families, where they acquired practical skills.

In Biard's case, it is certain that he would have known about Alpine life since he was born in Grenoble, the capital of Dauphiné.[63] In his *Relation* he explicitly compares the conditions he encountered in Canada with those he had experienced personally throughout the Jesuit Province of Lyons, including in the Dauphinois towns of Grenoble and Vienne,[64] and in Alpine mountain ranges in general and the Chartreuse (which rises immediately beside Grenoble) in particular.[65] That the Jesuits chose Biard as the theologian to lead disputes against Calvinist theologians in Alpine districts might also indicate that he was recognized as having experience of this region.[66] Furthermore, since they selected, from among the many volunteers presenting themselves for the Canadian Mission, a man already in his mid-forties, one imagines that the Jesuits considered him to be exceptionally well adapted to living in harsh climates. Biard and Massé contrasted starkly with their successors, those Jesuits who would write the later series of *Relations* (and the *Historia Canadensis* derived from them), on which historians have hitherto mainly relied. For both of these first missionaries sent by the Society of Jesus came from the Province of Lyons, covering the Alps and the Massif Central, and were therefore familiar with such tough environments and the skills developed by their inhabitants to exploit them; by contrast, their successors would come from the Province of France, being men brought up either in Paris itself or in the relatively flat lands around it, at farthest the rich farmlands of Normandy or the seaports of the North Coast, such as Dieppe.

A NEW EDEN

In presenting New France in terms of experiences that he shared with his readers, Biard not only described it through comparing it physically with the Old World but also assumed that the religious beliefs they held in common would inform any metatextual readings.

Throughout, Biard describes Canada – despite its wild and savage condition – in terms of a Paradise, or perhaps more precisely, in terms of a pre-Lapsarian Eden.[67] Despite the "extreme poverty" endured by all who lived there, including the Jesuits themselves, Biard deems life in Canada – although simple and lacking much that was taken for granted in France (e.g., proper homes, clothing and shoes, or wine and a variety of foodstuffs) – to be superior.[68] In Canada there was usually only water to drink, instead of wine, but it was "pure water,"[69] with all the waters found there being "very good"; likewise, he rates the air there as "very healthy."[70] Moreover, Biard sees the dearth of food and drink in positive terms, sparing those living in Canada from two major ills, namely excess consumption and, tacitly associated with this, sloth. Biard felt that, together, exercise and "a stomach not weighed down" served as "a good opiate"[71] – in other words, a cure for most ills.

Biard takes pains to describe – sometimes mouth-wateringly – the various fruits that grew untended in Canada. During the course of his travels, he found ripe grapes in one place and a different kind of wild grape *(lambruche)*[72] in another, trees for walnuts here and hazelnuts there.[73] He also discovered delicacies unknown in France, and he describes in some detail a wild root, called *chiquebi* by the Natives, which grew around oak trees:

> They are like truffles, but better, and grow underground attached to one another in the form of a rosary. There are lots of them in certain places; it is true that it is really difficult to go anywhere that the natives have not already dug [them up]: thus one hardly ever finds anything better than small ones, and even then, one has to work hard.[74]

On several occasions, Biard remarks on the fertility of the land – for instance, when presenting St.-Sauveur in terms of as perfect a site as anyone could wish for:

> This place is a pretty hill that rises gently, on the coast, and is watered on its sides by two springs. The earth there is divided into [sections of] 20 to 25 *arpents,*[75] covered with grass in some parts to the height of a man. It faces the South and East, almost at the mouth of the Pentegoet, into which flow several pleasant, fish-filled rivers. The earth is black, rich [*gras*], and fertile. The port and harbour are the most beautiful that can be seen and in the right place for commanding views over all the coast; the harbour in particular is protected by a lake and in addition is separated from the mountains [Monts Deserts] by a large island, and

> there are also some small islands that break up the waves and winds and thus strengthen its entrance. There is no fleet that it could not hold nor ships too high to approach the land to discharge cargo there.[76]

All in all, the generally high quality of the land found in New France provided a material argument for colonization that complemented the Jesuits' spiritual rationale. It was portrayed as

> another France in terms of celestial influences, and conditions, and in terms of the elements: in extent a land ten or twelve times larger [than France]; in quality, at least as good, if cultivated; in situation, on the other bank of our "river" [*rivage*, meaning here "the Atlantic"], capable of yielding us knowledge of, and dominion over, the sea and navigation.

Finally, New France was seen as "another France and another Spain [together] to cultivate."[77]

The Jesuit missionaries' commitment to colonization derived from premises radically at odds with those of the trader or soldier. Biard's labelling of the Native peoples he encountered as *sauvages* is likely to mislead us, as the seventeenth-century understanding of this word was closer to today's "Natives," denoting people much less aggressive than the English word "savages" suggests and is closer to today's usage of the term "primitive." He chose the word "sauvages" to signify these people's forest habitat and the exotic character of their lifestyle; as a later Jesuit missionary, Paul Ragueneau, would remark in 1646, "Although they live in the woods, they are nonetheless men."[78] Perhaps "sauvages" is best understood in the current context as denoting otherness and, moreover, best interpreted in terms of its function within a text anticipating otherness before the subject is even encountered.[79] In consequence of Biard's depiction of New France as an Eden, he portrays the Native peoples he encountered there not so much as some kind of lesser mortals but, on the contrary, as pre-Lapsarian creatures.[80] Regardless of their "extreme nudity of dress," they enjoyed noteworthy "riches of the soul."[81] Due to their dependence on hunting and fishing, they, in common with Adam prior to the Fall, "do not labour at all":

> This nation is one of *sauvages*, wanderers, unaccustomed to our way of life ... it is *sauvage*, running around in the forests, lacking literacy, government or good manners; it is one of restless wanderers, lacking houses, relationships, possessions, or fatherland.[82]

Like Adam, they therefore, quite explicitly, have all their needs provided for by Biard's God, with whom they implicitly live in harmony, even if they remain ignorant of His existence:

> The fatherly protection of our good God, who does not abandon even the sparrows, has in no way left these poor creatures, who are disposed toward recognizing Him, without provisions that they can hunt, provided for them month by month, since different game is provided for them in each season.[83]

Biard goes so far as to present these simple people as morally superior to educated, civilized westerners. He notes that these sauvages lacked any inclination toward theft,[84] to the extent that he felt safer living among them than he did in Paris; whereas there one had to bolt the door against robbers, in New France one had to close it only against the wind.[85] Elsewhere he remarks: "These good folk are far from this accursed greed that we see amongst ourselves, which in order to gain the wealth of the dead, desires and pursues the loss, and death, of the living."[86] Hence, he deduces, the absence of theft among these Natives. He also observes that divorce and adultery were rare among them,[87] adding that their women were modest *(pudique)* and did not indulge in any shameful *(honteuse)* behaviour, while the men were discreet (not *impudent*).[88] Indeed, the Natives possessed the virtues that Christians should have demonstrated but failed to:

> They are never in any way ungrateful [*ingrat*] toward one another; they share everything among themselves. None of them would ever dare to refuse another's request, showing him the door, nor eat without first sharing whatever he had with another.[89]

Overall, their whole demeanour reflected a state of pre-Lapsarian harmony, leaving them utterly without worry and able to live entirely in the present.[90] This tacitly excused them from thinking of the future or from preparing for anticipated hardships, with the effect that they failed to plan accordingly (for instance, they rarely stored food for winter).[91] Given the Christian piety common to author and reader alike, Biard's text seems calculated to evoke Christ's admonitions to his disciples, whose lack of faith made Him compare them unfavourably with the birds of the air or the lilies in the field, who trust God to provide for their needs. The message delivered implicitly through such an allusion is that "life is more than food and the body more than clothing" and, indeed, that whoever seeks the Kingdom of God will find their material needs provided for by their Divine Father.[92] The "Canadins" contrasted starkly with the French in never feeling the need to hurry:

> These Natives [*sauvages*] are hardly ever seen rushing about, as all their days are just beautiful pastimes. They never rush. Quite different from us, who never know how to do anything without hurry and worry [*presse et oppresse*]. I say "worry" because our desire enslaves us and banishes all peace from our activities.[93]

The Natives were not only better able to enjoy the divine creation than were sophisticated French Catholics but, in turn, also led lives more open to meditating upon it and thus to entering into communion with their Creator.

All in all, Biard effectively depicts these Natives in ways that make them appear to us like Rousseauian "noble savages."[94] He opens his chapter dealing specifically with the natural disposition *(le naturel)* of the Natives, along with their clothing, homes, and lifestyle, as follows:

> The natural condition of our Natives [*sauvages*] is to be generous [*liberal*] and in no way malicious: they have a mind that is quite lively [*gaillard*] and clear [*net*], and in whatever concerns the appraisal [*l'estime*] and discernment [*jugement*] of material or ordinary [*communes*] things, they deduce their reasonings [*raisons*] most agreeably [*gentiment*], always rendering them more piquant [*assaisonnant*] with some attractive similitude.[95]

The Natives' state of pre-Lapsarian purity was expressed through their appearance, "always beautiful and harmoniously composed [*bien prinse*], as if we remained at the state we had at the age of twenty five." Biard claims that he had never met an Indian who was "beer-bellied, hunchbacked or ill-made: leprous, gout-stricken, afflicted by gall-stones, or mad – they don't know what these are." By contrast, the Indians immediately remarked upon how they found the French who came to Canada "defective [*tarez*], for example, one-eyed, cross-eyed or squinting, pug-nosed, and so on."[96]

Consequently, Biard concludes: "You will see that these poor barbarians, regardless of their so great lack of political organization [*police*], power, letters, arts, and wealth, nevertheless hold such great account of themselves that they much despise us, magnifying themselves above us."[97] In Biard's terms, the Natives' outer beauty expressed an inner reality, the behaviour of these uneducated people putting that of the supposedly more civilized French to shame. The latter are deemed "most miserable" in comparison with the Native Canadians, for these Natives were "not at all inclined towards robbery." It therefore grieved

God that Christians who went to Canada behaved scandalously, such that the Natives said, "We aren't robbers like you."[98] Biard thereby attracts his readers' attention by reversing their expectations, presenting the sauvages as more virtuous than educated, civilized westerners, such as themselves.[99]

Biard even goes so far as to say, "For to see a group of French beyond reproach, and without mistrust, envy, and gossip among them, is as difficult as to see the sea without waves, to the extent that it is not within cloisters and monasteries that grace predominates over nature."[100] He thus implies that it was in the Canadian wilderness, in the persons of these Natives, that one could witness the triumph of divine grace, rather than in monks and nuns back in supposedly Christian France. The Jesuits' Thomist theology – in opposition to the Augustinian theology of contemporary Protestants and Jansenists alike – emphasized the human's innate goodness rather than his or her fallen nature, thereby allowing the possibility that a pagan could lead a good life – if not the best one – even in ignorance of the Christian God.[101] Biard emphasizes the friendly character of the Natives toward the French, commenting on how "this good-natured people ... stretch out their hands to us with an incredible desire, and so deep a sadness to see us rise to leave."[102] Although the later cruel torture and murder of Jesuits by Iroquois would inevitably modify their fellow missionaries' view thereafter of this tribe,[103] they would fundamentally retain Biard's view of the Natives in general as noble savages amiably disposed toward them.[104] Throughout, they would explain any misbehaviour by these Natives as resulting from their corruption by westerners. From the very outset, the Natives were friendly toward the Jesuits, except when other westerners had "interfered"; for instance, Biard came across one tribe, the "Excommuniqois" (Eskimos), who had turned implacably against all white men after having been swindled by Europeans in bartering goods with them.[105] In particular, the Jesuits would hold responsible those European traders who exploited Indian tribes as sources for furs and skins, bartered in exchange for alcohol and firearms; the acquisition of these powerful European weapons had led the Natives to kill their enemies more readily, instead of imprisoning and then ransoming them. Biard also notes the increased mortality among Natives due to their excessive consumption of wine and spirits, supplied to them by European traders, because the Natives were not used to alcohol.[106] Taken together, these goods acquired from Europeans wrought a disastrous change in the Natives' behaviour, leading to both internecine decimation and aggression against other foreigners; Biard hints that he feels it was with some justification that the Indians held those giving them these goods responsible for their subsequently delinquent behaviour. The Jesuits thus promulgated a view of the Native peoples very different from that held by the traders.

Hence the tension between Jesuits and traders and the discrepancies between their accounts, each trying to justify themselves at the expense of the other.

Biard concluded that, if one only considered their "temporal felicity" – their earthly state – the Canadian Natives were probably better off than the French because their innate state of happiness and contentment was worth more than the far greater quantity of material goods enjoyed by the French.[107] As a Jesuit, however, this consideration was outweighed by that of the Natives' natural – or eternal – felicity.

COLONIZATION AS REDEMPTION

From the outset, Biard introduces this perception of the Edenic state of New France and of the pre-Lapsarian condition of its Native inhabitants together with his belief that Catholic colonization offered the only way of redeeming this land for God and thereby of obtaining divine blessing for it. Catholic mission alone could simultaneously assure the fulfilment of the latent promise inherent in the land and in its Native people alike:

> Where can any Christian more effectively bring about the rise of good, than where their position brings bodily and spiritual felicity together to strengthen [those people]; and where else, as a great instrument for God, can it make a Paradise out of a desert?[108]

Significantly, Biard reiterates this message in his concluding chapter, devoted to arguing why the French should cultivate New France. He plays on the emotions of his readers, telling them that they should be moved by hearing how "we [French] leave poor New France untended, in the secular and spiritual domains alike, leaving it in barbarianism and paganism."[109]

Throughout, Biard states his belief in the need to cultivate the spiritual realm as well as the material "at the same time" and "in the same proportion."[110] His *Relation* concludes with a detailed argument justifying colonization on spiritual grounds. If the French Catholics didn't fulfil their religious duty there toward the Natives, they would put the Native Canadians in danger of falling into heresy, not least because of the presence of British and Breton Protestants fishing and trading skins. If the French did not support Catholic missions for "these poor people, these images of our God, like us, and capable of enjoying Him as much as we do," the blood of these Natives would be on their hands.[111]

It needs to be noted that Biard is arguing not simply for any kind of colonization but specifically for Christian (in fact, Catholic) colonization, a subject to which he devotes an entire – indeed, the concluding – chapter. He therefore criticizes the official policies, which in order to reduce state expenditure had offered private individuals advantages, such as title to land or commercial monopoly, in exchange for their promises of colonization:

> The worst would be when this mad vanity befalls folk who flee the ruin of their lands in France: since what infallibly happens when such covetous people are involved is not just that, half-blind they reign over the blind, but also that, being as blind as they are, they rush into the precipice of misery, where it would be possible to build instead a fortress of Christianity, [that they make] a cave of robbers, a nest of brigands, a receptacle of bandits [*escumeurs*],[112] a refuge for scoundrels [*pendarts*], a workshop for scandal and all kinds of wickedness.[113]

Hence the spiritual imperative for wealthy French Christians to sponsor the Mission proposed by the Jesuits.[114]

In Biard's vision for Canada, physical or material improvements were – not surprisingly – intrinsically linked with spiritual salvation. The Jesuit Mission would also bring the Natives "to some degree of perfection in the arts, sciences, and knowledge in general [*raison*]," successively improving their level of general thought *(philosophie),* then their civil government *(police),* their lifestyle, and finally, their material comfort.[115]

Biard was convinced of the need for the settlement of the Natives as a prerequisite to their redemption and, through this redemption, that of the land itself. Reading through Biard's *Relation,* one senses another biblical parallel being drawn – once more, tacitly – between the Natives' current nomadic lifestyle and that of the Children of Israel wandering in the wilderness. In both cases, the unsettled lifestyle of the hunter-gatherer tribe is seen as a period of preparation for the more evolved lifestyle of the settled agrarian cultivator, which will enable the fulfilment of the potential inherent in the people and their land alike. Throughout, Biard refers to the Canadian forests as "deserts"; for example, he asks his readers in a parenthesis, "Aren't these evidently deserts, all the land being nothing but an endless forest?"[116] In early-modern French, the word meant any place that was not yet settled and that was therefore uncultivated and by extension uncivilized; as Biard would probably have been aware, his compatriot Samuel de Champlain had already (in 1604) named the mountains near the Jesuit settlement of St.-Sauveur "Monts Desert," specifically because he found its peaks "all bare and rocky,"[117] and a century later French explorers would use the word *désert* in this way in referring to the bayous of Louisiana.

At the outset, Biard invokes this desert-like forest as a physical metaphor for a barren spiritual state, saying that in front of Satan lies a Paradise of delicacies (namely lands enlightened by Christianity), while behind him lies the solitude of the desert.[118] He reinforces this point by evoking the past glories of Greece and Palestine through allusion to the same metaphor: each had been "once a beautiful Eden, today a pitiful desert."[119]

Biard explicitly sets up an opposition between the state of bliss embodied in an existence within a garden setting, symbolic of Paradise, and that of misery inherent in the desert life, representing Hell.[120] One should recall here Biard's use of the word "inculte," meaning at once the uncultivated state of land and the uneducated, and by extension uncivilized, condition of its Native inhabitants. Hence the significance of his selection of metaphor to open his *Relation* – a metaphor at once agricultural and scriptural – namely harvest: it is "our holy faith, from which we cast some seeds in these New Lands, with hope for making from this a plentiful harvest."[121] Nevertheless, in the Christian tradition – from the Desert Fathers in Egypt, inspired by Christ's own forty day sojourn in the wilderness, onward – the desert was simultaneously viewed more positively, as a place of retreat from the manmade world and its distractions, a place where one could more easily encounter the Divine and be open to His calling. Moreover, deserts were seen as places with special potential for revealing the glory of God, such arid surroundings endowing any event set in them with a sense of the miraculous and thus with a demonstration of God's transformative – indeed, redemptive – powers. The Jesuit vision of colonization of such places was therefore radically different from that of other colonizers, whether commercial or royal, in that it was conceived as a means of making the Divine more visible, thus intrinsically constituting an effective means of mission.

Furthermore, coming from Grenoble, Biard would have been well aware of a related concept of "desert" – indeed, one specifically French and Catholic – namely that used by the Carthusians to denote their properties. Their famous mother house of the Grande Chartreuse was situated in the mountain range (the Chartreux) overlooking Grenoble.[122] In addition, this monastery, far from any other human settlement and accessible only on foot, was hidden within deep forests, a situation resonating with that in which he found himself in Canada. Effectively a Christian colony implanted into physically inhospitable but morally untainted territory, the Chartreuse would have provided him with a physical model for a hermetic community of individuals living in communion with God and – being dependent upon sustainable exploitation of its land – with His divine creation. In this case, a series of small houses, each with its own garden, was linked with a series of places for communal use (refectory, chapel, and so on), arranged so as to form a solid defence against external forces and resulting in such an iconic form as has proven capable of inspiring secular architects and planners right down to modern times.[123] Yet even without this particular model, colonization of the kind envisaged by the Jesuits thus became a spiritual imperative for French Christians, support of which could therefore help them to attain their own spiritual redemption.

THE JESUITS' CULTURAL BAGGAGE: "OUR WAY" OF SEEING AND THINKING

The worldview to which Lyonese Jesuits adhered in the seventeenth century – a Thomist one – underlay their own theories of perception and mental processing and therefore their interpretation of what they saw in New France. Their Thomism was an updated version of Thomas Aquinas's specific school of philosophy, developed within medieval Scholasticism. It was successful within such a Counter-Reformation cultural milieu because of its resolution of the intellectual problem of how to accommodate Christianity with ancient philosophy, in this case specifically that of Aristotle, who here acquired authority almost equal to that of Scripture itself. It seems more than coincidental that Aristotle is explicitly evoked as a principal authority in Biard's *Relation*.[124]

According to this philosophical standpoint, whatever is accessible to the physical senses (above all, to that of sight) through the material evidence provided by way of particular objects is a manifestation of some universal form(s) otherwise inaccessible to these physical senses, and thus also to the mind, since the latter depends upon such sensory data in order to perceive anything existing in the external, material world; in the technical terminology of Aristotelian philosophy, "form" can become accessible to the human mind only through "matter." Whatever is accessible to the physical senses is of secondary importance to these universal forms, but such forms depend upon their material manifestation through physical objects in order to be brought within the grasp of human minds. It is therefore important to learn to look correctly so as to be able to perceive the deeper meanings – indeed, the inner realities – incorporated in material things; hence the spiritual imperative to exploit visual imagery but to do so – as is exemplified by Ignatius of Loyola's Spiritual Exercises and other devotional practices developed by the early Jesuits – in order ultimately to "see God in all things."

The firsthand – or rather eyewitness – nature of the accounts of Canada written by Jesuit missionaries there ensured that these were thus automatically imbued with a special significance. For by relating their own observations of particular natural phenomena, the Jesuits were offering their readers divinely created images (thus they explicitly presented the Natives [*sauvages*] as "images of our God");[125] these therefore contained – hidden within and thus invisible to the physical eye – those qualities characterizing the imageless Creator. These Jesuits interpreted such material images in terms of their own theologically conditioned expectations of this creation, which differed somewhat from their Protestant counterparts' reading of the divine "Book of Nature," mainly because of the Catholic belief in the Christian's duty to work out his or her salvation through righteous deeds, as opposed to the Protestant reliance on divine grace alone. The Catholic perspective allowed a greater role for human intervention in fulfilling the divine plan for redeeming creation to its pre-Lapsarian state; indeed, it imposed a duty upon Catholics to take an active role in such a task – in this case, through mission and colonization.

The key issue here is that, for these Jesuits, the spiritual and divine were accessible only through material images since the human mind could not apprehend abstractions by any other means. In Thomism the paired terms "essence" and "accident" have specific, technical meanings. On the one hand, "essence" refers to the intrinsic nature or character of something, that which makes it what it is, whatever that thing must have in order not to be something else; on the other hand, "accident" refers to any property or quality not essential to a substance or object. Midway through his *Relation,* Biard explains that he has arranged it so as first (in the preceding sections) to present his observations in thematic and generalized form and then (in the following sections) to relate a chronological account of the Jesuits' experiences in New France in greater detail. His explicit intention here is thus to follow up his presentation of generalized observations with a series of specific examples through which the reader will be better able to grasp and remember underlying truths of a more universal nature, thus effectively moving from "essence" to "accident." Indeed, in this explanatory passage he carefully uses the word "accident" in this strictly technical sense: he says that in the sections to follow he will give his readers a detailed account of the Jesuits' activities in order to enable a better appreciation of the lands and their natural condition and that he will do so specifically as a means of aiding readers to appreciate the "accidents" of the Jesuits' particular Mission described here.

He then spells this out more clearly, saying that he will show the readers "events so numerous and so diverse, and such unforeseen outcomes [*fortunes*] and subjects [*articles*] that the reader will be able to conceive [*former*] knowledge of right conduct [*prudence*] from it":

> For in truth, it is one thing to philosophize theoretically, and quite another to work out a hypothesis in practice: [it is one thing] to mould [*mouler*] one's abstract ideas in the privacy of one's own room, and [another thing] to bring into daylight [*esclorre*] actualities in front of other men: [one thing] to work freely in abstract types, and then [another to] find oneself enslaved to any given place, time, persons, and a thousand other things, only of secondary importance, but which nevertheless very tightly tie one down; these lack any value, yet often force one to change one's mind, or force a change in one's condition. Well, knowledge of right conduct is acquired, and acted upon, through experiencing, and reacting to, such specific circumstances; not by cursory, nor generalized, glimpses, or apprehensions.[126]

Biard concludes in justifying the detailed description of the Jesuits' experiences that follows by stating that his ultimate rationale here is to enable the reader to "acknowledge God's truly fatherly, sweet and admirable providence toward those who call on Him for help and trust in Him through all the dangers and varied situations of this life, many of which will be seen here."[127]

In other words, by exploiting their experiences of Canada so as to create a series of vivid images in their readers' minds (a practice that the Jesuits taught in their colleges – *ekphrasis* being a rhetorical technique – and to Marian congregations alike), the Jesuits believed that they could move their French readers to act in ways leading toward their own salvation, that of the Canadins now becoming a means as much as an end. This strategy was deemed realistic because, in Thomism, images are held to have a greater ability than anything else to "delight" the mind, thereby literally animating their viewer and moving him or her to act.[128] Such an understanding of the efficacy of images equally underwrote the Jesuits' approach toward the Natives as potential converts. Biard therefore writes that he saw it as a Christian duty to "little by little tame the Natives' senses to the sight, use and fashion of Christianity, visiting them, and giving them some taste for piety, even if this was only fleeting."[129] He later recounts how he therefore "prayed to God in front of them, and showed them images, and signs [*marques*] of our belief."[130] Biard claims that showing the Natives such visual manifestations – enacted images – was effective, in the sense of moving them to attend his celebration of the Mass; in remarking that they did "not often [see] such spectacle," he hints that this further affected them.[131] He thus believed that one should first show Christianity, to the Natives' eyes and ears, before catechizing them in words. The Jesuits therefore catechized as much as possible without full use of language, "by eyes, and by ears" – in other words, "by making them see our usage and ceremonies, and getting them used to these." For instance, they encouraged the Natives to join in processions, letting the children walk in front of the cross and letting adults carry the lights.[132]

Thomist philosophy determined these Jesuits' psychology of mind, which they in turn applied again in anticipating the likely response both of the Native peoples whom they encountered in Canada and of their French readers. Within this particular model of human perception and conception, imagination *(phantaisie)* and memory are the mental faculties that are most easily trained and whose adequate development is a prerequisite for training the higher faculties of judgment and understanding. Within the Jesuits' model of mental processing, both imagination and memory rely upon manipulating "images" accessible to the five external senses – sight, hearing, smell, taste, and touch – whereas judgment and understanding depend instead upon a comparable ability to manipulate abstractions. In this model, the external senses transmit corporeal images (called *espèces*) to the mind (*esprit* or *phantaisie*), which then converts these into incorporeal images (called *phantosmes/phantasmes* or *images spirituelles*) in order to render them accessible to the soul or will. There is consequently ambiguity due to the French language of the time, the word *spirituel* primarily being the adjective derived from the noun *esprit,* meaning (among other things) "mind" but also already conveying something of its more common sense today, that of the English word "spiritual." From the standpoint of this model, only those who have been educated to a level where their faculties of judgment and understanding are sufficiently developed to enable them to manipulate abstractions – including the vital tenets of Christian doctrine, such as salvation, redemption, and so on – are capable of having their souls or wills moved and thus of attaining salvation; conversely, those incapable of manipulating abstractions implicitly lie beyond salvation.[133]

THE "NATURAL" MIND: THINKING DEPENDENT UPON IMAGES

Biard proceeds to argue so as to imply that the Natives' spiritual value equalled that of Europeans. Yet within the context of the Jesuits' beliefs and understandings of mental processing, together with their implications for Christian salvation, his description of the minds of the Canadian Natives he had met acquires a painful significance. For although they exhibited virtuoso skills in their dealing with material imagery, they totally lacked any ability to deal with abstractions:

> They have a very good memory for anything which is embodied, such as having seen you, or the qualities of a place where they have been, or of what has been

> done in front of them, [and memory of such things can go back] twenty ... [or even] thirty years. But to learn by heart, there lies the stumbling block [*l'escueil*]: there is no way of putting into their thick skulls [*caboche*] a logical sequence [*tirade rengée*] of [abstract] words.[134]

Given the spiritual implications of these underdeveloped mental faculties, one appreciates why the Jesuits, despite their belief in the redemptive power of colonization, accorded a higher priority to the education of Natives than to their settlement.

Biard had noted the paucity of abstraction in the Native languages and the intrinsic relation between this lack and their inadequacy for expressing his religion: "The Natives say that they believe in a god, but they have no specific word for god, using the same word as they do for the sun. They know no prayers, nor any rites for worship, simply turning towards the sun."[135] A little further on he notes that "the Natives believe in the immortality of the soul and the recompense of good or evil deeds," but their belief system extends no further than this because they are living in a subsistence economy, where survival is their sole preoccupation.[136]

The Jesuits' mission, already greatly hindered by this circumstance, was further exacerbated by their own ignorance of the Native languages. Their study of these revealed further shortcomings in them for the purpose of evangelization. Enough was known of the Natives' languages for simply bartering with them but not for the more complex issues presented in trying to explain spiritual truths.[137] Biard wrote that the Jesuits were

> forced to learn the language for themselves, interrogating the Natives as to how they called each thing. And the need for it was not at all painful, so long as whatever they asked could be touched or shown to the eye; a stone, a river, a house; to hit, to jump, to laugh, to sit down. But [when it came to] internal, and spiritual, activities, which cannot be shown to the senses, and to words that are called abstract, and universal, like to believe, to doubt, to hope, to debate, to apprehend, an animal ... a body, a substance, a spirit, virtue, vice, sin, reason, justice, etc. [words were lacking].[138]

The Jesuits realized that such study of the indigenous languages was absolutely crucial to their mission. Giving themselves to the study and apprenticeship of the Native *(sauvage)* language, the Jesuits deemed it a good means of forcing themselves to learn the use, and lifestyles, of the land. So they went and lived among these "natural" people, wandering and running around with them over mountains and through valleys and living in their style in terms of society and bodily needs.[139] In pursuit of this work, the fathers had "beat their brains," as the task seemed as difficult – and perhaps as futile – as the alchemist's search for the philosopher's stone.[140] Such difficulties further predisposed the Jesuits to use images, instead of words, in their evangelization of the Natives, a situation repeated – no doubt for similar reasons – in Jesuit missions to other "natural" peoples, whether in the southern Americas or the Indies. Moreover, the mere perception of images would not suffice since salvation depended upon a sensual engagement that drew the viewer into a more profound interaction with them, to the extent of moving his or her will. Consequently, only meaningful images *(images spirituelles)* had any value for this objective; yet all creation, being divine in origin, could potentially be used for this purpose, so long as viewers could be trained how to see it by engaging inner as well as outer eyes.

CONCLUSION: RE-VIEWING THE FRENCH CONSTRUCTION OF NEW FRANCE

The purpose of this chapter is to provide a contextualized (re)reading of the earliest Jesuit account of Canada so as to enable a re-viewing of those French perceptions and conceptions of this place that framed its (re)construction as New France. The original writer's state of shock on encountering this unknown place – its unimaginable otherness, both the natural wilderness and the minds of the "natural" people inhabiting it – would often "force a change" in his own mind and, he hoped, in those of his readers who were changed by the virtual experience of Canada provided by his book;[141] only subsequently, through their support, could the French Jesuits effect any change to the land and people that had so changed them. Meanwhile, and perhaps paradoxically, the mechanism employed for negotiating this state of shock was an attempt at normalizing the experience by trying to understand it through comparison with the known environment of the writer's homeland and by trying to convey it to his fellow citizens back home through familiar similitudes.

Having assumed comparability between France and New France on rational and scientific grounds, the French Jesuits attempted to transplant familiar agricultural techniques, simply adapting and modifying them pragmatically in response to climatic exigencies. It is in this context that we should therefore view the French importation to Canada of French vernacular architecture (likewise pragmatically modified in response to climate and to indigenous resources), which has been well documented by scholars such as Alan Gowans and Harold Kalman.[142] In other words, we should discern in the Jesuits' transfer of French models here the same tacit, normalizing belief in the essential comparability of the two "Frances."

For the French Jesuits, the key difference between these two places consisted not so much in physical factors as in conceptual – indeed, spiritual – ones; the crucial difference was not one immediately apparent to the physical senses, being an issue of one's state of harmony with the Divine. They did not see New France, with its seemingly primitive but innocent Natives, in terms of a Stone Age society, as it has usually appeared to recent historians. Instead, for them, it represented a pre-Lapsarian Eden, inhabited by "natural" people, now falling under threat of contamination by civilized but corrupted – and corrupting – Europeans. For spiritual reasons, it was vital to make Christian readers aware of the potential perils here so as to enable them to avoid unconsciously contributing toward engendering this peril and to encourage them instead to support the Jesuits' alternative. In expounding Canada in Edenic terms, the Jesuits presented it as offering Christians a second chance to fulfil God's original intention for man, of living in harmony with Him, as the Native Canadins thus appeared to do, and of working with Him as responsible stewards of His creation. The discovery of Canada opened up a new opportunity to Christians, that of continuing the Creator's work by working toward the fulfilment of this Eden's innate potential.

Colonization thus acquired a spiritual value in its potential not only to redeem Native people spiritually but equally to realize, and make manifest, the land's divine potential. In undertaking these tasks simultaneously, colonization promised that both the physical "desert" of endless forest and the metaphysical one of spirits – "minds and souls" – would blossom into the state intended for them in the divine vision for creation, the one providing the visible image necessary for expressing the other to human minds incapable of grasping abstractions (as Jesuits perceived Native minds to be). Moreover, the fact of realizing this within the forest wilderness – against the bleak background of a "desert" – would dramatize such an achievement, thus ensuring that it would make a greater impact upon Christians "viewing" it from the far side of the Atlantic. The French Jesuits' concern to prevent the usurping of French sovereignty in New France by Protestants (whether British or Dutch traders or French Huguenots) needs to be regarded within this holistic perspective rather than within the narrower one of making short-term improvements to the Natives' well-being or even converting individuals. Hence their concern not only to raise financial support from devout individuals but also to secure state or royal protection for their Canadian Missions or, more precisely, Catholic colonies.

The Jesuits' conviction that they needed to save these pure, pre-Lapsarian Natives from European corruption explains why they envisaged settling these Natives together with French Catholics but separate from other Europeans. In so doing, they would, however, not merely be preventing negative outcomes but also be attempting to create material images of their obedience to humankind's divinely appointed vocation, that of working in harmonious partnership with God to enable the fulfilment of divine creation. Consequently, the Jesuits' model for their communities could not be the town – a human response to the post-Lapsarian condition – but rather the garden, the original vision in which all creation lived in harmony, together, and with its Creator. Yet their consequent establishment of self-sustaining agricultural communities was at once visionary – in a prophetic sense too – and pragmatic, fitting the geographically dictated conditions of New France. Nevertheless, although the Society of Jesus would later be able to establish settlements, a variety of vested interests – the commercial ones of fur traders and political ones of the Crown – would combine to prevent the full realization of Biard's proposal, and the problems that had beset earlier French attempts at settling New France would recur.[143]

As for those Jesuit settlements that would subsequently be realized, their regular geometries should be read not merely in pragmatic terms, as optimal defence systems, but also in symbolic terms, as expressing divine – universal and ideal – harmony through visible order. They were after all being built by Jesuits as material images that would enable humans to accede to invisible and immaterial truths, to forms (in Thomist and Aristotelian terms) that would otherwise remain inaccessible to them. It might also be worth exploring whether this model of Catholic settlement owes any debt to the settlement of a wilderness close to Biard's birthplace, that of the Carthusian "desert."

Nevertheless, despite their self-imposed incentive to establish such settlements, the Jesuits accorded an even higher priority to establishing *seminaires:* colleges for Natives and French colonists, boys and girls. The building of such colleges was accorded greater resources than even churches, which, significantly, were often embedded within them. Again the Jesuits' procedure needs to be understood in symbolic terms, as articulating their theological beliefs, rather than in merely pragmatic ones. The material image they thus created – of college dominating the township – reflected their belief in the priority of education due to the need to develop certain mental faculties as a prerequisite to spiritual salvation and thence to co-working with God in the fulfilment of His divine plan for creation. The college buildings conformed as closely as possible to a pragmatically derived but universally applied, and therefore abstracted, ideal plan. Developed for use throughout France, this was then deemed appropriate for New France due to the perceived comparability of these two places. Furthermore, in realizing this model, as with that of the settlement, the Jesuits erected a material image through which one could access a universal truth otherwise inaccessible to bodily humans – in this case, that of the need to train the spirit in order to accede to the Divine.

The crucial role accorded to the image in Thomist theology and Ignatian spirituality alike, and thence in Jesuit mission, explains, in more than merely pragmatic terms, why the Jesuits treated their buildings as supports for symbolic decorations and as theatres for acting out rites at once significant and signifying. Given their Thomist and Aristotelian belief in how universal forms could be made manifest only through a diversity of material images, and consequently the exploitation of images in Ignatian devotional practices, we can now better appreciate their architecture from this early period, as conveyed to us through descriptions or, more rarely, depictions: simple, legible building types, often evoking well-known European models (notably the Jesuit college), with figurative decoration that was usually more indigenous in character. Faced with Natives who had proved incapable of understanding any abstractions, Jesuits deployed imagery so as to express Christian dogma through figures, notably indigenous ones, as these would render it most accessible to them.[144] Thomist theology's emphasis on the human's innate, divine image did not presuppose any inevitable superiority of European culture, so the Jesuits believed in the possibility of an indigenous Christian culture as much as that of its French equivalent.[145] They sought to change the Natives' religion and their level of civilization but not their culture, rather letting them retain as much of their own culture as was compatible with Christian doctrine and practice. In other words, Thomist theology permitted assimilation of Native imagery without compromise of Christian doctrine; more Augustinian Christians, notably Jansenists, would perceive this as evidence of excessive accommodation.

The enforced termination of the *Relations* is telling here. For in 1673 the publication of all Jesuit *Relations,* worldwide, was forbidden by Rome.[146] The reason for this was the Chinese-rites controversy, over the Jesuits' assimilation of elements from Native Chinese religion into Christianity, or rather the way in which the Jesuits' opponents – principally Jansenists – had, in the Jesuits' view, misunderstood and misrepresented this enterprise. Within this context, we should perhaps ask whether the paucity of extant decorative works from the early Jesuit Missions in Canada might be due not only to material decay but also to deliberate suppression of such evidence once it was realized how opponents might misunderstand it.

To conclude, what I have suggested here is that we might reread the fabrication of "New France" by sharing the early Jesuits' lens, through which they perceived this new territory and their intentions for it, having been themselves moulded by a particular theological training and devotional praxis. Having entered into such empathy with these fabricators, we shall be able to appreciate better the impact that their seminal writings made on the psyche of the French nation and how in turn its own fabrication of Canada was framed.

ACKNOWLEDGMENTS

I would like to thank Erik Oland, S.J. (Guelph, Ontario), John O'Malley, S.J. (Georgetown University, Washington, DC), and Thomas Worcester, S.J. (Holy Cross College, Worcester, Massachusetts), for their thoughtful and helpful comments on early drafts of this chapter, as well as Geoffrey Samuel (Cardiff University) for reading the final draft.

NOTES

All English translations are my own.

1 These *Relations* were published annually from 1632 to 1673 by Sébastian Cramoisy in Paris and then reprinted in Avignon (papal state) and Lille (imperial territory); see Elie de Comminges, "Les Récits de voyage des Jésuites en Nouvelle France: La Mission du Père Biard (1611-1613)," *French Review* 49, 6 (May 1976): 840, 842. Constituting an unsurpassed collection of contemporary material concerning the French discovery of eastern Canada that had become extremely rare, the series was republished in a three-volume set in Quebec in 1858. Since copies of this in turn became scarce, another edition appeared, this time incorporating much associated material, all with parallel English translation; see Reuben Gold Thwaites, ed., *The Jesuit Relations and Allied Documents: Travels and Explorations of the Jesuit Missionaries in New France, 1610-1791*, 73 vols. (Cleveland, OH: Burrows Bros., 1896-1901). This is now available as part of Early Canadiana Online, www.canadiana.org/ECO; the English translation (alone) is at http://puffin.creighton.edu/jesuit/relations. The appearance of Thwaites's magisterial edition led immediately to numerous review articles, which in turn encouraged much research exploiting this source. More recently, the late Lucien Campeau, S.J., edited nine successive volumes of the Society of Jesus's *Monumenta Novae Franciae* (Rome: Monumenta Historica Societatis Iesu, 1967-2003), containing this material and more, accompanied by fuller notes and critique than Thwaites could provide as an amateur and non-Jesuit; most of this material has in turn been translated into English by William Lonc (with George Topp) and published in eleven volumes in the series *The Jesuit Relations and Allied Documents, 1610-1791: Early Jesuit Missions in Canada* (Halifax: William Lonc, 2002-07).

2 The region called Acadia in the seventeenth (and eighteenth) centuries covered today's three maritime provinces of Canada – New Brunswick, Nova Scotia, and Prince Edward Island – and the State of Maine in the United States.

3 For instance, at the beginning of the twentieth century, Charles Colby (a far from uncritical historian) pointed out the extent to which even the Jesuits' enemies were obliged to rely substantially upon the *Relations*, concluding that "to write of the St. Lawrence Valley or the West without using the Jesuit *Relations* would be almost like writing the history of the Heptarchy without Bede. Their merits are decidedly more prominent than their incompleteness or their shortcomings"; see Charles Colby, "The Jesuit *Relations*," *American Historical Review* 7, 1 (October 1901): 44. Toward the end of the century, Elie de Comminges could still write (specifically of Biard's *Relation;* see below), "en tant que source historique, ces récits ont une valeur inégalable," adding that without them we would know little about

early Canada since the fur traders and loggers left no records; see de Comminges, "Les Récits de voyage," 843-44.

4 Anthropologists and ethnographers have long recognized the utility of the *Relations;* see, for example, Henry S. Spalding, "The Ethnologic Value of the Jesuit *Relations,*" *American Journal of Sociology* 34, 5 (March 1929): 882-89. Innumerable scholarly articles (notably in *Ethnohistory*) continue not only to cite but also to depend upon the *Relations,* which have become the prime authoritative source for seventeenth-century rural Canada (for some regions, they constitute the sole contemporary source). They have therefore become subject to various interpretations; for a good demonstration of this, see the series of articles on Native American demography in *Ethnohistory* 36, 3 (Summer 1989). Daniel Richter judged them to be "a more balanced record ... than might be expected," noting that "when treated with care the *Relations* provide significant insights into political and social aspects of encounters between missionaries and Indians"; see Daniel K. Richter, "Iroquois versus Iroquois: Jesuit Missions and Christianity in Village Politics, 1642-1686," *Ethnohistory* 32, 1 (Winter 1985): 2, 1. In other words, not only the Jesuits' firsthand observations but also their interpretation of them continue to offer a valuable resource to scholars.

5 Travel literature was the single most widely read, and sold, genre in seventeenth-century France; armchair readers became progressively more attracted to accounts of more distant lands due to their inherent exoticism; see François de Dainville, S.J., "Voyages," rev. Philippe Hourcade, in *Dictionnaire des lettres françaises: Le XVIIe siècle,* rev. ed., ed. Georges Grente, 1266-70 (Paris: Fayard, 1996). The classic text on this subject is Geoffroy Atkinson, *The Extraordinary Voyage in French Literature,* vol. 1, *Before 1700* (1920; reprint, New York: Benjamin Franklin, 1967), trans. as *Les relations de voyage du XVIIe siècle et l'évolution des idées, contribution à l'étude de la formation de l'esprit du XVIIe siècle* (1924; reprint, Geneva: Slatkine, 1972). On the impact of American accounts in particular, see Gilbert Chinard, *L'Amérique et le rêve exotique dans la littérature française au XVIIe et XVIIIe siècle* (1934; reprint, Geneva: Slatkine, 1970).

6 Charles Lal(l)ement also wrote *Divers entretiens sur la vie cachée de Jésus-Christ en l'Eucharistie* (Paris: Denys Bechet, 1657); Paul Le Jeune also wrote *Solitude des dix iours sur les plus solides veritez, et sur les plus saintes maximes de l'Evangile* (Paris: Florentin Lambert, 1664) and *Epistres Spirituelles* (Paris: Florentin Lambert, 1665); Jean de Brébeuf also compiled a Huron dictionary (unpublished) and translated into "Canadian" (presumably Huron) Diego de Ledesma's *Doctrine chrestienne* (Rouen: R. L'Allemant, 1630); Paul Ragueneau also wrote *La Vie de la Mere Catherine de Saint Avgustin* (Paris: Florentin Lambert, 1671); and Claude Dablon also wrote a *Relation des missions des évêques français aux royaumes de Siam de la Cochinchine et du Tonkin* (Paris: P. le Petit, 1674).

7 See, for instance, Spalding, "Ethnologic Value," 883; and Colby, "Jesuit *Relations,*" 53. Dainville, "Voyages," 1267, mentions the social range of readership specifically with regard to the *Relations* concerning the Jesuit Missions in Canada.

8 The authors of the *Relations* were Charles Lal(l)ement and Jérôme Lal(l)ement (1626), Paul Le Jeune (1632-41), Jean de Brébeuf (1636), Barthélemy Vimont (1640, 1642, 1643, 1645), Jérôme Lal(l)ement (1645-48), Paul Ragueneau (1650-52), François Le Mercier (1652-54), Jean Le Quen (1655-56), François Le Mercier (1656), Jean Le Quen (1657-58), Jérôme Lal(l)ement (1659-64), Paul Le Jeune (1660-61), François Le Mercier (1664-69), and Claude Dablon (1670-79).

9 These also drew on occasional reports submitted to Rome (see note 29) or private letters to the Jesuit Provincial (see notes 30, 83, 98).

10 The effect of the *Relations'* purpose upon their content is a point often made; for instance, see Richter, "Iroquois versus Iroquois."

11 See also Colby, "Jesuit *Relations,*" 39-41. In the following century (1702-76), the Jesuits' effective sequel to these *Relations* would actually be called *Lettres édifiantes et curieuses.*

12 Marcel Trudel, *The Beginnings of New France, 1524-1663* (Toronto: McClelland and Stewart, 1973), 184-89.

13 Ibid., 182.

14 Ibid., 209.

15 Ibid., 230-31.

16 Ibid., 233-35.

17 Ibid., 237-40.

18 Ibid., 241.

19 Although publication was suspended from 1673, the Jesuits continued to write *Relations* until the end of the 1670s, in anticipation of once more being permitted to publish them.

20 The central volumes are largely derived from the Annual Letters, supplemented by material drawn from Sagard's *Long Journey*. The first couple of volumes, covering the Jesuits' arrival in Canada and the period prior to it, also draw on the devout Champlain's *Voyages* (but not, of course, the work of the anti-Jesuit Lescarbot). The final volume depends heavily upon du Creux's conversations with the Jesuit missionaries Isaac Jogues and Giuseppe Bressani to supplement the material drawn from the *Relations*.

21 Pierre Biard, S.J., *Relation de la Nouvelle France, de ses terres, naturel du païs et de ses habitans; item du voyage des pères Jésuites ausdictes contrées, et de ce qu'ils y ont faict jusques à leur prinse par les Anglois* (Lyons: L. Muguet, 1616). This also appears in Thwaites, ed., *Jesuit Relations*, vol. 3, 21ff. In addition, Thwaites includes Biard's letters of 21 January and 11 June 1611 to Claudio Aquaviva, S.J., General of the Society of Jesus in Rome (vol. 1, 125-37, 188-92), his letter of 10 June 1611 to the Provincial in Paris (vol. 1, 138-83) and Ennemond Massé's of the same day to the Provincial (vol. 1, 184-87), his letters of 31 January 1612 to the Jesuit Provincial in Paris (vol. 2, 3-56) and to the Jesuit General in Rome (vol. 2, 57-118), his annual reports to the Provincial for 1613 and 1614 (vol. 2, 193-286), and his letter of 26 May 1614 to the General (vol. 3, 3-20); none of these is considered here since they were not available to the public in the seventeenth century and therefore could not influence the framing of its view of Canada, the subject of this chapter. Throughout, cited page numbers are from the original Lyonese edition of Biard's *Relation* (which also appear in Thwaites's edition), and the translations are my own, not Thwaites's.

22 Camille de Rochemonteix, S.J., *Les jésuites et la Nouvelle-France au XVIIe siècle*, vol. 1 (Paris: Letouzey and Ané, 1895), 1-84. This is an extremely well-documented study, based on wide archival research and thoroughly referenced throughout.

23 Trudel, *Beginnings of New France*, esp. 276-78.

24 The vernacular use of these two forms, according to season, by several North American tribes has been recognized by anthropologists for over half a century at least; see Cara Richards, "Of Vikings and Longhouses," *American Anthropologist*, n.s., 60, 6, part 1 (1958): 1200, citing articles by Robert Lowie and by John Murray (both writing in 1946).

25 Biard, *Relation*, 41.

26 Ibid., 200.

27 In one of the unpublished sources from which Biard subsequently derived his *Relation*, an account intended for the General of the Society of Jesus in Rome and therefore written in Latin, in place of the French *cabane* he uses the word *tuguriolum*, meaning a small form of *tugurium*, the latter being a hut or cottage such as shepherds or peasants might use; see Pierre Biard, *Missio Canadensis: Epistola ex Portu-Regali in Acadia* (Dillingen: Melchior Algeyer, 1611), 28, 30, reprinted in Thwaites, ed., *Jesuit Relations*, vol. 2, 94-97.

28 Biard, *Relation*, 140. It is worth comparing this with his original account, a private letter written on 10 June 1611, soon after arrival in Canada, to his order's Provincial in Paris. The way Biard rewrote his account in 1616, so as to appeal to a primarily Parisian audience, seems clearer in this passage than any other, as the earlier version is equally dramatic but lacks any specifically Parisian references: "Aucunes des glaces sembloient des isles, autres des petits bourgs, autres des grandes églises ou dômes bien haults, ou superbes chasteaux: toutes flottoient"; first published in Thwaites, ed., *Jesuit Relations*, vol. 1, 150-51.

29 Biard, *Relation,* viii.
30 Ibid., viii, 1-2, 9ff.
31 Ibid., for example, 31, 226. The site of St.-Sauveur was subsequently resettled and is now Bar Harbor, Maine.
32 This early in the century, science (or natural philosophy) was still largely, and in the case of Jesuits exclusively, Aristotelian in its philosophy and therefore emphasized careful and detailed observation of individual natural specimens, from which universal principles were to be deduced. Jesuits were therefore trained in such observation, which no doubt contributed to the appeal of their accounts.
33 Biard, *Relation,* 9-11.
34 Ibid., 10.
35 Ibid., 18.
36 This site later became today's Annapolis, in Maine.
37 Ibid., 11.
38 Ibid.
39 Ibid., 26.
40 Ibid., 31.
41 In early-modern French, a *faisole* was a kind of bean.
42 Ibid., 26-27.
43 Ibid., 19.
44 Ibid., 20.
45 Ibid., 10.
46 Ibid., 11.
47 Ibid., 23ff. In the original French text, the word translated here as "inlets" is an archaic French one, *seins,* which specifically means a gulf or small sea connected to the ocean only by means of a narrow passage.
48 Ibid., 24.
49 Ibid.
50 Ibid., 27.
51 Ibid., 24.
52 Ibid., 25.
53 Ibid., 25. Biard also notes elsewhere that if the land was inhabited, its mineral resources could also be exploited (ibid., 32).
54 Ibid., 30.
55 For example, ibid., 27-29.
56 Rochemonteix, *Jésuites et Nouvelle-France,* vol. 1, 23.
57 At Tournon, Biard taught scholastic theology (1600-04) and at Lyons moral theology (1604-06) and then scholastic theology, with Hebrew (1606-07) (ibid., vol. 1, 23). On returning from Canada, Biard briefly returned to teaching theology at Lyons before resuming his missionary vocation within France (ibid., vol. 1, 83).
58 For instance, Lescarbot, although hostile to the Jesuits, referred to Biard as an "homme fort sçavant," acknowledging that the "Premier Président du Bordeaux lui a fait bon récit" (cited in ibid., vol. 1, 24).
59 This was in fact apparent from the earliest days of the Society of Jesus, Ignatius stipulating that no charge should be made for teaching specifically so as to "répandre le plus possible l'enseignement, de la faire pénétrer dans toutes les classes sociales"; see Camille de Rochemonteix, S.J., *Un Collège de Jésuites aux XVIIè et XVIIIè siècles: Le Collège Henri IV de La Flèche,* vol. 1 (Le Mans: Leguicheux, 1889), 85. On supplementary education provided by Jesuits specifically for adult artisans, see Judi Loach, "Revolutionary Pedagogues? How Jesuits Used Education to Change Society," in *The Jesuits II: Cultures, Sciences, and the Arts, 1540-1773,* ed. John W. O'Malley, S.J., Gauvin Alexander Bailey, Steven J. Harris, and T. Frank Kennedy, S.J., 66-85 (Toronto: University of Toronto Press, 2006).

60 In fact, his father had been a baker; see Lugd. 36, fols. 195-96, Archivum Romanum Societatis Iesu, in Lucien Campeau, *La première mission d'Acadie (1602-16)* (Rome/Quebec: Archivum Romanum Societatis Iesu/Presses de l'Université Laval, 1967), 647-53. See also Rochemonteix, *Jésuites et Nouvelle-France,* vol. 1, 24.

61 Biard, *Relation,* 211.

62 Rochemonteix, *Jésuites et Nouvelle-France,* vol. 1, 83. Nevertheless, his missionary vocation would lead him to return to Canada in 1625-26 and again in 1633, remaining there until his death a decade later; see note 60 and Thwaites, ed., *Jesuit Relations,* vol. 39, 167-73.

63 Carlos Sommervogel, S.J., *Bibliothèque de la Compagnie de Jésus,* vol. 1 (Paris: Picard, 1890), col. 1440; Claude Breghot de Lut and Antoine Péricaud, *Catalogue des Lyonnais dignes de mèmoire* (Paris and Lyons: Techener and Giberton and Brut, 1839), 36. It is significant that Biard's *Relation* was not published in Paris, as is sometimes assumed (including by Thwaites in the "Contents" page of his edited *Jesuit Relations*), but in Lyons, the city where the Provincial of the Jesuit Province covering Grenoble (Biard's hometown) resided.

64 Biard, *Relation,* 9.

65 Ibid., 20.

66 Biard led such disputes in Embrun in 1616 and in Carpentras in 1619; see Rochemonteix, *Jésuites et Nouvelle-France,* vol. 1, 83.

67 See, for example, Biard, *Relation,* 73ff; see also viii.

68 Ibid., 12.

69 Ibid., 12-13.

70 Ibid., 13.

71 Ibid., 17.

72 The lambruche was a type of wild vine found in North America, producing large grapes that were good in flavour but had tough skins.

73 Ibid., 31-32.

74 Ibid., 212-13. It was sufficiently common, at least among the Indians of this region, for the French Canadians to call it the "MicMac potato"; see Thwaites, ed., *Jesuit Relations,* vol. 2, 307n77). It seems most likely that this was the Jerusalem artichoke, indigenous in North America and cultivated by Indians by this date (as Champlain observed in 1605 near Cape Cod and in 1606 at Gloucester); they would be brought to Europe by Italians and so were probably not yet known to the French (ibid., 298n35).

75 An arpent was a land measure roughly equivalent to today's acre.

76 Biard, *Relation,* 224-25.

77 Ibid., 332.

78 Thwaites, ed., *Jesuit Relations,* vol. 29, 281, cited in George R. Healy, "The French Jesuits and the Idea of the Noble Savage," *William and Mary Quarterly,* 3rd ser., 15, 2 (April 1958): 150.

79 Michel de Certeau, S.J., "Montaigne's 'Of Cannibals': The Savage 'I,'" in *Heterologies: Discourse on the Other,* 67-79 (Minneapolis: University of Minnesota Press, 1986). See also Frank Lestringant, *Le cannibale: Grandeur et décadence* (Paris: Perrin, 1994), trans. as *Cannibals: The Discovery and Representation of the Cannibal from Columbus to Jules Verne* (Berkeley: University of California Press, 1997).

80 For variants on this interpretation, see Healy, "French Jesuits"; and J.H. Kennedy, *Jesuit and Savage in New France* (New Haven, CT: Yale University Press, 1950).

81 Biard, *Relation,* ix.

82 Biard's earlier letter to the Jesuit Provincial in Paris, 10 June 1611, first published in Thwaites, ed., *Jesuit Relations,* vol. 1, 170-73.

83 Biard, *Relation,* 42; see also 47. In his unpublished letter (see note 82), Biard paints a less positive image of these Natives – "extremely lazy, greedy, irreligious, treacherous, cruel in their vengeance and given

over to all sorts of luxury" – and estimates that there are not enough of them to justify any missionary activity.

84 Biard, *Relation,* 71.

85 Ibid., 308.

86 Ibid., 92-93.

87 Ibid., 65.

88 Ibid., 66.

89 Ibid., 58.

90 Ibid., 69.

91 Ibid., 69-70.

92 Matthew 6:25, 33; Luke 12:23, 31.

93 Biard, *Relation,* 49.

94 See René Gonnard, *La légende du Bon Sauvage* (Paris: Librairie de Médici, 1946).

95 Biard, *Relation,* 36.

96 Ibid., 38.

97 Ibid., 39. Again, as per note 83, Biard rewrites – indeed, this time virtually contradicts – the views expressed in his initial letter written from Canada to persuade readers to support the Jesuit Mission. Here, he extols as virtuous a people whose behaviour he had previously condemned as being *glorieux,* in the sense of "vainglorious" (i.e., blind to their own faults while critical of those committed by the French); moreover, Biard had felt that they had been led astray by the devil, being blinded by "self-love" into not admitting that only a few of the French behaved so badly and not realizing that their own vices were worse; see Biard's letter to the Jesuit Provincial in Paris, 10 June 1611, first published in Thwaites, ed., *Jesuit Relations,* vol. 1, 138-83, quotations at 172-75.

98 Biard, *Relation,* 71.

99 Ibid., 57. Healy, "French Jesuits," 149, claims that those passages in the *Relations* describing Indians in terms of noble savages invariably relate to Catholic converts, without admitting this to be the case. Although this might be true for the later *Relations,* it is not so in Biard's *Relation,* where the vast majority of the Indians encountered were as yet unconverted.

100 Biard, *Relation,* 57.

101 Healy, "French Jesuits," 146-48, explains these theological underpinnings and their consequences well and in greater detail than space permits here.

102 Biard, *Relation,* 333.

103 In particular, the Jesuit missionaries martyred by the Iroquois from 1646 to 1649 were Isaac Jogues and Jean Lalande in 1646, Antoine Daniel in 1648, and Charles Garnier, Noël Chabanel, Jean de Brébeuf, and Gabriel Lalemant in 1649.

104 For instance, "This simplicity creates for us a golden age"; see Thwaites, ed., *Jesuit Relations,* vol. 18, 89, cited in Colby, "Jesuit *Relations,*" 46.

105 Biard, *Relation,* 33. In this, Biard was diplomatically deflecting attention from the root cause of Iroquois opposition to the French, namely Samuel de Champlain's alliance with the Hurons. Consequently, he defended the latter, with musket power, when the Iroquois attacked them, killing many Iroquois in the process; thereafter, that tribe considered all French to be their enemies.

The Native Abenaki name, Eskimatsie, was corrupted by the French into "Esquimaux" and by the Danes into "Eskimo"; see Thwaites, ed., *Jesuit Relations,* vol. 2, 293n10. The original meaning, "eater of raw flesh," combined with the other tribes' antagonism toward them and the French ignorance of them, was probably the reason why Biard thought they were cannibals (e.g., "Fera gens est, et ut dicatur Anthropophaga"). The French then dubbed them "Excommunicated" ("Excomminqui, sive, ut vulgus indigetat, Excommunicati"); see Biard, *Missio Canadensis,* 9, reprinted in Thwaites, ed., *Jesuit Relations,* vol. 2, 66-67.

106 Biard, *Relation,* 69.

107 Ibid., 97.

108 Ibid., xi.

109 Ibid., 331.

110 Ibid., 103.

111 Ibid., 334-37; see also ibid., Chapter 9, "On the means available to aid these nations to their eternal salvation," 98-101.

112 *Écumeurs* usually means "pirates," but a terrestrial version is presumably intended here.

113 Biard, *Relation,* 99-100.

114 Ibid., 101.

115 Ibid., 74.

116 Ibid., 4: "Deserts sont-ce voirement, tout le pays n'estant qu'une forest infinie?"

117 Champlain led the expedition that landed, on 5 September 1604, on the island now known as Mount Desert Island. He wrote in his journal, "Le so[m]met de la plus part d'icelles est desgarny d'arbres; parce que ce ne sont que rochers. Les bois ne sont que pins, sapins & boulleaux. Ie l'ay no[m]mée l'isle des Monts-deserts." In this context "desert" meant "treeless." See Samuel de Champlain, "Les Voyages du Sieur de Champlain" (Paris: Iean Berjon, 1613), in *The Works of Samuel Champlain,* vol. 1, ed. H.P. Biggar (Toronto: Champlain Society, 1922), 282-83.

118 Ibid., vi, ix.

119 Ibid., viii.

120 Ibid., ix. But this is also the overall message of all of the "Avant-Propos" (ibid., vi-xii).

121 Ibid., iii-iv. Agricultural metaphors are again applied later on, in a comparable reference to the need to work land before sowing it with seed (ibid., 107), reinforcing the hypothesis of Biard's own peasant roots.

122 The order, established by St. Bruno in the late eleventh century, drew its metaphorical usage of the word from a verse in Scripture: "Je vais la séduire, je la conduirais au désert et là je lui parlerai coeur à coeur" (Hosea 2:14). See also Philip Gröning's film of the Grande Chartreuse, *Die Grosse Stille* (2005).

123 The Counter-Reformation's internal renewal of the Catholic Church led to the order's expansion, with a monastery being founded immediately above Lyons, on the Croix-Rousse hill, in 1580; thus both French Jesuits – Biard and Massé – would have had firsthand knowledge of this order's communities. This model of settlement – balancing privacy and community while ensuring harmony with nature – has attracted architects, most notably in modern times Le Corbusier, for whom the Chartreuse at Ema in Italy became the model for his Unité d'habitation.

124 Biard, *Relation,* 30.

125 Ibid., 337.

126 Ibid., 120.

127 Ibid., 120-21.

128 This refers back in part to Horace and his triad of "docere" (teaching) and "delectare" (delighting) leading to "movere" (moving). It also refers to his concept of the parallel between verbal and visual expression, "ut pictura poesis" (usually translated then as "as in painting, so in poetry").

129 Biard, *Relation,* 175.

130 Ibid., 180.

131 Ibid., 177.

132 Ibid., 310.

133 It is from this belief that Biard argues that baptism must be preceded by catechism, and this in the Natives' own language, so that they can reply for themselves rather than via (French) godparents; ibid., 114.

134 Ibid., 36-37.

135 Ibid., 96.

136 Ibid., 96-97.

137 Ibid., 150.

138 Ibid., 150-51.

139 Ibid., 198-99.

140 Ibid., 153.

141 Ibid., 120.

142 Alan Gowans, *Church Architecture in New France* (New Brunswick, NJ: Rutgers University Press, 1955) and *Building Canada: An Architectural History of Canadian Life* (Toronto: Oxford University Press, 1966); Harold Kalman, *A History of Canadian Architecture* (Toronto: Oxford University Press, 1994).

143 Benjamin Sulte, review of *The Jesuit Relations and Allied Documents,* by Reuben Gold Thwaites, *American Historical Review* 2, 3 (1897): 526-27.

144 For a detailed and critical study of the way Jesuits used Indian imagery to impart Christian doctrine, see John Steckley, "The Warrior and the Lineage: Jesuit Use of Iroquoian Images to Communicate Christianity," *Ethnohistory* 39, 4 (Autumn 1992): 478-509.

145 For a similar interpretation, see Healy, "French Jesuits," 152-53.

146 In 1673 Clement X's brief *Creditae nobis caelitus* required all publications to be approved by cardinals at the Propaganda Fide. Due to Louis XIV's refusal to acknowledge the authority of Rome over the French Crown within his kingdom, Jesuits in France could not submit their writings to such censure. Meanwhile, the letters continued to be issued in New France until 1678.

Visibility, Symbolic Landscape, and Power
Jean-Baptiste-Louis Franquelin's View of Quebec City in 1688

MARC GRIGNON

One of the main issues that historians have raised about Canadian culture in the seventeenth century is the early emergence of a North American specificity. The encounter with a new environment and the Amerindian cultures is often believed to have required rapid adaptation on the part of the French colonist. This point of view has strongly influenced the history of Canadian architecture; sometimes formulated in a naive manner, such as in the belief in the spontaneous creativity of seventeenth-century builders, and sometimes formulated with greater sophistication, as in the argument about the clash between French academic models and the North American environment, it has remained a leitmotiv in the historiography of architecture in New France until today. In this view, the need to address the constraints of a new environment would have triggered a pragmatic attitude in builders and clients alike, and this attitude – be it a natural disposition or something imposed on colonists by circumstances – constituted the basis for the transformation of architecture in Canada.[1]

Emphasizing adaptation to material conditions, this perspective fails to seize the full importance of the symbolic dimension of culture, which is the main topic of this book. Indeed, such a heavy focus on the emergence of a distinct North American identity has played down the cultural continuity between France and Canada to an unrealistic degree. Canadian architectural historians naturally want to understand how architecture participated in the

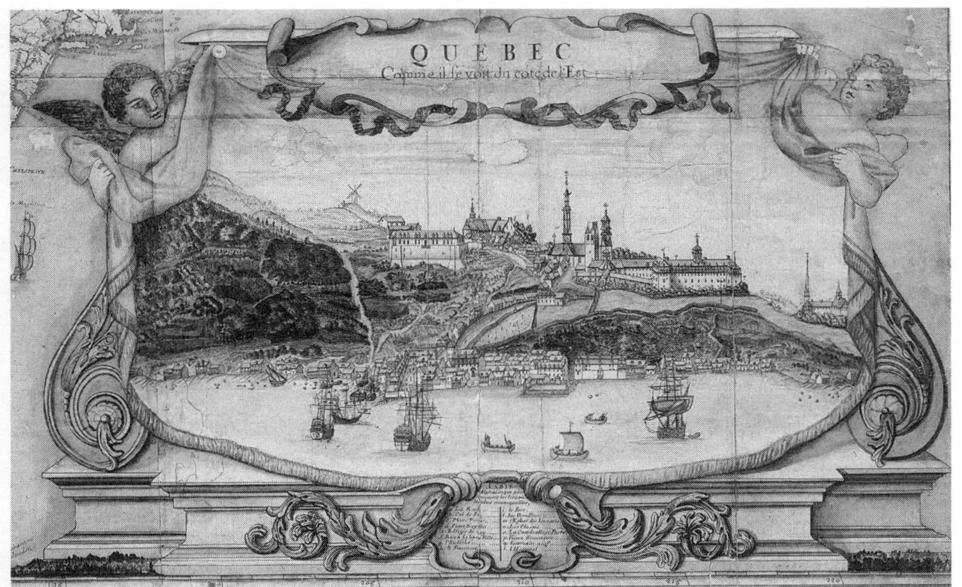

Figure 2.1 "Québec comme il se voit du côté de l'Est," 1688, by Jean-Baptiste-Louis Franquelin (detail from Figure 2.2). | © Service historique de la Défense, Département Marine, Vincennes.

formation of this country, but in their haste to do so, many have oversimplified the multifaceted relationship between the colony and the mother country. The symbolic aspect of French cultural references is something the colonists would not have dismissed very easily because of material conditions.

In this chapter, I focus on the symbolic dimension of the relationship between colony and mother country through the careful examination of a single document: Jean-Baptiste-Louis Franquelin's view of Quebec City in 1688 (Figure 2.1), which is set on a large map of New France preserved in the Service historique de la Défense in Vincennes (Figure 2.2). Obviously, such a limited case study can offer only hypothetical conclusions, but as we shall see, the historical characters and the events that revolve around the symbolic landscape of Quebec City, as it is represented in this single image, are quite significant. Moreover, in the past thirty years, the study of individual city views and maps has led to valuable insights into the urban culture of places such as Venice, Florence, and Paris, and the methods used in these studies, having contributed to a profound renewal in the history of cartography, can provide some guidance in the context of this chapter.[2]

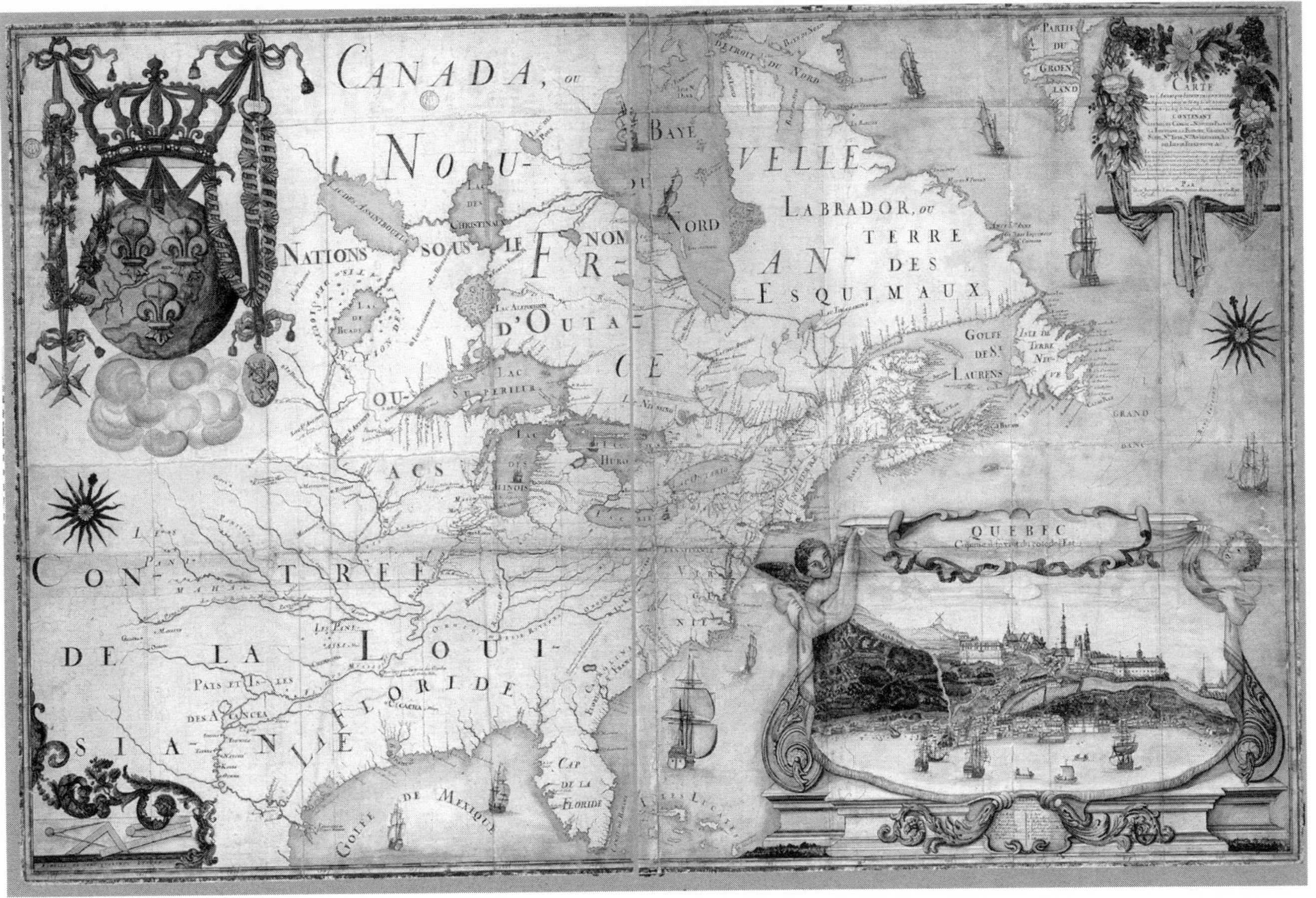

Figure 2.2 "Carte de l'Amerique septentrionnalle," 1688, by Jean-Baptiste-Louis Franquelin. | © Service historique de la Défense, Département Marine, Vincennes.

I hope to demonstrate that Canadian architecture in the seventeenth century largely followed the principles of what Norbert Elias has called the "court society" and that urban images, such as Franquelin's 1688 view of Quebec City, provide interesting clues to understanding this process. According to Elias, the social codes that bound the courtiers to the king in Versailles provide a socio-historical model useful in characterizing French *ancien régime* society as a whole.[3] In Versailles the rituals of *étiquette* and the ostentatious competition for prestige – which involved architecture as much as anything else in public life – became the cornerstone of absolutist rule. In my view, the competition for prestige that one can find in Quebec City between various colonial officials and religious institutions during the same period constitutes an extension of the court society in the colonial context, and prestige is an essential preoccupation in the field of architecture.

After an introductory discussion of Franquelin's 1688 map of New France as a whole, the chapter turns to the city view that lies in its lower right-hand corner, entitled "Québec comme il se voit du côté de l'Est." I examine how this image can be understood as a "symbolic landscape" – that is, as an expression of the meaning associated with the city established on the St. Lawrence River, standing more or less as a gateway to the French territories in North America. I also discuss the construction of some prominent buildings represented in the view in order to show how their design suggests an awareness of this symbolic landscape. According to this argument, buildings were conceived to fit not only into the physical environment of the city as such but also into the image of the city as it was perceived at the time. Finally, the chapter addresses the question of Franquelin's objectivity by arguing that his use of pictorial conventions played on the relative importance of buildings and of the institutions they represented but that it remained above all an attempt to raise the interest of the king in the true appearance of his colonial capital.

THE MAP AND THE MAPMAKER

Jean-Baptiste-Louis Franquelin had been drawing maps for colonial officials since approximately 1674, a few years after his arrival in Canada as a merchant.[4] His maps quickly became part of the continuous flow of documents – letters, reports, edicts, city plans, building plans, maps, and so on – that developed between the colony and the royal administration during the reign of Louis XIV. Franquelin's reputation as a mapmaker reached its peak in the mid-1680s, when he was appointed instructor of navigation and began signing his maps "hydrographe du roi" (royal hydrographer).[5] As historian Burke-Gaffney explains,

Jacques-René de Brisay de Denonville, governor of New France since 1685, also wanted Franquelin to plan city defences, and he tried to have him appointed military engineer in replacement of Robert de Villeneuve, with whom officials were dissatisfied.[6] Franquelin's responsibilities in the colonial administration kept increasing in this manner throughout the 1680s. However, obtaining a better pay turned out to be more difficult than he expected, in spite of Denonville's support. In these circumstances, Franquelin himself went to France in 1688 to make his case for a higher position, bringing with him the special map he had prepared as a demonstration of his cartographic skills. Enriched with colour washes and finely detailed decorative elements, this map reached an unprecedented quality in Franquelin's production. As a proof of his ability, it also held the promise of even better maps in the future, should the king agree to his requests.

From a strictly geographical perspective, the 1688 map is quite an ambitious document. It is believed to have been produced in response to the royal administration's standing demand for a map showing the borders between New France and the English colonies, and it is considered one of the earliest serious attempts at doing so. The area represented covers the whole of the eastern part of North America, from Hudson's Bay to the Gulf of Mexico, and the toponymy is extremely detailed. The map in fact represents the sum of Franquelin's considerable geographical knowledge, acquired through the compilation of documentation provided by numerous French explorers. As Conrad Heidenreich and Edward Dahl explain, "almost all known manuscript maps from this period of exploration passed through the hands of Louis Jolliet and the official cartographer for maps relating to New France, Jean-Baptiste-Louis Franquelin. From these compilers, the manuscripts were sent to France where others had access to them."[7]

The noncartographical elements drawn on the periphery contribute to underscoring the importance of this document and raise its status to a royal gift. In the upper left-hand corner, one finds the French royal emblems – three fleurs-de-lis topped with a royal crown – accompanied by the cross of the Ordre du Saint-Esprit and the medal of the Ordre de Saint-Michel.[8] It is interesting to note that, instead of the usual uniform blue background, Franquelin displayed the fleurs-de-lis over an image of the globe, with a particular emphasis on the oceans, clearly referring to French exploration and expansion overseas.[9] The title "Carte de l'Amerique septentrionnalle," positioned opposite the royal emblems in the upper right-hand corner, is surrounded with a garland of flowers and accompanied by the name and title of its author: "Jean-Baptiste-Louis Franquelin, hydrographe du Roy à Québec." In the lower left-hand corner are the mapmaker's instruments – the compass, the square, and two rulers laid in perspective on top of a table whose edge indicates the scale of the map – all proclaiming the author's professional standing and the reliability of the information provided. Finally, the well-known city view, "Québec comme il se voit du côté de l'Est," occupies a large portion of the map in the lower right-hand corner.

In addition to the map, Franquelin presented a new and ambitious cartographic project to the king, and he explained the details of it in a report addressed to the Marquis de Seignelay, minister of the navy, *ex officio* in charge of the colonies. In this text, Franquelin proposes surveying and mapping the French territories in North America with utmost precision and installing copper markers bearing the arms of the king – visible in the upper left-hand corner of the map – along the borderlines. Franquelin is not explicit about the method he would use for such an undertaking, but he obviously wanted to improve on the existing documentation by having aides directly on site. A passage in which Franquelin argues for the necessity of establishing a French toponymy leaves no ambiguity about the purpose of the whole project:

> It appears necessary to divide this large area into Provinces, establish their limits, and give them stable and permanent French names – the same for the rivers and specific places, thereby abolishing all savage names, which are only a source of confusion, since they change so often, and because every nation calls places and rivers in its own language, the result being that one single thing always has several names.[10]

It is interesting to note that, according to Franquelin, giving French names to places under French control would put an end to such toponymic confusion. This project would also contribute to making the French control over these areas more conspicuous: "This work would not only make the maps more intelligible, but it would also confirm the possession of the areas contained within them."[11] Clearly, the new cartographic project was conceived in direct continuity with the 1688 map, as it was meant further to improve on the mapping of North America and to develop the symbolic affirmation of French control over the lands depicted. Franquelin then goes on to argue that he is the only person living in Canada to have the knowledge required for this task, and he concludes his *mémoire* by requesting a salary he considered appropriate, that of a military engineer.

As we can see, the map that Franquelin presented to King Louis XIV in 1688 is an object with a carefully constructed meaning. Combined with a new mapping project, it proposes not only a way of improving on the existing geographical knowledge but also an appropriate way of displaying French colonial assets to European eyes. It is clear that Franquelin understood the symbolic role played by geographical images in the European courts at the time and that he was aware of Louis XIV's strong interest in them. As Louis Marin, Christian Jacob, and others have very well demonstrated, geographical images were central to Louis XIV's vision of the world, and cartographers working for the French monarch did not fail to conceive them as means of glorifying him. Maps, atlases, and globes had become a highly efficient way of exhibiting one's power in the seventeenth century and thereby constituted an exemplary gift for political and religious authorities.[12]

In the period with which we are concerned, the most famous of such gifts were probably the two globes fabricated by Vincenzo Coronelli between 1681 and 1683, which were offered to Louis XIV by Cardinal César d'Estrées.[13] These globes were so large that they required the construction a special pavillon to exhibit them at the Château de Marly. And it is also known that Louis XIV had special glasses made for himself to examine them. Jacob comments on the symbolism thus associated with the royal gaze: "The glasses symbolically underline the importance of the royal gaze, of which they are the prosthesis as well as the privilege. No one can hide from the telescopic eye of the sovereign, capable of seeing the entire globe as much as any of its regions or specific places."[14] The production of geographical images for Louis XIV thus responded in a very direct manner to this visual metaphor. Indeed, according to Louis XIV's own comments on the art of ruling, the capacity to see everything was essential to royal power:

> Everything that is most necessary for this task is at the same time pleasant; for it consists, in a word, my son, in keeping one's eyes open on the whole world, incessantly learning the news from every province and every nation, finding out the secrets of every court, the whims and weaknesses of every prince and every foreign minister, informing oneself on an endless number of matters of which we are believed ignorant and, likewise, seeing in our own surroundings what is most carefully concealed from us, discovering each of the views and the thoughts of our own courtiers.[15]

This association between geographical images, capacity of seeing, and political power is essential to the interpretation of Franquelin's 1688 map of North America because the significance of such documents is not limited to providing good information. Franquelin's "gift," meant to bring royal favour upon himself, proposed some means by which Louis XIV could display himself as the absolute ruler – or the virtuous and courageous knight, considering the medals surrounding the royal emblems – who controlled the territories depicted. The project of developing a better map of North America, in the same sense, can be seen as a response to the criticism adressed to Coronelli's globes. Indeed, even though Coronelli had access to a considerable amount of geographical documentation in the Bibliothèque royale in Paris, and even though he paid special attention to the North American continent, the scientific dimension of his work was very quickly called into question. In contrast, Franquelin's proposal takes into consideration the speed at which geographical knowledge developed in these years of exploration.[16]

We of course know that Franquelin's success in France was only partial, for although he was confirmed in his duties and put in charge of the new cartographic project, he did not obtain an increase in pay. His 1688 map may not have been as convincing as he hoped, or the king may not have liked the idea of leaving the production of symbolic maps to a colonial officer, but it is clear that Franquelin's role had to remain what it was: that of providing reliable and synthetic information that others could use in Europe. For the purpose of our discussion, however, it is enough to see how Franquelin's cartography was conceived in a way that binds together a strong claim of accuracy in mapmaking and the glorification of the French Crown. Throughout the text in which he explains his intentions, Franquelin portrays himself as indispensable to the affirmation of the king's authority and to the celebration of his power in North America.

SYMBOLIC LANDSCAPE

Turning now to the view of Quebec City (Figure 2.1), we can see that Franquelin chose to represent the site from the east (i.e., from the St. Lawrence River), and in doing so, he followed an established convention. Plans and views of Quebec City from the time of Samuel de Champlain had always emphasized the eastern facade of the city. Plans were systematically oriented toward the west, thus locating the east at the bottom of the page, as though the observer were looking at the site from that vantage point, and, similarly, views consistently looked from east to west.[17]

For example, Jean Bourdon, the military engineer who accompanied Champlain in Canada, always placed the St. Lawrence River at the bottom of his plans of Quebec, thereby giving them a westerly orientation. This convention

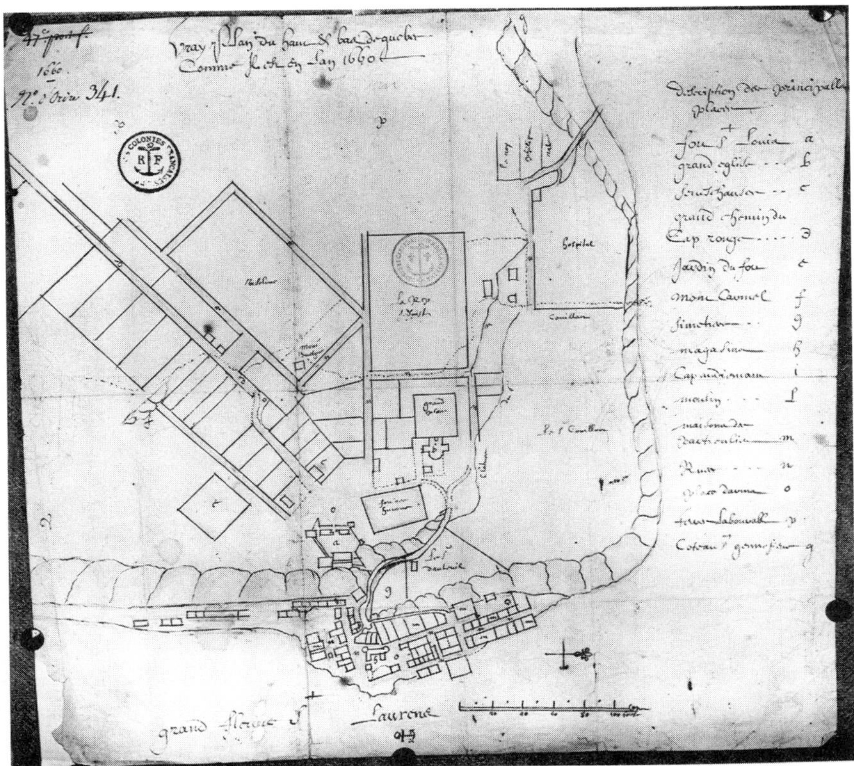

Figure 2.3 "Vray plan du haut et bas de Québec comme il est en l'an 1660," by Jean Bourdon. | No. 341 C, Amérique septentrionale, Dépôt des fortifications des colonies, Centre des archives d'outre mer, Aix-en-Provence.

can already be observed in the 1630s in a series of drawings and projects for the Quebec establishment.[18] The same convention is preserved in later plans showing the city as a whole, such as "Vray plan du haut et bas de Québec comme il est en l'an 1660," a plan that frames exactly the same area as Franquelin's view of 1688, from Cap-aux-Diamants on the left to the St. Charles River on the right (Figure 2.3).

The westerly orientation characterizing the French plans of Quebec City corresponds to the view people had when arriving by ship, and it also follows the orientation adopted for city views from very early on. Significantly, the two modes of representation – plans and views – are, from the early years of the colony, remarkably similar in this regard: they are co-ordinated like the plan and the elevation of a single building, the subjective dimension of city views imposing itself on the orientation of city plans.[19] The view of Champlain's

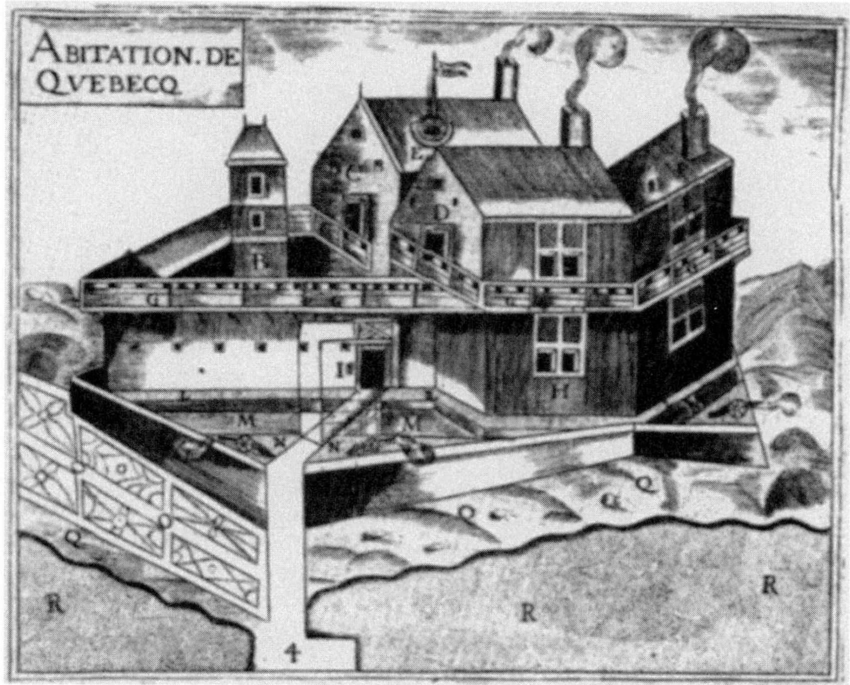

Figure 2.4 View of the fort at Quebec established by Champlain in 1608, anonymous. | From Samuel de Champlain, *Les voyages du Sieur de Champlain* (Paris: Jean Bergeon, 1613). National Library of Canada, Ottawa.

"Habitation," published in 1613, which may be considered the earliest known view of Quebec, established a type of representation that remained stable throughout the entire French regime: the observer is situated on the river and looks at the eastern side of the site, which appears more or less in elevation (Figure 2.4). Throughout the seventeenth century, the distance between the viewer and the site gradually increased to accommodate a larger field of vision, but the orientation remained constant.

In Franquelin's own work, the 1683 map-view of Fort St. Louis (Figure 2.5) is an important step leading to the view of Quebec City examined here. It shows the governor's palace sitting atop a cliff, with Lower Town situated below. As in a bird's-eye view, the observer hovers above all possible obstacles to contemplate the city from an ideal vantage point located over the St. Lawrence River, in midair. But the image also borrows from the conventions of city plans, as it shows the perimeter of Fort St. Louis more or less as it would appear when seen directly from above. Moreover, the drawing bears a compass rose, placing it

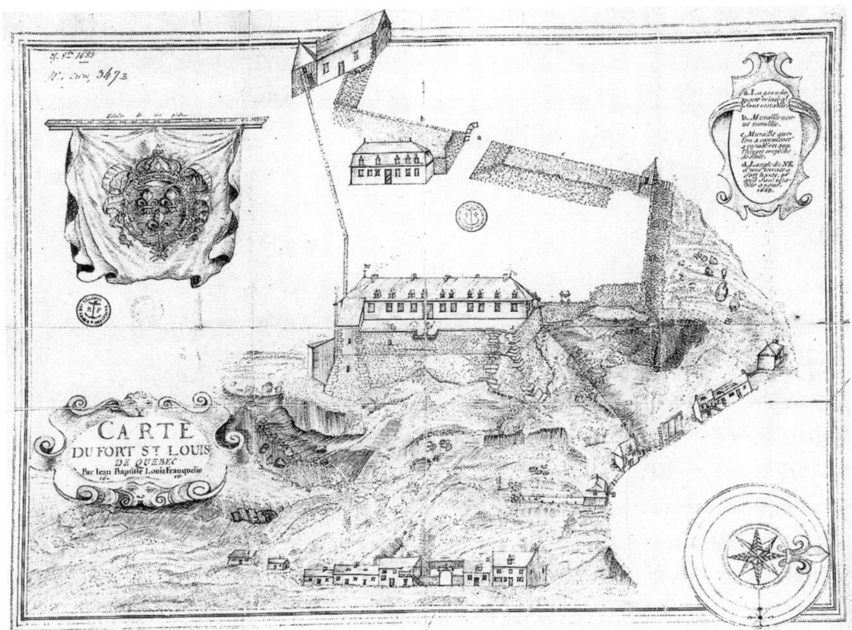

Figure 2.5 "Carte du fort Saint-Louis," 1683, by Jean-Baptiste-Louis Franquelin. | No. 347 B, Amérique septentrionale, Dépôt des fortifications des colonies, Centre des archives d'outre mer, Aix-en-Provence.

clearly in the field of cartography. North is located to the right of the image, and the westerly orientation of the plan coincides with the viewpoint chosen to represent the fort in profile.

In continuity with these earlier images, the view found on the 1688 map is based on conventions developed in Europe in the late sixteenth and early seventeenth centuries to represent cities in the context of geographical works. Most of these conventions find their source in Georg Braun and Frans Hogenberg's *Civitates Orbis Terrarum* (Amsterdam, 1572-1617), a six-volume work dedicated to providing the best possible images of more than 500 cities. Indeed, it was the ambition of Braun and Hogenberg to get rid of the stereotypical images that dominated publications until that time and to replace them with more realistic views. The means by which they aimed to achieve this objective included choosing the best point of view of any given city, representing the site in bird's-eye view, and specifying the cardinal orientation.[20] Significant buildings and topographical features were identified either directly on the image or in a legend with numbers or letters. In many cases, we know that Braun and Hogenberg decided to delay the inclusion of a certain city in their work in order to obtain a sufficiently good image. Topographical views became one of the most popular type of images in seventeenth-century Europe, after religious images, and several important printmakers and publishers made it a speciality.[21] In the context of France, artists such as Adam Pérelle (1640-95) and Israël Silvestre (1621-91) developed topographical art in a very creative manner. But numerous others simply popularized and perpetuated the standard one-page city view based on the schemes developed by Braun and Hogenberg, providing views of almost every average-size city in the kingdom.

Franquelin's 1688 view of Quebec City clearly proceeds from this tradition and uses familiar conventions: a viewpoint situated on the river, an emphasis on the legibility of topographical features, a certain exaggeration in the size of important buildings, and the identification of these buidings in a legend set under the image. The result is a view that brings out the particularities of Quebec City in quite an acute manner. As already mentioned, the viewpoint situated on the St. Lawrence River corresponds to the standard way of presenting the city since the time of Champlain. Franquelin also chose a tight frame that corresponds to the area generally represented in contemporary plans, and he completely ignored the background of mountains that would become a major feature in the "picturesque" images of the city one century later. The conventions that Franquelin used thus seem to convey the idea of an ideal prospect of the city. The view can be said to represent Quebec's "eidetic profile," to borrow a term from Louis Marin.[22] It is a partial image that stands for the whole, purporting to give a complete inventory of the city's most significant elements, something that is explicitly claimed in the legend: "Table alphabétique pour connoistre les lieux les plus remarquables." Franquelin's way of exaggerating the difference in size between official and religious buildings, on the one hand, and ordinary houses, on the other, in addition to his minute detailing of architectural elements, puts a clear emphasis on individual buildings and the institutions they represent. The legend allows for a quick identification of these buildings, silhouetted against an empty background, through a series of accompanying letters (Figures 2.6 and 2.7). Starting in the lower left-hand corner with the harbour, Franquelin lists buildings and urban features following a path that runs through Lower Town and climbs the hill to Fort St. Louis, official residence of the governor, identified by the letter I. Then, continuing from left to right, one can see the Ursuline monastery (L); the Jesuit church (M), exhibiting the highest spire in the city; the Seminary of Foreign Missions (N and Q); the cathedral (O); and Hôtel-Dieu hospital (R). The sum of these features thus gives a clear idea of the city's significance in the New World and clearly emphasizes its religious dimension.

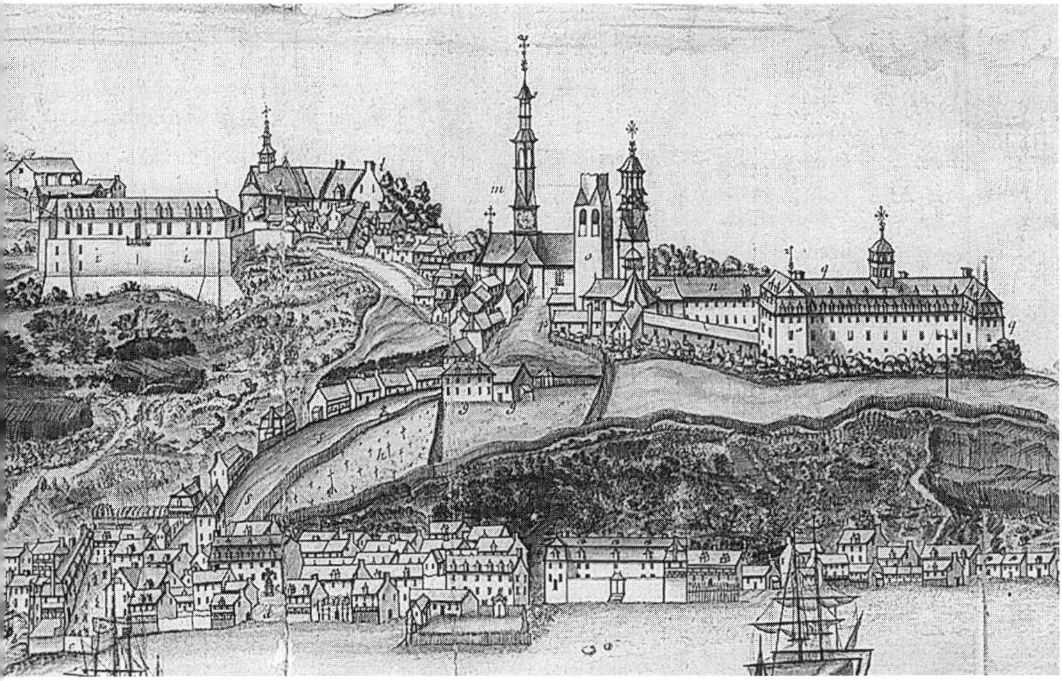

Figure 2.6 Detail of Upper Town and Lower Town in Franquelin's view of Quebec City, 1688 (detail from Figure 2.1). | © Service historique de la Défense, Département Marine, Vincennes.

Figure 2.7 Legend of Franquelin's view of Quebec City, 1688 (detail from Figure 2.1). | © Service historique de la Défense, Département Marine, Vincennes.

Taken as a whole, these various conventions – orientation toward the west, high viewpoint, tight framing, legibility of individual buildings (especially in Upper Town), index letters referring to a legend – establish a definite manner of looking at the city and constitute good evidence of the way Quebec City was perceived at the time. Indeed, Franquelin's 1688 view, as well as the other plans and views I have been discussing in parallel, are more than simple historical records that provide historians with a certain amount of factual information. Recent trends in the history of cartography demonstrate that such images correspond to a certain "way of seeing," and it is clear that the facade of Quebec City as seen from the St. Lawrence River was perceived as the most important, and perhaps its only real, facade.

Taking into consideration this tradition of always representing the city from the same viewpoint, I propose that many buildings in Quebec City were conceived with an acute sense of their role as identity markers in this visual landscape. Thus Franquelin's way of representing Quebec City would correspond to what was actually expected of buildings: that they should represent specific institutions and make their presence felt in the visual environment. Elias has shown that buildings were among the most important symbols of rank and prestige in court society and that, as such, they were absolutely central to the nobility and to those aspiring to it. This was undoubtedly also the case in Quebec City, as officials posted in the colonial capital cared for signs of prestige as much as they would have in France.[23] In Quebec City, however, certain additional factors must be taken into account in order to measure the full impact of these concerns on the city's visual landscape. If the social codes of court society had a significant impact on the architecture of French *hôtels* and *palais,* because of the prestige these buildings provided, the same kind of impact in Quebec City was necessarily mediated by local conditions and by the way the city's image was structured. Indeed, it is reasonable to think that because of the visibility it provided, the eastern facade played the most significant role in the city's development, and it can be demonstrated that the conspicuousness of public and religious buildings from this particular prospect was a top priority for many architectural clients. Thus a symbolic landscape developed essentially on the eastern side, facing the St. Lawrence River, and the idea that a monumental building would carry more prestige if appropriately situated from that particular view could influence important building projects. At least, this is what I will be arguing: visibility of a building from the river meant being part of the city's "image," and this situation explains many of the tensions and conflicts that developed between the members of an image-conscious ancien-régime elite.

BUILDING PROJECTS AND THE IMPACT OF VISIBILITY

In order to discuss the impact that the concern for visibility might have had on certain building projects in Quebec City, I first examine the simultaneous construction of two churches: the cathedral in Upper Town and an auxiliary chapel in Lower Town. Differences in the way construction priorities were set for these two buildings reveal important characteristics about the symbolic landscape of the city at the end of the seventeenth century.

In Franquelin's view, the cathedral appears as a strikingly incomplete building, prominently set in the middle of Upper Town (Figure 2.6). The small church seen from the apse is the old Notre-Dame-de-la-Paix, built in 1648, waiting to be incorporated into the fabric of the new cathedral. The large tower located next to it, and whose construction is discontinued in the upper parts, is also part of the projected building.[24] Although the spatial relationship between these two elements remains slightly unclear in the image, the size of the tower suggests that, once completed, the cathedral would become the single most imposing structure in the city.

What we know about the erection of the cathedral corresponds entirely to Franquelin's view. Construction began in 1683 with the approval of a modest project drawn by the architect Claude Baillif (Figure 2.8).[25] The work started with the facade and its two towers, set at some distance from the old church of Notre-Dame-de-la-Paix, to which it was meant to be connected by lengthening the existing nave. Although construction was partly under the authority of churchwardens (because the building still retained its status as a parish church), Bishop François de Laval necessarily had a strong influence on the projects concerning the cathedral. Thus, after the foundations of the new facade had been laid in the spring and summer of 1684, the project was suddenly enlarged to include a much bigger facade, with higher towers, in anticipation of a three-nave basilical church destined to replace the old one. It is also Laval who seems to be responsible for the way priorities were set during construction. In a letter he wrote to the Quebec Seminary in 1685, while in Paris, the bishop argued that the towers and the facade, being in a certain sense "unnecessary," should be erected with the first funds available. In this way, the king would be faced with the necessity of paying for the construction of the walls and the nave toward the end of the process and would therefore be obliged to keep sending money:

> If we should fail to complete the second tower before starting to build the walls of the church, it might happen that this second tower would remain unfinished,

Figure 2.8 Project for the reconstruction of the cathedral Notre-Dame de Québec, 1683, by Claude Baillif. | No. Z-114-3, collection "Archives du Séminaire de Québec," Musée de la Civilisation, Quebec City.

> something that will be very disgraceful and ugly to see, but this would not happen with the walls of the church, which appear to be of greater necessity than the completion of the second tower, which we can ultimately do without, but which is nevertheless greatly needed, if we think about it carefully.[26]

The construction thus proceeded with the facade and the two towers of an enlarged project (Figure 2.9), although it was later modified and made smaller again because of weaknesses in the foundations, designed for the smaller plan. Because of these difficulties, the facade remained half-completed for several years, and the old parish church stood undisturbed fifty feet away, just as it appears in 1688 in Franquelin's view.

The great importance that Laval gave to the towers and facade of the cathedral is clearly related to the question of the visibility of buildings located in Upper Town. In the letter already quoted above, Laval also writes: "Since we believe that we should continue the work on the Quebec church as early as next summer, so that the court may see that we spend the money given for that purpose, the first thing we ought to do is complete the second tower."[27] The completion of the towers was, according to Laval, the best demonstration that the grant he obtained from the king was being used appropriately. Theoretically, the construction of the nave could have achieved the same result, but conspicuous towers were thought to provide more visibility and send more echoes in the direction of the king.

Meanwhile, the bishop had been arguing since 1681 that an auxiliary chapel was needed in Lower Town, the most densely populated area of the city. Indeed, to attend services at any of the city's churches, parishioners had to climb to Upper Town, something that could become particularly difficult during winter, with the accumulation of ice and snow. Laval's continuing request to use the site of the *magasin du roi*, an abandoned royal warehouse located on the market square in the centre of Lower Town, to build this chapel therefore had a strong basis in practical considerations.

The construction of the chapel in Lower Town began in the summer of 1688, and for this reason it is not represented in Franquelin's view.[28] The contract awarded to Baillif in 1687 specified that he should erect "le commencement de la chapelle" (i.e., the first part of a chapel to be completed at a later date). And in contrast to the cathedral, construction here started with the apse and the nave: "two portions of walls measuring fifty feet, for the sides of the chapel, closed by a third wall at the end, where the altar shall be located."[29] Laval preferred to start construction of this church with the nave and to delay completion of the facade.

Figure 2.9 Revised project for the reconstruction of the cathedral Notre-Dame de Québec, [1684], by Claude Baillif. | No. Z-114-1, collection "Archives du Séminaire de Québec," Musée de la Civilisation, Quebec City.

Figure 2.10 "A View of the Church of Notre Dame de la Victoire," 1761, etching, by Antoine Benoist, after Richard Short. | No. 53.110, Musée national des Beaux Arts du Québec, Quebec City. Photo: Patrick Altman.

It is known that the chapel, later called the Church of Notre-Dame-des-Victoires, was closed using a temporary facade on the market square for several years. Only in 1723 was its length increased and a more permanent masonry facade added.[30] Completed in this manner, the church appears in Richard Short's 1759 view of Lower Town (Figure 2.10).

Such a radical difference in the way priorities were set is striking, and it is an important clue to the different ways in which visibility, or the lack of it, could influence a building project. Apparently, the funds that Bishop Laval and his successor, Bishop Saint-Vallier, could secure were insufficient to erect the cathedral in a single campaign. It is clear that Laval was entirely aware of the risk he was taking, but he was able to convince the churchwardens to direct the available funds toward the erection of the enlarged facade and its towers. The more essential parts of the building – those that would actually shelter the parishioners and the clergy during celebrations – would therefore be delayed. Of course, Laval hoped that the king would not let him down when the time came to complete the project, and he established priorities accordingly. With the chapel in Lower Town, however, a comparable situation was treated in a completely different manner, and priority was given to the nave. In a way, it could be argued that Bishop Laval was able to build but a single church in the city during that period, half of which was in Upper Town while the other half was in Lower Town. If the density of population explains why priority was given to the nave in Lower Town, the symbolic importance of the urban landscape explains the priority given to the facade and the towers in Upper Town. Upper Town, with its increased visibility reinforced by a tradition of images focusing on the east side, was the most obvious place to erect a building whose significance lay in its becoming part of the city's symbolic landscape.

Although every significant building represented in Franquelin's 1688 view could be examined in relation to the question of visibility, I will limit my comments to two more examples, which should suffice to demonstrate the idea. My next example, then, is the Ursuline monastery, which, in Franquelin's view, is composed of two wings set at a right angle to one another and is topped by a belfry at one end (Figure 2.6). In the view, these two wings are drawn larger than the urban houses around them, but they remain nevertheless small in comparison to other institutional buildings, such as the neighbouring Fort St. Louis or the Seminary. The size of the belfry is particularly modest in comparison to those punctuating other religious institutions.

The appearance of the Ursuline monastery in Franquelin's view corresponds to what can be concluded from building records. After being almost completely destroyed by a fire in December 1686, the monastery was partially rebuilt in 1687 and 1688. Two wings – Aile Sainte-Famille and Aile Saint-Augustin – existed by the summer of 1688, and although more buildings were needed, the construction would resume only several years later.

During the winter months of 1686-87, the chapter of the Quebec Ursulines discussed a variety of ideas about the reconstruction of their monastery, but, unable to make up their minds, the nuns referred the decision to a specially appointed committee.[31] This committee was composed of Louis Ango de Maizerets – Bishop Laval's vicar general and father superior of the Ursulines – and four Jesuits, one of whom had a fair amount of experience overseeing building projects in his own community. Instead of choosing among the solutions considered by the nuns, as they were asked to do, the five priests devised a solution of their own, and they insisted on the practical advantages of their plan. The committee's solution extensively re-utilizes the foundations of the old buildings, including those of the church, as was commonly done. However, they split the project into two distinct parts by moving one of the old wings away from the centre and erecting it on new foundations. This is the Aile Saint-Augustin, which holds the small belfry in Franquelin's view. In this way, their argument went, a gap would protect the church in case of another fire, and communication between the nuns' residence and the church would be made possible by a small covered passage.[32]

Although this plan was entirely justified by practical considerations, its effect on the general appearance of the buildings cannot have been overlooked. The idea of physically separating the monastery from the church, which goes against the most basic Classical principles, displeased a number of nuns, as other more monumental schemes were considered in the following years.[33] In the end, however, the practical considerations of the committee prevailed and a variation on their initial scheme was completed in the 1720s.

Although incomplete, the Ursuline monastery represented in Franquelin's view gives a good idea of the ensemble projected by the committee. In comparison to the buildings of the Jesuits and the Seminary, the Ursuline monastery is small and, apparently following the rules of étiquette, shows modesty and submission toward the two male religious communities that dominate the urban landscape. In support of this reading, Classical architectural theory has always positioned buildings conceived solely on practical grounds at the lower end of a symbolic hierarchy of types, not outside it.[34] In this manner, the practical argumentation of the five priests can be read on a symbolic level, and it is reasonable to say that it conveys an opinion about the place the nuns should be given in the image of the city.

The last case I would like to discuss in this section is an absent building: the hospice that Louis XIV granted the Récollet friars in 1681, which they installed in an old building located in front of Fort St. Louis.[35] If it had been represented in Franquelin's view, the Récollet hospice would have appeared in the open space between Fort St. Louis and the Ursuline monastery (Figure 2.6). But as the hospice is absent from the city view, the name of the Récollet friars has been omitted from the legend altogether, even though the order also owned a monastery in the vicinity of the city.[36] To understand why the hospice is not represented in 1688, we need to go back to the beginning of June 1683, when the Récollet friars crowned it with a small belfry. The event did not go unnoticed; as soon as he became aware of its addition, Bishop Laval ordered the Récollets to immediately demolish the belfry. When the Récollets refused, the conflict over the belfry quickly degenerated into a war of sanctions, letters, and reports, and it was settled only by appealing to King Louis XIV, who studied the whole case and rendered his decision in April 1684.

In 1681, when pleading for permission to open a hospice, the Récollets argued that they needed some kind of presence in "la ville la plus apparente du pays" (the most visible city in the country), something that their monastery did not provide because of its location.[37] Laval agreed to an infirmary, but when a belfry appeared on top of the building, he perceived the gesture as an intolerable abuse of the situation. The controversial belfry was finally demolished by order of the king in the fall of 1684, and the Récollets thus disappeared from the cityscape, although they were allowed to keep their hospice as a secondary building for temporary stays.

Contrary to the Ursulines, the Récollets were clearly unwanted in the upper town of Quebec City, and Bishop Laval was able to impose the destruction of the belfry that would have given them some presence in the symbolic landscape.[38] If the Récollets are not identified in Franquelin's view of 1688, in spite of the fact that the hospice remained in place, it is because they had to demolish the belfry that would have made them visible.

This situation of conflict between Bishop Laval and the Récollet friars, centred upon the visible mark of their presence in Upper Town, is another interesting clue indicating the structure of the symbolic landscape of Quebec City. Indeed, if a belfry is the most common sign of a religious building in the Christian world, the meaning of this sign is also linked to its location, as it signals the presence of an institution in a specific place. The Récollets wanted to put up this sign in the upper town of Quebec City, where it would be most visible (and audible), whereas the bishop – without refusing the actual presence of the friars in a building the size of an average house – could not accept a sign that would inscribe their presence on the symbolic landscape. Obviously, Franquelin could have identified the Récollets with a letter attached to their hospice, even without a belfry. However, he preferred simply to acknowledge the existing state of affairs: the Récollets' actual monastery, because of its location, could not be seen from the standard viewpoint on the river and therefore could be omitted.

THE QUESTION OF FRANQUELIN'S OBJECTIVITY

A remaining question concerns Franquelin's objectivity. From the previous discussion, it appears that Franquelin adopted an attitude that leaned toward the Jesuits' and Bishop Laval's "perception" of the city, with the Jesuits occupying the major position, the Ursulines showing respectful modesty, and the Récollets – the main competitors to the Jesuits in missionary work – completely invisible. However, this was more or less the "official order" of things in 1688, and any other attitude on Franquelin's part would have amounted to a purposeful manipulation. The most that can be said, therefore, is that Franquelin faithfully portrayed the equilibrium between the religious forces as it existed at that time. There is no doubt that the size of the different spires and the multiplicity of their levels has been altered in the view: for example, the height of the Jesuit spire has clearly been emphasized more than that of the Ursulines. But their relative importance and position appear to have been respected. This point is worth noting because, in contrast, Robert de Villeneuve did not remain as neutral in his representations.[39] It should be remembered that Franquelin was addressing King Louis XIV with the specific purpose of obtaining a better position. For that reason, neutrality, or a certain kind of "objectivity," was the best attitude he could adopt in his city view. Franquelin did not embellish Fort St. Louis, he did not try to include the Récollets' hospice, whose belfry had been destroyed by royal decree, nor did he complete the towers of the cathedral, as he could easily have done if his aim had simply been the promotion of the city. If King Louis XIV was able to see everything that happened in places as far away as Canada, it is because he had people who would report these things to him, and Franquelin is undoubtedly trying to present himself as a "reliable tool" of the king's vision. He is not trying to promote Bishop Laval's vision of the colonial order but is portraying the exact state of colonial affairs for the eyes of the king.[40]

There is one place, however, where Franquelin's neutrality can be questioned, and that is the square known as Place Royale. Franquelin, in his apparent readiness to celebrate Louis XIV, identified the market square of Lower Town, where a bust of the king had been installed a few years earlier, as "Place Royalle." He even made a second entry in the legend to point out the king's bust separately (Figures 2.6 and 2.7). These two distinct elements – corresponding to letters D ("Place Royalle") and E ("Effigie du Roy") – might again appear as the simple reflection of an existing reality, but the situation is in fact more complicated. A 1685 project for the transformation of the marketplace into a formal urban square had been blocked by the merchants, who wanted to preserve the public space just as it was since it was well suited to market activities. The installation of the royal bust was the only part of the transformation that was actually carried out in 1686, thanks to the initiative of Intendant Bochart de Champigny.[41] But in spite of the monument, the existence of Place Royale in Quebec City was not commonly recognized when Franquelin was preparing his map: the only drawing that shows the 1685 project simply calls the square "Place de Québec,"[42] and city maps from the 1680s and 1690s use a variety of other names for the square.[43] The bust itself did not stay very long on the market square. Considered a nuisance to market activities and circulation, the intendant's "gift" to the city was soon returned to him, and it was thereafter exhibited inside his *palais*. Afterward, we lose track of the bust around the time Bochart de Champigny returned to France in 1702.

On the basis of the available cartographic and topographical documents from the period, Franquelin thus seems exceptional in using the name Place Royale to designate the public square in Lower Town. Therefore, the choice of calling this square Place Royale was most likely motivated by his intention to create a "royal map," for it does not reflect a common practice of the time. In fact, this particular detail seems to be the most significant distortion of reality that Franquelin imposed on the city in his 1688 view of Quebec. He may have intended to suggest that the inhabitants of Quebec City saw no problem with the idea of having a public square dedicated to Louis XIV in their city, even though the merchants had directly petitioned the king against the transformation of the square a few years earlier. Louis XIV could indeed have remembered this event, in which he had to accept that his own approval of the project might be cancelled by local authorities because of the merchants' opposition. In this context, Franquelin's view seems to suggest that the inhabitants of the city were nevertheless keen on celebrating their monarch.

This situation brings us to argue that Franquelin's 1688 view still bears some influence on how people imagine Quebec City today. The current name of the square in Lower Town is Place Royale, a name that had not been used for more than two centuries, if it ever really was. The new appellation is the result of actions led by local historians and politicians in the first half of the twentieth century to review the toponymy of the city.[44] Interestingly, it is directly based on the evidence provided by Franquelin's view of 1688 and on a few other views he produced in the following years.[45] Even today, local publications rely on Franquelin's view as their main piece of evidence for the historical validity of the name Place Royale.[46] A more critical look at the documents, however, suggests that Franquelin attributed the name Place Royale independently from common usage.

Of course, this observation is not about a simple question of truth or falsehood in the way the 1688 view represents the city. Although opportunistic, Franquelin probably did not intend to give a false indication by choosing the name Place Royale. On the contrary, he may have sincerely hoped that his appellation would stick. Documents such as Franquelin's view can indeed contribute to modifying the reality they represent, just as toponymic commissions do when they produce new maps today. The problem, rather, lies in perceiving such documents as simple reflections, whether true or false, of an autonomous reality. That this dimension has not been taken into consideration may explain why, approximately 250 years after he made his famous view of Quebec City, Franquelin finally succeeded in his rhetoric, and the name Place Royale was officially adopted.

CONCLUSION

Urban images do not simply reflect – or fail to reflect – reality. Images can play a significant role in the development of symbolic landscapes, and symbolic landscapes indeed play a major role in the development of cities. The case of Quebec City, because of a particular conjunction of factors, simply magnifies the importance of a symbolic process that existed in the development of most cities in the Baroque age: Quebec City was the capital of New France, but a great distance separated it from Versailles, making it impossible for King Louis XIV to see it with his own eyes.

Cartographic documentation that was being sent to the royal administration as part of the regular correspondence between the colony and the mother country thus had more than a practical role to play, as it was almost sure to fall under the eyes of the king, or at least those of his minister. Mapmakers such as Bourdon and Franquelin were bringing a particular fragment of the world to the gaze of the king, and they thus participated in a symbolic enterprise to which contemporary geographers and cartographers dedicated considerable time and effort. Franquelin, in his position as royal hydrographer, took this role very seriously, and he produced the most striking views of Quebec City in the second half of the seventeenth century. As a major feature in the map with which he hoped further to improve his situation, Franquelin's 1688 view can be understood as a display of Louis XIV's dominating presence in North America. Emphasizing the institutional and, more specifically, the religious character of Quebec City with its numerous church spires, he also equated French control with the spread of the Catholic faith in the New World – an argument that could indeed be useful to the king in the European context. One of Franquelin's main preoccupations, in the map as in the view itself, apparently was the creation of images that could be useful to the king and his administration on a practical as well as on a symbolic level. For this reason, a certain neutrality toward the conflicts that existed in New France at the time probably appeared as the best attitude he could adopt.

Views such as Franquelin's also had an effect on the city itself, as they necessarily reinforced a certain way of looking at it and raised the stakes of representation by making this image visible all the way to Versailles. Indeed, it seems that by the 1680s, the members of Quebec City's elite had internalized a perception of the city that corresponded to the structure of such images. The symbolic dimension of the buildings they were erecting was therefore grounded in a specific way of looking at the city from a viewpoint located on the St. Lawrence River. The importance attributed to the visibility of a building in this symbolic landscape is demonstrated by the manner in which architectural elements such as towers, belfries, and facades participated in the competition for prestige – and for the attention of the king – that characterized the relations between them. Certainly, the material conditions of New France limited the means available to the colonial elite for the ostentatious display of social status, but this limitation did not automatically bring about new codes of conduct. On the contrary, the codes of court society were adapted to these new conditions and the reduced means available – such as the visibility of a building from a certain prospect of the city – became proportionately more critical and more contentious.

ACKNOWLEDGMENTS

This research is part of a project funded by the Social Sciences and Humanities Research Council of Canada. My thanks to Judi Loach and Rhodri Windsor Liscombe for their generous comments and suggestions on this chapter.

NOTES

1 For a more detailed discussion of this point, see M. Grignon, "Transformation et adaptation des formes architecturales européennes en Nouvelle-France aux XVIIe et XVIIIe siècles," *Perspective: La revue de l'INHA* 3 (2008): 551-64.

2 Juergen Schulz, "Jacopo de' Barbari's View of Venice: Map Making, City Views, and Moralized Geography before the Year 1500," *Art Bulletin* 60, 3 (1978): 425-74; Thomas Frangenberg, "Chorographies of Florence: The Use of City Views and City Plans in the Sixteenth Century," *Imago Mundi* 46 (1994): 41-64; Louis Marin, "Le roi et son géomètre," in *Le portrait du roi,* 209-20 (Paris: Éditions de Minuit, 1981); Louis Marin, "La ville dans sa carte et son portrait," in *De la représentation,* 204-18 (Paris: Gallimard, 1994). For a broader theoretical perspective, see also John Brian Harley, "Maps, Knowledge and Power," in *The Iconography of Landscape,* ed. Denis Cosgrove and Stephen Daniel, 277-312 (Cambridge, UK: Cambridge University Press, 1988); John Brian Harley, "Deconstructing the Map," *Cartographica* 26, 2 (1989): 1-20; and David Woodward, "La cartographie et la méthode artistique," *Préfaces* 5 (1987-88): 84-88.

3 Norbert Elias, *The Court Society* (London: Basil Blackwell, 1983), ch. 4. In the field of architectural history, Hilary Ballon uses the notion of "court society" to explain the size of large building projects in the Baroque age in Europe. See Hilary Ballon, "Architecture in the Seventeenth Century in Europe," in *The Triumph of the Baroque,* ed. Henry A. Millon (Washington, DC: National Gallery of Art, 1999), 86.

4 M.W. Burke-Gaffney, "Franquelin, Jean-Baptiste-Louis," in *Dictionary of Canadian Biography,* vol. 2, ed. George W. Brown (Toronto/Quebec City: University of Toronto Press/Presses de l'Université Laval, 1969), 228.

5 Jean-François Palomino, "Jean-Baptiste Franquelin: Un hydrographe du roi à Québec," in *Les villes françaises du Nouveau Monde,* ed. Laurent Vidal and Emilie d'Orgeix (Paris: Somogy, 1999), 164.

6 Burke-Gaffney, "Franquelin," 229. See also Gérard Morisset, "Villeneuve, Robert de," in *Dictionary of Canadian Biography,* vol. 1, ed. George W. Brown (Toronto/Quebec City: University of Toronto Press/ Presses de l'Université Laval, 1966), 663-64.

7 Conrad E. Heidenreich and Edward H. Dahl, "The French Mapping of North America in the Seventeenth Century," *Map Collector* 13 (1980): 8.

8 These were the two main chivalric orders in France, and the king was the grand master of both. The Ordre de Saint-Michel was instituted in 1469 by Louis XI, and the Ordre du Saint-Esprit was created in 1578 by Henri III. See François Bluche, *Dictionnaire du Grand Siècle* (Paris: Fayard, 1990), 1125-26, 1384, 1395.

9 This observation was first made by Jean-François Palomino, "L'image cartographique de la Nouvelle-France: Approche iconologique de l'œuvre de Jean-Baptiste-Louis Franquelin, 1678-1708" (MA thesis, Université Paris VII Denis-Diderot, 1998), 66.

10 My translation. "Il semblerait qu'il serait nécessaire de diviser ce grand terrain en Provinces, auxquelles on donneroit des limittes, et des noms françois stables, et permanants, aussy bien qu'aux rivières, et aux lieux particuliers, en abolissant tous les noms sauvages, qui ne font que de la confusion parce qu'ils changent très souvent, et que chaque nation nomme les lieux, et les rivières, en sa langue, ce qui fait qu'une mesme chose a toujours divers noms." J.B.L. Franquelin, "Mémoire de Mr Franquelin sur les limites des terres qui appartiennent aux français dans la N. F., et addition," 24, portfolio 124, Mémoires généraux, Amérique septentrionale, Dépôt des fortifications des colonies, Centre des archives d'outre mer, Aix-en-Provence.

11 My translation. "Ce travail non seullement rendroit les cartes plus intelligibles, mais confirmeroit encore la possession des pays qui y seroient contenus." Ibid.

12 Christian Jacob, *L'empire des cartes* (Paris: Albin Michel, 1992), 405.

13 See Monique Pelletier, "Les globes de Louis XIV: Les sources françaises de l'œuvre de Coronelli," *Imago Mundi* 34 (1982): 72-89.

14 My translation. "Les lunettes viennent souligner symboliquement l'importance du regard royal, dont elles sont la prothèse et le privilège ... Nul n'est à l'abri de l'oeil télescopique du souverain, capable de saisir l'ensemble du globe terrestre comme chacune des régions et tous ses lieux singulier." Jacob, *L'empire des cartes,* 411.

15 Quoted in Elias, *Court Society,* 128.

16 And Franquelin undoubtedly was in good position to make this proposal. His 1684 map of Louisiana already had corrected Coronelli on the course of the Mississippi River and its tributaries. See Pelletier, "Les Globes de Louis XIV," 84.

17 For a more complete discussion of this point, see Marc Grignon, "Comment s'est faite l'image d'une ville: Québec du XVIIe au XIXe siècle," in *Ville imaginaire, ville identitaire: Échos de Québec,* ed. Lucie K. Morisset, Luc Noppen, and Denis Saint-Jacques (Quebec: Nota Bene, 1999), 102-4.

18 These drawings are reproduced in *Plans of the French Settlements on the Saint Lawrence River, 1635-1642, by Jehan Bourdon* (Montreal: McGill University Library, 1958).

19 It should of course be mentioned that this relation between plans and views is not exceptional. Early plans of European cities such as Paris usually follow the orientation suggested in city views and become independent only when the more "scientific" north orientation is applied to them. In the case of Paris, this happens with the plan made by Albert Jouvin de Rochefort between 1672 and 1674. Interestingly, the famous plan by François Blondel and Pierre Bullet of 1676 retains the traditional orientation toward the east, used in the works of Sebastian Münster (1550) and Braun and Hogenberg (1572). This orientation corresponds to the common way of drawing views of the city, as in the view by Mathieu Merian (1615), an orientation that favours the visibility of important monuments such as Notre-Dame Cathedral and City Hall. Reproductions and a good discussion of these images can be found in Pierre Pinon and Bertrand Le Boudec, *Les plans de Paris: Histoire d'une capitale* (Paris: Bibliothèque nationale de France, 2004). In the case of Quebec City, plans oriented north appeared only with the English colonial regime after 1759. See Grignon, "Comment s'est faite l'image d'une ville," 111-12.

20 Although the volumes of *Civitates Orbis Terrarum* contain a variety of profile views, bird's-eye views, and plans, the authors clearly preferred bird's-eye views because they provided the most telling information in one single image. See Johannes Keunig, "The 'Civitates' of Braun and Hogenberg," *Imago Mundi* 17 (1963): 41-44.

21 See Marianne Grivel, *Le commerce de l'estampe à Paris au XVIIe siècle* (Geneva: Droz, 1986).

22 Marin, "La ville dans sa carte et son portrait," 212.

23 On this point, see Colin Coates, "Authority and Illegitimacy in New France: The Burial of Bishop Saint-Vallier and Madeleine de Verchères vs. the Priest of Batiscan," *Histoire sociale – Social History* 22, 43 (1989): 65-90.

24 The other tower, crowned with a belfry, situated directly in front of Notre-Dame-de-la-Paix, belongs to the facade of the Jesuit church and should not be confused with the cathedral.

25 See Marc Grignon, *"Loing du Soleil": Architectural Practice in Quebec City during the French Regime* (New York: Peter Lang, 1997), ch. 1.

26 My translation. "Si l'on achevait pas la ditte seconde tour avant que de commencer les murailles de l'église il pourrait arriver que cette seconde tour demeurerait en cet estat sans estre achevée, ce qui seroit très fascheux et extrêmement disgracié et vilain à voir ce qui n'arrivera pas au regard des murailles de l'église lesquelles paroistront d'une nécessité plus grande qui ne feroit pas d'achever la ditte seconde tour, de laquelle absolument l'on peut se passer, qui néanmoins à bien peser les choses est d'une grande nécessité." Bishop Laval to the Quebec Seminary, Paris, 1685, no. 130, Lettres N, Archives du Séminaire de Québec, Musée de l'Amérique française, Quebec City.

27 My translation. "Puisque l'on juge que l'on doibt continuer dès l'été prochain les travaux de l'église de Québec afin que la cour voye que l'on employe l'argent qu'elle donne à cet effet la première chose qu'il est nécessaire que l'on fasse est d'achever la seconde tour." Ibid.

28 The second bishop of New France, Jean-Baptiste de Saint-Vallier, arrived in Canada on 1 August 1688, and he also played a role in the construction of this church. But Laval, who had retired from his role as bishop, remained superior of the Seminary until his death in 1708. The chapel depended on the Seminary.

29 My translation. "Deux murailles de cinquante pieds de costé et d'autre sur la longueur de la dite chapelle; lesquelles seront fermées d'une troisième muraille du costé que doît estre l'autel." Contract between Claude Baillif, architect and building contractor, on the one hand, and François Dupré, parish priest and the churchwardens of Notre-Dame de Québec, on the other hand, "Marché pour la maçonnerie de l'église de la basse-ville," public notary François Genaple, 31 December 1687, Bibliothèque et Archives nationales du Québec, Quebec City.

30 Luc Noppen, *Notre-Dame-des-Victoires à la Place Royale de Québec* (Quebec: Ministère des affaires culturelles, 1974), 51-55.

31 The history of the Ursuline monastery was first examined by Ramsay Traquair, *The Old Architecture of Quebec* (Toronto: MacMillan, 1947), 29-33. A revised account of the reconstruction after the 1686 fire can be found in Grignon, *"Loing du Soleil,"* ch. 3.

32 "It has been decided that we should move back the aforesaid residence in such a way that the southwest wall will become that of the northeast, and, in this manner, it will be possible to rebuild the church in the place where it stood and to separate it entirely from the residence, to which it will be linked by no more than a small communicating passage, this arrangement aiming at preventing fire accidents" (my translation). "Il a esté conclu que l'on reculera entièrement le dit corps de logis, en sorte que la muraille, qui est entièrement au Sorouest sera celle du Nordest, et par ce moyen l'église pourra estre rebastie dans le mesme endroit, et estre entierement détachée du corps de logis, auquel elle ne sera conjointe que par une petite allée de communication, le tout pour prévenir les accidents de feu." Report of the decisions taken by Mr. Soumande and the Jesuit fathers, Construction papers, 3 March 1687, Archives of the Ursuline monastery, Quebec City.

33 These schemes included a two-courtyard design inspired from plans by Étienne Martellange for Jesuit colleges in France. See Grignon, *"Loing du Soleil,"* 111-19.

34 This point appears clearly in treatises that classify residences in relation to social hierarchy, such as Pierre Lemuet's *Manière de bien bastir pour toutes sortes de personnes* (1623, with new editions in 1647, 1664, and 1681). In the eighteenth century, Marc-Antoine Laugier explicitly recommended simplicity for the buildings of religious communities: "I say the same thing about seminaries or regular and secular communities. These kinds of buildings should always exhibit on the outside a simplicity appropriate to the condition of the persons living inside" (my translation). Original: "J'en dis autant à proportion des séminaires ou communautés séculières et régulières. Ces sortes d'édifices doivent toujours avoir à l'extérieur toute la simplicité convenable à l'état des personnes qui les habitent." Marc-Antoine Laugier, *Essai sur l'architecture* (Paris: Duchesne, 1755), 170.

35 See Grignon, *"Loing du Soleil,"* ch. 2.

36 This was the monastery of Notre-Dame-des-Anges, which would become the Hôpital Général in 1692.

37 "Eclaircissement nécessaire pour l'établissement d'un hospice que Sa Majesté nous a accordé dans la haute ville de Quebek," letter from the Quebec Récollets to the superiors of the order in France, 1681, published in Eugène Réveillaud, appendix to "Sixte le Tac," in *Histoire chronologique de la Nouvelle-France* (Paris: Eugène Réveillaud, 1888), 203.

38 This point, of course, should not be seen in an isolated manner. Bishop Laval was obviously worried about the number of people who could be drawn to the Récollets' chapel and might give alms to them instead of to other communities. Destruction of the Récollet belfry also meant the removal of the bell. As suggested to me by Judi Loach, the size of the church spires in the city view could evoke, in the seventeenth-century context, a specific soundscape, as higher towers would normally support more powerful bells.

39 See Marc Grignon, "Robert de Villeneuve and the Representation of Quebec City at the End of the Seventeenth Century," in *Circa 1700: Architecture in Europe and the Americas*, ed. Henry Millon, 187-206 (Washington, DC: National Gallery of Art, 2005).

40 Considering later views of Quebec City that Franquelin produced in his carreer, this conclusion becomes inescapable, as he continued to emphasize the official order, even after the Récollets were allowed to build a full-fledged monastery in Upper Town. Indeed, Laval's successor, Bishop Saint-Vallier, granted them this permisssion in 1691, and by the end of the century, the Récollet belfry dominated the eastern prospect. In a view drawn by Franquelin in 1699, the Récollet belfry occcupies the central position, and the Jesuit one is moved farther to the right. See Grignon, *"Loing du Soleil,"* 85.

41 See Marc Grignon, "La pratique architecturale de Claude Baillif," *Journal of Canadian Art History* 15 (1992): 19-21.

42 Ibid., 18.

43 Examples include Villeneuve's plan of 1690, "Place où est le buste du roy posé sur un pied d'estal en 1686 par M. de Champigny intendant"; Villeneuve's plan of 1692, "La place"; and Beaucours's plan of 1693, "La place au centre de laquelle est un piedestal portant le buste du roy."

44 The present copy of the original bust of Louis XIV is a gift offered by France in 1931. It was installed on the original spot in "remembrance" of the old one.

45 I am especially thinking about the 1699 view mentioned earlier (see note 40), which resembles that of 1688 very closely (including the name Place Royale), except for the fact that buildings have been updated. The 1699 view was traditionally attributed to Charles Bécart de Fonville because his signature appears on the map together with the title. But this map has been convincingly reattributed to Franquelin. See Palomino, "L'image cartographique de la Nouvelle-France," 73-75. Consequently, the 1699 view of Quebec does not provide an independent source confirming the validity of the name Place Royale.

46 See, for exemple, Renée Côté, *Place-Royale: Quatre siècles d'histoire* (Quebec: Ministère de la culture et des communications, 2000), 11.

PART 2
UPPER CANADIAN ARCHITECTURE

The powerful French intervention in Acadia was challenged and then constrained by British initiative. At first, this initiative was anchored in the maritime provinces but eventually centred on the capital of Upper Canada, York, later known as and referred to here as Toronto. The city became a particular focus for Loyalist identity but equally for Loyalist contestation, the latter partly due to the controversial provision of land for support of the established Anglican Church. Consequently, this part concentrates on the role of architectural design in the consolidation of colonial urban society at Toronto, notwithstanding the growth of British interests in such eastern seaboard towns as Halifax, Nova Scotia, Charlottetown, Prince Edward Island – where Confederation would be negotiated – and St. John's in the separate British colony of Newfoundland. It examines two building types. One was central to the social economy of colonial settlement: the church. The other was more utilitarian but equally basic to robust municipal growth and collective identity: the food market.

In "The Expansion of Religious Institution and Ontario's Economy, 1849-74: A Case Study of the Construction of Toronto's St. James Cathedral," Barry Magrill demonstrates the close relationship between economic and civic growth and religious architecture in mid-nineteenth-century Toronto – the result of intersecting networks of business and worship together with the sheer physical prominence afforded ecclesiastical structures. The enormous concern over the details of the commission and the ensuing complexities of the construction – both social and political – bring out the diverse agendas of those engaged in collegial undertakings. The erection of the church tower and steeple in particular demonstrates the extent to which architecture can resolve divergent forces toward an emblematic assertion of collective identity.

The agency of architect and patron is less of a factor in Sharon Vattay's similarly focused analysis of the food markets serving Toronto. Her chapter, "'For the benefit of the inhabitants': The Urban Market and City Planning in Toronto," reveals the importance of supposedly utilitarian infrastructure to the functioning, and thus self-awareness, of municipal societies, including the growing impact of urban centres on much wider geographies of resource and governance. Although less concerned with aesthetic display, the design and construction of markets such as those examined by Vattay enacted the intersection of commercial and bureaucratic systems underpinning civic, regional, and ultimately proto-national allegiance. Whereas the visibility of St. James was central to its religious (and socio-political) purpose and civic status, the effective working of the markets depended on relative invisibility. These markedly different architectures – church and market – illustrate the conceptual and material constituents of the everyday fabric of society. Their successive rebuilding reflected not only Toronto's changing demographic but also the persistent imprint of early planning decisions on long-term urban development.

The Expansion of Religious Institution and Ontario's Economy, 1849-74

A Case Study of the Construction of Toronto's St. James Cathedral

BARRY MAGRILL

"A RAPIDITY OF GROWTH AND STABILITY OF ENTERPRISE": CONTEXT FOR THE SPREAD OF ECONOMY AND RELIGION IN TORONTO

In May 1873 the view from the nearly complete spire of St. James Anglican Cathedral encompassed the increasing commercial and religious expansion of the City of Toronto (incorporated 1834) (Figure 3.1).

Briefly the tallest ecclesiastical structure in North America, the tower represented both the perceived robustness of this expansion and the unsustainable reality therein. Civic discourse had been preoccupied with discussion surrounding economic growth in Toronto for the subsequent two decades yet remained inconsistent with Toronto's actual economic situation; New York's economy had long outdistanced Toronto's, and New York's St. Patrick's Cathedral would surpass the height of St. James Cathedral in 1879. And growth endured as the dominant focus defining civic and group identities, despite the incontrovertible steady rise in the number of Toronto's poor throughout this same period. Indeed, growth stood as the chief measure used to define and shape civic identities, regardless of glaring cultural bias, social injustice, and economic unfairness.

This study of St. James Cathedral illustrates the social economy and culture of Toronto in the 1870s and the city's status as a place of architectural fashion in later Victorian Canada. The debates surrounding the construction of the monumental project demonstrate the interrelationships between the church's social life, federal politics, and the emerging modern urban lifestyle.[1] Indeed, Anglican church-building in Upper Canada largely constituted local colonial identities.[2] The Anglican Church in the Canadas was a significant agent of the British imperial regime, in spite of resistance from the Roman Catholic and Protestant denominations.[3] For these reasons, I adopt case study methodology in order to present specific sets of data that support this comparison without losing sight of significant contextual factors.

The civic growth represented by the completion of the St. James tower was not universally shared among Toronto's citizenry. Located at the corner of King and Church Streets, the St. James site was positioned between civic poverty and civic wealth. A buffer towering between affluent Torontonians and new immigrants, it stood a few blocks north of the city's first wharf and, in the 1850s, the Grand Trunk Railway yards. Although shipping and rail expansion brought the traffic of immigration and commercial goods to Toronto and neighbouring municipalities, the chief beneficiaries of this expansion were already economically privileged.[4] The wharf was also an entry point for sickness; in 1847 Irish immigrants fleeing the Potato Famine died on Toronto's docks of disease and starvation after disembarking their boats. Low-cost dwellings and drab merchant shops (owned by the Anglican Church) surrounded the broad, manicured church grounds, a far cry from the affluent residences farther north along tree-lined Jarvis and Sherbourne Streets. The rectory and the cathedral's south transept door stood as a bulwark against the encroachment of low-cost housing located to the immediate east. In the 1850s this south transept door was filled with bricks to reduce the visibility of the poor living in the deplorable conditions. The practice ran counter to the idea of a religious institution operating as a charitable foundation. Filling in the south transept doorway at St. James indicated that affluent Torontonians who funded church-building benefited from their privileged role at the expense of the poor they were publicly charged with aiding.

The poor had little expectation of social justice in this period. Any social and economic assistance that underprivileged Anglicans in Toronto could expect came from their affluent brethren and was delivered through the church. Cultural affiliation strongly linked social and economic privilege. For this reason, religion, no less than the politics and economy of Britain, and to a lesser extent of the United States, shaped regional self-identification in the Canadian provinces. This complex process was further compounded in Toronto because of the city's focus on outwardly portraying its growth instead of on improving its quality of life.

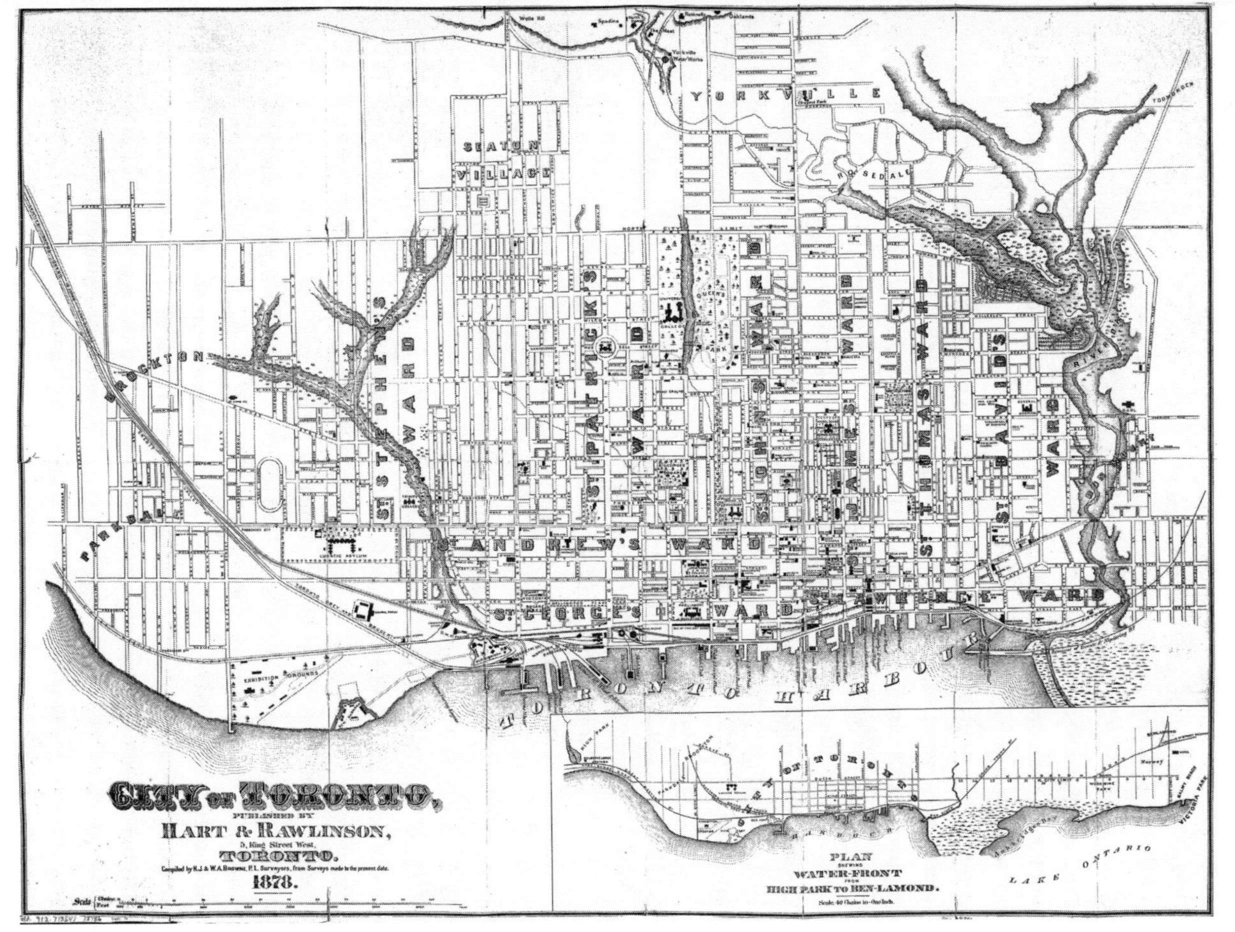

Figure 3.1 Map of Toronto, 1878. | Provided with permission from the Toronto Public Library Archives.

The outward appearance of St. James Cathedral exemplified Toronto's civic desire to identify with major European cities. The public was to view the cathedral as a symbol more of civic growth than of the city's spiritual qualities. The Toronto-based *Anglo-American Magazine* boasted of the city's expansion: "We assert ... a rapidity of growth and a stability produced by wholesome enterprise, as encouraging as it is remarkable."[5] However, the modest scale of Toronto's major buildings undercut the hubris; there was no dominant landmark or dominant structure in 1852. In that same year, the editors of the *Anglo-American Magazine* regretted that "there are no contiguous heights from which an extended prospect is afforded to the eye."[6] Thus upon its construction in 1874 the St. James spire, then the tallest structure in North America, immediately became the locus of civic identification. Local citizens identified the tower and spire of St. James Cathedral with economic prosperity even if the spire also signified an as yet deficient social and economic order. There was, as in all things, a price to pay for such an ambitious project, as the church concentrated its revenue on building and away from aiding Toronto's growing poor. Indeed, the continued visibility of urban poverty in Toronto shed a pall over the civic assertion of the positive effects of commerce.[7] Toronto's poor may have felt that the role of the great tower was not to uplift their spirits but to shroud the city's poverty and cast their needs into shadow.

The turbulent construction history of St. James Cathedral was closely linked to the fabrication of Toronto's self-image throughout this period. By 1839 St. James Church had been granted cathedral status in the newly formed Anglican diocese of Toronto. John Strachan, the inaugural bishop for this new diocese (1839-67), inherited an 1820s Georgian-style church that was a poor match for developing High Anglican liturgical-cum-architectural tastes, which favoured a sophisticated neo-Gothic mode (Figure 3.2). Fire destroyed the Georgian building along with a large sector of the city in 1849 and created the opportunity to rebuild the church in the current Gothic Revival fashion. A visible monument to Toronto's burgeoning prosperity was an understandably contentious project. Disputes within the congregation delayed completion of the main body for two years. The tower, topped by the spire, remained uncompleted until 1874 when its unparalleled height in North America marked a significant point in Torontonians' identification with major European and American cities. This new vantage point overlooking the city afforded Torontonians a much enhanced view of their environment and seemed to confirm their assertions of cosmopolitan status.

Toronto's self-image as an expanding commercial centre developed in tandem with the extension of religious institution and the syndication of

Figure 3.2 St. James Cathedral, 1840. | Provided with permission from the Toronto Public Library Archives.

Canadian economic and political interests. The spread of religious enterprise, especially church-building, was assisted by a "commerce of taste," more commonly termed "fashion," since church aesthetics were a marketable commodity. This so-called "commerce of taste" involved commercial expansion, which exploited a continual renewal of production and consumption, as exemplified by the renovation and rebuilding of churches. "Fashion" and taste were instruments used to legitimate the social claims and economic privileges taken by Anglicans as the dominant group. In a visual sense, they appropriated the enduring aspects of an ancient – mainly Gothic – architecture in order to visually assert their prestige. Taste, however, was also subject to the transience of fashion, and architects had to carefully market their designs as enduring without appearing "old-fashioned." In a complex network of dynamic group social interactions, expressed as architectural rivalries, taste was a commodity. And taste came at a cost. To invoke these visual associations with superior status, St. James Anglican Cathedral had to focus its revenue upon design and construction of this new church and away from its charitable works.

OF ARCHITECTONICS, ECONOMY, AND CHURCHMEN

Toronto's architectural regrowth following the Great Fire of 1849 was meant to put the city in league with a notional suite of European and US cities, including London, Chicago, and Seattle.[8] The reconstruction of St. James coincided with Toronto's fashioning itself as both an imperial and even a continental European city; efforts initially involved protracted debates on the way the new St. James should look, as well as on the sources of income needed to support its construction. Sporadic but intense negotiations took place from 1851 to 1853, between Bishop John Strachan and members of the vestry building committee, as to the choice of architect as well as the orientation of the new cathedral and its overall design. All of these matters related to building cost. Methods for financing the rebuilding became contentious, especially since some parties, particularly the bishop, favoured selling portions of the cathedral's churchyard that contained old gravesites. Despite significant cost overruns, which resulted in a prolonged building campaign, the congregation persevered in completing a monumental cathedral that they could not afford.

Religious faith and economic optimism, tempered by practical concerns, and interdenominational rivalry contributed to the building committee's decisions regarding the scale of the cathedral project. For the church was not trying simply to rebuild but was actively seeking to mark the Anglican faith as the dominant religion in this new, burgeoning metropolis of Toronto. The construction of monumental church architecture like St. James Cathedral satisfied the city's ambition to assure a leading role in regional politics. The scale of the cathedral, although small by European standards, was designed to fulfil Toronto's growing need to identify itself with the larger European cities and proved to be

Figure 3.3 Bishop Strachan. | Photograph by author.

a substantial economic burden for both the congregation and its bishop. Nevertheless, the cathedral – and its expression of current fashion in transatlantic ecclesiastical architecture – was a potent symbol of Bishop Strachan's belief that prestige ought to accrue to the established church. This position, one shared by a range of Anglican groups, saw the economic development of Canada as an outcome of Anglican effort and accomplishment. Thus multiple layers of Toronto's new, fashion-conscious civic self-image were linked in the building of a single cathedral.

A brief analysis of the political and business activities of the members of the St. James building committee explains their design selection and demonstrates how Anglican interests were closely linked to the social, economic, and cultural development of Canada West (the western portion of the Province of Canada, formerly Upper Canada). The building committee's chair was the lawyer, judge, conservative politician, and "Family Compact" member John Beverley Robinson (1791-1863). His conservative politics meant he maintained close personal ties with Bishop Strachan and Lieutenant-Governor Sir Peregrine Maitland. Robinson believed that respect for rank, privilege, and the power of wealth needed greater emphasis in Upper Canadian society. The other committee members held similar economic, social, and political ties, including Frederick Widder (1801-65), who became an official of the British land and colonizing venture the Canada Company upon his immigration from England. He was also active in the St. George's Society, was lay vice-president of the Anglican Diocesan Church Society, and later turned to railway promotion. Peter Paterson (1807-83) owned a successful hardware and dry goods business in Toronto, incorporated the British American Fire and Life Assurance Company (1834), founded the Consumer's Gas Company (1847), developed the Canada Permanent Building and Savings Society (1855, renamed the Canada Permanent Mortgage Co.), held a directorship with the Bank of Upper Canada (1861), and was active in the St. Andrew's Society. Sir J.H. Hogarty (1816-1900), born in Dublin, was a professor of law at Trinity College and a judge for forty-one years, as well as president of the St. Patrick's Society. Although this list of accomplishments is deliberately concise, it demonstrates the interconnection of commercial interests with nation building, politics, law, and religion.[9] A pervasive wish to extend Anglican influence motivated their decision to construct the cathedral and its tower, even though few of them lived to see the tower begun. Via these connections, the city and the Anglican officials jointly asserted that an iconic church tower was in the best interests of the poor.

Torontonians self-identified with architectural fashion and large-scale buildings as early as the 1850s. Church-building increased in line with the city's robust economy, causing a correspondent of the *Montreal Herald,* in 1853, to compare the opening of St. James with the "beauty of the principal streets."[10] This sentiment only increased during the ensuing two decades and spread among all denominations (almost exclusively Christian) but also among Jewish congregations, such as members of the Holy Blossom Temple (built in 1856) located on Eglinton Avenue. By the 1870s Toronto believed itself graced with important architectural works from every major religious denomination. In the vicinity of St. James was Metropolitan Methodist Church (referred to as the Cathedral to Methodism) constructed at the corner of Queen and Church Streets; Jarvis Street Baptist Church went up at the corner of Jarvis and Gerrard Streets; the Roman Catholic St. Michael's Cathedral at Bond and Shuter Streets represented the advanced social standing of Catholicism in Upper Canada; and Knox Presbyterian Church owned a large block of land framed by Queen, Bay, Richmond, and Yonge Streets. Surpassing all of these churches in height at 316 feet – if not also in controversies surrounding its design and construction – was the tower of the Anglican cathedral of St. James.

Accounting for the force of religion in Canada's modern urban development presents a fuller portrait of the Dominion's social formation. By using St. James Cathedral as a microcosm of these forces at work, we can see them take a wide variety of forms, including the social activities and networks of the chief architects: Fred Cumberland (1882-81), who provided the initial design of 1849-54; and Henry Langley (1836-1907), who redesigned the tower and spire in 1864 (completed 1874). Cumberland in particular exemplified the interconnections between religion and economy. He had a hand in railway management and development, a seat in the Ontario Legislature, and a voice in the Anglican Synod during the second half of the nineteenth century, not to mention a thriving drawing table.[11] As the Great Western Railway's chief engineer, Cumberland even accepted a $10,000 "under-the-table" payment from railway contractors in return for sanctioning their "speedy and careless efforts."[12] This questionable payment serves as an example of the notable lack of checks and balances yet to develop in Upper Canada's rapidly expanding economy. It also provides some insight into the personalities drawn into the project of rebuilding St. James Cathedral.

Henry Langley, the tower's designer, had a respected and active practice that not only graced Toronto with several fashionable domestic, civic, and religious structures but also bridged cultural and religious borders in Ontario.[13] Awarding Langley the commission to complete the St. James tower and spire was significant because he was particularly well known for finishing church towers, making him something of an architectural celebrity in religious circles.

Although periodically adversarial toward the building committee, Bishop Strachan (Figure 3.3) clearly supported the building of a monumental civic structure. Adding to this were Bishop Strachan's broad ideas on religious authority in civil society, which materialized architecturally in his founding of Trinity College (designed by Kivas Tully in 1852). The bishop believed that the moral development of the society of Canada West required religiously framed higher education, under the direction of an established Anglican Church.

METHODOLOGY OF CASE STUDY ANALYSIS

Case study methodology takes into account disparate social factors, such as economy, religion, and individual and collective identity, visualized as "organic, living systems," the components of which are flexible and adaptive.[14] Working through the lens of St. James Cathedral, case study can be used to show systems of enterprise operating socially, spatially, and temporally. Incorporating multiple narratives bounded together by all of the factors at play, it allows one to focus upon the relative positions of different social agents and forces. Analysis of the construction of St. James is well served by the case study approach. Such an analysis supports the contention that economy, especially commercial practice, contributed largely to the formation of Canadian civic identities and social interactions.

The factors that formed Canadian society are explored here in terms of spatial and reception theories, as well as discourse analysis. In particular, I apply social theorist Pierre Bourdieu's notion of "habitus" to this case study of St. James Cathedral. This notion holds that the dispositions and social actions that inform people's positions and identities synthesize multifarious economic, religious, and political factors – as evident in the construction of the cathedral.[15] Social and cultural development in mid- to late-nineteenth-century Toronto is examined through the emergence of new commercial practices. The growth of religious institution – as exemplified in church-building – was a commercial affair employing and exchanging vast amounts of economic, cultural, symbolic, and artistic capital.[16] In addition, Michel Foucault's observations of self-discipline around the panoptic device due to a subject's continual observation provide insight into the metaphoric views afforded by the St. James tower and spire.[17] I argue that the tower at St. James was a distant colonial metaphor for Jeremy Bentham's panoptic tower, in the sense that many Anglican clergy and parishioners believed the established church represented the moral conscience of the Dominion at large – and should thus be highly visible in the built environment of its major urban centres. The completion of the St. James tower in Toronto, indeed, coincided with the public's expectation of increased moral self-discipline beyond the doors of the Anglican Church.

Toronto's economy was both instigated and managed by a social interface of citizens. The roots of Toronto's commercial expansion reached back to the period between 1820 and 1840, when its role as a centre for grain distribution grew via entrepreneurial practice coupled with expanded banking facilities. Locating the Bank of Upper Canada (est. 1821) in Toronto, for instance, gave the city an advantage when business investment in Upper Canada increased over the next two decades. This was clearly reflected in the settlement patterns of Toronto and later Hamilton in Upper Canada.[18] The location and operation of financial institutions in both of these towns contributed to the development of each city's uniquely diverse economy and social structure, exemplified by the proximity of housing zones to industrial zones. With a growing capital base and system of investment, many affluent Toronto neighbourhoods developed farther from industrial land and closer to centres of commerce. The growth of these commercial centres was accompanied by increased church-building in adjacent residential areas.

ANGLICAN PRIVILEGE AND BRITISH CULTURAL AFFINITY IN TORONTO

Perched atop the "lofty" neo-Gothic spire of St. James Cathedral in 1874, an observer with a sharp eye – and a little faith – might believe Britain's cathedrals were visible across the Atlantic.[19] Indeed, a sense of "imagined community" continued to link Canada with Britain well beyond the period of official Confederation in 1867.[20] The phenomenon was particularly strong in church architecture, which Torontonians continued to believe paralleled similar stylistic movements in Britain. Prominent social and political figures connected to the established church included the governor-general of Upper Canada, Lord Durham (John Lambton, 1792-1840), and his successor, and son-in-law, Lord Elgin (James Bruce, 1811-63). Lord Durham's Report to the British Crown on the political state of the Dominion (1839), among other things, suggested that the French cultural issue be settled by creating a union of Upper and Lower Canada in order to place the French in minority.[21] Subsequently, Lord Elgin influenced the financial fate of the Anglican Church in Canada by recommending that the future of the Clergy Reserves be decided in the Canadian, not the British, Parliament. Whereas Lord Durham's action was beneficial to the established church – whose socio-political power belied its minority population – Lord Elgin's act imposed serious financial strain on the Anglican Church. The appointment of Lord Durham and Lord Elgin to superior posts in the Dominion enacted British policy across the Atlantic, even though both men championed the Dominion's responsible self-governance. At the same time, the proximity of the United States gradually shifted the economic and cultural perspective, as was evidenced in the increasing award of architectural competitions in the Dominion to American practitioners.[22] Consequently, the manner in which the Dominion chose to assert its identity in architectural terms that differed from the United States, while also being differentiated from Britain, became an issue linked to debates in the social and political arenas.

In actuality, modest but tangible architectural variations in church-building separated Canada West, particularly Toronto, from Britain. Some of this variation came from differences in economic capacity; the white brick of St. James Cathedral stands in stark opposition to the use of coloured brickwork in the constructional polychromy of William Butterfield's All Saints, Margaret Street, London (1849), a building that initiated a stylistic mode quickly accepted as progressive (Figure 3.4). Thus social practices and norms in the Canadas also developed subtle but meaningful differences from Britain. The nascent issue of the Dominion's identity was being worked out in architectural terms in tandem with the same debates in the socio-cultural and political arenas.

Nevertheless, the proliferation of the Gothic Revival in Canada reflected the personal and local networks that sustained British influence. The complexity of imperial/colonial relations meant that church builders in Upper Canada also asserted regional differences. For this reason, British architectural fashions came up against local, climatic, and economic conditions. This led to continued interest in transatlantic developments but also to the beginnings of an environmentally determined concept of "Canadian architectural style."[23] Awed and sometimes overwhelmed by the extreme Canadian climates, nineteenth-century church builders regularly referred to local climate as a factor in their choice and interpretation of architectural style.[24]

Historical, and even contemporaneous, discourse around architecture in Canada has placed climate over economy. Yet in reality, local economy played a more significant role than was supposed at the time in the aesthetics of churches. The layout of St. James Cathedral demonstrates how the commission of this large building was negotiated between Bishop Strachan and the building committee in order to maximize pew-rental income: the cathedral's size was subject to the financial restraints of large-scale construction. Given that the unevenness of civic and economic growth was perceived as generally acceptable, the architect Fred Cumberland was sent back to the drawing table on several

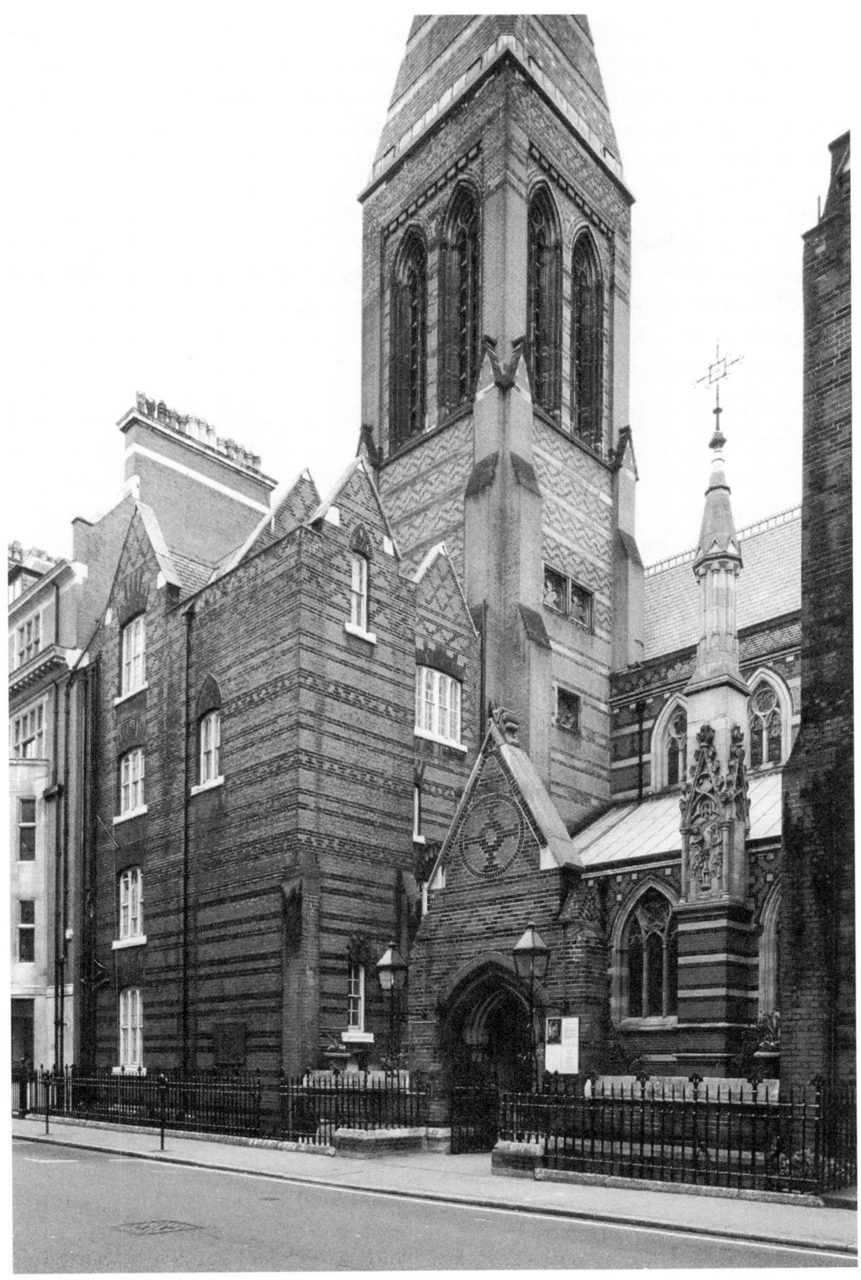

Figure 3.4 All Saints, Margaret Street, London, architect William Butterfield, 1849. | Photograph by author.

occasions to rework the relatively modest floor-plate so as to raise pew-rental income, while at the same time, the vestry building committee wanted to reduce costs where possible. In a counterproductive move, the bishop even attempted to inflate the number of pews. The arrangement of a western tower was a cost-saving device, which circumvented the need for massive supporting piers around the crossing area in the case of a more "fashionable" central or crossing tower.[25] Typical of the pragmatic concerns that faced colonial building initiatives, the cathedral was built onto the old Georgian foundation. The decision to use the old foundation was a cost-saving initiative that also sped rebuilding efforts. A rather squat layout for the cathedral resulted, later compensated for by the tower's elevation. As a result, the layout did not truly conform to the Ecclesiological principles advocated by the Cambridge Camden (later the Ecclesiological) Society, the purveyors of neo-Gothic taste (Figure 3.5). Cumberland's adaptation of fashionable neo-Gothic aesthetics to the proportions of a Georgian church illustrates how design practice conformed to Toronto's economic situation.

ARCHITECTURE AND SOCIAL PRIVILEGE

The close association of architecture and social privilege occurred even when privilege was imagined as opposed to statistically substantiated. The 1851 census returns show that the overall Anglican population in Upper and Lower Canada was only 14 percent, which put it behind Methodist, Presbyterian, and Roman Catholic groups.[26] Undeterred by these statistics, Anglican groups and individuals behaved as though they dominated the Dominion's social structure, and many tried to extend their advantage into greater state policy concessions and economic dispensations. In Toronto the Anglican enclave was greater, at roughly 25 percent, which accounts for the Church of England's increased demands on the political system.[27]

This Anglican predominance was reflected clearly in the height of the St. James tower. But perceived dominance and privilege were complicated matters and there were clear instances where Anglicans were irritated by the social and economic advancements of rival denominations, visibly manifested by new Catholic and Methodist churches. A significant architectural rival for the builders of St. James Cathedral was the Roman Catholic Church. The metaphorical bile of the Anglican spleen must have risen at the prospect that the Catholic congregation at St. Michael's Cathedral (at Bond and Shuter Streets) had completed a tower and spire ahead of St. James. By the time that St. Michael's had a completed spire around 1867, the tower of the Anglican cathedral had not

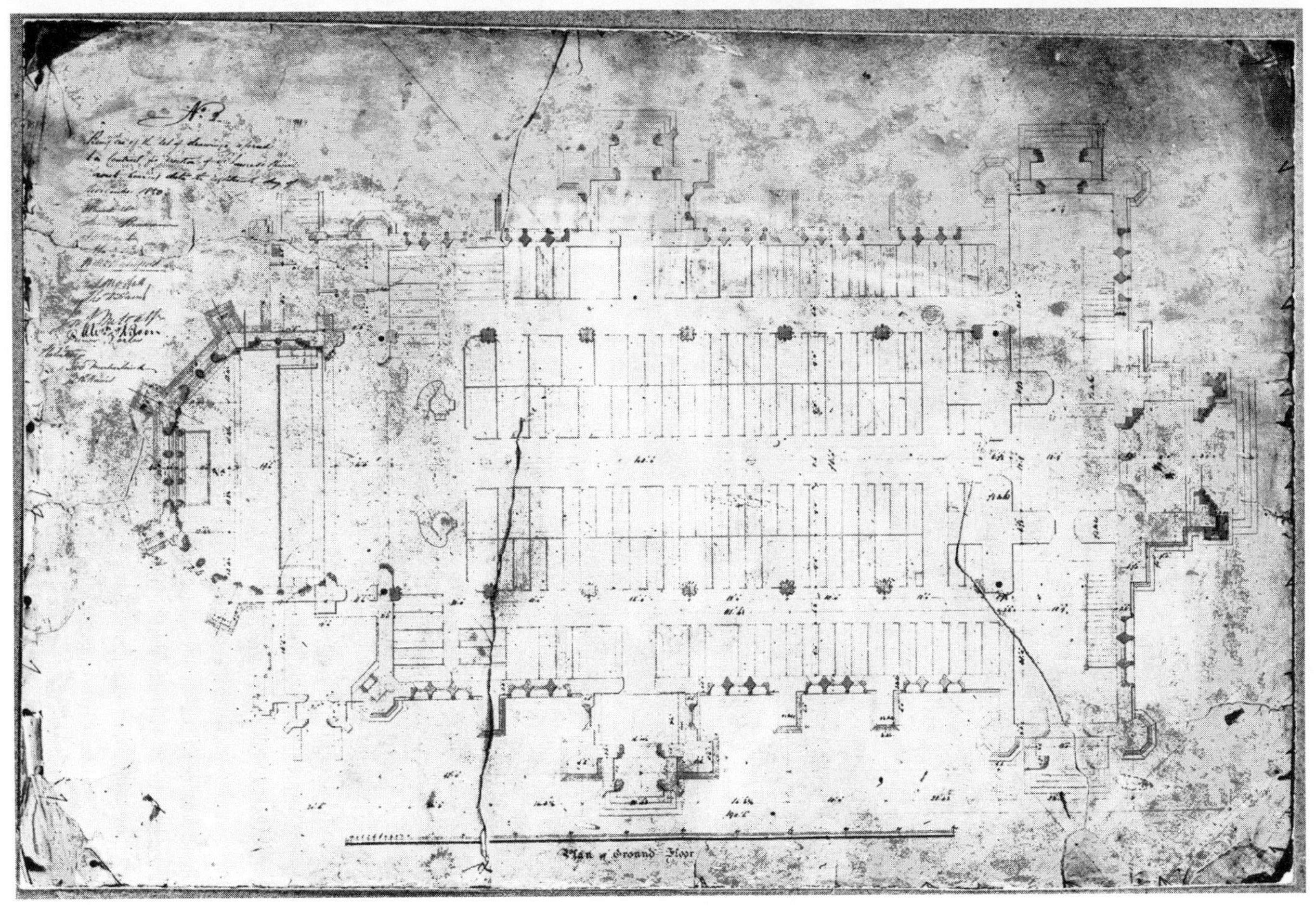

Figure 3.5 St. James Cathedral layout, by Fred Cumberland. | Provided with permission from the Toronto Public Library Archives.

Figure 3.6 St. James Cathedral, 1853. | Provided with permission from the Toronto Public Library Archives.

risen above the height of the nave roof (Figure 3.6). The Anglican congregation at St. James was spurred into action. Demonstrating that privilege formed a core component of identity, the Anglican congregation at St. James determined to construct the tallest spire in the Dominion; the vestry building committee even hired the architect of the St. Michael's tower, Henry Langley (Figure 3.7). Langley was especially respected for his practice's church towers, and his talents helped the Anglican congregation outstrip the St. Michael's spire by fifty-six feet.

The complex interchange between the social, economic, and cultural structures at work in Toronto had been made explicitly evident by the large-scale immigration of Scottish and Irish Protestants. Many were associated with the Orange Order established in Canada in 1830. The Orange Order was a powerful political force in Ontario at this time and its members often rose in public service, not the least of whom was Prime Minister John A. Macdonald.[28] Toronto

Figure 3.7 St. James Cathedral, Toronto. | Photograph by author.

was an "Orange" town, as exemplified by resistance to the 1837 Mackenzie Rebellion, wherein the mayor of Toronto had, at the last minute, enlisted 317 Orangemen into the militia. Often penniless and undernourished, the Irish Catholics escaping from the effects of the Potato Famine began arriving at the Toronto wharf alongside waves of new Orange immigrants. The situation heightened religious differences in the Canadas already complicated by the Fenian Movement centred south of the border. A large proportion of the Scottish and Irish attended Cooke's Presbyterian Church on Queen Street (rebuilt 1891, demolished 1984). A smaller group, many of whom were members of the Orange Order and only a few of whom were not well off, attended St. James Cathedral alongside the predominantly English immigrant congregation.

Bishop Strachan's attempts to maintain good relations among the quite diverse congregation at St. James may have been disrupted after the Fenian militia, which was associated with Irish Catholics and intended to destabilize the political situation in Britain, began conducting cross-border raids into Ontario, Quebec, and New Brunswick from America. Fred Cumberland, now retired from architecture and working in railway management, proposed that the railway transport militia regulars to counterpose the Fenian raids. Like the internal division that threatened to split the congregation at St. James over the cost of rebuilding the cathedral, the Fenian raids of 1866 tested them as well, perhaps also exposing the frayed edges of an embryonic "national tapestry." Indeed, the Fenian raids in the summer of 1866 triggered shifts in the Dominion's "official" policy on open immigration. Increased surveillance and an early form of cultural profiling became border protocol during this period. After the initial raids across the Quebec and New Brunswick borders in June 1866, the nascent Government of Canada became more sensitive to the potential for mass uprisings. For instance, Canadian authorities scrutinized the build-up of 14,000 Fenian supporters in Buffalo on 7 August 1866 as a potential staging ground for an incursion that could end up in Toronto.

At the same time, the Fenian raids aroused officially sanctioned intolerance. The collective attitude among the Dominion's citizenry varied between disgust and fascination. Just months after the Fenian raids, the combination of sectional intolerance versus collective identity translated into a rare business opportunity. W.C. Hewitt and Company of Toronto advertised the sale of private accounts of the raids complete with maps showing the route of the troops and the ground plan of the Lime Ridge Battle; purchasers paid twenty-five cents for the accounts in 1866.[29] Upper Canadians, and particularly Torontonians, were fascinated by their own controversies and adversities, especially when they could read about them in the press. In this sense, Toronto's civic identity was also constituted in the *Toronto Globe*'s initial report of the Great Fire of 1849, worth recalling: "With deep regret we announce that a dreadful fire that broke out about half past 1 o'clock this morning, in some outbuildings in the rear of Graham's Tavern ... St. James Cathedral has been entirely burnt down, and the valuable buildings adjoining on King Street."[30] Interestingly, the report recognized the economic value of the land on King Street, which Bishop Strachan also wanted to capitalize upon. These raids highlighted the already visible division in the St. James congregation and served as a reminder of the careful path Toronto would need to forge as it developed into a modern, urban centre.

REBUILDING ST. JAMES CATHEDRAL: A CASE STUDY IN A "COMMERCE OF RELIGION"

As further particulars of the fire were reported, a clearer picture of the city's re-forming began to emerge: "It is not easy to describe the gloom which this calamity has cast over the city, or the ruinous appearance of the ground so lately occupied by many respectable and industrious individuals, who by the work of four or five hours, were suddenly thrown out of business."[31] The report continued in an optimistic tone that demonstrated Torontonians' faith in progress: "There cannot be a doubt, however, that the activity and enterprise of the inhabitants will soon surmount the loss ... Many improvements will doubtless be introduced in the formation of new streets."[32] Not only was the loss of St. James a dramatic event, but the process of reconstruction was long and often contentious.

An ember had ignited the original wooden spire of St. James Church, causing its blackened frame to fall into the body of the cathedral below. Yet from tragedy came opportunity. Within two weeks, the congregation organized a building committee, which outlined and debated several issues about the cathedral's reconstruction. At issue in the building committee's meetings was the proposed sale of the churchyard located along King Street for commercial development.[33] With £5,000 insurance money matched by congregants' donations, the building committee still needed significantly more funds.[34] One faction of the building committee advocated reusing the old foundation, oriented north-south along Church Street, which would retain the sanctity of church land, leave graves undisturbed, and save money.[35] A petition among residents was also organized to block the lease of the Anglican Church's lands, a rare instance of public intervention in church affairs.

The cathedral's initial reconstruction was relatively rapid; the nave was completed in 1852, well in advance of the 1857 recession.[36] However, the ongoing internal debates over architect, cost, and design slowed the construction process.

Fred Cumberland had been awarded the commission through a competition with other leading British-trained practitioners, including Frank Wills, William Thomas, Kivas Tully and John Tully, John Ostell, and US resident Gervase Wheeler.[37] However, Cumberland had to struggle to retain the commission when Bishop Strachan attempted to have him replaced by Montreal architect George H. Smith, who had not even participated in the initial competition.

The bishop's belief that divine providence could overcome economic problems put him in league with Smith, who had suggested building a larger cruciform cathedral. Pragmatically, the bishop preferred Smith's layout. The larger cruciform plan would have added considerably to the old church's capacity of 2,000 seats. Smith's plan was achievable only by offsetting building expense with the sale of the churchyard. It ultimately proved too ambitious even for Bishop Strachan, so Cumberland's plan, with modifications, was fully adopted.[38]

Preventing the "legitimate" sale of the churchyard, in Bishop Strachan's mind, was the public's interpretation of the term "consecration." Although public opinion was divided – being strongly influenced by journalism, rumour, as well as beliefs rooted in tradition – there was vocal civic support for the preservation of the old graves at St. James. The opposition to the bishop's plan to move the graveyard was, in his own words, a source of "irritation."[39] To rally public support for the sale of the St. James churchyard, Bishop Strachan published and widely distributed a pamphlet in 1850 that illustrated his pragmatic approach to addressing the financial shortfall associated with building the new cathedral.[40]

Using the power of print media, the bishop argued that the preservation of consecrated land was important for the funding of a new, more prominent cathedral worthy of the prestige of the Anglican Church in Canada.[41] "Public opinion, as well as, the law," he further argued, "were against burying in churches or cities ... being injurious to health." Burial in the city was invented by modern custom and legitimized through ecclesiastical warrant rather than with reference to theology or hygiene.[42] However, removing burial grounds to places beyond the urban confines may not have been as practical a solution as Bishop Strachan advertised given the rapid expansion of Toronto. Economic growth made the city limits unstable, and the city boundary continued to spread to the north, west, and east as the growth of population was coupled with increased commercial practices.

In the pamphlet, Bishop Strachan claimed it was fashion – or public custom – not Scripture – that brought about the practice of urban burial.[43] He noted the link between the invention of new customs and the transience of fashion, which ran contrary to the "public opinion" that the bishop conjured to agree with his own views. Essentially, he claimed that the public taste already concurred with the removal of the graves, an opinion that gave his printed public address the quality of a decree rather than a public plea. Clearly, the letter showed how Bishop Strachan expected that religious rank and privilege equated with social and economic capital. He intimated that his authority permitted the deconsecration of the churchyard, as long as the dead were carefully removed. Furthermore, he stated that the churchyard ought to be sold because all available space was already allotted.[44] His functional logic serves to underline a mindset of what might be termed religious real estate. The pamphlet prompted building committee member "Bramhill" to state that consecrated ground could not be unconsecrated for commercial purposes.[45]

Many of the bishop's congregants at St. James appeared unmoved by civic responsibility. It was no surprise, then, when the *Globe* report on the 1849 fire included a plea for the "relief of those who are so reduced by the fire as to require public assistance."[46] Since the report had to invoke the "hope that the public will ... come forward with a liberal hand," it is possible to adduce that such responses were not often forthcoming.[47] The bishop acknowledged the situation in another way. He noted that his congregants tended to concern themselves with the size and location of their pews as opposed to the retention of an "old churchyard." But he was also aware of the politics involved in selling the churchyard, and he therefore determined to focus the pew holders' attention on issues of pew rental instead of the sale of the churchyard. When one congregant complained that his new pew was smaller and poorly located in the nave of the new cathedral, the architect, Fred Cumberland, was called upon to produce a letter illustrating the favourable appointment of the new pews.[48] Religious and political controversy captured public attention and continually worked counter to the bishop's favour. In 1851 Bishop Strachan was finally, officially, unsuccessful in obtaining allowance to sell the churchyard.

Controversy compounded the delays in construction, and the imminent loss of income from the Clergy Reserves caused the bishop to write disparagingly of the state of the Anglican Church. His temper ran higher yet when it came to the issue of the Clergy Reserves. By the mid-1850s, Canada's colonial government and the British Foreign Office had rescinded the offer of monies accruing from the sale of Clergy Reserves to the Anglican Church. These were massive tracts of land in Upper Canada and other provinces in British North America set aside to fund religious institutions – which for Strachan was the Anglican Church alone. In 1854 Bishop Strachan wrote a second letter complaining that the Anglican Church had been unfairly treated with respect to the dispositions of the Clergy Reserves. The letter was written in the year of the completion of the cathedral, when Strachan was disposed to be accommodating to other Christian denominations. At this stage, Strachan appeared to be collaborating with Roman Catholics in order to assure the Anglicans a share of the monies from the sale of the Clergy Reserves.[49]

Bishop Strachan collected his emotions in a letter to the Right Hon. Lord John Russell, member of the British Parliament and Reform advocate. The bishop complained, "we [Anglicans] have fallen into a state so extraordinary and humbling in a British colony."[50] The bishop's position – that "the Romish Church has increased in efficiency, wealth, and importance, with the growth of the Colony"[51] – was prescient considering the eventual architectural developments at St. Michael's Cathedral.

Beginning construction at the cathedral did not dissipate the bishop's problems. Tenders from builders were advertised in the *British Colonist,* the *Church,* and the *Patriot*. The contracting firm of Metcalfe, Wilson, and Forbes supplied the lowest bid at £16,500, 50 percent more than Cumberland had initially anticipated. Costs further overran to £18,803.17.7 with a balance owing of £9,335.17.7, and this was for an unimpressive building – very unlike a cathedral and not at all what either the bishop or the building committee wanted. Increasing the level of insult, in the minds of architecture-conscious Torontonians, the English religious press turned its eye to St. James to make a comparison that benefited Montreal's Christ Church (Frank Wills, 1857). The *Ecclesiologist* journal wrote: "Altogether Montreal Cathedral will, when completed, mark an epoch in transatlantic ecclesiology. It will be the largest completed cathedral in America of our communion; for though the new one at Toronto would, if completed, be larger, it is as yet unfinished, and on (we believe) a much inferior and less correct plan."[52] The cathedral was not the only project of Bishop Strachan that encountered adverse public reaction. His initiative to ally higher education and Anglican tradition, as exemplified by his founding of Trinity College, was being thwarted in the press and in the Ontario Legislature, chiefly by Egerton Ryerson.

Although the bishop's tone was initially conciliatory, tempered perhaps by the satisfaction of finishing the nave of his cathedral, the reaction from another of the Anglican brethren showed that yet deeper resentments had developed between religious and governmental institutions. When addressing the Anglican congregation of St. Peter's Church at Springfield, Elgin County, on the Clergy Reserve issue, Henry C. Cooper was not the least taciturn when he raised the topic of Roman Catholic violence:

> The Romanists will not passively yield up their church's rights and properties. They are a united body; they acknowledge no bond of union so abiding and binding as their church. For it and its endowments they will sacrifice everything; colonial union – British connexion – civil peace: and ... we may see the fearful forms of political convulsion, intestine anarchy and strife – the dislocation of the whole frame of our social fabric – the probable dismemberment of our colonial empire.[53]

The threat of civil uprising involving Roman Catholics was not entirely misplaced. Religious and cultural intolerance was building in Toronto, including from within the mixed St. James congregation.

Yet, and as a microcosm of the larger social organization, the building committee's British, Irish, Scots, and Canadian-born members managed to complete their task despite such cultural and political disagreement. They behaved as a collective out of the interests of economy and religion. Moreover, the cobbling together of a collective approach involved the suppression of violence stemming from coercion rather than the building of consensus. Periodically, however, violent clashes had proven uncontainable. In 1852, more than a decade before the Fenian raids of 1866, the *Anglo-American Magazine* reported that "in Hamilton a party of Orangemen who had assisted at the demonstration in Toronto, were attacked by a hostile body."[54] During the attack, an Orangeman called Thomas Campbell stabbed and killed a Roman Catholic named McPhillips. On account of the disturbance, the dead McPhillips was accorded the rites of burial by the Roman Catholic bishop of Toronto, Armand-François-Marie Comte de Charbonnel (1802-91). Even architectural objectives were thus implicated in the religious, ethnic, and economic factions that were at work in forming the urban society and built environment of Toronto.

Although Toronto newspapers used factional disputes to increase readership, the press was also cultivating the town's identity. The reporting of civic violence or of civic architectural development helped to fashion Toronto's identity. On 7 August 1874 a letter to the editor of the *Globe* expressed admiration for the St. James tower and spire, making positive comparisons with British and European church architecture. The writer produced a table illustrating the various heights of European cathedral spires, among which the St. James spire ranked fifteenth behind the leading example, Strasbourg Cathedral's of 466 feet. Toronto's Anglican cathedral was specified as being one foot taller than Britain's Norwich Cathedral, which placed sixteenth on the list. In a further expression of civic pride, the author stated:

> Although the spire of St. James Cathedral in this city is not so high as quite a number in Europe, it is sixteen feet higher than any structure in North America, ninety-six feet higher than the highest in Montreal, and seventy feet higher than any in Toronto. Let us hope that an edifice so lofty, and so much admired already, will in due time, with its expected illuminated clock, be brought to a thorough completion, and that no loss of life or serious harm will be sustained therewith.[55]

Until well into the twentieth century, the Montreal economy edged ahead of Toronto's, reflecting the ongoing importance of the St. Lawrence transportation system.[56] This began to change with the joint US and Canadian initiative in 1895 to deep-dredge the St. Lawrence and open up the Great Lakes to transatlantic shipping. The dredging proved to be an initial stage in the improvement of Toronto's relative economic position. Such shifts in relative economic power were manifested in the rising skyline of Toronto. And the construction of the tower and spire of St. James Cathedral represented a major episode in this mixture of religious, cultural, and economic ambition. Nevertheless, this architectural aspect of civic economic competition also revealed disparities in the local social order. One example of the disparities in economic status was dramatized in a letter to the editor of the *Globe*. The letter recalled an incident of 1839 in which a worker was killed by a fall from the scaffold used to construct the earlier tower of St. James. Through the height of the St. James spire, and even loss of life, Toronto could claim unofficial membership in a "club" of European architectural "marvels," such as Canterbury Cathedral, whose architect, William of Sens, fell to his death from its scaffold in the twelfth century.[57]

CONCLUSION

In Toronto, the St. James tower and spire demonstrated the popular association of economic growth with large-scale architectural construction, particularly in religious commissions. Expenditure on monumental architecture was seen as tantamount to superior civic status, despite the resultant diversion of church funds from the alleviation of urban poverty and the provision of economic opportunity for new immigrants. In a wider perspective, disputes about the rebuilding of St. James Cathedral therefore reflected the economic and social instability that surrounded the project. The threat of Fenian raiding parties, the periodic eruptions of religious-inspired violence, and the growth of urban poverty associated with an economic expansion were not solved by the imagery of civic social stability both claimed for and signified by the construction of the tower and spire.

The contribution of the 1874 tower and spire of the cathedral to Toronto's civic maturation was matched by the Anglican Church's inability to contend with civic instability emanating from expanding economy. At the time of the Orange disturbance in Hamilton in 1852, St. James Cathedral could not provide a "view" of the hostilities or, more importantly, an understanding of the complex ethnic and economic situation that underscored the tensions. In 1874, a decade and a half after the completion of the main body of the cathedral, the unprecedented height of the spire was unable to encompass a historical "perspective" of the greater hostilities associated with the Fenian raids of 1866. These raids appeared to be comprehended in the Toronto press only in terms of local violence in the streets, rather than in terms of a strategy to achieve a political result elsewhere in the world.[58] By 1874 the discourse in Toronto had returned to the subject of economy, profit, and progress.

During the 1870s St. James Cathedral became an icon for Toronto with the height of its tower and spire. The cathedral also became permanently associated with the figure of its first bishop. Bishop Strachan died in 1867 and was buried beneath the foundations of the cathedral in the year of Canada's official Confederation. By this time, the tower and spire of St. James Cathedral remained incomplete.

The case study of St. James Cathedral underscores how religion, economy, and taste were woven together in the construction of Canada's social fabric, especially in nineteenth-century colonial society. The notion of privilege, particularly in connection with the Anglican Church, played a role in architectural rivalries where groups that self-identified as dominant were overly conscious of their role in a commerce of taste and of stylistic fashion. Within this environment of interdenominational rivalry, Toronto's economy and religious institutions expanded, impacting the way Torontonians saw themselves. Toronto was riding a rail between a British imperial regime and growing US influence, thereby fashioning the Dominion of Canada's nascent transcontinental national identity. The completion of St. James Cathedral, and above all its spire, marked a significant, if conflicted, episode in Toronto's assertion of cosmopolitan identity.

NOTES

1 On lifestyle as an analytic construct in which reality is constituted by the manipulation of appearances, see David Chaney, *Lifestyles* (London: Routledge, 1996), 115.

2 A recent publication that centres on the way British identity continues to manifest itself, even through the spectre of empire, is Bill Nasson, *Britannia's Empire* (Stroud, UK: Tempus, 2004).

3 Basic sources for the story of Anglicanism in British North America are Philip Carrington, *The Anglican Church in Canada* (Toronto: Collins, 1963); Richard W. Vaudry, *Anglicans and the Atlantic World: High Churchmen, Evangelicals, and the Quebec Connection* (Montreal and Kingston: McGill-Queen's University Press, 2003); H.H. Walsh, *The Christian Church in Canada* (Toronto: Ryerson Press, 1956); and Frank A. Peake, *The Anglican Church in British Columbia* (Vancouver: Pitchell, 1959).

4 *Anglo-American Magazine* 1, 4 (July 1852): 3, reported that the line from Kingston to Buffalo, New York, via Toronto would positively affect business in Toronto.

5 *Anglo-American Magazine* 1, 1 (July 1852): 1. The article described Toronto's spread eastward to the Don Valley and its port development, as well as growth of the population, which increased from 900 living in Little York in 1812, to 4,000 in 1832, to 15,336 in 1842, and to 30,763 in 1852. The value of dutiable and free goods imported to the city merchants was reported as £694,597 with exports to the United States worth £409,206.

6 *Anglo-American Magazine* 1, 1 (July 1852): 4.

7 Lynne Marks, *Revivals and Roller Rinks: Religion, Leisure and Identity in Late Nineteenth Century Small Town Ontario* (Toronto: University of Toronto Press, 1996), 58.

8 London's Great Fire occurred on 2 September 1666, the Chicago Great Fire began on 8 October 1871, and Seattle burned on 6 June 1889. Each city marked the beginning of its civic maturity with its Great Fire. On Toronto's fire, see also Frederick Armstrong, "The First Great Fire of Toronto," *Ontario History* 53, 3 (September 1961): 201-21.

9 Other no less important members of the building committee were John George Howard, architect, surveyor, and civil engineer (1803-90); James Edward Small, lawyer, Reform politician, and judge (1798-1869); Henry Sherwood, lawyer, businessman, politician, and judge (1807-55); Philip M. Vonkoughnet, politician and judge (1822-69); John James Browne, architect, businessman, and justice of the peace (1837-93); George P. Ridout, merchant and Conservative politician (1807-73); as well as the rector, churchwardens, the Hon. Chief Justice William H. Draper, the mayor, the sheriff, and William Proudfoot, William Atkinson, Alexander Dixon, and John Duggan. See *Dictionary of Canadian Biography* online, http://www.biographi.ca/index2.html.

10 *Anglo-American Magazine* 3, 4 (August 1854): 362.

11 For a detailed account of the career of Fred Cumberland, see Geoffrey Simmins, *Fred Cumberland: Building the Victorian Dream* (Toronto: University of Toronto Press, 1997).

12 Graham D. Taylor and Peter A. Baskerville, eds., *A Concise History of Business in Canada* (Toronto: University of Toronto Press, 1994), 168.

13 In partnership with Thomas Gundry, Langley designed the tower and spire for St. Michael's Roman Catholic Cathedral in 1865, and he designed Metropolitan Methodist Church in 1869, as well as St. Peter's Anglican Church on Carlton Street in Toronto, dated 1865. See *Dictionary of Canadian Biography* online, http://www.biographi.ca/index2.html.

14 Sharan Merriam, *Case Study Research in Education: A Qualitative Approach* (Oxford: Jossey-Bass, 1990), 10-12, with added emphasis on 104-18, which deals with mining data from documents.

15 Pierre Bourdieu, *The Field of Cultural Production* (New York: Columbia University Press, 1993), 161-63, also esp. 61-73.

16 Ibid., 37-60.

17 On panoptic measures involved in social organization, see Michel Foucault, *Discipline and Punish: The Birth of the Prison* (New York: Vintage Books, 1978), 195-228.

18 Kenneth Norrie, Douglas Owram, and J.C. Herbert Emery, *A History of Canadian Economy* (Scarborough, ON: Nelson, Thomson, 2002), 116-17. See also Taylor and Baskerville, eds., *Concise History of Business in Canada,* 174-75.

19 The influence of an Ecclesiological Gothic Revival in the Canadas was assisted by imported architectural pattern books and particularly by polemic texts such as Augustus Welby Northmore Pugin, *Contrasts,*

or A Parallel between the Noble Edifices of the Middle Ages, and Similar Buildings of the Present Day, Shewing the Present Decay of Taste Accompanied by Appropriate Text, 2nd ed. (London: Charles Dolman, 1836); and Augustus Welby Northmore Pugin, *The True Principles of Pointed or Christian Architecture: Set Forth in Two Lectures Delivered at St. Marie's, Oscott* (London: John Weale, 1841). The architectural principles that Pugin derived essentially for Catholic consumption in the nineteenth century were adopted and adapted by the Cambridge Camden (later the Ecclesiological) Society for Anglican usage. The society successfully used print media to get its message across concerning the "correct" way to build churches. Its print publications included the quarterly journal the *Ecclesiologist* (1841-68) and a series of inexpensive pamphlets such as "A Few Words to Churchbuilders" that spoke directly to the people involved in designing, restoring, and maintaining Britain's churches. British-trained architects immigrating to the Canadas were well versed in the rules of neo-Gothic architecture, and print publication was intended to keep architects and their clients up to date on the latest fashions in Britain. However, local practitioners in the Canadas also had some independent ideas about how the Dominion's churches should look, which were often discussed in terms of climate. An essential source for the history of the Ecclesiological Society remains James F. White, *The Cambridge Movement: The Ecclesiologists and the Gothic Revival* (Cambridge, UK: Cambridge University Press, 1962), and a good source for the Gothic Revival in Canada is Mathilde Brosseau, *Gothic Revival in Canadian Architecture* (Ottawa: Parks Canada, 1980). On the intersection of religious and social structures in nineteenth-century Ontario, see William Westfall, *Two Worlds: The Protestant Culture of Nineteenth-Century Ontario* (Montreal and Kingston: McGill-Queen's University Press, 1989).

20 On the notion of a collective communion in nationalistic terms, see Benedict Anderson, *Imagined Communities,* rev. ed. (New York: Verso, 2000), 6-7. However, I do not share Anderson's larger view that nationalism replaced religion on the political world stage of the eighteenth and nineteenth centuries.

21 John Lambton (Lord Durham), *Lord Durham's Report on the Affairs of British North America* (1839; reprint, Oxford: Oxford University Press, 1912).

22 Kelly Crossman, *Architecture in Transition: From Art to Practice, 1885-1906* (Montreal and Kingston: McGill-Queen's University Press, 1987), 17-24, 36, 127. Crossman points out that the Ontario Association of Architects was formed around the idea that there needed to be architectural standards in Canada to counter the popularity of American architects and architectural fashions.

23 Ibid., 114-15. Kelly Crossman sites W.A. Langton's address to the Toronto Architectural Sketch Club in 1892 as evidence that there were Canadian practitioners who wished to end the perpetual repetition of borrowed styles. Unfortunately, Crossman falls back upon the idea that Canadian architecture was unique simply because good architects designed for the climate, citing Ottawa architect G.F. Stalker: "We certainly have not a Canadian style of architecture ... one cannot be struck with the want of consideration that has been shown to Dame climate ... to give it in our architecture that consideration and study which is its due and which shall give it a certain amount, at least, of national character to our building"; see Glenna Dunning, *Climatic Influences on Architecture: A Partially Annotated Bibliography* (Monticello, IL: Vance Bibliographies, 1988), 105.

24 William Hay, "Architecture for the Meridian of Canada," *Anglo-American Magazine* 2, 3 (March 1853): 253-55. Hay was living in Toronto when he wrote: "The Old English style of building is admirably adapted to the climate of Canada. Its high pitched roof, and weathered projections are just what are needed for protection against the snow and rain" (253).

25 Omitting the crossing tower was also a device for improving the sightlines to the chancel, and it improved the acoustics for those in the nave.

26 Canada, Board of Registration and Statistics, *Census of the Canadas, 1851-52* (Quebec: J. Lovell, 1853-54), sec. 2.3.

27 Ibid. Anglicans numbered 11,577, compared to the Roman Catholics' 7,940.

28 The Orangemen were named after King William III of England (1650-1702, stadtholder of Holland from 1672), who re-established the Protestant state after succeeding James II, who had tried to institute

Catholicism as eminent in England. William's political malaise gave strength to parliamentary procedure. See Mike Ashley, *A Brief History of British Kings and Queens* (London: Robinson, 2002), 330-33.

29 *Toronto Globe,* 9 August 1866, 2.

30 *Toronto Globe,* 7 April 1849, 3.

31 *Toronto Globe,* 11 April 1849, 2.

32 Ibid.

33 The building committee initially approved of the idea of selling the churchyard but left the matter in the hands of the vestry. See "Report of the Committee Appointed by the Vestry of St. James Church to Report on the Rebuilding of the Church," Toronto, 1849, Archives of St. James Anglican Cathedral. Later, the committee members withdrew their approval of the sale and openly opposed it. My grateful thanks to Nancy Hurn, archivist at the Anglican Diocese in Toronto, and Nancy Mallet, archivist for St. James Cathedral, for providing much needed material and support.

34 The financial books record that the insurance paid was £8,500, but monies owing on the former building totalled nearly £3,500, leaving an insurance payoff of £5,357.2.10. The building committee envisioned selling new pews to the same pew holders of the former church, but at one-third of the original price, in order to raise £2,276.13.4. Sales of new pews were expected to bring in £1,490, for a grand total of £9,123.16.12 at the end of a twelve-month period. See "Report of the Committee Appointed by the Vestry of St. James Church to Report on the Rebuilding of the Church," Toronto, 1849, Archives of St. James Anglican Cathedral. This left a £1,000 shortfall, which Bishop Strachan later offered to obtain from the Society for the Promotion of Christian Knowledge based in England if the building committee agreed to hire the bishop's preferred architect, George Smith.

35 In a second report of the building committee, dated 4 December 1849, motions were made to sack Cumberland in favour of Smith, and an agreement was reached to sell the churchyard. The decision to rent out the church land was rescinded on 9 March 1850 by a close vote of thirty-one to twenty-nine. As the committee recognized that pew sales might not be entirely forthcoming, only the insurance money and the funds from the Society for the Promotion of Christian Knowledge (see note 34) were to be counted upon, totalling just over £6,000. A subsequent meeting held in July 1850 approved different motions agreeing to locate the church facing King Street in a north-south orientation and approving costs of not more than £12,000. A letter in the Archives of St. James Cathedral from "F.R.S." to the *Toronto Globe* in 1849 explains why the Cumberland design was not approved immediately and how Smith managed to curry favour with the bishop; see Geoffrey Simmins, *Fred Cumberland: Building the Victorian Dream* (Toronto: University of Toronto Press, 1997), 124, n22.

36 "The commercial depression which began in 1857 has prostrated the whole country and paralysed all of our resources." Letter from Strachan to Hawkins, Archives of the Society for the Propagation of the Gospel in Foreign Parts, D series, 30 March 1860.

37 Frank Wills (1820-57) trained in London, likely under John Hayward, a neo-Gothic specialist working out of Exeter. William Thomas (1799-1860) started from humble architectural roots in England working under Richard Tutin, a builder-turned-architect, but found success after emigration to Ontario. Kivas Tully (1820-1905) emigrated from Ireland after receiving an education in the Royal Navy School at Camberwell and architectural training in the offices of W.H. Owen at Limerick. John Ostell (1813-92) emigrated from London to Montreal and successfully combined surveying with architecture. Although he was an Anglican, he chiefly worked for the Sulpicians. Gervase Wheeler (1815-72) immigrated to America from England, having studied under Richard Cromwell Carpenter, and enjoyed success despite some indiscretion regarding the author Charlotte Brontë that caused him to leave Philadelphia society for New York. In 1867 he became a fellow of the Royal Institute of British Architects.

38 For a detailed description of the machinations taken by Bishop Strachan and the vestry building committee, see Simmins, *Fred Cumberland,* 128-30.

39 Bishop John Strachan, *Thoughts on the Rebuilding of the Cathedral Church of St. James* (Toronto: Diocesan Press, 1850), 1.

40 Ibid.

41 Ibid., 2.

42 Ibid., 4.

43 Ibid.

44 Ibid., 2.

45 Bramhill's letter is found in the Archives of St. James Cathedral. He wrote, "If [consecration] is not a fiction ... then will no good churchman wish or dare to alienate one inch of ground consecrated not alone by this service of the Church, but consecrated and endeared by the dust of those who died in the faith."

46 *Toronto Globe,* 11 April 1849, 2.

47 Ibid.

48 See Letter no. 2, 11 January 1850, Archives of St. James Anglican Cathedral.

49 "Strachan Letter to the Hon. A.N. Morin on the Clergy Reserves," 20 October 1854, 4, Archives of St. James Anglican Cathedral. The printed letter carries a postscript that bears a very different tone since news had reached the bishop of the government's refusal to pay the established church on its claim of the monies. It is worth quoting a passage: "I was favoured with a copy of your bill, providing for the confiscation of the Clergy Reserves, and I declare, without hesitation, that it is the most atrocious specimen of oppressive legislation, that has appeared since the days of the French Convention. Can members of the United Church of England and Ireland be expected to submit calmly to this monstrous robbery? ... Are you not rejoicing in the hope that the voice of prayer, and praise, and the preaching of the Gospel, will soon cease to be heard in Upper Canada?"

50 Bishop John Strachan, *Letter to the Right Hon. Lord John Russell on the Present State of the Church in Canada* (London: George Bell, 1851), 1. The sale of the Clergy Reserves – 2 million acres of land once set aside by governments for the benefit of religious institutions in Canada – appeared both imminent and likely to accrue little to the Anglican Church.

51 Ibid., 10.

52 *Ecclesiologist* 18 (1854): 359.

53 Henry C. Cooper, "The Duty of the Members of the Church of England Respecting Clergy Reserves: Address Delivered in St. Peter's Church, Springfield, Jan. 10 1854," Archives of St. James Anglican Cathedral.

54 *Anglo-American Magazine* 1, 2 (August 1852): 178.

55 *Toronto Globe,* 10 August 1874, 4.

56 Norrie, Owram, and Emery, *History of Canadian Economy,* 289.

57 William of Sens was brought in to rebuild the choir at Canterbury after the 1174 fire. He died in a fall from a scaffold in 1179, although he had already succeeded in introducing the Gothic vocabulary to the British Isles from France. See Robert Willis, *Architectural History of Some English Cathedrals: A Collection in Two Parts Delivered during the Years 1842-1863* (reprint, Newport, CT: Pagnell Paul and P.B. Minet, 1972), 52-53.

58 Foucault, *Discipline and Punish,* 215.

4

"For the benefit of the inhabitants"
The Urban Market and City Planning in Toronto

SHARON VATTAY

In his book *The City Shaped,* Spiro Kostof seeks to illustrate that a city's form can be studied as a receptacle of meaning. In "reading" a city's built environment, we are provided with knowledge of the cultural contexts of the past. And, conversely, the more we know about a specific society, the better we are able to understand the urban form.[1] In an effort to better understand the growth of commercial culture and its impact on the Canadian architectural fabric, this chapter examines the evolution of the urban market and the typology of the market building – specifically in the City of Toronto.

Toronto serves well as a case study since its market has been permanently solidified within the urban fabric, having operated at the same central downtown location for over 200 years.[2] Whereas the move from an agrarian society to a capitalist economy resulted in the demise of many urban markets across the country, Toronto's market continues in situ into the twenty-first century.

Although often a relatively simple structure, the market building took on great importance in Canadian urban centres in the nineteenth century, revealing a "civic materialism,"[3] where the government's reputation was at stake. The market's success allowed citizens to measure the government's efficacy, and the authorities' responsiveness to the needs of the people was visibly gauged in the market's physical manifestation. Such buildings came to serve as concrete symbols of the government's commitment to a well-ordered public economy and to social policy. Thus this building type – its program, architecture, and form – has become embedded in the collective memory. For this reason, the peripheral role that this building type has played in the critical discourse on Canadian architecture should be reconsidered – a task that this chapter seeks in part to undertake.[4] Although market buildings are relatively nondescript, often vernacular and utilitarian in style and form, this building type is no less important than more celebrated civic structures such as city halls and courthouses, and historically it has been known to garner attention from prominent architectural theorists – most notably Antonio Averlino Filarete, Colen Campbell, and Jean-Nicolas Louis Durand.[5] Defined as an open place or a covered building where buyers and sellers convene for the sale of goods, the market has long been central in the layout of urban locales.

Although related to the mundane and the everyday, these buildings are nonetheless settings for important societal rituals and have a significant impact on the quality of urban life. Throughout history, this building type has been of utmost interest to governmental authorities. The urban market has ranked in importance – economically, socially, and culturally – with other civic institutions such as the courthouse, jail, church, hospital, and school, affording it prominent consideration during city planning; indeed, the market, or merchants' quarter, has often received the most desired allotment of land. In the case of Toronto, each of these ranking civic institutions was assigned its own six-acre lot, with the market conveniently positioned between the established residential area to the east and the new institutional zone to the west. This disposition of functional zones and the privileged standing of the market square in the urban structure reveal the relationship between the formal considerations of the town's layout and pragmatic social and economic considerations.

The location of the market was determined shortly after the founding of the Town of York (as Toronto was known from 1793 to 1834), and today the market remains in this location at King and Jarvis Streets, even as other functional zones, as defined in the original town plan (such as zones for the courthouse, jail, hospital, and school), have been redefined and relocated to meet the city's changing needs and forms. In this location, the market's built form has evolved over the decades, shaped by social, political, and cultural influences that have reflected not only the physical needs of the town, and later the city, but also the cultural perceptions of what a market should look like in an expanding urban centre in Canada. Thus changes in the city's composition, including increased population, social reforms, and urban evolution, have all played a significant role in changes to the built form and commercial environment.

Accordingly, this chapter has two primary goals: first, to analyze the environment of the emergent commercial economy as it pertains to the City of Toronto, thus uncovering the government's role in the resultant urban design and architecture; and second, to consider the typology of the market building, assessing its evolution through the nineteenth and twentieth centuries, which reveals transatlantic and cross-border influences. Ultimately, this chapter follows Kostof's approach and examines Toronto's market architecture in order to show how the built environment contributes to a larger understanding of Canadian culture.

Since the market made a crucial contribution to both the social and economic stability of a place, this institution was almost always closely identified with the state. Government involvement with publicly owned market facilities was multifaceted. In *The City Shaped,* Kostof notes that the government's zealous supervision of market business was justified through historical precedents, which suggested that, unless regulated, merchants would appropriate any public space for their purpose.[6] Quite simply, however, government involvement was largely precipitated by the authorities' sense of duty to provide their citizens with an adequate, safe, and affordable supply of food. This governmental moral duty is a concept that stems from ancient traditions – the Greeks and the Romans both had market spaces that served as the civic, social, and commercial centres of their towns. The Greeks regulated markets through special market boards, and the Romans believed that the government had a sovereign right to establish and control markets. Later, in Britain, the establishment of markets was the exclusive prerogative of the king.

The continuing importance of this vital institution in postcolonial Canada is evident in the example of Toronto. Responsibility for the urban food market was, from the outset, vested in government; managing the market was the purview first of the Government of Upper Canada, then of the district government, and finally, from 1834 on, of the municipal government.[7] The creation and regulation of a market was among one of the earliest acts of the municipal government in Toronto, and the market continued to be regulated well into the twentieth century.

Yet not only did governments, particularly at the municipal level, see market construction and management as part of their moral responsibility to increase food supply to the urban population in order to ensure a healthy environment, but they also benefited from these market spaces, which served as important economic generators, particularly during the nineteenth century with the emergence of middle-class culture. Renting spaces to farmers and food merchants was a profitable endeavour. And thus political-economic forces ultimately shaped the construction of market buildings. Governments were in a position to profit from a regulated food supply, and in order to capitalize on this position, they conceived, constructed, and managed the best urban markets within their means. They tore down and rebuilt cities' market buildings several times in the belief that the replacements would better serve a growing and evolving population. Often, as in the case of Toronto, the urban area adjacent to the market buildings attracted other commercial endeavours (those commonly associated with a rising urban community), and the political purveyance and profit extended to the contiguous lands as well. Markets can be added to the long list of public buildings designed and built under governmental patronage in the nineteenth century.

Regardless of governments' motives (whether fulfilling a moral obligation to their citizens or generating civic revenues), the physical form of market buildings came to be representative of the spatial-economic needs of each place. The forms these buildings took were outward expressions of an underlying method of operation. This method also governed the location and extent of the buildings. Market buildings could be large or small. They ranged from open-walled sheds to large, mixed-use buildings. Selling spaces were subdivided into smaller stalls, each rented out and operated by an individual vendor.

Thus the market buildings in Toronto (six in total from the date of the founding of York through to the current day) serve as physical examples of cultural norms and architectural expression, evolving from simple colonial building types to large-scale, innovative building forms. Through each rendition, the market building had to serve its purpose well, while at the same time concretely expressing the urbanity of this important commercial and governmental centre, showing the civic capacity of government, and keeping up with advancements in market architecture in Europe, Britain, and the United States.

THE ESTABLISHMENT OF A MARKET IN THE TOWN OF YORK

York's first official market took place on Saturday, 5 November 1803, following a proclamation by Lieutenant-Governor Peter Hunter: "Great prejudice hath arisen to the inhabitants of the Town and Township of York, and of other adjoining Townships from no place or day having been set apart or appointed for exposing publicly for Sale, Cattle, Sheep, Poultry and other Provisions, Goods and Merchandize, brought by Merchants, Farmers and Others for the necessary supply of the said Town of York."[8] The establishment of this institution by the provincial government was thus motivated by the perceived hardship of the citizens of York in the absence of a market.[9] Although there is evidence that some commercial activity took place on the designated Market Reserve prior to this decree, a regular, weekly market was officially established by the government only when the population had increased to such an extent that the need became critical.

At this early date, the sale of goods took place in the open air of the designated Market Reserve, at the southwest corner of King and Jarvis Streets, as allocated in the town plan of 1797.[10] By 1802 the most easterly portion of this original six-acre Market Reserve had been appropriated and vested by the Crown to a group of trustees who were to manage the lands "for the benefit of the inhabitants."[11]

The market space was not only used for the sale of goods but also served as a primary public space and was therefore one that fulfilled both economic and social functions. Public floggings had taken place in the vicinity since 1798, and stocks were set up there in 1804.[12] A well was dug in 1823 for "the convenience of the public," and occasionally, open-air auctions occurred.

With the establishment of a market, the provincial government had to undertake the management of this amenity. In 1814 an act was passed sanctioning control of the market by the county magistrates, empowering them to set certain days and hours for the market, and authorizing them to make rules and regulations for its conduct.[13] Such restrictions were intended to protect the citizens, and the pervasiveness and thoroughness of these laws can be read as a desire to establish a well-ordered society. The importance of the market regulations was revealed in their posting on the doors of the church and the courthouse – both church and state acknowledging the crucial contribution of the public market to the social and economic stability of the town.[14] Market laws were commonplace in North America and often restricted the sale of food outside the designated public market, which, in effect, gave the government-controlled market a monopoly on food sales by restricting alternative methods of buying and selling provisions.[15] Sales in the market were direct from producer to consumer, thus prohibiting illegal practices such as food speculation, hoarding, and forestalling (i.e., the selling of goods before they reached the marketplace).

Although the regulations were ostensibly for the good of the public, one cannot ignore that these laws also guaranteed a healthy economic return for the government. In an article on the regulation of public markets in Upper Canada, W. Thomas Matthews argues that officials felt no commitment to anything resembling "the moral economy of the poor," being preoccupied with the promotion of commercial enterprise, not the protection of consumers.[16] Similarly, in an article on markets in London, Ontario, Sean Gouglas argues that the regulations served to enhance the economic power of the civic and mercantile elite under the "pretense" of protecting the general populace.[17]

THE FIRST MARKET BUILDING IN YORK

Ultimately, a market building was the most visible proof of a government's commitment to the well-being of its citizens. The first evidence of a built structure to house the market in the Town of York dates to 1820, when a call for tenders appeared in the *Upper Canada Gazette*.[18] The design of this market building is known today only through textual references (written after the fact) and from an early town plan that denotes the building as a simple, rectangular form located centrally in the easterly portion of the original Market Reserve.[19]

This utilitarian building, described by one early historian as a primitive wooden structure, was most likely all that could be afforded at this early date in the Town of York.[20] Brick was not yet in plentiful supply, and there were no architects residing in the town. In the town's formative years, architecture, for the most part, was "designed" by surveyors or military engineers. However, this market shed probably needed no designer as such. The plain shed form was typical of many early markets in Europe and North America. The crude, often temporary structure involved minimal costs yet provided some protection from the elements. Regardless, the introduction of a built form in the Town of York, however primitive, was a step toward moving the market out of the streets – a highly desirable circumstance in a progressively urbanizing and civilized town.

As market spaces expanded and the buildings therein became more sophisticated structures, the management of these commercial endeavours became a more pressing issue. To implement the regulations and policies properly and efficiently, market clerks were appointed annually, in the same manner as all other town officials.[21] Similar to the British model, the market clerk in the Town of York was responsible for a range of tasks, which included enforcing weights and measures, ensuring that only licensed vendors sold their goods, and establishing and collecting rents.[22]

THE SECOND MARKET BUILDING: THE BRICK MARKET AND TOWN HALL, 1831

Under the auspices of the magistrates of the Home District, a resolution was passed in March 1830 to erect a larger market building – one that would better serve the population, which had increased fivefold in less than a decade.[23] Immigration to Upper Canada had accelerated into the 1830s, and Toronto was

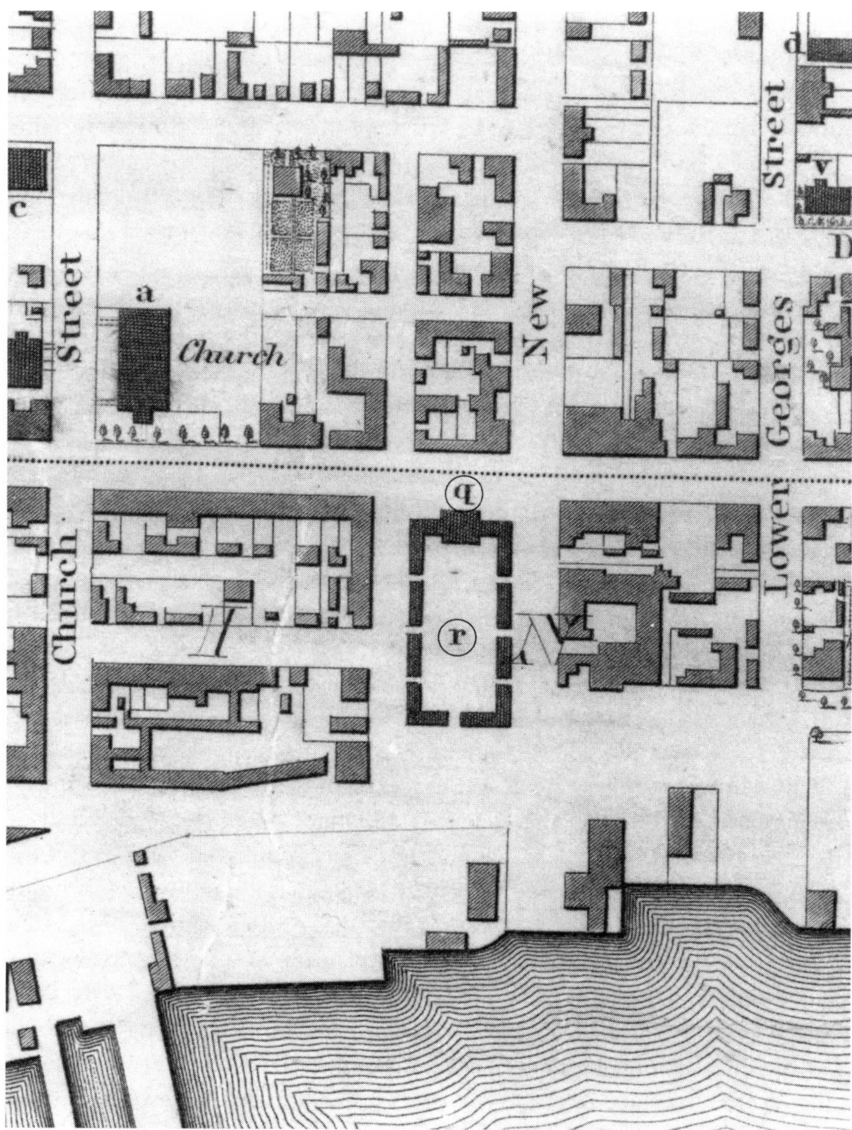

Figure 4.1 Detail of topographical plan of the City and Liberties of Toronto, by James Cane, 1842. The plan shows the footprint of the town hall (q) and market quadrangle (r). | City of Toronto Archives, MT00255.

the destination of about one-third of these immigrants – settlers who brought with them substantial amounts of cash that helped to spur the commercial market.[24] It was imperative that the government undertake an expansion of the urban market space at this time. Not only was the 1820s building far too small to serve the public and to accommodate the farmers, thus threatening a loss of market revenue, but public safety was also at risk, being exacerbated by health hazards in the town at the time. Revising the architectural form was seen as a remedy to the social crisis. The market shed also appeared architecturally inadequate when compared with other major governmental buildings in the town – by 1830 York had a number of substantial brick buildings, including the new courthouse and jail located just one block west of the Market Reserve.[25]

In procuring plans for the new market building, the district government, through a delegated building committee, insisted on two requirements: first, that the building be spacious (100 by 40 feet, or about twice the size of the current market shed); and second, that it be constructed of brick. Clearly, both capacity and image were of foremost concern to the government. In response to a call for plans, five local builders submitted proposals.[26] As when the previous market shed was erected, there were no architects residing in the town; eventually, a pragmatic design by the contractor James Cooper was chosen.[27] The building was completed by 1833.[28]

Once again, we are only able to surmise the appearance of York's second market building through textual references and town plans, although the building has been carefully recreated in model form.[29] Of particular interest is the plan of this early market and its program, both of which clearly reveal the increased complexity and rationality of the market-building type (Figures 4.1 and 4.2). The plan was based on a quadrangular configuration – commonly found throughout Britain, France, and North America – which allowed for an orderly and efficient layout.[30] Whereas the exterior walls on the east and west sides of the quadrangle were blank, the north range, which faced King Street, was designed to accommodate retail shop-fronts. The butchers' stalls were within the interior colonnade of the courtyard, and the large open area housed the farmers' wagons. Access to the market quadrangle was restricted though several sizable entrance archways located on all four ranges of the building, allowing the market clerk to monitor all who entered. A second-level, wooden gallery provided space for storage and granaries and served to shade the butchers' stalls below. For the first time in the history of the Town of York, the market was distinctly separated from other street activities, creating a physically defined arena for the sale of goods.

Figure 4.2 Model of the York market and town hall of 1831. | City of Toronto Archives, 1985-237-13.

Along with the open quadrangle, the building included a large meeting hall above the market entrance, and thus the architectural program followed a Western tradition dating back to the Middle Ages: the integration of market and town hall. In its dual role, the market portion of the building addressed the issue of orderly food distribution, and the town hall portion embodied public order. The connection of government to the equitable and safe distribution of food was made concretely apparent.

With this substantial brick market and town hall building, the district government achieved its objectives of providing a commodious, convenient, and efficient market space for the citizens while ensuring continued growth in revenue from the market rents.[31] And the building visually signified the town's progress since its founding forty years prior. A British visitor described it as a quadrangular building of great extent designed for the accommodation of a much larger enterprise and as having a "prospective reference" to the rapidly increasing population in the town. He was so impressed with the building that he wrote, "the convenience of this building, and the building itself, has no equal of the kind even in New York or in the States."[32] Another observer called the market the best of its kind in the province.[33] Clearly, the government had succeeded in enhancing both its and York's image through this built form.

Up to this point, the market in York came under the jurisdiction of the district government. However, upon incorporation of the City of Toronto in 1834, the lands and the management of the market were conveyed to the Corporation of the City of Toronto. This transference of responsibility from district to municipal government was common throughout Upper Canada as cities were incorporated – the city officials having much to gain from the continuation of traditional marketing practices.[34] The importance of this institution to the municipality of Toronto is immediately apparent through the numerous references to the market lands, buildings, and operations in the city's Act of Incorporation.

Indeed, the importance of the Market Reserve lands went beyond the market building proper, and, as was common in the development of urban form, there was a linear extension of commercial activity along adjacent streets – in this case, primarily on the western four acres of the original Market Reserve, running west along King Street as far as Church Street. Because of the economic power of the market as a magnet for commerce, the municipality also took control of these adjoining lands, designating this a central location for supplementary mercantile transactions. As with the market space proper, the lands were, through the Act of Incorporation, conveyed to and vested in the city for "public use."

The construction of the adjacent Market Block, as the commercial development west of the market building would become known, figured prominently in the municipal agenda. By 1836 this prime property had been subdivided into building lots and leased to various merchants. The former haphazard architectural developments on the property – wood-frame buildings that were a serious fire hazard – were razed and replaced with substantial brick buildings of a consistent architectural form. With this, the Market Block became the earliest unified urban design scheme in the City of Toronto, bringing much needed "embellishment and ornament" to the city.[35] It is relevant to note that the city played a leading role in the design and layout of this entire block, employing architects to ensure that the architecture was consistent with the image it wanted to convey.[36] Through architecture, the government was able to show its civic capacity by erecting an ensemble of commercial buildings meant to enhance the economic and social well-being of its citizens.

Meanwhile, under the superintendence of Mayor William Lyon Mackenzie, a number of alterations and improvements were being made to the 1831 market building. The former town hall portion was placed under the superintendence of the mayor, and sections of it were fitted up for use by the City Council and for the offices of the mayor, police clerk, and other government officials.[37] The council then turned its attention to the market portion of the building (the open quadrangle), which was proving inadequate and inappropriate for the people of the new City of Toronto. In April 1834 (one month after incorporation) the market clerk submitted an exhaustive report to the mayor outlining all of the shortcomings and inadequacies of the barely three-year-old brick market building, citing the damp and poorly ventilated cellars, the leaking roofs of the granaries on the second level, and the height of the encircling gallery, which in the summer unduly exposed the butchers' meat to the intense heat of the sun.[38] Although monies gained from market fees were technically for building repairs, it seems that this practice was rarely implemented and that market revenue simply went into the general city coffers. As a result of these deficiencies, the public interest was not being served.

The problem of physical deterioration was coupled with that of insufficient size as a result of increased market activity. The market was, at times, so crowded that farmers (some of whom had travelled great distances with their goods) had to be turned away. They were then induced to sell their goods to "hucksters" and grocers, which, according to the mayor, was a "serious evil" since it deflected revenues from the city coffers.[39] The relatively diminutive size of the market was also inadequate to support the increased number of consumers.[40] Two temporary solutions were found. Street vendors were accommodated along the western exterior wall on Market Street, expanding the number of rentable stalls, and a wooden, one-storey fish market was erected south of the current market buildings, directly on the water's edge.[41]

THE THIRD MARKET BUILDING: THE 1844-45 MARKET HOUSE AND TORONTO CITY HALL

Only ten years after market improvements were undertaken, the building was once again the subject of criticism and debate by the City Council. Whereas market fees generated £156 in 1834, by 1844 the amount had skyrocketed to over £1,000, and many believed this revenue could be considerably more if there were sufficient room in the building to accommodate all of the farmers who regularly made the trip to town.[42] To ensure the enforcement of the market regulations, which prohibited the sale of goods outside of the market space, and driven by the threat of financial loss, the council agreed in 1844 to undertake the erection of a new building – one that would supplement, rather than replace, the 1831 quadrangular market building.[43]

Although the potential loss of revenue was a major factor in the decision to erect a new market building, an equally pressing need in 1844 was to enlarge the adjoining Council Chamber. The council continued to meet, ten years after the city's formation, in the humble former town hall above the market entrance. The incentive to build a new City Hall at this time most likely stemmed from a need to compete with Kingston. At the time (1843), Kingston was building a new City Hall, having just been chosen the capital of the united Canadas in 1841, and evidently Toronto wanted to put forward an optimistic image of its continued strength and confidence despite the loss of its provincial governmental role.

To accommodate a larger, multipurpose market and city hall structure, while maintaining the existing market quadrangle, a relatively undeveloped water lot, directly to the south of the original Market Reserve and the existing building, was purchased.[44] The site was, however, problematic. It was situated on the damp shores of the harbour and sloped down significantly toward the water's edge.

For the first time in the city's history, the committee appointed to oversee the erection of the new market had at its disposal trained architects who could design a building in keeping with the advancements in architecture. By the 1840s several architects had emigrated from Britain.[45] Thus this building campaign for the new Market House and City Hall would mark the first opportunity for the government to achieve a market building that was "designed" in a high style of architecture – the previous two market buildings being decidedly vernacular in style.[46]

Of the eight designs submitted by local architects, the design prepared by the architect Henry Bowyer Lane was unanimously chosen, and the cornerstone for the building was laid in September 1844.[47] With current market revenue at £1,000 per annum, it was believed that increased revenue would quickly offset the cost of construction, estimated at £7,000. The works clerk, now with two buildings at his disposal, was able to organize an efficient commercial program with the older north market housing the butchers and the new south market accommodating vendors of fruits, vegetables, and poultry.

Figure 4.3 The Toronto Market House and City Hall of 1844-45. | City of Toronto Archives, fonds 231, item 98.

The design idiom for this new Market House and City Hall was vaguely Palladian, following the pattern of most late-Georgian public buildings in Canada. It was U-shaped and stretched south toward the harbour (Figures 4.3 and 4.4). The change in grade between Front Street and the water's edge allowed for the Corn Exchange to open toward the water.[48] The main portion of the building, part of which still stands today, was comprised of a three-storey, pedimented centre block containing the Council Chamber, flanked by wings of two storeys, which were divided into narrow shops. Later, a clock and bell tower were added to the central block, acting as a visual marker of the market in the urban setting. An arched entrance door in the centre of the facade led to the market behind and to the stairs that accessed the Council Chamber above. A truly multifunctional building, the front range also accommodated the police station, with jail cells in the basement.[49] Although the city may have wanted to

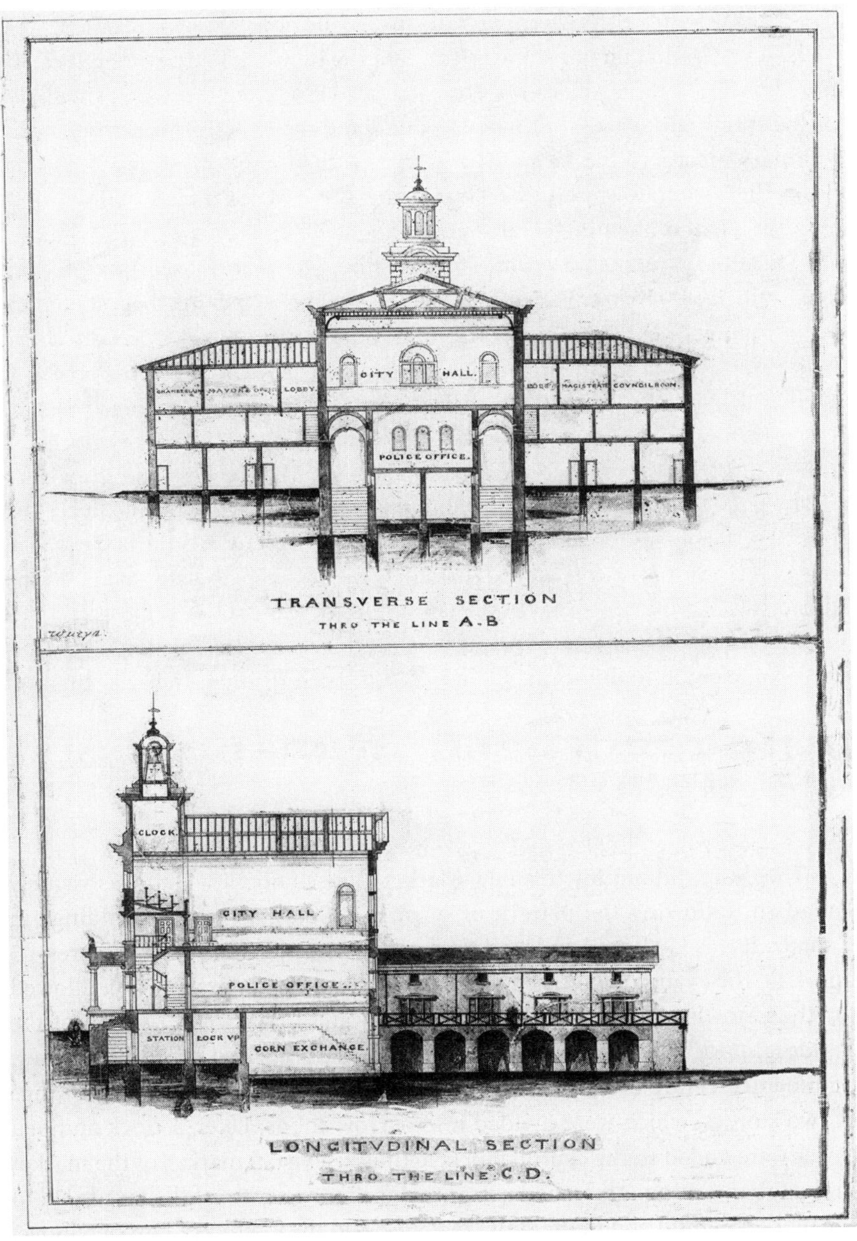

Figure 4.4 Toronto City Hall, 1844-45, transverse and longitudinal sections. | City of Toronto Archives, fonds 231, item 650.

express its urbanity through the architecture of the new Market House and City Hall, lack of availability of stone meant that the building had to be built of the more humble material of brick – stone was used sparingly, reserved principally for the entrance portico, window surrounds, and rusticated ground floor.[50] The building's most striking facade (with three arched windows detailed in buff brick) faced south toward the harbour, which was a major transportation route in the first half of the nineteenth century.

Since this was such a prominent building, one that housed not only the City Council but also the main urban market, it seems surprising that the council did not budget for a more impressive building. Indeed, the councillors chose to hire the cheapest contractor available, which may have been the prime reason for the numerous structural faults that were evident within six years of construction.[51] The building was also criticized from the outset for its lack of symmetry and its clumsiness, and the facade was redesigned only five years after construction to rectify some of the aesthetic and functional issues.[52] The frugality of the council probably stemmed from its desire to keep costs low in order to capitalize on gains from market revenue. Nevertheless, although the simplicity of the edifice was a product of the utilitarian nature of the market building, it still surpassed its predecessors in size and architectural expression and would thus bring some credit to the council that had instigated the building campaign.

THE FOURTH MARKET BUILDING: THE 1851 NORTH MARKET AND ST. LAWRENCE HALL

Shortly after the municipal offices and Council Chamber were relocated from the King Street range of the 1831 north market building to Lane's new Market House and City Hall, plans were underway to redesign the inadequate north market building. The substandard quality of the facilities had become even more evident by mid-century, reflecting the Victorian obsession with comfort and cleanliness – this as a mid-century cholera epidemic underscored the need for safer market spaces. The city's desire to improve market conditions at this time was also a manifestation of the ideas then current worldwide regarding spaces used for the sale and storage of foodstuffs. In Britain, for example, the Market and Fairs Clauses Act of 1847 laid down standards of cleanliness in an effort to provide citizens with more "respectable" streets.[53] One must realize that to be subjected to street peddlers was, in the Victorian mind, to risk unwanted exposure to bad language and habits.[54] Similarly, a Napoleonic campaign for sanitary markets transformed the building type in France, and many new,

Figure 4.5 The Toronto north market building, 1851. Photograph by F.W. Micklethwaite, c. 1890. | City of Toronto Archives, fonds 1248, item 21.

modern structures were developed between 1800 and 1850 to new standards.[55] All of these market reforms were part of a revolution in architectural form, most evident in the use of iron and glass technology.

Thus, at mid-century, to keep up with social and architectural reforms, the City Council proposed another multifunctional market building, one with retail shops, a grand public hall, and a newer, larger, and more up-to-date market to replace the 1831 quadrangular market building. Following an architectural competition, architect William Thomas's imposing design was approved by the council in 1845, although construction began only in 1850 after the Great Fire of 1849 had damaged the old market and town hall structure.[56] The St. Lawrence Hall and Market opened in April 1851 and comprised two distinct elements: the St. Lawrence Hall at the front and the Market Arcade behind. The impressive hall, which is still standing today, was built right up to the street, providing a prominent landmark on the major commercial thoroughfare of King Street. The three-storey building consisted of a number of modern shops at street level, flanking the entrance arches to the market behind, while above was located an impressive, two-storey public room. All was carefully ordered behind an imposing stone Palladian-style facade capped by a cupola that marked one of the highest points on the skyline at mid-century – the nearby Gothic Revival St. James Anglican Cathedral (1850-53) did not yet have a spire.

The entire north market complex took the form of an I-shaped building, with St. Lawrence Hall at the north end, a two-storey transept at the south end, and a 200-foot-long, two-storey arcade in between (Figure 4.5). The arcaded-market type was such that it provided pedestrian passage between two streets – in this case King and Front Streets – not unlike the fashionable nineteenth-century shopping arcades found in Europe and North America. Standing independently of other structures, the form allowed access to all sides of the building. The spatial arrangement of the market form was shaped internally by the business activities of the merchants, and its architectural expression conveyed the message that the building was to function as the prime location for the buying and selling of goods. The internal arcade had a range of stalls on both sides, occupied mainly by butchers, while street vendors (selling fruits and vegetables) rented food stands along the market building's outer walls.[57] Its orderly program was a reflection of an ordered society.[58]

In this arcaded form, the St. Lawrence Market Arcade took a similar configuration to the typical street market found throughout North America, the form and plan dictated by sanitary arrangements, the needs of increasingly convenience-oriented buyers and sellers, and the configuration of the site.[59] With the butchers' stalls being enclosed for the first time in the history of the market buildings in Toronto, not only were the goods protected from the elements (particularly sunlight), but the odours were also contained. A clerestory in the arcade allowed enough light to penetrate without subjecting the food to direct sunlight, while at the same time providing ventilation. All of these health-related advancements were accomplished through the new architectural form to better serve the citizens of Toronto.

The St. Lawrence Market Arcade, in serving as a public amenity more so than a public edifice, remained, as its predecessors, a fairly utilitarian structure, standing in contrast even to the high style of the Palladian St. Lawrence Hall portion, which stood on the north side. The construction costs of the arcade were purposely kept to a minimum with the expectation that the rents could then be kept low enough to attract more tenants and thus to generate more revenue. Aesthetics aside, the market was praised. One writer in the 1880s felt that Toronto enjoyed the reputation of having the best-supplied and most commodious market in the province.[60]

THE FIFTH MARKET BUILDING: THE NORTH AND SOUTH ST. LAWRENCE MARKET

Together, the north St. Lawrence Market Arcade (William Thomas, 1851) and the U-shaped south Market House and City Hall (Henry Bowyer Lane, 1844-45) served the needs of the city as the nineteenth century drew to a close. However, a number of instigating factors led to the full-scale rebuilding of Toronto's urban food market at the turn of the century. With a growing population, there was a corresponding increase in the number of wage earners with increased spending capacity and needs.[61] Health standards had evolved even further than was considered adequate at the mid-nineteenth century. And there was a marked change to the urban form of Toronto. The physical relocation of the City Council from the dual-purpose Market House and City Hall building on Front and Jarvis Streets to the newly completed Municipal Buildings (1888-99) on Queen Street West was just one example of the evolving morphology of the city at this time. As the physical area of the city expanded through annexations to the east, west, and north, distinctly residential zones developed farther away from the area of the original town plan and thus farther away from the Market Reserve. However, due to improvements in public infrastructure, such as road paving and transit lines, the city was more easily navigable. Nevertheless, supplementary market spaces were established in developing neighbourhoods elsewhere in the city. Simultaneously, warehouses and other commercial buildings now surrounded the original market at King and Jarvis Streets, having influenced land-use patterns.

To better cope with the complexities of urban expansion, the City of Toronto established a Board of Control and municipal commissioners to act as the city's executive – a kind of municipal reform movement that spread across Europe and America at the end of the nineteenth century.[62] A Market Commission was formed with a specific mandate to administer this important institution. And, for the first time since the 1830s, the market was physically autonomous from the City Hall function, providing an opportunity to focus solely on the commercial program of the building.

Although a proposal for the St. Lawrence Market's much needed improvements was introduced to the City Council as early as 1892, it was not until seven years later that the Property Committee was directed to proceed with the project.[63] In preparation for another architectural competition, a Market Commission was formed and a contingent from this commission, composed of a city alderman and the architect W.L. Symons, embarked on a tour of market buildings in the United States to ensure that the most up-to-date market was

Figure 4.6 Proposed improvements to the St. Lawrence Market, Toronto, March 1898. Drawing by W.L. Symons, architect, accompanying report of the Market Commission, 1898. | City of Toronto Archives, City Council Papers.

erected and that the most efficient operations were implemented.[64] A shift from British colonial architectural types to American influences and innovations was already prevalent in Toronto at the end of the nineteenth century, and this exploratory excursion was just one example of the cross-border influence.[65] The purpose of the tour, which included stops in Boston, New York, Philadelphia, Baltimore, Washington, Cleveland, and Buffalo, was to acquire information regarding the construction and management of successful markets, take the best of everything encountered there, and apply it to recommendations for the proposed enlargement of Toronto's market.

The importance of the market venture to the city is unmistakable, evidenced by the amount of time and money afforded to this investigative process. At the beginning of the twentieth century, the market continued to serve as a key civic institution – a prime economic generator – and as such it had to be operated and administered in the most credible fashion to ensure complete success. In addition, the physical building form that was to accommodate this important function had to be most efficient and appropriate.

An extensive report with recommendations for future development of the market complex was submitted to the council, complete with conceptual renderings by the architect Symons (Figure 4.6). The commission recommended the retention of William Thomas's St. Lawrence Hall on King Street, which would act as an anchor for a new extensive market complex comprising two large single-span sheds located north and south of Front Street, connected by a canopy. The report suggested that within the south market, the old Council Chamber could be retained "as a pleasing historical feature" and that it could serve as a produce exchange, fashioned after a successful example that the contingent had visited while in Boston.[66]

An important consideration put forth in the Market Commission Report was for proper modern cold storage. A rarity in public markets in the nineteenth century, refrigeration was probably the most important advancement in the relevant building technology.[67] The commission had seen the successful use of cold storage in Boston, Philadelphia, Washington, and Cleveland – mechanical refrigeration had only recently been introduced at Boston's Quincy Market. The report stated that the cold-storage area ought to yield a very handsome revenue "as in other centres this was a strong point of the whole system."[68]

Efficiency of design was stressed throughout the report, and all considerations were based on the most advanced ideas of market-building construction – bringing Toronto into the twentieth century with a proposal for buildings that went well beyond the city's humble beginnings.

In February 1899 the city engineer, Charles H. Rust, in collaboration with the well-known Toronto architect E.J. Lennox, used the Market Commission Report as the basis for drawing up the terms and conditions for an architectural competition.[69] The question arose whether or not the competition should be limited only to Toronto architects. In the end, most likely due to the importance of this building for the City of Toronto, it was agreed that the competition would be open to all Canadian architects.[70]

The competition jury, consisting of Rust, Lennox, and Robert McCallum (government engineer and architect), received four sets of plans.[71] The limited response was, according to one writer in the *Canadian Architect and Builder*, attributable to the minimal remuneration and the nominal monies allotted to the project by the council.[72] The City Council allotted only $150,000, which the jury members feared was not enough to erect a building of this magnitude. And since an architect's fee was based on a percentage of the total costs, the remuneration to the architect was not particularly attractive.[73] Once again, although the market was an important revenue generator – the Market Commission estimated a "handsome surplus" in 1898 based on an annual revenue of $38,000 – the money spent on the building was kept at a minimum to maintain high returns.[74] This frugality had been the trend throughout all of the successive market buildings in Toronto.

After considerable debate among the jury members, the design of architect John W. Siddal was chosen.[75] By the beginning of 1902 a substantial portion of the south market was ready for occupancy. This was Toronto's largest market to date with a roof structure eighty-two feet high spanning a large open space. One entered the modern market shed via Front Street through the arches of Lane's former City Hall structure, which was now virtually encased within the new building form. Reconstruction of the north market buildings began shortly after the opening of the south market, and the entire St. Lawrence Market complex was complete by 1904 – the north and south buildings being connected by an iron and glass canopy that covered the streetcar tracks on Front Street (the canopy was removed in 1954) (Figures 4.7 and 4.8).

Shunning historicism, the modern structures were utilitarian, or, as one contemporary reviewer commented, "business-like."[76] This aesthetic was

Figure 4.7 View of the south St. Lawrence Market with attached canopy, 1914. | City of Toronto Archives, 9.2.4.G1, item 51.

Figure 4.8 Postcard of St. Lawrence Hall with the attached north market in the background. | City of Toronto Archives, series 330, file 151, item 3.

directed by many factors, including the market's location in the urban context – namely the wholesaling district – and the minimal budget allotted to the civic project. Unadorned, battered brick piers, with stone dressing, ran down the east and west sides of the buildings. In the bays between the piers, the brick walls were opened up with large, multipaned, segmental-arched windows on the upper level and entrance doors below. The windows allowed in plenty of light, as did the continuous lanterns at the peak of the metal roof.

The most significant aspect of the newest market buildings in Toronto was their size. Each building was approximately 340 by 140 feet, made possible through the new building technologies. Like the late-eighteenth-century railway stations and exhibition halls, the market-building type encouraged the use of innovative construction methods and materials. Structural systems that provided wide-open spaces were much needed for this building type, as they provided programmatic flexibility within the building. Whereas brick, load-bearing columns formerly fragmented floor space and occupied valuable square footage on the market floor, the single-span, arched, metal roof created an open, column-free space.

Although iron and glass technology had been made popular in some of the grand market spaces of the mid-nineteenth century, particularly in Europe (e.g., Les Halles in Paris), it became evident that despite the need for natural light in the large, covered spaces, markets, by their very nature, could not tolerate overheating, which too often came with a fully glassed roof. In the Toronto example, metal was used for the roof sheathing, and the continuous lanterns and ranges of windows allowed for indirect lighting and adequate ventilation.

To maximize the return on market rents, the placement of stalls and the layout of aisles were critical. Using the traditional, three-aisle layout allowed for ease of movement, which not only encouraged the greatest amount of business but also ensured the health and safety of the buyer and seller alike. Programmatically, the two market buildings were divided into two distinct market functions. The north market was dedicated to wholesale trade and was opened only on Saturdays. The absence of fixed stalls inside allowed the building to be used for other purposes during the week and also permitted farmers to easily drive their wagons directly onto the concrete-slab market floor. The sleighs or wagons were left in the market, and for sanitary reasons, the horses were stabled in another location. The south market, with fixed stalls, operated daily and was dedicated to retailers of meat, poultry, fish, fruits, and vegetables. The basement in the south market was equipped with the most modern cold-storage facilities.

The municipality, through its Department of Property, continued to regulate and manage this new market in conjunction with the Farmers' Market Committee. Regulations had not changed drastically from the nineteenth century. These continued to prevent farmers from disposing of their goods for resale by grocers or butchers.[77] Weights and quality continued to be checked by the Department of Health. Rents were no longer collected by the market superintendent but were paid directly to the city treasurer.[78]

Following the opening of the new, "modern" market buildings, the loss of the "old" St. Lawrence Market building was lamented by some, and the latest market buildings were criticized for being less architecturally attractive.[79] Yet aesthetic considerations were secondary to economic factors, and there were great expectations for the new market, which was lauded as an impetus for renewing business activity in the area.[80] The city engineer was directed to reroute streetcars along Front Street in order to provide direct access to all citizens in anticipation of increased business. The city estimated that property values would increase in the neighbourhood, an outcome of interest especially to the city since it was the land owner of the blocks directly to the west of the market, which comprised the Market Block commercial development that the city had undertaken in the first half of the nineteenth century. And although the municipal offices were now several blocks away, a civic presence remained firmly ensconced in the urban form through this substantial market-building complex.

THE SIXTH ST. LAWRENCE MARKET: THE 1969 NORTH MARKET

St. Lawrence Market retained its status as the principal distribution centre for foodstuffs for Toronto's citizens well into the early decades of the twentieth century, continuing to generate a healthy revenue for the municipality. However, by mid-century the government-controlled monopoly on food sales was coming to an end, and the functionality of this central, urban market was being challenged. There are numerous reasons for the demise of the urban market, including changes in consumer patterns, demographics, and urban form. Among the main precipitators were certainly the move from an agrarian society toward a capitalist economy and the rise of the suburbs, which saw the market-building type supplanted by the modern grocery store, or supermarket. Scattered throughout the city, neighbourhood grocery stores, with substantial parking facilities, made the centralized, downtown government-controlled market an inefficient endeavour. With the changes in consumer trends, a more complex system of food distribution emerged and, with it, a new building typology.

By the mid-twentieth century, the St. Lawrence Market had evolved to become a place that served both retail and wholesale purposes – yet it served neither well by the 1960s. As a retail outlet, the market-building type, especially in its configuration of the large market shed, seemed to some to be archaic and old-fashioned in comparison to the new supermarket-building type – this at a time when most people were eager to embrace a more modern, convenient, up-to-date commercial realm. And for the wholesalers, the urban market was difficult to access, lacking raised loading docks and direct rail or highway links, and was inadequate in terms of size, with no room for expansion in the immediate area. The growing use of trucks to transport produce was also causing traffic congestion in the downtown core on market days.

Concerned about public health and safety at the aging market building, the provincial government, as part of its postwar policy to develop provincially regulated and operated produce marketing boards, passed the Ontario Food Terminal Act in 1946, demonstrating the province's role in the economy of agricultural distribution.[81] Government involvement in urban food distribution had come full circle, returning to the realm of the provincial government, where it had been in 1803 when the lieutenant-governor passed the proclamation to establish a market in the Town of York.

The erection of the Ontario Food Terminal Building in Toronto in 1954 was the ultimate solution to a number of problems. Governed by a board appointed by the Ministry of Agriculture, Food and Rural Affairs, the terminal became the primary venue for sale of local produce, improving farmers' access to the wholesale market – the Ontario Food Terminal being the central location for the sale of foodstuffs to supermarkets and greengrocers throughout southern Ontario.[82] The board, mandated to play a major role in the orderly marketing of fruits and vegetables in Ontario by providing this central market space, superseded the role formerly held by the municipal government.[83]

The decision to demolish and rebuild the north St. Lawrence Market in 1968 was a result of these changes in the consumer culture and urban form. By the second half of the twentieth century, market expenses were outrunning revenue, thus making the market one of the contributors to Toronto's fiscal problems at a time when city expenditures exceeded all previous levels of spending.[84] In an effort both to cut costs and to increase revenue in the downtown market building, the City of Toronto undertook the market's redevelopment, hoping to offer buyers and sellers a new, modernized facility.[85] In addition, with the relocation of the wholesaling function to the Ontario Food Terminal Building, which boasted appropriate transport access and cold storage, the urban market at Jarvis and King Streets no longer had to accommodate the transport trucks and large stalls. The market's building program was thus greatly altered at this time. For the farmers who would sell directly to the public, only a smaller-scale building was required.

The new north market, designed in-house by city architect J.G. Sutherland, followed in the emerging modernist architectural aesthetic. Ahistorical, and stripped of all architectural details, the new market building, which is still in use today (as of 2011), is a simple, flat-roofed, rectangular, brick building. Staid, two-storey, brick columns run along the east and west sides of the building, creating an overhang to shelter outdoor stalls. With concrete-block walls and a concrete floor and ceiling, the interior is sparse and utilitarian. The interior space was meant to be multipurpose, so there are no fixed stalls, and on days other than Saturday the market can be rented out for other uses, allowing the city to capitalize on rental potential.

Despite changes in food distribution, changing demographics in Toronto, and new urban forms, the municipality continued to fulfil its traditional mandate of protecting the common good by building and regulating spaces devoted to the urban food market, even if it did so in a capacity much reduced from previous decades.

CONCLUSION

The demolition of the 1904 north market and the erection of a modern replacement in the late 1960s spurred some public reaction. The criticisms are telling because they suggest that the typology of the urban food market was embedded in the collective memory – that there was a knowledge of and, perhaps, a nostalgia for the historic market-building form. A newspaper article printed upon the opening of the 1968 market building titled "Why Doesn't the St. Lawrence Market Look Like a Market?"[86] suggests not only that the market-building type was recognized as inherently different from the modern supermarket but also that there was a desire for it to remain distinct due to the market's very status as a unique commercial forum – the antithesis of the supermarket.

Today, urban markets are making a comeback in many Canadian cities. Historic markets and districts have been redeveloped, revealing that they can once again become instruments of economic returns. Although some market buildings are being replaced by imitations designed primarily to attract tourists, many others continue to function in their historical role, as is the case with the market in Toronto. And although the same political and economic drivers that founded the urban market are no longer at play in the twenty-first century, this phenomenon shows that the market continues to be a prime consideration in municipal planning and that its buildings continue to contribute to the urban landscape. By attracting people back to the public spaces of cities' urban cores, markets provide effective strategies for revitalizing communities, thus continuing to play an important social, cultural, and economic role.

As noted at the outset of this chapter, the peripheral role that this building type has played in the history of Canadian architecture should be reconsidered in light of the fact that the architectural and urban issues surrounding the market aid in the analysis of social, political, and cultural milieus in specific times and places. Even the mundane act of everyday food distribution has significant impacts on the moral and physical arrangement of public spaces. A city is never complete – it is perpetually changing.[87] Throughout all of its changes, the urban market in Toronto has survived and has continued to exist "for the benefit of the inhabitants."

NOTES

1 Spiro Kostof, *The City Shaped: Urban Patterns and Meanings through History* (Boston: Little, Brown, 1991), 9-10.

2 Although other public markets were erected in the City of Toronto serving specific neighbourhoods, the markets that are the subject of this chapter, those at King and Jarvis Streets, were always the primary distribution point.

3 Mary P. Ryan, *Civic Wars: Democracy and Public Life in the American City during the Nineteenth Century* (Berkeley: University of California Press, 1997).

4 The market buildings in Toronto have not formerly been the topic of scholarly debate. Since the market buildings have been rebuilt and replaced, many of the actual buildings are no longer extant, so the analysis undertaken in this chapter is based chiefly on primary historical sources such as government records (including City Council papers and minutes), historical accounts, and visual documents (such as maps, architectural drawings, and early photographs).

5 Filarete provided an example of an "Ideal Market" in his *Treatise on Architecture* (1460). Campbell provided a plan in *Vitruvius Brittanicus* (1720). And in his *Précis des leçons d'architecture* (1809), Durand wrote, "existing markets degrade our towns."

6 Kostof, *City Shaped*, 94-95.

7 From 1788 until 1850 southern Ontario was divided into districts, each having a Court of General Quarter Sessions of the Peace. The Town of York, later the City of Toronto, was within the Home District, which included the Counties of Durham, Lincoln, Norfolk, Northumberland, Simcoe, and York.

8 Proclamation of Peter Hunter, reprinted in *Upper Canada Gazette,* 5 November 1803.

9 Indeed, the lack of a market was an embarrassment for the governmental authorities, as suggested by Lord Selkirk when writing in his diary on the lack of progress in the Town of York. See *Lord Selkirk's Diary, 1803-04,* ed. Patrick C.T. White (Toronto: Champlain Society, 1958).

10 See "Plan Submitted by Order of His Honor the President for the Enlargement of York," 9 June 1797, D.W. Smith Papers, Toronto Public Library. King, Jarvis, Front, and Church Streets bound the six-acre reserve. See also letter from Peter Russell to John Graves Simcoe, 9 December 1797, Peter Russell Papers, Toronto Public Library.

11 Appendix to *Journal of the House of Assembly of Upper Canada*, 19 February 1831.

12 Henry Scadding, *Toronto of Old: Collections and Recollections* (Toronto: Adam, Stevenson, 1873), 17; David B. Read, *The Lives of the Judges of Upper Canada and Ontario from 1791 to the Present Time* (Toronto: Rowsell and Hutchison, 1888), 55.

13 Statutes of Upper Canada to the Time of the Union, 54th Geo. III, Chapter 15, "An Act to empower the Commissioners of the Peace for the Home District, in their Court of General Quarter Session assembled, to establish and regulate a Market in and for the Town of York, in the said District," passed 14 March 1814.

14 John Ross Robertson, *Landmarks of Toronto*, vol. 1 (Toronto: J.R. Robertson, 1894), 61.

15 Helen Tangires, *Public Markets and Civic Culture in Nineteenth-Century America* (Baltimore, MD, and London: Johns Hopkins University Press, 2003), 4.

16 W. Thomas Matthews, "Social Government and the Regulation of the Public Market in Upper Canada, 1800-1860: The Moral Economy of the Poor?" *Ontario History* 79, 4 (December 1987): 321-22.

17 Sean Gouglas, "Produce and Protection: Covent Garden Market, the Socioeconomic Elite, and the Downtown Core in London, Ontario, 1843-1915," *Urban History Review* 25 (October 1996): 3.

18 *Upper Canada Gazette*, 25 May 1820, 3.

19 See "Plan of the Town of York," by J.G. Chewett, 1827, copy in Toronto Public Library.

20 Henry Scadding and John Ross Robertson described the building as a primitive wooden structure. Scadding, *Toronto of Old*, 14, called it a wooden shambles measuring thirty-five by twenty-five feet. Robertson, *Landmarks of Toronto*, vol. 1, 61, gave the dimensions as forty-five by thirty feet and also included a conjectural sketch.

21 Up until 1831 the market clerk in the Town of York pocketed the fees he collected as remuneration for services rendered. However, with the passing of an act by the House of Assembly in that year, the market fees were collected by the clerk but then deposited directly into the government account. The clerk became instead a salaried employee. See *Journal of the House of Assembly of Upper Canada*, 19 February 1831, 57; and *British Colonist*, 6 September 1844, 2.

22 In Britain the market clerk was an officer of the Crown whose duty was to regulate the permanent market kept for the supply of the royal household. By the middle of the seventeenth century, however, his jurisdiction had been extended over the entire country. See William Addison, *English Fairs and Markets* (London: B.T. Batsford, 1953), 67.

23 Minutes of the Court of General Quarter Sessions of the Home District, 13 March 1830, Archives of Ontario.

24 Donald P. Kerr and Jacob Spelt, *The Changing Face of Toronto: A Study in Urban Geography* (Ottawa: Queen's Printer, 1965), 42.

25 A rendering of these buildings can be found in "View of King Street," 1835, reproduced in Harold Kalman, *A History of Canadian Architecture*, vol. 2 (Toronto: Oxford University Press, 1994), 664, Figure 12.16.

26 Submissions included those by James G. Chewett (a designer and surveyor) and James Cooper. See Minutes of the Court of General Quarter Sessions of the Home District, 31 January 1831, Archives of Ontario.

27 On Cooper, see Eric Arthur, *Toronto: No Mean City*, 3rd ed., rev. Stephen A. Otto (Toronto: University of Toronto Press, 1986), 63.

28 Minutes of the Court of General Quarter Sessions of the Home District, 31 January 1831, 21 July 1831, and 1 April 1833, Archives of Ontario. A request for funds to pave and flag the area around the market building suggests a completion date of around 1833.

29 A detailed description of the design can be found in Isaac Fidler, *Observations of Professions, Literature, Manners and Emigration in the United States and Canada, Made during a Residence There in 1832* (London: Whittaker, Treacher, 1833), 263-64. The model was constructed in 1985 by a team of students in the Department of Architectural Science/Landscape Architecture at Ryerson Polytechnical Institute. It is in the collection of the City of Toronto Archives.

30 An example of this type of market plan is the Royal Exchange, London, 1840. See Roger Dixon and Stefan Muthesius, *Victorian Architecture* (New York: Oxford University Press, 1978), 119.

31 A list of renters for the first market building was published in 1831 with twenty-two butchers' names. See Appendix to *Journal of the House of Assembly of Upper Canada,* 2 February 1831. This list expands significantly on a reference found in the city directory of 1834.

32 Fidler, *Observations of Professions,* 264.

33 "City of Toronto from the British Whig," *Christian Guardian,* 31 December 1834.

34 Matthews, "Social Government," 300, 310.

35 City Council Papers, "Report of the Select Committee," 5 December 1836, City of Toronto Archives.

36 This was, in fact, not the first instance of the government's interest in architecture and urban design. At the time of the founding of the Town of York, the lieutenant-governor directed the Executive Council to "adjust such regulations as may be expedient and not burthensome to give an architectural Uniformity to the Town, an object of very great importance in the Establishment of a new Province." Minutes of the Executive Council, 5 April 1796, Library and Archives Canada, R10875-2-1-E.

37 City Council Minutes, 8 April 1834, City of Toronto Archives; Robert B. Kellough, "Historical Outline of Toronto's Municipal Buildings, Prepared for the Committee on City Hall and Court House Requirements," 5 February 1952, City of Toronto Archives.

38 City Council Papers, "Report of Markets by the Clerk of the Markets, James McMillan," 14 April 1834, City of Toronto Archives.

39 *British Colonist,* 6 September 1844, 2. A huckster was someone who peddled goods outside of the market in the hope of avoiding the market fees.

40 This rapid growth continued, with the population rising from 1,719 in 1826 to 9,654 in 1834 and more than doubling by 1844 to 19,000. See *British Colonist,* 6 September 1844, 2.

41 For information on the expansion of stalls, see City Council Papers, "Correspondence from the Clerk of the Markets, James McMillan, to William Lyon Mackenzie," 20 May 1834, City of Toronto Archives. For information on the fish market, see Council Resolution, 30 May 1834, City of Toronto Archives. The fish market is defined on James Cane's "Topographical Plan of the City and Liberties of Toronto," 1842, City of Toronto Archives, reproduced in Arthur, *Toronto,* 81.

42 *British Colonist,* 6 September 1844, 2.

43 Although by this date other subsidiary markets in "suburban" neighbourhoods had been established and helped to alleviate some of the problems (such as St. Patrick's and St. Andrew's Markets in the west), the central market at King and Jarvis Streets was still the primary point of food distribution.

44 City By-Law No. 75, 6 November 1843. The Home District's Farmer Store was already located on this lot; see James Cane's 1842 map of Toronto. This company was the first farmers' co-operative organization in central Ontario, founded in 1824; see Kellough, "Historical Outline of Toronto's Municipal Buildings," 4.

45 Builders, engineers, surveyors, and amateur architects designed the earliest buildings in the Town of York. When a project demanded a more refined and sophisticated design, calls were sent to Kingston or abroad to Britain. The first architects to arrive in York/ Toronto include John George Howard, Thomas Young, William Thomas, John Tully, and Henry Bowyer Lane. See Sharon Vattay, "Architectural Practice in Nineteenth Century Toronto" (PhD diss., University of Toronto, 2001), 66-76.

46 The call for plans was published in the *Examiner,* 10 January 1844. The results were described in City Council Papers, "Report of the Committee on Public Markets," 4 March 1844, City of Toronto Archives.

47 City Council Papers, "Report of the Committee on Public Markets," 4 March 1844 and 26 August 1844, City of Toronto Archives. Full details of the competition and issues surrounding this building can be found in William Dendy, *Lost Toronto: Images of the City's Past* (Toronto: McClelland and Stewart, 1993), 64-67.

48 This configuration is comparable to the lower portion of Hungerford Market (1831-33) by Charles Fowler, which took the form of an open U-shaped courtyard oriented toward the river.

49 The building is illustrated in detail in Marion MacRae and Anthony Adamson, *Cornerstones of Order: Courthouses and Town Halls of Ontario, 1784-1914* (Toronto: Clarke, Irwin, 1983), 88-91.

50 Toronto itself did not have stone quarries. Stone had to be brought in from Queenston, Indiana, or from Britain, making this an expensive venture, whereas brickyards were plentiful in the city.

51 Dendy, *Lost Toronto,* 66.

52 In reference to the building, W.H. Smith wrote, "a very strange looking building and it was unfortunate for the reputation of the architect that he had not left the province before he completed the building instead of afterward." See W.H. Smith, *Canada: Past, Present and Future,* vol. 2 (Toronto: Thomas Maclear, 1852), 5. William Thomas undertook the reworking of the facade in 1850-51.

53 Dixon and Muthesius, *Victorian Architecture,* 119.

54 James Schmiechen and Kenneth Carls, *The British Market Hall: A Social and Architectural History* (New Haven, CT: Yale University Press, 1999), 55.

55 Nikolaus Pevsner, *A History of Building Types* (Princeton, NJ: Princeton University Press, 1976), 238.

56 Many of the same architects who had entered the 1844 competition for the south market submitted proposals for this north market complex. The architects included William Thomas, Henry Bowyer Lane, and Kivas Tully. See *British Colonist,* 11 February 1845, 1.

57 Robertson, *Landmarks of Toronto,* vol. 5, 144.

58 The idea that order in architecture bred order in society was put forth by many architectural theorists, including writer and landscape architect John Claudius Loudon, *Encyclopedia of Cottage, Farm and Villa Architecture and Furniture* (1833; rev. ed., London: Longman, Brown, Green and Longmans, 1836), 94.

59 This configuration is comparable to Baltimore's Lexington Market, which was 290 by 50 feet.

60 C. Pelham Mulvany, *Toronto: Past and Present, A Handbook of the City* (Toronto: W.E. Caiger, 1884), 142.

61 The number of wage earners increased from 12,708 in 1881 to 45,515 in 1901. See William Dendy and William Kilbourn, *Toronto Observed: Its Architecture, Patrons and History* (Toronto: Oxford University Press, 1986), 153.

62 Ibid.

63 *Canadian Architect and Builder* 5, 11 (November 1892): 106; City Council Minutes, 9 January 1899, City of Toronto Archives.

64 City Council Minutes, "Appendix C: Report of the Market Commission," 1898, 1, City of Toronto Archives.

65 Another well-known example is Toronto's Old City Hall. In the 1880s, prior to designing his Richardsonian, Romanesque Municipal Buildings in Toronto, architect E.J. Lennox travelled extensively throughout the eastern United States studying buildings of a similar type. See Dendy and Kilbourn, *Toronto Observed,* 148-51.

66 City Council Papers, "Report of the Market Commission," 1898, 8, City of Toronto Archives.

67 James Mayo, "The American Public Market," *Journal of Architectural Education* 45, 1 (November 1991): 51.

68 City Council Papers, "Report of the Market Commission," 1898, 9, City of Toronto Archives.

69 The City Council directed the city engineer to obtain the services of a competent architect to assist in the preparation. He chose Lennox, who was just then completing eleven years as architect of the new Municipal Buildings on Queen Street West; see Board of Control, "Report No. 4," 15 February 1899, City of Toronto Archives. See also City Council Reports, "Terms and Conditions to Govern Architects in the Preparation of Competition Plans for the Alteration and Improvement of St. Lawrence Market, Toronto," February 1899, City of Toronto Archives.

70 Board of Control, "Report No. 3," 3 February 1899, City of Toronto Archives.

71 Board of Control, "Report No. 4," 15 February 1899, City of Toronto Archives.

72 *Canadian Architect and Builder* 12, 4 (April 1899): 69.

73 Board of Control, "Report No. 2," 26 January 1899, and "Report No. 19," 13 May 1899, City of Toronto Archives.

74 City Council Papers, "Report of the Market Commission," 1898, 10, City of Toronto Archives.

75 Board of Control, "Report No. 36," 13 October 1899, City of Toronto Archives.

76 Robertson, *Landmarks of Toronto,* vol. 5, 149.

77 For example, one of the regulations in place in 1944 was that all persons wishing to sell at the market had to apply and declare that at least 75 percent of their merchandise was produced on their own farms.

78 Board of Control, "Extract," 1905, 1052, 1247, City of Toronto Archives.

79 Robertson, *Landmarks of Toronto,* vol. 5, 149.

80 By 1944 the north market accommodated, on average, 225 farmers, who came from places within a radius of twenty to twenty-five miles. See City Council Papers, Department of Property, "Report," 4 December 1944, 8, City of Toronto Archives.

81 By centralizing all wholesalers in one location, the Ontario Food Terminal was expected to facilitate governmental regulation by ensuring, for example, that low-quality produce would not be dumped on the Ontario market.

82 Toronto Food Policy Council, "A Wealth of Food: A Profile of Toronto's Food Economy," January 1999, 11-12. The Ontario Food Terminal is currently one of the largest fresh-produce entrepots in North America, making Toronto one of the continent's major food-distribution centres.

83 The board is the market regulator and manager of the facility, with specific responsibilities for maintaining standards of food safety. See Canadian Urban Institute, "Final Report: The Ontario Food Terminal: A Unique Asset in the Central Ontario Economy," June 2004, 3.

84 James Lemon, *Toronto since 1918: An Illustrated History* (Toronto: James Lorimer and National Museum of Man, National Museums of Canada, 1985), 147.

85 Board of Control, "Report No. 26A," 22 May 1968, City of Toronto Archives.

86 *Toronto Star,* 15 February 1969, 38.

87 Kostof, *The City Shaped,* 13.

PART 3
BUILDING THE CONFEDERATION

The fabric of Confederation was built architecturally as well as politically, socially, and economically. The allusion to building or construction is apt in the functional and ideological senses since, as has already been argued, the Canadian Confederation was a connecting of various components that remade spatial and material dimensions of polity and culture. This third part is therefore longest and deliberately addresses the confluence between architectural design and political, communal identity formation. It sets urban settlement – which continued to be the foundation for colonial and provincial expansion – in the broader context of the scripting and structuring of a national political and cultural fabric. The emerging Canadian nation was positioned in a distinct relation to Britain and the United States both by the establishment, even before the enactment of Confederation, of a transcontinental seat of government at the already thriving resource centre of Ottawa and by the building of a parliamentary edifice of remarkably impressive scale, plan, and iconography. This edifice openly declared the force of architecture and planning for Canadian publics well in advance of the establishment of a design profession in Canada. In "Shifting Soil: Agency and Building Type in Narratives of Canada's 'First' Parliament," Christopher Thomas explores the design agency of the architects Thomas Fuller and less acknowledged Chilion Jones in the execution of this extraordinarily large commission, quite on par with either the Houses of

Parliament at Westminster or the Capitol at Washington, DC. Thomas also reconsiders the spatial composition of the Canadian legislature as part of a broader understanding of the cultural politics and political culture of Confederation. As is well known, a core incentive for joining Confederation was the railway system linking the East and West Coasts – the old and new geographies of emergent nationalism. At the western terminus of this Canadian Pacific Railway was the volatile resource and port town of Vancouver, colloquially named Terminal City. Geoffrey Carr's "Stitching Vancouver's New Clothes: The World Building, Confederation, and the Making of Place" studies a single commission as an indicator of wider systems of commercial and cultural exchange forming collective identity. His account shows the imbrication of personal ambition and contesting community prejudices with the more patent financial and fiduciary factors driving speculation in real estate – a particular feature of colonial urban development, including in Vancouver, where advertisements by real estate agents predominated in early media. The communal and racial divisions Carr reveals as lurking behind the promotion of a unicultural civic and national facade were palliated to some extent by sporting spectacle and the contemporary cobbling together of a trans-Canada media, namely radio. Ice hockey, invented in the anglophone community of Montreal but rapidly regarded as the national game, took on an everyday pan-Canadian cultural reality largely through broadcasts from Toronto's Maple Leaf Gardens by the Canadian Broadcasting Corporation. In "Digging in the Gardens: Unearthing the Experience of Modernity in Interwar Toronto," Michael Windover traces the genealogy of the commercial network, architectural design, and media infrastructure of this now unused icon of Toronto's survival of the Depression. The Gardens also became a potent signifier of Canadian identity, fabricated from national initiative woven into the already changing weft and warp of power deployed by Britain and the United States (Canadian players won the Gold Medal in ice hockey for Britain at the 1936 Olympics, and the annual competition instigated by Governor-General Lord Stanley has become embedded in American sports culture).

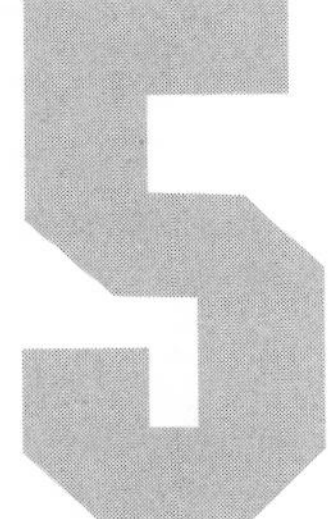

Shifting Soil
Agency and Building Type in Narratives of Canada's "First" Parliament

CHRISTOPHER THOMAS

Surely, in an anthology intended to illuminate the historiography and cultural politics of Canadian architecture, an indispensible topic of study is the legislative buildings and public offices erected from 1859 to 1876 to house and encode the federal government in the national capital (Figure 5.1). Often called Canada's "first" Parliament, since they antedate the present complex, rebuilt after fire in 1916,[1] these have been the subject of published accounts that tend, so far, to be structured chiefly by attention to the buildings' character as national symbols. The same observation can be made of the discursive webs that wrap national capitols generally.[2] Dell Upton notes, for example, that "Over the past two centuries, the builders of the United States Capitol" buildings, which as architecture are "rambling [and] ungainly," "have been more interested in building a mythology ... than a coherent formal composition."[3] Although the centre block in Ottawa always was – and is – more compact and unified than the Capitol in Washington (Figure 5.2) and the patriotic rhetoric around it has been less heated, still, John Ralston Saul reminds us, scholarly problems always arise, even in comparatively prosaic Canada, when mythology becomes confused with history.[4]

This is what I contend has happened in narratives of building the nineteenth-century Parliament at Ottawa.[5] In so saying, I recognize that history and myth are not as easily separated as we may wish – may not indeed, in a radical sense,

Figure 5.1 Parliament Buildings of Canada, Ottawa, main front as in April 1915, architects Thomas Fuller and Chilion Jones, 1859-66 (some elements finished later). | Photograph by A.W. Campbell. Library and Archives Canada, PA 130626.

Figure 5.2 "Panoramic View of Washington City: From the New Dome of the Capitol Looking West," by E. Sachse and Co., c. 1856. The lithograph shows architect T.U. Walter's additions to the Capitol, then in progress, as though complete. | Courtesy of the Library of Congress, Prints and Photographs Division.

be separable at all.[6] I also acknowledge that postmodern skepticism of Grand Narratives is just as prone to mythicism as other critical viewpoints have been. Yet this should not paralyze us in writing history nor prevent me, here, from challenging the accepted, "classic" accounts of Parliament's building.

An essential starting point for writing a fresh account of Parliament will be a historiography of what has been written, a task too ambitious to undertake here. Instead, I will raise just two questions that, I think, the classic narratives gloss over. One is: has the discipline of architectural history attributed too much initiative to the architects of Parliament, and what alternative causal agents might be identified? The second is: what is the origin of the building type the parliament house represents? These two questions by no means exhaust the potential for a critical architectural inquiry into Canada's Parliament; indeed, they suggest only how resistant to closure such an inquiry would be, especially since the answers ventured here, particularly the first, are quite tentative. I hope, however, the discussion will draw attention to some useful lines of questioning that could be pursued – lines that *should* be pursued, given that the central legislative buildings were charged with the responsibility to encode a sense of Canadian-Victorian collective identity.

What the classic historiography did do was to shape a certain canon of Canadian "greats" and document these factually.[7] That was invaluable, as I shall explain, and some mastery of the factual skeleton that architectural historians – including myself – have assembled is needed if the issues raised here are to make sense. Here is a thumbnail version of this history.[8] In 1857-58, after fifteen years of discord and inconvenience, Queen Victoria, on the advice of her governor-general, Sir Edmund Head, chose Ottawa (formerly Bytown) as the permanent seat of government of the United Province of Canada, comprising Canada East (Quebec) and Canada West (Ontario). This decision and a legislative appropriation of $225,000 led to the calling in May 1859 of a competition to solicit designs for a government complex on Barrack (or Barracks) Hill, now known as Parliament Hill – a sloping, slightly irregular terrace north of the town that dropped off steeply and spectacularly to the Ottawa River, behind, from a pleasingly bowed-out limestone cliff. The group would consist of "Buildings for the Provincial Parliament and Library," "Buildings for the Public Departments," and a "residence for the Governor General." Although the brief for these specified only "a plain, substantial style of architecture" and surely little more was expected, the entries chosen that summer by Public Works officials (assisted by Head) proved to be surprisingly advanced – *dernier cri,* actually – examples of the mode that is today called High Victorian Gothic, which avant-garde architects then called "civil" or "modern" Gothic, hoping to extend the style's previously rather limited revival to all areas of fast-changing contemporary life.[9] In Ottawa, the design chosen for the central block accommodating the Houses of Parliament proper – consisting of an appointed, advisory Council and an elected Assembly – was by the team of Fuller and Jones; and, for the flanking departmental (bureaucratic) blocks, by the firm Stent and Laver. (The viceregal residence was dropped from the program for the sake of economy.) The architects involved, excepting only Fuller's partner, Chilion Jones (a Canadian), had emigrated fairly recently from England, as many professionals then working in Canada had. Collectively, the two firms imagined a complex of ceremonial and bureaucratic buildings of highly English and Ruskinian character, very like work being pioneered at home by High Victorian architects such as George Gilbert Scott, George Edmund Street, and Alfred Waterhouse.

Eager to start work before winter set in and to discourage Canadian public officials and parliamentarians from changing their minds, yet again, about decamping to what many thought a glorified timber depot, the Department of Public Works launched construction work immediately and irreversibly. The heir apparent, Edward Prince of Wales, laid the cornerstone in September 1860 while visiting Canada. Just over a year later, however, work was halted when it became clear to legislators that costs, especially to excavate the surprisingly rocky hill, had gotten out of hand. A commission of inquiry was held, and construction recommenced in 1863 on a more restricted basis, with Thomas Fuller (1823-98) – the architect credited with the design of the parliament house – placed in charge of the entire building project, to be assisted by Charles Baillargé (1826-1906), of Quebec. The complex was near enough completion to allow the government departments to move to Ottawa in the fall of 1865 and Parliament to meet in its new chambers the following year – the only session held there before the provincial government transferred its authority to the new Dominion of Canada on 1 July 1867. Peripheral elements – the Victoria Tower anchoring Parliament's main facade, a neo-Gothic polygonal library at the rear (Figure 5.3), and an addition to the western departmental building – saw completion in the mid-1870s.

The centre block that housed Parliament (Figure 5.1), although famously splendid, was never more than a qualified functional success. An overcrowded firetrap almost from the start, it nevertheless met the needs of Parliament and its denizens middlingly well, given constant alteration and a considerable addition at the northwest corner (in 1906-07), until February 1916, when, at the nadir of the First World War, a spectacular nighttime blaze burnt the structure to a degree that made restoration unthinkable. Here at last was an opportunity to replace the old dowager. Only the splendid central-plan library attached to the original Parliament was left, although the fully detached east and west office blocks were relatively unscathed. The centre block was replaced by a new and larger version designed by John Pearson and J. Omer Marchand in an updated, twentieth-century version of neo-Gothic, which some thought soulless and mechanistic. The new block was substantially complete by 1927, even to the sleek Peace Tower on its front commemorating the Armistice. The Library of Parliament was reattached to the rear and remains today, in outer appearance if not inner and subterranean reality, much as Fuller designed it (Figure 5.3).[10]

This is the essence of what architectural historians (including myself) have told us of the building of Parliament's centre block, and for factual accuracy it represents a huge advance over what was known before. In poetic, romantic evocations of the building, writers of the early twentieth century had sometimes failed even to name the architects or to report basic facts about the building correctly.[11] The current, rather positivist account of Parliament is a product, mainly, of scholarship performed after the Second World War, when art history was introduced as a discipline in Canadian universities, sometimes with heavy emphasis on architecture, and when architectural education was systematized.[12] Factual accuracy and descriptive rigour have become the pillars of architectural

Figure 5.3 Library of Parliament, Ottawa, view from the east, architects Thomas Fuller and Chilion Jones, 1859-76. | Photograph by author.

history, and these must continue to stand; but the methodological contributions of the past quarter-century should not be dismissed either. These have had the effect of subjecting received architectural "stories" to critique across a number of axes.[13] In my view, existing explanations of Parliament omit too much and have become of limited interest. This is partly because the accounts deny the writers' ideological positioning – their subjectivity – which usually favours a certain kind of unitary Anglo-Canadian nationalism. Moreover, the writers, including myself, return to focus again and again on the surprising choice of style for Parliament, since style-history is the privileged domain of investigation in Canadian architectural history. Treatments of Parliament written so far, culminating in Carolyn Young's,[14] usually seek to answer the question: how did one of the most progressive Victorian Gothic public buildings in Euro-America, described by a former dean of American architectural historians, Henry-Russell Hitchcock, as "a major monumental group unrivalled for extent and complexity of organization in England,"[15] come to be built in what Goldwin Smith exaggeratedly called a "sub-arctic lumber village"?[16] This paradox rightly grips both patriots and modernists, if only because it suggests the way provincials can sometimes get away with what metropolitan sophisticates at the centre of empire cannot. But surely it is not the only and perhaps not even the main question to be asked of Parliament; indeed, it may not be answerable at all without investigating a number of other matters that cross the boundaries of art history into other disciplines and interdisciplines. What might some "missing" questions about Parliament be? Here, I suggest just two, acknowledging that even these may not at present admit of crisp answers.

First, in the area of *agency* as a narrative means to explain what causes buildings, architectural history has a constitutional preference to assign initiative to the architect, in particular the creative building designer. Frankly, I am embarrassed to realize how often I have thoughtlessly referred, in writing and teaching, to the Parliament Buildings – and other structures and projects – as "Fuller's," neglecting even to acknowledge his partner, Jones; in fact, this shorthand creeps in here, at times. Protracted and extensive training in architectural history long ago conditioned me to "think like" an architectural historian, causing me reflexively to throw a causal spotlight on the architect. In the case at hand, too, there are sound historical reasons to attribute the artistic aspect of Fuller and Jones's work to Thomas Fuller.[17] But to some degree, this is a circular defense, for, after all, why attend to architecture in the first place and, within architecture, to the element of artistic invention, as opposed to the wide range of functional, aesthetic, and financial issues and operations that occupy the architect (not to mention the host of agents and concerns that surround any public-building project)? Clearly, early-twentieth-century commentators did not have a similar prejudice: as we saw, they all but overlooked the architect as a causal agent. We are entitled to suspect that this change in narrative and scholarly convention owed much to the rise in the architect's professional status from the late nineteenth century to our own time.[18] Another point in my own defence for using "Fuller's building" as shorthand is that, in the circumstances of mid-nineteenth-century Canada, the Parliament Buildings *were,* in a concrete, demonstrable sense, "Fuller's" because at the time architects were few; British North America had seen no design competitions of a magnitude and sophistication comparable to the one conducted for the buildings on Barrack Hill; and the government, with little experience of collaborating with architects, was inclined to give them – especially an architect as confident and savvy as Fuller – a freer hand than it might have otherwise, or than a government at home might have done. As it happened, the Canadian government probably gave the architects *too much* latitude.[19] So in this case it is surely safe to infer that Fuller and the like-minded Stent and Laver were the instigators of a style revolution on Barrack Hill – something to keep in mind when considering that old chestnut: how did the Parliament Buildings come to be so advanced in style? In short, the building of the Parliament in Ottawa is probably one case where the architects did play a formative role.

Problems arise, however, when this assumption is made too quickly or unconsciously. Even in such a nuanced formulation as this, architectural history's attribution of agency to the architect – in this case, to two or three architects – has the effect of neglecting or downplaying many nonarchitectural agents and choices that require exploration if the story of Parliament's building is to make sense. Carolyn Young rightly observes, "The question of who was responsible for the layout of the complex and the administration of the competition remains unanswered";[20] yet that this observation appears in an endnote rather than in the body of the text suggests how little impact the uncertainties she expresses have made and how thoroughly the assumptions of canonical architectural history inform the accepted account.

The question arises, then: what other persons' initiatives may have determined the character, scale, and appearance of Parliament whose role or roles are not well understood? For example, who was behind the decision to erect in the new, allegedly backwoods capital of the United Province of Canada one of the largest complexes of public buildings on the North American continent? I say "allegedly" because the question of whether the City of Ottawa in 1859 *was* quite the primeval wilderness unhappy legislators and bureaucrats claimed is itself worth revisiting. Many modern nation-states have built "new" capitals, including Washington, Canberra, Soviet Moscow, New Delhi, Brasilia, and Chandigarh. It is practically a literary form to denounce newly minted or recycled capital cities as rustic, backward, and impossibly remote.[21] Not usually wrong in a simple sense, such withering views nonetheless commonly conceal defences of the interests and pretensions of elites in established, typically more conservative centres. In Ottawa's case, if Goldwin Smith's "sub-arctic" is justified – until the Soviet Union collapsed in the 1990s, spawning a clutch of new states, Ottawa had without exception the coldest winter of any capital city in the world, even Moscow – it bears noting that the city's winter is essentially identical to Montreal's, but less snowy; and, with a population of 10,000 to 15,000 at the end of the 1850s (having doubled in a decade), Ottawa was surely no village. It was eastern North America's largest lumbering centre; it was located at a strategic bend and portage on a major river artery having transcontinental potential; and the Ottawa Valley boasted a modest cultural and scientific life and a decades-old tradition of fine masonry construction.[22] With a transient population of river raftsmen, Ottawa could, it is true, be rough around the edges. If I perhaps digress, it is because I am trying to suggest the kinds of questions that should be asked, or asked again.

The question at hand here is: what larger cast of characters standing in the shadows of the spotlight of architectural history can be identified who may have contributed to the building of Parliament more than is usually recognized? Governor General Sir Edmund Head? The provincial legislature? Public Works officials, especially Frederick P. Rubidge, about whom a good deal is known but little is written in respect to the building of Parliament?[23] What is the connection between the project for Ottawa and one mooted earlier in the decade, involving architect-engineer Frederic William Cumberland, to build the provincial Parliament at Toronto instead?[24] Who first proposed $225,000 as the cost limit for the new legislative complex?[25] A great many questions may be asked, and I will tackle but one "test-patch" here, even if summarily.

Governor General Head's role in the parliamentary project, although often acknowledged, has not been well understood, even by his contemporaries, and it is possible, given his delicate position as governor-in-chief within the British Empire's pioneering foray into responsible government, that he intended the uncertainty. Anthony Trollope, however, left us a clue. In 1861 the popular London novelist, making a Grand Tour of North America, was shown around the construction site in Ottawa, and based on the visit, he wrote a panegyric of which later authors have made much: "The glory of Ottawa will be – and, indeed, already is – the set of public buildings which is now being erected on the rock which guards, as it were, the town from the river." There was, he believed, "no modern Gothic purer of its kind, or less sullied with fictitious ornamentation," nor an instance so picturesquely sited.[26] Although the passage about the Parliament's a-building goes on several pages, most authors quote only the section dealing with aesthetics and more or less ignore the rest. One particular point that bears on aesthetics, to be sure, merits attention, for it interfaces with politics. Trollope speculates, "How much of the excellence of these buildings may be due to the taste of Sir Edmund Head, the late Governor, I do not know."[27] This is a provocative lead that invites the sifting and weighing of a wide range of historical evidence. A probable answer, which I explore in detail elsewhere,[28] is that, although Head seems to have had plenty to do with the choice of the capital and the site for the public buildings, it is unlikely the building style was his choice. On its face, this far-from-exciting answer appears to take architectural history nowhere at all, but it exemplifies the kind of close, curious reading of the historical record the field needs.

A second example *can* be pursued in some detail here. It arises from architectural history's preoccupation with Parliament's aesthetic *style,* which has, I think, suppressed awareness of the novelty of the building's *type*. Building typology and the project's scale and ambition, seen against the backdrop of the critical late-Union period, are interwoven. Is it not remarkable that the civil-service mandarin Edmund Meredith, though horrified to move to such a "rough, wild, and unfinished" place as Ottawa, conceded that the east block in which he worked was (in Sandra Gwyn's words) "unquestionably the handsomest and most modern office building in the country" – even before its advanced hot-air heating system was working?[29] What explains the asymmetry between building and setting? Partly the rhetorical construction of Ottawa as a remote fastness, which I have noted; but more is at work than that. Not fully realized yet, I think, is the extent to which the government complex at Ottawa, especially its centre block, represented the invention of a new – to be precise, hybrid – building type, worlds away from the converted markets, hospitals, and palatial residences that by and large had served British North American legislatures in the colonial and early-Union periods (Figure 5.4).[30] The Ottawa Parliament, along with Cumberland's slightly earlier scheme for one in Toronto, represented not so much one increment in a graduated development as a quantum interrupter of the development. It was more like dropping Somerset House or the United States Treasury onto Barrack Hill than simply building one in a series of steadily grander, more explicitly symbolic parliament houses. The departure is especially startling in that, in the late 1850s, the province was being pulled under by recession and wracked with crippling canal and railway debt. By setting the then-enormous sum of $640,000 aside for new government buildings – a sum that proved inadequate – Canada was behaving like a spendthrift who seeks relief from anxiety about credit-card debt by going on a shopping spree!

The question of the scale and building type of Parliament at Ottawa is best understood, I think, when the project to build it is seen within an expanded field of historical explanation. First, consider the design challenge the program presented to the competing architects in spring 1859: what should Parliament's architectural form and character be? That the large, slightly sloping site was empty, giving them a clean slate, was helpful, but only negatively. British North America itself furnished no helpful precedents, and competitors appear to have drawn no inspiration whatever from what were then the largest new public buildings in Canada: a series of big municipal halls that often – as was traditional – combined market with meeting facilities, erected in the larger Canadian cities in the 1840s and 1850s, such as Kingston's imposing City Hall (Figure 5.5).[31] Anyway, a Romantic age would have dismissed as symbolically weak a national parliament that echoed a town hall, especially since the purpose of removing the capital to Ottawa rather than rebuilding the seat of government in an established centre was to challenge local loyalties, to draw into one the *whole* Canadian community, not that of one locale. As Young shows, architects who in the main hailed from Britain looked there for models, but, although architectural historians have emphasized the High Victorian Scott-and-Ruskin character of the designs selected, they have not much analyzed the building type. The newly rebuilt Houses of Parliament at Westminster had set a precedent by applying Gothic to the pre-eminent British national building – a lesson not lost on some of the architects in Canada, among them Fuller and Jones – but this situation was too particular and historically freighted to be of much help to designers in Canada. In a sense, they faced the opposite problem – for white Europeans – of insufficient historical resonance in an "empty" land. In London, Charles Barry had worked the complex around sacred surviving fragments of the Old Palace, one reason he fixed on a longitudinal processional axis as his compositional theme.[32] Fuller and Jones arrived at a very different *parti* – different in style-metaphor and in its insistent bilateral symmetry and air of abstract rationality throughout (Figure 5.6). Where did these qualities originate? A tight competition deadline of two and a half months from call to delivered design surely reinforced the unavoidable need to draw on established sources. Besides a century and more of symmetrical neo-Baroque and neo-Palladian design in British public building, the architects had access to current French models of what we call "Second Empire" character, which enjoyed great prestige among Anglo-Americans in the 1850s.[33] Did Thomas Fuller have in mind a more specific model than these?

A biographical answer might interest itself in the fact that Fuller's principal experience, to that point, of designing symmetrical public buildings was with schools, an important type in the reformist early-Victorian period.[34] To be sure, the prominence of the library in the Parliament's building program did give the Ottawa project a remarkably bookish, scholarly quality.[35] But since designs for

Figure 5.4 Ste-Anne Market, Montreal, architect George Browne, 1833, enlarged 1839. Rented by Union government as Canadian parliament building, 1844-49; burnt, 1849. | Augustus Kollner fonds / Library and Archives Canada, C-013425.

neo-Gothic public buildings, including one submitted to the competition in Ottawa, were sometimes criticized for being excessively collegiate in character,[36] it is unlikely Fuller and Jones looked chiefly to school designs for inspiration. So a concatenating, biographical explanation of the design for Parliament falters as an explanation of the radical change it represented. Where, then, did the designer(s) look?

Before I attempt an answer, let me pause to comment on the degree to which Fuller and Jones's symmetrical, rather loosely spread-out design, besides commanding a spacious site, succeeded in visually capturing the political and cultural character of the country it was to represent – Canada in the Union period (1841-67). By contrast, as I argue elsewhere,[37] a whole body of literature, much of it written in the 1950s, 1960s, and early 1970s – a period constellated around the federal Centennial of 1967 – sought to read into the complex the character of *post-Confederation* Canada. This makes the fact that the new

Figure 5.5 City Hall, Kingston, Ontario, early view of main front, architect George Browne, 1843-44. | Library and Archives Canada, Rifle Brigade album, PA-062174.

Parliament was actually built for the *province,* not the Dominion, a scholarly inconvenience of some magnitude. Up to now, moreover, contextual data marshalled to explain the building project have generally been confined to events viewed as directly causal – the settling of the long, troubling seat-of-government question and the calling of the building-design competition in early 1859. But consideration of a penumbra of other factors and developments, especially the character of the Union, may produce a broader understanding of the complex on Parliament Hill.[38]

The period of the Union can be understood in many ways; one is as that in which the province experienced the transition from a cosseted but restrictive status as a set of military and resource-rich colonies directly benefiting the mother country to that of a liberal, modern nation-state.[39] Modernity and processes of modernizing are key to this understanding. Like the so-called Middle Period in United States history (1814-61), in Canada the quarter-century after passage of the Act of Union in 1841 saw the scale grow not only of public building but of urban life in general, as patterns of politics and rule, trade, manufacture, and publishing were liberalized. Institutions of responsible government and rational bureaucratic administration were introduced in the Canadian province, perhaps nowhere more than in public works.[40] The changes were needed to support massive and, in the end, ruinously expensive "internal improvements" – the building of roads and canals, followed all too shortly by railways.

The character of the Union period also altered Canadians' cultural stance toward their position in North America. Despite the ascendancy of pro-British sentiment – in Anglo areas – and of emigration from the British Isles, Canada of the Union era was willy-nilly drawn into more "American" patterns of life than formerly, with changes in trade its impetus. Britain's adoption of imperial free trade in 1846 deprived its North American holdings of the protected markets they had enjoyed as colonies under mercantilism, and in the late 1840s some Canadians, especially in the commercial capital of Montreal, contemplated suing for annexation to the United States. Although a temporary return to prosperity quelled annexationist sentiment, trade reciprocity with the United States was successfully negotiated in 1854 – for the last time until the 1980s. Four years later, decimal currency replaced pounds sterling as the Canadian currency standard. Unsurprisingly, the entry of American goods, rail lines, and publications, including the popular illustrated magazines of the day, markedly altered British North American culture during the later 1850s – for the worse, conservatives thought. (How contemporary that rings!) During Trollope's visit early in the following decade, Canadians' free-and-easy manner of speech and socializing, without regard for class or occupation, made his eyebrows arch in disapproval and surprise that familiarity of that kind, which had been on the rise in Canada since the 1830s, had made such inroads on British-held soil.[41] The changing Canadian temperament goes far in explaining why Governor-General Head, though a vigorous and progressive executive, proved less effective in his post than he might have been: egalitarian Canadians took umbrage at what they felt to be Head's air of arrogant presumption.[42]

"Americanism" literally changed how Canadians imagined their country, perhaps even impelling them to imagine it *as* a country.[43] Eastern Americans' overland drive to the Pacific in Oregon and California during the 1840s and 1850s encouraged some Canadians, especially Ontarians, to imagine a "greater Canada" stretching from sea to sea.[44] Among those who began to think this way was Head himself, who by 1856, at least, had come to favour a broad confederation of the British North American provinces, extending to include even Vancouver Island.[45] Pronounced echoes of American Manifest Destiny rhetoric are heard in George Browne's calls during the 1850s in the *Toronto Globe* for Canada to annex Hudson's Bay Company lands in the Northwest as the prelude to establishing an agricultural subempire into which southern Ontario farmers, fast running out of *Lebensraum,* could spread.[46] Even at that early date, the sense existed that Canada should exist to benefit (primarily) Ontario's business concerns, especially those based in Toronto. It was not the Canada of the limited East-West Union formed in 1841, then, but the imaginary of a "greater," transcontinental Canada for which the Parliament Buildings on Ottawa's Barrack Hill were built. If this statement seems to contradict a point made earlier, let me note that the pan-Canadian, or subimperial, sentiment referred to here was an ambition felt under the Union, before Confederation generated its own kind of pride. The scope of the Union-era territorial ambition helps to explain the seemingly mad budget and legislative obsession devoted to the project in Ottawa, and to this degree the historiographic bias of earlier writers – including myself – is well founded.

Recognition of the changes occurring in Canada goes far to understanding not only Fuller and Jones's design for Parliament but Thomas Fuller's decision to immigrate to Canada in 1857. In a year of worldwide depression, deciding to leave his native Bath for Toronto was understandable; still, Fuller's professional standing in the West Country before he left is not yet fully clear.[47] Nevertheless, a picture of him is emerging, by the middle 1850s, as a leading regional designer in and around Bath and Bristol and in south Wales, particu-

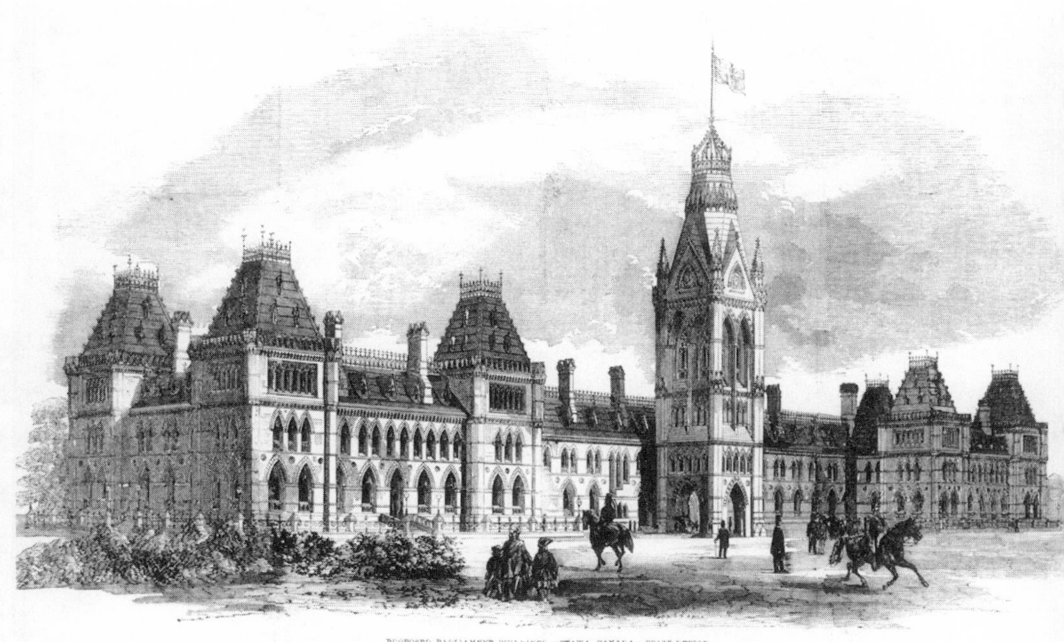

Figure 5.6 Engraving after Thomas Fuller and Chilion Jones's design for the Canadian Parliament Buildings, perspective view. | *Illustrated London News,* 5 November 1859.

larly well connected to Bath's civic and business leadership.[48] The "picture" shows an architect animated by neo-Gothic architectural ideology and in possession of a mature, well-digested design language. At the receiving-end, another picture is apparent – that of a professional circle of builders and architects who emigrated, more or less en masse, from various counties in southwest England to Canada in the middle years of the decade.[49] Fuller was probably induced to join them – at first temporarily, perhaps – by invitations from friends in that group who had already emigrated, although an absence of correspondence and second-hand testimony permits only informed conjecture as to his motives. Fundamentally, what drew him to Toronto, metropolis of Canada West, was the professional opportunities available in the expansive if somewhat uncouth Canadian proto-country, which was to be sure Americanizing but was still heavily Anglophile, with probably more British and Irish accents than native-born heard daily in city streets. The new scale and ambition of the government complex proposed two years later embodied those of the country itself: in its frontal symmetry and horizontal spread, Fuller and Jones's parliamentary block

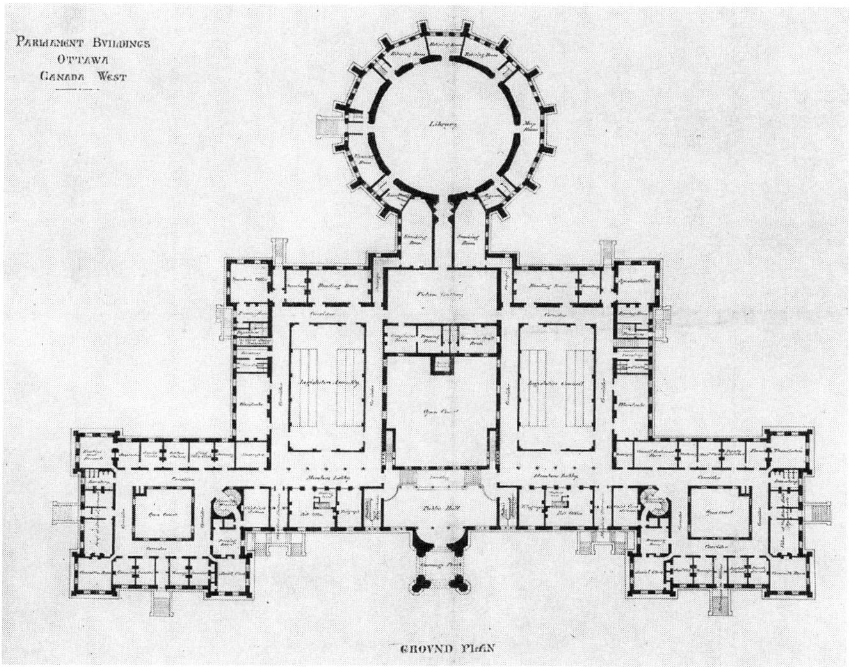

Figure 5.7 Floor plan of Canadian Parliament Buildings, Ottawa, architects Thomas Fuller and Chilion Jones, 1859. | Library and Archives Canada, C-005410.

captured the optimistic egalitarianism of Canadian life in a liberal period, despite the province's limited prospects at the end of the 1850s.

Let me return to the question of Fuller and Jones's compositional model for their parliament house. This model *could not* be British, for no well established public-building type placing twin ceremonial chambers astride a central spatial element, as in the Ottawa scheme (Figure 5.7), was to be found there. Parliament at Westminster offered a spatial expression of the principle of legislative bicamerality, but I have commented on its differences from the arrangement at Ottawa. Yet symmetrical spatial bicamerality – strict if theoretical equality of the elected and appointed chambers – is what Fuller and Jones's spatial symmetry most insistently proclaimed (Figures 5.6 and 5.7). This fact should not be overlooked. However Britannic, neo-Medieval, and Ruskinian in its detail, the parliament house at Ottawa was to be a three-dimensional exposition of the character and institutions of colonial responsible government within the British Empire. No Victorian town hall, no law courts of which I am aware – not even Alfred Waterhouse's Manchester Assize Courts (Figure 5.8), practically identical

Figure 5.8 Design for Assize Courts, Manchester, England, perspective view, architect Alfred Waterhouse, 1859. | *Builder,* 14 May 1859. Photograph in Toronto Public Library.

in style and date of design to the Ottawa building and furnished with a design statement that Fuller and Jones pilfered in their own[50] – none of these set in parallel two assembly chambers of equal size to either side of a central spatial element, in this case a square light-court. In this regard, the Gothic Revival offered Fuller and Jones no compositional precedent for their Houses of Parliament. The absence of such models in Britain is the very reason that High Victorian designers such as George Gilbert Scott, when they won commissions for public buildings and, like Fuller, sought to give them commanding, symmetrical frontal elevations, turned for sources to early-Modern German or Flemish town halls or guild halls, where symmetry *had* ruled, and to recent French symmetrically composed public buildings, especially the wings newly added to the Louvre in the early 1850s.[51] Fuller drew from the German-and-

Flemish well some of his wall details and tower forms, but copybook borrowing does not account for his overall *parti*.

I ask again: what reasonably close and similar building type incorporated a symmetrical pair of assembly chambers? Framed thus, the question all but answers itself – the American capitol type, which by Fuller's time had crystallized into definitive form.[52] By 1859, when Fuller and Jones conceived their design for Ottawa, a massive project by T.U. Walter to enlarge the arch-exemplar of the type, the federal Capitol in Washington, was far advanced (Figure 5.2),[53] and both project and building were extensively published, thanks to advances in commercial printing and photography. (The decade was crucial in the emergence of the modern illustrated magazine.) The federal capitol project attracted particular attention because, with the United States on the brink of almost certain collapse over slavery and Free Soil, the aggrandizement of the building that symbolized its federal union and constitution exercised urgent cultural poignancy. With filial piety of diverse sorts convulsing their neighbours, Canadians – including ones recently arrived from Britain – were unavoidably moved. Of what more logical, resonant model would the architect of a large North American legislature avail himself at that moment, given the neo-Palladian heritage in both countries' public architecture and the common descent of their governmental systems from British colonial rule by council and assembly?

If my conjecture is accurate, Fuller disguised the actual nature of his typological debt within a building having an apparently most British of envelopes executed in the High Victorian "civil" Gothic of Scott, Street, and John Ruskin, a mode with which he was by then thoroughly comfortable (Figures 5.1 and 5.6).[54] For the Jeffersonian sequence of staircase, columned portico, and domed rotunda, Fuller and Jones substituted a salient tower, lobby, and light-court. They stepped the building's side walls inward toward the rear, echoing and accommodating the line of the cliff and emphasizing the design's picturesquely irregular character. For the same reason and from practical need, they employed a centralized, sixteen-sided form for the Library of Parliament (Figure 5.3).[55] On the exterior, the library climaxed the formal sequence, but access to it from the inside was made tortuous, in keeping with a guiding intention to separate the building's public or quasi-public frontal range from the secluded, club-like spaces behind it.[56] In fact, such tonal separation is a major respect in which Fuller and Jones altered what I argue was their American prototype, whose design – especially its focus on a monumental rotunda – underlined the public's right to enter, observe, and *know*. In Washington, Walter even gave his huge new House and Senate blocks to either side great frontal staircases! This is something British North American provincial authorities would not have considered doing, even if Ottawa's severe winters had not made staircases of the kind impractical.

It is true that my evidence for the derivation of the parliamentary design is circumstantial, but it is also convergent and, I submit, in historical context persuasive. So many factors point in the same direction: the speed with which a *parti* had to be adopted; the suddenness with which, for Canada, a radically new building form appeared, expressive of the institutions of "responsible" government in an imperial framework; the dearth of relevant compositional models in Britain; the Americanization of Canadian culture in the 1850s under the stimulus of reciprocal trade; the wide attention paid in the popular and professional press to the enlargement of the US Capitol before the American Civil War; and – most decisive – a basic similarity to be observed in the two legislatures' spatial layouts. Accepting the explanation given here does not exclude inferences that other sources were at work in the Canadian Parliament emanating from English or French, neo-Classical or neo-Medieval, sources – causation is rarely simple – but it does imply the operation of a spatial prime mover appropriately located on this continent, with its then relatively liberal political culture. Specifying the process by which Fuller and Jones assembled their sources into a persuasive design, however, will require further architectural, interdisciplinary, and perhaps archival analysis.

The argument made here is fundamentally based on formal analysis, but with this difference: that a reading of the architecture of the Canadian Parliament as typologically indebted to a model in the United States violates a cultural taboo many Canadians hold and harbours an alternate reading of the character of Canadian culture in 1860. My argument is that, however Ruskinian, Puginian, or Streetian in detail, however indebted in form to a Flemish cloth-hall or an English monastic kitchen, the Parliament Buildings at Ottawa were actually a thoroughgoing product of Modernity, imbricated in the transoceanic and transborder development of large, novel, rational building types intended to serve and represent new, international "Victorian" publics constituted by new social, cultural, and political relations.

This argument sheds new light on a fact that has, up to now, been something of a historiographical embarrassment: that even as the work of constructing Parliament in Ottawa was taking place, Canada's "national," or proto-national, architect Thomas Fuller entered and won (as Fuller and Jones) a competition for perhaps the leading American state capitol of the immediate post–Civil War period, that of New York at Albany, and with a team that included another

English-trained veteran of Ottawa's Parliament Hill, Augustus Laver, partly built it.[57] An awareness that Fuller and Jones had already designed for Ottawa what I have called "an extraordinary fusion of types – a Victorian Gothic parliamentary capitol,"[58] permits us to see in Fuller's venture of the following decade an exercise politically and stylistically different from, but typologically continuous with, the project of building Parliament. Far from seeming disconcertingly unpatriotic – to the degree a *patria* yet existed – the move now seems entirely natural. This observation suggests, in turn, a need to reframe the historiographic portrayal of Thomas Fuller from that of the arch-Canadian architect celebrated in the period of the national Centennial to that of an Anglo-American Victorian architect who, partly by chance, met his best opportunities in Canada.

NOTES

1 See, for example, the subtitle of the book now thought definitive on the project, Carolyn A. Young, *The Glory of Ottawa: Canada's First Parliament Buildings* (Montreal and Kingston: McGill-Queen's University Press, 1995).

2 See Lawrence J. Vale, *Architecture, Power, and National Identity* (Cambridge, MA: MIT Press, 1992).

3 Dell Upton, *Architecture in the United States* (New York: Oxford University Press, 1998), 75.

4 John Ralston Saul, *Reflections of a Siamese Twin: Canada at the End of the Twentieth Century* (Toronto: Penguin, 1997), esp. ch. 1.

5 This article extends an argument built up chain-fashion in two earlier ones: Christopher A. Thomas, "Slippery Talk of Parliament's Architecture: Canadian, Canadian British, or Anglo-American?" *RACAR (Revue d'art canadienne/Canadian Art Review)* 29, 1-2 (2004): 14-27; and Christopher Thomas, "'Canadian Castles'? The Question of National Styles in Architecture Revisited," *Journal of Canadian Studies* 32, 1 (1997): 5-27.

6 How radically this point can be made is apparent from reading Hayden White, "The Fictions of Factual Representation," reprinted in *Reading Architectural History*, ed. Dana Arnold, 24-33 (London: Routledge, 2002). See also Dana Arnold, "Reading the Past," in ibid., 1-13.

7 See Thomas, "Slippery Talk," 15.

8 For a more complete version and bibliography, see Young, *The Glory of Ottawa;* and Harold Kalman, *A History of Canadian Architecture*, vol. 2 (Toronto: Oxford University Press, 1994), 534-41. The single most accurate, comprehensive chronology of building activity on Parliament Hill is Audrey Dubé, comp., "Historical Chronology of the Parliament Buildings," unpublished, under auspices of the Library of Parliament, Information and Reference Branch, 1985.

9 See Chris Brooks, *The Gothic Revival* (London: Phaidon, 1999), ch. 10.

10 A current, indeed continually updated, survey of the buildings of Parliament Hill appears in *A Legacy for Future Generations: The Long Term Vision and Plan*, http://www.parliamenthill.gc.ca (follow link "Vision and Plan"). A major campaign of expansion and renovation of the "Parliamentary precinct" was undertaken in 2001, and by the time of writing (summer 2006) the Library of Parliament had reopened after renovation, and restoration of the heavily compromised west block had begun. The building of an additional structure on the hill's west flank, near the corner of Bank and Wellington Streets, was also being contemplated but had not been decided on.

11 The downplaying of architects' roles in building projects was due partly to their generally low professional status until the mid-twentieth century. James David Edgar's lengthy account of the buildings in *Canada and Its Capital* (Toronto: G.M. Morang, 1898), chs. 5-6, neglected to identify the architects;

in 1916 Thomas Fuller was identified as the designer, merely "a Toronto architect," by M.O. Hammond, "Ashes of History: Events Recalled by the Parliament Buildings Fire at Ottawa," *Canadian Magazine* 46 (1916): 474. Other elementary facts got lost, too: architect W.A. Langton, relying on an informant who had lived through the construction, nonetheless supposed the choice of Gothic for Parliament to have been "no doubt decreed"; see W.A. Langton, "Canada's National Buildings," *Construction* 2 (1908): 47.

12 On the historiography of Canadian architecture, see Annmarie Adams, "The Monumental and the Mundane: Architectural History in Canada," *Acadiensis,* 30, 2 (2001): 149-59; Annmarie Adams, with Martin Bressani, "Canada: The Edge Condition," *Journal of the Society of Architectural Historians* 62, 1 (2003): 75-83; and Thomas, "Slippery Talk," 15, 24n8.

13 A voluminous literature on the current state of the field includes *Architectural History, 1999-2000,* special issue of *Journal of the Society of Architectural Historians* 58 (1999); and Arnold, "Reading the Past."

14 Young, *Glory of Ottawa,* esp. 4.

15 Henry-Russell Hitchcock, *Architecture: Nineteenth and Twentieth Centuries* (Harmondsworth, UK: Penguin, 1958), 195. In this, Hitchcock was echoing widely shared nineteenth-century opinion: Lord Frederic Hamilton (Governor-General Lord Lansdowne's brother-in-law) ranked the Ottawa Parliament with the United States Capitol as "the most successful group of buildings erected anywhere during the nineteenth century." See Lord Frederic Hamilton, *The Days before Yesterday,* 27th ed. (London: Hodder and Stoughton, 1930), 253.

16 Goldwin Smith, quoted in Wilfrid Eggleston, *The Queen's Choice: A Story of Canada's Capital* (Ottawa: Queen's Printer, 1961), 131. On the seat-of-government controversy as a whole, see David B. Knight, *Choosing Canada's Capital: Conflict Resolution in a Parliamentary System* (Ottawa: Carleton University Press, 1991).

17 Until the appearance of Dorothy Mindenhall's full-length biography, currently in manuscript, with the working title "Thomas Fuller: Architect for a Nation," probably the best introduction to the career of Thomas Fuller (1823-98) remains my article on him in *Dictionary of Canadian Biography (DCB),* vol. 12, 343-46, where, however, on page 344 I slip – from one paragraph to the next – from "Fuller and Jones's design" to "Fuller's design for the Parliament Buildings."

18 See David Watkin's survey *The Rise of Architectural History* (London: Architectural Press, 1980). Canadian architects' struggle for professional recognition is treated in Kelly Crossman, *Architecture in Transition: From Art to Practice, 1885-1906* (Montreal and Kingston: McGill-Queen's University Press, 1987).

19 The findings of the commission of inquiry of 1862-63 were distinctly unflattering to the architects; see Young, *Glory of Ottawa,* 85-86. It should be noted that the Canadian architectural profession was in a nascent, highly volatile state, its development closely intertwined with that of the profession in Britain, whose professional institute was then just twenty-five years old.

20 Young, *Glory of Ottawa,* 154n30.

21 Critical, often satirical commentary of nineteenth-century foreign (chiefly British) visitors to Washington is sampled in John W. Reps, *Monumental Washington: The Planning and Development of the Capital Center* (Princeton, NJ: Princeton University Press, 1967), 38-41.

22 See Suzanne Zeller, *Inventing Canada: Early Victorian Science and the Idea of a Transcontinental Nation* (Toronto: University of Toronto Press, 1987), 98-99; and R.H. Hubbard, "Land of the Stone Gable," *RACAR (Revue d'art canadienne/Canadian Art Review)* 2, 1 (1975): 23-32. Histories of Ottawa, besides Eggleston's *Queen's Choice,* are Lucien Brault, *Ottawa Old and New* (Ottawa: Ottawa Historical Information Institute, 1946); Robert Haig, *Ottawa, City of the Big Ears: The Intimate, Living Story of a City and a Capital* (Ottawa: Haig and Haig, 1975); Shirley E. Woods Jr., *Ottawa: The Capital of Canada* (Toronto: Doubleday Canada, 1980); and John H. Taylor, *Ottawa: An Illustrated History* (Toronto: James Lorimer and Canadian Museum of Civilization, 1986). For advice on this bibliography, I am grateful to Thomas Rooney of the Ottawa Public Library.

23 On Rubidge, and on Samuel Keefer, whose influence on the project seems mainly to have been later, see Young, *Glory of Ottawa,* 18, 154nn28-31; Douglas Owram, *Building for Canadians: A History of the Department of Public Works, 1840-1960* (Ottawa: Public Works Canada, Public Relations and Information Services, 1979), chs. 2-4 (re Keefer); Janet Wright, *Crown Assets: The Architecture of the Department of Public Works, 1867-1967* (Toronto: University of Toronto Press, 1997), 7-8 (re Rubidge), 278n12 (re Keefer); and *DCB,* vol. 12, 930-31 (re Rubidge), and vol. 11, 463-65 (re Keefer).

24 See Geoffrey Simmins, *Fred Cumberland: Building the Victorian Dream* (Toronto: University of Toronto Press, 1997), 225-33.

25 Legislative Assembly of Canada, *Journals* 130, 4 (24 March 1857).

26 Anthony Trollope, *North America,* vol. 1 (1862; reprint of 1869 ed., London: Dawsons of Pall Mall, 1968), 83-84. The passage is quoted in, for example, Douglas Richardson, "The Spirit of the Place: Canadian Architecture in the Victorian Era," *Canadian Collector* 10, 5 (1975): 27-28; Christopher Alexander Thomas, "Dominion Architecture: Fuller's Canadian Post Offices, 1881-96," (MA thesis, University of Toronto, 1978), 66, 69; Kalman, *History of Canadian Architecture,* vol. 2, 541; and Young, *Glory of Ottawa,* book title, 90, 93.

27 Trollope, *North America,* vol. 1, 84.

28 Thomas, "Slippery Talk," 21-22.

29 Sandra Gwyn, *The Private Capital: Ambition and Love in the Age of Macdonald and Laurier* (Toronto: McClelland and Stewart, 1984), 90. "Rough, wild, and unfinished" is Meredith's phrase (quoted in ibid., 35-36).

30 Since 1841 buildings in Kingston, Montreal, Toronto, and Quebec had been used or seconded for parliamentary purposes; the reuse of the Ste-Anne Market at Montreal (Figure 5.4) was typical. The grandest of the lot, until Ottawa's complex, were the Parliament Buildings in Quebec, originally the bishop's palace but expanded and renovated between the 1830s and the 1850s for parliamentary purposes. See Charles P. De Volpi, *Québec, A Pictorial Record: Historical Prints and Illustrations ... 1608-1875* ([Toronto]: Longman Canada, 1971), plates 17, 71, 126; and Luc Noppen and Gaston Deschênes et al., *Québec's Parliament Building: Witness to History* (Quebec: Gouvernement du Québec, 1986), 35-38 (incl. illustrations of parliament buildings in all four cities named).

31 The known competition entries for Ottawa are described and illustrated in Young, *Glory of Ottawa,* ch. 2. The flurry of civic building in Canada emulated a wave of such building in Britain following the passage of reform legislation in the 1830s; see Colin Cunningham, *Victorian and Edwardian Town Halls* (London: Routledge and Kegan Paul, 1981), esp. ch. 1. Besides Kingston City Hall (Figure 5.5), the Canadian buildings I have in mind are exemplified by Montreal's Bonsecours Market (William Footner, 1844-47) and St. Lawrence Hall, Toronto (William Thomas, 1849-50); see Kalman, *History of Canadian Architecture,* vol. 1, fig. 6.56 (Bonsecours); and Eric Arthur, *Toronto: No Mean City,* 3rd ed., rev. Stephen A. Otto (Toronto: University of Toronto Press, 1986), figs. 4.78-80 (St. Lawrence).

32 See Brooks, *Gothic Revival,* 209-14.

33 Leading examples of neo-Palladian public design at home were Somerset House, London, by architect William Chambers (1776-86), and James Gandon's Custom House, Dublin (1781-91); see Sir John Summerson, *Architecture in Britain, 1530-1830,* 7th ed. (Harmondsworth, UK: Penguin, 1983), figs. 336-38 and 356, respectively. On the prestige of Second Empire, see M.H. Port, *Imperial London: Civil Government Building in London, 1850-1915* (New Haven, CT: Yale University Press, 1995), 14.

34 Variously, on his own or in partnership with William B. Gingell or on behalf of James Wilson of Bath, Fuller had been involved in the construction of probably six or more school buildings before he emigrated to Canada in 1857. These were located mainly in Wales and southwest England. Not all had symmetrical fronts; still fewer can have had symmetrical floor plans. But an underlying (if often Gothicized) preference for neo-Palladian frontal symmetry was a general theme of most of these school designs, on which I am grateful to Dorothy Mindenhall and Julian Orbach for research material.

35 Young, *Glory of Ottawa,* 20-24.

36 Ibid., 46-47.

37 See my comments in "Slippery Talk," 14-16, which are based on readings of the work of Alan Gowans, R.H. Hubbard, John Bland, Northrop Frye, and myself (writing in 1978).

38 For a robust defence of studies of "context," see John Harris, *The New Art History: A Critical Introduction* (London: Routledge, 2001), 26-28.

39 On the Union – as much a cultural as a political system – see J.M.S. Careless, *The Union of the Canadas: The Growth of Canadian Institutions, 1841-1857* (Toronto: McClelland and Stewart, 1967); and J.M. Bumsted, *The Peoples of Canada: A Pre-Confederation History* (Toronto: Oxford University Press, 1992), chs. 10-12.

40 See Owram, *Building for Canadians*, chs. 2-4.

41 Trollope, *North America*, vol. 1, 89-90.

42 On Head, see the biography by James A. Gibson in *DCB*, vol. 9, 381-86; and D.G.G. Kerr, assisted by J.A. Gibson, *Sir Edmund Head: A Scholarly Governor* (Toronto: University of Toronto Press, 1954). Head's arrogance also receives comment in Douglas Richardson, with J.M.S. Careless et al., *A Not Unsightly Building: University College and Its History* (Oakville, ON: Mosaic Press for University College, 1990), 13 and passim.

43 On the countries' relationship at a slightly later period, but with important implications for the one considered here, see Robin W. Winks, *The Civil War Years: Canada and the United States*, 4th ed. (Montreal and Kingston: McGill-Queen's University Press, 1998).

44 See Zeller, *Inventing Canada;* and Suzanne Zeller, *Land of Promise, Promised Land: The Culture of Victorian Science in Canada*, Canadian Historical Association Historical Booklet No. 56 (Ottawa: Canadian Historical Association, 1996).

45 See sources on Head cited in note 42. As early as 1848-49, Head had envisioned a sea-to-sea nation, self-governing within the British Empire, which at that moment showed little interest in its colonies. By late 1856, when negotiations began for the transfer to Canada of Hudson's Bay Company lands, he was firm in this belief and in a conviction that the seat-of-government question must be settled, as it shortly was.

46 See J.M.S. Careless, *Brown of the Globe*, 2 vols. (Toronto: Macmillan, 1960-63), esp. vol. 1, 305-28, and vol. 2, ch. 4.

47 My entry on Fuller in *DCB* (see note 17) reflects the state of knowledge as it was in the mid-1980s. The entry lists a number of British commissions but gives no sense of his status in his society or profession. Recently, Dorothy Mindenhall (see note 17) has turned up a number of new connections and commissions and elucidated others, including the schools listed here.

48 His father, also Thomas Fuller, served on Bath's municipal council for thirty-three years and served as mayor in 1861-62; see Alexandra E. Kolaczkowski, "The Politics of Civic Improvement, Bath, 1835-1879, with special reference to the career of Sir Jerom Murch" (PhD diss., University of Bath, 1995), 524. I am grateful to Dorothy Mindenhall for this reference.

49 This picture owes much to the research of Stephen A. Otto, who suggests that Fuller and Thomas Stent, considered the lead designer of the east and west departmental blocks at Ottawa, met during their architectural training in Bath and thereafter remained in contact. A sworn statement by Stent of August 1862 dates his own arrival "in this Province" about 1855; see *A Report of the Commissioners Appointed to Inquire into Matters Connected with the Public Buildings at Ottawa* (Quebec: Hunter, Rose and Co., 1863), 31.

50 See Young, *Glory of Ottawa*, 32-35. In turn, both architects were indebted to ideas George Gilbert Scott had formulated during the Public Offices Affair in London in the previous three years. See ibid.; and Thomas, "Slippery Talk," 20-21.

51 See David B. Brownlee, "That 'regular mongrel affair': G.G. Scott's Design for the Government Offices," *Architectural History* 28 (1985): 164 (re Hamburg Town Hall), 165 (re Louvre).

52 On American capitols, near-universally marked by neo-Classical bilateral symmetry, see Henry-Russell Hitchcock and William Seale, *Temples of Democracy: The State Capitols of the U.S.A.* (New York:

Harcourt Brace and Jovanovich, 1976), esp. chs. 3 and 4. On the US Capitol see William C. Allen, *History of the United States Capitol: A Chronicle of Design, Construction, and Politics* (Washington, DC: Government Printing Office, 2001).

53 Between 1851 and 1863 a long campaign based largely (but not entirely) on designs by Walter added two large, new chambers (opened in 1857 and 1859), attached by hyphens to the original ones flanking the central rotunda. The same campaign anchored the lengthened complex with an appropriately large and symbolically fitting central feature – the familiar, huge, cast-iron dome over the rotunda. See Allen, *History of the United States Capitol,* chs. 6-9.

54 See my entry on Fuller in *DCB* (cited at note 17). In southwest England, Fuller had distinguished himself as a partisan of the doctrinaire yet eclectic High Victorian phase of the Gothic Revival, had been associated as James Wilson's partner with the campaign to apply the revived Gothic to the religious architecture of Nonconformism, and individually had designed several neo-Gothic schools and chapels.

55 The library, although apparently at first an afterthought, was the segment of the program that received the most deliberate a priori thought, from parliamentary librarian Alpheus Todd. A leader in scientific librarianship, Todd was familiar with all major international libraries and the principles on which they were planned. He insisted on supplying the competing architects with a supplementary memorandum covering the planning of the library that, in effect, mandated a fireproof, centralized design; see Young, *Glory of Ottawa,* 20-24. On Todd, who was also a scholar of constitutional history, see *DCB,* vol. 11, 883-85.

56 On the club or country-house character of Parliament, see Vanessa Reid, "Ladies in the House: Gendered Space in the Parlours of Parliament" (MA thesis, McGill University, 1997), esp. 46-54. I am grateful to Annmarie Adams for drawing this excellent thesis to my attention. An order-in-council in 1868 halted construction of the library, which did not resume until two years later and was consequently not finished – with the largest all-iron roof structure in Canada – until 1876; see Dubé, comp., "Historical Chronology," 10-11. To a degree, Todd foiled exclusionary intentions by opening the library to the people of Ottawa when Parliament was not in session, but how long the practice lasted is not clear; see Marjory A. Bolick, *An Observation Study of the Library of Parliament, Ottawa, Canada* (Ottawa: Canadian Library Association, 1966), 15-16, and Appendix 1 (re early rules), a reference for which I gratefully acknowledge Thomas Rooney.

57 By 1867 Fuller and Laver were on a design team with Arthur D. Gilman, of Boston, and Nichols and Brown, of Albany (the latter, presumably a local front for the English architects). The team built its design for the Capitol only partway before the intervention of a commission of inquiry held in 1875-76 led to the appointment of three Americans to complete the project, H.H. Richardson, Leopold Eidlitz, and Frederic Law Olmsted; see John Coolidge, "Designing the Capitol – The Roles of Fuller, Gilman, Richardson and Eidlitz," in *Proceedings of the New York State Capitol Symposium,* ed. Temporary Commission on the Restoration of the Capitol, 21-27 (Albany, NY: Temporary State Commission on the Restoration of the Capitol, 1983).

58 My own phrases, in a review of Young, *Glory of Ottawa,* in *Journal of the Society of Architectural Historians* 56, 2 (1997): 234.

Stitching Vancouver's New Clothes
The World Building, Confederation, and the Making of Place

GEOFFREY CARR

In 1912 the tallest building in post-Confederation Canada, and indeed, the British Empire, stood in fledgling Vancouver. Designed by William Tuff Whiteway (1856-1940), the World Building (1911-12) – now known as the Sun Tower – only briefly remained the tallest building in the empire (Figure 6.1).[1] Yet this fleeting architectural achievement bolstered the civic pride of a city that, since its incorporation, had struggled to define its identity. The World Building was completed when Vancouver bore the moniker "Terminal City," among the first in a series of such sometimes pejorative epithets – Hollywood North, Hongcouver, Vansterdam – that imply a relational identity, a place defined by being at the edge of or akin to somewhere else. The sense of placelessness implied by these nicknames suggests a mercurial nature that has animated the city since incorporation. From its founding in 1886, Vancouver has served as the western terminus for the Canadian Pacific Railway's transcontinental line binding British Columbia into Confederation, at once a destination and point of departure, the end of the line and a gate. The speed of the city's many transformations has also troubled any stable sense of place. Chronicles of Vancouver's brief history, with titles such as "From Mill Town to Metropolis" or "Primordial to Prim Order," rightly trace a frenetic and, at times, unruly growth.[2] Soon after the turn of the century, Emily Carr noted that "Vancouver was growing hard," bemoaning as a "hideous transition" the cairns of charred stumps and brackish fens that dotted

Figure 6.1 The Bekins Building (a.k.a. World Building), 1931. Photograph by Leonard Frank. | Courtesy of Vancouver Public Library, accession #4658.

the city's new landscape.[3] Of interest in this chapter are the desires, motives, and tactics fuelling early efforts to put the city "on the map" – to better understand, through contemporary theorizations of place, Vancouver's enduring and often anxious project of place-making.

By the time workers poured the foundations for the World Building in 1911, Vancouver was in the throes of "instant urbanism," morphing from a colonial outpost housing some 1,000 residents at incorporation to a city of 100,000.[4] This burgeoning brought with it pronounced social stratification that partitioned Terminal City along class, ethnic, and racial lines – producing more or less elite places, with all the typical perceptions of who belonged where.[5] Stitching the city's fabric into discrete pockets depended on both clearing land for the development of new neighbourhoods and raising symbolically significant structures, edifices literally constructing a particular sense of place. I argue that the site of the World Building can be read as a definitive, if unsuccessful, attempt to construct, in a moment of turbulent change, a seminal place promising to help define and fix Vancouver's uncertain identity.

An analysis of the mongrel architectural genealogy of the World Building, in particular its less-than-accurate labelling as Beaux Arts, will help to shed light on the perceived placelessness in which this iconic structure was built. Like most Canadian contemporary architects, William Tuff Whiteway likely apprenticed in a form of pupilage rather that attending an architectural school.[6] By contrast with those studying in the United States, especially after the entrenchment of Beaux Arts teaching methods in the 1880s, Canadian students underwent little training in advanced design, architectural history, or theory, generally focusing instead on draftsmanship.[7] As a consequence, Western Canadian architects responsible for major civic and commercial structures like the World Building tended to favour an eclectic approach. Imported from Britain, the Edwardian vocabulary (or so-called "free" style) was less regulated by a common set of guiding design principles. Thus it allowed for flexible interpretations of historical forms and motifs. Edwardian buildings above all were meant to be visually striking; as such, structural issues tended not to determine their design.[8] This fondness for eclecticism and ornateness led to a loose borrowing from Beaux Arts practice in the United States and Europe, a hybridization that may explain the stylistic mislabelling of the World Building.[9]

Formal analysis of the World Building reveals a lack of legibility and fluency uncharacteristic of the Beaux Arts. For instance, the arcading under the cornice spanning the building's broad base fails to articulate clearly its relationship to the tower, thus contradicting the formal consistency sought in Beaux Arts *partis*. Moreover, the caryatids under the shallow roof cornice are not load-bearing and appear awkwardly pasted to the wall. They also break the cornice for no apparent reason, again untypical of Beaux Arts design practice (Figure 6.2). The entrance, with its pared-down, sporadic application of Classical motifs, similarly differs from Beaux Arts principles. Perhaps the most convincing proof is the poor circulation system in the tower, a programmatic oversight unthinkable to Beaux Arts architects and designers. Classifying the World Building as

Figure 6.2 The Sun Tower (a.k.a. World Building), detail. | Photograph by author.

Edwardian rather than Beaux Arts better recalls the socio-cultural sense of place in which it was built. The amateurish use of Classical aesthetics not only shows Vancouver's architectural culture as somewhat parochial but also suggests, in keeping with its British connections, a quest for an enduring identity through a regional variant of imperial architecture. And this localization of British and international practice in Vancouver – a monumental tower built with local bricks and with wood hewn from ancient forests nearby – seems apt in a fledgling city consciously in pursuit of legitimacy.

CONSTRUCTING PLACE

The process of place-making in Vancouver bears the mark of material exigencies and economic opportunism. For example, many of Vancouver's West End streets were laid out near creeks or springs to ensure that loggers and their horses received adequate water. This initial sense of place, produced by practical need, radically shifted with the subsequent erection of many opulent homes in the area. But such factors cannot completely explain how places become constituted.[10] At the nexus of subjectivity and the built environment, the production of place also depends upon a reciprocal sense of belonging, familiarity, and ease among its citizenry. As importantly, sensing place involves the encounter, bodily or psychologically, with a perceived absence, with a nonplace, or *atopos*. The urban wasteground, the uncharted wilderness, the prison, or the refugee camp – each connotes for most a space without place and, as a consequence, helps to locate place. But of course this dialectic is too simplistic since notions of place or nonplace never operate consistently: any precinct can afford comfort and well-being for one, fear and alienation for another. Moreover, the imagined borderlines between places cannot be regarded as firm in any objective sense. Thus any conceptualizing of place must account both for its polysemy and for its uncertain confines. With this in mind, I argue that the World Building produced a locus that beamed certain colonial ideals of material progress and moral rectitude, an *axis mundi,* around which a new identity for the city would circumambulate. In addition, this identity was formulated against an apparent atopos, associated with, on the one hand, the "undeveloped" indigenous landscape and, on the other, communities of nonwhite and non-Anglo-Saxon settlers.

My phrase "certain colonial ideals" acknowledges the disparate ideas of place within Vancouver's white-settler community. Such disparity can be demonstrated in the career of Louis D. Taylor, the man who promoted the World Building project.[11] Taylor reached Vancouver in 1899 penniless, a fugitive from fraud charges in his native America and a refugee from the Klondike gold rush. Despite this humble beginning, he concocted a successful career, as both the owner/editor of the *Vancouver Daily World* newspaper and as the city's mayor. He fervently championed the cause of labour and, less consistently, moral reforms.[12] His slogans of "Fair Play" and "A Full Dinner Pail" appealed to working-class voters, enabling him in 1910 to win the first of eight mayoral elections.[13] Significantly, however, fair play in the mayor's view extended only to white residents. A member of the Asian Exclusion League and a virulent opponent to immigrants from China, Japan, and India, Taylor's views differed little from those of many other white settlers. His editorials routinely enjoined the need to "preserve British Columbia for the white people" against "invasions" of Asian immigrants – inflammatory rhetoric that likely played a significant role in inciting Vancouver's most notorious race riot on 7 September 1907. In the days leading up to the riot, the *Daily World* reported on its front page the story of residents in Bellingham forcing some 500 Sikhs and Hindus north toward the Canadian border. Their forced displacement into the Lower Mainland was attributed by Taylor to the loss of white jobs to Indian men and to minor attacks on white women. Taylor, speaking at an anti-Asian rally, picked up on the theme of the Bellingham refugees, inflaming the passions of the crowd shortly before the riot erupted.[14]

The racial unrest fomented by Taylor and others worried members of Vancouver's moneyed elite, owing to sharp criticisms from the federal government and London of the city's inability to contain racial tensions. Taylor's pro-union position further alienated him from Vancouver's more affluent citizens. Economic growth at the turn of the century exacerbated labour disputes: from 1903 to 1914 seventy-six strikes erupted in British Columbia. In response, local business interests (headed by the Canadian Pacific Railway) developed sophisticated means to resist unionization, resorting to espionage, strike-breaking, and violent attacks on labour leaders.[15] This class conflict inflamed rhetoric between Taylor and his conservative political opponents, many of whom labelled him "socialist" because he advocated reducing the workday for civic employees from ten hours to eight. In response, he replied, "If a Socialist is a man who stands by what he thinks is right and does not fear to express his opinions irrespective of monopolies [and] corporations ... who dares to speak on behalf of the masses of the people, then I am a Socialist."[16] His most vexing and vociferous adversary was Roger Nichol, the owner and editor of the *Vancouver Daily Province* newspaper. Well heeled and well connected to the Conservative Party, Nichol never tired of sniping at his Liberal rival. Their vendetta played out in plain view, editorial barb for barb. Nichol, receiving word in 1913 of Taylor's financial woes, gleefully ran the story on the front page. Two years later, as a worsening recession gripped the city, Taylor filed for bankruptcy, gave up control of the newspaper, and lost ownership of the World Building.

Yet, however briefly, Taylor's World Building stood as a monument to his own and the city's boosterism.[17] By erecting the World Building and, thereby, raising the ire of members of the city's financial elite, he produced – albeit temporarily – a highly visible icon for white settlers of the middle and working classes. The actual and imaginary dimensions of this symbol and, indeed, the *genius loci* it helped to produce were formed proactively and reactively. On one boundary, for Taylor, were the exclusive business and social networks to which he could never gain entry, typified by the "At Home" days – those semiformal summer gatherings in West End mansions frequented by Vancouver's socialites, by the "wearers of purple and fine linen."[18] However, this is not to assert that any imagined topos or atopos finds discrete correspondence to the urban fabric; instead, it is to reiterate that the space shared by subjectivity and built places embodies contradiction and ambiguity. The semantic juxtaposition of "a full dinner pail" with the tower's Edwardian Classicism and seminude caryatids underscores this point. But such contradictions do not negate the worth of attempting to discern the course of place-making; rather, they present productive points of tension for analysis, shifting attention from intended to unintended layers of meaning.

Such contradictions and conflicts seem to be a major feature in the constitution of place. Places, especially urban ones in the modern era, rarely assume stable form. Neither are they confined to singular identities or hermetic boundaries, nor reliant upon some internalized history for definition. On the contrary, their boundaries appear porous, ephemeral, and mobile, opening rather than occluding multivalent or hybrid meanings. As Doreen Massey suggests,

> Instead of thinking of places as areas with boundaries around, they can be imagined as articulated moments in networks of social relations and understandings ... [Moreover,] if places can be conceptualized in terms of the social interactions which they tie together, then it is also the case that these places themselves are not static. They are processes.[19]

Understanding what defines the character of a particular place and, more specifically, the making of a place such as that associated with the World Building involves explicating not its inherent qualities but the particular ways it links to the social interactions of other locales beyond.

PLACING THE WORLD BUILDING

Up to this point, the analysis has focused on the formal presence of the World Building in relation to class conflicts between Louis Taylor and his social "betters." His enterprises in real estate and journalism coincidentally reflect more general colonial operations that served to establish commonality between the various classes of white settlers. The "networks of social relations" opened at the site of the World Building can be considered in the light of what anthropologist Nicholas Thomas calls a "colonial project." The term "project," rather than "discourse," outlines a methodology that seeks to ground theorization of the colonial experience in the particular, to conflate rather than polarize material and cultural forces. According to Thomas, the word *project* "draws attention not towards a totality such as a culture ... but rather to a socially-transformative endeavour that is localized, politicized, and partial, yet also engendered by longer historical developments and ways of narrating them."[20] The World Building affords an apt example of the relations between the material and cultural in both colonialism and the formation of place.[21]

Today, the site and the sense of place attaching to the World Building may seem somewhat of a back eddy. But during the time of its construction (1911-12), the neighborhood promised to become one the city's most important areas of development. The north side of False Creek had already attracted investment, in large part owing to the invidious interest of rail companies looking to break the Canadian Pacific Railway's exclusive access to downtown. In 1904 the Vancouver, Westminster and Yukon Railway established a terminal on Dupont Street (now East Pender Street) in Chinatown. Six years later the Great Northern Railway purchased this station, filled in a portion of False Creek, and laid rails on this reclaimed land connecting downtown to its tracks south to Seattle.[22] In 1912, three blocks from the World Building, the BC Electric Company built a lavish Richardsonian, Romanesque-styled streetcar depot, designed by the prominent firm of Somervell and Putnam, serving as a central terminus for its interurban network. And since 1907 the city had made concerted efforts, some under the direction of Taylor himself, to upgrade the infrastructure of the blocks surrounding the World Building. This structure, towering over Vancouver's emerging transportation hub, literally indicated the establishment of urban infrastructure and forged the formation of civic place with its corporate neighbours through common, speculative goals. Both forms of economic expansion, tracks traversing and towers ascending, produce spatial hierarchies, which in geographer Derek Gregory's phrase create a "grid wiring metropolitan circuits of action to their colonial ground."[23]

The railway stations, the streetcar terminus, and the World Building were sites of connected and, sometimes, competing economic interests. Together, they articulated a desire felt across the Confederation: to subdue and reconstitute a supposedly alien landscape, to establish a garrison of place in what has been called "Canadian space."[24] Richard Cavell has further argued that colonizing cultures in Canada have deemed their geographical environs to be desolate, an absence of place. This perception of absence often affects a denigration of the landscape beyond its resource capacity alongside a felt need to realize a utopic community. In this dichotomous tension, a powerful contradiction of empire appears: "Empire," Cavell asserts, "is never where it seems to be, or is always somewhere other than where it is ... The totalizing project of empire means that it is never fully present to itself – if its centre is absent ... so must its periphery be."[25] The cutting of rail through Vancouver's wooded areas and the soaring height of the World Building register, as *colonial projects,* the material as well as ideological act of place-making. Seeking to negate the presumption of non-place, each attempts to centre or circumscribe empire.

This more recent definition of "Canadian space" also informs Louis Taylor's 1907 editorial for the *Daily World* entitled "The Early History of British Columbia." Although praising the beauty of the province's scenery, he claimed that it was bereft of a "background of tradition," that most of the local topography, however aesthetically pleasing, remained untamed as unnamed and therefore uncivilized. The genesis of British Columbia's history, for Taylor, coincided with the arrival of Captain Cook on the shores of Vancouver Island's west coast. He flatly dismissed First Nations histories – what he called the "Indian story" – since "in truth there is no very definite story before the coming of the white man."[26] He insisted that without the intercession of the missionaries "among the degraded races on the frontiers," the fate of British Columbia's indigenes would have been "one, long, cruel misfortune." Clearly, these are prejudiced claims. Yet they were central to the colonial imaginary that occluded the cultural and geographic taxonomies of indigenous peoples. Moreover, as sociologists Geoffrey Bowker and Susan Star suggest, "things *perceived* as real are real in their consequences."[27] By asserting that the landscape takes on historical and cultural dimensions only with the arrival of settlers, Taylor substitutes an actual colonial binary (settler/indigene) with a fictive one (settler/*terra nova*) so as to disavow the primary role of colonizing violence. However, to be truly effective, ethnocentrisms such as Taylor's require a means of bearing in the built environment, an anchoring place.[28]

Personal or cultural egocentrisms tend to be centred both in consciousness and in material form. Although the impetus for self-centredness likely originates in the subject, more sophisticated and entrenched transpositions occur on a collective level with the expressed or tacit agreement of a wider community. Max Robinson argues that the form of the tower represents a manifestation of collective centring, a centripetal archetype, or axis mundi. Juxtaposing a horizon plane with an ascendant vertical axis describes "the simplest model of man's existential space ... It structures both the intellectual and physical content of our environment into a complete, unified vision by providing the means to distinguish a particular location and to empower it as a referential object."[29] In this light, erecting the tallest building in the empire in a small city with large undeveloped tracts cannot be a consequence of functional need. Rather, by delineating a site of difference, a space apart, this edifice established a new, hierarchical point of reference. It was a place deposing proverbial no-place, heralding new colonial urban development. The World Building stood at the birth of a spectacular new world.

A 1911 photograph, depicting the annual review of the 72nd Seaforth Highlanders marching past the partially constructed World Building, reveals the importance of spectacle in infusing a sense of place into landscape (Figure 6.3). The Seaforths were named for a British regiment whose uniform and ceremonial were closely adopted in Vancouver. Within this extravagant moment of imperial ritual, the homologous functions and purposes linking these surrounding locales become legible. Both parade ground and tower display allegiances to Britain, yet both endeavour to stand apart, to forge and carve out a new surrogate centre of imperial force. Only a structural-steel skeleton in 1911, its skin yet to be fitted, the World Building looms large over the parade square, as if it were a distant general soberly surveying the troops. (It seems telling that the Union Jack suffers cropping, whereas the tower occupies a prominent position.) The local militia regiment, mainly, but not exclusively, recruited from Scots descent, is also a skeletal framing (of British colonial control of a vast territory). Moreover, both display elaborate regalia – although the tower has yet to be dressed – defining a feeling of place through performative enactments of distinct yet collectivized colonial identities. This inscription of a distinctly *local,* yet also imperial, sense of identity onto the burgeoning urban environment effectively entrenches a sense of place. In this way, both tower and ceremonial gesturally enforce a spectacle of unified purpose and, in doing so, actualize instrumental regime.[30] Yet many of those marching in 1911 would experience a radically different iteration of empire on the battlefields of the Somme, Passchendaele, and Vimy Ridge, enduring traumas physical, psychological, and spiritual. The World Building, however, would survive as a cultural instrument, a colonial project imperiously dominating the skyline of Vancouver until after the Second World War.

Figure 6.3 The 72nd Seaforth Highlanders on the Cambie Parade Grounds, 1911. | Courtesy of City of Vancouver Archives, Mil P314.4.

Through its very survival, Taylor's Edwardian Classical office building would constitute yet another perception of place, settler/axis mundi, a binarism still standing today, fallaciously, as a legible point of contemporary culture, a place to be preserved and even revered. I am not suggesting that the World Building does not possess heritage value and should not be maintained as a heritage property. I want to call attention, rather, to its function as, to use Massey's term, "an articulated moment in networks of social relations." It is not a defunct artefact of the historical past but rather an urban structure that continues to function commercially as well as to focus a perceived sense of place. At the most obvious level, this building provides an aesthetic pleasure and a sense of history to many local citizens and visitors. Yet this structure, like a magic lantern, still projects the deeply conflictual motives at work in settler nations, transmitting across the expanding urban space of Vancouver an image of original colonial hubris.

LIEUTENANT WORLD

This exercise of economic and cultural authority becomes more apparent by an analysis of the relation between the World Building and its immediate neighbour,

Chinatown. The proximity, yet contrast, between these precincts also underscores the ways that colonial projects are realized ideologically no less than instrumentally. As David Lai demonstrates in his book *Chinatowns: Towns within Cities in Canada,* there is nothing arbitrary about the location of Canadian Chinatowns. Typically, Chinese immigrants gained permission to occupy land of little perceived value. If the real estate values did appreciate suddenly, its residents often fell prone to evictions. For example, Calgary's two Chinatowns suffered rapid displacement after the announcement in 1910 that the Canadian National Railway planned to build a hotel nearby.[31] In Vancouver, shortly after the disastrous fire of 13 June 1886, the city allowed Chinese workers to camp rent-free on the north shore of False Creek – owing to the need for cheap labour to clear land for new settlers, roads, and, soon after, streetcar lines.[32] This area, located as it was on a marshy tidal flat far from the centre of town, not surprisingly, held little promise for development. And very soon after, the geographic shortcomings of this place would reinforce the intolerant attitudes of whites toward the new Chinese community.

Consequently, Chinatown's main thoroughfare, Dupont Street, resting on piles to stave off the flooding from False Creek's highest tides, signified a boundary between places deemed either respectable or disreputable. The absence of effective storm or sewer lines led to an unpleasant odour that further stigmatized those who lived in the Chinatown district. As early as 1887, the *Vancouver News* printed a story warning that in the "nucleus of the pest-producing Chinese quarter ... strict surveillance by the City will be necessary to prevent the spread of this curse."[33] Chinese merchants and landowners repeatedly but unsuccessfully petitioned the city to improve the neighbourhood's infrastructure; the only relief came in the form of condemning and, often, burning buildings considered threats to public health. This process reinforces but also modifies the stress on visuality and the power of the gaze in postcolonial discourse. As this comparison between the development of the World Building and of Chinatown shows, the force of colonial authority is manifest not only through visuality but also through the "corporeality of landscape." In other words, the experience of place or non-place is a visceral one. Geographer Jennifer Dubow proposes that a fuller comprehension of this experience requires a methodological shift away from "landscape as a static visual image or 'snapshot' and towards a concern for the embodied 'passages' and 'procedures' by means of which perception and representation of landscape is arrived at."[34] The process of othering marginal groups and urban locales depends on a wide set of exclusionary practices, each fuelled by anxieties informed by material encounters, from the economic to the bodily, and especially around concerns of health and hygiene.

Fear of contagion was compounded in the minds of many by anxieties over moral contaminants – gambling, prostitution, drugs – thought to emanate from Chinatown's "underworld." Without doubt, these social ills did flourish there. But just as those solicitous about the area's squalor ignored the impact of civic policy, so too did those censuring Chinatown's "social evil" overlook the white settler's participation in the sex trade and the city's role in licensing opium factories in Chinatown. Commonly, Chinatown was represented as a dark, dangerous place, inhabited by shadowy figures able to elude the grasp of the law by escaping through trapdoors or tunnels running under the streets. No locale elicited more moral panic than the opium den.[35] Under the byline "Worst Joint Underground," a reporter for the *Daily World* related how behind a "sinister doorway" leading to a "subterranean apartment" he encountered the "darkest, vilest opium den in town."[36] The caption accompanying an illustration of a supine Chinese opium smoker reads, "The opium fiend *at home,* in Vancouver's Chinatown" (Figure 6.4) (emphasis added). By conflating the wretchedness of a drug den with the homes of those in the Chinese community, such representations fed the abjection of Chinatown as a nonplace fit only for less-than-worthy residents of the city, while concurrently inscribing a clearer outline of decorous places.

There exists a rather obvious semantic contrast between the perceived baseness of Chinatown and the apparent ascendancy of the World Building, towering over the city as a beacon of the Confederation's technological and cultural progress. But this binary masks the dialectic between the World Building and Chinatown. Most accounts of Vancouver's xenophobic past focus on violent events, exclusionary laws, or partitioned spaces, while overlooking the more generative interaction between edifices such as the World Building and surrounding, differentiated spaces like Chinatown. In this instance, these become evident by examining bylaws enacted to aid or to limit the development of local real estate. What is also made plain though this line of interrogation is the difficulty in isolating the motives – economic, pragmatic, moralistic, or racial (among others) – for producing place.

As has been argued, Louis Taylor shared with many other white settlers in Vancouver a virulent disregard for Asian newcomers and residents. City bureaucrats frequently enforced regulations to prevent Chinese businesses from migrating out of Chinatown north toward Hastings Street – at that time the civic and business centre of Vancouver.[37] In 1910, two years before completion of the World Building, Mayor Taylor and other local civic officials appealed, unsuccessfully, to the provincial legislature for more sweeping powers to pass and enforce new bylaws in Chinatown. Among these were the right to search and seizure

Figure 6.4 "The opium fiend at home, in Vancouver's Chinatown." | *Vancouver Daily World,* 10 February 1912.

without warrant.[38] Two years later Taylor's *Daily World* supported demands to "force them [Chinatown residents] to more respectable quarters."[39] These demands disclose a shift in intention – from containing and controlling Chinatown to displacing it altogether. The demolition in 1911 of dozens of buildings on East Pender and Carrall Streets, to lay tracks for the Great Northern Railway Company, was intended to alter the economic and social topography of East Pender. The real estate transactions completed by Taylor prior to erecting the World Building similarly suggest that this new building played a key role in this new approach to Chinatown. Not only would this new tower house the *Daily World* offices, but it would also act as a lieutenant – in the original French meaning as "placeholder" – in the proposed white-settler real estate development in Chinatown.[40]

As mayor, editor of the *Daily World,* and builder of the World Building, Taylor doubtless inflated his impact on Vancouver. Indeed, contrary to all fact,

Taylor would claim in his editorials that during his mayoralty "social evil was little heard of."[41] Taylor's reputation, in fact, fell under attack on several occasions. The worst scandals involved allegations that Taylor pushed through bylaws favourable to shareholders in his development company, World Building Limited.[42] City Council minutes from 20 July 1910 record a similar instance of conflict of interest: in this case, an abortive scheme to displace Chinese businesses and residents to make room for a new, white business district. The minutes state that, under the advisement of the city engineer on 14 July 1910, the south side of Pender Street was to be widened by twenty-four feet. The first lot trimmed was the future site of the World Building, and for conceding this portion of its property, World Building Limited received compensation. Chinese businesses and residents farther east were forced to accept settlements and vacate. That the city chose to widen the south – and predominantly Chinese – side of the street cannot reasonably be seen as a coincidence but should, instead, be considered as a sophistication of earlier strong-arm tactics. In early January 1912, soon after workers topped out the tower's steel frame, the *Daily World* ran a special on "World Progress and Building," celebrating the economic and architectural development in the city. The World Building, not surprisingly, figured prominently. One especially telling photograph, with the dome of the tower breaching the upper register of the vignette frame, proclaims that the fledgling tower stands as "the pioneer structure" in a "new business district" on Pender Street (Figure 6.5). The *Daily World*'s claim, however, overlooked the continued vibrancy of Chinese-owned businesses on East Pender. This appears, once more, to be a reiteration of the topos/atopos binary, wherein the axis mundi confirms the nascence of place where before none existed.

This sort of exercise of power never occurs without opening spaces of and for dissent. One of Vancouver's most novel structures, the Sam Kee Building (1913), stands as a consequence of such oppositional tactics. After the city appropriated twenty-four feet of his thirty-foot East Pender Street lot, Chang Toy, its principal owner, chose to build the "world's narrowest" commercial structure (Figure 6.6).[43] Chang, according to popular lore, raised this architectural sliver – a mere six feet wide – to spite the City Council, which had failed to compensate him fairly. City records, however, suggest the opposite. Chang appealed for and received extra compensation above what other landowners received.[44] In 1911 Chang hired the architectural firm of Brown and Gillam (which would eventually design the Sam Kee Building) to survey the remainder of the lot, well before the settlement from the city was finalized.[45] The choice, then, to erect the Sam Kee Building should be regarded as a sound business decision, one that yielded more than profits (incidentally, the Sam Kee Building

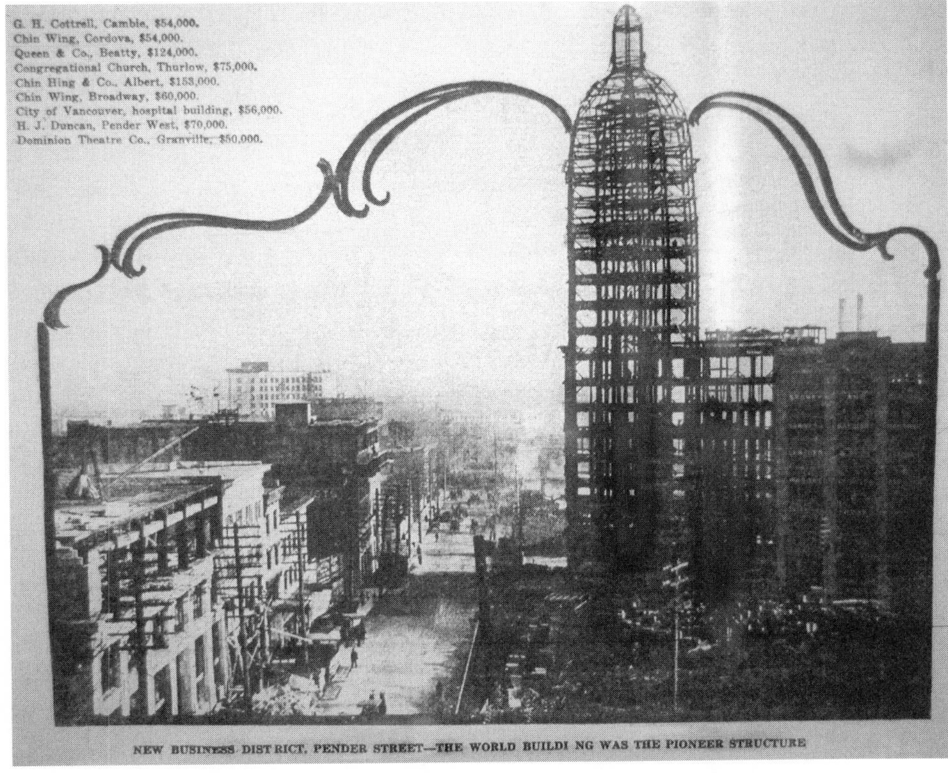

Figure 6.5 The World Building. | *Vancouver Daily World,* Business and Progress Edition, 6 January 1912.

to this day remains well maintained and fully occupied). Chang managed to maintain a presence on East Pender and to turn a profit – a surprising outcome that played out under the encroaching shadow of the World Building. Spite would have been too crude and extravagant a method to repulse efforts to displace the Chinese-owned businesses from Chinatown; instead, they managed to stay afloat by capitalizing, as did those seeking their removal, upon a booming economy. Moreover, as historian Paul Yee insists, Chinese entrepreneurs such as Chang never conducted business to "test white racism."[46]

THE WORLD TODAY

Walking north today through the bustle of Chinatown to the adjacent, forlorn stretch of East Hastings, entire blocks of once-proud businesses sit boarded up. Many people wracked by addiction and abuse walk these streets, throwing into

Figure 6.6 The Sam Kee Building, 1913, with the World Building in the background. | Photograph by author.

high relief the profound failure of those, including Taylor, who sought to locate and preserve their idea of the "good city" by dislocating a perceived nonplace. Taylor's new business district never materialized on East Pender; instead, the World Building continues to mark a site of uncertain identity, a liminal zone between the financial district to the west, Chinatown to the east, and the Downtown Eastside to the north, Canada's poorest neighbourhood.

Vancouver, at the time of the World Building's construction, was "growing hard," as Emily Carr had complained. Much of today's city looked like pasture, forest, or clearcut. The rapid influx of multinational and multi-ethnic residents resulted not only in the displacement of First Nations communities from waterfront areas but also in the partitioning of the city's precincts according to biases of class, race, and ethnicity. Such partitioning imbued each part with a sense of place, yet this often depended on the encounter with a perceived nonplace, or atopos. For example, William Whiteway's use of the Edwardian vocabulary for the World Building's design, utilizing the signifiers and systems of building native to Britain, reflected a widespread desire in Vancouver to identify with this distant, yet pervasive, imperial authority – and to be counted as a player in the subimperial regime of Canadian Confederation. The manner in which these loyalties to Britain shaped place, however, differed remarkably across class lines, evidenced by Louis Taylor's social estrangement from the clubs and events of the city's elites, as well as in his promethean ambitions to build the tallest tower in the empire.

In other ways, however, the World Building participated in a more general set of economic and socio-cultural exchanges, facilitating the broader aims of white-settler cultures. The tower functioned – by virtue of its sheer scale – as a symbolic marker, a highly prominent focal point, an axis mundi aiding the larger project of occupying and filling the "empty" landscape. This new assertion of place depended as much on a perceived sense of progress, legitimate regime, and spectacle as it did upon an anxious contrast with its immediate neighbour, Chinatown. Mayor Taylor's hope to establish a new business district replacing Chinatown relied both upon the image of economic and social advancement projected by the World Building and upon the associated appropriations and relocations of Chinese businesses and landowners facilitated by the development of the World Building site. Owing to its part in the project of reconfiguring the social and economic topography of this sector of Vancouver, the World Building should be seen not merely as an aesthetically pleasing marker of the past but also as a veritable instrument of imperial and Confederation systems, a needle sewing a thread of colonial discourse through the fabric of land, human flesh, and cultures.

NOTES

1 In 1914 it was surpassed by Toronto's twenty-storey Royal Bank Building.

2 Alan Morely, *Vancouver: From Milltown to Metropolis* (Vancouver: Mitchell Press, 1974); Timothy Oke, M. North, Olav Slaymaker, and J. Ryder, "Primordial to Prim Order: A Century of Environmental Change," in *Vancouver and Its Region,* ed. Graeme Wynn and Timothy Oke, 146-70 (Vancouver: UBC Press, 1992).

3 Heather Conn and Henry Ewert, *Vancouver's Glory Years: Public Transit, 1890-1915* (North Vancouver: Whitecap Books, 2003), 144.

4 Lance Berelowitz characterizes both Vancouver and Los Angeles as sites of "instant urbanism," as places of intensive development without the benefit of sophisticated planning models. See Lance Berelowitz, *Dream City: Vancouver and the Global Imagination* (Vancouver: Douglas and McIntyre, 2005), 4.

5 The early history of Vancouver's social and economic development is reviewed in Robert A.J. McDonald, *Making Vancouver: Class, Status, and Social Boundaries, 1863-1913* (Vancouver: UBC Press, 1996); and more generally in Graeme Wynn and Timothy Oke, eds., *Vancouver and Its Region* (Vancouver: UBC Press, 1992).

6 For a brief account of Whiteway's career, see Donald Luxton, *Building the West: The Early Architects of British Columbia* (Vancouver: Talon, 2003).

7 Kelly Crossman, *Architecture in Transition: From Art to Practice, 1885-1906* (Montreal and Kingston: McGill-Queen's University Press, 1987), 95. For the Western context, see Anthony A. Barrett and Rhodri Windsor Liscombe, *Francis Rattenbury and British Columbia: Architecture and Challenge in the Imperial Age* (Vancouver: UBC Press, 1983).

8 For a discussion of Edwardian architecture in relation to ornamentation, space and organization, and civic expansion at the turn of the twentieth century, see Richard Fellows, *Edwardian Civic Structures and Their Details* (Oxford: Architectural Press, 1999); see also Rhodri Windsor Liscombe, "Fabricating the Legalities of State in the Imperial West: The Social Work of the Courthouse in Late Victorian and Edwardian British Columbia," *Law Text Culture* 8 (2004): 57-82.

9 The World Building is mislabelled Beaux Arts both by the building's heritage designation plaque and by Harold Kalman's seminal text *Exploring Vancouver*. See Harold Kalman, *Exploring Vancouver 2: Ten Tours of the City and Its Buildings* (Vancouver: UBC Press, 1978), 40.

10 But neither of these early places nor the economic or social forces forging them can explain the contemporary sense of place enjoyed by Vancouver's gay community. Clearly, as this example illustrates, the constitution of place also depends on disruption, chance, and voices from the margins.

11 For a comprehensive account of Louis Taylor's political career and personal life, see Daniel Francis, *L.D.: Mayor Louis Taylor and the Rise of Vancouver* (Vancouver: Arsenal Pulp, 2004). See also Mary Rawson, "Eight Times Mayor of Vancouver," *BC Historical News* 34 (2000-01): 22-26.

12 Francis, *L.D.,* 35, 57.

13 McDonald, *Making Vancouver,* 177.

14 See *Vancouver Daily World,* 5 September 1907. Taylor's role in the riot is briefly outlined in Francis, *L.D.,* 63. For a detailed account of the riot, see Michael Barnholden, *Reading the Riot Act: A Brief History of Riots in Vancouver* (Vancouver: Anvil, 2005).

15 McDonald, *Making Vancouver,* 109.

16 Quoted in ibid., 178.

17 Both beliefs, with the onset of recession, became his undoing; as the *Daily World* took an increasingly nonpartisan position, he lost support from the Liberals, who had provided significant funding to his paper. Also, he relied on near-maximum occupancy of the World Building to cover the property's mortgage. His pockets were not deep enough to survive the vacancies brought by the economic downturn.

18 The extent of Mayor Taylor's exclusion from the city's business circles was never clearer than in 1915 when members of the city's Board of Trade failed to invite Taylor to an official reception for a visit from Theodore Roosevelt and his wife. To his credit, Taylor discovered their plan and boarded Roosevelt's train before they disembarked and took them on a tour of the city; cited in Chuck Davis, *The Greater Vancouver Book: An Urban Encyclopedia* (Vancouver: Linkman, 1997). For a discussion of the social activities of Vancouver's elite during this period, see Graeme Wynn, "The Rise of Vancouver," in *Vancouver and Its Region,* ed. Timothy Oke and Graeme Wynn, 69-148 (Vancouver: UBC Press, 1992).

19 Doreen Massey, "Power Geometry and a Progressive Sense of Place," in *Mapping the Futures: Local Cultures, Global Change,* ed. Jon Bird, Barry Curtis, Tim Putnam, George Robertson, and Lisa Tickner (London and New York: Routledge, 1993), 66.

20 Quoted in Mark Crinson, *Empire Building: Orientalism and Victorian Architecture* (London and New York: Routledge, 1996), 6.

21 Neil Besner argues for the value of regional studies of colonialism by championing the importance of "a thick sense of particular place and particular histories," a methodology that does not preclude understanding the national or international spheres, as all three interpenetrate and inform each other; see Neil Besner, "What Resides in the Question, 'Is Canada Postcolonial?'" in *Is Canada Postcolonial? Unsettling Canadian Literature,* ed. Laura Moss (Waterloo, ON: Wilfred Laurier University Press, 2003), 46.

22 D.M. Churchill, "False Creek Development" (MA thesis, University of British Columbia, 1953), 81. For a summary of the Canadian Pacific Railway's activities in Vancouver in this period, see Norbert Macdonald, "C.P.R. Town: The City-Building Process in Vancouver, 1860-1914," in *Shaping the Urban Landscape: Aspects of the Canadian City-Building Process,* ed. Gilbert A. Shelter and Alan Artibise, 382-412 (Ottawa, ON: Carleton University Press, 1982).

23 Derek Gregory, "Edward Said's Imaginative Geographies," in *Thinking Space,* ed. Mike Crang and Nigel Thrift (London and New York: Routledge, 2000), 325.

24 Richard Cavell examines why much modern, Canadian theorization of space fails to account for its social dimension, for a sense of place. For Cavell, this lacuna between place and space finds its origins in the colonial spatial imagination, where Canadian space was never full but always a "space without place." See Richard Cavell, "Theorizing Canadian Space: Postcolonial Articulations," in *Canada: Theoretical Discourse,* ed. Terry Goldie, Carmen Lambert, and Rowland Lorimer, 75-104 (Montreal: Association for Canadian Studies, 1994).

25 Ibid., 83. Of course, this absence of centre/periphery exists in further contradiction beside the definite material presence of both a remote and local imperial form of governance, registered in law, real estate practices, and the built environment.

26 Louis Taylor, "The Early History of British Columbia," editorial, *Vancouver Daily World,* 13 July 1907.

27 Geoffrey Bowker and Susan Star, *Sorting Things Out: Classification and Its Consequences* (Cambridge, MA: MIT Press, 1999), 53.

28 The establishment of colonial places and the consequent displacement of First Nations peoples relied to a large extent on the passing of bylaws. For instance, on 23 October 1907 the city requested that the chief of police enforce a recently passed bylaw meant to "abate the nuisance caused by [the] camping of Indians ... on the waterfront." These evictions forced indigenes from ancestral village sites located, with few exceptions, on shorelines surrounding the city; see City of Vancouver Archives, Council Minutes, MCR-1-15 (6/27). For a detailed account of the construction of place at Stanley Park and the removal of First Nations and immigrant communities, see Jean Barman, *Stanley Park's Secret: The Forgotten Families of Whoi Whoi, Kanaka Ranch, and Brockton Point* (Madeira Park, BC: Harbour, 2005).

29 Max Robinson, "Place Making: The Notion of Center," in *Constructing Place: Mind and Matter* (London and New York: Routledge, 2003), 149.

30 Two other key, well-photographed moments of spectacle define Vancouver's sense of place: Harry Gardiner, known as the Human Fly, free-climbed the World Building in 1918, drawing the largest crowd then assembled in the city's history; and two years later Harry Houdini thrilled crowds by escaping from a straightjacket as he dangled upside down from the top of the building's lantern.

31 David Chuenyan Lai, *Chinatowns: Towns within Cities in Canada* (Vancouver: UBC Press, 1988), 89.

32 Ibid., 79.

33 Quoted in Kay J. Anderson, *Vancouver's Chinatown: Racial Discourse in Canada, 1875-1980* (Montreal and Kingston: McGill-Queen's University Press, 1991), 82.

34 Quoted in Heidi V. Scott, "Rethinking Landscape and Colonialism in the Context of Early Spanish Peru," *Environment and Planning D: Society and Space* 24 (2006): 481-96.

35 Dread of white women frequenting opium dens was especially acute in this period, creating what Victor Burin has termed a "paranoiac space," an outcome of the jealous fear that white women could not only suffer addiction and fall into prostitution but also grow receptive to the advances of men from other races; see Victor Burgin, "Paranoiac Space," *New Formations* 12 (Winter 1990): 61-75.

36 "Worst Joint Underground," *Vancouver Daily World,* 10 February 1912.

37 For example, in the early 1900s, Vancouver's chief health inspector Robert Marrion protected the interests of xenophobic Hastings Street businessmen by taking to court those owners operating Chinese boarding houses located on the northern fringes of Chinatown. See Lai, *Chinatowns,* 83.

38 *Vancouver Daily World,* Business and Progress Edition, 27 January 1910.

39 Editorial, *Vancouver Daily World,* 10 February 1912.

40 The term "lieutenant" is not meant to connote any sense of the subaltern; rather, the World Building is posited as an agent facilitating the incursion of an invasive force.

41 Francis, *L.D.,* 86.

42 Perhaps the most damaging defamation to Taylor's character involved railway magnate James T. Hill's financing of the World Building concurrent to successful negotiations between the city and Hill's Great Northern Railway over the rail company's right-of-way in False Creek. See Francis, *L.D.,* 100.

43 Although the superlative claim to "world's narrowest" commercial structure, applied to the Sam Kee Building by the *Guinness Book of World Records,* acts as a tourist draw, this status remains uncertain, as the Skinny Building in Pittsburgh, at only five feet, two inches, appears narrower still.

44 The owners of the Sam Kee Company received $7,000 in addition to the $45,000 disbursed to other landowners. See City of Vancouver Archives, Sam Kee letter files, 566-E-7.

45 Ibid.

46 Paul Yee, "Sam Kee: An Early Business in Early Vancouver," in *Vancouver Past: Essays in Social History,* ed. Robert A.J. McDonald and Jean Barman (Vancouver: UBC Press, 1986), 92.

Digging in the Gardens
Unearthing the Experience of Modernity in Interwar Toronto

MICHAEL WINDOVER

When Maple Leaf Gardens was constructed in an astonishing five months and twelve days, it immediately became a locus of identification for Torontonians as well as for many Canadians across the country (Figure 7.1). The building, echoing the rapidity with which it was constructed, played host to the "fastest game on earth," ice hockey – a sport often identified as Canada's national game or as somehow intrinsic to "Canadianness."[1] The Art Deco styling of the Gardens alluded to this sense of speed as well as to modern notions of progress and technological efficiency, while unapologetically announcing the building's place within Toronto's emergent consumer culture. The history of this civic institution lays bare the complicated interpenetration of the process of modernization with its own representations in everyday life both physically on/in the Gardens and virtually on the airwaves, in the pages of the popular press, and on the lips of many Canadians.

What seems odd initially when considering this Art Deco arena is that in its singular form it is referred to in the plural (Maple Leaf Gardens rather than Maple Leaf Garden).[2] This grammatical transgression could be read as pertaining to the multiple, intersecting, spatial-temporal relationships engendered by the space. The building of the "modernistic" arena coincided with a critical moment in the shaping of an imagined Canadian identity, fuelled in part by technological

Figure 7.1 View of Maple Leaf Gardens, Toronto, 28 November 1931, gelatin silver print mounted on canvas. | Ross and Macdonald Fonds, Canadian Centre for Architecture, Montreal, ARCH33235.

advances in communications (particularly radio) as well as in transportation, which together compressed time and space. For Torontonians, however, it also marked the cityscape, becoming a place of civic belongingness. So at once the Gardens operated as an earth-bound, physical place and as an imagined ("unearthed") site within the everyday landscape – a duality that exposes for us a distinctly modern signification of identity.

Central to the experience of modernity and the creation of modern identities are the conceptions of situatedness and placelessness within the context of consumer culture. Although stadiums and arenas have been regarded as insignificant architectural sites given their obvious affiliation with consumerism, and no doubt also their proximity to the supposed less-cultured "masses," their study provides a prime example of the interface of these notions. Anne de Fort-Menares, who objected to the designation of Maple Leaf Gardens as an Ontario heritage site during the debates of the 1980s, opined that hockey, as a recreational activity, should be considered social history and would be better commemorated by video rather than architecture.[3] She saw the Gardens primarily as a broadcasting centre of "planned repetitive low context" events, meaning that architecturally speaking the Gardens had little to do with the actual events produced within. Yet, as Neil Leach has argued, repetition is essential to the establishment of an identification with place.[4] He asserts that in order to ascertain how people develop a sense of belonging to place, we must consider not only the form of a building but also its use – how space is performed or, following psychoanalytic film theory, how users see themselves projected in the space and how the space is absorbed into them visually and haptically, particularly through the incorporation of habits and creation of memories associated with the experience of the place.

De Fort-Menares's view has been countered by recent theorizations of the stadium as a metaphor of modernity, as an extension of the city, and as a means of exploring the interweaving of social relationships on an everyday level.[5] With these conceptualizations in mind, I investigate the Gardens along the lines suggested by Michel de Certeau. He is concerned with how a place – what he calls a concrete and "proper" location that connotes a sense of stability – can become a space bound to "the operations that orient it, situate it, temporalize it, and make it function in a polyvalent unity of conflictual programs or contractual proximities" in everyday life.[6] "In short," he explains, "*space* is a *practiced place*."[7] I contend that we need to consider as well the construction of virtual place as space in this sense, the spilling over of the "proper" locations into day-to-day life outside of their physical sites. It is through their engagement with the physical structures of the city and the virtual constructions of them in everyday life that citizens garner a sense of belongingness and community.[8] The invocation here of the wider notion of place as a multivalent locus might be understood as adding the concrete physicality of place to Jody Berland's useful discussion of *topos* – a flexible term that takes into account the narratives/myths constructed and reinforced in/around/by place.[9] The simultaneously "placeless" and "placed" space of the Gardens becomes an ideal location from which to investigate the fragmented and stable, individual and collective, "earthed" and "unearthed" experience of modernity in interwar Toronto.

HISTORICITY OF THE GARDENS: STAGING THE CITY

At the time of the opening of Maple Leaf Gardens on 12 November 1931, Toronto had briefly witnessed enormous economic development, to which the building projects of the late 1920s attest. In an era of biggest, tallest, and fastest,

Figure 7.2 View looking north on Church Street, Maple Leaf Gardens, Toronto, 1931. | From Sinaiticus, "Maple Leaf Gardens, Toronto," *Construction* 24 (December 1931): 370. Courtesy of the Toronto Public Library.

particularly evident in the erection of Art Deco skyscrapers in Manhattan, Toronto asserted its new, modern identity on the international stage with the construction of the largest hotel (the Royal York, opened in 1929) and tallest building (the Canadian Bank of Commerce Building, completed in 1931) in the British Empire.[10] Toronto's T. Eaton Company, the eighth largest retailer in the world at the time, evinced this enthusiasm with its College Street store – an enterprise planned in an epoch of optimism but poleaxed by the Depression.[11] Due in large part to the opening of new prairie settlements and the discovery of abundant mineral deposits in northern Ontario, rich investments that reinforced the development of financial and legal operations, Toronto began to rival Montreal as the economic hub of Canada.[12] It was in this atmosphere of prosperity and pronounced civic identity that, in 1927, Conn Smythe bought the Toronto St. Pats and renamed them the Toronto Maple Leafs.[13] Shortly thereafter, he began to think about moving the team from its Mutual Street location to a larger arena, situated on land owned by the T. Eaton Company on Carlton Street, visible from the new College Street store.[14] Smythe, a colourful Toronto native who had fought in the First World War, understood well the growing patriotism and civic pride associated with professional sports and capitalized on producing what would become English Canada's rival to the Montreal Canadiens by planting the Gardens in the burgeoning, modern city.

Despite the hardships of the Depression, "Sinaiticus," a regular contributor to the local commercial journal *Construction*, retained the excitement aroused by the building projects in the Gardens' neighbourhood. So great were recent developments that

> any former Torontonian, absent from his native shores for the past half-a-decade, and suddenly precipitated from the modern equivalent of a magic carpet into this area would find extreme difficulty in identifying his [*sic*] surroundings. Facing the west-bound traveller is the completed first unit of the T. Eaton Co.'s new store – only a portion of what is still to be and yet already most imposing. Upon the north-east corner of Carlton and Yonge is a block of stores faced in Tyndall stone and striking in the simplicity. Just south of Carlton upon the east side of Yonge is a new stone-faced commercial building of modern design, while upon the opposite side of the street are several other excellent examples of modern architectural expression. Coming eastward along Carlton Street from Yonge one discovers the steam shovels to be hard at work in the excavation for the new Hydro Building.[15]

These new buildings, he argued, were illustrative of the "easy-going Toronto of the now," in sharp contrast to the "now despised mid-Victorian era" structures characteristic of the city at the time (e.g., see the houses around the Gardens visible in Figure 7.2).[16] Sinaiticus's pronouncements, read widely by the "makers" of the civic fabric, pointed to the dynamism of his urban milieu. Although infused with an enthusiasm characteristic of the modern spirit of change, his observations suggest a more pragmatic response to modernity, one that did not conceal the commercial intentions fuelling development with utopian theoretical posturing. The Gardens' physical presence was seen as cut from the same cloth as contemporary edifices in the imagined modern city.

The architecture of the building spoke to conflicting tendencies of modernity: the ephemeral and permanent, imaginary and concrete. Unlike much architecture of the Modern Movement that sought a visual separation from history with the removal of historicizing ornament, the Art Deco Gardens evoked the desire to appear fashionable and new, progressive and efficient, yet blended these concerns visually with Classical and localized building traditions. The result was an architecture that embodied Janus-faced modernity; an architecture that displayed the embeddedness of modernization in tradition; an architecture that made evident the collision of commerce, communication, and culture in its construction. We might agree with Tim Benton that, as an example of Art Deco, it captured perhaps better than Modernist architecture the complicated interplay of the fleeting and fragmentary with the universal.[17] Art Deco responded to modernity in a sensual, humanistic manner that appealed to the consumerist love of spectacle.[18]

Although more staid than many Art Deco buildings in terms of its ornament and certainly less glamorous in its materiality, the Gardens attracted consumers in the heart of the Depression with its fusion of Classical design elements, local building tradition, and modern engineering. Perhaps Conn Smythe was hoping to imbue the building with the sense of stability evident in the Beaux Arts banks and insurance buildings of the time, and even in Eaton's College Street store.[19] The allusion to classicizing motifs may have helped to garner a sense of trust, which was particularly important during the uncertain economic climate of the time. The elongated, flat-headed windows, which recede into the Carlton Street facade, are interrupted by fluted, columnar elements banded with five horizontal lines in white stone (Figure 7.3). Rather than providing support, these decorative motifs float over the open space of the vertical windows. In alluding to traditionally structural elements in a strictly decorative manner, the facade might be read as referring to the lack of structural supports on the interior: columns have actually been replaced by a large, open expanse. Maple Leaf Gardens, designed for a mass audience, was the first of the National Hockey League's (NHL) arenas to offer spectators an unobstructed view of the ice surface from every seat.[20] The modern stability established here was thus tied to technology and efficiency (as well as to maximizing revenue), was associated with openness and expansiveness, and was offered in a "user-friendly" style through allusion to popular recognition of Classical visual vocabulary. Indeed, William Greer (who argued for the historical designation of the arena in the controversial heritage debate noted above) argued that the Classical detailing related to the materiality of concrete and layers of yellow brick, which reinforced the horizontal thrust of the building.[21] But he also pointed out that the use of brick was characteristic of Toronto's urban landscape and was part of a well-established southern Ontario building tradition.[22] The Gardens thus acknowledged the modern strains of the universal, capitalizing on contemporary advances in engineering and interest in representing functionality to create a timeless, potentially placeless location, as well as a recognition of locality grounded in regional building practices and materials.

The topos of the Gardens prefigured the actual built place. Like clever lawyers who introduce inadmissible material in the courtroom only to have it

Figure 7.3 Detail of window above entrance, Maple Leaf Gardens, Toronto. | Photograph by author.

THE TORONTO DAILY STAR, THURSDAY, MARCH 5, 1931

Maple Leaf Gardens to Be Erected at Church and Carlton Streets

PROPOSED NEW HOCKEY ARENA FOR NATIONAL HOCKEY LEAGUE AND O.H.A. HOCKEY

Figure 7.4 Proposed plan for Maple Leaf Gardens. | *Toronto Daily Star,* 5 March 1931. Reprinted with permission of Torstar Syndication Services.

stricken from the record, Smythe had an architectural drawing from the firm Ross and Macdonald released to local newspapers on 5 March 1931, influencing the reading and understanding of the building (Figure 7.4).[23] This image ignited popular interest in the building, projected a particular vision of the modern, and set in motion the virtual existence of the arena.[24] The proposed plan emphasized the vertical with dramatic set-backs and pronounced projections, as well as a more active facade, mirroring the skyscraper drawn in the background.[25] The narrow, elongated fenestration and decoration toward the top of the facade produced an upward thrust, a sensibility retained (albeit somewhat muted) in the completed building. The horizontal banding, which figured so prominently in the finished Gardens and lent the building its more earthbound weightiness, was present only in the upper storeys of the building drawn. No doubt, the realities of the Depression led to a scaling-back of the original plan, as was the case with the unfinished College Street store.[26] The built Gardens maintained a sense of gradual projection and accession as the eye moved from either corner to the main portals in the centre of the Carlton Street facade. This horizontal movement was emphasized by the banding and acknowledged the streamlining trends coming into fashion at the time of its construction – a kind of visual representation of efficiency. The parallel horizontal lines also conjured notions of speed, echoing the movement of the street cars and traffic, as well as alluding to the energetic sport housed beyond the imposing facade.

The reference to transportation and speed was particularly important given their role in the construction of the modern city as well as the modern nation, not to mention in the transcontinental growth of professional sports. Crucial to the development of the modern city, transportation infrastructure, including not only the streetcar, subway, bus, and rail but also the automobile, was discussed widely by urban planners in the West, including in Toronto.[27] Built in a period characterized by accelerating time-space compression, the importance of transportation was particularly acute for Canada, a nation whose Confederation owed much of its constitutional definition to the promises of railway linkage. Modern transportation was also central to the expansion of professional sports and was of primary concern to Conn Smythe when choosing the property for his "temple to hockey." Colin Howell notes that although the infrastructure was laid prior to the First World War, the "explosion of sports" in the interwar period stemmed from the expansion of urban transportation networks, especially electric-tram services and railways.[28] The streetcar line – its tracks and cables visible in Figure 7.1 – was the most significant factor in Smythe's decision, besides the discounted price of the land.[29] Efficient transportation and communication between cities was also critical to the establishment of professional sports. Both the city/country and professional sports required transportation and media infrastructure (e.g., newspapers and radio) to compress time and space and weave together citizens/consumers based around a common set of identifications (whether with "Canadianness" or with the Maple Leafs). Transportation and communications development fuelled not only a larger "imagined community," to borrow Benedict Anderson's phrase, but also an intensified identification with place and the local.[30]

In a sense, as the community's showplace and large-scale meeting centre, the arena was built of the community itself. Beyond abstract civic connections, however, the use of brick illustrated the economic realities of the time. Although an expensive stone frontage would have appeared more congruent with the downtown skyscrapers and banks and a more affluent audience, the use of brick acted as a visual signifier for the class of spectators who would predominantly attend games at the Gardens. As I discuss below, Conn Smythe sought to bring respectability to hockey and his arena by catering in part to Toronto's elite, but the chief patrons, the ones who filled the blue, green, and especially the grey sections, were from the middle and working classes. Many of the hundreds who worked on the project – a rare opportunity in the Depression – no doubt occupied these seats.[31] Because of a shortage of some $200,000, Frank Selke,

Conn Smythe's assistant, convinced all those working on the job, both individually and through unions, from bricklayers, carpenters, and masons to electricians, plumbers, and steelworkers, to take 20 percent of their wages in Gardens stock.[32] Many of them had to sell off their shares at the time; however, those who hung on to them did well thanks to the economic viability of the arena.[33] The Gardens was thus owned by the community, a fact that lends more credence to a reading of the stadium as a staging of the city.

Niels Kayser Nielsen takes up this idea of the stadium as civic stage, contending that it "is an extension of the city's streets and street life, while, at the same time, it differs in that, as in the duality found in the theatre, it provides on the one hand a distinct, formalized and aesthetic staging, and, on the other, an arena for the 'agon,' which in the city streets is silently expressed."[34] As a centre where teams representing cities met for competition, the Gardens became a site of civic identification. Richard Gruneau and David Whitson suggest that although in larger urban centres, such as Toronto, people tended to identify with subcommunities built on class, racial, and/or ethnic differences, the development of sports teams that represented the city was one of the ways that a broader sense of shared belonging to the city was inculcated.[35] As Austin "Casey" Ryan, a loyal supporter of the Toronto Maple Leafs, recalls, "Everyone wanted tickets when the Canadiens or Detroit was playing."[36] The arena thus staged difference, with the local Maple Leafs (and by extension the city) juxtaposed against visitors' cities.

The flexibility of the interior, which allowed for the transformation from ice rink to concert hall, meant that the Gardens was used for religious meetings, political rallies, circuses, ice shows, big band concerts, operas, as well as other sports, including boxing, wrestling, track and field, and tennis.[37] The sense of place, the self-conscious space for belonging that responded to certain modern conceptions of civic identity seen in the built and imagined cityscape, secured the Gardens a central position within everyday life in Toronto. At the same time, the Gardens was necessarily a placeless location, affording the flexibility to stage events that met the other political, social, and economic interests of Torontonians.

ON THE POWER PLAY

The Gardens, understood as a practised place, became a locus where social architecture met built architectural form. In relating the stadium to Georg Simmel's understanding of the city as "a sociological entity that is formed spatially," Joseph Maguire argues that we should read the arena as a set of social relationships – an example of "social geometry" – where we can see the interweaving of different kinds of interactions between different groups.[38] This affords a view of the production of space in the stadium, including the disciplining of the docile body of the modern citizen in Foucaultian terms, as demonstrating these social interrelationships. In a similar vein, Nielsen views the stadium's evolution as the rationalization of a landscape, where mono-functionality supplants multifunctional landscapes.[39] He combines Robert David Sack's notion of "territoriality" – understood not as static, defended landscapes but as a social process by which "a limited area is bound together by dispositions of power" – with Michel Foucault's assertion that bodies are disciplined and behavioural patterns established by "certain spatial distribution."[40] The body is confined essentially to a single space (a designated seat) for a limited amount of time, as the stadium remains closed for much of the week, opened only to the public when events are staged. The mechanized precision and rational organization of the seats echoes mass production, which Nielsen argues is the "prerequisite for the understanding of the democratic mass-citizen."[41] The patrons have a certain amount of "free space" and freedom of activity but are confined spatially and temporally. Conflict between classes and individuals is reduced as patrons become spectators of the sports activity – a substitution for violence, as some theorists contend, following the argument that sports are a "civilizing force."[42]

Like the organization of the department store or ocean liner, the architectural layout of the Gardens reinforced a societal hierarchy, albeit arranged visually in reverse.[43] Rather than a bargain basement leading up to a high-end restaurant and society meeting area, the stadium's lower tiers were reserved for the wealthy, while the seats at the top (the farthest from the action) were left to those of lesser means. In Maple Leaf Gardens these were clearly delineated by a gradual reduction in comfort as one moved from the rink to the rafters by coloured sections (red boxes to blue ones and green seats to grey benches), making visible in a single view the distinctions of class that were obscured in other commercial spaces of everyday life, such as the department store.[44] Lou Marsh, sports editor for the *Toronto Daily Star,* offered a tongue-in-cheek impression of opening night at Maple Leaf Gardens, commenting on the explicit hierarchy:

> Isn't it wonderful? ... Look at the size of it ... Looks like a cathedral ... How'll they ever fill all those seats? ... My aren't those red leather seats smart? ... Do I get a red seat? ... No, you don't ... You have to have evening clothes to sit down there ... Well, why didn't you put on your lodge suit so we could go down there? ... No, the blue seats are not as nice ...[45]

Although, as Russell Field notes, this critique was not echoed widely, Marsh's commentary does indicate an awareness of a social hierarchy spatially reinforced in the Gardens' architecture.[46] Returning to Nielsen's discussion, we can see the tension between the freedom of leisure time and the capitalist power relationships circumscribing it. The apparent similarity of the spectators' positions – all classes joined together watching the game in unison – simultaneously enforced differentiation.

Gruneau and Whitson, recounting the impact of the communications and transportation development combined with the vast economic expansion of the early twentieth century in Canada, note that "the Canadian city was becoming a symbolic monument to technology and progress," a point enunciated by the architecture and construction of the Gardens, as well as by the narratives created around it.[47] The speed at which the building was raised proved to be a modern feat of engineering. Despite being riveted rather than arc-welded, the construction of the roof was quite advanced.[48] The domed roof, which covered an area of 207 by 225 feet and was crowned by a Modern-style lantern seen in Figure 7.2, needed the support of enormous trusses "too large to be shipped intact from the fabricating shop to the site [thereby requiring] considerable [portions] of the fabrication [to be] done at the job," as the *Contract Record* reported.[49] One corner was pinned while the other three rested on metal rollers in order to absorb the expansion and contraction of the metal roof.[50] Working eight-hour shifts and sometimes through the night thanks to the use of floodlighting, employees saw their labour materialize into a place that would help regiment their leisure time in the years to come. The building also contained the most up-to-date broadcasting and public-announcement system, as well as the SporTimer clock, which regulated the game and created a suspenseful atmosphere, especially in the dying moments of a period or game. The narrative of the building's construction, like the early rendering published in local papers, helped to establish the very modern characteristics of the Gardens in the public imagination. This set the stage for the equally modern narrative of commodified practice that would take place with the Gardens' opening.

Sparse in decoration, the lobby spoke to a controlled economy of space and rationality, as well as to the modernist concern for hygiene and sterility (Figure 7.5). Upon the Gardens' closure, Trent Frayne described Conn Smythe's insistence that the Gardens appear pristine at all times: "Two painters were on the job year-round, splashing hundreds of gallons on the seats and walls. Every day all winter, 35 staff workmen scoured the interior with vacuum cleaners, mops, brooms, brushes and dust cloths."[51] This stress on cleanliness created an atmosphere of timelessness as it attempted to efface the uncontrollable aspects (the

Figure 7.5 Lobby of main entrance, Maple Leaf Gardens, Toronto, 1931. | From Sinaiticus, "Maple Leaf Gardens, Toronto," *Construction* 24 (December 1931): 369. Courtesy of the Toronto Public Library.

"everyday" presence) of the crowd, reinforcing notions of sameness and thus stability. In addition, this focus on hygiene supported the disavowal of abject poverty facing many Torontonians at the time. Between 1931 and January 1933, the rate of unemployment rose from 17 to 30 percent, and by 1935, one-quarter of Torontonians and those living in the suburbs were on relief.[52] Indeed, on the occasion of the centennial luncheon in 1934, Lieutenant-Governor Herbert Bruce called for a plan of action to deal with the growing slum districts in the city, a reality expunged from the Gardens' interior.[53]

The Gardens became a clean slate for the inscription of a particular "living history." Nielsen describes how the stadium is a prime location "where the city and its inhabitants inherit themselves,"[54] producing collective memory

> by demonstrating through routine and repetitive action that one belongs to a certain place, in a certain time; that is to say, one is specific in a temporal and spatial 'historicity'; one creates history rather than just being created by history; and history is created with the body substantial. The crowd may be an historic product, yet, in its crowding together – such as at the stadium – it dismisses this

Figure 7.6 Interior of rink, Maple Leaf Gardens, Toronto, 21 January 1933. | Toronto Reference Library/ Special Collections, acc. 979-38-2, repro. T 10161. Courtesy of the Toronto Public Library.

> product-likeness and recreates it(self), not as mere distributed nitwits, but as an historic being making its presence known and making a great fuss about it.[55]

The rink thus becomes, like the city, a highly ambiguous site where the rationality that brings about the timeless stages for the practices of everyday life and the approbation of a modern subjectivity collides with this very subjectivity. The subjectivity, in itself, seeks to assert its difference and timeliness and physical situatedness within the placeless and timeless confines of the arena, free from the grit and danger of the streets outside.

The planned unexpectedness of this encounter is heightened by the design of the edifice. From the street level, the arena appears to rise only five or six storeys but could actually house a ten-storey building in its interior beneath the lantern. This design works as a metaphor for the experience of the everyday event. The arena seems integrated into the everyday cityscape yet contains within it the space of the extraordinary. On the interior, the rather low, sloping ceilings of the lobby and corridors act as a foil for the expansiveness of the rink and seating area (see Figure 7.6). For Sinaiticus, "The initial impressions derived from the interior of the arena itself are those of size, scale and colour."[56] He goes on to observe that "standing on either side of the rink and looking across the smooth, blue-white expanse of ice and up past the tiers of seating, one is impressed not only with the vastness of the place, but by its striking colourful effect."[57] We must remember that this aesthetic effect represented and reinforced the distinctions of class. With an unobstructed view across the ice surface, neighbours could see each other, as well as strangers, forming an ordered mass spectatorship and collective identity thanks to the efficiency of modern building techniques and design. The building thus points to the contradictory experience of modernity – of rationality or orderliness alongside the unplanned (this is the key difference between theatre and modern sports spectatorship), of being at once a member of a community and an anonymous stranger. If we can read the Gardens as a microcosm of the modern city producing a collective identity, this collective identity should be understood to be as unified as it is fractured. After all, although the place offered a space of gathering for many, it simultaneously enforced difference and exclusivity. It promoted the dominance of a primarily male, Caucasian identity, as some scholars have rightly pointed out.[58]

HE SELLS! HE SCORES!

Of significance to the arena, of course, was the technology that brought about the rationalization of the landscape necessary for the commercialization of the sport: the ice-making facilities. Ten miles of 1¼-inch Stelco pipe were required to cool the ice surface and maintain its integrity.[59] This feature intrigued broadcaster Foster Hewitt, who outlines the cooling process in his multiply reprinted book *Hockey Night in Canada: The Maple Leafs' Story*.[60] After describing the impossibility of maintaining the coloured lines and circles necessary for playing the game "in the natural-ice age," he argues that "with only man-made ice, hockey would be a Victorian era sport. With refrigerated ice, players train earlier, seasons last longer, the surface is keen at all times, spectators dress normally, and hockey has become big business. The scientist has made it possible for Canada to retain world supremacy in her favourite sport."[61] Here, Hewitt suggests that modern science, thanks in no small part to developments in consumer capitalism, had created a modern sport for Canadians that was quite distinct from its earlier Victorian roots. The amateur game, developed out of a blend of folk traditions along with the British ideals of discipline, order, fair play, and manliness encouraged in the elite public schools, had "matured" into a professional sport.[62] Professionalism in hockey, as with other sports, did not gain respectability until well into the first quarter of the twentieth century. Amateurism was upheld by the moral elites of the country who felt that the "civilizing" effects of the sport would be corrupted with the introduction of paid players. Money made through sports speculating was associated with gambling, and even team sports had proven corruptible by the lure of economic gain, as the infamous Cincinnati-Chicago World Series of 1919 exposed.[63] Despite this, professionalism in hockey had gained acceptance certainly by the time the NHL was established in 1917.[64] As Canada's urban centres became hotbeds for consumption, leisure time and entertainment, including professional sports, became big business. Frederick B. Edwards observed in 1927,

> Hockey, which began its career as a rough and ready game played by small boys on home-made skating rinks in a thousand Canadian vacant lots, and grew up to be Canada's national pastime, is Big Business, now ...
>
> Millionaires back the organizations, fine ladies in evening gowns applaud the efforts of the skating roughnecks with polite patting of gloved palms, ticket speculators buy out the seating accommodations for the crucial games, and the Wall Street commission houses handle bets on the results.
>
> Hockey has put on a high hat.[65]

An evolving professionalism in hockey placed greater emphasis on individual skills, which required more training and practice as well as rationalized landscapes where this could be executed.[66] Maple Leaf Gardens as the home of successful professional hockey, imbued with the patriotism of Hewitt's commentaries, ultimately commemorated the growing commodification of hockey at the time.

Conn Smythe, who had worked for the New York Rangers until his dismissal before the team's first season, had witnessed firsthand the revenue that hockey as a professional sport had generated following the construction of Madison Square Garden with its 17,000-seat capacity.[67] The Montreal Canadiens club had initiated a building spree in the NHL with the erection of the Forum in 1924, which was followed by Madison Square Garden (1926), Detroit Olympia (1927), Boston Garden (1927), and Chicago Stadium (1929).[68] The old Toronto Mutual Street Arena, designed by Ross and Macdonald and built in 1912, accommodated only about 7,000 spectators, a base number too low to cover the expenses of icing a top-level professional team.[69] Field argues that this rink, erected before the widespread acceptability of professional hockey and predating the NHL by five years, should be considered a "vernacular sports space" – one that was intended for community use rather than one envisioned for mass consumption. The 15,000-seat Gardens, on the other hand, was designed to support a professional hockey team first and foremost.[70]

To finance the purchase of the Toronto Maple Leafs in 1927 and the Gardens four years later, Smythe depended on the patronage of Toronto's elite.[71] To fill his new arena at slightly higher ticket prices, Smythe sought to alter the prevailing sentiment around professional hockey by appealing to the elite, selling hockey, when played in his rink, as a form of respectable entertainment. He led a publicity campaign that played into civic pride, suggesting that Toronto needed to be competitive with Boston, Detroit, Chicago, Montreal, and New York. Furthermore, he insisted that his patrons dress up for the game, rather than don old sweaters: "We need a place where people can go in evening clothes."[72] Even the seats, described as "folding seats of the opera type," implied the growing prestige of sports spectatorship.[73] Although part of the impetus behind building the Gardens was certainly to attract Toronto's upper class, Smythe did not want to dissuade the club's loyal supporters. The principal goal in attracting the well-off, as Field notes, was to see "this new attitude towards hockey and spectatorship ... become entrenched and result in increased long-term profits."[74]

That the spectator of modern sports was positioned as a consumer was apparent in the design of the Gardens. The arena worked visually and viscerally to reinforce mass consumption, not only by selling products but also through the production of a collective identity built around the experience of winning. The Gardens' architects incorporated shopping directly in their design with ten shops along its south and east sides (see Figure 7.1).[75] Shopping and entertainment thus were conjoined, marking the space of leisure time as consumptive. Like the experience of cinema-going, viewing hockey games was not a singular activity. Buying food, either from the street vendors outside the entrance or inside, as "Casey" Ryan remembers,[76] was part of going to the Gardens – reinforcing the spectator's role as consumer.

The very activity of sports consumption should not be seen as a passive experience, as Field claims. Although the excitement of the game and personalities of the players did account for much of the experience, the thousands of spectators cheering the local team on to victory were also significant. Indeed, Garry Crawford, investigating fans and their role in the consumption of sport, argues that the audience should be seen not as a product or by-product but as a "constitute part of the text itself."[77] This is in keeping with de Certeau's description of "consumer production," which seeks to highlight the agency inherent in consumption and how users of space "make do" with their material conditions by inscribing their own trajectories onto places.[78]

The Gardens acted as a place of community meeting and social activity. As Gruneau and Whitson explain, with the development of professional sports in the consumer culture climate, "a sense of community identification with particular teams or entertainers could suddenly be purchased with a portion of one's wages."[79] Particularly on the eve of large-scale tournaments, such as the Stanley Cup series in the NHL, the World Cup for football/soccer, or the Olympics, spectators often enter into a collective-identity dynamic according to the success of their team, which produces a powerful sense of belongingness. The enactment of this identity is far from passive, harbouring instead distinctly active attitudes and outward behaviours toward an imagined community. John Hannigan, in his discussion of the Leafs' move from the Gardens to the Air Canada Centre in 1999, describes the conscious conflation of nationalist sentiment with team branding as producing a "mediated community," one that I would argue was mobilized by Symthe as early as 1927 when he exchanged the Irish St. Pats image for the Canadian Maple Leaf.[80]

It is also important to note that part of successfully professionalizing hockey in Toronto was producing women consumers. After all, Smythe envisioned the Gardens as a place where the traditionally male audience could "be proud to take their wives or girl friends."[81] This appeal to women for sport spectatorship aimed at bringing "respectability" to the game and was linked to consumerism, itself seen at the time as associated with the feminine.[82] Integral to the new arena were women's lounges. As Field notes, promotional booklets that sought support for the construction of the Gardens contained cartoons of ladies commenting on the features, including lounges, adding another modern dimension to the image of the arena in the discourse around the rink.[83] The creation of these exclusive spaces for women suggested the production of a different kind of sports place in terms of the experience of spectatorship. Part of the vision of the modern embedded both in the pre-existing narrative of the Gardens as well as in its very structure was a call for equality, despite the reinforcement of difference along class lines noted above. The sense of equality striven for was fuelled by a desire for maximized and sustained profit. However, the move to include women in the design did widen the appeal of the building as a place of identification.

As in the case of cinema-going, and shopping for that matter, sports consumption occurs as much in the "live" venue as outside the building. Crawford argues that "sport is not just something that takes place at a specific location and time, but lives on in people's imagination and conversations, through their social networks, friendships, mass media and consumer good use, and in their very identity."[84] He draws a parallel between the identification of the cinema-goer with the movie star and that of the sports fan with the professional athlete.[85] The advent of modern sport and the growth of professionalization witnessed the expansion of sporting-equipment suppliers.[86] Although set in rural Quebec in the 1950s, Roch Carrier's *The Hockey Sweater*, a story of a boy's identification with a hockey player (Maurice Richard) and the central role of the sweater in the child's fantasy projection, which allows him access to a certain subculture, exemplifies the importance of various commodities associated with hockey (from equipment to sweaters).[87] The knowledge of a sport can act as a form of cultural capital that can transcend normal class boundaries.[88] This cultural capital flowed not only from viewing hockey games live but also from newspapers and radio reports, which ultimately helped to increase audience numbers at games by acting as advertisements.[89] As John Herd Thompson and Allen Seager note, "a new kind of journalist called a sportswriter fabricated larger-than-life heroes" out of professional athletes, beginning with American baseball stars who quickly became heroes to Canadians, echoing the development of Hollywood stars.[90] This identification with the pros fuelled dreams of social mobility given that professional sports provided economic opportunities for talented working-class athletes, in contrast to amateur sports played predominantly by the upper and middle classes. The Gardens provided a kind of dreamscape for some, a topos where the best of the best met in competition regardless of socio-economic background.

"HELLO CANADA AND HOCKEY FANS IN THE UNITED STATES AND NEWFOUNDLAND": RADIO, PLACE, AND CITIZENSHIP

Conn Smythe understood the potential market reached by radio broadcasts of hockey games and thus made room in Maple Leaf Gardens for a broadcasting "gondola," hung high above the ice surface for Foster Hewitt's *Hockey Night in Canada* broadcasts.[91] He recalled that, when approached by Jack MacLaren of MacLaren Advertising in 1929 and offered money for hockey broadcasts, "it was then that I believed the story about manna from heaven."[92] With the corporate sponsorship of General Motors in 1931, regular Saturday night broadcasts of *Hockey Night in Canada* began, and by 1933 games could be heard from coast to coast.[93] By the time of the Second World War, the number of Canadians tuning in to *Hockey Night in Canada* (sponsored then by Imperial Oil) had nearly doubled to 2 million from 1934.[94] By linking the Dominion together, the radio broadcasts dovetailed with a growing sense of nationalism in the country, presenting one aspect of Canadianness.[95] We see here how the notion of the modern citizen blends with that of consumer, a tendency recognized in the American context as early as 1924 by philosopher Samuel Strauss.[96] Indeed, the liberal form of citizenship owed much to the introduction of a market economy in terms of highlighting the importance of equality between citizens with all its accompanying rights and freedoms, including the freedom to desire and consume.[97] Like the radio, which was hailed by many as a democratizing technology, the arena was available to anyone, regardless of class, provided the spectator paid for a ticket.

Although there were concerns about the Americanization of the NHL at the time, particularly among Anglo Canada's intellectual elites, most Canadians "were happily incorporating the new continental popular culture into the rhythms of local and regional life."[98] That the majority of NHL players were Canadian and that some were becoming stars in American cities on par with baseball heroes Babe Ruth and Jack Dempsey diffused some nationalist concerns and, instead, led to expanded marketing of civic (even nationalistic) identity and a unique sense of place through repetition of place names on the airwaves and in newspapers.[99] Gruneau and Whitson argue that because of this popular coverage on Canadian radio, the NHL appeared to be essentially a Canadian league, despite icing only four of the league's ten teams during the 1930s.[100]

Because of its prominent place in the country's mythology of hockey, Maple Leaf Gardens became a shrine for hockey enthusiasts and a popular tourist attraction in Toronto, suggesting a strong sense of place as well as imagined community for Canadians outside the city.[101] Jack Warner, from Carlyle, Saskatchewan, remembers, "During the thirties ... we'd gather around the radio on Saturday nights and listen to Foster Hewitt's broadcasts from the Gardens. Even though we couldn't see what he was talking about, we seemed to know what it all looked like: the game, the building, the players."[102] It is significant that listeners, such as Warner, could envision the Gardens without having entered it, for it illustrates the simultaneous quality of "placelessness" and particularity, unity over space and difference (highlighting the local). It also indicates the power of the medium to facilitate a rich space for listeners to escape into during the Depression. Just as the interior of the Gardens was kept pristine at all times, the radio, whether broadcasting hockey games or Jack Benny, rarely acknowledged the "real" world, as an anonymous Canadian remembered:

> Do you recall any one of [the popular radio personalities], just once, ever mentioning the Depression, that times were tough, millions out of work, kids sleeping

> in ditches and barns? Can you ever recall one of them mentioning just once all these terrible things which were happening around them? Think about it. Kind of scary, isn't it? There were two worlds in those days, the real one and the fantasy one.[103]

The games played in the Gardens and broadcast across the country might be conceptualized as part of the "fantasy" world described here, yet they were "real" in evoking shared sentiments and a sense of community. Listeners as much as spectators entered the Gardens for a period of time, displacing their anxieties for the spectacle of the game, which would then possibly inform other aspects of their everyday life.

Maple Leaf Gardens thus existed both as a physical place in the Toronto urban landscape and as a virtual space for Torontonians and Canadians across the country, enhancing the sense of "placelessness" inherent to stadiums.[104] Arenas by necessity were similarly organized. The ice surface needed to be roughly the same dimensions as the other NHL rinks, as did the arrangement of the blue lines, goal lines, and circles because of the standardization of the game. The rationalized mass-produced seating and the sterility of the interior also produced a timeless quality, which would be placed in time for the duration of games or events. The placelessness, or interchangeability of place, was further heightened by the radio broadcasting of the game, where the sport quite literally could exist anywhere. Given the role of hockey in popular culture and its representation and repetition in daily life (whether in the newspaper, on radio, in conversation, or enacted by children on their local park's skating rink), the game became an everyday event, something perhaps outside routine – that is, not necessarily physically enacted – but seemingly ubiquitous, an everyday occurrence but an event of potential significance and therefore worth cultural capital in some circles. In essence, Maple Leaf Gardens existed physically and virtually as a main stage for everyday events, and this, I contend, was symptomatic of the experience of modernity. The Gardens was as physical as it was virtual, a site of history as much as a site of the ever-effacing present, and it produced an identity that was as corporeal as it was imagined.

CONCLUSION

Maple Leaf Gardens in its plural and singular form reads as a metaphor for the experience of modernity in Toronto. The building played host simultaneously to the enactment of community identity and the performance of individual consumer acts, intermingling the imagined and the material in complicated ways. On the one hand, its Art Deco styling invoked the speed and efficiency of the construction techniques and modern technology that brought about the professional game fleetingly played within, and on the other hand, the building connoted stability and order with its monumental presence and timeless hygiene. The Gardens staged the city physically, in terms of its material situation within the city's urban fabric and as a site of gathering together mass crowds, and virtually, given its place within the larger national imagination carried by the mass media. The building and its presence in daily life activities emphasized the modern duality of placelessness and situatedness. Although the building was open only for short periods of time, the Gardens existed very much in the everyday consciousness of Torontonians at large, whether discussed by adults at work or imagined by children playing hockey on their local park's outdoor rink. The Gardens contributed to the imagining of the modern Canadian citizen, promoting the place as a locus of civic identification; however, it was a mass citizen, demarked visually in the interior by status. Intertwined with the conception of this modern identity was the role of the citizen as consumer. The space reinforced capitalist power dynamics and trained fans to be good consumers. The infrastructure necessary for the successful incorporation of the National Hockey League, which produced active fans, was likewise a means of creating a wider sense of belongingness on a national scale.

Highlighting some of the aspects of the modern experience engendered in this space as a practised place affords a more complicated understanding of the space and "Canadianness" that begs further exploration. How did the Gardens act as a social filter in the construction of "Canadianness" (i.e., how was it both a place of inclusion and exclusion along gender, ethnic, and racial lines)? The startling charges in 1997 of sexual abuse against minors carried out by long-time employees in empty offices of the Gardens from the late 1960s through the 1980s revealed another darker side of this civic monument, one demanding further investigation into usage and power relations embedded in spaces like stadiums.

Despite this chapter in its life, Maple Leaf Gardens continues to exert an important presence in Toronto today as a locus of identification. Following the Maple Leafs' move to the Air Canada Centre in 1999, the future of the Gardens was uncertain. Even after its purchase by the grocery-store chain Loblaw's in 2004, plans to renovate the facility made little progress. In the fall of 2009, with the partnership of Loblaw's, the federal government, and Ryerson University, it was announced that the heritage-protected Maple Leaf Gardens would be revitalized for the university and surrounding community as a commercial and recreation centre containing a large-scale grocery store, rink, and athletic facility.[105]

Ironically, it took another serious economic crisis to give the Gardens a new life. It will no doubt become even more deeply ingrained, albeit differently, in contemporary practices of everyday life.

ACKNOWLEDGMENTS

This chapter is dedicated to the memory of Austin "Casey" Ryan and Elizabeth Scott. Their conversations with me provided an invaluable perspective on the experience of living in the Toronto of the 1930s. I would like to acknowledge the support of the Social Science and Humanities Research Council of Canada, the Ontario Graduate Scholarship program, the University of Western Ontario, and the University of British Columbia. I would also like to extend a special thanks to Rhodri Windsor Liscombe and Bridget Elliott, as well as to Geoffrey Carr, Barry Magrill, and Chris Bilton, for their thoughtful insights and comments.

NOTES

1 Rallying behind hockey as being indicative of "Canadianness" can be seen in the Canadian Broadcasting Corporation's documentary *Hockey: A People's History,* a social history centred on the sport, which aired in the fall of 2006. For perhaps the most comprehensive scholarly discussion of hockey culture in Canada, see Richard Gruneau and David Whitson, *Hockey Night in Canada: Sport, Identities, and Cultural Politics,* Culture and Communications in Canada Series (Toronto: Garamond, 1993). They argue that "hockey is not, as some commentators have implied, the result of a cultural manifest destiny rooted in Canadians' struggle for survival in the vast spaces of a rugged northern country. Rather, the sport we call hockey has emerged out of a series of clashes of cultures and traditions that have occurred against the backdrop of Canada's development as an industrial and consumer society" (6). For a concise historiography of hockey culture, see David Whitson and Richard Gruneau, "Introduction," in *Artificial Ice: Hockey, Culture and Commerce,* ed. David Whitson and Richard Gruneau, 1-25 (Peterborough, ON: Broadview Press, 2006).

2 In this, the Gardens is unlike its Manhattan precursor, Madison Square Garden. However, there was a local precedent in the Mutual Street Arena, which was known prior to 1938 as the Arena Gardens, as Mike Filey points out in his "The Gardens on Mutual," in *Toronto Sketches: The Way We Were* (Toronto: Dundurn, 1992), 73.

3 The decision by the City of Toronto to make the arena into a heritage site met opposition from Maple Leaf Gardens Limited, the company that owned the building and presumably felt that the property value had more potential than the arena itself. The sports complex had been recommended to the City of Toronto for heritage designation under Part 4 of the Ontario Heritage Act by the Toronto Historical Board on 23 March 1988, which the City Council adopted on 18 and 19 May 1989. The Conservation Review Board, after considering the arguments at a public hearing on 7 and 8 December 1989, recommended on 25 January 1990 that the property receive heritage designation. See Toronto Historical Board, "Report of Conservation Review Board of Ontario Regarding the Proposed Designation of Maple Leaf Gardens as a Heritage Site," August 1990, 1-13, http://www.culture.gov.on.ca/english/culdiv/heritage/crb/toronto_mapleleaf-gardens.pdf. Anne de Fort-Menares's opinions are found in this document at page 11.

4 Neil Leach, "Belonging: Towards a Theory of Identification with Place," *Perspecta* 33 (2002): 126-33.

5 Of particular note is the work of John Bale, including *Sport, Space and the City* (London: Routledge, 1993), as well as two collections of essays: John Bale and Olof Moen, eds., *The Stadium and the City*

(Keele: Keele University Press, 1995); and Patricia Vertinsky and John Bale, eds., *Sites of Sport: Space, Place, Experience* (London: Routledge, 2004). In this chapter, I look primarily to Joseph Maguire, "Sport, the Stadium and Metropolitan Life," in *Stadium and the City,* 45-57; Niels Kayser Nielsen, "The Stadium in the City: A Modern Story," in *Stadium and the City,* 21-44; John Bale, "The Stadium as Theatre: A Metaphor for our Times," in *Stadium and the City,* 311-22; and Patricia Vertinsky, "Locating a 'Sense of Place': Space, Place and Gender in the Gymnasium," in *Sites of Sport,* 8-24.

6 Michel de Certeau, *The Practice of Everyday Life,* trans. Steven Rendall (Berkeley: University of California Press, 1984), 117. For example, he cites how streets are transformed by pedestrians into space. Patricia Vertinsky takes up this idea in discussing issues of gender at the War Memorial Gymnasium at the University of British Columbia.

7 De Certeau, *Practice of Everyday Life,* 117, original emphasis.

8 Benedict Anderson describes how print capitalism (which I would consider a virtual means of connection between citizens) was instrumental in the constitution of the modern subject and thus national identity. See his *Imagined Communities: Reflections on the Origins and Spread of Nationalism* (London: Verso, 1991).

9 Jody Berland develops this term, borrowed from Keith Belton's work, and situates it within a Canadian context. She describes it as "the layering of historically and chronotopically diverse narratives over a topography that shapes and is shaped by such narratives" in her article "After the Fact: Spatial Narratives in the Canadian Imaginary," *New Formations* 57, special issue on *The Spatial Imaginary* (Winter 2005-06): 41.

10 William Dendy and William Kilbourn, *Toronto Observed: Its Architecture, Patrons, and History* (Toronto: Oxford University Press, 1986), 200. For brief descriptions and photographs of the Royal York and the Canadian Bank of Commerce Building, including their dominant place on the Toronto skyline, see Charis Cotter, *Toronto between the Wars: Life in the City, 1918-1939* (Richmond Hill, ON: Firefly Books, 2004), 29, 32-33, 35, 46-47. The buildings garnered attention from local and national journals; see, for example, "The Royal York Hotel, Toronto," *Royal Architectural Institute of Canada Journal* 6, 8 (August 1929): 246-67, and "The New Canadian Bank of Commerce Building, Toronto," *Royal Architectural Institute of Canada Journal* 8, 4 (April 1931): 134-53. But the buildings were also noticed internationally; see, for example, Parker Morse Hooper, "The New Hotel," *Architectural Forum* 51, 6 (December 1929): 582-601. See also *Architectural Forum* 52, 6 (June 1930), which is dedicated to skyscraper design and includes an image of the Canadian Bank of Commerce (797).

11 Although the structure reached only seven storeys, the building captured the optimism of the period with its enormous triumphal entrance along Yonge Street. According to the original plan, the building was to be some forty-eight storeys high, covering more than two city blocks, and to become the corporate symbol and flagship store for Eaton's. For more on the College Street store, see Cynthia Jane Wright, "'The Most Prominent Rendezvous of the Feminine Toronto': Eaton's College Street and the Organization of Shopping in Toronto, 1920-1950" (PhD diss., University of Toronto, 1993); and William Dendy, *Lost Toronto* (Toronto: Oxford University Press, 1978), 157.

12 In 1939 the *Toronto Financial Post* proclaimed that Toronto had "passed Montréal as a centre of finance, commerce and industry," a boast perhaps better founded than the *Toronto Globe*'s comparable claim made in 1906, as James Lemon notes in his *Toronto since 1918: An Illustrated History* (Toronto: James Lorimer and National Museum of Man, National Museums of Canada, 1985), 64. Although Toronto did make advances economically throughout the Depression, it would not surpass Montreal definitively as the economic centre of Canada for a few more decades.

13 Smythe chose the maple leaf emblem based on that worn by soldiers who had fought in the First World War. For more on the purchase of the St. Pats and the raising of funds partially through gambling, see Conn Smythe, with Scott Young, *If You Can't Beat 'Em in the Alley* (Toronto: McClelland and Stewart, 1981), 83-86.

14 Apparently, Eaton's vice-president, J.J. Vaughan, was not initially enthused with Smythe's proposal to build the Gardens on the corner of Carlton and Church Streets, but he was convinced by Smythe that

the thousands attending hockey games would pass by the new College Street store, providing higher visibility to the new department store. See Smythe, with Young, *If You Can't Beat 'Em,* 104.

15 Sinaiticus, "Maple Leaf Gardens, Toronto," *Construction* 24 (December 1931): 369.

16 Ibid.

17 Tim Benton, "Art Deco Architecture," in *Art Deco, 1910-1939,* ed. Charlotte Benton, Tim Benton, and Ghislaine Wood (London: Victoria and Albert, 2003), 259. Charles Baudelaire famously described modernity as "the ephemeral, the fleeting, the contingent, the half of art whose other half is the eternal and immutable."

18 Ibid., 258-59. On approaching modern architecture as competing discourses (i.e., responses to modernity), see Sarah Williams Goldhagen, "Something to Talk About: Modernism, Discourse, Style," *Journal of the Society of Architectural Historians* 64, 2 (June 2005): 144-67. Absent in Goldhagen's engaging discussion is the place of Art Deco as a competing narrative. Deco is read often as a "reflectionist" style by the likes of Benton in keeping with Bevis Hillier's pioneering work on the topic, which argues that we read Deco as a "total style"; see Bevis Hillier and Stephen Escritt, *Art Deco Style* (London: Phaidon, 1997). Rather than approach Art Deco from a "reflectionist" position, I argue in "Aestheticizing Mobilities: Art Deco and the Fashioning of Interwar Public Cultures" (PhD diss., University of British Columbia, 2009), that the style actively reinscribed pre-existing social hierarchies and thus was a statement of some socio-political import.

19 It is not surprising that he employed the same architectural firm as the T. Eaton Company. Ross and Macdonald were significant architects in the period, having carried out a number of large-scale projects in Toronto and "erected a 'skyscraper' upon every important corner in Montréal," as reported by Sinaiticus, "Maple Leaf Gardens, Toronto," 369.

20 For more on the construction of the Gardens, see "Rapid Construction Features Erection of Large Toronto Arena," *Contract Record and Engineering Review* 45, 41 (14 October 1931): 1235-38, 1248; and "An Outstanding Construction Accomplishment – Erection of Large Sports Arena in Five Months," *Contract Record and Engineering Review* 45, 42 (11 November 1931): 1341-53, 1357.

21 Toronto Historical Board, "Report of Conservation Review Board of Ontario," 5.

22 Ibid.

23 See *Toronto Daily Star,* 5 March 1931, News section, 15; and *Toronto Globe,* 5 March 1931, News section, 11. The associate architects for the Gardens were Jack Ryrie and Mackenzie Waters of Toronto.

24 Conn Smythe must have known well the power of the newspaper as his father had written for the *Toronto World.* Ross and Macdonald were also savvy in their understanding of how to garner trust and support for architectural projects during the Depression. In fact, according to Smythe, it was these reputable architects who pitched the idea of the arena to Montreal-based insurance company Sun Life. It was securing Sun Life's support that gave local investors the confidence to put their money behind the project. See Smythe, with Young, *If You Can't Beat 'Em,* 13, 103.

25 This background skyscraper represented the proposed Toronto Hydro Building by local architectural firm Chapman and Oxley (1931-33). For more on the Toronto Hydro Building, see *Art in Architecture: Toronto Landmarks, 1920-1940,* exhibition catalogue (Toronto: Department of the City Clerk, 1988), 22-23; and A.H. Chapman, "The New Toronto Hydro-Electric Building," *Royal Architectural Institute of Canada Journal* 10, 9 (September 1933): 152-56.

26 As Lemon reports in *Toronto since 1918,* 76, the construction industry was hit very hard in Toronto, resulting in fewer changes to its skyline in the 1930s than in any other decade.

27 See Dendy, *Lost Toronto,* 142-47, for more on the proposed Federal Avenue by John Lyle (1911), as well as the updated schemes for Cambrai Avenue and Vimy Circle dating from 1929. The plans for broad avenues and a unified architectural program were thwarted by the onset of the Depression, leaving only Union Station on Front Street and the Parker Pen Company Building (1933) and the Canada Life Building (1929-31) on University Avenue as evidence of the initial conception.

28 Colin D. Howell, *Blood, Sweat, and Cheers: Sport and the Making of Modern Canada* (Toronto: University of Toronto Press, 2001), 65, notes that "railways offered excursion fares that enabled fans to follow

their teams from town to town; this heightened urban rivalries and stimulated community boosterism." As well as the movement of fans, particularly for special matches, railways, like the Canadian Pacific Railway, looked to supporting the transportation of professional sports leagues as sure sources of income (65-66).

29 Smythe had considered a location on the waterfront, which would have involved a large parking lot and tunnel connecting it to the arena, as well as a location on Spadina Avenue. See Stan Obodiac, *Maple Leaf Gardens: Fifty Years of History* (Toronto: Van Nostrand Reinhold, 1981), 10-12.

30 See Anderson, *Imagined Communities,* as well as David Harvey, *The Condition of Postmodernity* (Oxford and Cambridge, MA: Basil Blackwell, 1989), esp. "Time-Space Compression and the Rise of Modernism as a Cultural Force," 260-83.

31 Smythe observed on opening night hundreds of the workers who had built the place in the crowd; see Smythe, with Young, *If You Can't Beat 'Em,* 108. As Stan Obodiac notes in *Maple Leaf Gardens,* 12, at times some 1,300 workers were employed. Wage earners, including most of the construction industry, were hit the hardest during the Depression, whereas Toronto's salaried middle and upper classes, in many cases, prospered given the lower costs of goods, as Lemon observes in *Toronto since 1918,* 60, 64.

32 Foster Hewitt, *Hockey Night in Canada: The Maple Leafs' Story,* 10th ed. (Toronto: Ryerson Press, 1968), 96-97. This was also remembered by Conn Smythe in his autobiography; see Smythe, with Young, *If You Can't Beat 'Em,* 106.

33 Obodiac, *Maple Leaf Gardens,* 15, reports that "preferred shares eventually rose to $12.50 and common stock to over $80 each, before the shares were split four to one and then three to one." He also notes, writing in 1981, that every Maple Leafs game had been sold out since 1946 (7).

34 Nielsen, "Stadium in the City," 21.

35 Gruneau and Whitson, *Hockey Night in Canada,* 68.

36 Austin "Casey" Ryan, interview by author, 12 May 2005.

37 See Obodiac, *Maple Leaf Gardens;* and Lance Hornby, *The Story of Maple Leaf Gardens: 100 Memories at Church and Carlton* (Champaign, IL: Sports Publishing, 1998). Both books outline many of the nonhockey events that took place at the Gardens.

38 Maguire, "Sport, the Stadium and Metropolitan Life," 45, 49.

39 Nielsen, "Stadium in the City," 22.

40 Ibid., 22-23.

41 Ibid., 23.

42 Gruneau and Whitson, *Hockey Night in Canada,* 12-18, outline some of the work on the civilizing effects of sports, beginning with Johan Huizinga's *Homo Ludens* and including Michael Novak's *The Joy of Sports.*

43 For a discussion of the organization of department stores, see Susan Porter Benson, *Counter Cultures: Saleswomen, Managers, and Customers in American Department Stores, 1890-1940* (Urbana: University of Illinois Press, 1986), 90.

44 In the red boxes, closest to the ice, red padded-leather seats with arms and a width of nineteen to twenty inches were filled by the top-paying patrons. The seats in the blue, green, and grey sections were wooden and eighteen inches in width. Although the blue section had hinged seats, the second tier (greens) had fixed seats and separate backs, and the top rows (greys) were comprised of bench-style seats with backs. See Russell Field, "Passive Participation: The Selling of Spectacle and the Construction of Maple Leaf Gardens, 1931," *Sport History Review* 33 (2002): 44. The costs of tickets were as follows: $3 for reds, $2.50 for blues, $1.75 for greens, and $0.90 for greys, as Trent Frayne observes in "Goodbye to the Gardens," *Maclean's,* 15 February 1999, 54. These prices do not appear substantial compared to the $122, $93, $53, and $26.50 for tickets sold in the last year the Gardens hosted the Leafs.

45 Lou Marsh, "Lamping the arena opening with the frau – and others," *Toronto Daily Star,* 13 November 1931, News section, 10. Also quoted in Field, "Passive Participation," 45.

46 The stratification of society was also implicitly noted by Bert Perry, "Chihawks Victorious as Great New Arena Gets Official Start," *Toronto Globe*, 13 November 1931, News section, 1. He described the red boxes as being "where society was well represented by patrons in evening dress."

47 Gruneau and Whitson, *Hockey Night in Canada*, 79.

48 Anne de Fort-Menares argued that, as a result, the Gardens should not be considered technologically advanced. See Toronto Historical Board, "Report of Conservation Review Board of Ontario," 7.

49 "Outstanding Construction Accomplishment," 1349.

50 Toronto Historical Board, "Report of Conservation Review Board of Ontario," 3-4.

51 Frayne, "Goodbye to the Gardens," 55.

52 Lemon, *Toronto since 1918*, 59. As Lemon notes, Toronto was hit hard by the Depression, but the suburbs experienced much worse conditions. Toronto, making up 8 percent of the population of the country, contributed 19 percent of the bill for relief; however, in 1936, for example, the residents of East York contributed approximately one week's pay for relief, whereas Torontonians, on average, contributed one day's pay (62).

53 Ibid., 59. Bruce's comments inspired the Board of Control's Bruce Report, issued in the fall of 1934. For more on this report, see ibid., 65-68.

54 Nielsen, "Stadium in the City," 30.

55 Ibid., 34. Quoted also in Chris Gaffney and John Bale, "Sensing the Stadium," in *Sites of Sport*, ed. Vertinsky and Bale, 35.

56 Sinaiticus, "Maple Leaf Gardens, Toronto," 370.

57 Ibid.

58 This point was made by Anne de Fort-Menares in the heritage debate discussed above. For more on hockey as being an exclusionary activity, see Mary Louise Adams, "The Game of Whose Lives? Gender, Race, and Entitlement in Canada's 'National' Game," in *Artificial Ice: Hockey, Culture and Commerce*, ed. David Whitson and Richard Gruneau, 71-84 (Peterborough, ON: Broadview Press, 2006). Adams's article speaks primarily to contemporary issues of gender and race in relation to the construction of hockey as a national sport. There is more work to be done on the history of the space of arenas and exclusivity at the level of audience as well as sports participation.

59 See "Outstanding Construction Accomplishment," 1349-51.

60 Hewitt, *Hockey Night in Canada*, 63-64.

61 Ibid., 64.

62 For a history of the sport and the development of professionalism in sports in Canada, see in particular Gruneau and Whitson, *Hockey Night in Canada*, chs. 2-4; and Howell, *Blood, Sweat, and Cheers*, chs. 2-3. The first professional hockey league in Canada emerged in 1908; however, it was not until well into the 1920s that professionalism gained prestige. It should be noted that although professionalism became acceptable in the 1920s, amateur leagues continued to flourish, particularly in western Canada, which was unable to sustain a professional league during the 1920s.

63 John Herd Thompson, with Allen Seager, *Canada, 1922-1939: Decades of Discord*, Canadian Centenary Series (Toronto: McClelland and Stewart, 1985), 187.

64 Gruneau and Whitson, *Hockey Night in Canada*, 57. Gambling, however, had never left the realm of professional sports and, in fact, was instrumental in Smythe's purchase and construction of the Maple Leafs and the Gardens.

65 Frederick B. Edwards, "High Hat Hockey," *Maclean's*, 15 December 1927, 5.

66 Gruneau and Whitson explore the subculture of the professional athlete in *Hockey Night in Canada*, 109-13.

67 Field, "Passive Participation," 41-42.

68 Ibid., 35.

69 Field, ibid., 48n16, notes the controversy surrounding the number of people the Mutual Street Arena actually held, with numbers varying from 7,000 to 9,000, which included standees.

70 Although I do not question that the Gardens was built specifically with capitalist interests in mind, I would argue that the Mutual Street Arena, too, was built at least partially for commercial purposes and that the ideal "vernacular sports space" for hockey was the outdoor rink.

71 Field, "Passive Participation," 50n44, lists Smythe's directors – a veritable who's-who list of Toronto's social elite. They included Sir John Aird (president, Canadian Bank of Commerce), A.L. Ellsworth (president, British American Oil), George H. Gooderham (president, Northop-Strong Securities), Harry McGee (vice-president, T. Eaton Company), J.Y. Murdoch (president, Noranda Mines), Frank A. Rolph (president, Imperial Bank of Canada), Victor Ross (vice-president, Imperial Oil), R. Home Smith (chairman of the board, Algoma Steel), and John A. Tory (supervisor for western Ontario, Sun Life Assurance).

72 Smythe, with Young, *If You Can't Beat 'Em,* 102-3. In an interview by the author (12 May 2005), Austin "Casey" Ryan remembered that "most people in them days, even young guys ... [like himself] wore a suit and tie" to hockey games at the Gardens.

73 Sinaiticus, "Maple Leaf Gardens, Toronto," 370. For a reaction to the Gardens on its opening, see Perry, "Chihawks Victorious as Great New Arena Gets Official Start," 1, 8.

74 Field, "Passive Participation," 45.

75 Field, ibid., 44, notes that originally twenty-two shops had been planned for the Gardens, with ten along the north side of the building.

76 Austin "Casey" Ryan, interview by author, 12 May 2005.

77 Garry Crawford, *Consuming Sport: Fans, Sport and Culture* (London: Routledge, 2004), 3.

78 De Certeau, *Practice of Everyday Life,* xii-xxii.

79 Gruneau and Whitson, *Hockey Night in Canada,* 61.

80 John Hannigan, "From Maple Leaf Gardens to the Air Canada Centre: The Downtown Entertainment Economy in 'World Class' Toronto," in *Artificial Ice: Hockey, Culture and Commerce,* ed. David Whitson and Richard Gruneau, 71-84 (Peterborough, ON: Broadview Press, 2006), 205.

81 Smythe, with Young, *If You Can't Beat 'Em,* 102-3.

82 For a discussion of the coding of consumption as feminine in Toronto, see Wright, "'The Most Prominent Rendezvous,'" 21-72.

83 Field, "Passive Participation," 42.

84 Crawford, *Consuming Sport,* 106.

85 Ibid.

86 Gruneau and Whitson, *Hockey Night in Canada,* 61. For example, they cite the American company Spalding, which sold equipment to Canadians across the country.

87 Roch Carrier, with illustrations by Sheldon Cohen, *The Hockey Sweater,* trans. Sheila Fischman (Montreal: Tundra, 1984).

88 Crawford, *Consuming Sport,* 107, makes this point in reference to studies of conversations in the Canadian workplace by B. Erickson, "Culture, Class and Consciousness," *American Journal of Sociology* 102 (1996): 217-51. The concept of cultural, or symbolic, capital is based on the work of sociologist Pierre Bourdieu, notably his *Distinction: A Social Critique of the Judgement of Taste,* trans. Richard Nice (Cambridge, MA: Harvard University Press, 1984).

89 Gruneau and Whitson, *Hockey Night in Canada,* 81, report that in the last quarter of the nineteenth century, the number of newspapers tripled with the advent of "people's journals."

90 Thompson, with Seager, *Canada, 1922-1939,* 186. Writing about teams was supplanted by tales of individual stars by the 1920s, Gruneau and Whitson observe in *Hockey Night in Canada,* 84.

91 See Gruneau and Whitson's discussion of the role of the media in shaping hockey in Canada in *Hockey Night in Canada,* 70-106.

92 Quoted in ibid., 97.

93 Ibid., 100.

94 Ibid., 101.

95 Berland, "After the Fact," 44-45, explores radio in relation to notions of citizenship and Canadian nationalism, as well as how it marked a border rather than circumventing one, as in the case of US commercial radio.

96 In his discussion of "consumptionism," Strauss argued that "the problem before us to-day is not how to produce the goods, but how to produce the customers. Consumptionism is the science of compelling men [*sic*] to use more and more things. Consumptionism is bringing it about that the American citizen's first importance to his [*sic*] country is no longer that of citizen but that of consumer." See Samuel Strauss, "'Things Are in the Saddle,'" *Atlantic Monthly* 134, 5 (November 1924): 579.

97 For a discussion of the liberal tradition of citizenship in relation to capitalism, see Derek Heater, *What Is Citizenship?* (Malden, MA: Polity, 1999), 7-10.

98 Gruneau and Whitson, *Hockey Night in Canada,* 101-2.

99 Ibid., 100. See Berland, "After the Fact," 52, for a discussion of the repetition of place names in radio and its impact on reproducing memories as well as a broader sense of place.

100 Gruneau and Whitson, *Hockey Night in Canada,* 100. By the end of the 1930s, only two Canadian teams had survived the Depression – the Montreal Maroons and the Ottawa Senators folded due to economic hardships, as did the New York Americans and the Pittsburgh Pirates. This left the Original Six: Boston Bruins, New York Rangers, Detroit Red Wings, Chicago Blackhawks, Montreal Canadiens, and Toronto Maple Leafs.

101 It is interesting to note that during the Depression, tourism in the city actually went up, beginning in 1933; see Lemon, *Toronto since 1918,* 64. Despite not housing the Maple Leafs for over a decade, the Gardens continues to draw tourists today.

102 Quoted in Charles Wilkins, "Maple Leaf Gardens: What Fate Awaits This Icon of Canadian Culture?" *Canadian Geographic* 114, 1 (1994): 33.

103 Barry Broadfoot, *Ten Lost Years, 1929-1939: Memories of Canadians Who Survived the Depression* (Toronto: Doubleday Canada, 1973), 250.

104 For a discussion of "placelessness," or "sameness," see Nielsen, "Stadium in the City," 23-24; and Bale, "Stadium as Theatre," 318.

105 The renovated facility – Ryerson University Sports and Recreation Centre at Maple Leaf Gardens – is scheduled to open in 2011. For more on the plans by BBB Architects, see "Play Called for Renos at Maple Leaf Gardens," *Toronto Globe and Mail,* 9 March 2010, B8.

PART 4
RECONSTRUCTING CANADA

"Reconstruction" is a Canadian and British Commonwealth term that describes policies for national renewal formulated during the Second World War. It is particularly associated with urban redevelopment and programs of institutional building. In Canada these policies were compiled by a series of advisory committees, the fourth of which was devoted to Housing and Community Planning. The report of this latter committee led to the creation in 1947 of the Central [later Canada] Mortgage and Housing Corporation (CMHC), charged with the provision of loans for private and corporate residential construction and ownership as well as the improvement of architectural design, town planning, and the building industry across Canada. The CMHC was one of several government interventions into the economic and cultural life of Canadians, the latter being epitomized by the 1951 Massey-Lévesque Commission, which expanded academic research and public access to the creative and performing arts. Most associated with the political career of C.D. Howe and the governments of Louis St. Laurent (1948-57), Lester Pearson (1963-68), and to a lesser degree John Diefenbaker (1957-63), the Reconstruction ethos paralleled the positivist early-postwar phase of the transatlantic Modern Movement in architecture and planning. It did so by privileging standardized analytic solutions that corresponded with widespread enthusiasm for universal social norms and new socio-cultural collectivities. Thus governmental policy and popular media framed a new national independence but also an international, especially North American, consciousness. Both the buoyant economy, sustained by a retooling of the industrial-military complex, and increased and ethnically diversified immigration contributed to the consolidation of national economies of finance, culture, and identity. Yet the growth of consumerism also led to renewed regionalism and fractured urbanism, best described as surbomodernism or auto-conurbation. Central to these coalescing and diversifying conditions was the engine of housing – whether the compounding commodification of single-family dwellings or public/corporate residential construction.

Lucie Morisset links the several levels of the economic system operating to enlarge personal consumption in Quebec with the province's emergent secular popular culture in "A Modern Heritage House of Memories: The Quebec Bungalow." She summons up the intriguing archaeology of this particular version of old, colonial typology by identifying it as a site for the individualist reconfiguring of collective Modernist aesthetic and modern marketing-media practices. The distinctive societal fabric she diagnoses contrasts with the standardized, if climatically attuned, community planning project Alan Marcus contextualizes in "Place with No Dawn: A Town's Evolution and Erskine's Arctic Utopia." Arctic sovereignty became a major objective during the Second World War and a major policy plank during the ministry of John Diefenbaker. Marcus relates the dystopic aspects of the modernization of the Canadian North – notably the enforced relocation of the Inuit (echoed in the residential schooling of Aboriginal children across Canada or in Joey Smallwood's push to remove outpost communities to urban centres in post-Confederation Newfoundland) – to the environmental and socio-cultural sensibility Ralph Erskine brought to making a modern community at Qausuittuq, the former Resolute Bay. He maps the appropriations of Modernist ideal and utopic urban design onto the later phases of Canadian endeavour to weld the far northern landmass and seas onto the country's national system.

A Modern Heritage House of Memories
The Quebec Bungalow

LUCIE K. MORISSET

Nowhere in Canada – or anywhere else, for that matter – is post–Second World War residential architecture commonly associated with the idea of memory, identity, or heritage. In Canada, Wartime Housing Limited and its successor, the Canada Mortgage and Housing Corporation (CMHC, formerly the Central Mortgage and Housing Corporation), are instead credited with developing the stock plans and models of easily and rapidly built homes that popularized the relatively homogeneous and shoddily constructed "small house" that broke with its occupants' previous lifestyles. Similar reasons are used to discredit "modern heritage," although experts and activists more commonly use this designation to refer to works of the Modern Movement that are attributable to well-known designers and clearly distinguishable in the built landscape. Critics of modernity in architecture, whether that of Le Corbusier or the North American suburbs, generally point to a variety of constructive flaws, whether an internationalizing pretension contrary to today's quest for local or regional individuality or some form of break (voluntary, at that) with the past. In short, for average citizens, the architectural productions of the twentieth century – particularly the second half – are said to be hardly conducive to the anchoring of identity that "heritage" produces in communities. To the extent that many of these productions, which also occupy a significant portion of the Canadian landscape, also belong to the residential domain – that is, to a world inherently resistant to the collectivization typical of heritage recognition (heritage being extracted from the *private* sphere for the *common* good) – we might go so far as to say that Canada will have little to pass on to the world heritage of humanity, whether in terms of the CMHC's small houses or Quebec's famous "bungalow." When the president of the Commission des biens culturels du Québec was asked recently about the heritage value of this notable figure of our suburbs – by a film director gifted with rare intuition who did not hide her desire that the bungalow be assigned historic-monument status – she cautiously indicated that "the assignment ... of national status ... helps ensure the property itself is preserved to some degree. [However,] you can classify a bungalow, you can classify a neighborhood; but you have to be sure to conserve the meaning of the property in question, in addition to its material features."[1]

The bungalow is nevertheless a "famous" yardstick for the Canadian residential market and, at least in Quebec, the favoured dwelling of a very large number of residents.[2] Since heritage, like its shades of identity, is much more a matter of representation than an invocation of the material labelled as "heritage," it may be worthwhile – in the broader context of an exploration of contemporary modalities for building identity and in full awareness of today's "all-heritage" trend – to try to see how this object that is inherently modern, banal, and private might or might not deserve the exceptional and collective title of "heritage." In this regard, this chapter asserts that the Quebec bungalow, like the sacrosanct eighteenth-century "Canadian house" (sometimes called the "Quebec house"), is one of Quebec's most emblematic features. This can be demonstrated thanks to the Quebec bungalow's physical configurations and verified in the domain of the imagination, where the "Canadian house" prevails but where the bungalow instead produces a "counterrepresentation" (Figure 8.1).

We must therefore trace two parallel histories, the first being that of the bungalow in the imagination. This includes cultural, musical, theatrical, and cinematographic representations like *Deux femmes en or,* a film viewed by nearly one in three Quebecers in 1970, which tells the epic tale of two neighbours who fight the boredom of their daily lives (spent in bungalows) by seducing all sorts of repair and deliverymen; *Les voisins,* a satirical comedy that criticizes the artificiality of a Quebec society that inhabits and cherishes bungalows; *Le Québec moderne,* a documentary that uses bungalow-construction scenes to show the extent to which 1960s Quebec had lost its "true" values; *Une chaumière, un cœur,* the unfortunate story of a couple who purchase a bungalow and are cheated by its builder; and *Elvis Gratton,* a cult film about an average Quebecer depicted as a sort of happy idiot whose home is a bungalow, of course.

Figure 8.1 Dion family bungalow on Rue Bilodeau in Saint-Rédempteur, Lévis. The occupants of this South Shore Quebec City bungalow call it a "Canadian house" without any form of reference to the eighteenth-century house this name normally signifies. Confusion or lucid intuition? | Photograph by author.

Parallel to these representations is the history of the bungalow itself, which helps us to understand why and how it became "Quebecois"; this history is little known, which probably explains why – for lack of deeper exploration – it becomes secondary to the "other" history woven by the imagination and unrooted in any material considerations. Let us therefore begin with this history of the "bungalow itself"[3] and its highly characteristic and cliché representation in the imagery of "modern Quebec."

WHAT IS THIS BUNGALOW?

Although in Quebec the term "bungalow" designates the post–Second World War single-family suburban home, we should probably differentiate it more

Figure 8.2 The "bungalow" discovered in the colonies, here by Tintin. | Excerpt from Hergé (Georges Rémi), *Les cigares du pharaon,* 1st ed. (Tournai, Belgium: Casterman, 1934).

Figure 8.3 "Rêve d'Or" (Gold Dream) bungalow model by architect Antoine Ragot. | Published under the title "Bungalow, transposition du plain-pied français" in the French magazine *Vie à la Campagne* in 1928.

clearly from the "bungalow" found in the rest of the world (e.g., the Canadian Style Bungalow sold by Sonier LLC among its Log Home Kits).[4] "This house type," states John E. Traister, "has a long international history."[5] However, it is not certain that "bungalow" automatically refers to the same *type* of house, or even the same *idea,* at different times and in different places. Across the Atlantic, the word generally refers more or less to a vacation dwelling,[6] as its etymological root is apparently borrowed from *bangla* (in Hindi, "from Bengal," seventeenth century) or *bangollo* (in Bengali, "Bengal house," eighteenth century), which the British and Dutch discovered in their Indian colonies and were strongly associated with exoticism in the typical vacationer's imagination. Characterized first and foremost by its veranda (a word itself borrowed from Indian vocabulary), this picturesque house came to represent "the East" that Tintin discovered in 1934 under the pen of his Belgian creator Hergé (Figure 8.2),[7] as well as the "jungle where the mighty tiger lies" roamed by the Beatles' "Bungalow Bill" in 1968.[8] This is roughly the same bungalow found in *Maisons de campagne sans étage* and described in the French magazine *Vie à la campagne* in 1928 as a "charming single-storey house that is very livable and easy to maintain ... often built from wood, thereby simplifying and speeding construction" (Figure 8.3).[9]

Probably due to the common French view of wood construction as unreliable and not very durable, the term referred to the simple beach huts where bathers change clothing (Figure 8.4) – thus maintaining the association with vacationing. By and large – and to get back to its most common depiction – it is a "one-story house with veranda. Sometimes the attic is finished as a second story," states Anthony King in a highly exhaustive history that describes the *typical bungalow* as a mechanism of social distinction (as Marc Boyer describes resorts).[10] King indicates that this dwelling, although associated with suburban development, generally refers to a "vacation house" that is secondary to the main urban dwelling.[11] This explains why the public cottage built in 1915 in St. John's Bowring Park in Newfoundland, with its characteristic veranda, is called the Bowring Park Bungalow (Figure 8.5).

Having migrated through the Arts and Crafts style of Charles Greene and Henri Greene (Figure 8.6), a picturesque connotation of the bungalow also materialized, first in the large villas designed by the architect brothers at the turn of the twentieth century, then before and after the First World War in a variety of rich wood emulators that in recent years have caught the fancy of US readers of *American Bungalow* magazine – considered "one of the 50 best magazines" by the *Chicago Tribune* – or many "mainstream" publications and historic reprints, from *Bungalow Style* to *California Bungalows of the Twenties*.[12] Of course, these early models – with craftsman bungalows since that time often confused with the ranch house in certain typologies – were to be used much less for vacation purposes than to allow more people to live in an affordable house like the bungalow farmhouse. Peter Ward credits the British Columbia government with introducing this one-storey, 864-square-foot house with a front veranda on the short side of the rectangular plan to Canada in 1916 "based

Figure 8.4 (*right*) "Bungalows" in Douarnenez, Brittany. As elsewhere in France, these "bungalows" are fragile beach structures where bathers can change, in some sense bringing together the popular representation of a wooden structure (less durable than stone) and that of a vacation home. | Photograph by Luc Noppen.

Figure 8.5 (*facing page*) Bowring Park Bungalow shortly after its construction, St. John's. | Heritage Foundation of Newfoundland and Labrador.

on California prototypes developed at the turn of the century."[13] However, just like the "Bungalow Camps in the Canadian Pacific Rockies" – midway between settler and resort imagination (Figure 8.7) – that the Canadian Pacific Railway Company promoted in 1924,[14] they retained from their etymological origin a common aesthetic feature: a form of "artistic beauty and cozy convenience."[15] This feature was similarly credited in 1917 to William Coaker's "bungalow" in Port Union, Newfoundland, which was said to add "to the picturesque appearance of the settlement"[16] (Figure 8.8).

This structure bore no inherent relation either to the yardstick of the real estate market that the bungalow in Canada now *also* represents or to the "typical *no frills,* functional bungalow,"[17] described in a recent advertisement by a Quebec family wishing to trade their home.

This Quebec bungalow, more or less pejoratively called "Volksbungalow" in certain forums,[18] has considerably less to do with the bungalow of Tintin and other adventurers than with the post–Second World War era. As mentioned in

(Counterclockwise, from top left)

Figure 8.6 Gamble House, Pasadena, the "dream" bungalow in the United States, architects Charles Greene and Henri Greene, 1908. | Photograph by Luc Noppen.

Figure 8.7 "The Bungalow, Banff, Alberta," Department of Mines and Technical Surveys, 1902. | Photograph by J. Smith, Library and Archives Canada, PA-020464.

Figure 8.8 "The Bungalow," Port Union house of William Coaker, founder of Fisherman's Union Trading Company. | Photograph by Rhona Goodspeed, Historical Services Branch, Parks Canada, 1998.

the introduction to this chapter, they arose from efforts by the Central Mortgage and Housing Corporation to properly house Canadian families. In Montreal nearly 1,500 families lived in hangars or garages or shared an apartment at a time when the population was skyrocketing;[19] in Quebec, for example, the population doubled between 1941 and 1971. Yet these 3 million Quebec baby boomers and their parents shared the dream of a North America marked by the absence of urban culture, especially since most Quebecers had never known villages made of townhouses. For these spiritual heirs of Frank Lloyd Wright's Broadacre City – he proposed dividing US land equally in order to give each family a one-acre lot – the CMHC, drawing on the expertise of its predecessor, the Wartime Housing Corporation, began in 1947 to compile catalogues of

Figure 8.9 Central Mortgage and Housing Corporation, cover page of *Small House Designs: Bungalows*, c. 1955, one of the catalogues of plans "designed especially by Canadian architects for Canadian requirements."

inexpensive and easy-to-build single-family units (Figure 8.9). In the late 1940s the federal corporation – possibly inspired at the time by the Royal Institute of British Architects (RIBA) and the Small House Bureau of the United States[20] – gave these particularly popular single-storey *small houses* the name "bungalow."[21] What is more, the National Film Board had already used this name in 1944 to document certain productions by Loxtave Homes Prefabricated Buildings and the Wartime Housing Corporation in British Columbia:

> PREFABRICATED HOMES, VANCOUVER. Rome wasn't built in a day but that was probably because the Romans didn't have prefabricated houses like this four-room bungalow which was erected, painted, water and electricity connected, and lawns landscaped between 9:00 a.m. and 6:20 p.m. one day in an orchard in the Vancouver area. War workers Mr. and Mrs. Harry Kalek moved in at 6:30 p.m. the same day.[22]

Therefore, a major difference should exist between Tintin's bungalow and the Canadian bungalow due to the mass production – light years away from any idea of picturesque charm or distinctive exoticism – of the uniformity generally attributed to postwar North American suburbs, bungalow kingdoms that would be especially prolific in Quebec. From 1941 to 1971 Quebec's built territory occupied by dwellings doubled, as did the number of municipalities in just the fifteen years following the Second World War. Over a half-million new houses were built, each on its own lot. They certainly met the segregation requirements of the Athens Charter but were even more in line with the Anglo-Saxon ideal of individual/family development. This is one reason – but not the only one – why it may be dangerous to quickly conclude that these bungalows actually fit a serial, homogeneous, boring, "average" image – in short, that due to their conveyance of current cultural representations or even due to the use of pan-Canadian catalogues and models, all bungalows have multiple twins from coast to coast.

WHEN THE BUNGALOW MEETS QUEBEC'S CULTURAL TOPOGRAPHY: THE REBUILDING OF A COLLECTIVE MEMORY

Although it is certainly possible that the CMHC borrowed from the "original" bungalow only its noble name, perhaps inspired by the idea of a single-storey wood structure, this does not mean that the post–Second World War Quebec bungalow lacks the aesthetics or originality that elevated its "ancestor" into a work of art. It is true that it is often described generically, in functional terms – as in the catalogues – particularly by drawing a distinction between private spaces (the bedroom area) and public spaces (the living room area). A generic profile definitely seems to exist, namely the single-storey house that literally devours the yard by presenting its long side to the street rather than its short side.

Yet this profile already strays from the principles promoted by the CMHC, which at the time questioned the wisdom of presenting a model that was by and large not very cost-effective, at least in terms of land use, since it inherently required a lot that was wider than it was deep. However, this is "the house of the people" *(la maison du peuple)*, as it soon came to be called, that spread in Quebec. Despite its standardized origins, there quickly appeared an incredible number of variations as different from each other as the long-front bungalow prevalent in Quebec and the small-facade bungalow (as one might describe the more elongated structure with narrower frontage already adopted in 1916 by the British Columbia "bungalow farmhouse"),[23] apparently more common in the rest of Canada.[24]

Several authors have already indicated certain characteristics in Quebec that gave rise to these long-front bungalows, specifically with respect to the construction of these new houses in new suburbs. In particular, the structure of the residential housing market in Quebec is different from in the rest of Canada since "the supply of new house lots [in Quebec] is not in the hands of a few large firms and no substantial land banks have been identified," even in Montreal, where "housing ... is still provided by hundreds of small builders-entrepreneurs, as it was in other [Canadian] cities before ... the mid-fifties."[25] In Quebec in the days of Maurice Duplessis during the so-called Great Darkness,[26] the small municipalities that sprang up like weeds made it their practice to take charge of the development of new subdivisions, which were charged to municipal taxpayers, rather than to employ the developers of "corporate suburbs" and other new suburbs as in the rest of Canada. As unbridled competition arose between young Quebec municipalities due to the lack of a management framework or subsequent urban-planning regulations, this situation – which analysts believe earned Quebec the distinction of having the lowest-priced suburban lots in Canada[27] – was directly responsible for the popularization of the long-front bungalow and, consequently, the appearance of a "Quebec bungalow" with this profile: a house that has about forty feet of frontage and is twenty-five feet deep, which is often extended by a carport and features a kitchen/dining room, three bedrooms, and a recreation room in the basement.

Unlike promoters in the rest of Canada (not to say the Western world) who had to bear the cost of street systems in their developments, the Quebec municipalities that literally paved the way for the long-front bungalow were less concerned with the additional development costs arising from this "gluttonous" shape (which requires longer yards and streets) since the property taxes they received were calculated, as we know, according to frontage. But there is more: this situation in the municipalities, which was particularly favourable to residential construction, simultaneously kept alive a construction practice dating to before the war, even to previous centuries. Accordingly, skilled tradesmen, without the resources accumulated by developers of the time or the restrictions developers faced in paying for sewerage and waterlines, streets, and sidewalks in new neighborhoods, built home after home and financed each one with funds received on the previous sale. In Quebec these *contracteurs* (from the English "contractor") are generally distinguished from *entrepreneurs,* who assign and oversee development tasks, whereas "contractors" by trade often do their own work. These contractors joined with municipalities to host bungalow

Figure 8.10 Crowds at a "parade" of bungalows in Sainte-Foy, near Quebec City, in the early 1960s. | *Bâtiment*, December 1964, 34.

"parades" – part celebration, part exhibition – where, between truck processions and a cocktail reception hosted by the municipal government, hundreds of thousands of Quebecers and their children discovered these "houses of the people." Arms loaded with kites, comic strips, and other tantalizing freebies, they visited these bungalows like one visits a museum, according to articles of the time (Figure 8.10).

It is therefore not surprising that scientific literature and architects in particular still hold the bungalow in contempt. Apart from rarer yet remarkable "architect works," particularly in Modernism-friendly regions like the Saguenay, the Quebec bungalow escapes the theatre of architecture, whose key players do not hesitate to lament, "Even if we could and wanted to, we wouldn't try to create a work of art or, in any case, an original work, since we don't know who would buy it."[28] "It is instead the builder," adds an urban planner in 1963,

> who takes the initiative to build a certain number of single-family or rental homes in large subdivisions and then sells them using techniques like model homes, monster ad campaigns, and elaborate grand openings with political and religious figures. Since a certain degree of product standardization is required for production efficiency, builders try to make their product stand out by creating an artificial market with as English-sounding a pretentious name as possible, generally featuring a coat of arms or symbols clients value, i.e., "City of Dreams," "St-Eiderdown, the Green Suburb," etc.[29]

Possibly starting with some plan by some architect that became a stock model in CMHC catalogues, the bungalow – by becoming the "house of the people," as it was called at the time – entered the world of contractor know-how and local vernacular that made it distinctively Quebecois and gave rise to a wide variety of expressions.

For contractors, the "product standardization" criticized by some architects and urban planners cannot be reduced to factory-built half-houses and other prefabricated creations that began invading the Canadian market. Instead, standardized *materials* – the 2-by-4-inch studs, 4-by-8-feet panels, and other pieces typical of wood-frame construction – gave rise to each successive "easy-to-build" bungalow (*"d'érection facile,"* as they were sometimes described) because they enabled builders to assemble two walls and determine the dimensions of an opening without a plan. Yet these "meccano houses" allowed tradesmen to freely transpose their inner vernacular architectural history, as seen, for example, in *pièce-sur-pièce* bungalows.[30] More in-depth research (an issue further discussed below) would certainly uncover other remaining regional or local building traditions. Probably for this reason, the well-known *Dictionnaire Visuel*, by Montreal publisher Québec-Amérique, illustrates the building of a house with a diagram of a cross-braced floor in which the joists are spaced not using simple separators but with *croix de Saint-André* bridging that clearly speaks of the ancestral art of roof framing, recycled here by a tradesman in a so-called "cost-efficient" bungalow but without forsaking *"le bel ouvrage."*

Through the figure and character of the contractor, the bungalow transformed Quebec's built landscape house by house. The massive popularization of the model, supported by the standardization of North American materials that facilitated assembly without a plan but rather "as built," led to diversification – the opposite of the banalization that the bungalow's rapid proliferation led some to imagine.

WHEN AND HOW STANDARDIZATION PRODUCES DIVERSITY (AND MEMORY)

> That's one heck of nice place you got yourself there! I was comin' down the street and watchin' and almost all the houses were the same. Must be confusing at first, but you get used to it. And you're close to everything! I really, really like it. I like how it's not the country, but it's not the city either, and still, it's really nice.
>
> – Yvon Deschamps praising the bungalow in the film *Deux femmes en or*, my translation

The uniformity ascribed to bungalow suburbs seems to arise more from the imagination than from reality. In this regard, it should be noted that in North

America and particularly Quebec standardization was already known to support construction of multiple inexpensive dwellings. By 1926 in the industrial town of Arvida (the ancestor of Kitimat, British Columbia, born at about the same time as the Quebec bungalow), the Aluminum Company of America developed sixty different models for the 270 houses it built for its workers.[31] This type of response to the quest for individuality of the idealized home of Wright's Broadacre City, renewed and popularized in postwar-era Levitt Towns, was based on a simple principle: wood rather than concrete construction, for example, enabled the production of many architectural variations by swapping or inverting a limited number of components – windows, doors, cornices, and so on. This being the case, the standardization of materials beginning in the 1940s led the way to a multitude of variations and more personalized models than ever before.

A product of this standardization, the bungalow is eminently flexible. The "repetition of some models" set off a chain of events: suburban municipalities wished to attract residents, residents wanted the option of personalizing their environment, and contractors wanted to sell their bungalows. Consequently, "parades" showcasing enticingly novel bungalows were held, and little by little, with each event and family outing, bungalows were etched into the imagination of Quebecers as modern, distinctive dwellings. But to be distinctive, they had to be distinguishable; "modernity" became a symbol of "appropriation."

The Quebec bungalow took a position midway between the know-how of new owners and that of contractors, who built on each owner's desire for personalization. Quebecers were also in the habit of appropriation; in an environment woven from vernacular architecture after the Second World War, many had lived in temporary Wartime Housing Corporation dwellings that they had to move, set on foundations, or expand, such as by adding a floor. In a recently urbanized society still close to its farming roots,[32] "do it yourself" was such a deeply rooted habit that contractors often delivered "unfinished" bungalows.

Landscaping, particularly of the backyard – an "unfinished" showplace free of regulatory constraints – demonstrates the predilection for personalization that seized hold of the bungalow. Although winter prevented its use except for two or three months a year, hundreds of "family chores" still mark the memory of Quebecers who put time and energy into landscaping, lawns, fountains, flowerbeds, and "patios."[33] Of course, this effort is not exclusive to Quebecers or the bungalow, but the popular rumour since that time – that Quebec is the kingdom of the "above-ground pool" – eloquently testifies to the symbolic nature of the (bungalow) backyard in the Quebec perception of property and suburbs.

Figure 8.11 Bungalow model and variants (different coverings, with or without carport), Rue Toronto, Sainte-Foy. | Photographs by author and *L'appel*, 14 September 1961.

The standardization of materials that enabled the popularization and personalization of bungalows – and, consequently, their "Quebecization" – had an even greater impact on the architectural configuration of the house itself: plywood, shingles, and aluminum soon provided dozens of possible bungalow designs and as many different coverings. In a line-up of apparently homogeneous bungalows, an insertion was added during construction to one, and the placement angle was varied on another. A single model would therefore generate three, five, or ten variants (Figure 8.11). Then personalization spread to the interior: "ultrawall," "fiesta," "arborite," "masonite," and "formica" covered *"salles de lavage,"* children's bedrooms, and living rooms that could be modified to taste (Figure 8.12).

Admittedly, this breakdown of formal references, just like the "bathroom revolution" announced in 1963,[34] is part of the North American commercial environment – or even a universal modernity; it is not specific to Quebec. However, since it is tied to appropriation in Quebec, modernization of the interior focuses on use: don't Quebecers who are eager to personalize their backyards spend three-quarters of the year *inside* their bungalows?

In somewhat the same way as tradition superimposed itself on bungalow construction and its cross-braced floor, the proximity relationship between *one* contractor and *one* owner (rather than between one developer and two hundred buyers) brought local customs into the spatial organization of the Quebec bungalow. As the domain of the "queen of the household," to whom baby-boomer homes were supposedly dedicated,[35] the kitchen was the main catalyst of this "Quebecization" (Figure 8.13).

Thanks to the bungalow's malleability, the traditional space of old homes and small "settlement houses" was reworked: the "family room" transformed the kitchen. It is significant that whereas "family room" designated the main living area in 1950s and 1960s Canadian and US English-language publications, "family room" in Quebec automatically meant the kitchen (Figure 8.14). It should be noted that this penetration of tradition into the bungalow was combined with a desire at that time to see Quebec women return to the home that they had left during the war.[36] The kitchen/family room represented the bungalow's offering to the good Catholic homemakers of French Canada.

With even less industry support than for bathrooms, for example, Quebec contractors competed to create a multitude of creative combinations of materials and colours in the "favorite room of the French Canadian family."[37] The kitchen soon became the focal point of the Quebec bungalow at the risk of overshadowing the rest of the house.[38] It was therefore hardly surprising that most

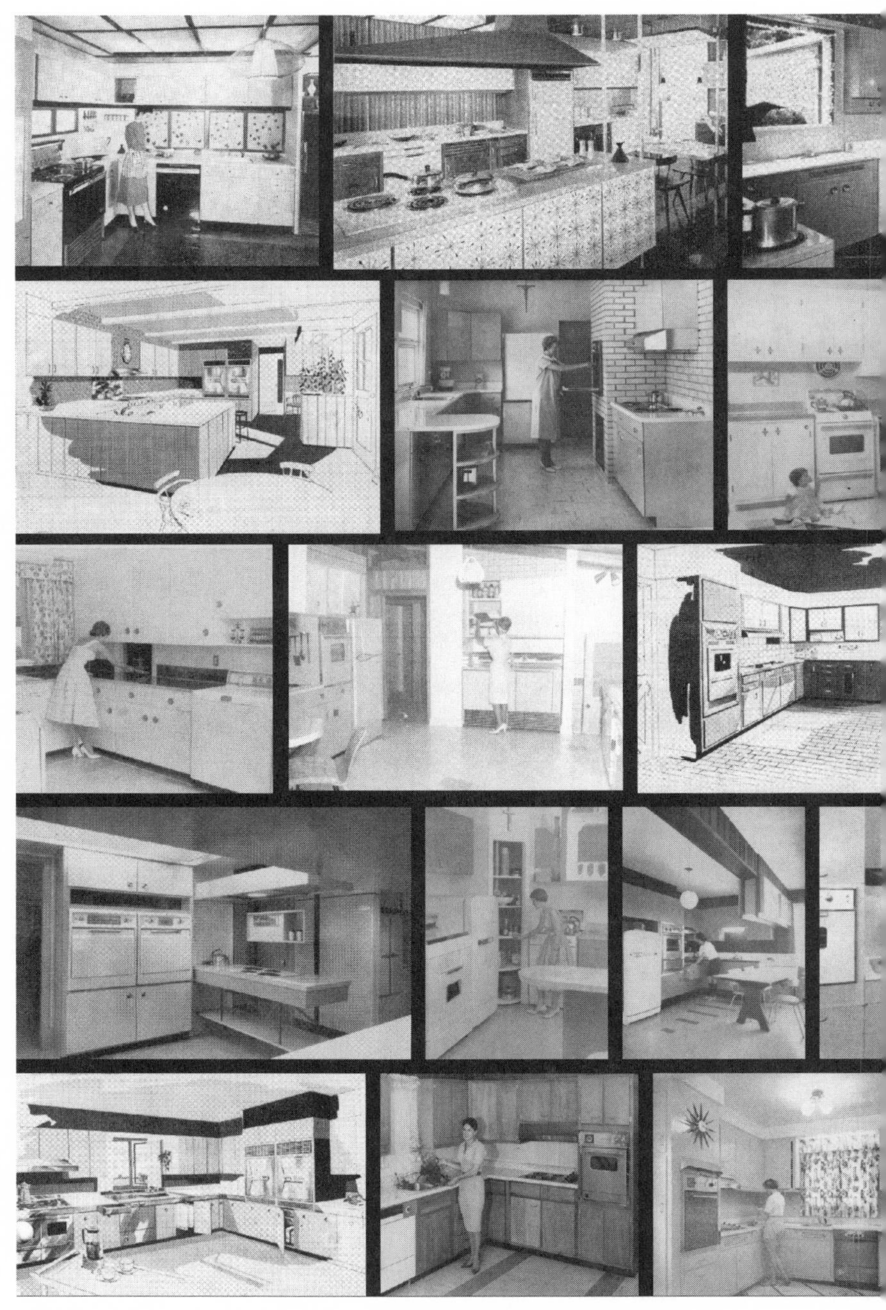

Figure 8.12 Photomontage of bungalow images published in the 1950s and 1960s (repeats are exclusively kitchens). | Published in the magazine *Bâtiment*.

Figure 8.13 The "new homemaker" in her bungalow, featured in a plywood ad describing an "outsider's" perspective of "our" bungalow: "Carla Maria Valez is a new Canadian ... ravishing ... sophisticated ... beaming ... radiant." | Published in *Bâtiment*, October 1963, 22, my translation.

Figure 8.14 Family room of the French Canadian home enshrined in the kitchen of the Quebec bungalow. | Photograph by Office du film du Québec, Bibliothéque et Archives nationales du Québec, E6,S7,P7141768.

1950s kitchens were renovated in the 1960s, once people had a knack for redoing them *"à la québécoise."*

From diversification to personalization, the bungalow became increasingly Quebecois in nature.

EASY TO BUILD, EASY TO REMODEL: FROM ADAPTATION TO "QUEBECIZATION"

Central to daily life in Quebec, the bungalow's many transformations could fuel conversations – as evidenced by a number of films and plays, some satirical, from the 1960s to the 1980s.[39] As easy to build as it was to change, the bungalow increasingly penetrated the Quebec landscape and imagination while, conversely, Quebec producers, materials, and needs converged in the bungalow. Beyond the kitchen – called the "soul of the home"[40] – two particular spaces began to be personalized: the carport and the basement.

In the 1960s the carport became the bungalow's forced companion as its contribution to the automobile, without which neither the suburbs nor the elongated long-front bungalow (nor the interminable suburban streets that this shape generated) would have arisen. In Quebec, however, something special occurred. As the winters passed, the carport gradually shifted the house's front entrance to the side, off the kitchen – the centre of the Quebec bungalow. The main entrance therefore fell into disuse. The predominance the side entrance acquired is certainly not limited to the Quebec bungalow, as it may be observed in a number of Canadian regions, particularly smaller communities whose proximity relationships also evoke the original suburbs of the Quebec bungalow – where it is well known that anyone who approaches via the "main" door is a stranger.

However, in Quebec it was even easier to stop using this main door – which became buried under the snow during the long winter months – when the vestibule was removed to give space to the living room, reduced to its simplest expression to make way for the larger kitchen/family room. Then access to the basement – from the inside of traditional homes due to the winter – was moved near the now main entrance in the kitchen, where the "homemaker" could supervise the backyard, go about her daily chores, and observe household comings and goings.

Carports became so popular that most first-generation bungalows were lengthened with this new appendage. But the evolution did not stop there: perhaps partially due to the climate, people also began closing off all these carports (Figure 8.15), which were originally simplified garages, turning them "back," so to speak, into garages but now also a space dedicated to fatherly pursuits. The garage was the masculine counterpart to the family room in a matriarchal society. Cars were sent outside, and furnished garages equipped with workbenches, barbecues, musical instruments, weights, and refrigerators have since continued to increase. Again, of course, this use of the suburban garage is common throughout North America.[41] However, the mess that seems to characterize the Quebec bungalow garage (more than any activity it is used for)[42] may have something to do with the memory of the "Quebec do-it-yourselfer" who channelled the self-sufficiency once rooted in the land into the habit of working on his bungalow.

While carports and then garages further "Quebecized" the bungalow, the basement stairs that carports polarized took on new importance. The basement *(sous-sol),* even more than the carport, became the archetypal space of

Figure 8.15 Bungalows with open carport or garage conversion, Sainte-Foy. | Photographs by author.

the Quebec bungalow for a number of reasons. On the one hand, Quebecers' habit of building deep foundations (below the frost line) and storing furnaces and fuel in this underground space gave the household additional room with the introduction of smaller heating devices; Quebec's nationalization of hydroelectricity in 1963 probably sped the "liberation" of the basement. On the other hand, contractors took an increasing interest in the basement, certainly because indoor work helped to stabilize their jobs during the winter but also because the unregulated Quebec market – although it permitted their existence and ensured their survival – was dangerously close to saturation by the early 1960s. Basement finishing and renovation became the leitmotiv of Quebec owners and contractors as the *chambre de bonne* (au pair suite), game rooms, sewing rooms, ping-pong rooms, bars, and discos once again proved the bungalow's infinite adaptability.[43] Few Quebecers do not still remember fondly an intimate evening, a special meeting, the freedom they experienced in basements. A participant in the documentary *Éloge du bungalow* revealed, not without humour, "I lived my entire life in a basement. And I'm still in a basement. Everything happens in the basement. And when you got here, I was in the basement. Cleaning the basement."[44] Those who spent much of their teenage years in the basement might tell us, "I thought the basement was the centre of the world."

It should be noted that in addition to architectural models and habits that added value to the bungalow, the "Parent Report," released in 1964, suddenly reformed the Quebec education system by abolishing boarding schools, concentrating institutions of higher education in cities, and moving high schools into the suburbs.[45] This occurred at a time when "everyone," according to contractor magazine *Bâtiment,* "was clamouring for a finished basement"[46] (e.g., to accommodate a student from a remote region). A new entryway was then added to the bungalow near the entrance to the garage or carport. Or the garage was simply converted into a student apartment.

As the basement became somewhat of a seasonal replacement for the backyard, the residual storage space of the "unfinished" basement disappeared. What, then, could homeowners do with large appliances, mowers, gardening implements, and pool maintenance equipment that in summer brought the activity of the Quebec household into the backyard? The answer was the *cabanon,* or shed, a Quebec backyard essential, as evidenced by its many laudatory and satirical representations from *Bâtiment* magazine to the film *Elvis Gratton* and, even more typically, in Quebec advertising, notably by IKEA. For the grand opening of a new store in Montreal's southern suburbs in March 2003, the famous Swedish chain ran a special contest in which competitors were invited to live in "my hut at IKEA," a cabanon made inhabitable thanks to IKEA furniture and the design efforts of a group of young guest artists (Figure 8.16).

Figure 8.16 "My hut at IKEA," interior design of a shed made "inhabitable," Antoine Laverdière, 2003. | Photographs by Antoine Laverdière.

HIDE THIS BUNGALOW THAT I OUGHT NOT SEE

> Mais c'est la France! Quoi, Français, nous renversons
> Ce qui reste debout sur les noirs horizons?
>
> –Victor Hugo, "Les Deux Trophées"

These are not the words of some Quebecer regarding the bungalow, of course, but of Victor Hugo regarding what we could now call the "political aspects" of heritage long, long ago when the Communards threatened to do away with the Arc de Triomphe and Vendôme column. Yet the sentiment applies today: the monumental, now eminently Quebecois bungalow is advertised online as a "typical no frills, functional bungalow"[47] in an apparent attempt to close a sale by neutralizing the imagination with insult.

However, between 1951 and 1961, 1.2 million Quebecers – more than one out of five – turned fourteen. Practically anyone who grew up or got married in Quebec still has memories of being a child, teenager, or new parent in a bungalow garage, family room, or basement. And with the "bungalow do-it-yourself" habit ingrained in all these Quebecers, the bungalow took on many faces over the course of ten or twenty years. Notwithstanding its reputation for uniformity, we no longer find bungalows that resemble other bungalows; rather than the bungalow's form, it is instead the image deeply etched in Quebec's collective memory that produces today's generic image and the sense that all bungalows are the same. That some Quebecers call their bungalow a "Canadian house"[48] (Figure 8.1) – a designation specific to the vernacular eighteenth-century house – shows that the bungalow is part of Quebec's landscape and customs. Through the bungalow, construction practices and housing remained distinctively Quebecois after the Second World War as they were recycled into a new and local architectural form. In the twentieth century, the bungalow became the equivalent of the famous eighteenth-century "Canadian house." But the bungalow now occupies a significantly larger portion of the built landscape.

It is therefore worthwhile to revisit accusations that have been made against this archetypal figure. Elevated into a symbolic "house of the people" in 1960s advertisements,[49] the bungalow has since been associated by some scholars with a form of materialism that should be combated or with a decline in the environment or even Quebec society. Disregarding the common lawn/pesticide association that ecologists attach to its beloved landscaping, the bungalow would seem to illustrate – or be – the "problem of the Quebec left":

> I grew up in a family that could be compared to the typical "settler." Suburban bungalow, television constantly on, poor diet. I saw lawn tractor races in the street in front of my house each summer. Men were constantly washing their cars on their asphalt driveways while the neighborhood slowly deadened their minds in front of the cathode screen of shame. I continually faced these experiences that discouraged me.[50]

In Ontario, Valerie J. Korinek recently pondered the odd defect that seems to afflict the suburban built landscape; apparently, in Quebec bungalows "parents fear for the safety of their loved ones,"[51] and a doctor was killed in a bungalow that was inevitably "poorly decorated."[52] "What does it mean," writes Korinek, "if fiction stories highlight traumas and conflicts within the suburban bungalow, rather than the joys of marital bliss?"[53] It is true that in the rest of Canada, as in Quebec, the bungalow's pervasiveness – whatever the home's actual form – works against it: once built in the outskirts where people are now demanding densification, this model of contemptible rurbanization is incurring the wrath of modernization. A result of its economical construction, the bungalow's limited life expectancy – the term of its twenty-year mortgage – adds to the imminence of a new cycle of the sort of perpetual transformations it has brought upon itself; current interest in the bungalow is aimed only at making it *something other* than a bungalow.[54]

Apart from the environmental or social objectives now spurring the bungalow's transformation and eventual disappearance, and beyond the avant-garde perspective of the suburbs and rurbanization – which probably includes the Canadian "anti-bungalow" syndrome described by Korinek – there seems to be more to the "Quebec bungalow" both in its distinctive features and in the imagination, which too often holds it in contempt. More than the setting of a happy or unhappy story, the bungalow in Quebec has become a symbol of "what not to be" contained entirely in its name alone. Whereas elsewhere in the world the word "bungalow" still evokes a form of exoticism, in Quebec folk songs, including "En berne" by Les Cowboys fringants (2002), it is used to denounce the mindlessness of contemporary Quebec society:

> J'suis né dans les années 1970
> Dans un Québec en plein changement
> Où l'emblème de la fleur de lys
> Donnait un peu d'espoir aux gens
> Mais quand je r'garde ça aujourd'hui
> J'suis donc pas fier de ma patrie

Ça dort au gaz dans les bungalows
Le cul assis sur'l'*statu quo*[55]

Worse than banal, the bungalow thus appears evil; the low materialism it represents contrasts with "high" materialism or the veneration of the sacrosanct eighteenth-century "Canadian house" and the "ancestral way of life" of this house with a "French spirit."[56] Representations of the bungalow in Quebec are clear in this regard: the symptom of a "quiet defeat"[57] and the result of a family sacrifice,[58] the bungalow is modern, hence American. Consequently, bungalows exist in Quebec "because you gotta hand it to those Americans,"[59] in the words of Elvis Gratton, cult character of the film by the same name.

The image replaces the object, and for lack of a more sophisticated characterization that would reveal its secrets – since the one attempted here generally concerns only the bungalow of the Quebec City area – the little twentieth-century "Quebec house" is buried under an exogenous interpretation. The following description, for example, is often attached to the Canadian bungalow: "While this house type has a long international history, the Canadian version was based on California prototypes developed at the turn of the century."[60] Although certainly valid in other cases, the sentence is still final and without appeal in Quebec: not only is the bungalow not *old,* but worse it *is American.* "It is the worst example of doing our best to copy what they were doing in the United States," pronounced the president of Conseil des monuments et sites du Québec on the issue.[61] The neglected Quebec bungalow is up against the wall of identity more than the melting pot of modernity. Although archetypal, the bungalow does not fit the image of a unique Quebec defined by its "distinct identity."

The current "elevated bungalow" trend could be explained as follows: to avoid being "American," homes are being built "French style," "Italian style," or another "style of the week" extolled by the various dailies.[62] Instead of a landscape of bungalows that is believed to be standardized and uniform but that, in the end, gave rise to a varied environment closely woven into Quebec culture, we find a growing number of these "fashionable cottages" that immediately or ultimately claim diversity, from turrets to roof crests. But these "cottages," delivered "finished," including landscaping, oddly give rise to a perfectly homogeneous landscape resistant to personalization, in accordance with the increasing requirements of overall planned development and urban regulations (Figure 8.17).

Four out of five new homes built in Quebec in the 1950s and 1960s were "bungalows." We can therefore understand today that their presence in the collective memory is increasing as their total number and physical presence in the

Figure 8.17 The future? "Elevated" bungalow in Ancienne-Lorette, 2003. | Photograph by author.

built landscape dwindles. Could the bungalow, threatened with extinction, join the body of heritage established several centuries ago by virtue of our "Christian religion of traces"?[63] Probably not. In the imaginary world of heritage – built, as we know, on the sum of our representations, which are filtered by a few qualified and institutionalized "values" regarding age, art, use, materiality, and position – there is a conflict between what is exceptional and what is "genuinely" vernacular.[64] In other words, beyond the identity constraints that banish it to the collective imagination of early-twenty-first-century Quebecers, the Quebec bungalow – without the "age value" that would probably save it through the appearance of oldness or a sampling effect – seems bound to disappear in the very multitude of its pervasive expressions. All bear witness to an era, which certainly gives them an "age," whether respectable or not. Some reflect now bygone Quebec household customs; others reveal the "craftsmanship" of a contractor in a *croix de Saint-André* here, a *pièce-sur-pièce* wall there; still others feature gleaming arborite and other modern materials. In short, one or all bungalows could be ascribed any number of the "heritage values" that have led the Western institution to identify monuments since the nineteenth century. Yet isolating one of them for all these reasons – if that were even possible, since the bungalow archetype contrasts with the appropriation that defines it (and distorts it over time) – would erect an insignificant monument.

The conflict between exceptional and genuinely vernacular ("genuinely" because it remains to this day the continuously appropriated Volksbungalow) mentioned above lifts the veil, as a backdrop to the bungalow, on a deeper antithesis between the expertise from above that identified heritage and the "historic monument," particularly in the twentieth century, and the representations of the "people" who, from below, are fond of "their" bungalow, "their" property, and the melting pot of "their" memories.[65] There is therefore a contrast between the old "experts' heritage" and today's "proximity heritage." Furthermore, the bungalow, as heritage, is less a generally ascribed "state that exists" than a state of becoming, a future in gestation that is nearer to the definition of heritage (that which is passed down or projected in the future) than are current practices of relative museumification. In the end, the Quebec bungalow probably illustrates the boundaries of heritage, at least the notion of heritage we have developed for the purpose of "protection." As the cradle of modernity and a disregarded showcase of identity, will the Quebec bungalow go so far as to overturn our idea of heritage?

NOTES

1 Louise Brunelle-Lavoie, in Danielle Pigeon, dir., *Éloge du bungalow,* documentary (Productions Virage, 2003), my translation.

2 *Le Soleil* (Quebec City), 20 October 1988, A11, featuring the results of a survey conducted jointly by Société d'habitation du Québec and Association provinciale des constructeurs d'habitations du Québec.

3 In the interest of conciseness, however, this chapter summarizes this history that is "material" to that of the bungalow of the Quebec City area and eastern Quebec, particularly because – in the absence of a massive densification of the outskirts – it remained faithful longer to the original 1940s and 1950s design. In the Montreal area – which remains to be studied in this regard – the bungalow seems to have appeared as, or has more rapidly become, a "split-level" dwelling; the long-front bungalow nevertheless remains sufficiently representative of the Quebec bungalow, both to be "imitated" by many split-levels and used in films, plays, and other melting pots of collective memory.

For a more detailed history of the evolution of this physical configuration and the appearance of the bungalow at that particular time in Quebec, which is touched on here, see Lucie K. Morisset and Luc Noppen, "Le bungalow québécois, monument vernaculaire: De l'espace urbain à l'identité domestique," *Cahiers de géographie du Québec* 48, 134 (September 2004): 127-54; and Lucie K. Morisset and Luc Noppen, "Le bungalow québécois, monument vernaculaire: La naissance d'un nouveau type," *Cahiers de géographie du Québec* 48, 133 (April 2004): 7-32. I mention the history of the bungalow from another angle in Lucie K. Morisset, "Du banal au local: *Carport,* piscine hors-terre et sous-sol fini – Le bungalow québécois," in *Construire dans la diversité,* ed. Daniel Le Couédic and Jean-François Simon, 85-98 (Rennes, France: Presses universitaires de Rennes, 2005).

4 "La Belle Maison Shows That New Log Homes Have It All," *Franklin Focus,* June 2005, 16.

5 John E. Traister, *Illustrated Dictionary for Building Construction* (Lilburn, GA: Fairmont, 1993).

6 Although the Oxford Dictionary defines it as a one-storey house, this *idea* of the bungalow is the most common, as described by Anthony King, *The Bungalow: The Production of a Global Culture* (Oxford: Oxford University Press, 1995).

7 Hergé (Georges Rémi), *Les cigares du pharaon,* 1st ed. (Tournai, Belgium: Casterman, 1934). A colour edition appeared in 1955, and the first English translation was published in 1971.

8 The Beatles, "The Continuing Story of Bungalow Bill," *The White Album,* 1968.

9 Georges-Benoît Lévy, *Maisons de campagne sans étage et bungalows* (Paris: n.p., [19??]); "Du plain-pied traditionnel au bungalow moderne," *Vie à la campagne,* 15 August 1928, my translation.

10 King, *Bungalow;* Marc Boyer, *Histoire générale du tourisme: Du XVIe au XXIe siècle* (Paris: L'Harmattan, 2005).

11 King, *Bungalow,* 259.

12 *Chicago Tribune,* quoted at the very comprehensive website of *American Bungalow,* published "in the interest of preserving and restoring the modest American 20th century home, the Bungalow, and the rich lifestyle that it affords," http://www.ambungalow.com/AmBungalow/home.htm; April Halberstadt, *Bungalow Style* (New York: Friedman/Fairfax, 2000); Henry L. Wilson, *California Bungalows of the Twenties* (New York: Dover, 1993).

13 Peter Ward, *A History of Domestic Space: Privacy and the Canadian Home* (Vancouver: UBC Press, 1999), 38.

14 In a promotional brochure written by Betty Thornley.

15 Henry L. Wilson, *The Bungalow Book: A Short Sketch of the Evolution of the Bungalow from Its Primitive Crudeness to Its Present State of Artistic Beauty and Cozy Convenience* (Los Angeles: H.L. Wilson, 1908).

16 J.H. Scammell, "Port Union: Observation and Description," *Evening Advocate,* 22 December 1917, http://www.ucs.mun.ca/~melbaker/scammellpu.html.

17 http://www3.sympatico.ca/annie.morey/public/quebec.html, consulted 4 January 2006, emphasis added.

18 http://carnets.ixmedia.com/magellan/archives/003930.html, consulted 28 December 2005.

19 On the use of hangars or garages, see, for example, Marc Choko, Jean-Pierre Collin, and Annick Germain, "Le logement et les enjeux de la transformation de l'espace urbain: Montréal, 1940-1960," *Revue d'histoire urbaine/Urban History Review* 15, 2 (October 1986): 128.

20 In 1932 and again in 1934, RIBA fellow Frederick Chatterton published a catalogue entitled *Small Houses and Bungalows* (London: Architectural Press); in 1937, apparently in the same post-Depression context (following the stock market crash of 1929), the Architect's Small House Service Bureau of the United States published *Bungalows: Seventy-Three Small Homes, Bungalows, and Story-and-a-Half Homes* (Minneapolis).

21 Central Mortgage and Housing Corporation, *Small House Designs: Bungalows* (Ottawa: CMHC, 1949).

22 Photo report by the National Film Board, Vancouver, May 1944, Library and Archives Canada, acc. 1971-271.

23 See Ward, *History of Domestic Space,* 41. This rectangular-plan house had its facade on the shorter side of the rectangle and also had the sacrosanct veranda common to vacation homes (which did not become popular in Quebec as such until second-generation bungalows, namely those that adopted regionalist and neo-Canadian features).

24 In some respects, this model was recently reintroduced by Sonier LLC, whose Log Home Kits include a "Canadian Style Bungalow": a 24-by-36-foot (864-square-foot), one-storey house with a central facade entrance opening into a vestibule and a Palladian plan divided roughly symmetrically into four equally sized rooms (two bedrooms, a kitchen/dining room, and a living room). See "La Belle Maison Shows That New Log Homes Have It All," *Franklin Focus,* June 2005, 16.

25 James Lorimer and Evelyn Ross, eds., *The Second City Book: Studies of Urban and Suburban Canada* (Toronto: James Lorimer, 1977), 57-61, 28.

Regarding this development context and for further references, see the two-part article by Lucie K. Morisset and Luc Noppen cited at note 3, in which the history of the bungalow that is suggested here was first explored.

26 Maurice Le Noblet Duplessis (1890-1959) was the Union Nationale party leader and Quebec premier from 1936 to 1939 and from 1944 until his death in 1959. Most historians refer to this period of Quebec history marked by conservatism and a reification of so-called traditional values, rurality, and Catholicism as the Great Darkness (Grande Noirceur), which some do not hesitate to liken to a form of fascism. As regards the issues of interest to us here, the Great Darkness was also marked by various manifestations of nepotism that delayed the establishment of a legislative framework for regulating urban growth.

27 Researchers also emphasize that the high price of suburban lots continued outside Quebec, throughout Canada, where developer oligopolies were rampant, but to a lesser degree in Halifax and Saskatoon due to the impact of public-land reserves on these markets; see Lorimer and Ross, eds., *Second City Book,* 120. It would be worth looking at the actual predominance of long-front bungalows in these cities, where they seem at first glance to be more common than in the rest of Canada. This would, in turn, support my explanation of the situation in Quebec.

28 "Le point de vue de l'architecte M. Edgar Tornay," *Bâtiment,* March 1969, 32, my translation.

29 Claude Langlois, "La bonne maison au bon prix au bon endroit?" *Bâtiment,* December 1963, 35, my translation.

30 Sometimes called in English "log construction," "pièce-sur-pièce," which is described as "a variant of frame construction" by Linda Haud, refers to walls made of beams one on top of the other. See Linda Haud, "Pièce-Sur-Pièce Construction," *Historians, Preliminary Architectural Studies,* vol. 1, unpublished report HG 02, Louisbourg, 1972, http://fortress.uccb.ns.ca/search/HG020104.htm.

31 See Lucie K. Morisset, *Arvida, cité industrielle: Une épopée urbaine en Amérique* (Quebec: Septentrion, 1998), 251.

32 Paul-André Linteau and colleagues note that the urbanization rate of the Quebec population rose from 61.2 percent in 1941 to 74.3 percent in 1961; it was only 36 percent in 1901 and 51.8 percent in 1921. See Paul-André Linteau, René Durocher, Jean-Claude Robert, and François Ricard, *Histoire du Québec contemporain,* vol. 2, *Le Québec depuis 1930* (Montreal: Boréal, 1989), 55, 275; and Paul-André Linteau, René Durocher, and Jean-Claude Robert, *Histoire du Québec contemporain,* vol. 1, *De la Confédération à la Crise* (Montreal: Boréal, 1989), 470.

33 Originally designating an inner courtyard, "patio" in Quebec generally refers to a finished (e.g., paved) space in the yard that is often adjacent to the house and may include the "barbecue" of the famous "bungalow, above-ground pool, barbecue" trio cited recently by François Cardinal, "Bungalow + piscine hors terre + barbecue = banlieue: La mutation de Bungalowpolis," *Le Devoir* (Montreal), 14 and 15 September 2002, my translation.

34 "Nouvel élément-clé dans la vente des maisons ... Les salles de bains," *Bâtiment,* September 1963, 28-32.

35 A host of articles and features sing the praises of the "stairless" bungalow, which is supposedly "less tiring" for "homemakers." See Central Mortgage and Housing Corporation, *Choosing a House Design* (1960).

36 See in particular Louise Fradet, "Femmes, cuisines et consommation de masse au Québec, 1945-1960" (MA thesis, Université Laval, 1989), 34-36.

37 "Pourquoi la cuisine est un outil précieux pour vendre votre maison," *Bâtiment-Génie-Construction,* August 1957, 24-29.

38 Apart from so-called "women's" publications, few North American magazines have discussed kitchens as much as the virile *Bâtiment* for Quebec builders.

39 Take, for example, this lighthearted banter on renovations from the film *Les voisins,* directed by Micheline Guertin, Claude Meunier, and Louis Saïa (Montreal: Radio-Québec, 1987), my translation, based on the hit play by the same name:

"Have you put in your basement washroom yet?"
"Not yet, but don't mention it to Janine, it's supposed to be her present."
"Didya move the living room?"
"Sure did. It used to be where the dining room is."
"Oh! It's beautiful. You'd swear it's not the same place [...]"
"I didn't tell you, either, I totally redid my kitchen [...]"
"Oh! It must be pretty!"
"We innovated [*sic*] Susie's room too. And look here, I put wallpaper on the stove wall. Makes it look like a real proper kitchen."
"I know what you mean. You had just the perfect wall for wallpaper, I can tell!"

40 "Une décoratrice de renom démontre que la cuisine est l'âme de la maison," *Bâtiment,* September 1960, 67.
41 For example, an important portion of the film *American Beauty,* directed by Sam Mendes (1999), takes place in a garage in the suburbs.
42 See, for example, Pierre Falardeau, dir., *Elvis Gratton* (Lions Gate, 1985).
43 "Un énorme marché s'ouvre aux constructeurs: Finition et rénovation de sous-sols," *Bâtiment,* December 1963, 26-27.
44 Pigeon, dir., *Éloge du bungalow,* my translation.
45 Government of Quebec, *Report by the Royal Commission of Inquiry on Education in the Province of Quebec* (1964).
46 "Un énorme marché s'ouvre aux constructeurs," 26, my translation.
47 http://www3.sympatico.ca/annie.morey/public/quebec.html, consulted 1 February 2006.
48 Stéphanie Dion, the occupant of a bungalow on Rue Bilodeau, Saint-Rédempteur, Quebec, interview by author, 19 June 2003.
49 *Le Soleil* (Quebec City), 1 October 1955.
50 Marie-Noëlle Clermont, "Le problème de la gauche au Québec," *Le Devoir* (Montreal), 9 August 2002, my translation.
51 "The ill are sent to foster families in suburban *bungalows,* into the hands of people who have neither the necessary training nor the resources." Isabelle Paré, "Des parents craignent pour la sécurité de leurs proches," *Le Devoir* (Montreal), 1 and 2 March 2003.
52 A new sound stage is described as being in "an enormous, unoccupied, and poorly decorated *bungalow* that belonged to a former doctor who was killed there ten years earlier. You don't make up stories like that" (my translation). Paul Cauchon, "Victoriaville sur l'acide," *Le Devoir* (Montreal), 10 and 11 May 2003.
53 Valerie J. Korinek, *Roughing It in the Suburbs* (Toronto: University of Toronto Press, 2000), 26.
54 See, for example, Andrée Fortin, Carole Després, and Geneviève Vachon, eds., *La banlieue revisitée* (Quebec: Nota Bene, 2002). This work, as well as the research on which it is based, looks at the bungalow's transformation vis-à-vis the needs of an aging suburban population, particularly its adaptation for "intergenerational cohabitation."
55 Here, *statu quo* (status quo) refers to the political view that Quebec should remain a part of the Quebec federation, in opposition to "separatist" aims.
56 In the same tone, see Michel Lessard and Huguette Marquis, *Encyclopédie de la maison québécoise: 3 siècles d'habitations* (Montreal: Les Éditions de l'Homme, 1972), 468.
57 This is at least Jean-Pierre Guay's interpretation of it in his *Bungalow: Le journal* (Montreal: Les Herbes Rouges, 1995).
58 Line from Philippe Hauterive, dir., *Le Québec moderne* (1978), my translation: "We sacrificed big families for the bungalow."

59 Falardeau, dir., *Elvis Gratton,* my translation. In the colourful language of Elvis Gratton, the phrase means that the Americans in question know what they are doing and are superior to Quebecers: "Parce qu'eux autres ils l'ont l'affaire, les Américains."

60 Ward, *History of Domestic Space,* 38.

61 France Gagnon-Pratte, in Pigeon, dir., *Éloge du bungalow,* my translation.

62 Gilles Angers, "Du bungalow au cottage," *Le Soleil* (Quebec City), 9 August 2003, E2, my translation: "The elevated bungalow is an interesting way to live," and "the bungalow isn't much to look at."

63 See the origin of this interpretation in Jean-Yves Andrieux, *Patrimoine et histoire* (Paris: Belin, 1997), 213.

64 The idea of "monumental values" with regard to heritage is first found in the historic work of Alois Riegl. I and my colleague Luc Noppen have proposed a systematic, bipolar model for analyzing heritage according to five values. We have validated this model in a number of case studies in Luc Noppen and Lucie K. Morisset, "De la production des monuments: Paradigmes et processus de la reconnaissance," in *Les espaces de l'identité,* 23-52 (Quebec: Presses de l'Université Laval, 1997). This system was updated and redeployed in Luc Noppen and Lucie K. Morisset, *Les églises du Québec: Un patrimoine à réinventer* (Quebec: Presses de l'Université du Québec, 2005), 456.

65 The tremendous popularity of the documentary *Éloge du bungalow,* directed by Daniel Pigeon, is enough to show the widespread affection for this "little Quebec house." Broadcast on several occasions during prime time (then rebroadcast) on Quebec and European networks, the documentary was also selected for screening at many festivals, many times drawing full houses.

Place with No Dawn
A Town's Evolution and Erskine's Arctic Utopia

ALAN MARCUS

THE ARCHITECT AND THE HUNTER

In the early 1970s a paradigmatic enterprise was initiated by the government in which a northern-town design by one of the world's leading architects was commissioned in order to spearhead attempts to provide a Modernist architectural and social fabrication above the Arctic Circle. The architect was Ralph Erskine, and the town was Resolute Bay, or Qausuittuq, on Cornwallis Island in the Canadian High Arctic archipelago. In the early 1990s, I sat in two different living rooms – one in the expansive, Modernist home of Ralph Erskine in Drottningholm, on the island of Lovön outside Stockholm, and the other in the house of Simeonie Amagoalik, an elder in the small Inuit community of Qausuittuq.[1] The architectural spaces around these two rooms and their living circumstances were innately connected.

Amagoalik's home is not an Erskine design, yet its placement was due to Erskine's involvement. It resembles a number of the other older houses in the settlement, now increasingly being replaced by better-insulated, triple-glazed, double-storey box homes. Sitting at his kitchen table, Simeonie paused in conversation to lift his binoculars and look out in the direction of the sea. I asked if he was admiring the distant view, with the sea ice floating in the bay? No, he said, he was trying to see his boat down by the water's edge. The community of

some 250 people is located on the side of a hill, a little over one mile back from the shoreline (Figure 9.1). Since most other Canadian Inuit communities hug the seashore to permit ease of access for marine hunting activities, upon which their diet and livelihood in part depend, the placement of the town on a hillside seems a curious one. Although Erskine's and Amagoalik's communities are located in northern latitudes, Simeonie contends with a far more demanding climatic environment; after all, his town's name, Qausuittuq, means "place with no dawn."

This chapter investigates the origins and evolution of the architectural design of Resolute Bay, and the government's plans for creating a model new community. The new town design proposed by Ralph Erskine is examined in detail and considered in terms of both its intertextual relationship to his other work and the legacy of the project once it went into construction in the mid-1970s (Figure 9.2).[2] Reviewed are issues of social engineering associated with the relocation of the Inuit population in the early 1950s when the original community was established, and again in the 1970s when the site for the settlement was moved to Erskine's new location.[3] The importance of Erskine's design

Figure 9.1 Resolute Bay community, 1997. | Photograph by Ansgar Walk.

Figure 9.2 Drawing for Resolute Bay new town, 1975. | By Ralph Erskine.

as a prototype for cold-climate architecture is discussed, together with its viability for a northern Canadian context. "My question is," argued Erskine, "do the cities and buildings of the north well serve the needs of their inhabitants? My answer is No."[4]

RALPH ERSKINE AND THE CANADIAN PROJECT

> Ralph was a true humanist. His buildings radiate optimism, appropriateness and wit, which endear them to many. His philosophy of work accommodated the climate and the context together with the social and humanistic needs of people. He was concerned that the expression of buildings should engage the general public interest, generate a sense of ownership and appeal to genuine participation.[5]

Ralph Erskine, a prominent figure in the Modernist Movement in Sweden and a successful architect on the international stage, died at the age of ninety-one on 16 March 2005. His initial engagement with Canadian architecture transpired at an important time in his career when he was a visiting professor at McGill University in 1967-68. Erskine designed a large number of homes, office buildings, and townscapes, lectured widely, and received numerous honours in recognition of his contributions to the field. He was made an honorary fellow of the American Institute of Architects (1966), a fellow of the Swedish Royal Academy of Arts (1972), and a Commander of the Order of the British Empire (1979), and he was awarded the Canadian Gold Medal from the Royal Architectural Institute of Canada (1983), the Wolf Prize for Architecture (1984), and the Royal Gold Medal for Architecture from the Royal Institute of British Architects (1987).

Born in Mill Hill in North London on 24 February 1914, Erskine was educated at The Friend's School in Saffron Walden. The Fabian socialist ideals of his Scottish father, a Presbyterian minister, and his university-educated mother, coupled with Erskine's Quaker beliefs acquired at Saffron Walden, made a discernible impact on his later approach to architectural design. These beliefs were borne out in statements he made and in the way he engaged with clients and executed his designs. "Architecture and urban planning," he stated, "be it at macro or micro level, a private villa or an office block – must not only be a showpiece of design and technology, but also give expression to those democratic ideals of respect for human dignity, equality and freedom that are fostered in our society."[6] In 1939 Erskine immigrated to Sweden, arriving with just a bicycle, rucksack, and sleeping bag, drawn by the socialist appeal of the country's embryonic welfare state and its influence on new thinking for town planning. Continuing his studies at the Swedish Royal Academy of Art, Erskine was intrigued with the work of leading Swedish architects, including Gunnar Asplund (1885-1940), known for his provocative Modernist design for the Stockholm Public Library, Sigurd Lewerentz (1885-1975), and Sven Markelius (1889-1972),

Figure 9.3 Ralph Erskine, Svappavaara new town, Sweden, 1965. | Courtesy of Ralph Erskine.

fathers of Swedish Functionalism. Following the 1930 Stockholm exhibition, the country became a nexus for experiments in humanistic Functionalist design.

In his many national and international projects, Ralph Erskine developed as an integral part of his design philosophy a reputation for working closely with the future inhabitants of his buildings to ensure that the schemes met the needs of the users. Some of his best-known designs were constructed for cold-climate habitation, a subject upon which he published and for which he became well known. An example was the ski hotel at Borgafjäll (1948), which was integrated into the landscape to the extent that guests could ski off the roof and down the slope. He went on to design large-scale complexes comprising multi-unit dwellings, offices, and shops, such as at Kiruna (1961-66), above the Arctic Circle in northern Sweden. In particular, his designs for the Svappavaara housing and community plan (1963-64) in northern Sweden and for the University of Cambridge's new postgraduate college, Clare Hall (1968-69), together with the massive Byker housing estate with 2,317 dwellings (1969-81) in Newcastle upon

Tyne in northern England, provided precursors for his Canadian project, as will be discussed later (Figure 9.3). Erskine's more recent works have included the Ark (1990) housing design built in Hammersmith, London, and the large-scale Millennium Village in Greenwich, begun in 1998, featuring 1,377 houses and flats, near the London Dome site.

In the early 1970s, Resolute Bay was the major supply airbase for the High Arctic and was being considered for an expansion of resource exploration and extraction operations. Aware of Ralph Erskine's reputation for progressive urban planning tailored for cold climates, the Canadian government commissioned him to design a new town for Resolute Bay. The scheme was intended to racially integrate the Inuit community of some 140 inhabitants consisting of 32 households, with the transient white population housed at the base, which alternated between 250 and 600 persons, depending on the time of the year. The remit called for a new town with housing for 1,200 people and further plans to expand it to accommodate a population of up to 3,000. Following a number of site visits from Stockholm and approval of his design, the project moved to the construction phase.

"I try to base my work on that seasonal rhythm of the north which I find so enthralling, and form communities which encompass all its richness of contrasting experiences," remarked Erskine.[7] "I hope that we architects could give such a dwelling a form, make a space with a potential for contentment. But in the final count it is the inhabitants who will give the same dwelling its meaning and will change our architectural space to place."[8] Erskine's Resolute design called for moving the existing Inuit community from what became known as "the old village" (even though it was created just twenty years earlier) to a new site perched on the rise of a hill five miles away. A principal feature of the new town was a horseshoe-like perimeter "living wall" containing apartments, which would encircle detached family units – some models intriguingly shaped like spaceships, raised off the ground on stilts so as not to adversely affect the permafrost (Figure 9.4). The plan replicates the formation of a medieval walled town, such as those in Britain like Conwy in North Wales, Arundel in West Sussex, and Alnwick in Northumberland. In place of the traditional castle, an enclosed communal area with shops, restaurant, library, a swimming pool, and an indoor botanical garden would be created, attached to the apex of the horseshoe and sealed off from the severe climate by a bubble roof (Figure 9.5). Instead of possible invaders, the foe was the weather. The chief difference between the concepts was that Erskine's town was open at the bottom to reveal the view. With its back to the slope, much like the design for his Borgafjäll hotel, it was intended that the natural contours of the land would provide an element of

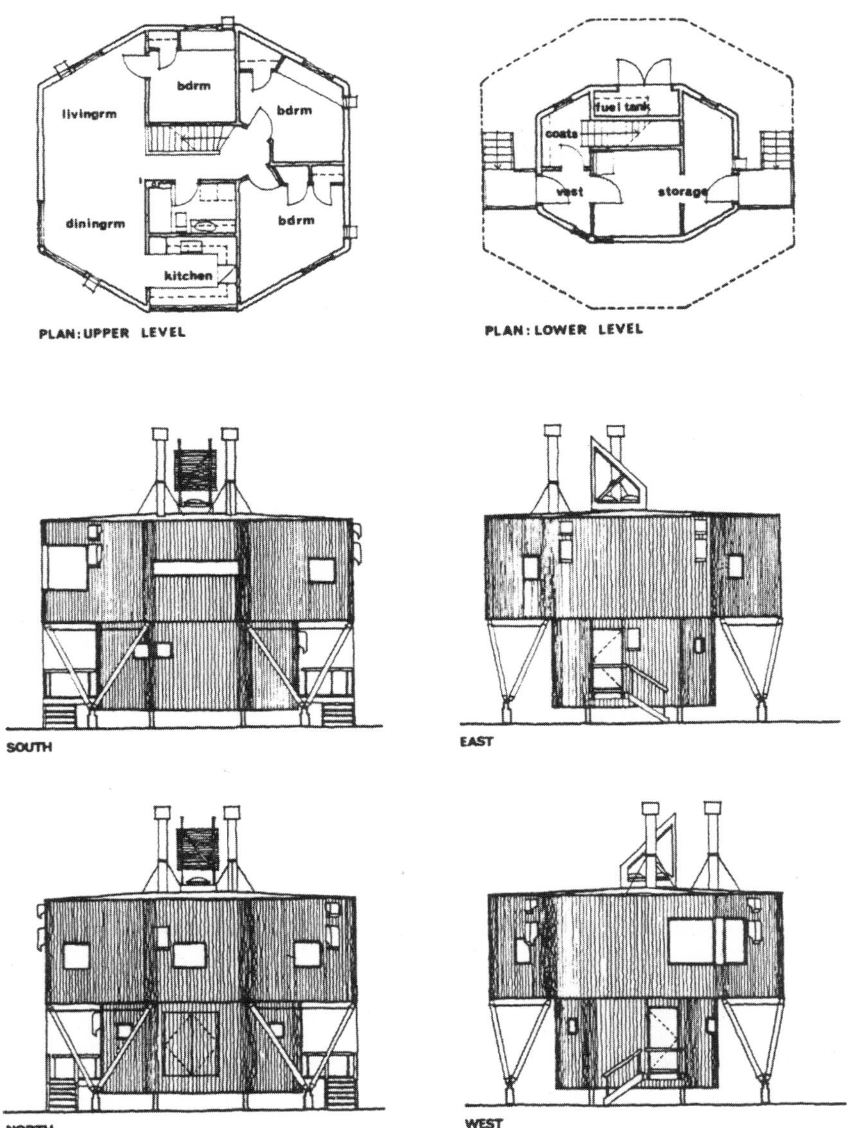

Figure 9.4 Design for Resolute Bay detached house. | By Ralph Erskine.

Figure 9.5 Drawing for Resolute Bay indoor town centre. | By Ralph Erskine.

protection from the winds and drifting snow. Five possible sites were tested for microclimate and other conditions before Erskine and his team settled on the final choice.

Although Erskine attached importance to building a dialogue with residents of his urban planning schemes, especially as with the case of the Byker estate and Resolute where they were being rehoused, the issue of the Inuit giving their informed consent is complicated by previous events. This group had been moved once before when in 1953 the Inuit community was first established. The Canadian government selected a collection of families from Inukjuak (then known as Port Harrison) in Arctic Quebec, together with several families from Pond Inlet on Baffin Island, and relocated them to the new colony at Resolute Bay. An additional group was moved at the same time to Grise Fiord on Ellesmere Island, followed by a second relocation of Inuit to both communities in 1955. Later efforts were made by officials to recruit young women in Inukjuak to move up to Resolute to increase the mating pool, but these were unsuccessful. The background of the 1953-55 moves and the influences it had on the new town resettlement and functions twenty years later are closely interlinked.

THE ESTABLISHMENT OF RESOLUTE BAY

At Resolute Bay's airport there was an old sign that read, "Resolute, pronounced Desolate." The community had a reputation in the North of being an environmentally unpleasant place to live, with a paucity of fauna, poor weather conditions, and terminally overcast skies. The United States and Canadian military first established a weather station and airport at Resolute in 1947, and a number of airplane crash-sites eerily litter the area around the airstrip. Resolute Bay was named after the ship HMS *Resolute,* which wintered in the area in 1850-51 while searching for Sir John Franklin's lost expedition of 1845. The circumstances surrounding the establishment of the Inuit settlement at Resolute in 1953 have been the subject of much debate, controversy, and study.[9] To appreciate the context for the town's resettlement during Erskine's involvement in the mid-1970s, it is important to understand the relationship of the Inuit and the government to the community since its origin twenty years earlier. This issue is particularly pertinent in light of the fact that a community that was originally moved to the site without any initial investment in the siting of the community was then subjected to a second move – in both cases the choice of location being the final decision of officials. In addition, key aspects of Ralph Erskine's design for the new town suggest a form of implicit social engineering aimed at creating an ethnically integrated community and arranging the different forms of accommodation to promote a refashioned Canadian architectural fabric. This element closely relates to the original remit for the establishment of the community and to an inherited identity derived from the sense that the inhabitants were part of an ongoing social experiment.

The 1953 relocation, implemented by the Royal Canadian Mounted Police (RCMP), was referred to as an "Eskimo Rehabilitation Experiment." The move was also taken by the federal government to demonstrate "effective occupation" of the area. The intention was to use the first settlers as a forerunner for "seeding" the Canadian High Arctic with an Inuit population. Superintendent Henry Larsen, head of the RCMP's operation in the Northwest Territories in the 1950s, had a utopian vision for creating Inuit settlements in the High Arctic. This view embraced an element of history and folklore. When selecting the locations

Figure 9.6 Inuit winter houses, Port Harrison (Inukjuak), 1948. | Richard Harrington/Library and Archives Canada, PA-146917.

for the Resolute and Grise Fiord camps, he chose sites where there was clear archaeological evidence of previous habitation.[10] Both of the new colonies on Cornwallis and Ellesmere Islands were next to the archaeological remains of Thule Eskimo encampments over 500 years old. Detailed knowledge of these sites was published for the first time in the year before the relocation plan was developed.[11]

The site Larsen selected for the relocatees was a raised beach beside a row of nine stone and whale-bone houses, which the Inuit called *qarmartalik,* "old ruins." These were part of the largest collection of permanent house sites on the island. The Thule Inuit had left the area during either the first phase of the Little Ice Age, 1450-1520, or the third phase, 1600-1750. Occupation of the region, as elsewhere throughout the Arctic during periods of population expansion and contraction, was influenced by changing climatic conditions. As winters became intolerably cold, the caribou, muskox, and other game migrated southward, the people followed, and the land was left uninhabited.[12] Nevertheless, Larsen felt that if their "ancestors" had been able to survive here at one time, perhaps the relocatees could do so as well.

The Inuit to be selected for the relocation in 1953 to establish the new colony came from two communities. The plan was that the smaller group of Pond Inlet Inuit would be able to assist the Port Harrison Inuit in adapting to life in the High Arctic, which was considerably different from what they were used to. The community selected by officials for "rehabilitation" and the move north was one that had featured previously in the best-known film about the Inuit. This community, later given its Inuit name of Inukjuak, first came to international attention when it was the subject of Robert Flaherty's classic feature documentary *Nanook of the North* (1922). When the hunter who played the role of Nanook reportedly died of starvation two years after the film was made, his death was mourned as far away as China.[13] In Western popular culture, *Nanook of the North* remains the quintessential iconographic representation of Inuit life. Although the face of Nanook became known and was marketed around the world, the Inukjuamiut continued their lives in much the same way as before Flaherty's visit, with little or no knowledge of their widespread fame (Figure 9.6).

Thirty years after the making of the film, the Inukjuamiut and other Inuit living in northern Quebec were no longer regarded by officials as "happy-go-lucky Eskimos" but rather as an economically depressed people living in an "overpopulated area."[14] It was the transformation of the Eskimo from the "noble savage" of the 1920s, presented in *Nanook of the North,* to the welfare-dependent "white man's burden" of the 1950s that altered the government's essential relationship with the Inuit. By replacing its former policy of minimal social intervention with one of financial provision, Ottawa was no longer responsible to the Inuit but became responsible for them. To claim state aid was to relinquish one's private freedom, allowing the state to exert control over those who had come to depend on its resources for their survival.[15] Within the context of "welfare colonialism," the government now felt it had a prerogative to organize resettlement projects in order to ameliorate the Inuit's standard of living and reduce their dependency on the state.[16] At the 1952 Conference on Eskimo Affairs, it was suggested that the federal Department of Northern Affairs should develop an Inuit relocation policy: "Movements could be initiated from overpopulated or depleted districts," the conference concluded, "to areas not presently occupied or where the natural resources could support a greater number of people."[17] That year, Inuit from Arctic Quebec were selected for relocation to the High Arctic.

HIGH ARCTIC COLONIZATION AND "NEW HOMES" FOR THE INUIT

In a popular magazine article, senior Department of Northern Affairs official Bob Phillips called the Inuit "slum dwellers of the wide-open spaces."[18] Featuring a picture of a small makeshift wooden dwelling, Phillips's article stated: "Except for those who have built shacks like this one from refuse, no Canadian Eskimo owns a home. Most are forced to live in the cold and damp of igloo and tent." Minnie Allakariallak, whose husband Johnnie Echalook was a lay preacher, arrived in Resolute Bay in 1955, feeling that "God has placed us here, and we were imagining a place where there's plenty of vegetation."[19] However, she soon discovered that the area's vegetation was far less than that near Inukjuak. The area chosen for relocation made the "rehabilitation experience" exceptionally difficult, as the climatic differences between Port Harrison and Resolute Bay are pronounced. Port Harrison is at latitude 58°27' north in the southern Arctic, whereas Resolute Bay is at 74°42' north in the High Arctic.

Port Harrison is 900 kilometres south of the Arctic Circle and thus never experiences continual winter darkness, whereas at Resolute Bay there is no daylight from late October until mid-February. During the dark period the snow surface reflects the moonlight and provides limited visibility. The relocatees also had to adjust to four months of continual daylight, from the end of April to the end of August. Temperatures averaging –34°C in February and +5°C in July, with an annual daily temperature of –16°C, are also much colder, and weather conditions are more severe in Resolute Bay and for longer durations than in Port Harrison. Due to ice cover, a supply vessel can enter the bay in front of Resolute only between mid-August and mid-September (Figure 9.7).

Just as Robert Flaherty tried to recapture the character and images of "traditional" Inuit life, so the Department of Northern Affairs in the early 1950s envisaged a relocation project that would rehabilitate and socially transform a group of Inuit so that they could live like the idealized Nanook. Ironically, Robert Flaherty's own illegitimate Inuit son was selected by officials to be relocated to the High Arctic as part of this rehabilitation experiment. Joseph Flaherty and other Quebec families were transported to a land completely foreign to them. Although the officials may have seen the Inuit relocatees as migrants and volunteers, those relocated to the High Arctic in 1953-55 have consistently described themselves as "exiles" (the term of reference also employed by the Royal Commission on Aboriginal Peoples in their investigating report).[20] These contrasting labels indicate the key distinction between Inuit and former official views on the issue and how participants wish to see these events represented.

Figure 9.7 The CGS *C.D. Howe* rendezvousing with the CGS *d'Iberville* at Craig Harbour, Ellesmere Island, 29 August 1953. | Wilfred Doucette/Library and Archives Canada/National Film Board, PA-176810.

The notion of feeling exiled from one's homeland also complicated later efforts by Ralph Erskine to design a new town – one in which the majority of inhabitants, Inuit and white, would not have an innate sense of ownership, having been permanently or temporarily displaced there from their indigenous homes down south.

Despite newspaper stories of "new homes" for families in the High Arctic, such as appeared in the *Montreal Gazette,* housing remained a serious problem for the Inuit at Resolute.[21] The homes for most relocatees were initially old tents. In his inspection report of the Resolute Bay camp, C.J. Marshall noted that many of the relocatees' tents were in poor condition.[22] In northern Quebec they were able to build an igloo *(illu)* around November, whereas in Resolute Bay the Inukjuamiut discovered that despite colder temperatures, snowfall was sparse and they might not be able to construct igloos until January. During the month of December, snowfall averages only 1 inch in Resolute Bay, whereas Port Harrison receives an average of 9.3 inches. Elijah Nutaraq recounted his adjustment to the colder climate: "We had to live in tents all winter because there was not enough snow to build a snow house. I remember waking up every morning rolled up like a ball because it was so cold! Today, I am glad I did not have a wife then – it would have been very difficult for a young couple's relationship to survive in that severe climate."[23]

Ross Gibson, the RCMP constable in charge of overseeing the new Inuit camp, admitted that "the cold was something the Quebec Eskimos had never endured the like of."[24] Gibson's observation reflects the notion that a scientific experiment appears to invoke nature as an independent judge.[25] From Gibson's comments and those of the relocatees, one can assume that the environmental conditions in themselves would have caused the relocation experiment to fail. Thus Gibson declared: "I am sure they would have all gone home right then if they could."[26] Shortly before he died, Larsen warned: "I shudder to think of the criticism which will be levelled at us in another fifty years time."[27] No wooden dwellings were built for the relocatees until they started building shacks for themselves in 1954 using packing cases discarded from the annual sealift (Figure 9.8). Not providing houses for the relocatees was consistent with the project's rehabilitation ideology, which discouraged the adoption of nontraditional practices. When in 1959 the RCMP submitted a plan for low-cost housing at Grise Fiord, the administrator of the Arctic, Alex Stevenson, was not supportive and advised that "the existence is marginal here and it may be more practicable to use this settlement for experimental purposes."[28] His decision illustrates the extent to which the laboratory metaphor was being perpetuated, which would have further ramifications when Erskine later implemented his experimental town plan.

RESOLUTE BAY AND SOCIAL INTEGRATION

One aspect of Ralph Erskine's remit for designing a new town at Resolute Bay was to amalgamate the Inuit and transient white populations, who by the 1970s had often worked together at the airbase facilities and in resource-exploration activities but who remained in segregated living accommodation. At that point, the twenty-year history of their interactions and segregation was complex. One of the most important functions of the military airbase at Resolute was to supply the five weather stations (Resolute, Mould Bay, Isachsen, Eureka, and Alert) jointly operated by Canada and the United States. In view of these activities, the Department of Northern Affairs envisaged a growing need at Resolute Bay

Figure 9.8 Sarah Salluviniq, Jaybeddie Amagoalik, Mawa Iqaluk, Anknowya, George Echalook, and John Amagoalik, Resolute Bay, 1956. | Courtesy of Jaybeddie Amagoalik.

for manual labour. After their initial objections to the project, base officials and government agencies operating out of Resolute soon came to realize the advantages of having a Native labour pool to draw upon. The Inuit could be employed part-time as equipment operators, refuse removers, cleaners, and general handymen. The department proposed the second-stage relocation to Resolute Bay in 1955 to meet a growing demand for casual labour to unload supplies during airlifts and during the summer resupply.[29] The Inuit, however, were still left to find their own shelter and to feed themselves from the land. Gibson concurred that the government had brought the Inuit families to Resolute Bay "hoping they'd kill enough polar bear and seal to keep going. That way, men would be available to load aircraft and do other chores."[30]

The Inuit lived in the original community established for them near the Thule ruins by the beach, and the whites lived on the base. This separation evolved from the origination of the Inuit community. At the outset, Gibson was instructed by his superiors that the military base was out of bounds for the Inuit, as was the base dump. There was to be complete segregation.

Larsen agreed that such a practice was necessary if they were to keep the Inuit pure; otherwise, "had Gibson allowed everybody to run about as they liked, those Eskimos would have been ruined the first winter."[31] He was particularly concerned about "indiscriminate association" between the whites and the Inuit women. Base personnel were informed that they were not to approach the Inuit camp, and any request to do so had to be approved by the constable.[32] Gibson pinned a note on the bulletin board in the base recreation room stating that he would give guided tours of the Inuit camp so that personnel could take pictures of the relocatees.[33] The Inuit called the base *aupartualuk,* meaning "the big red one," because of its red buildings. Thus Gibson, nicknamed Auparttuq, "Red," lived in quarters at the aupartualuk.

A party of senior officials, including two air commodores and department official Ben Sivertz, visited Resolute Bay a few days after the Inuit arrived on 7 September 1953. In a report on the trip, the arrival of the Inuit was discussed, together with the initial problems associated with their encampment at Resolute: "The reasons for moving this family are grounded in an attempt to keep the Eskimo in his native state and to preserve that culture as primitive as it is. However, by moving the Eskimos to an area where they come into intimate contact with white men destroys the basis of this reasoning while leaving them untrained to cope with the problems presented by this contact."[34] The report's author commented on the view, widely held at the time, that Inuit relations with military and transient civilian personnel should be closely monitored and discouraged. He suggested that by placing Inuit near the Resolute base, the project's objective of preserving "Nativeness" was being jeopardized. The report therefore advised that legislation should be considered to make Inuit settlements out of bounds to non-Inuit. In light of what one might characterize as a "keep the Eskimo an Eskimo" approach to social development at Resolute Bay, it is interesting to note the paradoxical statement by Jean Lesage, minister of the Department of Northern Affairs at the time of the second relocation to the High Arctic in 1955: "the preservation of the Eskimo in his primitive state is not a real alternative ... It would involve segregation and isolation [and] denial of the most humane services."[35] In this case, the social policy that the department was advocating in public did not accord with what it was putting into practice.

Two years after the relocation, Gibson recorded in a report to his superiors: "The native camp at Resolute Bay continues to survive."[36] To survive, the relocatees had to hunt and scavenge, regardless of the weather conditions. John Amagoalik remembers "being very excited when any military airplane arrived in Resolute, because we knew that the people on those airplanes had box lunches. We used to rush to the dump five miles away in the middle of winter to go and get those boxes of half-finished sandwiches."[37] Lizzie Amagoalik recalls that they "were always hungry. We had to look through the white man's garbage for food for our children. We had to take clothes that had been thrown away, for our children. When the policemen found out that we were living off their garbage, they got very angry at us and told us to stop. We asked, how are we going to eat?"[38]

Supplementing the Inuit diet of country food with leftovers from the white man's dump became a contentious issue between the RCMP officers and officials at the Department of Northern Affairs. This situation undermined a basic tenet of the rehabilitation project, namely that if relief was abolished the poor would become self-reliant.[39] Gibson was intent on adhering to the guidelines established for the rehabilitation project and insisted that the group should comply with isolation measures. Gibson therefore reported, "strict instructions were given the natives that they were not to carry away any articles found in the dump."[40] Department planner Ben Sivertz cautioned his deputy minister about the implications "of the growing problem of Eskimos scrounging from garbage dumps." He was particularly concerned about the public's perception of such activity since "it is the sort of thing which can give rise to embarrassing publicity ... It is our view that, if Eskimos are really destitute, they must, as a temporary measure, be provided with relief and proper food. We must not be put in the position of providing garbage as relief rations for Canadian citizens, which is exactly what is happening in some places."[41] Yet this was still the situation in 1964, when Constable G.D. Lucko at the Resolute Bay detachment commented on the source of building materials the Inuit were using. As before, they needed to resort to "what they obtained for themselves from the local dump."[42]

COMMUNITY GROWTH, SHAPING SPACE, AND ERSKINE'S PARADIGM

Further colonization of the High Arctic islands was still being considered by the Department of Northern Affairs in the 1960s. Ben Sivertz, who had become commissioner of the Northwest Territories, was interested in establishing new colonies at Mould Bay, Isachsen, Eureka, and Alert. The plan was to use Resolute Bay as a hub community, servicing a number of satellite Inuit colonies throughout the archipelago. Ultimately, the project was not implemented. Perhaps the government realized that the old problem of welfare dependency might recur but in even more distant locations. In the 1960s, the cost of providing schools and facilities, teachers, mechanics, and other necessary personnel for the colonies outweighed the possible advantages of redistributing the Inuit in the High Arctic islands. Resolute Bay developed a symbiotic relationship between the Inuit settlement and the base, with opportunities for menial employment and various forms of ongoing interaction. It underwent a dramatic conversion, however, in the mid-1960s, from model community to what some viewed as a dystopian environment, when RCMP paternalism was moderated and Inuit relations with the airbase changed. Alcoholism and prostitution became commonplace, and Resolute developed a reputation as a town with serious social problems.

By the early 1970s, due to improved economic conditions, a rise in oil revenues, and potential for enhanced opportunities for resource extraction in the Far North, the government decided that Resolute Bay would benefit from a completely new vision. It was at this point that Ralph Erskine was hired to offer this inspiration, and his design for the Resolute Bay new town presented a culmination of his ideas on cold-climate urban design. Reviewing the project in an article in *Canadian Geographic,* Michael Dear and Shirley Clark observe that "the Resolute new town was to have been a significant experiment in physical and social planning, and planners intended to set a precedent for future land-use and social programs throughout the North."[43] The town would also be a prototype for an ethnically integrated Arctic community. When contracted to devise an imaginative new town for Resolute, Erskine's brief included finding a housing solution for amalgamating the permanent Inuit population and the transient white personnel, who worked at the airbase – most of whom were on seasonal contracts engaged in scientific and resource-exploration activities. In photographs and Erskine's own accounts, we also see the architect deeply immersed in conversation with the Inuit inhabitants, discussing the merits of the plan in an effort to assumedly incorporate their suggestions (Figure 9.9). A central query, however, especially given the community's prior history of being relocated, is to what extent the appearance of participation and empowerment of consultation becomes in itself another "instrument for managed intervention."[44]

At the heart of his design was a horseshoe-shaped "living wall," which would consist of apartments and townhouses, in which most of the whites would live, encircling the detached Inuit family homes. The master design was an elaboration and refinement of an earlier conceptual idea that Erskine had implemented both in his plans for Svappavaara in northern Sweden and in two British projects, Clare Hall at Cambridge and the Byker housing estate at Newcastle. All four

Figure 9.9 Ralph Erskine in discussions with Inuit inhabitants of Resolute Bay, c. 1973. | Courtesy of Ralph Erskine.

large-scale plans called for a combination of single-unit and family accommodation and for the overlapping of private and communal spaces. Erskine's intention was to use architecture to create an attractive environment that promoted interaction in a myriad of ways.

In all four designs, the living wall formed a castle-like structure that both provided climatic shelter and created a sense of inner sanctum. At Svappavaara, which was only partially completed, and in the Resolute plan, the wall formed a shoulder against the prevailing wind and snow. In the Newcastle development, what became known as "the Byker Wall" provided insulation for the community from winds off the North Sea and a sound barrier against a planned motorway. At Clare Hall, the outer buildings provided a genuine sense of enclosure and community. The blueprints for the four designs bear a catalogue of strong similarities, particularly in the overall shape of Svappavaara and Byker as forerunners for Resolute, with similar humanizing influences of materials, including wooden porches and suspended balconies. The adaptation of functionalist design principles incorporating an aesthetic use of colour and the presence of prominent design features such as air vents, rain-water chutes, and railings are almost identical in each plan. These elements can also be seen in earlier works, such

Figure 9.10 Drawing for ski hotel at Borgafjäll, Sweden, 1948. | By Ralph Erskine.

as the use of a curved outer wall and air intakes on a factory he designed for the manufacture of cardboard at Avesta, Sweden (1950-53), and the hanging balconies, which were a feature of his housing development at Brittgården (1959), in Tibro, Sweden.

Like the later design for Resolute Bay, the seven-year Brittgården project also had a mix of dwellings, with 85 family houses and 255 flats that ranged from studio to three-bedroom units. As envisaged for Resolute, an emphasis was placed on social integration, with the intention, as seen at Brittgården, of catering to a full range of inhabitants by creating a community whose buildings included old people's houses and homes specially designed for the handicapped. For the late 1950s, the design was considered highly progressive in that it was pedestrian-friendly, keeping roads and car parks at the perimeter of the townsite to ensure greater freedom for children to roam. The notion of an egalitarian environment was fundamental even to the University of Cambridge's Clare Hall project, where in collaboration with the future dons, there was no allowance for a high table in the dining room or even a porter's lodge. In this late-1960s design, the intention was to create spaces that broke down social barriers between students and faculty and allowed for communal spaces that invited ease of mixing. Even the college president's house at Clare Hall is carefully folded into the overall design, such that its more spacious interior is undetectable from adjoining buildings.[45]

One of the aspects that immediately strikes one about Erskine's hand-drawn rendition of the new town for Resolute is not just the quizzical addition of the hot air balloon (a signature item in his drawings) but also the way the town design relaxes its form into the contours of the landscape. It was Erskine's early association with Gordon Cullen (1914-94), founder of the Townscape Movement, whom he met at the outset of his architectural career in England, who instilled in him the need to strive for a harmonious relationship between buildings and their environment. In Erskine's early Swedish design work – whether the Borgafjäll ski hotel (Figure 9.10); the church at Segato, southern Rhodesia (1960), whose roof mirrored the native fan-shaped trees but was not considered "Swedish-looking" enough for the local priests to be approved; or the Gadelius house (1961) on Lidingö, Sweden, built into the sloping terrain and adorned with a grassed roof – his instinct for integrating the built environment with the natural environment is immediately apparent.

In fact, the earliest precursor for the Resolute new townscape is revealed in a design he drew for a hypothetical Arctic town in 1958, with its characteristic south-facing slope, which he was invited to present to the Congrès Internationaux d'Architecture Moderne in Holland.[46] Many of these designs are helpfully illustrated in Peter Collymore's invaluable *The Architecture of Ralph Erskine*.[47] Further cold-climate experimentations include his whimsical design for an igloo-shaped home built of aluminum: the Engstrom house on Lisö Island in

Sorunda, Sweden (1955-56). Even here, however, he has carefully accommodated the needs of the owner, creating an enormous igloo with four children's bedrooms and the master bedroom radiating like spokes off the core, and still with spacious living and dining rooms, all contained within the dome and set in extensive, well-wooded grounds. Even before getting to the Arctic, in this early design work Erskine betrays his fascination for indigenous forms of cold-climate architecture.

A hallmark of Erskine's approach to urban design methodology, as previously noted, was the involvement of the end user in the conceptualization process. Even within his architectural firm, Erskine developed an ethos for democratic discussion. This approach was based on the informal egalitarian format of a Quaker meeting, which originated from his experiences at the school in Saffron Walden. Upon embarking on initial consultation meetings at Resolute with white personnel at the airbase and with Inuit, Erskine recorded in his diary on 2 September 1973:

> I was impressed by the high level of involved interest and understanding shown both in the Base and in the village. This was (due to language) easiest to assess in the Base, but attendance at meetings was highest in the village ... Common to both was quick assessment of the town plans and models and rejection of all that might lead to segregation of the Eskimo and white communities. There was an immediate and very profound will for integration.[48]

However, in the development of the blueprint for Resolute Bay and in the design discussions involving Inuit and whites, systemic flaws appear to have been overlooked. A reason for moving the Inuit community from its "old village" location next to the shoreline to the new site up on a hill was that in its former position the town was underneath the runway approach to the airport, which was deemed unsafe. In the formal report that Erskine's team prepared, the rationale was further advanced:

> Low clouds forced the aircraft to fly low over the village when landing. The site was noisy and felt to be dangerous. The site collected an abnormal amount of drifting snow, and the access road was regularly drifted in during the 9 or 10 month long winter ... The unions and private companies supported the proposal and all parts wished to avoid racial and social segregation.[49]

A report on the community prepared for the Department of Indian and Northern Affairs also recorded that the selected site offered an improved view of the coastline.[50] As the majority of the intended residents were to be whites, this aesthetic consideration was viewed as more appealing. All Inuit communities are adjacent to water because of the need for ready access to boats used for hunting and transport. The decision adopted at Resolute reduced Inuit engagement with the natural resources over a period of time, promoting greater reliance on the foodstuffs offered in the new town's stores. Hence, even at this early planning stage, a strategic decision was taken that was inherently at odds with the utilitarian needs and cultural practices of the Inuit community.

The horseshoe design of the apartment complex actually meant that the Inuit's detached homes would be placed in the centre, clustered around a freestanding church and school, with the whites occupying the encircling apartments, inadvertently looking down on the Inuit's homes in a panoptic surveillance configuration. In an attempt to encourage racial integration, the risk was that the communities would still be largely segregated, except in public areas, but the metaphorical layout of a white circle with the Inuit in the middle could potentially create an even more problematic dynamic. With the whites staring out of their windows at the Inuit in the inner courtyard, the sense of being watched from above might have been untenable and exacerbated cultural difference. Animals in a zoo is another uncomfortable analogy. Erskine's intention, however, as with those he consulted, was to achieve the opposite with this town plan, as he records: "Much interest was shown in this factor i.e. that the town should not sub-divide into white and Eskimo township and that there should be no obvious 'snob hill' situation."[51] Erskine's design had created a paradox. What was the alternative to this shaping of space? Keeping the detached homes separated from the horseshoe and placing them on their own in a quasi suburb of the main town would have defeated the basic premise of providing a protective wall against the winds and promoting an integrated community.

With regards to the wall, one report observed that "the Eskimos were unanimously more interested in reducing the snow clearing problems (i.e., allowing the wind to penetrate the development), than in creating a wind shelter. 'Wind is part of Arctic life.' The whites were, on the other hand, very eager to get wind shelter."[52] If Erskine had placed the Inuit community down by the shore and the whites up on the hillside where the view was more favourable for them and where they were closer to the base, the Inuit would have remained a ghettoized community. His remit was to try to accommodate both groups' wishes (although, of course, those whites included in the consultation would have left the area by the time the new town had been built), while realizing his own longstanding design ambitions for creating an Arctic urban paradigm.

Although the Inuit were an important component of the new community, their small numbers meant that they would have been dwarfed by the white population, especially as transient workers' numbers were expected to expand. Unlike most other communities in the Canadian Arctic, where Inuit substantially outnumber whites, in Resolute the process would have been inverted at a ratio of anything from 5:1 to 20:1 if resource-development activities in the High Arctic ballooned as projected. Erskine's ultimate decision to site the town not on the seashore but on the side of the hill was therefore potentially prompted more by the ideals and needs of the white community than by those of the Inuit. This balance echoed the colonial paradigm, which in the past had resulted in marginalized living conditions for Inuit who gathered near white sites of habitation, such as military facilities – although in this instance the wish was to ameliorate their previous circumstances. Even at an early stage in the process, immediately prior to his consultation meeting with inhabitants, Erskine recorded in his diary on 21 August 1973: "I suggest that this study should include a siting nearer the hill than the site already tested."[53]

In an effort to accelerate the building program for the new town and to manage costs, a decision was made to move the old Inuit homes to the new location once the townsite was levelled rather than to construct new homes. Work was also commenced on the periphery apartment building. Only one end section of the horseshoe townhouses was actually completed when the government decided in 1978 to abandon the project. The reason given was a change in the market for natural resources, which meant that the expected substantial influx of transient workers would now not materialize. In his diary, Erskine noted the Inuit's prophetic observation when they met with him in the summer of 1973 at the outset of the project: "Great interest in central facilities and, as in the Base, emphasis on their importance. Question in both places: Will it really happen?"[54]

The apartment block, finished inside in a high-design Swedish style, was nonetheless uninhabitable without necessary plumbing and was soon boarded up (see Figure 9.11). Few communal facilities were initially provided, and most whites remained in accommodation at the airbase, which meant that the much-discussed plans for social integration did not come to fruition. Further underscoring the tenuousness of the town's existence, when Erskine returned to Sweden and reflected on the project in December 1973, still in the early part of the design process, he noted, "we would try to avoid the risk of creating in the future another 'throw away' ghost town [and] should a reduction or moving of the township become essential, there might at least be the chance that (as with

Figure 9.11 Uncompleted townhouses designed by Ralph Erskine, Resolute Bay, as in 1991. | Photograph by author.

the present Eskimo village?) people who have to move might be able to take with them some familiar furnishings, buildings and social institutions."[55]

A number of the Inuit presently living in Resolute Bay were young children at the time of the initial relocations or were born in the High Arctic. In 1988 the Department of Indian and Northern Affairs finally acknowledged that thirty-five years earlier it had made a two-year promise of return and agreed to pay the transportation costs of those people who wanted to move back to Inukjuak. By the 1990s most of the original elders had returned to Inukjuak. The three who remained have stayed primarily because their children live there. Yet, fifty years since its inception, the town of Qausuittuq remains one of the two northernmost communities in North America. Its existence and strategic position provided Erskine with an opportunity, made complex by the somewhat unusual history of the community and policy reversals of the government, to put his philosophy of integrated town planning and Arctic architecture to the test.

When reviewing the legacy of the project and the image of the forlorn boarded-up townhouses in 2002, Erskine expressed dismay that the current inhabitants of the community should have realized few of the benefits of his original design. Instead, their lives were made more complicated by their premature movement to the hill, which was missing the necessary infrastructure and modern dwellings promised them by the government. "Neither in Canada, Alaska, Scandinavia nor Siberia will I find communities intelligently and inventively built to give pleasing and effective comfort and protection in the specific conditions of the north," recorded Erskine in 1967 while a visiting professor at McGill University.[56] Industrial economic fluctuations undermined the construction of both Svappavaara and Resolute Bay, but the promise his design held out may still one day be achieved as world climate continues to change and as populations expand into new regions.

NOTES

1 The author interviewed Simeonie Amagoalik and other Inuit at Resolute Bay in 1991 and interviewed Ralph Erskine twice at his home in Drottningholm, in 1992 and 2002.

2 See also Rhodri Windsor Liscombe, "Modernist Ultimate Thule," *RACAR (Revue d'art Canadienne/Canadian Art Review)* 31, 1-2 (2006): 64-80.

3 Passages detailing the 1953-55 relocations initially appeared in Alan Marcus, *Relocating Eden: The Images and Politics of Inuit Exile in the Canadian Arctic* (Hanover, NH: University Press of New England, 1995).

4 Ralph Erskine, "Architecture and Town Planning in the North," *Polar Record* 14, 89 (1968): 165.

5 Ralph Erskine website, http://www.erskine.se/e_biografi.htm.

6 Architecture Week Great Buildings Collection, http://www.greatbuildings.com/architects/Ralph_Erskine.html.

7 Erskine, "Architecture and Town Planning," 165.

8 Ibid.

9 See Alan Marcus, "Out in the Cold: Canada's Experimental Inuit Relocation to Grise Fiord and Resolute Bay," *Polar Record* 27, 163 (1991): 285-96; Frank J. Tester and Peter Kulchyski, *Tammarniit (Mistakes): Inuit Relocation in the Eastern Arctic* (Vancouver: UBC Press, 1994); Royal Commission on Aboriginal Peoples, *The High Arctic Relocation,* 3 vols. (Ottawa: Ministry of Supply and Services, 1994); Marcus, *Relocating Eden.*

10 Henry Larsen, *Memoirs,* unpublished manuscript in the private collection of Doreen Riedel (n.d.); M. Maxwell, *Prehistory of the Eastern Arctic* (New York: Academic Press, 1985).

11 H. Collins, "Excavations of Thule and Dorset Culture Sites at Resolute Bay, Cornwallis Island, NWT," in *Annual Report of the National Museum of Canada for the Fiscal Year 1953-54,* Bulletin No. 136 (Ottawa: Department of Resources and Development, 1955), 22.

12 Guy Mary-Rousselière, *Qitdlarssuaq: The Story of a Polar Migration* (Winnipeg: Wuerz, 1991), 160.
13 Hugh Brody, *Living Arctic* (London: Faber and Faber, 1987), 21.
14 "Summary of the Proceedings at a Meeting on Eskimo Affairs Held 19 and 20 May 1952, in the Board Room of the Confederation Building, Ottawa" (1952), RCMP Information Access Directorate, D1512-2-4-Q-27.
15 Francis Piven and Richard Cloward, *Regulating the Poor* (London: Tavistock, 1972), 22; D. Garland, *Punishment and Welfare* (Aldershot: Gower, 1985), 48.
16 Robert Paine, *The White Arctic,* Newfoundland Social and Economic Papers No. 7 (St. John's: Institute of Social and Economic Research, Memorial University of Newfoundland, 1977).
17 "Summary of the Proceedings," 4.
18 Robert Phillips, "Slum Dwellers of the Wide-Open Spaces," *Weekend Magazine* 9, 15 (1959): 20.
19 "Transcripts of a Public Hearing Held in Ottawa by the Royal Commission on Aboriginal Peoples on the High Arctic Exiles," 5-8 April 1993, 39. Available from the commission, Ottawa.
20 Ibid.
21 "New Homes for Eskimos Said Success," *Montreal Gazette,* 26 October 1954.
22 C.J. Marshall, "Report to Graham Rowley, Secretary, Advisory Committee on Northern Development, DRD," 9 November 1953, Library and Archives Canada, RG22/254/40-8-1/4.
23 "Interviews with High Arctic Exiles," *Makivik News* 15 (1989): 15.
24 F. Ross Gibson, letter to Bob Pilot, 24 September 1983, author's personal collection.
25 David Gooding et al., *The Uses of Experiment* (Cambridge, UK: Cambridge University Press, 1989), xv.
26 F. Ross Gibson, letter to Bob Pilot, 24 September 1983, author's personal collection.
27 Larsen, *Memoirs,* 1004.
28 Alex Stevenson, memorandum to Mr. Bolger, "Eskimo Loan," 4 February 1959, Library and Archives Canada, RG85/1474-251-2/8.
29 "Agenda for the fourth meeting of the Committee on Eskimo Affairs to be held in room 304, Langevin Block, Ottawa, on Monday, May 10, 1954 at 10:00 A.M.," 1954, Library and Archives Canada, RG22/298/40-8-1/5.
30 A.H. Brown, "Weather from the White North," *National Geographic,* April 1955, 543-72.
31 Larsen, *Memoirs,* 48.
32 F. Ross Gibson, personal communication with the author, 1991.
33 Larsen, *Memoirs,* 47.
34 G.W. Stead, "Report on Tour of the Arctic Islands, September 8-12," 1953, 6, Library and Archives Canada, RG22/176/40-2-20/3.
35 Jean Lesage, "Obligations of the White Race to the Eskimos," *Ottawa Journal,* 23 March 1955.
36 F. Ross Gibson, "Conditions amongst Eskimos – Resolute Bay, NWT," RCMP Resolute Bay detachment report, 22 March 1955, Library and Archives Canada, RG18, acc. no. 8586-048, box 55, TA-500-8-1-14.
37 "Evidence given at a hearing before the House of Commons committee on Aboriginal Affairs, Ottawa," 19 March 1990. Available from the House of Commons, Ottawa.
38 "Interviews with High Arctic Exiles," *Makivik News* 13 (1989): 9.
39 Hugh Johnston, *British Emigration Policy, 1815-1830: 'Shovelling out Paupers'* (Oxford: Clarendon, 1972), 11.
40 Gibson, "Conditions amongst Eskimos – Resolute Bay, NWT," RCMP Resolute Bay detachment report, 26 March 1954, Library and Archives Canada, RG18, acc. no. 8586-048, box 55, TA-500-8-1-14.
41 Ben Sivertz, memorandum to the deputy minister, "Garbage Dumps," 19 May 1958, Library and Archives Canada, RG22/485/40-8-1/9.
42 G.D. Lucko, "Conditions amongst Eskimos generally – annual report – year ending 31 Dec. 1964," RCMP Resolute Bay detachment report, 1964, Library and Archives Canada, RG18, acc. no. 8586-048, box 55, TA-500-8-1-14.

43 Michael Dear and Shirley Clark, "Planning a New Arctic Town at Resolute," *Canadian Geographic* 97, 3 (1979): 46.

44 Andrea Cornwall, *Making Spaces, Changing Places: Situating Participation in Development,* IDS Working Paper No. 170 (Brighton, UK: Institute of Development Studies, University of Sussex, 2002), 3.

45 One of my former tutors at Cambridge University, Dr. Terrence Armstrong, was one of the first fellows at Clare Hall and provided useful information about his discussions with Erskine during the design and early-use periods. I was also a visiting fellow at Clare Hall in 2001 and while living in the college had the opportunity to explore and experience its egalitarian and communal design features firsthand.

46 Peter Collymore, *The Architecture of Ralph Erskine* (London: Granada, 1982), 22.

47 Ibid.

48 Ralph Erskine, unpublished diary, 19 August to 1 November 1973 (Drottningholm: Ralph Erskine's Arkitektkontor AD), 7.

49 Ralph Erskine, "Resolute Bay New Town," unpublished report, c. 1978, 7.

50 Underwood McLellan and Associates, *General Development Plan Resolute Bay, NWT,* Escom Report No. AI-33 (Ottawa: Department of Indian and Northern Affairs, 1980), 14.

51 Ibid., 8.

52 Boris Culjat, *Climate and the Built Environment in the North* (Stockholm: Avdelningen för Arkitektur, 1975), 92.

53 Ibid., 1.

54 Ibid., 9.

55 Ibid., 33.

56 Erskine, "Architecture and Town Planning," 166.

PART 5
STYLING MODERN NATIONHOOD

The force of Modernist, and nationalist, agendas in Canada reached an apogee with the staging at Montreal in 1967 of Canada's World Exposition. Thereafter, the dynamic for normative modernization and nationalism would be maintained professionally and politically but against a growing scale and range of resistance or contestation. The standardized, abstract, functionalist Modernist design paradigms commanded increasingly less professional and popular support. One species of Modernist architectural design that seemed to offer greater formal variety and visual interest was the forceful aestheticization of functional purpose and structure, particularly in concrete, denominated Brutalism. A comparable emboldening of complex but unifying national polity was articulated through the equally dramatic legislation enacted by Prime Minister Lester B. Pearson and even more so by Pierre Elliott Trudeau: from the 1965 vote to institute the Maple Leaf flag to the 1969 Official Languages [Bilingual], 1982 Constitution, and 1985 Multicultural Acts. Reflecting such legislative fabrication of nationhood, Réjean Legault situates the beginning of "The Idea of Brutalism in Canadian Architecture" at the Fathers of Confederation Memorial Building in Charlottetown, Prince Edward Island. He reads the narrative of the many Brutalist-styled civic and cultural buildings erected across Canada between 1960 and 1970 against the designation in 1973 of the Confederation Memorial Building as a National Historic Site. Legault vividly illuminates the ambiguities and anxieties at play in the architectural and nationalist discourse of that era. The ongoing ascription of symbolic and practical capacity to architecture in national-identity formation was manifest in Trudeau's direct intervention in the final realization of long-delayed schemes for a National Art Gallery and a National Museum. Clearly, Laura Hanks argues, Trudeau recognized the significance of art and ethnographic collections to the creation of the (later) modern nation-state but also saw them as repositories of the kind of cultural capital necessary to external recognition of nation-states. Such capital is allied by Hanks with the later phases of building up the national capital through erection of the National Gallery and National Museum on sites in Ottawa and Hull, below and facing Parliament Hill. The title of her chapter encapsulates the hubris and also anxiety underlying the architectures of national identity: "Nation, City, Place: Rethinking Nationalism at the Canadian Museum of Civilization." The commissioning of the museum involved a burgeoning recognition of the precontact heritage of Canadian identity realized through the building of traditional Aboriginal precepts into advanced technological processes by the Métis architect of the museum, Douglas Cardinal.

10

The Idea of Brutalism in Canadian Architecture

RÉJEAN LEGAULT

Thirty-nine years after its inauguration in October 1964, the Fathers of Confederation Memorial Building in Charlottetown, Prince Edward Island, was declared a Canadian National Historic Site.[1] The complex – now called the Confederation Centre of the Arts – is the first modern architectural project of the 1960s to be given such a designation (Figure 10.1).[2] In a 2005 article that focuses on the building's new status – a text we might take as an official statement – Parks Canada historian Geneviève Charrois explains that the designation was based on three primary attributes.[3] The first is that the Confederation Centre "exemplifies Canadian cultural complexes of the 1960s dedicated to the performing arts, many of which were built to mark Canada's centennial celebrations."[4] The second is that it showcases a number of significant technological advances. The third attribute, the one of most concern in this chapter, is that the building is a "superior example of Brutalist architecture in Canada."[5]

Well aware that Brutalism may not be a familiar notion to the general reader, Charrois provides the necessary clarification. After outlining the origins of the term, she explains, "Brutalist architecture rejected the luminous, ethereal qualities of the International Style in favour of more monolithic forms with a focus on the rough beauty and strength of concrete."[6] She then summarizes the key characteristics of Brutalist architecture, such as the emphasis on wall textures

Figure 10.1 Confederation Centre of the Arts, Charlottetown, architects Dimitri Dimakopoulos and the firm Affleck, Desbarats, Dimakopoulos, Lebensold and Sise, 1961-64. | © Barrett and MacKay Photo.

and limited fenestration that accentuate the building mass, the complex plans expressed through external irregularity and overlapping volumes, and the flexibility of layout that enables simultaneous activities. Yet most significant for our investigation is her statement that "the Brutalist Style influenced the architecture of many civic and cultural complexes in Canada between 1960 and 1970,"[7] a claim that gives Brutalism a central place in the history of the country's post–Second World War architecture.

Terms like "Brutalist" and "Brutalism" have long been used in specialized architectural discourse. From the 1960s onward, critics and historians have employed these expressions to qualify works of architecture built during the postwar period. As a result, the descriptors "Brutalist" and "Brutalism" have become valid as well as evocative categories in architectural criticism and historiography.[8] But they are also etymologically related to the adjectives "brutal" and "brutality," a negative connotation encouraged by the growing critique of

Modern architecture during the 1970s.[9] To complicate matters, these expressions have since entered popular architectural discourse, this time fully weighted with pejorative associations, to describe what has been found to be wrong with postwar Modernism. As a consequence, the use of terms like "Brutalist" and "Brutalism" in architectural historiography is at once wholly legitimate and fraught with ambiguity.

The designation of the Confederation Centre as a "superior example of Brutalist architecture in Canada" thus raises a number of questions about the definition of "Brutalism," the idea of style, and the interpretation of Modern architecture in Canada. Based on an examination of the Brutalist trajectory in postwar architecture, as well as a close reading of both discourses and buildings associated with Brutalism in Canada, this chapter explores how the idea of Brutalism has come to play such a strategic role in the interpretation of Canadian Modern architecture.

Figure 10.2 Hunstanton School, Norfolk, architects Alison Smithson and Peter Smithson, 1946-54. | Photograph by Michael J. Waters. Courtesy of the photographer.

NEW BRUTALISM AS AN ARCHITECTURAL MOVEMENT

As many critics and historians have noted, the origins of the term "Brutalist" are anything but clear.[10] For some, it derives from Le Corbusier's *béton brut,* for others, from Jean Dubuffet's *art brut,* and for others still, from "Brutus," the nickname given to the British architect Peter Smithson. But if the etymological sources of the term are uncertain, the origin of the discourse on Brutalism is well established: it is rooted in the British architectural movement called "New Brutalism."[11] The inaugural statement on the movement appeared in the British journal *Architectural Design* in January 1955,[12] in which the editor, Theo Crosby, singled out the Hunstanton School (1946-54) by Alison Smithson and Peter Smithson as an illustration of the New Brutalism.[13] Completed in 1954, the school was undeniably Miesian in inspiration (Figure 10.2). But what distinguished it from Mies's work was its matter-of-fact use of off-the-shelf components, where the materials are left in their raw, industrial state, and its frank display of the building's support systems. In these respects, it exemplified one of the Smithsons' key concepts of the time: the idea of the "as found."

Less than a year later, in December 1955, Reyner Banham published the first account of the new architectural movement.[14] Working as an art and architecture critic, Banham was deeply involved with some of the young architects associated with the group. Establishing the Smithsons as the founders of New Brutalism and Hunstanton School as the paradigm of Brutalist architecture, Banham moved on to define the basic characteristics of the movement's architecture. After a long discussion of a few examples, among them Louis Kahn's recently completed Yale Art Gallery (1951-53), Banham concluded that the qualities of a Brutalist project were: (1) memorability as an image, (2) clear exhibition of structure, and (3) valuation of materials for their inherent qualities "as found."[15]

Banham's formulation of the principles of New Brutalism was seminal. But it was not to remain unchallenged. Works by other architects soon began to inflect the definition of the movement's architecture. Central to this change of perspective was the lingering influence of Le Corbusier's béton brut, or raw concrete, a theme that was first brought to the fore with his Unité d'habitation of Marseilles (1946-52). Confronted with poor workmanship and unable to

Figure 10.3 Maisons Jaoul, Neuilly, architect Le Corbusier, 1951-55. | Photograph by Caroline Maniaque. Courtesy of the photographer.

obtain the desired quality of finishes, Le Corbusier decided that the concrete should be left in its rough state. The strategy adopted was to leave the concrete *brut de décoffrage* – that is, rough after the removal of the wooden formwork. The result was what Le Corbusier dubbed béton brut, a concrete whose surface bore the traces of the grain of the wooden moulds, the imprint of the production process. He further explored the idea to leave building materials in their rough state in his Maisons Jaoul in Neuilly, completed in 1955 (Figure 10.3). In this project, he combined béton brut with rough bricks and thick cement bonding. But here the expression of rawness was not left only to chance. The architect asked that the bricks be specifically selected for their imperfections and required that the workers laying the bricks be changed regularly so as to avoid too much regularity in the wall surface.[16] In his attempt to return to a pre-industrial, almost archaic material expression, Le Corbusier was far from the "as found" ideal advocated by the New Brutalists. But his exploration of the poetics of *matériaux bruts* was so influential that from then on the use of rough materials was generally read as the sign of a Brutalist intention.

In Britain, however, the architecture of New Brutalism was not yet framed by the poetics of rough materials. A case in point is the Engineering Building at Leicester University (1959-63) by James Stirling and James Gowan (Figure 10.4). With its various functions expressed by specific building forms, and its contrasting use of standard industrial materials, the school was hailed as a major Brutalist accomplishment.[17] Stirling himself did not wish to use the term, keeping the promoters of the New Brutalism at arm's length. But the building's formal and material expression was nevertheless in line with the original ideals of Brutalism conceived as a design attitude that sought a frank expression of the program and the creation of a "memorable image."

The contrast between various projects associated with Brutalism did not go unnoticed. In a 1964 article assessing recent developments of New Brutalism in architecture, the German critic and historian Jürgen Joedicke warned his readers, "We must be careful, in fact, to make a distinction between brutalism in the narrower sense, as it was generally represented in Smithson's circle and England as a whole, and the brutalism which later developed at an international level."[18] It is with this warning in mind that Banham, just a decade after his first statement on the New Brutalism, was to offer the first critical assessment of the history and fate of the movement. Published in 1966, the book is entitled *The New Brutalism: Ethic or Aesthetic?* and reiterates Banham's belief that New Brutalism had been primarily a design approach motivated by an ethical attitude toward architecture.[19] But his survey, which examines the British contribution to the development of Brutalism as well as its manifestations in many countries,

Figure 10.4 Engineering Building, Leicester University, Leicester, architects James Stirling and James Gowan, 1959-63. | Photograph by Richard Einzig. Courtesy of Arcaid.

is less optimistic about the future. In the book's conclusion, Banham suggests that by the mid-1960s the spirit of Brutalism had moved from Europe to America.[20] It is also clear to him that in this journey, the movement lost its ethical value, having been reduced to a limited and limiting aesthetic approach.[21]

FROM NEW BRUTALISM TO BRUTALISM

It was not until the end of the 1960s that American historians entered the discussion. But their interpretation of Brutalism was to be very different from that of their European counterparts. Most notable is the work of architectural historian Marcus Whiffen.[22] In his 1969 book *American Architecture since 1780: A Guide to the Styles,* Whiffen offers what is probably the first rereading of Brutalism in terms of an architectural style.[23] In his guide, Whiffen explains that the most recent trend in American architecture is called Brutalism. Significantly, he talks about Brutalism, not New Brutalism. And his description of the style focuses on formal considerations, not planning or program. "Brutalist buildings," he writes, "have a look of weight and massiveness that immediately sets them apart from those predominantly rectangular, flat-roofed styles ... Concrete is the favorite material; it is always left exposed."[24] Whiffen is acutely aware of the limitation inherent in the use of the notion of style, recognizing that buildings classified under the same style "differ from each other in more noticeable ways than they resemble each other."[25] Yet in spite of the deficiencies of architectural taxonomy, he nonetheless believes in the validity of the knowledge acquired through the classification of buildings in terms of their visual characteristics.

Whiffen recounts the history of Brutalism as it was written by Banham, correctly stressing that in its early phase it was less a style than a philosophy of design. He also underlines that "*béton brut* became so much part of the image conjured up by the term Brutalism" that many may think the term came from it.[26] Yet after this clarification, he goes on to explain the specificity of American Brutalism: "In America exposed concrete left in its rough state – or sometimes, as in Paul Rudolph's Art and Architecture Building at Yale (completed 1963), artificially roughened – is common to a great many, if not most, of the buildings by which the adjective Brutalist comes to be applied" (Figure 10.5).[27] Seemingly aware of the radical difference between Le Corbusier's and Rudolph's treatment of the material, Whiffen rightly points to the artificial roughness of the School of Art and Architecture's textured concrete, where the vertical ribs were hand-hammered to expose the aggregates.[28] In his conclusion, he is careful to note

Figure 10.5 School of Art and Architecture, Yale University, New Haven, architect Paul Rudolph, 1958-63. | Photograph by author.

that not all buildings with an exposed concrete envelope are "Brutalist" in the full sense of the term and that American architects have been less inclined to adopt the type of planning favoured by their English colleagues. But he concludes that "it is convenient to have a name for the style of mass, weight, roughness, and solidity that has become the most frequent medium of 'advanced' architectural expression."[29]

Whiffen's stylistic definition is evidence of a major change in the understanding of Brutalism in architecture. First, echoing Banham's conclusion, Whiffen's definition affirms the move from ethical to aesthetic considerations. Second, it highlights the semantic shift from the ideal of the "as found" to the idea of the "rough," or material roughness. Third, and more important, it confirms the move away from the prospective program of architects and toward the retrospective reading of historians. Given Whiffen's taxonomic goal, it is not surprising that Brutalism came to be framed as a stylistic category. But it also confirmed that Brutalism had unmistakably entered the realm of architecture's recent history.

BRUTALISM AND CANADIAN ARCHITECTURE

The trajectory I have just described shows that Brutalism, both as concept and as architecture, has been the subject of various, contrasting interpretations. It should come as no surprise, therefore, that in Canada the understanding of Brutalism was also subjected to a similar flux. To explore this question further, it is necessary to look at a few examples that show how critics and historians approached the idea of Brutalism in Canadian architecture.

The first case is Scarborough College in Toronto (1963-65), designed by the Australian architect John Andrews in collaboration with the Toronto firm of Page and Steele. Situated along a ridge overlooking a heavily wooded valley and a small river, the college comprises two wings of differing heights and shapes that are connected to a central plaza by broad vaulted pedestrian streets. The whole building is made of poured-in-place textured concrete left exposed both inside and out. In 1972 British historian Philip Drew argued that Scarborough College was "one of the most brutally frank buildings of the decade" and embodied a number of New Brutalist ideals, including its "tough-minded functionalism."[30] By the early 1980s, however, the functionalist reading had fallen away, and Canadian historians were to focus instead on the building's formal traits. In the 1981 *International Handbook of Contemporary Developments in Architecture*, the historian Claude Bergeron writes that Scarborough College displays the "Brutalist fad for heavy, sculptural supports and stair towers,"[31] and another critic refers to the building as a "fortress-like, Brutalist complex."[32] Seemingly oblivious to the historicity of the definitions of "Brutalism," these authors end up employing the term as a limited – and faintly pejorative – epithet, confirming that by then the expression had already started to acquire its negative connotation.

Equally revealing is the reception of the Brantford City Hall (1964-68) by Michael M. Kopsa, an ensemble of two buildings organized around a central court. Each exterior shape reflects the diversity of interior functions, like the stairs located in rounded towers. Box-like sun visors project from the building's surface to frame individual office windows, protecting them against sun and rain. The building is finished with poured-in-place textured concrete. In his *Modern Canadian Architecture* of 1983, historian Leon Whiteson writes that "local government welcomed official buildings executed in a radically Modernist manner, such as Kopsa's boldly Brutalist raw concrete city hall."[33] Here, it is the building's materiality that conjures up the idea of Brutalism, specifically that of Rudolph's textured concrete.

The same is true of the Centennial Planetarium in Calgary (1965-68) by architects Jack Long and Hugh McMillan. Designed to accommodate a set of programmatic needs, including a planetarium chamber, lecture theatres, and an observation deck, the building is treated as a sculptural shape composed of hard-edged walls that have a dramatic presence within the landscape. The complex is again made of poured-in-place concrete, but this time the concrete is left in its raw state. Commenting on the planetarium, the critic Trevor Boddy wrote in 1987, "The building combines the board-formed, rough concrete *béton brut,* with forms that clearly allude to medieval castles, so loved by Le Corbusier. The official stylistic label for the stream of Modern architecture utilizing rough-edged concrete building is the poetically apt 'Brutalist.'"[34]

Yet of all the examples of Brutalist architecture noted in the historiography, the most commonly cited is Place Bonaventure in Montreal (1964-68) by Raymond Affleck of the firm later known as ARCOP (Figure 10.6).[35] Place Bonaventure is a multipurpose building containing a shopping arcade, an exhibition hall, a five-level merchandise mart, an international trade centre, and a 400-room hotel on the roof. One of the most distinctive features of the building is its highly textured concrete exterior envelope. So close were the visual connections to Paul Rudolph's work that in a 1968 review Kenneth Frampton did not hesitate to call it "Rudolphian corduroy concrete."[36]

It is important to note that none of the reviews published around the time of Place Bonaventure's inauguration made any connection with Brutalist architecture.[37] Significantly, even Banham avoided any mention of Brutalism in his 1976 analysis of the complex.[38] It was only in the 1980s that the Canadian discourse took a decisive pro-Brutalist turn. In the 1981 *International Handbook,* Place Bonaventure is described as a "Brutalist concrete building."[39] Two years later, Whiteson referred to the building's "daunting Brutalist idiom."[40] But the most authoritative interpretation of Place Bonaventure as a Brutalist building appears in Harold Kalman's well-known *A History of Canadian Architecture,* published in 1994.[41] In a passage on the building, Kalman asserts: "Its weighty and massive appearance, and the textured, monolithic surfaces, make Place Bonaventure a representative of 'Brutalism.'"[42] In Kalman's description, the category of Brutalism is clearly associated with the formal appearance and textured surfaces of the building, an interpretation in line with the notion of Brutalist style developed by Whiffen. Yet what is most interesting about Kalman's description is what comes next, for he writes that Brutalism is "a style associated

Figure 10.6 Place Bonaventure, Montreal, architects Raymond Affleck and the firm Affleck, Desbarats, Dimakopoulos, Lebensold and Sise, 1964-68. | Photographer unknown. From Alexander Tzonis, Liane Lefaivre, and Richard Diamond, *Architecture in North America since 1960* (Boston: Bulfinch, 1995), 121.

with the work of Scottish architect James Stirling, American architect Paul Rudolph, and the English husband-and-wife architectural team of Peter and Alison Smithson."[43] By placing side by side the names of Stirling, Rudolph, and the Smithsons, this passage reveals the difficulty Kalman encountered in trying to identify the sources of Brutalism in Canada.

In 2000 Kalman's book was republished in a more concise version.[44] In the new version, the description of Place Bonaventure remains the same. But its architectural affiliations have been substantially edited. Dropping the references to Stirling and the Smithsons, Kalman now writes that Brutalism is "a style associated with the work of American architect Paul Rudolph."[45] Perhaps realizing the difficulty of making a convincing visual comparison with the canons of New Brutalism – the Smithsons' Hunstanton School and Stirling's Engineering Building – Kalman resorted to mentioning only the most obvious visual connection: that of the work of Paul Rudolph.

Based on these few examples, it would be fair to say that by the 1990s Brutalism was part of Canadian architectural discourse. But these cases also reveal two things: first, that these references to Brutalism were evidently not grounded in any in-depth probing of the notion; and second, that it was a very specific idea of Brutalism (a Brutalism primarily associated with weight, massive appearance, and rough concrete) that had taken root in the Canadian imagination.

TOWARD A DEFINITION OF THE "BRUTALIST STYLE" IN CANADA

By focusing on exposed concrete – in all of its forms – as the common denominator of Brutalism, Canadian critics and historians were mostly indebted to the American interpretation of this architectural trend. But in Canada the notion of Brutalism would also acquire an additional layer of meaning. This other dimension of the Brutalist idiom was brought to the fore in *A Guide to Canadian Architectural Styles,* a book first published in 1992. Written by three architectural historians – Leslie Maitland, Jacqueline Hucker, and Shannon Ricketts – the book proposes an overview of Canadian architecture from the seventeenth to the twentieth century.[46] It divides the postwar period into four architectural styles: International, Expressionist, Brutalist, and post-Modern. The importance of this book for my discussion rests on the fact that it offers the first full-fledged definition of "Brutalism" in the context of Canadian architecture. In their entry on the Brutalist style, the authors – following Whiffen's example – insist on associating the style with a specific building material, namely concrete:

> While the International Style explored the diaphanous aesthetic of glass and steel, Brutalism examines the beauty and power of concrete. Often, walls are constructed of load-bearing concrete; texture plays an important part in these surfaces and exaggerates the sense of mass. The surface of the concrete is often left with the patterns of the wooden mold, expressing the appeal of less highly machined finishes.[47]

In contrast to Whiffen, however, the authors of the Canadian guide go beyond the mere identification of visual characteristics to comment on the assumed intentions of the designers:

> Architects rejected the impersonalized machine aesthetic and responded to the need for a sense of privacy, individuality and human scale by designing buildings that used more varied massing and highly textured materials. Learning from new approaches in Europe – namely the English Brutalist movement and the

> Dutch Structuralist movement – Canadian architects produced a variety of structures that reflected a return to a more organic approach to design and an architecture that attempted to be more sensitive to community values.[48]

In other words, Canadian architects absorbed and blended clearly distinct design approaches to create a unique brand of Brutalism imbued with particular values. The authors do not stop there, for Brutalism in Canada is associated with another distinctive trait, that of a specific building type: the civic and performing arts centres that were built across the country in the 1960s. The wording cannot be clearer: "In Canada the style often influenced the design of civic complexes whose large scale was appropriately expressed in massive, irregular profiles constructed of raw concrete."[49] In fact, four of the six examples illustrated in the book are civic centres sponsored by the federal government to celebrate the Centennial of the Canadian Confederation: the National Arts Centre in Ottawa (1964-69) (Figure 10.7), the Grand Théâtre in Quebec City (1964-69), the Manitoba Theatre Centre in Winnipeg (1970), and the Confederation Centre of the Arts in Charlottetown (Figure 10.8).[50]

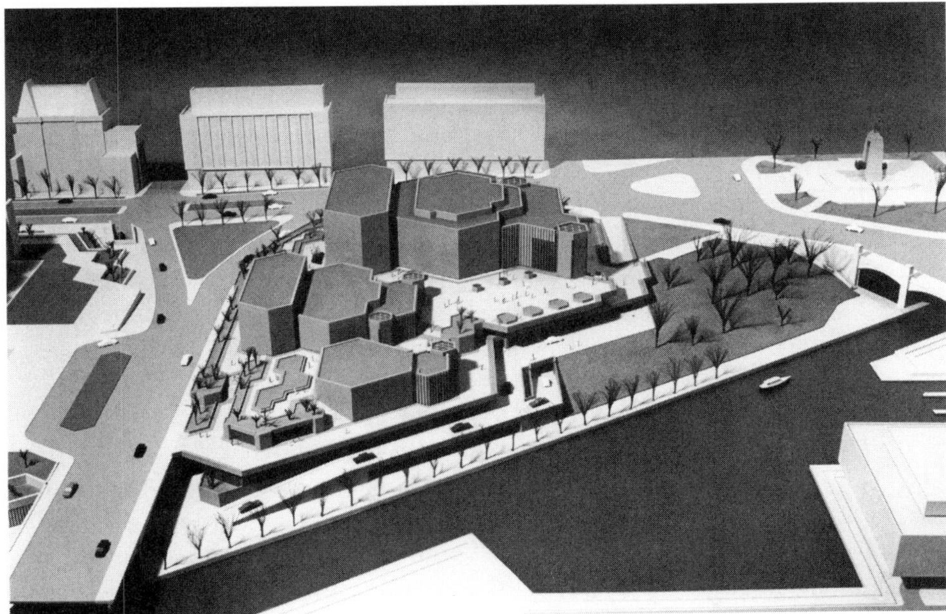

Figure 10.7 Architectural model of the National Arts Centre, Ottawa, architects Fred Lebensold and the firm Affleck, Desbarats, Dimakopoulos, Lebensold and Sise, 1964-69. | Photograph by Roger Jewett. Courtesy of the National Arts Centre (NAC Archives, CMPLX-1965-14).

Figure 10.8 Architectural model of the Confederation Centre of the Arts, Charlottetown, architects Dimitri Dimakopoulos and the firm Affleck, Desbarats, Dimakopoulos, Lebensold and Sise, 1961-64. | Photographer unknown. Courtesy of the Confederation Centre of the Arts.

Given that the Confederation Centre is finished with a veneer of Wallace sandstone rather than concrete, it may come as a surprise that the building is even included in the list. But this major discrepancy is clearly offset by the criteria of client and the program. With this reading, Brutalism is not merely a stylistic category in twentieth-century architecture but also becomes – surreptitiously – the marker of a set of buildings that can be distinguished both by the humanistic approach underlying their design and by the origin of the commission. In this narrative, the Brutalist style has come to stand for a specific genre of modern architecture associated with the Canadian government's cultural policies.

THE SOCIOLOGY OF CANADIAN BRUTALISM

Interestingly, this linkage of Brutalism with Canadian civic architecture is not totally original. In a fascinating, if not particularly well-known, study on Canadian architecture of the 1960s – "L'affaire du brutalisme" – the French critic Marcel Cornu argues for the existence of a Brutalism that is specifically Canadian.[51] Published in 1971 in the French journal *Architecture Mouvement Continuité,* the essay is based on personal observations made by the author during a long stay in Canada in 1970.

According to Cornu, the signs of this new architectural trend in Canada are the rejection of the model of the skyscraper, with its focus on lightness and glass, in favour of an architecture that emphasizes low, massive volumes made out of concrete. Whereas the former is translucent and open, the latter is consciously opaque and closed, a posture highlighted by the buildings' "brutal" exteriors. Citing these specific features, Cornu argues that it is an architecture that could and should be called Brutalist. Cornu is well aware of the dangers of such a comparison. He also understands the difficulty of defining what is specifically Canadian about this movement that makes it more than a mere translation of international or American trends. But he maintains the existence of the Brutalist fact in Canada and postulates its sociological importance. For Cornu, this Brutalist idiom is nowhere more present than in the public buildings commissioned by the Canadian government to commemorate the Centennial of the Confederation. As a sociologist, Cornu is interested in what this phenomenon says about an emerging Canadian identity.

To develop his argument, Cornu looks closely at three examples of civic buildings financially supported by the federal government: the Ontario Science Centre in Toronto (1964-69), the Grand Théâtre in Quebec City, and the National Arts Centre in Ottawa. He argues that one of the key characteristics of these Brutalist buildings is the specific relationship each establishes with its site. These buildings do not simply rest on the site or in any way negate its specific qualities. They instead address the site head-on, with the brutal frankness characteristic of British Brutalism.

A second aspect of Cornu's analysis considers the perceived materiality of these civic buildings. He underlines the roughness, starkness, and massiveness in the appearance of each of the buildings, adding that they seem to be made of an "immutable concrete."[52] Cornu is aware that these traits refer to the received, popular conception of Brutalism as an aesthetic category. But it is an interpretation so pervasive as to be granted full acceptance. In fact, Cornu's attention to concrete is of such intensity that, in his reading, the material almost becomes a metaphor for Brutalism. Noting the widespread employment of a concrete moulded with deep ridges, he comes to the conclusion that "in the end, this 'textured' concrete, object of predilection of Canadian Brutalism, appears as a sort of national material."[53] Not unlike marble in Italy or granite in Finland, for Cornu textured concrete in Canada has acquired a national identity.[54]

In his final point, Cornu insists on the "fortress-like" character of these civic buildings, a defensive image he finds evoked by the large round towers of the Ontario Science Centre, the tall crenellated walls of Quebec City's Grand

Théâtre, and the blind hexagonal towers of Ottawa's National Arts Centre.[55] Working from a sociological point of view, Cornu argues that this aesthetic trend has a social underpinning. To the question of why this Brutalist figuration acquired a national character, Cornu offers a long answer that may be summarized as follows: because it was functionally reassuring and seemed to offer a protective environment.

Cornu's idea of a protective, fortress-like architecture is reminiscent of Northrop Frye's oft-repeated idea about the "garrison mentality" of Canadian culture. In his conclusion to the *Literary History of Canada*, published in 1965, Frye uses this expression to describe the "closely knit and beleaguered society at odds with its environment."[56] Alhough Cornu does not mention Frye, his idea of a fortress-like architecture evokes the myth of Canadian nature as a menacing space that calls for the building of protective, fortified places. In his concluding remarks, Cornu – who was deeply aware of the growing tension between the country's two founding nations – underlines that Brutalist architecture is common to both French and English Canada, an observation that brings him to assert the belief that the Brutalist idiom has a national character and is revealing of the will to define a Canadian identity.[57]

Cornu's analysis did not receive much attention outside of France and, as far as I know, has never been mentioned in any study on modern architecture in Canada.[58] But his captivating argument surprisingly anticipates the narrative that was to be developed twenty years later by the authors of the *Guide to Canadian Architectural Styles*. As noted above, both relate Brutalism to the architecture of Canadian civic centres. But the similarities do not stop there: both stress the connection between Brutalism and concrete, and both underline that Brutalist buildings have complex plans that are "expressed on the exterior in irregular, juxtaposed masses."[59] Yet most significant for my analysis is that the authors of the *Guide* emphasize the effect the building may have on its users: "The rugged surfaces of these buildings are punctured by very few windows, which are often sealed, further accentuating the sense of an enclosed, protective environment."[60] Echoing Cornu's idea of a fortress-like architecture, the authors of the *Guide* are eager to draw the connection between the architecture's formal appearance and its "psychological" impact.

The *Guide*'s connection between Brutalism and the idea of a "protective environment" derives from an analysis that is primarily formal rather than sociological. But this psychological reading of the forms of these civic centres partakes of a similar attempt to define the "Canadian" character of the style. Unlike Cornu, the authors of the *Guide* do not explicitly state that the Brutalist idiom has a national character. But they do not hesitate to recognize that the buildings they have selected to discuss reveal a collective intent, an interpretation that unequivocally points in the same direction.

FROM RAW CONCRETE TO FINISHED STONE

The *Guide to Canadian Architectural Styles* has done much to codify Brutalism in Canada. But the course of the Brutalist trajectory does not stop there. The 2003 nomination of Charlottetown's Confederation Centre of the Arts as a National Historic Site was to have an unexpected impact on the definition of Brutalism, a change registered in the revised edition of the *Guide* published in 2004. In the 1992 edition, the authors insisted that Brutalism was a style that "examines the beauty and power of concrete."[61] But this description became untenable when a building made of finished sandstone was declared the pre-eminent example of Brutalist architecture in Canada. The 2004 edition wisely solves the problem. De-emphasizing the importance of concrete, the authors now state that Brutalism "examines the solidity and power of masonry."[62] The text also adds that variations on this theme include "buildings with more highly finished surfaces."[63] This slight change in the definition was immediately echoed in contemporary statements about the Confederation Centre itself. In her essay on the building, Charrois writes that "pure Brutalist expression was not devoid of more finely worked material, some with detailed surfaces and carvings."[64] She adds in a bracketed statement: "Charlottetown's Confederation Centre is itself just such a building with its exterior of stone, rather than concrete, expressing a refined form of the genre."[65]

This is, admittedly, a very minute change. But it is significant. With such a statement, the early definition of New Brutalism as an architectural movement that focused on the use of raw, industrial materials "as found" has completely disappeared. Moreover, rough concrete itself, the feature that occupied the central role in the discourses on Brutalism in North America for almost three decades, has now receded into the background, replaced in favour of masonry as a more general and more inclusive category. Yet most significant for this investigation is the consequence of these changes on the construction of Brutalism. Out of both necessity and coherence, writers on the Confederation Centre felt the need to adjust the definition of "Brutalism" to the features of the nominated building. With this operation, however, it is now the building that helps to characterize the style, rather than the opposite, giving "Brutalism" a definition that has enhanced national "content." Different from either the British or the American conceptions of the trend, "Brutalism" has now acquired a meaning that is specifically Canadian.

A "BRUTALIST STYLE"?

This change in the definition of "Brutalism" brings me to the notion of "style" and to the "Brutalist style." Needless to say, discussions on the concept of "style" in art and architecture have a long tradition.[66] Searching for a theoretical model of change in the history of art, the German art historian Heinrich Wölfflin defined style "as a collective approach to artistic conventions, materials, and techniques in which a more or less stable and definable formal pattern emerges."[67] But the notion of style has never been easy to deal with, triggering endless theoretical discussions.[68] Whereas some scholars have chosen to reject it altogether, others have felt compelled to make some important clarifications. Writing about painting and pictorial style, the art historian Richard Wollheim proposes the broad but necessary distinction between *general style* and *individual style*.[69] In a discussion of a painter's individual style, he explains that this problem must be approached in terms of a *generative conception* as opposed to a merely *taxonomic conception* of style. While the generative model seeks to describe and explain the processes and the principles that guided the artist, the taxonomic model proposes instead to describe the (mostly) formal features common to a group of works.[70]

The stylistic paradigm has been equally important for architecture. For James Ackerman – who has primarily worked on the Renaissance – style is used as "a way of characterizing relationships among works of art that were made at the same time and/or place, or by the same person or group."[71] In other words, it provides a structure for the history of art and architecture. Style was also central to the analysis of early historians of modern architecture like Siegfried Giedion, Henry-Russell Hitchcock, and Nikolaus Pevsner. But which conception of style did they adopt? When talking about Modern Movement architecture or the International Style, did they hold a *generative* or a *taxonomic* conception of style? Did they focus on the processes and principles guiding the design of the works or on their formal features? A cursory examination of canonical texts shows that architectural historians have overwhelmingly adopted a taxonomic conception of style. But is this approach still valid today?

In a brilliant contribution to this debate, Sarah Williams Goldhagen offers a thorough critique of the use of the notion of style in the interpretation of Modernism in architecture.[72] According to Goldhagen, it is the paradigm of style – as Modernism's unifying feature – that still governs the work of contemporary historians and theorists of modern architecture. She admits that the paradigm has served them well, for it helped to explain and analyze how progressive architectural and urban practices in the twentieth century constitute a profound change from those of the nineteenth century. But she also argues that this paradigm has been unable to account for anomalies (works that fall outside of stylistic boundaries) or to propose a coherent periodization. "It has become clear," Goldhagen writes, "that employing style even as the lowest or only common-denominator measure of modernism is akin to mistaking only chairs for all furniture or only houses for all architecture: it simply misconstrues the role of style in twentieth-century architecture and its conceptual place in modernism's domain."[73]

Goldhagen's essay focuses on architectural modernism as a whole. But her critique is equally valid for the analysis of the subcategory that has been called Brutalism. Problems of anomalies and periodization also appear in the discussion of the Brutalist style. Yet the most crucial problem remains the one of definition: how can we characterize a Brutalist building? Should such a characterization rely on a discussion of the approach of the designer (i.e., intentions, process, principles) or on a retrospective reading of the features of the work? If we adopt the latter, how are we to define the taxonomic traits of the Brutalist style: its planning approach, its formal expression, its materials treatment, its visual effect, its symbolic content? As Goldhagen explains, stylistic homologies can mask greatly divergent aims. And conversely, "differences in style can obscure common aims and common ethical agendas."[74] These should be sufficient reasons to be skeptical about the notion's cognitive efficiency.

Not unlike the International Style, Brutalism is a notion that has been used to group together broad sets of buildings under a single unified rubric. But the criteria chosen for this selection process are varied and rarely homogeneous: they may be formal, organizational, or material traits or even design attitudes. The result is often a heterogeneous collection of buildings that fits uncomfortably under the stylistic denominator. That the Smithsons' Hunstanton School, Le Corbusier's Maisons Jaoul, Rudolph's School of Art and Architecture, Stirling and Gowan's Engineering Building, Affleck's Place Bonaventure, and now Dimakopoulos's Confederation Centre have all qualified as Brutalist buildings should prove the point.[75] It reveals, in the end, that taxonomic style remains a weak paradigm to discuss Brutalism in architecture.

BRUTALISM AND THE IDENTITY OF CANADIAN ARCHITECTURE

In light of this discussion, what are we to make of the need to summon the notion of style to discuss the issue of Brutalism in Canadian architecture? Informed by Cornu's stimulating essay, I would argue that it has primarily to do with recurrent attempts to define the identity of Canadian architecture.

Needless to say, discussions about the nature of the Canadian identity abound.[76] Likewise, the identity of Canadian architecture has been the subject of numerous studies. If the issue was almost a constant source of debate from the turn of the twentieth century onward, it took on even more importance in the postwar period. The release of the Massey Commission's report in 1951 with its stated goal to foster the development of a Canadian culture distinct from that of its southern neighbour coincided with the growing acceptance of modern architecture in the country. The commission identified a significant role for architecture.[77] In his seminal essay *Looking at Architecture in Canada* (1958), Alan Gowans took up the issue and argued that it was possible to have a modern architecture that was truly Canadian.[78] In the 1960s and 1970s many writers wrestled with the difficult task of pinning down what this specificity might be. Focusing on works of the 1960s, Carol Moore Ede suggests that although they are all responses to worldwide concerns and universal needs, they also share common traits, a "Canadianism" – she argues – that is reflected through geography rather than "style."[79] Other writers have singled out the specificity of either context or ideology.[80] Over the past three decades, historiographic explorations have oscillated uneasily between Modern architecture in Canada and Canadian Modern architecture.[81] But the drive to address the specificity – and thus identity – of Canadian architecture remains unabated. It is in this light, I believe, that we should read the ongoing search for the definition of "Brutalism."

In parallel with their American counterparts, Canadian historians first associated Brutalism with an architecture of weight, massive appearance, and textured concrete. But they did not limit themselves to the identification of general aesthetic traits. For the authors of the *Guide,* Brutalism also became the common denominator of a design attitude embodied in a specific building program sponsored by the Canadian government. Viewed in this light, Brutalism became the unofficial code word to designate the architecture of the civic centres built to celebrate the Centennial of the Confederation. Brutalism, in other words, was turned into a marker of Canadian architecture's modern identity.[82]

This semantic shift represents a major historiographic turn. Overcoming the negative connotation often associated with Brutalism, proponents of this interpretation instead acknowledge that the term could be used in a positive way to distinguish a set of buildings produced during a highly symbolic period in Canadian architectural and cultural development (i.e., the country's Centennial). However, this operation is not without consequences for Canadian historiography. For if it rightly establishes a connection between buildings that have the same institutional sponsor and comparable programs, it may also

Figure 10.9 National Arts Centre, Ottawa, architects Fred Lebensold and the firm Affleck, Desbarats, Dimakopoulos, Lebensold and Sise, 1964-69. | Photograph by Roger Jewett. Courtesy of City of Ottawa Archives (MG 011 / National Arts Centre, 15 January 1979).

conceal significant differences in terms of either plans, forms, or materials as well as design ideals and intentions. Given that Charlottetown's Confederation Centre of the Arts and Ottawa's National Arts Centre were designed by the same firm during the same period, it may seem perfectly logical to bring them both under the Brutalist label (Figure 10.9).[83] But what are we to make of their significant differences in terms of planning (volumetric versus geometric), siting (axial versus asymmetrical), topography (podium versus terraced landscape), or materiality (finished stone veneer versus prefabricated textured concrete)? In such instances, the stylistic paradigm is mobilized at the expense of the specificity and uniqueness of the architectural objects themselves.

In Canadian architecture – as in the rest of the Western world – the adjective "Brutalist" has become so pervasive as to warrant special attention. Like the International Style, to which it is so often opposed, the designation has become part of our critical vocabulary. Yet as this chapter's brief excursus should make clear, Brutalism has already been the subject of many different, not to say divergent, interpretations. In short, it is a historical category whose definition is still in need of serious critical examination. Yet in Canada, use of the term also seems to be fraught with a persistent ambiguity. This mood is nowhere more perceptible than in the text drafted for the Confederation Centre's official designation. The bronze plaque unveiled by the governor-general of Canada in November 2005 reads, "With its monolithic outward appearance and extensive terracing, the Confederation Centre of the Arts is a notable example of 'Brutalist' architecture in Canada."[84] Here, the punctuation marks that bracket the word "Brutalist" – imprinted as they are on the bronze plaque – confirm the irresolution attached to the term. It is an ambiguity that reveals, more than anything else, the anxious connection between Modernist historiography and national identity in Canadian architecture.

ACKNOWLEDGMENTS

My first exploration of this topic was done in the context of a presentation for the 2002-03 Green Lecture Series, St. John's College, University of British Columbia. I would like to thank Rhodri Windsor Liscombe for inviting me to participate in this series and for his editorial suggestions. I would also like to thank Cammie McAtee for her insightful comments and suggestions on this chapter. Part of the research for this work was supported by a research grant from the Fonds Québécois de recherche sur la société et la culture. I would like to thank Colin Ripley, Michael J. Waters, and Caroline Maniaque for the photographs they provided me.

NOTES

1 The building was granted the status of National Historic Site on 3 June 2003. See Parks Canada, Directory of Designations of National Historic Significance of Canada, http://www.pc.gc.ca.

2 Commissioned to memorialize the Centennial of the first Confederation Conference held in that city, the complex was designed by the Montreal architectural firm Affleck, Desbarats, Dimakopoulos, Lebensold and Sise, with Dimitri Dimakopoulos as the partner in charge.

3 Geneviève Charrois, "Confederation Centre for the Arts: A 1960s National Historic Site," *Heritage* 8, 2 (2005): 11-13.

4 Ibid., 13.

5 Ibid.

6 Ibid.

7 Ibid.

8 For the most recent contribution on this historical category, see B.M. Boyle, "Brutalism," in *Encyclopedia of 20th-Century Architecture,* vol. 1, ed. R. Stephen Sennott, 180-82 (New York: Fitzroy Dearborn, 2004).

9 One such critic was Vincent Scully, who blamed Brutalist architecture for having encouraged the destruction of the street and the city; see Vincent Scully, "Le Corbusier, 1922-1965," in *The Le Corbusier Archives,* vol. 2, ed. H. Allen Brooks, 47-55 (New York and London: Garland, 1983). More recently, authors like Robert Twombly have strongly denounced Brutalism for its nefarious architectural intentions and results; see Robert Twombly, "Architecture," in *Encyclopedia of the United States in the Twentieth Century,* ed. Stanley L. Kutler (New York: Charles Scribner's Sons, 1996), 1689.

10 Most contributions on Brutalism start with a discussion on the origin of the term. For the most compelling explanation, see Reyner Banham, *The New Brutalism: Ethic or Aesthetic?* (London: Architectural Press, 1966).

11 For a recent study on Brutalism in England, see Noah Chasin, "Ethics and Aesthetics: New Brutalism, Team 10, and Architectural Change in the 1950s" (PhD diss., City University of New York, May 2002).

12 The first mention of the term in print, however, was in a 1953 article by Peter Smithson, "House in Soho, London," *Architectural Design* 23, 12 (1953): 342.

13 [Theo Crosby], "The New Brutalism," *Architectural Design* 25, 1 (1955): 1.

14 Reyner Banham, "The New Brutalism," *Architectural Review* 118, 12 (December 1955): 354-61. For a thorough discussion of Banham's contribution to the discourse on New Brutalism, see Nigel Whiteley, *Reyner Banham: Historian of the Immediate Future* (Cambridge, MA: MIT Press, 2002).

15 Banham "New Brutalism," 361.

16 Pierre Joly, *Le Corbusier à Paris* (Paris: La manufacture, 1987), 212. See also Caroline Maniaque, *Le Corbusier et les Maisons Jaoul* (Paris: Picard, 2005).

17 See Kenneth Frampton, "New Brutalism and the Architecture of the Welfare State: England 1949-59," in *Modern Architecture: A Critical History* (London: Thames and Hudson, 1980), 262-68.

18 Jürgen Joedicke, "New Brutalism – Brutalism in Architecture," *Bauen+Wohnen* 11 (1964), English summary, n.p.

19 Banham, *New Brutalism: Ethic*. The book was an extension of Banham's brief retrospective assessment of the movement published in German three years earlier. See Banham, "Brutalism," in *Knaurs Lexikon der Modernen Architektur* (Munich and Zurich: Droemersche Verlagsanstalt, 1963).

20 Banham, *New Brutalism: Ethic,* 135. Interestingly, Banham sustains this argument in spite of the fact that the only American project mentioned in the book is Paul Rudolph's married students' housing at Yale University, New Haven (1959-62).

21 He writes, "The Johnsons, Johansens and Rudolphs of the American scene were quicker than I was to see that the Brutalists were really their allies, not mine; committed to the classical tradition, not the technological." See Banham, *New Brutalism: Ethic,* 135.

22 Although born and educated in England, Marcus Whiffen (1916-2003) was most productive after his move to the United States in 1952. As a result, his books, among them the well-known *American Architecture, 1607-1976* (Cambridge, MA: MIT Press, 1981), can be considered the work of an American historian.

23 Marcus Whiffen, *American Architecture since 1780: A Guide to the Styles* (Cambridge, MA: MIT Press, 1969). Given that the introduction was dated January 1968, the book was most likely written in 1967.

24 Ibid., 275.

25 Ibid., vii.

26 Ibid., 276.

27 Ibid., 279.

28 On Rudolph's treatment of concrete, see Réjean Legault, "The Semantics of Exposed Concrete," in *Liquid Stone: New Architecture in Concrete,* ed. Jean-Louis Cohen and G. Martin Moeller, 46-56 (New York: Princeton Architectural Press, 2006).

29 Whiffen, *American Architecture since 1780,* 279.

30 Philip Drew, *Third Generation: The Changing Meaning of Architecture* (New York: Frederick A. Praeger, 1972), 144. Australian writer Jennifer Taylor, together with John Andrews, proposes a similar interpretation in *John Andrews: Architecture, A Performing Art* (New York: Oxford University Press, 1982).

31 Claude Bergeron, "Canada," in *International Handbook of Contemporary Developments in Architecture,* ed. Warren Sanderson (Westport, CT: Greenwood Press, 1981), 188.

32 Edith Sanderson, "Canada," in *International Handbook of Contemporary Developments in Architecture,* ed. Warren Sanderson (Westport, CT: Greenwood Press, 1981), 197.

33 Leon Whiteson, *Canadian Modern Architecture* (Edmonton: Hurtig, 1983), 14.

34 Trevor Boddy, *Modern Architecture in Alberta* (Regina: Alberta Culture and Multiculturalism and Canadian Plains Research Centre, 1987), 93.
35 The firm, which practised under the name Affleck, Desbarats, Dimakopoulos, Lebensold and Sise between 1955 and 1970, changed to ARCOP Associates in 1970 (a contraction of Architects in Copartnership). Raymond Affleck was the partner in charge of the project.
36 Kenneth Frampton, "Place Bonaventure," *Architectural Design* 38, 1 (1968): 42.
37 This is the case if we do not take into consideration André Corboz's article, which was published six years after the building's inauguration. See André Corboz, "Place Bonaventure: Kraak de l'import-export," *Archithèse* 10 (1974): 34-40.
38 Reyner Banham, *Megastructure: Urban Futures of the Recent Past* (London: Thames and Hudson, 1976), 120-25.
39 Sanderson, "Canada," 200.
40 Whiteson, *Canadian Modern Architecture,* 215.
41 Harold Kalman, *A History of Canadian Architecture,* 2 vols. (Toronto: Oxford University Press, 1994). This work is important, for Kalman is the first historian since Alan Gowans to take on the daunting task of writing a comprehensive history of Canadian architecture.
42 Ibid., 832.
43 Ibid.
44 Harold Kalman, *A Concise History of Canadian Architecture* (Toronto: Oxford University Press, 2000).
45 Ibid., 588. In all fairness, I must add that Kalman mentions Stirling elsewhere in the book, this time in the context of Crown Life Place in Vancouver (1976-78), making reference to "the new 'Brutalist' style associated with the British architect James Stirling (1926-93)" (568).
46 Leslie Maitland, Jacqueline Hucker, and Shannon Ricketts, *A Guide to Canadian Architectural Styles* (Peterborough, ON: Broadview, 1992).
47 Ibid., 185.
48 Ibid., 109. This passage ends with the following statement: "These buildings, with their blocky profiles and rough walls, were dubbed Brutalist." Although aware of Brutalism's historical pedigree, the authors are drawn into saying that the buildings selected were "dubbed" Brutalist, revealing a persistent ambiguity in the meaning of the term.
49 Ibid., 185. The authors further write, "During the late 1960s and early 1970s, scores of civic and performing arts centres were built across Canada in the Brutalist style" (188).
50 On the Centennial Commission's architectural program, see Peter H. Aykroyd, *The Anniversary Compulsion: Canada's Centennial Celebrations, A Model Mega-Anniversary* (Toronto: Dundurn, 1992).
51 Marcel Cornu, "L'affaire du brutalisme," *Architecture Mouvement Continuité* 21, 4 (1971): 15-42. Although he considered himself an amateur, Marcel Cornu (1909-2001) wrote extensively on architecture and urban issues and was on the editorial board of *Urbanisme* for more than twenty years.
52 Ibid., 23.
53 He writes, "En somme, ce béton 'texturé,' objet de dilection du brutalisme canadien, apparaît comme une sorte de matériau national" (ibid., 31).
54 For the identity of materials in Scandinavian countries, see Barbara Miller Lane, *National Romanticism and Modern Architecture in Germany and the Scandinavian Countries* (Cambridge, UK: Cambridge University Press, 2000).
55 Cornu adds that this fortress-like architecture can also be found in some commercial ventures, as exemplified by the "impregnable high walls of Montreal's Place Bonaventure." See Cornu, "L'affaire du brutalisme," 29.
56 Northrop Frye, *The Bush Garden: Essays on the Canadian Imagination* (Toronto: Anansi, 1971), 225-26.
57 Dated December 1970, the essay was completed at the time of the October Crisis, a traumatic event that exacerbated the rift between Quebec and the rest of Canada.

58 Cornu is quoted by Michel Ragon in the revised edition of his *Histoire de l'architecture et de l'urbanisme modernes,* 3 vols. (Paris: Casterman, 1986).

59 Maitland, Hucker, and Ricketts, *Guide* (1992), 185.

60 Ibid.

61 Ibid.

62 Leslie Maitland, Jacqueline Hucker, and Shannon Ricketts, *A Guide to Canadian Architectural Style,* rev. ed. (Peterborough, ON: Broadview, 2004), 203. In addition, the caption under the building's illustration explains that the reinforced concrete frame was faced with Wallace sandstone "instead of concrete" (208).

63 It must be noted that the 1992 definition already mentioned masonry in connection with Brutalism: "Brutalist architecture rejects the light, insubstantial quality of the International style in favour of weightier, monolithic masonry forms." It also included the proviso that Brutalist buildings could have "more highly finished surfaces." See Maitland, Hucker, and Ricketts, *Guide* (1992), 185. But the nomination of the Charlottetown Confederation Centre encouraged the authors to foreground these aspects in the 2004 edition.

64 Charrois, "Confederation Centre for the Arts," 13.

65 Ibid.

66 For a synthetic summary of these developments, see Sarah Williams Goldhagen, "Something to Talk About: Modernism, Discourse, Style," *Journal of the Society of Architectural Historians* 64, 2 (June 2005): 144-67.

67 Quoted in ibid., 146.

68 See, among others, Berel Lang, ed., *The Concept of Style* (Philadelphia: University of Pennsylvania Press, 1979); and C. Van Eck, J. McAllister, and R. Van De Vall, eds., *The Question of Style in Philosophy and the Arts* (Cambridge, UK: Cambridge University Press, 1995).

69 Richard Wollheim, "Pictorial Style: Two Views," in *The Concept of Style,* 129-45 (Philadelphia: University of Pennsylvania Press, 1979).

70 Wollheim is critical of the taxonomic approach, for it is prone to extreme relativization in the sense that "style-descriptions can be written and rewritten unconstrained by anything except prevailing art historical interests" (ibid., 140).

71 James Ackerman, "A Theory of Style," *Journal of Aesthetics and Art Criticism* 20 (1962): 227-37. In a 1991 postscript to his article on style, Ackerman writes that the intense discussion of the issue "has called attention to the problems inherent in the use of labels that imply a unity, that encourage unwarranted exclusions, and that discourage the formulation of new and better ways to place artifacts in time." See James S. Ackerman, "Style," in *Distance Points* (Cambridge, MA: MIT Press, 1991), 21.

72 Goldhagen, "Something to Talk About."

73 Ibid., 155.

74 Ibid., 157.

75 It may be useful at this juncture to mention that for the historian Harold Kalman a building like Charlottetown's Confederation Centre of the Arts is rather associated with the International Style: "In its serenity, clarity of form, abstract composition, and curtain-wall construction (albeit they are stone walls), the Centre displays the features of the International Style." See Kalman, *Concise History,* 585.

76 Among the many studies on this topic, see especially W.L. Morton, *The Canadian Identity,* 2nd ed. (Toronto: University of Toronto Press, 1972).

77 Government of Canada, *Royal Commission on National Development in the Arts, Letters and Sciences, 1949-1951,* report (Ottawa: King's Printer, 1951), ch. 15. One outcome of the commission's recommendations was the creation in 1960 of the Massey Medals for Architecture supported by the Massey Foundation.

78 Alan Gowans, *Looking at Architecture in Canada* (Toronto: Oxford University Press, 1958). In the section entitled "The Fifties: Towards a Canadian Architecture," Gowans writes, "If, therefore, there is such a thing as a distinctively Canadian culture, its likely expression will be architectural" (216).

79 Carol Moore Ede, "Preface," in *Canadian Architecture, 1960/70* (Toronto: Burns and McEachren, 1971), 6.

80 On context, see John Dixon Morris, ed., "Canada: A View from the South," *Progressive Architecture*, September 1972, 87. On ideology, see Ching-Yu Chang, ed., "A Perspective of Modern Canadian Architecture," *Process: Architecture*, no. 5, May 1978, 4.

81 See, among others, Whiteson, *Canadian Modern Architecture*.

82 For a challenging interpretation on this issue, see Colin Ripley, "Emptiness and Landscape: National Identity in Canada's Centennial Projects," *Architecture in Canada* 30, 1 (2005): 37-45.

83 This connection is forcefully made by Parks Canada historian Janet Wright: "Designed in the Brutalist style, both reflect the trend away from the glass boxes of the International Style in favour of a more solid and sculptural architecture built upon asymmetrical compositions of irregular concrete masses treated in a variety of surface textures." See Janet Wright, "Government Building," in *The Canadian Encyclopedia* (2005), http://www.thecanadianencyclopedia.com.

84 For the text of the plaque, see the Confederation Centre's website, http://www.confederationcentre.com.

Nation, City, Place
Rethinking Nationalism at the Canadian Museum of Civilization

LAURA HOURSTON HANKS

With "the creation of a symbol of national pride and identity" as the main programmatic objective, no late-twentieth-century Canadian building project reveals a stronger agenda of homogeneous nation building than the Canadian Museum of Civilization at Ottawa.[1] Since opening in 1989, the museum building has received a largely favourable reception from both press and profession. However, within the multi-ethnic context of late-twentieth-century Canada, the creation of a physical monument to symbolize a cohesive or unilateral national imagination was undeniably both challenging and contentious. In common with the other contributions to this volume, this chapter exists at the confluence of architectural and national design and considers the reflection and/or creation of national consciousness. The analysis begins with the curatorial policies applied to the display of the museum's collections. It then explores the uniting agency of the architectural fabric in terms of the larger national project. A particular aspect of the design is argued to be the representation of concepts of national identity in relation both to its immediate urban, civic context and to the wider geographical and cultural context. Beyond representation, the devices of re-presentation and ultimately fabrication employed in the architectural design of the museum are also acknowledged, as is their role in the pursuit of the more universal project of fabricating nation.

The nation-state is a construct of the modern age, with the later eighteenth and nineteenth centuries witnessing the great era of nation building. The French Revolution gave a "new impetus to the notion of a fatherland," with nationalism filling a void left by the downfall of the church and monarchy.[2] In the physical realm, borders were laid down, transportation routes were forged, and capital cities were aggrandized through a nationalized architectural project of institution building.[3] Less tangibly, political and economic boundaries were established, and collective identity was engendered through cultural means. The national public museum became an integral part of a state's ideology, as with both a physical presence and a politicized cultural agenda, its collections and fabric exemplified this project of creating or fabricating a cohesive national identity. The public national museum has been a strategic agency in the construction, symbolization, and promotion of the modern nation-state and its collective identity, occupying the imagined and invented space of nation. As Sharon Macdonald and Gordon Fyfe contend, "museums are products of modernity and their development is deeply implicated in the formation of the modern nation-state."[4] The museum institution has both informed and reflected national consciousness and is inseparable from the nationalist urge, being an important site for the depiction of national unity and for the ritual performance of citizenship.[5] If, as Jacob Burkhardt maintains, "the character of whole nations, cultures and epochs speaks through the totality of architecture, which is the outward shell of their being," then as one part of this totality, the museum began to reveal insightful glimpses into national character.[6]

By the closing decades of the twentieth century, the familiar schema of modern nationalism had come to be challenged on many fronts. Competing pressures of globalization and supranational organizations, in opposition and addition to ethnic separatism, had called into question the construct of the nation-state – a process aided by the characteristic plurality of postmodernism. It is in this late-twentieth-century context that the chapter is located: here, the *nation* of the title is Canada, the *city,* Ottawa, and the *place,* the Canadian Museum of Civilization. These three scales are inextricably interconnected, with national and civic identities finding expression in the exhibition and architectural design of the Museum of Civilization. In the Canadian nation's capital at the end of the twentieth century, exhibition and architectural design were primary cultural vehicles in the expression of the national imagination. However, do the museum building and its displays conform to the familiar schema of modern nationalism, exploiting the imaginings and desires of homogeneous subjecthood, or are they located within the postnational era of decentred identities and multiple subjective positions?

CONTEXT

The territories of modern-day Canada were originally inhabited by scores of autonomous First Nations tribes, each with their own distinct language, culture, and collective identity. This ethnic diversity was broadened first by the French and British colonizers and subsequently by a multiplicity of different settler groups. The Dominion of Canada was established in 1867, and this political homogenization demanded a new social and cultural cohesion around the construct of nation. By the final decades of the twentieth century, Canada was one of the most ethno-culturally diverse and mature countries in the world. In Will Kymlicka's assessment, "Canada is a world leader in three of the most important areas of ethnocultural relations: immigration, indigenous peoples, and the accommodation of minority nationalisms."[7] It was within this potentially paradoxical landscape of actual diversity and attempted cohesion that the Canadian Museum of Civilization was born, and the response it exhibits to this complex climate is intriguing.

Situated on the border between the Provinces of Ontario and Quebec, Ottawa was named capital of the Province of Canada by the British Cabinet in consultation with Queen Victoria in 1857.[8] The government, keen to legitimize the move, expediently established many symbols of state in Ottawa – this program beginning with the new Parliament Buildings, completed in 1866. The construction of the Victoria Memorial Museum, begun in 1904 and itself a forerunner of the Museum of Civilization, was another component of this wider strategy. It had been lobbied for by the country's academic and scientific communities, as an increasingly necessary showcase for the nation's natural and historic treasures, and became symbolic of the nation's emerging confidence.[9] The Museum of Civilization's fortunes, even at this early stage of its development, were bound to the prevalent political agenda of nation building. This strong association between national development and the new public museum, as played out in Ottawa, was typical. Tony Bennett reminds us that "the public museum, as is well known, acquired its modern form during the late eighteenth and early nineteenth centuries," which is exactly coincidental with the great era of nation formation.[10] The symbolic cultural capital of the museum was of paramount importance to these nascent nations, and, as Sharon Macdonald and Gordon Fyfe advance, both nation and museum were products of the same classificatory urge: "museums are ... technologies of classification, and, as such, they have historically played significant roles in the modernist and nationalist quest for order and mapped boundaries."[11]

By the later twentieth century, a new building for what would become the Museum of Civilization was desperately needed, and again the political climate was conducive to this. Having been voted back to power in the election of 1980, Prime Minister Pierre Elliott Trudeau oversaw the Constitution Act of 1982. This act ensured patriation and incorporated a charter of rights,[12] but the new constitutional deal was rejected and ultimately never signed by the Quebec government. Trudeau was then keen to concretize this achievement and his own legacy through the creation of lasting and symbolic cultural projects. Two new buildings were sanctioned: the National Gallery, designed by Moshe Safdie; and the Canadian Museum of Civilization. The design commission for the new home for the museum was secured by the architect Douglas Cardinal and his firm TSE in a 1983 architectural competition.[13] The Canadian Museum of Civilization was opened in Hull, on the Quebec side of the Ottawa River, in 1989 and has been described as "one of the best ... buildings that form the architectural embodiments of the best of the Trudeau era: three-dimensional representations of a century or more of our hopes and frailties."[14] Indeed, from the outset, Cardinal had been charged with creating architecture capable of engendering "national understanding and identity" – a key directive of the *Architectural Programme – Synopsis*.[15] Did he succeed in producing "a symbol of national pride and identity," as instructed in the project brief, and if so, what form did this take, and what significance had this objective and its relative achievement in the wider context of late-twentieth-century Canada?[16]

CONTENT

At its inception, the Museum of Civilization was given a prodigious brief: to recount the story of the Canadian "nation" and its people from prehistoric times to the present day,[17] in order "to generate interest in the Canadian legacy, to foster national understanding and identity, and to enrich the lives of Canadians and others."[18] The most effective vehicle for this engendering of shared national identity was not the architecture, however, but the museum's collection itself, and in turn the exhibitions fashioned around these material artefacts: "The national heritage is our collective identity."[19] However, as Rhodri Windsor Liscombe asserts in the introduction to this volume, it is here in the museum's displays that the contestations involved in this historical evolution of nation are also uppermost.

The museum's collection, at the time of rehousing, comprised almost 3 million individual artefacts of incredibly diverse character. Many of these had been appropriated through the Geological Survey of Canada, begun in 1842.

The survey was mandated to provide information regarding the natural history of Canada, as well as Canadian Native and Inuit life. It largely followed the British model of imperial science in its endeavours to map the land and harness its resources, and the systematic collection of ethnographic objects demonstrates instrumental colonialism. The accommodation had already been separated by Cardinal into two distinct blocks – the display and curatorial wings – and the latter of these acted as a "treasure-house" in which the reserve collections were also stored.[20] Only a small proportion of the total artefacts could be housed in the adjacent display wing, and these were allocated to the following main display spaces: the Grand Hall, the First Peoples Hall, the History Hall, the Native Art Gallery, the Arts and Traditions Hall, and the Special Exhibitions Hall. The first three of these galleries were to make up over three-quarters of the total exhibition floor area, and when completed they revealed most about the curatorial agendas and about approaches to the depiction and promotion of ethnic and national identities.

The Grand Hall, as its name suggests, is the most pivotal and iconic space within the museum. It is visible from the main entrance space above and from all levels of the public wing, while also providing spectacular views back across the river to Ottawa through its impressive floor-to-ceiling window-wall. It acts as an orientation and circulation core, and source of natural light, as well as providing an ideal space for a variety of functions.[21] Although not envisaged in the architectural program, it was decided that the length of the hall opposite the river should house a dioramic display; an imposing environmental reconstruction of a composite "village" of houses representing six Pacific Coast Indian tribes (Figure 11.1).[22] It was the curators' intention that, "as visitors pass down the Grand Hall, with the village to their right, they will travel northwards along the Canadian Pacific Coast through the different cultural regions. In this direction the houses represent Coast Salish, West Coast, Kwakiutl, Bella Coola, Haida, and Tsimshian cultures."[23] The "village," which was informed by key ethnological accounts and photographic evidence, recreates the period from the 1850s to the 1890s and provides the background for the in-situ display of original and reproduction artefacts from the collection, some of which are monumental in both scale and cultural significance.[24] Despite the lack of synchronization between curatorial and architectural schedules, the built form reinforces the displays. The interior roof of the Grand Hall was intended to resemble the contours of a canoe – an object of great practical paramountcy and prestige in Native society, if also associated with trade and settlement of colonizers. This allusion is unambiguous, and to heighten the analogy, the fins, or columns, of the hall's glazed facade, when seen in profile, resemble canoe oars (Figure 11.2).

Figure 11.1 Pacific Coast "village" dioramic display in the Grand Hall, Canadian Museum of Civilization. | Front cover of Andrea Laforet, *The Book of the Grand Hall* (Hull: Canadian Museum of Civilization, 1992).

Significantly, the use and import of the canoe was not confined to Native groups, with European explorers, traders, bureaucrats, and missionaries all having used the canoe to penetrate the heart of the country. Indeed, the canoe looms large in Canadian history and has undoubtedly entered its folklore: "The canoe emerges as the mother image of our national dreamlife, the symbol of our oneness with a rugged northern landscape, the vessel in which we are recreated as Canadians."[25]

The First Peoples Hall is the largest exhibition space in the museum and is contiguous with the end of the Grand Hall.[26] Following a multimedia introductory presentation, a central circulation route defines the display, and subhalls opening from this route address different themes in greater depth. The museum's first director, George Macdonald, set ambitious goals:

> Goals ... relate to CMC's concern for intercultural understanding. One is to demolish stereotypes of native peoples ... Also to be discredited are the common misconceptions that: all natives are the same, reflected in the blanket term 'Indian'

Figure 11.2 Glazed facade of the Grand Hall with oar-shaped fins, Canadian Museum of Civilization. | Photograph by author.

> used for the many different peoples; that their cultures had been static until changed by the advent of Europeans; or that their belief systems are merely unsophisticated responses to their physical environment. It is important ... to demonstrate that native peoples do have a history and rich oral culture, and to illustrate the changes on their cultures over time. Native peoples today are the result of the merging of their past, their traditions, and contemporary society of Western civilization. The exhibition is really about the modern Indian. It will therefore constantly reflect current issues of concern to native peoples.[27]

At the top of the public display wing beneath the great copper roof vault, the History Hall is another substantial display space.[28] Here, the curatorial challenge was to depict the stories of those who ventured to the new land of present-day Canada from the eleventh century onward, and therefore the narration largely excludes the histories of Canada's indigenous peoples.[29] Again, the architecture was ostensibly presented to the curators as a fait accompli, and again, its long and relatively narrow proportions, along with a maximum ceiling height of five storeys,[30] suggested a streetscape approach to the exhibition design.[31] Full-scale reconstructions of typical buildings were utilized to create an accurately detailed and representative cross-section of Canadian architecture.[32] To ensure the environments avoided appearing static, various techniques and programs – such as performances, live animation, light, sound, and special effects – were incorporated to provide them with a sense of habitation and change. The circulation pattern also enhanced the spatial animation here, for although the overall route was designed to be relatively simple and linear,[33] the ability of visitors to penetrate the environmental reconstructions "increased the potential for that participation and interactivity which enhances both the enjoyment and the learning process."[34] In her essay "Ritual Space in the Canadian Museum of Civilization," Jill Delaney critiques MacDonald's attribution of power and identity formation to the History Hall, writing that he "conceives of the CMC and the History Hall as an essential part of the process of the development of 'good' Canadian citizens, a virtual rite of initiation into Canadianism. A visit to the museum will allow the purchase of this essential commodity of Canadian knowledge and identity, and allow it in a single, easy stop."[35]

Clearly, then, the curators used *ethnicity* as an initial and key classificatory tool in the large-scale conceptualization of the museum's exhibits. The Grand and First Peoples Halls were given the remit of representing the country's indigenous cultures, whereas the History Hall was to address the colonial legacies that shaped the course of national life and the collective character. In contrast to the History Hall's portrayal of the interaction of all non-Native cultures within

Canada (which, it is stressed, "has both changed those cultures and produced at their meeting-point – their crossroads – our national community and national identity"), the separation of colonial and indigenous stories remained largely unbridged here.[36]

However, this division, along with its spatial realization, was at odds with the core of the museum's mission: to enhance cultural understanding. Thus it became apparent

> what was needed was a more interdisciplinary or holistic treatment, to show the integral role of all cultural elements in the formation of the Canadian identity. There was also a concern that the spatial organization might seem to symbolize a stereotypical cultural hierarchy reflecting concepts of superiority and dominance, with the culture of Canada's two official language groups at the highest level of the hierarchy/building, native peoples at the lowest, and other cultural minorities somewhere in-between. This connotation was never intended, although the spatial organization was designed to represent a temporal progression, from distant past to recent past.[37]

In light of these contradictions, and in an effort to achieve a more integrated national narrative, it was decided to depict indigenous life and culture in the museum's Grand Hall at a time *after* the arrival of European settlers. This forced the curators to address contentious and sensitive issues arising from this meeting of New World and Old World cultures, such as the decimation of the Native population through the introduction of European diseases: "The arrival of explorers, followed by fur traders, missionaries, the British Navy, and settlers, brought tragedy, opportunity and dilemmas to every family on the coast. The last years of the eighteenth century, and the nineteenth and twentieth centuries represent a period of innovation, change, resistance, loss, recovery and ultimately, survival."[38] The underlying theme of the exhibition – the disjunction in beliefs, values, and expectations between the two cultures – was approached from the "bottom up," through the voices of many individuals, and consultation with Native groups meant that their experience, knowledge, perspectives, and skills fundamentally informed the finished displays: "All the reconstructions of native houses and their decoration will be done in close association with natives, who will also animate the habitats with their presence."[39] As a result, it was hoped that the exhibition may help to

> pave the way towards a resolution, by allowing visitors – both those with their roots in the Old World and native peoples themselves – to explore and apprehend

> the complexity and richness of Pacific Coast Indian culture and also the effect on that culture of the encounter with Europeans, to examine stereotypes from our past, and to reach an appreciation of the value of native cultures to the national culture.[40]

Here, diversity is acknowledged and accommodated, but as a contributory factor to a singular "national culture."

Collective and contested identity is also germane at the smaller scale of the individual artefact. When Europeans encountered the "other" material culture of the indigenous Northwest Coast peoples in the nineteenth century, they were presented with the difficulty of how to classify and understand such "alien" artefacts. This new material made its way almost exclusively into anthropological museums and ethnographic collections, where it could be "apprehended in terms of Western epistemologies ... alongside other objects according to the macro-classifications of the museum system."[41] In this way, these artefacts were shoe-horned into the Western cultural construct of the museum, and in this process their original values were often lost, while additional layers of meaning were attached to the objects via history, museum institutions, ethnographers, and curators.[42] Within this historical context, it is perhaps unsurprising that an acute awareness of traditional Eurocentric ideas and treatment of Native artefacts, as well as a strong desire to avoid any repetition or continuation of this colonial hegemony, appear to have influenced the creation of the Grand Hall exhibition.[43] This influence is indicated in the museum literature on the Grand Hall and also at the very different scales of activity within it – from the life-size environmentally reconstructed village houses down to the treatment of individual artefacts. Consultation with and participation of indigenous Northwest Coast groups were critical in this awareness: "An ... important goal is to present native cultures in a way with which native peoples themselves feel comfortable. CMC will obtain their cooperation in presenting their perspectives in person."[44] Indeed, cultural sensitivity was uppermost, with "rigorous ... ritual correctness [being] employed in the construction of the houses" of the Grand Hall village.[45] Similar measures were put in place for smaller artefacts, such as the partial obscuration of certain Native masks, in accordance with their traditional supernatural significance.[46]

THE CITY

As a largely urban construct, the museum constitutes a major artefact within the city. Many theorists have commented upon the civic role of the urban museum, from David Michael Levin's observation that "it makes a cultural statement which goes beyond its own place in history"[47] to Didier Maleuvre's assertion that the museum is "a formidable model of civic membership."[48] Lewis Mumford declared that the museum represents "the most typical institution of the metropolis," and this connection between the museum and its urban context is pertinent here.[49]

Routes

The two adjacent wings of the Museum of Civilization are monumentally scaled and allowed to repose on their spacious site, with a large plaza between and landscaping sloping down to the river's edge. The buildings read as grand cultural objects in space, the seeming antithesis of contextualized architecture tightly woven into the grain of the urban fabric. However, the museum's site is tangibly and strategically linked into the city through the national ceremonial route, or Confederation Boulevard. This avenue was imagined and constructed by the National Capital Commission to incorporate various political, cultural, and diplomatic landmarks into one civic and national promenade, and most significantly it includes the Parliament Buildings, Confederation Square, the Château Laurier, the Rideau Locks, the Bytown Museum, the Supreme Court, the National Library, the National Archives, the National Arts Centre, and the National Gallery of Canada, as well as the Canadian Museum of Civilization.[50] The edifices are to be viewed individually and sequentially in a carefully choreographed route and celebration of the civic, but also national, realm.

When, in the 1980s, the projects for both the National Gallery and Museum of Civilization were under development, a politically strategic decision was made – against a backdrop of the struggle for Quebecois separatism – that the Ontario and Quebec sides of the river in Ottawa should be granted one institution each. Moshe Safdie's National Gallery was to occupy a prime site in affluent Ottawa, while the Museum of Civilization would redress the balance. Looking across the river toward the city centre from its Brewery Creek site in the commercial district of Hull, this new flagship museum was intended to improve both the economy and perception of its surrounding area. The subsequent routing of Confederation Boulevard past the museum site and through Hull can therefore be seen as part of a wider political agenda: a physical "stitching" together, symbolic of a desire to retain national cohesion. Excepting the National Gallery and Museum of Civilization, the other edifices along the national ceremonial route all date from the later nineteenth and early twentieth centuries when the Enlightenment project of Canadian nation building was at its peak, and taking its place within such a strong chain of national symbols, the museum itself becomes a part of this politicized agenda. Confederation Boulevard powerfully "link[s] the principal images every visitor to the capital is likely to retain of national symbols," thereby promoting the authority and cohesion of the traditional national construct.[51] Here, the physical order is manipulated to bolster the constructed order of nation.

Vistas

The Canadian Museum of Civilization has a strong physical prominence in Hull and a formidable visual impact from Ottawa. However, like Karl Friedrich Schinkel's type-defining Altes Museum, which attempted to dissolve the distinction between museum building and Berlin cityscape, the vistas composed from the Canadian museum's building were crucial. The architect opted to separate the curatorial and exhibition accommodation in order to admit fine views between these two wings and across to the nation's Parliament Buildings, which, as Christopher Thomas reveals in this volume, rapidly became a potent cultural and spiritual symbol of the nation and proved to be a thoroughgoing product of Modernity. The Parliament Buildings were also used at a more integral planning level, with an axis linking the centre of the museum's plaza to the Parliament's Peace Tower (Figure 11.3). Such ritual symbolism physically and metaphorically aligns the museum with a most potent image of the Canadian nation-state, and this connection was iconized on the national one-dollar bill produced for the museum's inauguration in 1989 (Figure 11.4). Here, a contemporary structure of the Canadian nation was used to frame the historic home of Canadian democracy in a resonant layering of imagery and ideas.

THE NATION

So far, we have seen how the Museum of Civilization's displays and immediate urban, civic context have provided opportunities for the affirmation of nation, but the wider geographical context was also an inspiration to Cardinal. As Carter Hammett explains, "Geography and identity. These two words seem to best describe the ebb-and-flow of Douglas Cardinal's ... Canadian Museum of Civilization."[52]

Topography

The country's natural environment was the privileged metaphor for the architecture of the Museum of Civilization, with Cardinal explaining how, "instead of viewing the museum as a sculptural problem, instead of identifying all the historical forms and making them the vocabulary for my solutions, I prefer to

Figure 11.3 View-lines of ritual symbolism linking the nation's Parliament Buildings with the Canadian Museum of Civilization. | In George Macdonald and Stephen Alsford, *Museum for the Global Village* (Hull: Canadian Museum of Civilization, 1989), 27.

Figure 11.4 Iconic view of Parliament Hill framed by the Canadian Museum of Civilization, on the reverse of the national dollar bill. | In George Macdonald and Stephen Alsford, *Museum for the Global Village* (Hull: Canadian Museum of Civilization, 1989), 10.

Figure 11.5 Canadian Museum of Civilization, overhang on the Laurier Street facade. | Photograph by author.

take a walk in nature, observe how nature has solved its problems, and let it be an inspiration to me in solving mine."[53] In poetic language he traced the history of the Canadian landscape, determining that the museum's form was to be symbolic of glacial forces and the geological formations they carved over thousands of years. Specifically, the Canadian Shield, the glaciers, and the Great Plains were to be abstractly represented in the curatorial wing, the exhibition wing, and the plaza respectively.

Within the museum's curatorial wing, horizontality is sharply emphasized by the narrow and unbroken strip windows, the glazing of which is dark in contrast to the building's Tyndall [Manitoba] limestone cladding. These pronounced horizontal bands were designed to evoke the strata of coloured aggregates found within the multilayered Canadian Shield. The stepped and cantilevered construction of the building accentuates this analogy to the very bedrock upon which the nation was founded (Figure 11.5). The overall sculptural mass of the building was also conceived to resemble land carved by glaciers: "The convoluted swirls shaped by glacial action are reflected in the rounded, sinuous forms of the main Exhibition Hall."[54] The most dramatic feature of the museum's display wing, the large glazed window that faces the Ottawa River and encases the Grand Hall, is emblematic of the great wall of the melting glacier, and the green copper roof vaults represent the eskers and drumlins of gravel and glacial till. Outside, a watercourse, consisting of a series of stepped pools, flows down between the two wings. This is to evoke the mass of melt water that flowed away from the glaciers and cut into the rock shelf beneath.[55] Finally, the design rationalization contends that the vast, flat Canadian plains are symbolized through the parkland incorporated in the interstitial space between museum wings.

That some of these allusions are obvious or even clumsy, while others are dubious and possibly postrationalized, is largely irrelevant to this analysis. It is the meaning of their deployment that is of interest. The country's geological landscape is undoubtedly the primary leitmotiv in the architecture of the museum, but why was this theme deemed appropriate for the creation of "a symbol of national pride and identity"?[56] To whom does it speak, and can it be seen to adhere to a national or postnational model?

The first stage in a search for explanations is the positivistic bond between a country's natural landscape and its inhabitants' sense of collective identity. The physical characteristics of a country are key determinants of the nation's political, social, and economic development. These threads intertwine, contributing to the creation of a national self-image. In this empirical explanation of the link between landscape and identity, aspects of nation directly influenced by a country's terrain, such as security and prosperity, in turn influence the national "personality." However, this explanation is problematic, most notably in its assumption of homogeneity both within the nation's inhabitants and their responses to their land, and within the land itself. Stretching for thousands of miles, the Canadian landscape is in reality as startlingly diverse as the population that inhabits it.

As distinct from these positivistic connections, it is a more abstract, aesthetic, and emotional tie to the landscape of his "home" upon which the architect drew in his design for the museum. From his Albertan childhood to the later embrace of his indigenous roots, the land had always been essential to Cardinal. As Windsor Liscombe concurs, Cardinal synthesized the great compositional themes of North American landscape into an expression of nationhood inspired by his own reverence for nature. Indeed, as his biographer Trevor Boddy points out, "not since ... the 1920s and 1930s ... has a Canadian architect so openly appealed to our national connection with the natural order, [and] addressed himself squarely to the ghost of the wilderness that haunts our collective psyche."[57] Although intrinsically personal, this naturalistic vision of Cardinal's

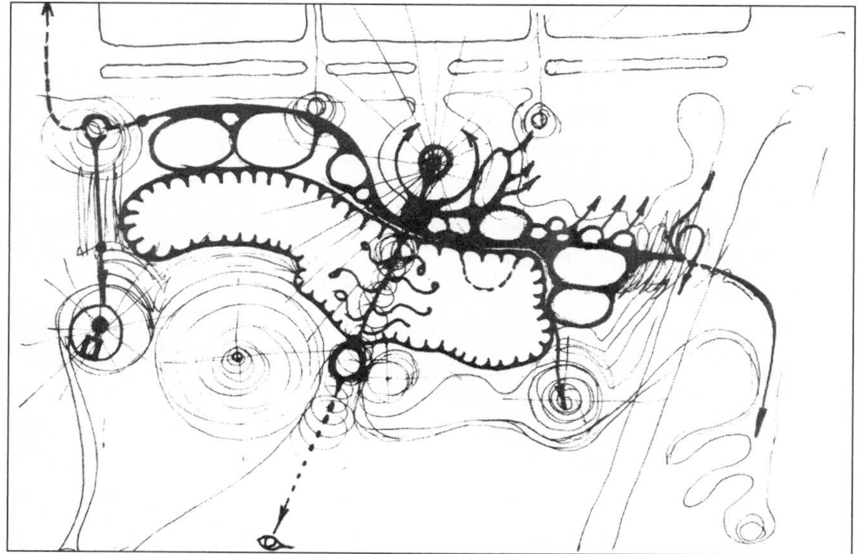

Figure 11.6 An early organic sketch plan by Douglas Cardinal for the Canadian Museum of Civilization. | In George Macdonald and Stephen Alsford, *Museum for the Global Village* (Hull: Canadian Museum of Civilization, 1989), 13.

also has wider resonance. In Michael Hough's terms, "the drama of the natural scenery strikes a primeval chord in *all* of us."[58] Importantly here, this "primeval chord" struck by the physicality (whether experienced, imagined, or mythologized) of the country's landscape is enduring for both Canada's indigenous and colonial ethnicities.

As for the indigenous population, "Canadians have always identified Aboriginal people with the wilderness, believing that Aboriginals enjoyed a special, some believe mystical, relationship with the land."[59] This prevalent European belief was presumably due to the ability demonstrated by these communities to survive and adapt to often extreme terrains and climatic conditions, along with their use of the natural world as inspiration for their mythical worldviews. Cardinal's creation may even be seen as an abstract interpretation of the natural worldviews of some First Nations peoples. In opposition to the progressive linearity of Western Christian ideology, many First Nations peoples adhere to social and spiritual schemas or worldviews that are inherently cyclical, as evidenced by the potlatch culture of some West Coast nations. Within this context, the curvilinear organicism of Cardinal's architecture may begin to take on new meaning – as a portrayal of the circular, recurrent pattern of much indigenous Canadian thought and belief (Figure 11.6). Indeed, "although Cardinal's Métis background was not a factor in the selection process, ... his architectural ideas – deeply influenced by the natural landscape and the elements – cannot be understood without reference to the native world-view."[60]

Landscape was also a critical and defining factor in the colonists' experiences of Canada, although this encounter was perceived quite differently. The European explorers saw themselves as distinct from nature and charged with imposing their will upon it in order to gain possession of it.[61] The ultimate symbol of this colonial struggle against the enormity and wildness of its territory is surely the Canadian Pacific Railway, which "permitted more than the physical linking of a territory. Apart from joining the country to facilitate commercial intercourse and political administration, the CPR offered the possibility of developing a mythic rhetoric of national origin."[62] The primacy of and respect for nature in the psyche of non-Native Canadians is traceable in some part, then, to this epic struggle against the harshness and magnitude of the terrain. Art, like technology, has forged a connection between European Canadians and the natural landscape, most notably in the work of the Group of Seven. In painting the drama and magnitude of Canada's northern territory, the Group of Seven promoted an appreciation for wild scenery and in so doing forged a powerful and lasting fusion between art, landscape, and nationalism in the colonial consciousness.

CONCLUSION

Ernest Gellner proclaimed in *Nations and Nationalism* that "nations as a natural God-given way of classifying men, as an inherent though long-delayed political destiny, are a myth," and the cultural capital of artefacts and architecture has been used to sustain this myth.[63] At the Canadian Museum of Civilization, the myth of nation is clearly sustained with reference to material culture and to both immediate and wider cultural and natural landscapes. Paradoxically, although ethnic difference was taken as a starting point for the design of the exhibitions, it is ethnic cohesion that is the overriding message of the displays. The self-conscious plurality of postmodern narratives – designed to promote intercultural understanding – were intended to coalesce into one principal, overarching story: the story of the nation. In its relation to the adjacent civic realm, the museum shows marked similarities to its nineteenth-century forebears. It is locked into the physical civic order of Confederation Boulevard and, by this association with the other monuments, to the conceptual construct of nation. The link to the most iconic and mythologized edifice in this choreographed sequence, the

Canadian Parliament Buildings, is then strengthened through the wilful manipulation of axes and vistas. That this framed view has been elevated to the iconography of the one-dollar bill only reinforces the symbiosis between nation, architecture, and the museum (Figure 11.4).[64] Broader natural references are also apparent in the museum's architecture. In attempting to evoke the Canadian Shield and Great Plains upon which the nation was built, as well as the robust glacial forces that carved the land, Cardinal attempted to exploit both Native and European Canadians' innate, powerful consciousness of their own piece of and place in the natural world; as Boddy asserts, "the winding shell in resonance and sometimes in competition with its displays, redolent with the history of this country, acts as a memory chamber, a device that filters and amplifies history and ethnicity in unpredicted ways."[65]

This geological symbolization of nation is astute; a poll conducted by the Centre for Research and Information on Canada in 2003 reported that 88 percent of Canadians claimed to be very proud to be Canadian, notably because of "the vastness and the beauty of the land."[66] However, Douglas Cardinal's nature-inspired architecture is also open to criticism on two fronts. First, the originality of the design inspiration is questionable, as "the form and characteristics of the surrounding natural world [have become] not only a predominant concern, but also a consuming inspiration for architects in Canada."[67] This may not be problematic, but Cardinal's congruous architectural response to the Museum of the Native American Indian in Washington, DC, is more so. Here, Cardinal's design again featured a limestone-clad curvilinear building, with the appearance of a stratified stone mass that has been carved by wind and water. The conditions of site, program, and most important, identity were very different here than in Ottawa, but the very similar handling of the two commissions potentially undermines the validity of each. Second, the architecture of the Canadian Museum of Civilization may be charged with the promotion of a nostalgic national Romantic "myth" at the expense of contemporary cultural and societal self-awareness and development. Douglas Cardinal has explicitly turned to the myth of wilderness in the belief that Canadians' link to the land is a defining national characteristic.

Although still pervasive, the ongoing usefulness of this post-Enlightenment, national Romantic myth of landscape is questionable. It has long contributed to and reinforced a romanticized collective imagining of nation, and its success has ensured its longevity. However, the place of this myth in the modern urbanized landscape of contemporary Canada is highly equivocal, representing as it does a nostalgic longing for the nation's past, rather than an accurate and effective understanding of it.[68] It would seem to be time, therefore, to challenge the old, comfortable myths and imagine them anew; as Daniel Francis explains, "there is consolation in nostalgia, the glance behind to a better time when the world seemed to make sense ... but there is also danger. If a nation is a group of people who share the same illusions about themselves, then Canadians need some new illusions. It is wrong to think that the old ones have the necessary power to imagine solutions to contemporary problems."[69] It would seem that myths for collective imagining and identity formation must combine both resonance and relevance if they are to produce resonant, relevant conceptions of nation.

George Macdonald has asserted that "a building is not, of itself, a museum: but neither is it merely a container for a museum. It is a living expression of a culture and as inseparable from the museum programming as is body from soul, or (as [Marshall] McLuhan pointed out) as is medium from message."[70] No late-twentieth-century Canadian building reveals a stronger agenda of homogeneous nation building or national fabrication than the Canadian Museum of Civilization, and this agenda is visible in both the exhibition and architectural design. Indeed, even the reference to a singular "civilization" within the museum's title attests to this desire for homogeneity, just as the very nature of the project attests to the desire for a monolithic national museum institution. This singular identity was locked into the architectural brief in its call for "the creation of *a symbol* of national pride and identity,"[71] and to meet this requirement, Cardinal integrated elements into the design from both the adjacent historical civic realm and the wider national topographical context. Within the multi-ethnic context of late-twentieth-century Canada, this imagining of a unilateral symbol of nation for the museum was both challenging and contentious. Cardinal's decision to use landscape as design inspiration was intelligent in its inclusivity, speaking as it does to both indigenous and European experience. However, other, newer Canadian identities may be implicitly excluded from this connection. Without doubt, however, here in the Canadian nation's capital at the end of the twentieth century, architecture was a primary cultural vehicle in the expression and fabrication of a unified national imagination; an objective squarely located within the familiar schema of modern nationalism, with its easy acceptance of a singular subjecthood.

NOTES

1 Architecture and Planning Group, *National Museum of Man: Architectural Program* (Ottawa: National Museums of Canada, 1983), 14.

2 B. Bergdoll, *European Architecture, 1750-1890* (Oxford and New York: Oxford University Press, 2000), 140. See also B. Anderson, *Imagined Communities: Reflections on the Origin and Spread of Nationalism*

(London: Verso, 2006); E. Hobsbawm, *Nations and Nationalism since 1780: Programme, Myth, Reality* (Cambridge, UK: Cambridge University Press, 1990); H. Seton-Watson, *Nations and States: An Enquiry into the Origins of Nations and the Politics of Nationalism* (Boulder, CO: Methuen Young, 1977); E. Gellner, *Nations and Nationalism: New Perspectives on the Past* (Oxford: Basil Blackwell, 1983).

3 This theme is critically explored in Christopher Thomas's chapter, "Shifting Soil," in which he re-addresses the architectural history of Canada's "first" Parliament in Ottawa.

4 S. Macdonald and G. Fyfe, *Theorizing Museums: Representing Identity and Diversity in a Changing World* (Oxford and Cambridge, UK: Blackwell, 1996), 7.

5 Duncan writes that museums "made (and still make) the state look good: progressive, concerned about the spiritual life of its citizens, a preserver of past achievements and a provider for the common good." C. Duncan, "Art Museums and the Ritual of Citizenship," in N. Prior, *Museums and Modernity: Art Galleries and the Making of Modern Culture* (Oxford: Berg, 2002), 4.

6 J. Burkhardt, *Weltgeschite Bretrachtungen,* translated as *Reflections on History* (London, 1943), cited in Bergdoll, *European Architecture,* 139.

7 W. Kymlicka, *Finding Our Way: Rethinking Ethnocultural Relations in Canada* (Don Mills, ON: Oxford University Press, 1998), 2-3.

8 The city was formerly named Bytown.

9 Canadian Museum of Nature, http://www.nature.ca.

10 T. Bennett, *The Birth of the Museum: History, Theory, Politics* (London and New York: Routledge, 1996), 19.

11 Macdonald and Fyfe, *Theorizing Museums,* 7.

12 Patriation meant the transfer of responsibility for the Canadian Constitution (as enshrined in the British North America Act of 1867) from the British Parliament to the Canadian Parliament.

13 Douglas Joseph Henry Cardinal was born in Calgary in 1934. He was partly of Blackfoot origin, although his family never acknowledged this ancestry, being fully integrated into the non-Native community. It was not until the early 1970s that he seriously addressed his Native roots, engaging with "Indian" and Métis political issues and exploring Native religion.

14 T. Boddy, *The Architecture of Douglas Cardinal* (Edmonton: NeWest, 1989), 95.

15 Architecture and Planning Group, *Architectural Programme – Synopsis* (Ottawa: National Museums of Canada, 1983), 2. In 1980 the National Museum of Man changed its name to the Canadian Museum of Civilization to quell unrest over what was increasingly being seen as an inappropriately male-centric title.

16 Ibid., 14.

17 For the vast majority of its history, the concept of the Canadian "nation," even in the loosest sense of premodern ethnies, was either embryonic or nonexistent.

18 Ibid., 2. This aspiration was reiterated throughout the museum's developmental and marketing literature.

19 G. Macdonald and S. Alsford, *A Museum for the Global Village* (Hull: Canadian Museum of Civilization, 1989), 101.

20 These were stored in the core of the building, protected by a buffering ring of surrounding offices.

21 The hall measures 112 metres in length and 23 metres across at the widest part of its elliptical form. It rises to a height of 15 metres and provides a total floor area of 1,782 square metres.

22 Macdonald and Alsford, *Museum for the Global Village,* 78. In this environmental reconstruction, the alternately coarse-grained and polished marble floor of the Grand Hall represents the Pacific Ocean, while the rainforest is recreated via layers of scrim, and the whole is animated through lighting and audio special effects.

23 Ibid., 82.

24 Ibid., 80.

25 D. Francis, *National Dreams: Myth, Memory, and Canadian History* (Vancouver: Arsenal Pulp, 2003), 129. Another design allusion is apparent in the nearby rippling stone projection of the main entrance,

which is clearly evocative of a face, with light-coloured protruding stonework and dark-coloured recessed windows representing eyes, a nose, and a mouth. The favoured readings of this feature as totem face, Native mask, or mythical thunderbird all promote this connection between the architectural form of the museum and Native culture, with its supposed intimate associations with the natural world.

26 It has a floor area of 5,574 square metres.

27 Macdonald and Alsford, *Museum for the Global Village,* 86.

28 This floor space totals 4,046 square metres, divided between structural floor and mezzanine levels.

29 "A thousand years of history is covered in the History Hall. Its organizing theme is 'New Beginnings,' the story of how generations of Canadians have faced new and challenging situations as they moved from one frontier to another: the waves of immigration, the spread of people from many cultural backgrounds across a wilderness, the growth of settlements, the adaptations to the environment, and the far-reaching changes in technology and in the character of society." Macdonald and Alsford, *Museum for the Global Village,* 98.

30 This rises to seventeen metres.

31 This lack of co-ordination between the architects and curators, which came about for a variety of reasons, is evidenced by the retrospective strengthening of areas of the hall's floor with steel plates to enable it to carry the requisite loads.

32 These reconstructed buildings were created using authentic construction materials on the ground-floor level, with lightweight synthetic materials above, and were divided into three types of "environments": *realistic, stylized,* and *symbolic.*

33 Albeit with several break-outs to the mezzanines.

34 Macdonald and Alsford, *Museum for the Global Village,* 96.

35 J. Delaney, "Ritual Space in the Canadian Museum of Civilization: Consuming Canadian Identity," in *Lifestyle Shopping: The Subject of Consumption,* ed. R. Shields (London: Routledge, 1992), 140.

36 Ibid., 99. The lack of interchange between Cardinal and the History Hall display team was one, not wholly avoidable, causal factor in this failure to produce a fully integrated exhibition narrative.

37 Ibid., 69.

38 Canadian Museum of Civilization text, the Grand Hall.

39 Macdonald and Alsford, *Museum for the Global Village,* 86.

40 Ibid., 80.

41 L. Jessup, "Hard Inclusion," in *On Aboriginal Representation in the Gallery* (Ottawa: Canadian Museum of Civilization, 2000), xiv-xv.

42 Therefore, in addition to an artefact's original and immutable cultural specificity, over time it is imbued with additional layers of meaning: "Value and meaning in artwork are thus altered with regards to time, different perspectives, various institutions, value systems and systems of thought." C. Mah, "The Exhibition of Culture: Understanding the Art of the Other," paper presented at the University of British Columbia, April 2006, 2.

43 The mass collection, and in some cases confiscation, of Native artefacts was common, especially after 1922 with more vigorous enforcement of the Potlatch ban of 1884. Ibid., 6.

44 Macdonald and Alsford, *Museum for the Global Village,* 86.

45 R. Phillips and M. Salber Phillips, "Double Take: Contesting Time, Place, and Nation in the First Peoples Hall of the Canadian Museum of Civilization," *American Anthropologist* 107, 4 (2005): 694-705.

46 However, some of the literature surrounding the exhibition brings into question the achievement of true integration and influence, being still framed around "them" and "us": "It is vital to present to visitors the core features of the world-view, or cosmology, of each native group, since this feature provided group-members' orientation within *their* specific culture. Parts of *their* world-view are reflected in each piece of *their* material culture – tools, weapons, clothing, personal adornments, etc.; but all these messages are brought together in *their* houses. The very form and orientation of *their*

dwellings reveals much about *their* world-view and which elements of it *they* consider paramount." Macdonald and Alsford, *Museum for the Global Village,* 86, emphasis added.

47 D.M. Levin, *The Modern Museum: Temple or Showroom* (Jerusalem: Dvir, 1983), 1, quoted in M. Giebelhausen, ed., *The Architecture of the Museum: Symbolic Structures, Urban Contexts* (Manchester and New York: Manchester University Press, 2003), 2.

48 D. Maleuvre, *Museum Memories: History, Technology, Art* (Stanford, CA: Stanford University Press, 1999), 3, quoted in Giebelhausen, ed., *Architecture of the Museum,* 4.

49 L. Mumford, *The City in History* (Harmondsworth, UK: Penguin, 1975), 639, quoted in Giebelhausen, ed., *Architecture of the Museum,* 4.

50 This device of freestanding monumental public buildings, linked by grand tree-lined boulevards, finds its precedent in the Viennese Ringstrasse and has been replicated across the world.

51 Macdonald and Alsford, *Museum for the Global Village,* 10.

52 C. Hammett, "The Building of an Architect," *Metro,* May 1989, 1.

53 G. Macdonald and D.J. Cardinal, "Building Canada's National Museum of Man: An Interpersonal Dialogue," *Museum* 149 (1986): 14.

54 D.J. Cardinal, *A Vision for the National Museum of Man* (Hull: Canadian Museum of Civilization, 1983), 22.

55 With its source at the top of the plaza between the two buildings, this feature gives the effect of having eroded a single rock form into the two discrete wings of the buildings.

56 Architecture and Planning Group, *Architectural Programme,* 14.

57 Boddy, *Architecture of Douglas Cardinal,* 95.

58 M. Hough, *Out of Place: Restoring Identity to the Regional Landscape* (New Haven, CT, and London: Yale University Press, 1990), 20, original emphasis.

59 Francis, *National Dreams,* 147.

60 Boddy, *Architecture of Douglas Cardinal,* 10. The second assertion here seems indisputable, but it seems probable that Cardinal's ethnicity may have had some political bearing upon his appointment. However, Macdonald and Alsford echo the official reassurances: "It seems appropriate that a museum housing collections of Indian artefacts of national importance should be designed by someone with roots in Canada's native culture, although this was not a factor in the selection decision." Macdonald and Alsford, *Museum for the Global Village,* 14.

61 Rather appropriately, the Canadian Museum of Civilization owes its very presence to this colonial desire for knowledge and appropriation of the land, with exhibits from the country's Geological Survey forming the basis of the collection of its forerunner, the National Museum of Canada.

62 M. Charland, "Technological Nationalism," *Canadian Journal of Political and Social Theory* 10, 1-2 (1986): 200.

63 Gellner, *Nations and Nationalism,* 48-49.

64 Indeed, the role of the museum's plaza in civic and national life recalls the public squares of the modern age, in which public man performed acts of ritual citizenship within the public realm.

65 Boddy, *Architecture of Douglas Cardinal,* 105.

66 International Council for Canadian Studies, http://www.iccs-ciec.ca.

67 B. Carter, "An Architecture of Difference: Celebrating Contemporary Canadian Architecture," *Canada Academic: Canada House Lecture Series* 64 (1998): 3.

68 In his chapter of the present volume, Michael McMordie also draws attention to this discrepancy between the rural perception and urbanized reality of contemporary Canada, noting Brian Carter and Annette Lecuyer's contention that by 2004, 78 percent of the Canadian population lived in cities.

69 Francis, *National Dreams,* 176.

70 George MacDonald, quoted in Boddy, *Architecture of Douglas Cardinal,* 2. See also R. Cavell, *McLuhan in Space: A Cultural Geography* (Toronto: University of Toronto Press, 2002).

71 Architecture and Planning Group, *Architectural Programme,* 14, emphasis added.

PART 6
FABRICATING CANADIAN SPACES IN THE LATE/POSTMODERN ERA

The still partial rehabilitation, or positive repositioning, of Aboriginal society centrally in Canada's cultural politics has accompanied repositionings of the nation itself in the larger global order eventuated since the Constitution Act. The harsh and volatile, rather than humane and stable, conditions of globalization were predicted by the most prominent Canadian public intellectual, Marshall McLuhan, who coincidentally had a particular interest in urban design. McLuhan's contribution to the discourse of socio-cultural modernity is measured by Richard Cavell in "From Earth City to Global Village: McLuhan, Media, and the Cosmopolis." Cavell cleverly connects the evolution of McLuhan's concept of changed cultural and urban fabric with two major events held in Vancouver aimed at palliating homelessness and environmental degradation. Cavell's broad theoretical and historical span positions the Canadian discourse of urban design within these larger international governmental and critical projects of societal reform – projects that are increasingly concentrated on the conservation of natural resources rather than, as during most phases of the coalescing of the Canadian nation, their exploitation. Two very different forms of the introvert societal production Cavell detects in late-modern cosmopolitanism figure in the succeeding chapters in this part – each, by way of completing the geographic consolidation of Canada, also located on the West Coast. Once again, these disclose the international connectivity of late-modern

Canada but also the reconfiguration of nationalist praxis. The heightened nationalism of postcolonial independent states contrasts with the increasingly multicultural/ethnic and devolutionist policies of older nations, played against the backdrop of the contradictory nationalist ploys aimed at trade and financial advantage operating in the globalized economy. Justin McGrail takes on major instantiation in the built environment of outlets of cheap food or manufactured products. "Big-Box Land: New Retail Format Architecture and Consumption in Canada" adeptly articulates the evacuation of conventional ideas of urban planning and architectural design involved in the filling up of the spaces and shelves in big-box stores. The absence of architectural or civic identification, beyond signage and parking, betray the new economic logic of the post-postmodern era: a nowhere with everything except an authentically placed and produced social culture. McGrail effectively positions the big-box store in the politics of community, including First Nations land claims, the culture of commerce, and the theorization of social practice. The novel manifestation of prior, more contained financial and societal systems – Canada has some of the earliest auto-Modernist shopping malls – applies to the post–Expo '86 redevelopment of Vancouver. In "Archi-tizing: Architecture, Advertising, and the Commodification of Urban Community," Liscombe places the current marketing of condominium property in Vancouver within the tradition of architectural publications but more so of advertising media, the cultural force of which was particularly discerned by McLuhan. He argues that the messaging frequently inverts the ethos of critical theory, diminishes the agency of architects, and promotes individuated, instead of communal, urban culture.

From Earth City to Global Village
McLuhan, Media, and the Cosmopolis

RICHARD CAVELL

> Henceforth this planet is a single city.
>
> – Marshall McLuhan, *The Mechanical Bride* (1951)

> The metropolis is almost everywhere.
>
> – Peirce Lewis, *Beyond the Urban Fringe* (1983)

> To date, this country has been slow to get it. Cities matter. Indeed, the relative vibrancy, economic vitality and social cohesion of our major cities will determine, in large part, how this country will survive in a global economy.
>
> – John Honderich, "Getting Smart about Cities" (2006)[1]

The World Urban Forum (WUF), which took place in Vancouver, 19-23 June 2006, provides an appropriate vehicle to reflect on the built fabric of the Canadian city, in theory and in practice. The WUF is aptly named: within the next fifty years, at some unpredictable moment, a massive tectonic shift will take place that will see more than half the earth's population living in cities.[2] The implications of this shift are immense: they will affect our understanding of the nation-state and thus our social, political, and cultural identities; they will present unavoidable implications for sustainability; and they will require a rethinking of what it means to be a citizen.

In 1976, at Habitat, the first major attempt of the United Nations to consider such issues, which was also hosted in Vancouver (where I write), the notion of a global city, if present at all, tended to take the form of the megalopolis, the great urban sprawl that was beginning to make itself felt in such conurbations as the one extending along the East Coast of the United States, from Boston to New York, Atlanta, and Miami. Here, the question was how we were to survive in such a "sprawl" – a term made into a generic marker by Vancouver novelist William Gibson in *Neuromancer* (1984), where he writes, "Home was BAMA, the Sprawl, the Boston-Atlanta-Metropolitan Axis"[3] – with one answer being to move out to the suburbs and their promise of peace, quiet, and fresh air. It was the late Jane Jacobs who took issue with this notion, arguing that to abandon the city was precisely what *not* to do if one wished to keep the city alive, and this position has come to dominate the debate on the sustainability of the city (although not without raising issues around gentrification and the related issues of race and class).

The megalopolis, however, is not the global city, which presents a new set of problems and possibilities in ways that are counterintuitive with regard to traditional urban planning and our notion of what a city is and does, largely because the issues the global city asks us to deal with are not present in the way that urban sprawl, for example, is present. Of course, the concept of a global city is not new; Ernest Hébrard proposed a "world city" in the early 1900s,[4] an idea that resonates within the utopian tradition, from Augustine's *City of God* (which, significantly, supplied the epigraph to the single most important cultural document in Canadian history, the 1951 Massey Report) to Tommaso Campanella's *Città del Sole,* as well as in the dystopian tradition, and one thinks here of the movie *Blade Runner,* based on a story written by Philip K. Dick when he was marooned in Vancouver. Whether these cities are the products of practising architects, however, or of philosophers, they emerge as uniformly static concepts, and this is one of the central challenges to thinking the city – not the city of the future but the city of the all-too-present: how to accommodate the dynamism that characterizes the global city, a dynamism that seeks to accommodate not only the various demands of work and leisure but also the local demands of an increasingly globalized culture and economy.

These observations provide my point of entry to an examination of Marshall McLuhan's notion of the "global village" (a term he coined circa 1959) not only as a key concept of post-1950s thought (extending beyond architecture and civic planning to the domain of cultural production generally) but also as a pragmatic guide to thinking the global city. McLuhan's earliest notion of what he would later famously call the global village made its debut in his 1954 broadside *Counterblast* (not to be confused with the 1969 book of the same title), where McLuhan argues that a new sense of the urban has emerged as one of the effects of electronic media: "The new media are not ways of relating us to the old 'real' world; they *are* the real world and they reshape what remains of the old world at will ... Technological art takes the whole earth and its population as its *material,* not as its form."[5] This "Earth City," as McLuhan calls it, constitutes a new articulation of space; indeed, it is one of the "new spaces created by the new media."[6] The first point McLuhan wishes to make about this articulation is to suggest that it provides a new basis for our understanding of what it means to be cosmopolitan. Hence his comment that "Europeans cannot imagine the Earth City" since a major effect of electronic mediation is to unmoor cosmopolitanism from the old, established centres: "any highway eatery with its TV set, newspaper, and magazine is as cosmopolitan as New York or Paris."[7]

McLuhan's "earth city" was significantly in advance of Saskia Sassen's 1991 notion of the "global city" (a term McLuhan had used four decades earlier), with its major communications infrastructure that facilitates transnational economic and cultural exchanges. McLuhan's notion is more complex, however, in that it is not limited to alpha cities such as London and New York but is fundamentally dynamic in that it shifts ground with the flow of information. All cities, for McLuhan, were two cities (at least) since the traditional role and functions of a metropolis were now reproducible outside the metropolis. He theorized this relationship dynamically as one between the local (referred to in terms of a "village" in order to bring out the spatial complexities of the relationship) and the global, which was independent of a mappable delimitation – "Globes make my head spin," he wrote at the beginning of *War and Peace in the Global Village* (1968); "by the time I locate the place, they've changed the boundaries."[8] For McLuhan, the global village is here *and* there at one and the same time. As an interface, or flashpoint, it would become the site of enormous creative vibrancy as well as of terror and tribulation, as he put it at the end of *The Gutenberg Galaxy* (1962).[9]

Post 11 September 2001, and post the Madrid and London bombings of 2004 and 2005 respectively, the contours of McLuhan's global village have become more discernible. In a recent article on counterterrorism in the United Kingdom, Christopher Caldwell notes that "culturally and politically (and theologically and gastronomically), London ranks among the capitals of the Muslim world and is certainly its chief point of contact with the United States and the rest of the West" – "Londonistan," as some now call it.[10] We have entered a cultural shift similar to the one experienced in the Renaissance with the discovery of the New World, at which point the Mediterranean could no longer be understood as occupying a space in the middle of the earth – William Shakespeare's *The Tempest* places Prospero's island at once in the Mediterranean and mapped onto the "Bermudas." This sense of location as a factor of dislocation is very much a media effect (the proliferation of easily and rapidly produced pamphlets in Shakespeare's time), and in this context we must remember that even a traditional medium, such as the newspaper, is now a product of digitization and wireless transmission, which is how I am able to have my copy of the *New York Times* in Vancouver at about the same time as it's being read in the West Village (or at exactly the same time if I want to log on to the newspaper's website). As Caldwell notes, "global media" play a role in the local/global tensions that have arisen in places such as London, which is

> one of six cities in which *The Daily Jang*, Pakistan's largest paper, is published, so the second-generation tube rider who 20 years ago would have been absorbed in the county cricket scores in his *Evening Standard* is now preoccupied with the conduct of India in Kashmir and with what Pakistani Muslims ought to do about it. Many South Asian immigrants get their news from Urdu television stations, and, despite the language barrier, from Al Jazeera.[11]

Indeed, Caldwell goes on to state, "when you talk to many Muslim leaders in Britain, you hear them focus almost obsessively on international politics, to the exclusion of religious, social and local political issues." This leads to the sort of paradox that McLuhan intuited: "The 'national' government wants to talk about local integration and facilities and role models, while 'local' representatives want to talk about the West Bank."[12] Indeed, the arrest of seventeen men in Ontario on suspicion of planning terrorist attacks in Canada served to further demonstrate "how hard it is to separate the fight at home and the fight abroad. In the Yorkshire town of Dewsbury, ... the teenage grandson of a prominent British Muslim scholar was arrested for links to the ... conspiracy."[13]

The notion of the global village came out of McLuhan's experience as a Canadian, which is to say within a colonized nation whose history was (and is) precisely that of seeking to assert a cultural identity in the face of hegemonic cultural production. What he proposed, interestingly, was not resistance (of the classic, Gramscian sort) but a form of post-hegemony, a position he occupied by virtue of his status as a postmodernist *avant la lettre*.

Jon Beasley-Murray's discussion of post-hegemony argues that

> the state has come to be directly responsive to the demands made of it by (what was once) the people; but those responses are provided according to the terms of capital accumulation, and in the name of pure command ... that responsiveness has been divorced from any sense of responsibility ... Has there been any better instantiation of the society of control than Vladimiro Montesino's almost invisible permeation of the socius by means of video technology in what was nominally Fujimori's Peru?[14]

The question gives considerable poignancy to the classic political dilemma (as Beasley-Murray rightly terms it) of why the oppressed participate in their oppression. McLuhan proposed one possible response in his foundational study *Understanding Media* (1964), a response that provides a profound insight into the structure of his thought:

> Physiologically, man in the normal use of technology (or his variously extended body) is perpetually modified by it and in turn finds ever new ways of modifying his technology. Man becomes, as it were, the sex organs of the machine world, as the bee of the plant world, enabling it to fecundate and to evolve ever new forms. The machine world reciprocates man's love by expediting his wishes and desires, namely in providing him with wealth.[15]

McLuhan cautions, however, that

> once we have surrendered our senses and nervous systems to the private manipulation of those who would try to benefit from taking a lease on our eyes and ears and nerves, we don't really have any rights left. Leasing our eyes and ears and nerves to commercial interests is like handing over the common speech to a private corporation, or like giving the earth's atmosphere to a company as a monopoly.[16]

These comments were born from McLuhan's profound realization that, with the end of the Second World War, the era of Mars was giving way to that of Venus. This was not, however, simply a prophetic insight into the age of sex and consumerism that would characterize the 1960s, when, not so coincidentally, McLuhan achieved the height of his fame, becoming the most quoted person on earth through the power of a mediated network he had theorized in masterworks such as *The Gutenberg Galaxy* and *Understanding Media*. Rather, McLuhan was proposing that the world's economic engine had exhausted itself in the war effort and reconfigured itself as a libidinal economy, a vast desiring machine, in which consumption was at once the product and the goal in a feedback loop of endless consumerism. A third world war, he suggested, would be fought with credit cards.[17] He wrote about this libidinal economy in his 1951 book *The Mechanical Bride,* in which the bride is the automobile, which embodies the displaced libido of a culture whose sexual identity has been profoundly disrupted by the war. This libidinal model of economic and cultural configuration was thus founded upon a notion of mediation as bio-technological. According to McLuhan, all "media" – and by this he meant cities and cars as well as the more traditional understanding of the term as referring to newspapers and television – were extensions of the body, and these extensions simultaneously amputated the extended organ, such that the massive increase in power afforded by our prosthetic extensions was likewise the site of a profound alienation. The electronic globe was now one vastly distended body, but this body was outside of us.

This sense of mass as a vector of power (influenced, no doubt, by Albert Einstein's famous theorem), coupled with the notion of bio-technology (and here we can draw a parallel with Antonio Negri's reference to the "biopolitical ... mass"),[18] intrigued McLuhan immensely, and his interest in it finds resonance with the post-hegemonic notion that there has been a cultural and political shift toward the *affective,* toward "the order of bodies rather than the order of signification."[19] If, as Beasley-Murray argues, this affective social order can be understood "topographically"[20] in terms of the "undulations and intensities of affective investment that (immanently) constitute a social landscape,"[21] then this formulation goes some way toward helping us to understand what McLuhan meant by the global village. It is a notion that defines itself through intersubjectivity (i.e., dialogue; hence the insistence on the metaphor of the village) and one in which the mass has come to be the central social actant. Here, Michael Hardt and Antonio Negri supply the apposite comment that "through circulation the multitude reappropriates space and constitutes itself as an active subject. When we look closer at how this constitutive process of subjectivity operates, we can see that the new spaces are described by unusual topographies, by subterranean and containable rhizomes – by geographical mythologies that mark the new paths of destiny."[22]

Beasley-Murray argues that, in this new, post-Marxist configuration, the "fundamental labour [of society] is the work of producing society itself."[23] McLuhan seized on a similar notion, arguing that the fundamental response to consumerism must be creativity, and hence he valorized very highly the role of the artist as the person for whom creativity is paramount. As McLuhan put it in *Through the Vanishing Point* (1968), "the artist can be regarded as a navigator who gives adequate compass bearings in spite of magnetic deflections of the needle by the changing play of forces. So understood, the artist is not a peddler of ideals or lofty experiences. He is rather the indispensable aid to action and reflection alike."[24] Although McLuhan sought to expand the role of the artist such that everyone engaging critically with their society took on this mantle, he was lamenting as early as 1958 that "the public [did] not rally with enthusiasm to the creator role" because "we had been only too successful in creating a consumer-oriented public that expected all articles presented to it to be fully processed for immediate use."[25] Hence McLuhan's valorization of intersubjectivity and interactivity and his love of the artistic form known as the Happening – the spontaneous (re)production of space. What is significant in McLuhan's formulation is that a marketplace, for example, could be understood as the site of Happenings; this is typical of his expansion of the notion of the Happening beyond an exclusively artistic context. Thus he writes of Toronto's Kensington Market that its "world of unenclosed space ... invites us to open the doors of perception ... The nearby play-ground is another unenclosed space necessary to the very existence of play, a spontaneous environment."[26] The notion is picked up in Richard Florida's account of "creative" cities,[27] and this account is placed in a specifically Canadian context by John Lorinc in *The New City: How the Crisis of Canada's Urban Centres is Reshaping the Nation* (2006). Lorinc writes that a "critical mass of such [creative] individuals gives rise to the kind of frisson that emerges from local social and professional networks, the presence of leading universities and other higher-learning institutions, and even random interactions in public or semi-public spaces."[28]

One form that this urban creativity took in McLuhan's case was the making of a film. In the early 1970s, Toronto was threatened with an archetypal urban calamity of the period: the proposed building of a freeway through the heart of the city. In this case, the freeway was to be built along the north-south axis of Spadina Avenue, effectively dividing the city in half (in much the same way that Highway 99 divides Seattle). McLuhan, like many Torontonians, was horrified by the prospect, especially since the freeway would come very close to his beloved Wychwood Park home. Deciding that a film would be the best way to address this prospect, he called on Jane Jacobs, who lived near him:

> "We need a movie about the Spadina Expressway! [he said to Jacobs, who recounts the story]. You and I can do the script."

I said, "But I don't know a thing about scriptwriting. I won't be any use."

"Oh, I've never written one either," he said, "but we can easily do it together. Come on down to my office and we'll get to work."[29]

Titled *A Burning Would* and directed by Christopher Chapman, the film was shown internationally. As for the Spadina freeway, it was not built.

McLuhan had arrived at his notions about the city by bringing together a number of his interests and influences, particularly those he derived from the work of Siegfried Giedion, the author of *Space, Time and Architecture* (1941), which McLuhan called "one of the great events of my lifetime."[30] As McLuhan goes on to note, "Giedion began to study the environment as a structural, artistic work – he saw language in streets, buildings, the very texture of form."[31] McLuhan was particularly influenced by Giedion's insistence on organic interconnections among cultural phenomena, which McLuhan understood in terms of dialogue; hence his praise for the fact that Toronto had so many Victorian buildings in addition to its Miesian towers.[32] For him, this "dialogic design"[33] was crucial to Toronto's success as a city, where dialogue was as much about the intersubjective production of space as it was about McLuhan's notion that "not only [are] words and metaphors ... mass media but buildings and cities as well."[34]

McLuhan was furnished with the opportunity to connect Giedion's notions about space to his own ideas about media through the unanticipated intervention of a Greek architect named Constantin Doxiadis, who in 1963 invited a number of key cultural thinkers to join him on an Aegean cruise, during which time they would discuss major issues having to do with town planning that were facing the world. McLuhan had been brought to the attention of Doxiadis by Jacqueline Tyrwhitt,[35] who had worked with Doxiadis in India in 1950 before studying architecture in London and being appointed to the Graduate School of Architecture at the University of Toronto in 1951 and to the planning department of the School of Architecture at that university in 1954. McLuhan befriended her, making her an associate editor of the journal *Explorations,* which he and anthropologist Edmund Carpenter were co-editing at that time.[36] By 1955 Tyrwhitt had accepted an appointment at Harvard University (where Giedion taught), but she remained in touch with McLuhan.

Tyrwhitt and Giedion were on the Aegean cruise, as well as Buckminster Fuller, but McLuhan dominated the gathering – even on the dance floor – according to a number of witnesses. As Mark Wigley has written, what captured the attention of those attending the seminar was McLuhan's notion that media were bio-technological: "McLuhan's argument was that electronics is actually biological, an organic system with particular effects. The evolution of technology is the evolution of the human body. Networks of communication, like any technology, are prosthetic extensions of the body. They are new body parts and constitute a new organism, a new spatial system, and a new architecture."[37] This notion took the meeting by storm, and the remainder of the cruise was devoted to unpacking its implications, especially McLuhan's idea that "electronics presents new challenges to city planners because this latest prosthetic extension of the body defines an entirely new form of space."[38] Here, in essence, we have McLuhan's notion of the global village: that it is at once a prosthetic extension, bio-technologically, and, in direct dynamic relationship, a shrinking-down into the sort of confluences associated with village life. As he wrote to Jacqueline Tyrwhitt on 23 December 1960,

> Now that by electricity we have externalized *all* of our senses, we are in the desperate position of not having any *sensus communis* [meaning that our senses no longer function as a unity and, relatedly, that we lack a sense of community]. Prior to electricity, the city was the sensus communis for such specialized and externalized senses as technology had developed. From Aristotle onward, the traditional function of the sensus communis is to translate each sense into the other senses, so that a unified, integral image is offered at all times to the mind. The city performs that function for the scattered and distracted senses, and spaces and times, of agrarian cultures. Today with electronics we have discovered that we live in a global village, and the job is to create a global city as centre for the village margins. *The parameters of this task are by no means positional. With electronics, any marginal area can become centre, and marginal experiences can be had at any centre* [emphasis added]. Perhaps the city needed to coordinate and concert the distracted sense programs of our global village will have to be built by computers in the way in which a big airport has to coordinate multiple flights ... Whatever we may wish in the matter, we can no longer live in Euclidean space under electronic conditions, and this means that the divisions between inner and outer, private and communal, whatever they may have been for a literate culture, are simply *not there* for an electric one.[39]

It was in the 1960s that McLuhan developed the notion of the global village specifically within the context of architectural publications. In 1961 he published "Inside the Five Sense Sensorium" in *The Canadian Architect*. McLuhan argues there that visual (linear) space is the product of print culture and that after 500 years of the book, we are entering into a new phase that is being created by electronic media and their tendency to collapse space and time into a space-time that is at once local and global, thus breaking down the distancing characteristics of perspectival space. McLuhan calls this new space "acoustic"; unlike visual space, acoustic space engages all of the senses in a way that is much more involving and interactive than that afforded by visual space. McLuhan adjures architects and city planners to take this space seriously: "It seems quite obvious that the lineality that invaded every kind of spatial organization from the 16th century onwards had as its archetype and matrix the metal lines of Gutenberg's uniform and repeatable types." He then asks: "How to breathe life into the lineal forms of the past 5 centuries while admitting the relevance of the new organic forms of spatial organization, what we have referred to as acoustic space – is this not the task of the architect at present?"[40]

The second of these articles was published in *Perspecta: The Yale Architectural Journal* in 1965 and was given the enigmatic title "Environment: The Future of an Erosion,"[41] which refers to the erosion of visual space under the onslaught of electronic media; in McLuhan's formulation, electronic media are not visual but audile. His title alludes to Sigmund Freud's 1927 essay "The Future of an Illusion" (and the reference to Freud brings us back to McLuhan's notion of media as constituting a libidinal economy), where Freud writes that "human creations are easily destroyed, and science and technology, which have built them up, can also be used for their annihilation."[42] McLuhan calls these scientific and technological domains "environments" and argues that we are largely unconscious of them since they constitute our total experience of the world around us – the fish, he liked to point out, knows nothing about water. As an unconscious domain, the built environment takes on the guise of a vast dream world. The city, in these terms, is not just a product but is itself productive, a locus of transformation.

In Ann Bowman and Michael Pagano's formulation, the "landscape of the contemporary horizontal city is no longer a place-making or a condensing medium. Instead, it is fragmented and chaotically spread, escaping wholeness, objectivity, and public awareness – *terra incognita*."[43] Hence the apposite allusion McLuhan makes to Freud, whose critical program, however, he reverses: rather than probing our unconscious, argues McLuhan, the cultural theorist (or artist/critic) must wake us up, bringing us to consciousness. Otherwise, as he put it, we dream awake, living in a vast phantasmagoria of our own invention that we take as natural, or environmental, when, ironically, even nature has become a medium that we constantly fine-tune. In fact, McLuhan argues that technology stands at the heart of humanity itself. Hence his "humanist" take on technology is double-edged, for it represents not only a humanizing of technology but also a recognition that technology is the *precondition* of our being human – that we are human *through* our technologies: we are watching *ourselves* on television; we are processing *ourselves* on the computer; and we are speaking *ourselves* in our cities, such that architecture must be understood as comprising not only built fabric but also the spatial relations this fabric produces.

Subsequent to these articulations, McLuhan developed his ideas about the city in a book that is little read today. *Take Today: The Executive as Dropout* (a title that gains significant resonance in the era of Bill Gates and Mark Zuckerberg) was published in 1972, putatively as a text in management studies, although one that quotes more from Shakespeare and James Joyce than from Peter Drucker. The book works out the implications of the *corporate,* a notion that McLuhan took literally: we were all corporate, insofar as we were embodied through mediation as a mass (Hardt and Negri's multitude). What McLuhan sought to retrieve through the idea of the corporate was its humanist legacy; language, for McLuhan, was the ultimate expression of the corporate. Hence the emphasis on culture throughout the book: the executive must "drop out" of the corporate grid in order to rediscover the humanist cycle. "The natural interval between the wheel and axle," he writes, "is where action and 'play' are one. The aware executive is the one who 'steps down' when the action begins to 'seize up.' He maintains his autonomy and his flexibility."[44] McLuhan traces a similar breakdown among categories of work and play. "The creative worker is never more powerful or more at leisure, never more the dropout from the specialist job, than when using all his faculties."[45]

It is in this context that McLuhan writes about Jane Jacobs, noting how, in *The Economy of Cities,* she argues that "cities foster many service activities in ever-proliferating patterns." What was significant for McLuhan in this comment was the notion that the city is a process and, like all processes, dynamic: "Today we live in an age of simultaneity rather than of sequence";[46] sequence was pre-eminently the domain of alphabetic culture, but electronic culture happens all at once. Thus separating living spaces from working and entertainment spaces was nonfunctional within an electronic cityscape. "Today, the utmost degree of social fragmentation achieved by the vertical city streets of high-rise units makes it obvious that the entire social strategy is ready for reversal. When the housing unity itself becomes the environment, *i.e.,* when *figure* becomes *ground,* there is no more interplay to create community." In the same section, McLuhan writes that the 1969 opposition to the Manhattan Throughway, and that to the Spadina Expressway, were attempts "to preserve human scale in a superhuman environment. The city is a place for the heightening of human awareness by providing the greatest possible range and diversity of space for dialogue."[47]

The problem, as McLuhan saw it, was that the "technocrats persist in their strategy of homogenization, which fosters a filling-in of all the older 'spaces' of the city with massive structures, obliterating all intervals of human scale."[48] Thus "Gottmann's megalopolis extends the 'asphalt jungle' to an urban strip." But suburbia, as exemplified by the garden city, was not a valid solution, according to McLuhan. "The pseudoquality of the Garden City of Ebenezer Howard is that it is all *figure* minus *ground* ... The Garden City is low-level homogenization of space and sensory life. The megalopolis is the high-rise level of homogenization and intense specialism of sensory life."[49]

Because television is a decentralizing medium (you are wherever it is), it has an alienating effect on those who live in "hardware" cities; yet planners, McLuhan laments, are stuck with their hardware ideas. "The recent pronouncements of Lewis Mumford *(The Urban Prospect)* show that he still sees core cities surrounded by satellites as an ideal regional pattern." In response to this notion, McLuhan argues that "in the jet age, every 'city' in the world is a suburban 'satellite' to every other city. The only possible regional environment for existing or prospective cities, large or small, is the planet itself."[50] Hence the global village, or as he puts it here the

> *Global Caravansary*
>
> The suburban or satellite city created by the decentralizing power of that private "space bubble," the *auto*mobile, now must yield to "instant" mobile cities such as the Woodstock and Mariposa festivals or the "disposable" cities we associate with World's Fairs since 1851. Airports and trailer parks are faint intimations of the return of nomadic communities. Business is conducted in restaurants and recreation spots around the world. In the information age of the "magnetic city" all "hardware" city forms are obsolescent and tend toward the status of tourist attractions and museums. The old "hardware" form is made vivid by the new "software" frame, or information surround.[51]

One is reminded here of the architectural collective Archigram, which derived its fame from projects, such as the modular "Plug-In City," that were (unbuilt) responses to the city as flow of information.[52] In fact, these unbuilt projects were for McLuhan the form the city of the future would take:

> The housing and city styles of the immediate future will be as flexible and as programmed to taste as cassettes. This trend became visible with the great World Exposition of 1851 and its Crystal Palace. These "instant" festival cities were

> programmed in every respect. Today, as work becomes play through depth involvement in knowledge, only festival cities will be meaningful to the new citizen of the global theater. Spaceship Earth will demand a perpetual renewal of repertory for its Phoenix Playhouse.[53]

The fungible quality of the new city arises from the notion that the

> magnetic city is our own nervous system put outside as an environment of information. This gesture of self-awareness scoffs at all the previous dimensions of "hardware" planning and "hardware" scale. When a child in a playpen can have access to universal knowledge and experience, the scale of the largest city or building in the world is puny and meaningless. The TV set is a kind of restoration of the reading carrel of the ancient scholar, a little Echoland in which all dimensions of word and being resonate. Under instant conditions, megalopolis is a bad joke, a garbage dump that is useful only as a resource for designing magnetic cities.[54]

Canada's particular advantage in this urban scenario was its "backwardness – its inadvertent retention of human scale in its urban environments. In the nineteenth century it did not commit very much of its space or working life to the fragmented assembly-line processes that were frantically pursued in more advanced areas in England and the United States."[55] McLuhan thus celebrated the Victorian remnants of Toronto as providing the sort of interface (in this case architectural, juxtaposing two different ways of configuring space) that was crucial to a successful city.

McLuhan's last major meditation on the metropolis was his book *City as Classroom* (1977). Here, the key word is "community," whereby the city has become its social interrelationships – the *production* of space, in Lefebvrian terms.[56] The city has become a classroom because it teaches in the nonsequential way of electronic culture: "Today's societies encompass an immense amount of information. Most of this information has to be acquired by all the inhabitants of a particular society so that they can survive there. Your society exists in a man-made environment, a huge warehouse of information, a vast resource to be mined free of charge. If you take time to think about your society's man-made environment, you will probably find that you already know a great deal about it, not because you have studied it in school, but just because you have lived in it."[57] In these terms, the city has become a vast Bauhaus project for (re)education, the place where we learn to live in a world that is characterized by a profound sense of (dis)location.

Although the notion of the global village struck a profound chord that resonates to the present day, it has also been deeply criticized, especially for the apparently utopian element encoded in the concept of "village" that it invokes, which has suggested that McLuhan believed in a naive form of communitarianism or else that he failed to understand the negative aspects of globalization. When such critiques were made by contemporaries, such as George Steiner, McLuhan reacted with amazement:

> There is amazing confusion of mind here on the part of Mr. Steiner ... The more you create village conditions, the more discontinuity and division and diversity. The global village absolutely insures maximal disagreement on all points. It never occurred to me that uniformity and tranquility were the properties of the global village ... The spaces and times are pulled out from between people. A world in which people encounter each other in depth all the time. The tribal-global village is far more divisive – full of fighting – than any nationalism ever was. Village is fission, not fusion, in depth ... Nationalism came out of print and provided an extraordinary relief from global village conditions.[58]

Regardless of such protestations, the phrase "global village" was considered to lack critical value and tended to be read through the 1970s and 1980s as the mantra of media triumphalism.

With Theodore Levitt's 1983 popularizing of the term "globalization," however, the notion of the global village, with its suggestion of uneven development, of scalar differences, of rapid shifts from margin to centre, has garnered new interest.[59] Gayatri Spivak, for example, has written that the use of the term "global" in McLuhan's formulation is "counter-intuitive: You walk from one end of the earth to the other and it remains flat," she writes. "It is a scientific abstraction inaccessible to experience. No one lives in the *global* village. The only relationship accessible to the globe so far is that of the gaze."[60] Spivak's comment fails to take into account that the visual domain no longer reigns supreme in the era of the Internet, where one's relationship to the globe can be via e-mail, the web, and Twitter, media through which the subaltern increasingly speaks. Spivak's blindness to the political potential of the new media (powerfully demonstrated in the Arab world at the beginning of 2011) stems from a failure to understand media as material. Yet, as McLuhan noted, we live increasingly in a world of *invisibilia* that has much more in common with acoustic space than with the visual space invoked by Spivak, and for McLuhan, acoustic space was profoundly material. As he put it in a 1974 letter, "the acoustic is just as material as the visual."[61]

The displacement of the visual domain that print had inaugurated by the acoustic domain of electronic media was to be deeply agonistic. If this displacement promised enhanced communicational possibilities by creating broad new media configurations, it also promised to place such possibilities in crisis through an intensification of local dialects. The notion of the global village is meant to signal this dynamic interrelationship of the global and the local; the medium of this interrelationship was what McLuhan termed the "environment," the technologized prosthesis of our human nature, and, as such, the epistemic stage of mediation succeeding modernism, feedback replacing progress. The global, in other words, is taking us back to a nature that we now discover to be ourselves, a world coterminous with our vastly expanded prosthetic body. Paradoxically, this embodiment is outside us – we now experience our humanity *corporately*, as a mass medium. This is the new environment, and we are related to it precisely through the dynamic that energizes the global village. Just as we are at once here and there in the global village, so in the technologized environment we are at once inside and outside, driving our sports utility vehicles through the canyons of the city and plugging our barbecues into the electric outlets conveniently provided in the old growth forest.

The concept of the global village, then, does not encapsulate a theory of "globalization" in the sense that the term is naively used today. Rather, it represents a theory of the interficiality, the interrelatedness, of the local and the global. As Mark Rakatansky puts it in an essay provocatively titled "Why Architecture Is Neither Here nor There,"

> architecture is neither purely specific nor purely abstract, neither purely social nor purely formal, neither purely local nor purely global. Architecture, all architecture, is here *and* there, specific *and* abstract, local *and* global ... These uncanny doublings of spatialized cultures ... unlike human binocular vision, which achieves depth at the cost of resolving difference, ... most productively achieve depth by putting into play sameness and difference ... enact[ing] the constitution of self and community through the engaged and conflictual interactions of identities, public and private, domestic and urban.[62]

It is in this sense that the notion of the global village has been taken up by those wishing to theorize a new cosmopolitanism. The task has particular urgency in the present context, given that the cosmopolitan attempts to rethink the citizen in terms of the city rather than the nation. Kwame Anthony Appiah has written most compellingly of the challenges posed by this new cosmopolitanism. As he states in *The Ethics of Identity*, our increasing interconnectedness – and our growing awareness of it – has not, of course, made us into denizens of a single community, the proverbial "global village." Everyone knows you cannot have face-to-face relations with six billion people. But you cannot have face-to-face relations with ten million or a million or a hundred thousand people (with your fellow Swazis or Swahilis or Swedes) either; and we humans have long had practice in identifying, in nations, cities, and towns, with groups on this grander scale.[63]

Yet, as Appiah goes on to write, a "cosmopolitan should – etymologically, at least – be someone who thinks that the world is, so to speak, our shared hometown, reproducing something very like the *self-conscious oxymoron* of the 'global village.'"[64] As this suggests, a major point inherent in the notion of the global village is that it expresses an imagined community (as Benedict Anderson, drawing on McLuhan's *The Gutenberg Galaxy,* has argued)[65] yet one that is "rooted," as Appiah puts it. As McLuhan's term suggests, the global must be understood not as free-floating but as *located.* Thus, as Appiah suggests in a subsequent book, globalization threatens homogenization as much as it promotes it.[66]

A number of these concerns reappear as urban planning issues in an editorial for the *Harvard Design Magazine.* Titled "Yes, Urban Villages (But What about Their Design?)," the editorial states that the problems with "single-use zoning and free-market development" are now well known and that a number of cities are taking on alternative goals: "to make and support multi-centred, mixed-use, dense, transit-supported, walkable, self-sufficient 'village' settlement patterns for cities, suburbia, and the countryside." The editorial goes on to suggest that "the sole exemplary large-scale environment depicted in this *HDM* is Vancouver, Canada, in which dense high-rise living has been humanized by street-level vibrant public life, with local stores, parks, and row houses fronting the towers."[67]

The two planners who dominated this period of growth in Vancouver, Larry Beasley and Ann McAfee, devoted their attention to the downtown core and to Vancouver's twenty-two neighbourhoods, respectively. Beasley calls his approach "experiential planning," meaning that (in the words of Gary Mason) "you need to look at a city's downtown core as a living, breathing organism ... It needed to be seen as an organic whole, which reached its full potential only when all the various parts were working together."[68] As Beasley puts it, "The key was tapping into the visceral experience a citizen has,"[69] and the metaphor of embodiment (as opposed to one of visuality) is crucial here, as it was to McLuhan's theorizing of the city of the future. Beasley's approach resulted in the reversal of the exodus to the suburbs; over the past decade, 90,000 people have moved into the downtown core. They are doing so not to work (there is a dearth of head offices in the core) but to *live*. As Mason notes, "Many businesses can be located anywhere today,"[70] with quality of life often being the deciding factor; the notion of a static centre no longer holds.

The confluences of these planning pragmatics with McLuhan's theories about the global village suggest that his theories have a deeply material and pragmatic dimension to them. If the global village can be said to be at all utopian, it is perhaps so in the critical sense used by Fredric Jameson in his book *Archaeologies of the Future*, where he argues that "utopia ... now better expresses our relationship to a genuinely better political future than any current program of action."[71] A place that is both here and not here, real and irreal, the global village presents the city in all its lived, terrible reality, as well as the dialogical possibility of another place, not here. As Reinhold Martin has recently written, we must avoid "the elementary mistake of assuming that reality is entirely real – that is, pre-existent, fixed, and therefore exempt from critical re-imagination." To address this irreality of the real, it is necessary, argues Martin, to reintroduce the idea of utopia "as the 'non-place' written into its etymological origins that is 'no-where' not because it is ideal and inaccessible, but because, in perfect mirrored symmetry, it is also 'everywhere.'"[72] As McLuhan put it, "every-where is now-here."[73]

NOTES

1 The epigraphs are from Marshall McLuhan, *The Mechanical Bride: Folklore of Industrial Man* (New York: Vanguard, 1951), 4; Pierce Lewis, *Beyond the Urban Fringe: Land Issues of Nonmetropolitan America* (Minneapolis: University of Minnesota Press, 1983), 221; and John Honderich, "Getting Smart about Cities," *Literary Review of Canada* 14, 4 (May 2006): 25-27.

2 John Lorinc, "The Cities of Dreadful Night" (review of Mike Davis, *Planet of Slums* [New York: Verso, 2006]), *Toronto Globe and Mail*, 27 May 2006, D10. Slavoj Žižek puts the situation more dramatically: "Since, sometime very soon (or maybe, given the imprecision of Third World censuses, it has already happened), the urban population of the earth will outnumber the rural population, and since slum-dwellers will make up the majority of the urban population, we are by no means dealing with a marginal phenomenon. We are thus witnessing the rapid growth of a population outside state control, living in conditions half outside the law, in dire need of minimal forms of self-organization." See Slavoj Žižek, *The Parallax View* (Cambridge, MA: MIT Press, 2006), 268.

3 William Gibson, *Neuromancer* (New York: Berkeley, 1984), 44.

4 On Ernest Hébrard, see Mark Mazower, *Salonica: City of Ghosts* (New York: Knopf, 2005), 304-5. Hébrard had been invited to Salonica, Greece, to help rebuild it after a devastating fire, a task that Thomas Mawson had abandoned after three months. Mawson had come to Salonica from Vancouver, which serves to remind us that, by the end of the nineteenth century, international travel had already inaugurated the diasporic flows of the contemporary city.

5 Marshall McLuhan, *Counterblast*, broadside (Toronto, 1954), [13], emphases added.

6 Ibid.
7 Ibid., [15].
8 Marshall McLuhan, *War and Peace in the Global Village* (New York: McGraw-Hill, 1968), epigraph.
9 Marshall McLuhan, *The Gutenberg Galaxy: The Making of Typographic Man* (Toronto: University of Toronto Press, 1962).
10 Christopher Caldwell, "The Lessons of Londonistan," *New York Times Magazine,* 25 June 2006, 42, 46.
11 Ibid., 47.
12 Ibid.
13 Ibid., 75.
14 Jon Beasley-Murray, "On Posthegemony," *Bulletin of Latin American Research* 22, 1 (2003): 119.
15 Marshall McLuhan, *Understanding Media: The Extensions of Man* (New York: McGraw-Hill, 1964), 46.
16 Ibid., 68.
17 Marshall McLuhan, *Culture Is Our Business* (New York: McGraw-Hill, 1970), 66; I paraphrase greatly.
18 Antonio Negri, quoted in Beasley-Murray, "On Posthegemony," 122.
19 Beasley-Murray, "On Posthegemony," 120.
20 The geographical metaphor is significant, as I argue generally in Richard Cavell, *McLuhan in Space: A Cultural Geography* (Toronto: University of Toronto Press, 2002).
21 Beasley-Murray, "On Posthegemony," 120.
22 Michael Hardt and Antonio Negri, *Empire* (Cambridge, MA: Harvard University Press, 2000), 397.
23 Beasley-Murray, "On Posthegemony," 121.
24 Marshall McLuhan and Harley Parker, *Through the Vanishing Point: Space in Poetry and Painting* (New York: Harper and Row, 1968), 238. The book appeared in the World Perspectives series, which had previously published Walter Gropius, Lewis Mumford, Werner Heisenberg, and Georg Lukács, among others.
25 Marshall McLuhan, "Media Alchemy in Art and Society," *Journal of Communication* 8, 2 (1958): 66. McLuhan makes this comment in a discussion of Richard Neutra's *Survival through Design,* which he states is "representative of the full recognition today of the power of the messages from interior and exterior design in buildings to pattern general awareness and to affect even physiological states" (64).
26 Marshall McLuhan, "McLuhan's Toronto," *Toronto Life,* September 1967, 26.
27 Richard Florida, *Cities and the Creative Class* (New York: Routledge, 2005); see also Richard Florida, *The Rise of the Creative Class* (New York: Basic Books, 2002).
28 John Lorinc, *The New City: How the Crisis of Canada's Urban Centres Is Reshaping the Nation* (Toronto: Penguin, 2006).
29 Jane Jacobs, "Making a Movie with McLuhan," in *Marshall McLuhan: The Man and His Message,* ed. George Sanderson and Frank Macdonald (Golden, CO: Fulcrum, 1989), 121. Also published as a special issue of *Antigonish Review* 74-75 (1988).
30 Marshall McLuhan, "A Dialogue with Gerald E. Stearn," in *McLuhan Hot and Cool,* ed. Gerald E. Stearn (New York: Dial, 1967), 269.
31 Ibid., 270.
32 Marshall McLuhan, with Barrington Nevitt, *Take Today: The Executive as Dropout* (Don Mills, ON: Longman, 1972), 33.
33 William S. Saunders, "Dialogic Design," *Harvard Design Magazine* 23 (2005-06): 4. This is a special issue on the reuse of buildings titled "Design as Dialogue, Building as Transformation."
34 Marshall McLuhan, "Culture without Literacy," *Explorations* 1 (1953): 125.
35 For an analysis of Tyrwhitt's significance, see Rhodri Windsor Liscombe, "Perceptions in the Conception of the Modernist Urban Environment: Canadian Perspectives on the Spatial Theory of Jacqueline Tyrwhitt," in *Man-Made Future: Planning, Education and Design in Mid-Twentieth-Century Britain,* ed. Iain Boyd White, 78-98 (London: Routledge, 2007).

36 As Douglas Coupland remarks in his recent bio-fiction, *Marshall McLuhan* (Toronto: Penguin, 2009), 140, Tyrwhitt was "a rare female given admittance into Marshall's academic universe."

37 Mark Wigley, "Network Fever," *Grey Room* 4 (Summer 2001): 86.

38 Ibid., 97.

39 Marshall McLuhan, *Letters,* ed. Matie Molinaro et al. (Toronto: Oxford University Press, 1987), 277-78.

40 Marshall McLuhan, "Inside the Five-Sense Sensorium," *Canadian Architect* 6, 6 (1961): 54.

41 Marshall McLuhan, "Environment: The Future of an Erosion," *Perspecta* 11 (1965): 165.

42 Sigmund Freud, "The Future of an Illusion," in *The Freud Reader,* ed. Peter Gay (New York: Norton, 1989), 687.

43 A. Bowman and M. Pagano, *Terra Incognita: Vacant Land and Urban Strategies* (Washington, DC: Georgetown University Press, 2004), quoted by Alan Berger, "Urban Land Is a Natural Thing to Waste: Seeing and Appreciating Drosscapes," *Harvard Design Magazine* 23 (2005-06): 51.

44 McLuhan, with Nevitt, *Take Today,* 4.

45 Ibid., 5.

46 Ibid., 27.

47 Ibid., 29, original emphasis.

48 Ibid., 31.

49 Ibid., 32.

50 Ibid., 34.

51 Ibid., original emphasis.

52 Peter Cook, the *force animateur* of Archigram, was steeped in McLuhan's ideas, referring in his writing to the *Perspecta* article discussed above and cited at note 39. See Cavell, *McLuhan in Space,* 290n100.

53 McLuhan, with Nevitt, *Take Today,* 35. As McLuhan puts it in "McLuhan's Toronto," "At night the city appears as a World Fair. At electric speeds the globe itself becomes a kind of Expo, or World Fair ... The usual forms of the city, dwellings, high-rise, and sky scrapers – these are already nostalgic and romantic relics of our mechanical and industrial past. The city of the present and the future already exists in the photographic and video forms that make up our immediate experience" (23).

54 McLuhan, with Nevitt, *Take Today,* 35.

55 Ibid., 33.

56 Henri Lefebvre, in *The Production of Space,* trans. Donald Nicholson-Smith (1974; reprint, Oxford: Blackwell, 1991), acknowledges McLuhan's contribution to a theory of the production of space.

57 McLuhan, with Kathryn Hutchon and Eric McLuhan, *City as Classroom* (Agincourt, ON: Book Society, 1977), 149.

58 McLuhan, "Dialogue with Gerald E. Stearn," 279-80.

59 See Theodore Levitt, "Globalization and Markets," *Harvard Business Review,* May-June 1983, 92-101.

60 Gayatri Spivak, "Cultural Talks in the Hot Peace: Revisiting the Global Village," in *Cosmoplitics: Thinking and Feeling beyond the Nation,* ed. Pheng Cheah and Bruce Robbins (Minneapolis: University of Minnesota Press, 1998), 331.

61 McLuhan, *Letters,* 489.

62 Mark Rakatansky, "Why Architecture Is Neither Here nor There," in *Drifting: Architecture and Migrancy,* ed. Stephen Cairns (London: Routledge, 2004), 99, 107, 109.

63 Kwame Anthony Appiah, *The Ethics of Identity* (Princeton, NJ: Princeton University Press, 2005), 216-17.

64 Ibid., 217, emphasis added.

65 As Appiah comments, "*Imagined,* as Benedict Anderson would insist, doesn't mean unreal: nothing could be more powerful than the human imagination" (ibid., 242, original emphasis).

66 Kwame Anthony Appiah, *Cosmopolitanism: Ethics in a World of Strangers* (New York: Norton, 2006); see particularly the section "Global Villages," 101-5.

67 William S. Saunders, "Yes, Urban Villages (But What about Their Design?)," *Harvard Design Magazine* 22 (2005): 3.

68 Gary Mason, "Vancouver Braces for Departure of Urban Design's Dynamic Duo," *Toronto Globe and Mail,* 20 June 2006, S1.

69 Quoted in ibid., S2.

70 Ibid.

71 Fredric Jameson, *Archaeologies of the Future: The Desire Called Utopia and Other Science Fictions* (London: Verso, 2005), 8.

72 Reinhold Martin, "Critical of What? Toward a Utopian Realism," *Harvard Design Magazine* 22 (2005): 109.

73 McLuhan, with Nevitt, *Take Today,* 297.

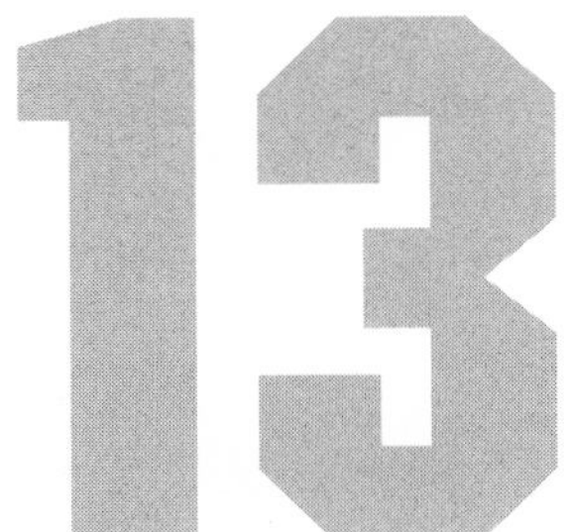

Big-Box Land

New Retail Format Architecture and Consumption in Canada

JUSTIN MCGRAIL

When considered in terms of production and consumption, identity is an everyday affair. Our sense of self and of nation is created and experienced in and through the habits, rhythms, and routines of daily life. For most Canadians, such life is urban. The architectural spaces that are most regularly encountered are often the most important yet least examined of all buildings in our lives. The chapters in this anthology use both spectacular and mundane examples in their explorations of architecture and the fabrication of Canadian identities. Sharon Vattay and Lucie Morisset, in particular, focus on common building types: the urban market and the single detached house, respectively. The authors describe the degree to which private and public identities in past historic situations were produced and represented in vernacular urban spaces. By doing so, Vattay and Morisset draw attention to the extraordinary elements hidden within the ordinary spaces of Toronto's public markets and the bungalows of Quebec City. This co-existence of the spectacular and the mundane is one characteristic of everyday life. Although our locations and activities may be fixed by daily routines, they also remain part of larger, and sometimes smaller, social processes that are not entirely predictable. Neither static nor monolithic, shared customs and identities are produced and reproduced, imagined, and experienced, and in the process they are fabricated by Canadians literally one day at a time. Major sites, such as Parliament Hill or Maple Leaf Gardens, are spectacular and undoubtedly produce an intense experience of feeling Canadian. However, such sites are visited by most only on special occasions and perhaps but once in a lifetime. By contrast, houses, cafes, schools, offices, and shops are experienced on a daily basis and are considered mundane. However, these are the buildings in which Canadians actually spend their lives, which makes them the central sites for the production and consumption of our social and cultural identities.

This chapter considers one such everyday and mundane building type: the big-box store. Since first appearing in 1984, big-box stores in Canada have seen prodigious growth. Between 1990 and 1999 the Greater Toronto Area, for instance, witnessed a 378 percent growth in big-box stores, increasing from 93 to 445 sites.[1] Big-box stores, also known as warehouse-format stores or "New Retail Formats" (NRFs), have been built in, and are identified with, the semirural and suburban areas around Canadian cities. Yet they are not confined to the suburbs. Increasingly, big-box stores are appearing in other urban areas, such as redeveloped shopping centres and downtown shopping streets. Some of these operations are Canadian, founded and owned, but most are US chains. This chapter examines the short history and typology of big-box stores in Canada, with examples drawn from Vancouver Island's Capital Regional District (CRD), particularly the City of Langford.

Common and yet controversial, big-box stores are now key centres for value retail and the distribution of commodities in Canada. It's clear that the main attraction of these sites to shoppers is the price of the goods for sale. The success of warehouse clubs and discount retailers, such as Costco and Walmart, is based squarely on the promise of bargains, typically meaning large quantities for low prices. This promise is vividly symbolized by the architecture and interior design of the buildings themselves. Through size, material, and often exposed structural elements, NRFs appear at once to be similar to the products they shelter – big and cheap. However, as described below, there are in fact also elements of decoration and architectural pastiche to be found in the big-box store.

Through the habits and expectations they engender in everyday life, big-box stores have come to play an important role in Canadian cities. This is most clearly seen in municipal politics, particularly in urban and regional planning. More than just places to shop, they are also where Canadians can find their place in the social and economic order of globalization. Although consumption is promoted as an economic and political expression of freedom and as a means of identity formation, contemporary retail produces widespread conformity. A criticism often heard at community meetings and public forums is that big-box stores make every place look the same. This production of sameness, and the eradication of cultural differences, is one of the most commonly voiced criticisms of consumer culture and globalization in general. The big-box store, ubiquitous and homogeneous, contributes to, and symbolizes, this conformity. In its physical appearance and operations, NRFs contribute to ongoing practices of conformity in Canadian suburbs as described by Richard Harris.[2] Some retailers and shopping centre developers have responded to these concerns of homogenization by incorporating local or postmodern themes into the facades of their locations.

CANADIAN ARCHITECTURE VERSUS BIG-BOX LAND

To mark the year 2000, the Royal Architectural Institute of Canada (RAIC) organized "The Millennium Celebration of Canadian Architecture," centred on a survey of the architecture Canadians value the most.[3] For one month, the RAIC received nominations of buildings from across the country that contributors were attached to or that they "believed to have been significant in shaping our built environment."[4] Dominated by locations in Ontario, British Columbia, and Quebec, the list of 482 buildings is nonetheless impressive in length and diversity. The list features the familiar icons of Canadian architecture, several of which are considered in this anthology, along with numerous rural churches, public buildings, and houses. Although some vernacular buildings made the list, including four shopping centres, big-box stores did not. This unsurprising fact was emphasized by RAIC officials at the press launch. Atlantic regional director John Emmett lamented, "so much of our built environment, particularly the big box store, is a product rather than a creation, slapped together to keep the rain out and sell a product."[5] Ron Keenberg, Ontario East regional director, was starker in his observations: "In the land of the big box, there is no community."[6] Aesthetically, socially, and culturally, for the RAIC, the big-box store is clearly the antithesis of the architecture most valued by Canadians. Worse, it seems that Canadian architecture is in danger of being lost amid the spreading growth of big-box land.

The RAIC survey is a good place to start exploring the big-box store. That no one nominated a big-box store for the list is unsurprising. The buildings are generally considered functional, undistinguished, and impermanent, qualities conveyed in Emmett's description of "a product rather than a creation." Retail buildings are especially subject to trends and fashions, which results in cyclical renovations and/or total replacement. In the words of Daniel Herman, "Shopping buildings don't age; they die young."[7] Emmett's "product"

Figure 13.1 Staples, Langford. | Photograph by author.

and "creation" also order the built environment into categories reminiscent of Nikolaus Pevsner's distinction between "architecture" (Lincoln Cathedral) and "building" (bicycle shed).[8] Like Pevsner, Emmett argues a creation (architecture) is meant to be visually consumed and is full of cultural value and historical significance, whereas a product (building) is functional yet symbolically empty. At the start of the twenty-first century, this categorization seems extremely old-fashioned.

For Pevsner, architecture refers to buildings designed with aesthetic appeal, ones meant to be looked at.[9] However, all buildings are looked at, and how they are looked at is beyond the control of the architect or academic. Further, Pevsner (like Emmett) uses the word "architecture" not as a category description but as a mark of quality or distinction. Why is it not possible to view architecture as a broad category of built objects of which there are simply good and bad examples? Perhaps it is because this division separates architects from ugly or unpopular architecture. When sites don't merit the title of "architecture," how can architects be responsible for them? However, big-box stores are designed by architects, are featured in architectural magazines, and even win architectural awards. Vancouver's Abbarch Partnership, for example, is an award-winning firm primarily engaged in retail projects whose clients include Walmart Sam's Clubs and Save-On-Foods grocery stores.[10] We might not think big-box stores are meant to be looked at, but their size, location, and signs perhaps argue

Figure 13.2 Walmart, Langford. | Photograph by author.

against us here. In terms of marketing and business, they are of course meant to be seen. The buildings' size and distinctive colours and design features house and advertise the operation. For instance, a Staples store is identifiable from a distance because the exterior of each site is divided into two horizontal bands of white and red (Figure 13.1). The Staples' colour scheme and form are reminiscent of one of its basic stock items: Xerox paper, sold in white boxes with red lids. Each building is branded and instantly recognizable. Further, when looked at closely, big-box stores can be seen to feature architectural forms and decorations, such as the open pilasters and coloured string-courses on the east facade of the Walmart in Langford (Figure 13.2). Although these features might not be the stuff the RAIC dreams about, the big-box store is clearly a work of architecture.

Whereas Emmett appears resigned to big-box stores, Keenberg is clearly opposed to them. To him, big-box stores are simply bad for communities. Of course, Keenberg has a specific idea of community in mind, and it is one that does not, and cannot, include big-box stores. In this position, he is not alone. Many critics of suburbs, sprawl, and consumption argue that big-box stores present environmental, social, economic, and cultural threats to existing communities.[11] The stores are characterized as engines of traffic, pollution, and environmentally destructive development. The big-box store is also the site of mass consumption, the sustainability of which is highly questioned. Opposing these criticisms are retailers, developers, investors, and politicians, who argue that big-box stores, on balance, contribute positively to their surrounding communities. For instance, city officials from Langford, which is considered in detail below, argue big-box stores have fuelled commercial growth, funded city works, and made their community stronger and a better place to live. Odd as it may seem to some, Langford is a community some local politicians claim big-box stores are helping to build.

The size of big-box stores and the scale of their operations – along with their impact on municipal politics, urban planning, and community life – make them one of today's quintessential building types. Their presence in suburban and urban areas further illustrates socio-economic discourses and priorities of twenty-first-century Canada in action. It thus seems appropriate to include them among this volume's histories of Canadian architecture.

NEW RETAIL FORMATS IN CANADA

Big-box stores and value retailers need to be included when considering the role of architectural space in the fabrication of Canadian identities in the twenty-first century. The size and scale, new patterns of land use and ownership, consumer shifts to value consumption, ever larger warehouse-style facilities, and community protests have pushed these buildings into the public spotlight. This underlines the political and economic significance of consumption. Retail activity is among the most influential factors in the economy and social organization of Canada. In 2000 commercial activities, defined as businesses serving consumers, became, at almost 40 percent, the single most important component of the Canadian economy, measured in jobs, capital investment, and contributions to gross domestic product (GDP).[12] Figures from 2004 showed these numbers had increased to 47.9 percent (jobs) and 48.3 percent (contribution to GDP).[13] Retail activity constitutes the second largest component of commercial activity, and Statistics Canada estimates that large retailers (i.e., supermarkets, department stores, and big-box stores) represent 35 percent of total annual sales.[14] As of 2005, there were 2,298 shopping centres in Canada, providing 423,459,125 square feet of retail space, which generated $242.6 billion in sales and $16.2 billion in provincial sales-tax revenue.[15] Within these numbers, big-box stores dominate in terms of new investment and construction.[16] For the present, they are very much the face of consumer capitalism in urban Canada.

Big-box stores are also part of everyday life in Canada. It is now widely accepted that consumption, particularly shopping, has become a key form of and location for social life. In much postmodern literature, the postindustrial city is often identified by the socio-economic shift from production to consumption services.[17] In such cities, geographer Jon Goss observes, "shopping has become the dominant mode of contemporary public life," one that shapes the citizen's identity as much as, if not more than, work or family.[18] This is especially true of everyday consumption. Sociologist Steven Miles writes, "How we consume, why we consume and the parameters laid down for us within which we consume have become increasingly significant influences on how we construct our everyday lives."[19] This includes the gathering of small items, such as food, played out daily in supermarkets and corner stores. Here, item selection is shaped by repetition and variation, influenced by personal notions of loyalty and value, and motivated by immediate or long-term needs. As our habits of consumption become regularized and customary, we become customers, as in, "I'll have the usual, Anne."[20] In this production of shopping customs, the dynamics of agency and structure are not sharply defined, and elements of either can be apparent and hidden. Analyzing the "bureaucratic society of controlled consumption," Henri Lefebvre stresses that this dialectic of individual agency and institutional structure can be a source of alternative actions and resistance.[21] For Lefebvre, everyday life is both the setting and the subject for capitalist structures of consumption: "The everyday is therefore the most universal and the most unique condition, the most social and the most individuated, the most obvious and the best hidden. A condition stipulated for the legibility of forms, ordained by means of functions, inscribed within structures, the everyday constitutes the platform upon which the bureaucratic society of controlled consumption is erected."[22] Lefebvre is interested in the spaces of resistance created in the daily routines of production and consumption and articulated in personal choices and statements of difference. The latter are of course unpredictable, which is why retailers and authors identify them as part of "the mystery of consumer behaviour."[23] Studying consumption in everyday life attempts to account for these personal and unpredictable elements in the consumer. It also recognizes the complexity of choice and expression played out in even the simplest acts of shopping. Consumers in their everyday life are both predictable and unpredictable, a consideration that challenges typical generalizations about shoppers. In their everyday lives, consumers are subject to controlling structures of consumption, yet they are not necessarily controlled. Recognizing agency promotes the view that consumers are creative and active: they individualize commodities, evade media manipulation, and make choices that are central expressions of self-image.[24] This is the "savvy" consumer, as opposed to the

Figure 13.3 Future Shop, Langford. | Photograph by author.

"sucker."[25] However, no amount of creativity can completely free the consumer from participation in the controlling discourses and social structures of market capitalism. This is what Miles has called the "consumer paradox" – any individual expression or personal fulfilment obtained through consumption is offset by the conformity of shopping practices and the manipulation of desire and taste.[26] The consumer, it seems, is free within a limited freedom.

The name "big-box store" describes both the buildings and the types of retail operation they house. In professional writing, these operations have been called New Retail, Warehouse-style Retail, Value Retail, and Power Retail, and the buildings have been identified as warehouse-format stores and New Retail Formats.[27] Both building and operation are distinguished from other retailers on the basis of size, location, merchandise category, and age.[28] They range in size from 50,000 to 250,000 square feet, are mainly found in suburban areas with highway access, and offer a large stock of either general or specialized merchandise, and their construction largely dates from the 1980s.[29] The basic design is that of a single-storey warehouse, with tilt-up concrete walls enclosing a post-and-truss frame that supports a corrugated ceiling and flat, asphalt roof (Figure 13.3). Similar to that of a warehouse, the structural system of a big-box store is usually left exposed. However, some retailers do use finishing surfaces, a feature determined by the goods for sale. Concrete floors and steel posts fit with Home Depot's product range (home-renovation supplies) in a way that does not suit either La Vie en Rose (lingerie) or Future Shop (electronics and DVDs). The merchandise category determines much, but not all, of the building's appearance.

Although "big-box store" is used in general to describe the locations, there are different NRF types. The most relevant here are: category killers, discount department stores, membership warehouse clubs, and power centres.[30] The differences between the types are again size and product range. A category killer, also called a category warehouse store, is a retailer specializing in one market area, such as home supplies, stationery goods, or furniture. Home Depot, The Brick, and Future Shop are examples of category killers, so named after their tendency to dominate their market and either devour or drive under area competitors. The first Toys R Us location, opened in Washington, DC, in 1957, is usually identified as the first example of this retail type.[31] However, this overlooks the fact that Canadian Tire, a retailer specialized in automotive supplies, was founded in 1927 and had 120 dealer-owner locations open across Canada by 1953.[32] It was arguably the first category killer in Canadian retail. Either way, the category killer is not a recent innovation at the end of the twentieth century. A discount department store is a general merchandiser, like Walmart or Kmart, that offers an extremely broad range of low-priced goods, carrying between 50,000 and 80,000 products.[33] Membership warehouse clubs are the largest big-box stores in terms of size, although they offer a smaller range of goods.[34] The clubs stock groceries, office supplies, jewellery, clothing, home supplies, appliances, hardware, electronics, sporting goods, and furniture, making them rivals to the department store, the discount store, the supermarket, and the shopping centre. These operations have their origins as wholesalers to restaurants and service-providers in the 1960s in the United States and central Canada.[35] In the United States, Price Club opened to nonbusiness members in 1976, followed by Costco in the 1980s; the two retailers would merge in 1993.[36] Warehouse clubs have proven especially popular with consumers. In Canada, Costco's sixty-one locations do an estimated $8 billion in annual sales, making the company the third largest retailer in the country, and the company plans to add twenty-nine additional locations by 2013.[37] A power centre is a grouping of big-box stores, often sharing parking facilities and access roads. The power centre developed almost simultaneously in the United States and Canada, with the first examples built in Colma, California, in 1986 and North York, Ontario, in 1987.[38] There are examples of each of these NRF types in the Langford study area.

The big-box store is a high-profile location for "value consumption," shopping characterized by good quality, low prices, broad selection, and decent service, in contrast to the high quality and prices, limited selection, and specialized service of luxury consumption. Value consumption is the "new" in NRFs – the expansion of bulk, discount selling of everyday items that began in the early 1980s.[39] The popularity of value consumption and the expansion of discount retailers have been blamed for closing department stores and shopping centres. Although there are certainly cases of this happening with Eaton's and Woolco, it is not always the case that big-box stores have this impact. Some NRFs have failed, and some older shopping centres have continued along, changing their retail mix with regular renovations and bringing big-box retailers to their malls, such as in the case of Victoria's Mayfair Shopping Centre, to which a Toys R Us store was attached in 1994.

Visiting a big-box store seems at first to confirm Emmett's description of the building as "slapped together." The sites provide the bare minimum of shelter required for the products, staff, and consumers. The interiors are of course dominated by the commodities for sale. This focus – similar to one NRF ancestor, the bargain basement – creates a no-frills atmosphere, strengthened by the high visibility of cardboard boxes and packing crates. These are also present because, although big-box stores maintain large inventories, they have little backroom storage. The store floor is also the warehouse floor. Product shelves tower above consumers, simultaneously displaying and storing goods. This storage-on-display approach strikingly conveys a sense of abundance and the possibility of near-limitless consumption. There are of course variations depending on the NRF type and the retailer itself. In Costco, for instance, products are sold in only one size: extra-large. Although this prevents comparison-shopping, Costco shoppers seem to accept the single size with an understanding that everything in Costco is as inexpensive as possible. The single size is a sign of this value. Costco members purchase large quantities that are expensive yet are represented as cost-effective when compared to the costs of numerous purchases of the same items in smaller quantities. This economic formula is a key rationale in value consumption and points to why people like big-box stores – maximum size for minimal price. Unlike that of the shopping centre, big-box pleasure is derived not from the architectural or entertainment spectacle but from the consumption of value.

DEBATING FOR AND AGAINST THE BIG-BOX STORE

Passionate debates and protests have accompanied NRF construction across North America. Opponents of big-box stores have multiple concerns, including: urban sprawl; preservation of regional, usually rural, character; protection of local retailers, small businesses, and agricultural land; and opposition to capitalism and globalization. NRF criticism has, of course, grown in size and scale alongside the big-box store. Two early, and different, responses to the big-box store were both written in 1994. In a report for the Ontario Ministry of Municipal Affairs, the NRF debate is described as follows: "Much of the debate concentrates on the nature of competition between established and incoming uses, on equality of planning treatment, on the fairness of the perceived advantages available to one competitor over another through land use designations through the description of uses and property taxation."[40] The authors perceive controversy only in terms of business practices and the operations of free-market capitalism, although they do acknowledge the potential for local business closures.[41] Constance Beaumont of the National Trust for Historic Preservation in the United States gives a much more alarming impression of the big-box debate. She acknowledges that NRFs offer affordable merchandise, create local jobs, and produce property and sales-tax revenues for local governments. However, Beaumont argues that such benefits are outweighed by the negative impacts of environmental destruction, increased sprawl, the collapse of local retailers, and the erosion of community uniqueness.[42] These arguments remain at the core of NRF opposition and have been augmented by numerous authors since Beaumont.[43]

In British Columbia, community opposition groups have met with both success and failure fighting developments in recent years. In 2005 Vancouver city councillors voted down a proposed Walmart, citing community-based opposition along with concerns about traffic, road costs, and the socio-economic impact on the South Marine neighbourhoods. This despite the fact the proposal called for a "Green Walmart," designed by the firm Busby, Perkins, and Will and incorporating sustainable design features, including rainwater collection, green roofing, and wind turbines to power mechanical systems.[44] Over a year later, and following municipal elections that saw the left-wing majority on council replaced by a right-wing party, Walmart reapplied and the proposal was accepted.[45] In reaction to a proposed Walmart of 116,000 square feet, Sunshine Coast Regional District directors recently proposed zoning changes to restrict retail developments to a new maximum size of 25,000 square feet.[46] Although not all big-box applications or operations succeed, clearly many do, supported by politicians and citizens.

Journalists and authors have praised and defended value retail, as in Steve Maich's widely discussed article "Why Wal-Mart Is Good," Larry Stevenson's *Power Retail,* and the vaguely hagiographical *What I Learned from Sam Walton* by Michael Bergdahl.[47] For growth-machine supporters, big-box stores represent major market opportunities.[48] Competition between cities for retail developments can be intense and is fuelled by retailers looking for concessions and/or subsidies.[49] This is an important part of the "new urban politics," which developed in response to the decline of industrial production in North American cities and the recession of the late 1980s.[50] Municipalities, under pressure from fiscally conservative provincial and federal governments, sought to attract development and investment by promoting themselves as business-friendly.

Intercity competition and business-friendly promotions accompanied the arrival of NRFs in the Capital Regional District. Costco tried to place the municipalities of Sidney and Central Saanich into competition by filing simultaneous development applications in both in 1995.[51] In the end, both applications were rejected, and in 1999 Costco instead opened in Langford, where, Mayor Stewart Young likes to remind opponents, Costco now contributes an annual average of $400,000 in city taxes.[52] In 1998 View Royal City Council turned down a proposed Home Depot of 125,000 square feet. Langford promptly invited the retailer to a Millstream Road development site, offering a smooth process with a fast approval timeline of six months.[53] Two years later, View Royal approved a Canadian Tire of 72,000 square feet for the same location proposed by Home Depot.[54] Fearing the loss of another major development, growth-machine councillors worked with Canadian Tire officials to sell the deal to council, over the vocal objections of nearby residents.

Equally significant to such intercity competitions have been the attempts by Walmart to partner with BC First Nations in retail development. At a time of limited investment and economic development, and slow progress on treaty negotiations, such development proposals represent profitable opportunities for First Nations. For Walmart, such partnerships reduce the normally lengthy approval process and mean no city council vote, no public meetings, and no municipal taxes.[55] In 2004 Walmart entered into negotiations with two BC First Nations: the Adams Lake Band of Salmon Arm and the Cowichan Tribes Band of Duncan. In both cases, the municipalities were alarmed and dismayed by the prospect of lost tax revenue and major developments constructed outside planning regimes yet requiring infrastructure servicing. Amid the resulting conflicts between the bands and local governments over jurisdiction and planning, the negotiations with Walmart stalled and, in both cases, had collapsed by 2006. In 2007 the Tsawout First Nation of the Saanich Peninsula announced a proposed power centre for lands adjacent to the Patricia Bay Highway in Central Saanich.[56] The Tsawout argued the project was a means toward financial independence and participation in the regional market economy, as well as improved social services and living conditions on the reserve.[57] However, along with being on Tsawout land, the proposed location was also part of the Agricultural Land Reserve, a provincial jurisdiction meant to protect farmland and green spaces. This is highly significant in Central and North Saanich, where there are large amounts of working farmland and where preservation of the agricultural economy and rural character is a long-established principle of governance. There was also neighbourhood opposition to new big-box stores in this part of the Capital Regional District. The Tsawout power centre proposal seemed unlikely to succeed in the face of this social and legal opposition, an opposition that potentially put local and provincial officials in the difficult position of denying economic opportunities to First Nations people. However, it was a legal dispute over reserve boundaries (a federal jurisdiction) that in the end stalled and eventually, in the opinion of Graham Powell of the First Nations Land Management Resource Centre, killed the proposed development.[58]

In these cases, the big-box store strangely operates as a capitalist, postcolonial vehicle for First Nations financial and political independence. This holds true even in the case of failure, as these proposals spotlight the many unresolved issues between First Nations and Canadian governments. It is worth noting that, currently, the BC Treaty Commission is in negotiations with fifty-eight First Nations, including the Cowichan Tribes Band.[59] The Tsawout, on the other hand, are signatories to one of the earliest, and least fair, treaties negotiated in the 1850s by BC governor James Douglas.[60] Although the big-box store can be a bargaining chip used by First Nations in treaty negotiations, it also comes with risks. Along with potential business and investment failure, the big-box store is a vehicle for cultural conformity via its promotion of mainstream modes of consumption. Any increase in political and economic freedom achieved with the big-box includes deeper ties to, and increased participation in, Lefebvre's "bureaucratic society of controlled consumption," whose institutions produce, and reproduce, practices of conformity. For both First Nations and organizations opposed to NRFs, this production of physical and social sameness is one of the least desirable effects of big-box development.

THE CASE OF LANGFORD

Here, I consider the big-box store in more specific terms by looking at examples from the city of Langford, one of thirteen municipalities in the Capital Regional District. Regularly labelled in the media "The Big-Box Capital" of Vancouver Island,[61] Langford covers forty-two square kilometres and has a population of close to 19,000, living on farms and in subdivisions.[62] Well known for its pro-development City Council, the city is home to the majority of value retailers in the CRD. Five-term mayor Stewart Young is a growth-machine politician well known for vigorously courting retail developments. He has been outspoken in his impatience regarding impact studies and public consultations that accompany development. As he told one reporter, "Democracy kills free enterprise. The most important thing for any politician is to get things done."[63] For Young and his councillors, this equals local economic development, especially projects that contribute enough to city revenues to offset, according to the mayor, the need to increase taxes. His support of commercial growth has been unwavering over his thirteen years in power. In response to concerns from environmentalists about the big-box developments in 1997, Young's answer is a good example of the populist rhetoric that characterizes new urban politics: "If we say we don't want trees cut down, we don't get any jobs and we'll have a community where we're all stuck on welfare."[64] Presumably to avoid this, Young's government implemented a stream-lined, fast-tracked approval process for commercial developments. Since 1997 Langford has become home to Costco, Home Depot, Staples, Future Shop, Home Outfitters, Canadian Tire, Rona, The Brick, Great Canadian Super Store, and Walmart. In terms of architecture, Langford provides an excellent range of recently constructed NRFs, as stand-alones and in groups, concentrated in the two commercial nodes of Millstream Road and the Westshore Town Centre, formerly CanWest Mall.

Langford's big-box stores have their origins in 1997, just three years after the municipality was incorporated. Langford's first City Council, led by Mayor Young, was dominated by growth-machine advocates who were actively seeking new business development for the city.[65] One of their goals was to bring in money needed for infrastructure and other urban improvements – specifically, at the time, new sewers – without having to raise property taxes.[66] One of the solutions they chose was to promote large retail development around the established CanWest shopping centre and on Millstream Road north of the Trans-Canada Highway. The latter area had been recently transformed by a new highway interchange, making it highly desirable to NRFs. The first big-box retailer in the Millstream Road area was Costco, which was approved by council in April 1998.[67] Local activists, led by the Garry Oak Meadow Preservation Society, protested the environmental destruction, particularly the clearing of a Garry oak meadow that occupied part of the Costco worksite.[68] On 19 May 1998 five environmentalists chained themselves to logging equipment and managed to delay operations for several hours before being arrested.[69] Despite this controversial beginning, other big-box stores followed Costco to Langford: Home Depot (1999), Staples (2000), Future Shop (2001), and Home Outfitters (2002). Surprisingly, opposition was muted during public hearings for Home Depot, despite the fact the project would be built over four hectares of arbutus and fir forest.[70] As Mayor Young continued to argue that big-box stores are funding city projects, including the acquisition of parkland, Millstream Road became the centre of value retailing, and value consumption, in the CRD.

The big-box stores of Millstream Road present a subtle variety in appearance (Figure 13.4). The general form – a massive, horizontal warehouse – is repeated, but the more one examines these outlets, the more details emerge. For instance, a review of the images provided in this chapter shows that each operation employs distinctive colour schemes and surface treatments. The exterior walls are not blank but instead feature horizontal bands, vertical grooves, and raised surfaces. In the language of architectural history, the walls are organized by simple string-courses, blind bays at regular intervals, and engaged pilasters. Costco has all of these features, along with an entrance marked by large pillars, a frieze, and entablature (Figure 13.5). Although hardly grand, it is also hardly blank. In fact, one of the conditions of approval imposed by Langford's Planning and Zoning Committee was that the developers "add more architectural features to the west wall of the building."[71] The effect was to make sure the surface-wall organization continued all the way around the building. In a nod to domestic architecture, Home Depot, identified by its orange and white colour scheme, uses a gable to mark the entrance and carry the main sign. Fittingly, Future Shop features high-tech-influenced surfaces and materials, which preview the colours and shapes of the commodities found inside. Home Outfitters is more traditional, with exterior walls organized by colossal pilasters and string-courses and pierced by bay windows serving as display spaces. Despite the reputation for functional efficiency, the big-box stores are actually decorated. This trend has increased in more recent buildings, such as with the Millstream Village Mall, which opened in 2006. This is a new power centre featuring off-price outlets for high-end brands and a grocery store. Unlike a typical power centre, the NRFs here are not stand-alone units but instead share facades and

Figure 13.4 Millstream Road shopping node, Langford. | Photograph by author.

Figure 13.5 Costco, Langford. | Photograph by author.

curtain walls, similar to the strip malls and exterior shopping centres of the 1950s (Figure 13.6). In a further difference, the Millstream Village Mall features facades and porticoes decorated with bungalow-inspired surfaces, alluding to some nearby buildings that predate the big-box era on Millstream Road.

The Millstream Road NRFs are popular and seemingly fixed into the retail structure of the CRD. In Langford, city officials continue to cite big-box stores as economic vehicles for urban redevelopment and improved amenities. In 2005, at a conference hosted by the Planning Institute of British Columbia, Langford planner Rob Buchan led a workshop entitled "Leveraging Opportunity for Community Benefit" on the lessons to be learned from Langford's negotiations with value retailers.[72] Buchan, like Mayor Young, argued that the economic contributions of the NRFs counterbalance their negatives. Although the stores may be ugly, they helped to pay for the city's first purchases of public art.[73] This promotion of the "Langford model" received a further boost when McGill University's Avi Friedman, a national expert on urban planning, met with Mayor Young while in the CRD for a conference, toured Langford, and applauded the urban improvements funded by commercial taxes.[74] After seeing the Millstream Road area, Friedman proposed adding residential floors to the NRFs in order

Figure 13.6 Millstream Village Mall, Langford. | Photograph by author.

to create density and vibrancy. Although mixed-use developments involving big-box stores are occurring in Canada and the United States, it remains to be seen if this will happen in Langford.

AMERICANIZATION OR NANAIMOIZATION?

Retail architecture better illustrates the way Canadians live their social and cultural values on an everyday basis than all the picturesque rural churches and post offices put together. The latter are nostalgic elements of a real and imaginary Canada, a cultural mythology shared across the country and primarily characterized by the ideas of the North and of Canadians' nordicity.[75] The "True North" is a key national image despite the fact nearly all Canadians live in the South and have little experience of travelling in northern Canada.[76] The North to most Canadians is thus an imagined place or one experienced through photography and film. It serves to counter the realities of urban Canada and the strong cultural influence of the United States, and it is present in many national and popular symbols: the Inuit, the *voyageur,* the tragic and frostbitten explorer, and, the beer-drinking hoser of SCTV's *Great White North*. In between the myths of the North and the realities of the South, everyday life is produced in Canada, forming itself out of this cultural-geographical dialectic. In terms of architectural symbols, the big-box store seems as good a representative of the South as the igloo is of the North. The symbols of the North maintain their power even as Canadians pursue lifestyles in cities and suburbs that increasingly resemble the lifestyles pursued in American cities and suburbs. We might dream of a snowy True North, but we spend our waking hours stuck in traffic and shopping for bargains all the same. Given the similarities across North America in retailing, urban politics, and consumption trends, Canadians today may need to admit that, despite trying to be different, we're really just citizens of, with a nod to Lizabeth Cohen, a "Consumer's Dominion."[77]

The big-box store is in fact an excellent symbol of the South and of American influence. Category killers, warehouse clubs, and power centres are vividly associated in Canada with the arrival and expansion of US retail chains in the late 1980s and 1990s. Writing in 2001, geographers Ken Jones and Michael Doucet of the Centre for the Study of Commercial Activity described this NRF growth as the "Americanization of the Canadian retail sector."[78] This process, beyond the entrance of new retailers into Canada, entailed fundamental changes to the structures of distribution, demand, and marketing, which were based on innovations developed in the United States. One example is Walmart's barcode technology and computerized inventories, which adjust stock numbers with each purchase and alert suppliers automatically when a target number of sales is reached and new stock is needed. The growth of American chains was visible in terms of new construction and had major impacts on Canadian retailers, suppliers, and consumers. The 1990s saw the closure of several Canadian retailers, including Eaton's, Woolco, and Consumer's Distributing.[79] Although the causal relationship is debated, the everyday perception is that American big-box retailers seemed to be replacing Canadian stores.[80] Such was the case with 122 Woolco stores bought, refurbished, and then occupied by Walmart in 1994. The perception that big-box stores were American was felt by their Canadian imitators. Larry Stevenson, past CEO of Chapters, experienced this during his company's expansion in the 1990s: "A lot of people think I'm American and that Chapters is American. I think it's because we're new and we're big and people assume that all of the big new stores are American, as they mostly are. We've been caught up in that sweep."[81] This perception was also due to Chapters' business practices, which are strongly associated with US retailers such as Walmart and with book giants like Barnes and Noble. In *Power Retail,* Stevenson summarizes the essential principles of big-box retailing: domination of geographic markets and categories; operation of a highly efficient management of employees, technology, and costs; openness to change and reinvention; and delivery of a superior shopping experience based on selection, convenience, and price.[82] These approaches characterize all big-box retailers and are strategies usually credited to Sam Walton of Walmart and to Sol Price of Price Club (later Costco). However, these characteristics were not entirely unheard of in Canada before Walmart and Costco arrived. Neither were sprawl and criticisms of overconsumption. At an anti-Costco rally in Langford in 1998, one sign read: "Stop the Nanaimoization of Victoria," referring to Nanaimo's reputation as Vancouver Island's sprawling "city of malls."[83]

The big-box store actually developed in both Canada and the United States. One of Canada's first big-box operations, recognized in hindsight, was Knob Hill Farms, which opened a bare-bones facility of 19,000 square feet in Markham in 1963.[84] Two early examples of warehouse-style retail are The Brick in Edmonton (1971) and Leon's Furniture in Toronto (1973); the latter is a location of 150,000 square feet that the company promotes as Canada's first big-box store.[85] The category killer has a strong forerunner in Canada: Canadian Tire.

As mentioned earlier, Canadian Tire was founded in 1927 in Toronto as an operation focused on a single retail category.[86] Building on the growth of catalogue sales in the 1930s, Canadian Tire expanded to three categories, adding housewares and sporting goods. The founders of Canadian Tire, William Jackson Billes and Alfred Jackson Billes, were competitive retailers who fought with wholesalers and suppliers and built a reputation for cornering markets and offering regular low prices. The Billes brothers began franchising their stores in 1934 as dealer-owner operations, and in 1958 they created one of the first customer-loyalty programs with the issuing of Canadian Tire Money. By the late 1980s, on the eve of the arrival of American big-box chains, Canadian Tire could claim that 80 percent of Canadians lived within fifteen minutes of a store, and of these Canadians, 80 percent visited these stores once every six weeks.[87] Canadian Tire vigorously promotes itself as a distinctly Canadian retail establishment by stressing ties to the True North. In its television advertisements for snow blowers or ice-resistant windshield wipers, Canadian Tire customers are portrayed as plucky, can-do folks trying their best to master the challenges of life in a northern climate. Canadian Tire is also a major retailer of hockey equipment. The latter is, of course, especially powerful in economic and symbolic terms in Canada, and not insignificantly, Canadian Tire is a television sponsor of CBC's *Hockey Night in Canada*. Despite these image priorities and its strong market presence, Canadian Tire hired Stephen Bachand, an American, as CEO in 1993 to help the company compete with US retailers. Bachand did this by aggressively adopting new store formats and expanding into power centres.[88] In 2000 Canadian Tire opened forty-five "new generation" stores across Canada, the company's name for big-box stores.[89] In its history and current retail format, Canadian Tire proves that big-box stores are not uniquely American in origin.

If ever a nation was created through the operations of commodity consumption and retail structures, surely it was ours. Codfish, beaver pelts, lumber, gold, and the Hudson's Bay Company – all are irreducible elements in the historical development and image of the country. As Harold Innis first argued, the fur industry largely determined the borders of Canada while also shaping the unique character of its socio-political institutions.[90] This is particularly evident to those of us, including myself, who live in cities that began as Hudson's Bay Company forts and trading posts. In the fabric of everyday life, the history of Canada has been, and continues to be, the consumption of Canada.

NOTES

1 Ken Jones and Michael Doucet, "The Big Box, the Flagship, and Beyond: Impacts and Trends in the Greater Toronto Area," *Canadian Geographer* 45, 4 (2001): 495.
2 Richard Harris, *Creeping Conformity: How Canada Became Suburban, 1900-1960* (Toronto: University of Toronto Press, 2004), 173.
3 Essy Baniassad, ed., *Millennium Celebration of Canadian Architecture* (Ottawa: Royal Architectural Institute of Canada, 2000), 2.
4 Ibid.
5 Patricia Bailey, "Canadians Love Churches, Tolerate Boxes," *Victoria Times-Colonist,* 6 May 2000, F3.
6 Ibid.
7 Daniel Herman, "The Next Big Thing," in *Harvard School of Design Guide to Shopping: Project on the City 2,* ed. C. Chung, J. Inaba, R. Koolhaas, and S. Leong (New York: Taschen, 2001), 531.
8 Nikolaus Pevsner, *An Outline of European Architecture* (Harmondsworth, UK: Penguin, 1963), 15.
9 Ibid.
10 Greg Potter, "The Abbarch Partnership Architects: Striking a Balance between Retail Vicissitudes and Aesthetic Verities," *Award Magazine,* August 2005, 8-9.
11 The essential arguments can be found in Dolores Hayden, *Building Suburbia: Green Fields and Urban Growth, 1820-2000* (New York: Pantheon, 2003); Andres Duany, Elizabeth Plater-Zybeck, and Jeff Speck, *Suburban Nation: The Rise of Sprawl and the Decline of the American Dream* (New York: North Point, 2000); Constance Beaumont, *Superstore Sprawl Can Harm Communities: And What Citizens Can Do about It* (Washington, DC: National Trust for Historic Preservation, 1994).
12 Jim Simmons and Shizue Kamikihara, *Commercial Activity in Canada, 2000* (Toronto: Centre for the Study of Commercial Activity, Ryerson Polytechnic Institute, 2001), 9.
13 Jim Simmons and Shizue Kamikihara, *Commercial Activity in Canada, 2004* (Toronto: Centre for the Study of Commercial Activity, Ryerson Polytechnic Institute, 2005), 9.
14 "Monthly Survey of Large Retailers (LMR), March 2007," *Statistics Canada Report #5027,* May 2007.

15 Jean Lambert, "The Canadian Shopping Center Industry in 2005," International Council of Shopping Centers, http://www.icsc.org/srch/rsrch/researchquarterly/current/rr2006133/Canada.pdf.
16 Simmons and Kamikihara, *Commercial Activity in Canada, 2000,* 9-12.
17 Mark Jayne, *Cities and Consumption* (New York: Routledge, 2006), 58-65.
18 Jon Goss, "The Magic of the Mall: An Analysis of Form, Function, and Meaning in the Contemporary Retail Built Environment," *Annals of the Association of American Geographers* 83, 1 (1993): 18-47.
19 Steven Miles, *Consumerism as a Way of Life* (London: Sage, 1998), 1.
20 Raymond Williams examines the etymological and cultural roots of "customer" and "consumer" in *Keywords: A Vocabulary of Culture and Society* (London: Fontana, 1973), 78-79.
21 Henri Lefebvre, *Everyday Life in the Modern World,* trans. Sacha Rabinovitch (London: Athlone, 1984), 68.
22 Henri Lefebvre, "The Everyday and Everydayness," trans. Christine Levich, in *Architecture of the Everyday,* ed. Steven Harris and Deborah Berke (New York: Princeton Architectural Press, 1997), 33.
23 Ken Jones and Jim Simmons, *Location, Location, Location: Analyzing the Retail Environment* (Toronto: Methuen, 1987), 86.
24 The creative consumer is discussed in Lefebvre, *Everyday Life in the Modern World;* Jayne, *Cities and Consumption;* and Mark Paterson, *Consumption and Everyday Life* (New York: Routledge, 2006).
25 Paterson, *Consumption,* 6-7.
26 Jayne, *Cities and Consumption,* 18-19; Miles, *Consumerism,* 147.
27 Professional and scholarly publications have established a broadly accepted set of definitions for contemporary retail. Sources include John R. White and Kevin D. Gray, eds., *Shopping Centers and Other Retail Properties: Investment, Developing, Financing, and Management* (New York: Wiley and Sons, 1996); Jon Goss, "Once-upon-a-Time in the Commodity World: An Unofficial Guide to Mall of America," *Annals of the Association of American Geographers* 89, 1 (1999): 45-75; Dolores Hayden, *Field Guide to Sprawl* (New York: Norton, 2004); N. Barry Lyon Consultants Ltd., in association with Emrik Suichies and Associates for the Provincial Facilitator, *New Format Retailing and the Public Interest* (Toronto: Ontario Ministry of Municipal Affairs, 1994).
28 Eric Genest-Laplante, "Specialized Big Box Stores." Analytical Paper Series No. 29 (Ottawa: Statistics Canada, 2000), 1.
29 In retail literature, area is still described in square footage.
30 Hayden, *Field Guide,* 24, 30, 80.
31 Sze Tsung Leong, "Evolution," in *Harvard School of Design Guide to Shopping: Project on the City 2,* ed. C. Chung, J. Inaba, R. Koolhaas, and S. Leong (New York: Taschen, 2001), 35.
32 Ian Brown, *Freewheeling: The Feuds, Broods, and Outrageous Fortunes of the Billes Family and Canada's Favourite Company* (Toronto: HarperCollins, 1989), 19-20, 42-43.
33 Marina Strauss, "A Looming Warehouse War Keeping Costco on Its Toes," *Toronto Globe and Mail,* 18 October 2003, B4.
34 Ibid.
35 Howard C. Gelbtuch, "The Formats Employed in New Retail Strategies," in *Shopping Centers,* ed. White and Gray, 173.
36 Sze Tsung Leong, "Evolution," 35.
37 Marina Strauss, "Retailers Brace to Battle Sam's Club," *Toronto Globe and Mail,* 27 October 2003, B3.
38 Jones and Doucet, "Big Box," 499.
39 Gelbtuch, "Formats Employed," 173.
40 N. Barry Lyon Consultants Ltd., *New Format Retailing,* 5.
41 Ibid., 7-8.
42 Beaumont, *Superstore Sprawl,* 7-12.
43 Constance Beaumont and Leslie Tucker, "Big Box Sprawl (and How to Control It)," *Municipal Lawyer* 43, 2 (2002): 6-9, 30-31; Deborah Curran, *Challenging the Sprawl of Big Box Retail: The Smart Growth Approach to "Zone It and They Will Come" Development* (Victoria: Polis Project on Ecological

Governance and Smart Growth BC, 2002); Stacy Mitchell, *Big-Box Swindle: The True Cost of Mega-Retailers and the Fight for America's Independent Businesses* (Boston: Beacon, 2006).

44 Lynda Challis, "Policy Report, Development and Building: CD1 – Rezoning 86 SE Marine Drive/ 101 East 69th Ave (Wal-Mart)," City of Vancouver, 29 April 2005, 8.

45 Glenn Bohn, "Wal-Mart Prepares to Submit Proposal," *Vancouver Sun*, 19 July 2006, B1.

46 Randy Shore, "New Zoning Bylaws to Thwart Wal-Mart," *Vancouver Sun*, 3 March 2007, B5.

47 Steve Maich, "Why Wal-Mart Is Good," *Maclean's Magazine*, 25 July 2005; Lawrence Stevenson, Joseph Shlesinger, and Michael Pearce, *Power Retail: Winning Strategies from Chapters and Other Leading Retailers in Canada* (Toronto: McGraw Hill, 1999); Michael Bergdahl, *What I Learned from Sam Walton: How to Compete and Thrive in a Wal-Mart World* (Hoboken, NJ: Wiley and Sons, 2004).

48 Harvey Molotch, "The City as a Growth Machine: Toward a Political Economy of Place," *American Journal of Sociology* 82, 2 (1976): 309-32.

49 Intercity competition is addressed in Beaumont and Tucker, "Big Box Sprawl"; and David Harvey, "From Space to Place and Back Again: Reflections on the Condition of Postmodernity," in *Mapping the Futures: Local Cultures, Global Change*, ed. Jon Bird (New York: Routledge, 1993), 7-8.

50 Jayne, *Cities and Consumption*, 58-65.

51 Bill Smith, "Costco Wins One, Waits for Choice," *Victoria-Times Colonist*, 3 May 1995, B3.

52 Bill Cleverley, "New Life for Langford," *Victoria Times-Colonist*, 14 November 2000, A2.

53 Ian Dutton, "Home Depot Goes Shopping in Langford," *Victoria Times-Colonist*, 11 November 1998, B2.

54 Sarah Cox, "B.C.'s Big-Box Backlash," *Georgia Straight* 35, 1733 (2001): 17-18.

55 Sarah Cox, "Wal-Mart on the Rez," *The Tyee*, 7 June 2004, http://www.tyee.ca.

56 "Big-Box Dreams on the Peninsula," *Victoria Times-Colonist*, 11 February 2007, D2.

57 Ibid.

58 Richard Foot, "First Nations Blame Ottawa for Continued Poverty on Reserves," *Vancouver Sun*, 15 October 2010, A11.

59 BC Treaty Commission, "Negotiation Update," 15 June 2007, http://www.bctreaty.net.

60 Robin Fisher, *Contact and Conflict: Indian-European Relations in British Columbia, 1774-1890* (Vancouver: UBC Press, 1992), 66-68.

61 Judith Lavoie, "West Ready for Boom in Building," *Victoria Times-Colonist*, 20 August 1997, A1.

62 Regional Planning Office, "Capital Regional District 2001 Statistics," in *Comprehensive Annual Financial Report* (Victoria: Capital Regional District, 2001), 6.

63 Jody Paterson, "Langford Reborn," *Victoria Times-Colonist*, 21 April 2002, C7.

64 Judith Lavoie, "Mayor Backs Costco Store Plans Despite Worries about Meadow," *Victoria Times-Colonist*, 7 August 1997, A4.

65 Norman Gidney, "The New Langford: Model of Livability," *Victoria Times-Colonist*, 22 April 2005, B1.

66 Ibid; Lavoie, "West Ready for Boom," A1.

67 City of Langford, "Minutes of the Regular Meeting of Council," 20 April 1998, http://www.cityoflangford.ca/documents.

68 Curran, *Challenging the Sprawl*, 10.

69 Bill Cleverley, "Activists Battle with Costco," *Victoria Times-Colonist*, 20 May 1997, A3.

70 Curran, *Challenging the Sprawl*, 10; Dutton, "Home Depot Goes Shopping," B2.

71 City of Langford, "Minutes of the Planning and Zoning Committee," 14 April 1998, http://www.cityoflangford.ca/documents.

72 Gidney, "New Langford," B1.

73 Ibid.

74 Joanne Hatherly, "Thinking outside the Box," *Victoria Times-Colonist*, 20 February 2006, B3.

75 Rob Shields, "The True North Strong and Free," in *Places on the Margins: Alternative Geographies of Modernity* (New York: Routledge, 1992), 162-99.

76 Ibid., 163-65.

77 Lizabeth Cohen, *A Consumer's Republic: The Politics of Mass-Consumption in Postwar America* (New York: Knopf, 2003).
78 Jones and Doucet, "Big Box," 506.
79 Ibid., 498.
80 Jim Simmons, "The Economic Impact of Wal-Mart Stores," report (Toronto: Centre for the Study of Commercial Activity, 2001).
81 Quoted in Jones and Doucet, "Big Box," 495.
82 Stevenson, Shlesinger, and Pearce, *Power Retail,* 3.
83 Martha Tropea, "From Corner Stores to Malls," *Nanaimo Daily News,* 11 August 2006, A3.
84 Ibid.
85 See the section "Our History" on the Leon's Furniture website: http://www.leons.ca.
86 Brown, *Freewheeling,* 19-20.
87 Ibid., 87.
88 Jones and Doucet, "Big Box," 505.
89 Sarah Cox, "Chain Reaction," *Monday Magazine,* 30 November 2000, 10.
90 Harold Innis, *The Fur Trade in Canada* (Toronto: University of Toronto Press, 1967), 391-92.

14

Archi-tizing
Architecture, Advertising, and the Commodification of Urban Community

RHODRI WINDSOR LISCOMBE

The status of architecture and its force within the social order have always been variable. But presently, in Canada at least, this status suffers the proverbial worst of all worlds. The tremendous pace of construction and publicity around a selection of major public or corporate commissions masks the exclusion of architects from designing much of the built environment. This represents a considerable reduction even since the Royal Architectural Institute of Canada's May 1960 "Report on Housing," written by Vancouver architect Charles E. "Ned" Pratt. More recently, Vancouver has become a particular site of this further diminution in architectural agency. Ironically, however, this phase in the subjugation or exclusion of architects is occurring through the marketing and promotion of high-end buildings often commissioned from celebrated architects. Besides subjugating the specific design form and the architect's specific design contribution, the sophisticated textual and visual rhetoric in the marketing of effects inverts the critical strategies associated with postmodern/structural/colonial discourses in which architecture has been accorded greater significance.[1]

The case of Vancouver, as argued briefly in the introduction to this volume, is representative of Canadian and international conditions in the late-modern, globalized era.[2] Its real estate is the object of offshore investment, one popular

Figure 14.1 View of Vancouver from Point Grey, 2007. | Photograph by author.

epithet for the city being "Switzerland of the Pacific." Its recent built environment and associated claims to leadership in "greening" urban development are an object of international professional attention (Figure 14.1). And its popular civic image is the object of many meanings ascribed to lifestyle.[3] In particular, Vancouver's contemporary manifestation demonstrates the entanglement of collective identity and individual subjectivity in the commercialization of social relations and the commodification of personal experience: life as shopping and self-identity as acquisition within a shifting scenery of spectacular or utilitarian architectural scenery.[4] The particular period under scrutiny here is the prelude to the global economic crisis of 2008-09 and the 2010 Winter Olympic-Paralympic Games that completed the rebranding of Vancouver as a world city.

This often chaotic juxtapositioning of imposed, and interiorized, ideas of self and society with the acquisition economy is manifest in journalistic publicity for property development in the Vancouver region.[5] The formerly hippie, now mildly counterculture *Georgia Straight* in its summer 2007 insert "Living" carried an advertisement for an apartment block called Watercolors with the caption, "Sometimes the world does revolve around you." Earlier, on 17 February 2007, the front page of the *Vancouver Sun*'s "Westcoast News" section carried two main stories symptomatic of the current place of property in narratives of excess, exploitation no less than environmentalism: "Credit-card fraud charges follow raid on luxury homes" and "Mayor backs green cabs." Buildings and planning have, indeed, become staples of the regional urban debate, and architecture has become an incident in the wording and imaging of ordinary city life. In particular, each reflects the monetary discrepancies within urban society and the volatile financial linkage of the local to the global marketplace.[6]

The rootlessness of money, or, more truly, its anxious search for stable investment, is manifest in the selling of condominium Vancouver. The same *Georgia Straight* "Living" insert carried a full-page-spread advertisement by Rennie Marketing Systems (its logo here emblazoned with the word "Green," picking up on Vancouver's self-branding as "Sustainability City"). The advertisement was for "Vancouver's Truly Green Waterfront Community/MILLENNIUM WATER.COM/A WORLD ADDRESS," which would serve initially as the Athlete's Village for the 2010 Winter Games. About the same time, the "Business" section of the *Vancouver Sun* of 3 May 2007 printed a headline that, doubtless unintentionally, exposed the profound discontent lurking in the "Vancouver Achievement."[7] The headline read, "April house prices rise 11.9 percent in Greater Vancouver over 2006. Hotel Georgia [downtown condominium development] attracts international celebrity level interest."

The harsh contrast between glitzy, green world city and decrepit, disadvantaged downtown – castigated in the United Nations Population Fund's June 2007 report – is most obvious in the Woodward's Redevelopment. The marketing (begun in 2005 by Rennie Marketing Systems) seized on the occupancy of one part of the complex by a unit of Simon Fraser University in an otherwise predominantly market-driven commercial and residential development to sell the project as "Intellectual Property." In a comparable artifice of redefinition, the promotional material sanitized the surrounding Downtown Eastside area as the Woodward's District. The existing residents will have less chance of remaining in their community, not least since the ratio of social (low-income) to market housing in the complex has contracted during the course of moving from design to construction. The decking-out with trees of the new lower and high-rise towers surrounding the single preserved section of the original Woodward's department store only partially moderates the conventional nature of the architectural design and the monetary focus of the project. The difficulty of resolving the radically divergent claims and demands of the public and the private sectors is evident in the compilation of an apologia by the project architects, Henriquez Partners Architects, with the interesting title *Towards an Ethical Architecture*.[8]

The mobilization of architectural knowledge and of the architect's creativity for social prestige, professional promotion, or corporate profit has a long history. Arguably, this began with respect to the Mediterranean-Atlantic tradition with the Roman architect and historian Vitruvius when he completed his *Ten Books on Architecture*. Still in currency to this day, Vitruvius both deployed and appropriated technical and aesthetic knowledge, originally to his own reward and reputation.[9] But his treatise also served to reinforce and project conventions of design value that could be exploited by individuals, institutions, and regimes seeking self-legitimation. These would include even Alfred Speer's megalomaniac neo-Classical National Socialist scheme for rebuilding Berlin as a material symbol of Adolf Hitler's thousand-year Reich.[10] Across this historical trajectory, architects helped to construct the fabric of modern capitalist and later-modern consumerist economies while also engaging in aspects of the commerce of knowledge. Their engagement ranged from the publication of pattern books (mainly for middle-class domestic or religious architecture) to collaborations with entrepreneurial and institutional real estate development.[11]

Especially during the 1950s and particularly in North America, architects briefly operated both radically and conservatively.[12] On the one hand, architects worked in the vanguard of comprehensive urban planning; on the other, they became agents in the reconfiguration of the social idealism of the Modern Movement into the socialization of conspicuous consumption through the domestic appliance and mechanized suburb. In these arenas, nevertheless, they increasingly lost design authority. In addition, the re-emergence of compounding socio-economic disparity returned architecture to its historical role as signifier of prestige and power, now mainly associated with financial enterprise. In turn, the realm of higher culture, centred on engines of monetary and social privilege such as the museum, art gallery, and opera or concert hall, returned to dependence on private patronage. The aesthetic domain – in some respects invented as a component of Enlightenment antiquarianism with its aura of transcendent value actually embedded in the selling of historical fragments and compendiums of simulacra – is once again a mode of social promotion through investment in institutional cultural capital.[13] But the resurgence of individuation in the neoliberal agenda has accompanied the late-modern deconstruction of public practice and private intention.

This deep disjunction effects the condition here described as *archi-tizing*, in which the architect and architecture operate as incidental justification for the mobilization of civic space for the marriage of elitist profit with singular desire. Instead of being foregrounded in the interplay of meaning between text and image – as in, say, the Adam brothers' *Works in Architecture of Robert and James Adam* (1773, 1779, and 1822) or at a more popular and local level the newspaper publicity for the second Hotel Vancouver (1901), designed by Francis Rattenbury, as "A Palace for the Public ... Equal to Any in Canada" – each is integrated into the background amalgam of opportunistic titillation and virtual possession.[14] Architecture and architects thus figure as incidental rather than as central agents of the economy of ownership and status. And the theoretical dimensions of design and cultural expression are constrained to instrumental purposes. Similarly, the critical edge of more recent academic discourse concerning both the political economy of the social order (especially questions of gender, ethnicity, subjectivity, and hierarchy) and the politics of culture (especially poststructural and postcolonial critique) is not only dulled but also reconstructed as positivist verbo-visual rhetoric – a veritable inversion of the communicative strategies first investigated effectively by Marshall McLuhan *and* of the intellectual underpinning of the multicultural ethos and populist pluralism so bruited in Canada, particularly with respect to Vancouver.[15] As a consequence, the work of both architecture and cultural criticism has been appropriated with great sophistication to the singular end of selling strata-title ownership and a discrete species of urban living.

At its foundation is a system of removal or reconstitution of actual place and conditions. Such alteration of physical attributes, especially of location and materiality, has something of a genealogy in Vancouver following the termination in 1956 of restrictions on building height in the West End precinct.[16] Even by then the collectivist approach to urban development embodied in the newly established Vancouver Planing Department was under siege. In 1956 the mayor was the entrepreneur and philanthropist Frederick Hume. He differed from the majority of mayors in being concerned with issues of low-income housing rather than representing real estate interests in the governance and construction of the city; at the time of Vancouver's incorporation in 1886, advertisements for real estate brokers predominated in the local press.[17] Without slipping into predictable moralizing about the power of property in civil society, it is worth remarking that advertisements from late-1950s and early-1960s Vancouver initiated a process that promoted the topographical advantages of singular buildings without regard to their impact on the surroundings and adjacent dwellings. But architectural qualities and features were still paramount. For example, the publicity material for Ocean Towers, erected on Beach Avenue in the West End to designs by Rex Reinecke in 1957-58, still lists "Building Design" among its distinctive features. View and amenities, including appliances, are also emphasized in the selling campaign but through quite simple verbal tactics as in the contemporary advert for Chilco Towers, also in the West End but designed by the more celebrated firm of Semmens Simpson (Figure 14.2).

Clearly, the advertisements for Chilco and Ocean Towers represent the less sophisticated and less aggressive mores of the day, as well as the practices of contemporary commercial promotion.[18] But the advertisement, being aimed at

Figure 14.2 Advertisement for Chilco Towers Apartment, Vancouver, architects Semmens Simpson, 1957-58. | Published in *Western Homes and Living*, January 1958.

engaging the, admittedly better-paid, public represents the lineament of usual culture. By "usual culture" is meant the social and spatial intermingling of a broad range of values and assumptions acting upon everyday living – a sphere investigated by such notable members of the Paris School of Continental Theory as Jean Baudrillard, Michel de Certeau, and Henri Lefebvre.[19] The imprimatur of an architect, and a sense of architectural form and its creation of spatial effect, obviously remained important. Move ahead almost fifty years to Vancouver as Pacific San Gimignano and internationally recognized as an exemplar of high-rise, high-density, downtown-core residential living. Compare the 2005 promotional literature for the Carina in the Coal Harbour precinct. The term "literature" is apposite since major residential developments involve the hiring of marketing firms to produce expensive booklets/flyers and project pamphlets together with much more extensive newspaper advertisements. Among the most adept is Rennie Marketing Systems, which, interestingly, is directed by a former real estate agent who also has a notable collection of contemporary visual art, including works from the school of conceptual photo-based production particularly associated with Vancouver. On average, the expenditure on the services of such marketing firms amounts to approximately 14 percent

Figure 14.3 Brochure for Carina Condominium, Coal Harbour, Vancouver. | Prepared by Delta Realty Services, 2005.

Figure 14.4 Brochure for Corus Condominium, University of British Columbia, Vancouver. | Prepared for Bastion Development Company, 2005.

of total development budget as against approximately 2 percent for all design activity. Delta Realty Services commanded equally talented copywriters and photographers in compiling the brochure for the Carina high-end condominiums. Both strata development and promotional literature are aimed at a client market among equally literate consumers of late-modern cultural economy. Their attention is directed to an array of features, chiefly topographical and functional, for which the architecture and even the projected building itself act as facilitation or foil (Figure 14.3).

Lest the Carina campaign appear exceptional, go to one of its satellite legatees. In this case, consider the Corus apartment tower built in 2007 as one component of the University Town development at the University of British Columbia (UBC). Alike informed by more than merely financial objectives – the most commendable being maximum livable construction toward a 50 percent live-work community at the Point Grey campus – the Corus is a high-rise, leasehold, strata-title apartment tower. Leaving aside the partial irony of situating expensive property development in the theological neighbourhood at UBC, given New Testament stricture against conspicuous consumption and usury, Corus is sold almost entirely around peripheral features. These are the view across English Bay and toward the Strait of Georgia but without reference to the adjacent and undistinguished Gage Towers student housing (Figure 14.4). The vistas in the advertisements distributed to nearby well-heeled inner-city suburbanites are carefully represented. Building and location are detached in inverse proportion to the virtual engagement of the design with nearby celebrity architecture: Sharp and Thompson's Iona Building (1946-51), Bing Thom's Chan Centre for the Performing Arts (1993-94), and Arthur Erickson's Museum of Anthropology (1974-76) (Figure 14.5). At a more profound level, the repositioning embodies the species of cognitive erasure that constitutes a benign parallel to the displacement of the Musqueam Nation from the Point Grey site to erect the university from 1914.

The iconic status of Erickson in Vancouver has, indeed, been appropriated as both aesthetic and investment commodity in recent developments where he also acted as project designer.[20] The phenomenon is remarkably multivalent in selling the Choklit neighbourhood condominium built on the site of a former chocolate manufactory. Reading the stylish brochure, Erickson's architectural reputation appears more significant than his design service. One page of the brochure is, indeed, devoted to a brief resume of his major commissions. And on another, the printing of his name literally performs as an emblem of quality. Much in the manner of the osmosis of creative quality ascribed to even casts

Figure 14.5 Brochure for Corus Condominium, University of British Columbia, Vancouver. | Prepared for Bastion Development Company, 2005.

Figure 14.6 Brochure for the Shangri-La Hotel and Condominium, Vancouver, architect James Cheng, 2005-08. | From "Living Shangri-La," brochure published by Rennie and Associates, 2006.

of antique sculpture or engravings of ancient and medieval monuments in eighteenth- and nineteenth-century Revivalism, the simulation of Erickson's creative ability carries greater force than its application. The plans of the Choklit units – reconstituted as neighbourhood in yet a further appropriation from Modernist planning history – occupy a subsidiary position to the literary and sensual fabrication of the visceral experience of occupying the barely described fabric. The tally of reasons deployed to buy at Choklit culminates in a page of highly informative phrases beginning with "Wake up Choklit" and climaxing with "Want Choklit."

The discourse of desire is one trajectory investigated in the compendium of deconstructive critical strategies associated with postmodernism. But most have become inverted into the covetous grist of the mill of condominium sales in Vancouver and increasingly in major North American cities. The inversion of critical strategy is most evident, and subtle, in the Rennie Marketing Systems campaign for the Shangri-La Hotel and Condominium. Initial proof resides in the very name assigned to the residential and hotel complex completed in 2009 on West Georgia Street in the extended downtown core of Vancouver. "Shangri-La" refers to the high-end hotel established in Hong Kong when many of the cheaper products of the Crown colony were sold in Britain through the US-controlled Woolworth chain stores as "Empire Made." Such naming is part of a little-studied if significant feature of the postcolonial era: nostalgia for imperial order and retrospective imperialist snobbery. The name Shangri-La deliberately invokes while repositioning the era of imperial privilege and ethnic hierarchy. Even more ironically for Vancouver as a reformed racist community (city officials excluded or relocated Asian immigrants wherever possible until the 1950s), it ascribes positive meaning to the heritage of exploitation disclosed in Orientalist and postcolonial criticism.[21] The name additionally summons up the exoticized othering of distant peoples or the romantic invention of unreality. The expensively produced brochure, "Living Shangri-La," lists the "dream team" of those responsible for this multimillion-dollar project early on. In it, the developers, promoters, and specialist designers appear above the architect, James Cheng. In the brochure Cheng's now extensive list of downtown towers is cited more as proof of financial utility than of architectural distinction. And his completed apartment towers figure as diagrammatic profiles virtually composing the Vancouver skyline that some might regard as phallic surrogates of architectural sublimity (Figure 14.6).

There is nothing new about the opportunistic use of the serious and trivial weft and warp of current culture either to convey meaning or, more so, to market goods. But, as already indicated, the currency of real estate promotion, exemplified by the Vancouver scene, presents a remarkable picture of intellectual discourse and architectural design reconstituted as sales pitch. The discursive critiques of postmodern scholarship can each be identified in the stylish visual and textual rhetoric of development advertising. Besides erasure, simulation, and Orientalism, there are aestheticization of utility, gender and irony inversion, preoccupation with spectacle, fictions of identity, and above all else, appropriation. These coalesce with especial force – and appeal – in the campaign for the Shangri-La. Illustrative of the substitution of simulation for substance and of the virtual for the real in a literal screening of life, the Shangri-La campaign began over two years before construction. Admittedly, architecture has always been as much about projects and schemes as about commissions and buildings – and often counter to the purport in the title of a 2005 exhibition of recent Canadian architecture (at the Belkin Art Gallery of the University of British Columbia), "Spectacle [has frequently triumphed] over Substance."[22] Nevertheless, the extent of the reconfiguration of cultural meaning and professional agency is remarkable. It corresponds with the fate of the radical social agenda of the Modern Movement typified by the Shangri-la commission: Cheng, in company with many architects, applies its aesthetic lineaments for elitist and exclusive rather than egalitarian and inclusive societal objectives.

In the promotion of Shangri-La, architect and architecture are almost tertiary. The *parti,* or concept, is primarily a packaged experience and secondarily a packaging of appliances and consumables. The commerce of culture traditionally affecting architecture has become a culture of commerce. In this culture of commerce architecture assumes a yet more subsidiary role in which the collusion between essential and exchange value are vaunted rather than latent. Expensive goods such as Bentley and BMW automobiles and high-end kitchen and bath wares determine the visual aesthetic of the building more than its architectural design – except as a vehicle for the display of an exotic or expressive lifestyle. And the clever wording and imaging of the building-to-be play upon Marshall McLuhan no less than Martin Heidegger. The play alike detaches interest from articulation. For example, McLuhan's verbo-visual-vico idea of late-modern space articulated in a June 1961 *Canadian Architect* article, and concentrated in the phrase "the street tries to become the city," could be revised in reference to the Shangri-La to read, "residence tries to become domicile."[23] Heidegger's negative exposure of the divide between essence and appearance becomes a positive mode of stimulating acquisitive desire.[24]

Arguably, the most remarkable process of inversion occurs around tropes of sensual appeal. In the major Shangri-La brochure, the narrative of want begins with a photograph of a woman, or rather of her leg, emerging from a luxury automobile, carrying the monogram of the hotel component of the complex. She wears stiletto heels, attire which has served as a longstanding emblem of the eroticized female body. Images of an exoticized young female, Asian of physiognomy and dress, courses through the brochure and the ongoing newspaper campaign. This is the female of colonialist literature, and of the representation of the colonized, the sexually subject woman criticized in Orientalist scholarship. Especially in the promotional linkage of hotel with apartments, these perform as erotic-exotic cyphers of male desire, mastery, and servicing. Yet, in a significant illustration of the opportunism of sophisticated marketing campaigns, the symbolism is reversed in a picture of a young woman being massaged by a masseur. The core dynamic is sensation toward heightened desire for acquisition.

The interpretation can be corroborated by reference to a new development, named Generations, in the less-fashionable adjoining municipality of Burnaby. The Generations advertisements cite complimentary alliterative attributes, "Exclusive, Expansive, Exceptional," that are purported to be transferred, or complementary, with the deeds of ownership. Such superfice indicates the positive interpretation of affect, transience, and titillation customary in late-modern culture. Even more interestingly, the really expensive strata-title condominiums – cleverly represented as *estates* (that is, extensive grounds and isolated buildings) in the latest Shangri-La newspaper advertisements – sell ownership as status bereft of owner visibility. Quite opposite to the historical work of architect and architecture as fabricator of elevated status and of manifest elite presence in public space and view, advertising for the Wall Centre Tower, 1996-98, designed by Peter Busby, typified the Vancouver situation in stressing the anonymity of possession. Owning an apartment at the Wall included ownership of secure and unseen occupation, ingress, and egress.

Now, this security component is a consequence of contemporary neuroses about safety; in this respect, its presence in real estate promotion and publicity further underscores the critical significance of apparently transient, even trivial, cultural production. All the promotional campaigns assert uncomplicated consumption of the city's amenities and, particularly in Vancouver, its remarkable topography. Once again, this aspect of the contemporary condition of architectural practice is not novel. Even at the height of respect for the comprehensive planning theory of the Modernists in the immediate post–Second World War era, architecture remained a singular process, wherein building after building was essentially conceived with limited reference to specific context. But the exclusion or erasure of the impact of buildings and building complexes has become much greater. The positivist irony involved in such erasure is evident in its most stylish mode in the photography and captioning of the Shangri-La hotel/apartment advertisements. Floor plans overlay obscuring and romanticizing night-time images of Vancouver's West End. Not surprisingly, these privilege the preferred views to sea and mountain, while eradicating the noisier and messier downtown surroundings. One page carries the heading "Take Shelter," which quite unconsciously, yet significantly, parodies both the conventions of grounded habitation and the inner-city shelters necessitated by the harsher social ethos of the neoliberal economy triumphant in most North American cities.

The parodic process is accompanied by equally ironic appropriations. The Shangri-La will house an outpost of the Vancouver Art Gallery, in an obvious conceit on the traditional interappropriation of wealth and culture. Its future legitimating, and titillating, presence is signified by a photograph of the upper, domed section of the Vancouver Art Gallery (converted in 1978-79 by Arthur Erickson from the third Vancouver Courthouse built to the designs of Francis Rattenbury, 1906-11).

The photograph shows two of the four vessels in the sculptural group *Four Boats Stranded: Red and Yellow, Black and White,* most prominently the Haida-inspired canoe, installed by Ken Lum. As noted in the introduction to this volume, these vessels represent the displacement of indigenous and would-be Asian migrants, but no aspects of a potentially more benign interpretation of more recent immigration policy is intimated in the accompanying text. Ironic critique is thus transformed into parodic commercialization, perhaps paralleling the interplay of Greenspeak with Greenwash in the development industry. Similarly, the everyday ritual and acts of living become transposed into the sensations of ownership signified through stylish photographs of the surfaces of appliances and furnishings. The structure and spaces are incidental to external and internal scenery.

The main record of the impact of such developments lies in other forms of promotion and commerce. The assessment of architectural and urban design is subsidiary to the self-congratulating rhetoric of civic improvement. In Vancouver this takes the form of the celebration of the greening of streetscapes and espousal of sustainability objectives while the tougher issues of public housing, transit, and welfare or preservation of agricultural land and pollution reduction receive less effective policy enactment.[25] A more substantive indicator of structural impact (i.e., of both construction and social economy) is the reporting of real estate commerce. Three examples will suffice. Two are from the *Vancouver Sun* of 2 October 2004. These acknowledge a modicum of the outcomes of economies of competitive development: "Shangri-La may have company" and "Shangri-La to ante up $17m." The third is the full-page advertisement printed in the 20 August 2005 *Sun* publicizing the various Lower Mainland developments by Polygon. With the odd caption "Homes for Everyone" for domiciles well beyond the average income, the advertising copy makes no reference to an architect or to architectural characteristics beyond a questionable allusion to the work of Frank Lloyd Wright; the sidelining of architects in the company's design process is especially interesting since its president is a high-profile enthusiast of the contemporary arts. Once again, these celebrate rather than consider the operation of civic civil society as primarily the promotion of property profit. The fictions inherent in this cultural practice, including the emasculation of architectural agency, revolve around the fabrication of consumer subjectivity.

The reconstruction of the deconstruction of the processes involved in this aspect of contemporary society are nicely summarized in a final instance of archi-tizing. This occurs in the promotional advertising for a less expensive condominium in Vancouver. The complex is shown only as a bird's-eye view, subservient to an artist's perspective of an interior and a landscape photograph. The most telling sentence in the captioning is "Find Yourself in Victoria Hall." Doubtless only unconsciously, the copywriter resolves Franz Kafka in retrieving John Locke – the anxieties of existence being capable of subjugation through the making of self by deed both as personal action and property contract.[26] Here is proof of the commercial appropriation of postmodern discourse and of the redirection rather than demise of Modernism as defined by the architect-theorists Claude Parent and Paul Virilio in the term "critical modernity." Alas, the role of architect and architecture in this phenomenon is often as not incidental and illusory. Lest this seem an exaggerated assertion, let the developmental advertising copy speak for itself. With undeniable wit yet candour, the header on the front page of the 2005 Choklit mail-out reads, "Architectural Eye Candy."

NOTES

1 The place of architecture in postmodern discourse is examined by Heinrich Klotz, *The History of Post Modern Architecture* (Cambridge, MA: MIT Press, 1988); and by Neil Leach, ed., *Rethinking Architecture: A Reader in Cultural Theory* (London: Routledge, 1997). A local perspective is presented in Rhodri Windsor Liscombe, "Conditions of Modernity: Si[gh]tings from Vancouver," *Journal of the Society for the Study of Architecture in Canada* 25, 1 (2000): 3-15, making reference to Paul Delaney, ed., *Vancouver: Representing the Postmodern City* (Vancouver: Arsenal Pulp, 1994).

2 Besides the argument in the introduction to this volume, the "global" place of Vancouver is discussed by Lance Berelowitz, *Dream City: Vancouver and the Global Imagination* (Vancouver: Douglas and

McIntyre, 2005). It has also entered into the work of local writers such as Douglas Coupland, author of *City of Glass* (Vancouver: Douglas and McIntyre, 2009).

3 The literature on lifestyle is as extensive as on postmodern, poststructural, and postcolonial theory and is exemplified by Rob Shields, ed., *Lifestyle Shopping: The Subject of Consumption* (London: Routledge, 1992), and by David Chaney, *Lifestyles* (London: Routledge, 1996), each with excellent bibliographies. An interesting historical perspective is provided by Janet Ward, *Weimar Surfaces: Urban Visual Culture in 1920s Germany* (Berkeley: University of California Press, 2001).

4 On these aspects, see Anthony Giddens, *Modernity and Self-Identity: Self and Society in the Late Modern Age* (Cambridge, UK: Polity, 1991); Scott Lash and John Urry, *The End of Organized Capitalism* (Cambridge, UK: Polity, 1987); Scott Lash and John Urry, *Economics of Signs and Spaces* (London: Sage, 1994); and James Finkelstein, *The Fashioned Self* (Philadelphia, PA: Temple University Press, 1991). See also Jonathan Beller, *The Cinematic Mode of Production: Attention Economy and the Society of the Spectacle* (Hanover, NH: Dartmouth College Press, 2006); and for the question of identity, Charles Taylor, *Sources of the Self: The Making of Modern Identity* (Cambridge, MA: Harvard University Press, 1989).

5 A shorter version of this chapter was published as "Archi-tizing," *Canadian Architect* 51, 8 (August 2006): 26-28. The linkage between architectural design and media in the modern period is examined by Beatriz Colomina, *Privacy and Publicity: Modern Architecture and Mass Media* (Cambridge, MA: MIT Press, 1994).

6 The cultural as well as socio-economic dimensions of the new global order have been studied by, among other scholars, David Harvey in *Spaces of Hope* (Berkeley: University of California Press, 2000) and in *The Conditions of Postmodernity* (Oxford: Blackwell, 1989); and Arjun Appadurue, *Modernity at Large: Cultural Dimensions of Globalization* (Minneapolis: University of Minnesota, 2003). The origins of both the phenomena and critical analyses are examined in Susan Buck-Morss, *The Dialectic of Seeing: Walter Benjamin and the Arcades Project* (Cambridge, MA: MIT Press, 1989).

7 This alludes to John Punter, *The Vancouver Achievement: Urban Planning and Design* (Vancouver: UBC Press, 2003).

8 Gregory Henriquez et al., *Towards an Ethical Architecture: Issues within the Work of Gregory Henriquez* (Vancouver: Simply Read Books and Blue Imprint, 2006). The development and the book are reviewed by Helen Grdadolnik, "Crosstown Examined," *Canadian Architect* 51, 1 (January 2006): 91-104.

9 For Vitruvius and his impact, see Indra McEwen, *Vitruvius: Writing the Body of Architecture* (Cambridge, MA: MIT Press, 2003). For architectural visualization, including through modern media, see Kester Rattenbury, ed., *This Is Not Architecture: Media Constructions* (London: Routledge, 2002), esp. Neil Leach, "Wallpaper* Person: Notes on the Behaviour of a New Species," 231-43.

10 The scheme is discussed by Iain Boyd Whyte and Dawn Ades, *Art and Power: Europe under the Dictators, 1930-45* (London: Hayward Art Gallery, 1995).

11 One instance is examined in Rhodri Windsor Liscombe, "The Commodification of Civic Culture in Early Nineteenth-Century London," *London Journal* 29, 2 (2004): 17-32.

12 The changing social status of the architect is examined by Andrew Saint, *The Image of the Architect* (New Haven, CT: Yale University Press, 1983).

13 The emergence of aesthetic discourse and connoisseurship in relation to new types of commerce in art objects is studied by Alex Potts, *Flesh and the Ideal: Winckelmann and the Origin of Art History* (New Haven, CT: Yale University Press, 1994). See also Pierre Bourdieu, *The Field of Cultural Production: Essays on Art and Literature,* trans. R. Johnson (Cambridge, UK: Polity, 1993); and N. McKendrick, J. Brewer, and J.H. Plumb, *The Birth of a Consumer Society: The Commercialization of Eighteenth-Century England* (London: Hutchinson, 1983).

14 For Robert Adam's literary and architectural work, see Geoffrey Beard, *The Work of Robert Adam* (New York: Arco, 1978); the publicity for the Hotel Vancouver is illustrated in Anthony Barrett and Rhodri Windsor Liscombe, *Francis Rattenbury and British Columbia: Architecture and Challenge in the Imperial Age* (Vancouver: UBC Press, 1983), 42.

15 McLuhan's study of print and popular culture is analyzed by Richard Cavell, *McLuhan in Space: A Cultural Geography* (Toronto: University of Toronto Press, 2002); and Judith Stamps, *Unthinking Modernity: Innis, McLuhan, and the Frankfurt School* (Montreal and Kingston: McGill-Queen's University Press, 1995). The multicultural policies, most associated with Canada, and discourse are scrutinized in Keith Banting and Will Kymlicka, *Multiculturalism and the Welfare State: Recognition and Redistribution in Contemporary Society* (Oxford: Oxford University Press, 2006); and Andrew Robinson, *Multiculturalism and the Foundations of Meaningful Life: Reconciling Autonomy, Identity, and Community* (Vancouver: UBC Press, 2007).

16 The planning and related architectural history are examined in Rhodri Windsor Liscombe, *The New Spirit: Modern Architecture in Vancouver, 1938-1963* (Montreal/Vancouver: Canadian Centre for Architecture/Douglas and McIntyre, 1997); and Rhodri Windsor Liscombe, "A Study in Modern[ist] Urbanism: Planning Vancouver, 1945-1965," *Urban History* 38, 1 (2011): 124-49.

17 The early architectural and social history of the city is studied in Don Luxton et al., *Building the West: Early Architects of British Columbia* (Vancouver: Talon, 2003); see also Rhodri Windsor Liscombe, "Fabricating a Place for Vancouver in the Pacific Northwest," in *Regionalism in the Age of Globalism 2: Forms of Regionalism*, ed. Lothar Honninghausen, Anke Ortlepp, James Peacock, and Niklaus Steiner, 195-208 (Madison: University of Wisconsin Press, 2005).

18 The development, impact, and constitution of advertising are reviewed in Roland Marchand, *Advertising the American Dream: Making Way for Modernity, 1920-1940* (Berkeley: University of California Press, 1985). See also Gilles Lipovetsky, *The Empire of Fashion: Dressing Modern Democracy*, trans. C. Porter (Princeton, NJ: Princeton University Press, 1994); Stephen Grundle and Clio Castelli, *The Glamour System* (Houndmills, UK: Palgrave Macmillan, 2006); and with respect to such urban architecture in Vancouver, and including an extensive bibliography, Rhodri Windsor Liscombe, "The Fe-Male Spaces of Modernism: A Western Canadian Perspective," *Prospects* 26 (2001): 667-700.

19 Their main books are respectively Jean Baudrillard, *System of Objects* (New York: Verso, 1996), and *Mass, Identity, Architecture: Architectural Writings of Jean Baudrillard* (Chichester, UK: Wiley, 2003); Michel de Certeau, *The Practice of Everyday Life*, trans. S. Rendall (Berkeley: University of California Press, 1984); and Henri Lefebvre, *The Production of Space*, trans. D. Nicholson-Smith (Oxford: Blackwell, 1991). See also Jurgen Habermass, *The Structural Transformation of the Public Sphere* (Cambridge, MA: Harvard University Press, 1989). The idea of usual culture is argued by Rhodri Windsor Liscombe, "Usual Culture: The Jet," *TOPIA: Canadian Journal of Cultural Studies* 11 (2004): 83-99.

20 Erickson's repute and architecture are considered in Nicholas Olsberg and Ricardo Castro, *Arthur Erickson: Critical Works* (Vancouver: Douglas and McIntyre, 2006).

21 The relevant texts include Edward Said, *Orientalism* (New York: Vintage, 1978); and David Cannandine, *Ornamentalism: How the British Saw Their Empire* (London: Allen Lane, 2001).

22 Andrew Gruft, *Substance over Spectacle: Contemporary Canadian Architecture* (Vancouver: Arsenal Pulp, 2005).

23 Marshall McLuhan, "Inside the Five Sense Sensorium," *Canadian Architect* 6, 6 (June 1961): 49-54.

24 This disjunction is examined on several occasions by Martin Heidegger, including in *Identity and Difference*, trans. J. Stambaugh (New York: Harper and Row, 1969); *Existence and Being*, trans. W. Brock (South Bend, IL: Gateway, 1975); and *Of Time and Being*, trans. J. Stambaugh (Chicago: University of Chicago Press, 2002).

25 Among a series of such publications are City of Vancouver, "The Climate-Friendly City: A Community Climate Change Action Plan for the City of Vancouver" (2004); and Greater Vancouver Regional District, "Sustainable Region Initiative" (2002).

26 For Kafka, see Stanley Corngold, ed. and trans., *Kafka's Selected Stories: New Translations, Backgrounds and Contexts* (New York: Norton, 2007); and for Locke, who developed his concept of the individual citizen in *Two Treatises of Government* (1689), see Maurice Cranston, *Locke on Politics, Religion and Education* (New York: Collier, 1965).

PART 7
IDENTITIES OF CANADIAN ARCHITECTURE

This final part returns to the literary and Aboriginal origins that opened this volume. The first chapter picks up on the relative lack of either internationally celebrated Canadian architects or a strong Canadian presence in the pantheon of architecture (or indeed, of architectural historiography). Although Frank Gehry, recipient of the Pritzker Prize and possessed of a global reputation, was born in Canada, his career and fame are associated with the United States. The naturalized Canadian architect Carlos Ott, who won the international competition for the Bastille Opera House at Paris in 1983 (opened 1989) is one in a series of Canadian designers with major overseas commissions. Another exception is Arthur Erickson, who was awarded the Gold Medals of the Royal Institute of British Architecture and of the American Institute of Architects. Besides distinguished architectural commissions or projects across several continents, he was tasked with giving architectural visage to Canadian national purpose overseas. The foundation and form of his repute are surveyed perceptively in "Canada's Greatest Architect" by Nicholas Olsberg, a former director of the highly influential Canadian Centre for Architecture, established by the internationally renowned champion of architectural culture Phyllis Lambert. Olsberg commands an array of literary and critical lenses to propose the creative capacities that have merited Erickson's accolade. Similarly, retaining investigative potency is the discourse of identity, one sharing origins with that of nation but also modification through fuller recognition of the determining forces of power, money, and ideology upon all forms of cultural performance and social process. Hence the value of Michael McMordie's bold treatment of the question of Canadian architectural identity in this volume's revisiting of the nation-building work of architecture. In "A Question of Identity," he nicely weighs the resilient aspects of architectural contribution against the impact of new orders of economy and allegiance consequent upon globalization. One site for observation is Calgary. The latest oil boom (and tar sands controversy) has transformed the city's national geographical and actual politico-economic place, with correspondingly radical changes in its social culture and built environment. The Calgary archi-scape presents a much more generic character than the innovatory lamination of traditional current methods by Aboriginal communities. In "Memory, the Architecture of First Nations, and the Problem with History," Daniel Millette mobilizes theories of history and memory to concretize the legacy of Aboriginal architectural activity across the lands now forming the national geography. His argument for an inserting of traditional into supposedly empirical historical knowledge affords means to acknowledge the sophistication of Aboriginal architectural patrimony. His choice of the ancient and the modern longhouses erected by the Tsawwassen nation, south of Vancouver, recalls the monumental scale and complex social function of ritual by Aboriginal builder-architects. Not only does Millette retrieve the indigenous tradition in Canada and complete the geo-temporal travel of the chapters in this volume, but he also, quite properly, returns to the larger issues of nation and architecture that frame the anthology.

15

"Canada's Greatest Architect"

NICHOLAS OLSBERG

> Surely the language of Churchill and Shakespeare and Milton, ignited with a careful mix of reason and passion, could win him a mere immigration visa.
>
> So he had written a paean to Canada, its awe-inspiring geography, its people, its place in the world, and the munificence of Canada's multicultural policy, a policy that in the beauty of its wisdom did not demand the jettisoning of the old before letting them share in the new. He had written that much had been made about the American dream and its melting pot, which, in his opinion, was ... a crude image ... No, the mosaic vision of the Canadian dream was far superior – a mosaic demanded imagination and patience and artistry, an aesthetic.
>
> – Rohinton Mistry, *Family Matters*

Certain ancient or peculiar cultures shadow those who work from within them like great painted parasols, colouring all that is made beneath in the light we believe is cast by their national spirit or tradition. Other national umbrellas, no less odd or imperial or brutal or burdened with a weight of history, are somehow oddly neutral, colourless, or universal. This national labelling is the phenomenon that makes James Joyce, the polyglot Parisian exile, someone who will always be "Irish," whereas the nearly unilingual Marcel Proust is never especially

"French." So Luis Barragan is a "Mexican architect" and Hassan Fathy an "Egyptian." So insistent is this exoticizing that certain countries are believed to scent their artists and thinkers with an unshakeable national aroma, whereas others are said to secrete no odour at all. Pity especially the artist from Russia, whence no great wine can be drunk – whether from the vats of Tschaikovsky or Chekhov or from the bottles of Nijinsky or Melnikhov – without first savouring a purported bouquet of potent, distinctive, rough, direct, and raucous national perfume. Yet the labelling is inconsistent. We would think it utterly bizarre to cast Renzo Piano with Giuseppe Verdi and Dante Alighieri. And perceptions shift: sometimes between fields – Villa-Lobos and the Tropical Movement are ineradicably Brazilian, whereas Oscar Niemeyer, Lo Bardi, and Burle Marx are equally firmly international; sometimes by epoch – for the first half of the last century no architect was more "American" to the world than Louis Sullivan, Henry Hobson Richardson, or Frank Lloyd Wright, but for the second there were no "American" architects at all (qualify Peter Eisenman, Thom Mayne, or even Paul Rudolph and Louis Kahn in that way, and see how absurd it feels).

No country in these respects is quite like Canada, where this native odour has been scented quite pungently on about half of her exportable cultural products but only very faintly or not at all on the rest. The distinction appears to lie in degrees of solemnity and absence of glamour. The more sanctimonious, homely, humourless, or banal the product – Northrop Frye, Leonard Cohen, Anne Murray, Marshall McLuhan, Glenn Gould – the more recognizably and unavoidably "Canadian" it becomes. Wryer, more romantic, and more weary voices like those of Neil Young, Diana Krall, and Joni Mitchell somehow gain leave to be housed forever in a vaguely defined North American no-man's-land.[1] The reason Canadians enjoy this unique and radical dichotomy between being decisively from somewhere and indistinctly from nowhere is that both conditions – being Canadian or not being so – are marked by the same supposed stamp of anodyne. This readiness on the part of the rest of the world to detect the scent of vanilla in everything Canadian is tantamount to race libel, and we would readily recognize its injustice if we did not do so much to encourage it ourselves. Where else – in a world that has christened its national architectural magazines with such names as the *Record, Review, Forum, Revue Générale, Architecture Aujourd'hui, Arquitectura, Wohnhaus, Domus,* and *Casabella* – can we find anything as apologetically titled as *Canadian Architect* or its even more sheepish predecessor *Architecture in Canada?*

This may sound playful; but it points out that there is equal wrongness both in casting people into a native stereotype and in refusing to grant them a native context. Both prejudices fail to recognize that there are mutating cultural genetics in the world at large, that those mutations work upon us all, and that a peculiarly native set of circumstances and aspirations mediates those changes. Architecture, in particular, can never stand apart from this dialogue between the general and particular – first, because, although absolutely international as a discipline, it can take shape and rise from the ground as a practice only if a complicated cluster of local collaborations come into play; second, because in its expression it is a branch of rhetoric, and both the pride of nationhood and the pieties of universality feed equally and voraciously on the sustenance of the rhetorical. In light of this, it is quite right to compare, say, Frank Lloyd Wright with a poet like Wallace Stevens or a composer like Charles Ives, because the same Emersonian mutterings and the same mix of American longings and Germanic Idealism can be heard beneath the noble gestures of each.

We must also recognize the potent and highly specific native forces at play between a political economy, a group's self-consciousness, and the architecture that together they produce. Adolf Loos and Josef Hofmann, for example, were inextricably linked to a new Jewish middle class in Austria that was eager for a luxurious domestic language with no visible ties to a native princely history, while their contemporaries Stanford White and Cass Gilbert served a class of parvenu industrial magnates who wanted to authenticate an assumed authority with ornate echoes of a landed aristocracy who ruled by right. Similarly, Otto Wagner could not have reclothed Vienna in the vestments of spaciously modern metropolitan grandeur without an equally grand new imperial political agenda that wanted such a representation of itself and had the autocratic powers to will that picture into being.

The wonderfully various Arthur Erickson trained first in the visual arts and through them, and through his mentor – the ecumenical Lawren Harris – both grounded himself in an inquiry into nature and touched on the quest to grasp the ineffable. He then moved into the humanities and social sciences and from there into Oriental studies as part linguist and part political economist; served in south Asia in the military secret service, running and frustrating codes; and only from there, quite late in his twenties, proceeded to study architecture at McGill University. McGill was then at the height of a Corbusian rationalism that suffused his training and has never left his work. But Erickson was also drawn to a quite antagonistic set of aesthetic principles – based in the instinct for play and in the play of instinct – that his graphics teacher Gordon Webber had taken from László Moholy-Nagy. At the same time, he remained faithful to a Frank Lloyd Wright whose "charged spaces" had drawn him to the field and faithful to Wright's notion that the purpose of architecture lay in exploiting its power to reveal – not only natural forces and structures but also the ways we perceive and relate to them. With the two years of travel that followed McGill, some of it with Webber and Guy Desbarats (whom we will meet again) at his side, Erickson added to this open-minded panoply of ideas a set of "memories of space" – almost visceral mind pictures of the fall of the sun on a wall, or a wall on the street, or a marvel of sitting – and of the different mental and social worlds they serve and portray. Ten years later, these "memories of space" began to inform, yet never to shape, the work he made in a New World landscape for a new society.

For one with such a catholic mind, and for one who has stayed so consistently and uniquely open to architectural cultures remote from his own, it seems at first unconscionable that Erickson should be limited by the constantly repeated rubric "Canada's greatest architect." I cannot think of another nation that has been awarded one. Is Le Corbusier France's or Niemeyer Brazil's? Is Vaslav Nijinsky Russia's greatest dancer, or Diego Velazquez Spain's greatest painter? And would they not be diminished if they were so described? In a subtler sense, however, the characterization is absolutely just. Erickson, whether working at home or in China, in the United States or the Middle East, not only represents a distinctly Canadian ethic and draws on a peculiarly Canadian determination to embrace a broader world but also produces something inextricably linked to the national political conditions and aspirations of his times. Nearly all of his most important expressions – from his new universities and Expo pavilions of 1963-70, through the Bank of Canada, Museum of Anthropology, and Robson Square, and on to Roy Thomson Hall and the Canadian Chancery – have been works with a marked civic or national agenda, prompted and nurtured by government or its corporate allies and derived from commissions governed by arbitrary and wilful political acts of selection.

We misread Erickson if we forget that, seductive as his dwellings are, large public works are the heart of his oeuvre. Indeed, so eager for them has he been that he has quite innocently complained – despite the overwhelming evidence to the contrary – that he never gets any. In many ways, the much-admired houses are simply proving grounds for ideas that gather scale and presence in more probing and difficult works for the civic arena. The concrete knees of Robson Square were tested at Helmut Eppich's house in 1972-74; the steel vaulting that organizes the San Diego Convention Center of 1984 began at Hugo Eppich's house five years earlier; and his Canadian pavilion at the Tokyo fair of 1964 drew on the idea of wooden cross-beams tried early that year for Gordon Smith. Similarly, Erickson's varied approaches to terracing, sitting, and the topographies of hardscape that mark his public space all developed through experiments at the domestic scale and in private landscapes – from the Danto and Graham houses in the early 1960s to Hilborn and Bagley Wright over ten years later. Often sitting houses deep into the western terrain and working with its horizons, Erickson used the more intimate inquiries into relationships between the forest and its clearings or the prairie and its shelter to develop arguments at Simon Fraser, Lethbridge, and Red Deer. He then carried this creation of complex topographies into city works like Robson Square and the Expo pavilions. These are even more firmly fixed on the Canadian dialogue between civilization and wilderness, sheltered and open worlds, personal and communal space. They are works whose first intent is to find an aesthetic that, in his own words, "can generate the fundaments of a social culture," settle "man into his community," and bring into the terms of our time the ancient discourse between man and nature.

Indeed, taken together, the public works lay out an amazingly varied and powerful portrait of a possible "Canada." They are particularly tied to the new, culturally embracing, nature-conscious, world-aware Canadianism that emerged in the mid-1950s with resistance to the Suez Canal and the celebration of Lester Pearson's Nobel Prize and that reached its rhetorical high point during the Liberal hegemony of Pearson and Pierre Elliott Trudeau. This was an ethical perspective rather than a political agenda. It was studiedly distanced both from the conflictual, metropolitan ideologies of Europe and the United States and from the emerging statism of the non-Aligned; it was an aesthetic posture toward society rather than a social policy, and it revolved around optimism: faith in the force of nature and its vast resources to sustain us; trust in the power of technology to humanize us; and belief in the goodwill of a "community of nations" and "family of man" to protect and enrich us. Its very vagueness cried out not for words but for a felt aesthetic to express it, and this is why the concrete work of building carried this expression so effectively. In the decade from Simon Fraser (1963) to the Museum of Anthropology (1974), when he was commissioned to design everything from new universities, courthouses, and Sikh temples to the national exposition pavilions, the national bank, and the private offices of his friend the prime minister, it was the architect Arthur Erickson who laid out this national aesthetic.

The persistence of Erickson's national themes – all of which hover about the notion of reconciliation – and the radical variety of ways to capture them show most eloquently in the two great Exposition pavilions of 1967 (designed in 1965) and 1970 (designed in 1967). Canada's pavilion at Expo '67 took the

Figure 15.1 "I am a Canadian, open to the wide world." Erickson's theme pavilion for Expo '67 used the metaphor of a clearing in the forest to extend the "family of man" internationalism, the Pearsonian ideology behind the fair, into a dialogue with nature. Called "Man in His Community," a huge climbing ziggurat of wooden beams drew light down to an irregular social space, suggesting a political microclimate in which humans create a casual civil topography within a vast protective planetary pattern. | Photograph in Nicholas Olsberg and Ricardo L. Castro, *Arthur Erickson: Critical Works* (Vancouver: Douglas and McIntyre, 2006), 9.

wooden beams of the Tokyo Fair and simply laid them up like a building toy into a pyramid, or ziggurat. Set up against the light, as the photograph in Figure 15.1 shows, these man-hewed forest forms offer a glimpse of the cellular and celestial geometries of which our greater universe is made. And they cast this light to the ground like shafts to a forest clearing where figures – as in Erickson's sketch – would be both isolate in nature and congregate in community. Amid the noisy, plastic, steely circus of transport and communication technology that marked this fair, it must have brought a startling stillness that offered moments

Figure 15.2 At the Osaka Exposition of 1970, Erickson's prizewinning national pavilion was a transcendental reflection on the idea of Canada as uniquely expressive of the place of man in a wider universe. Here, he surrounded an open meeting space with reflective walls and covered it with spinning discs of captured light. The diffusion and shifting colours of these mirrored skies were meant to suggest both the vast expanse of Canada and the power of its majestic scale to refract the spectrum of flags and peoples, as they mingled within its spacious shelter, into equally vivid but less distinctive and more fluid patterns of its own. | Photograph in Nicholas Olsberg and Ricardo L. Castro, *Arthur Erickson: Critical Works* (Vancouver: Douglas and McIntyre, 2006), 135.

of repose in nature, of awareness of others, and of the possibility that space, movement, community – perhaps a nation – could mediate between the vast and the personal. At Osaka (see Figure 15.2), Erickson, taking the crowd with its jumble of colours and its cacophony for granted, laid out what is in effect simply a huge open-ended plaza whose reflections mingle with those of the sky. The symbolism of Osaka was meant quite consciously to suggest Canada's capacity to be at once vast and hospitable, a landscape large enough to welcome, observant enough to recognize difference, but, like a kaleidoscope, able to sort its many colours into the civilizing patterns of a common culture.

Even Simon Fraser University (1963-67) – although prompted by a Social Credit government – was conceived as an acropolis of learning that would extend a booming city on to a wilderness promontory. There it would shine as a lantern of civilization, gathering light in from nature to cultivate the human campus and casting that light out again, transfigured, to the unlearned or unenlightened. It is at once Canada's Brasilia – a deliberate stretching of faith in the modern out to the frontier – and an homage to the peculiarly Canadian and peculiarly innocent belief in the integrity and continuity of knowledge, nature, and imagination. This was the spirit that allowed the prairie engineer Marshall McLuhan to recognize kinships first with Thomas Nashe and the literature of the Renaissance and then with T.S. Eliot and James Joyce and, through them all, to see communications as a composite of the technical and the intuitive. In the same way, at a moment when Europe was hopelessly obsessed with the divorce of cultures – scientific from humanistic, high from low, rational from intuitive – Erickson, like McLuhan, clearly believed that there was nothing between mind and spirit that required reconciliation. Indeed, his theory of design, mingling Webber with Le Corbusier, held that rational and structural truths and cultural and social appropriateness would emerge from the playful exercise of the private imagination.

This defiance of binary European traditions, of the persistent Manichean heresy, and of the insistence on a dialectic between branches of knowledge is even more evident in Lethbridge University. This great prairie schooner is in love with the exigencies of the western winter and the subtle undulations of the plain. But it transfers to them the relaxed democratic space of the ancient Islamic university community of the desert lands and the sheltered indoor streets – the wandering sunlit stoas – of Greece. At Lethbridge, built in the near-revolutionary year 1968, Erickson followed Frye, refusing to distinguish between different faces of a great tradition and setting up space and movement that encouraged the same tolerance and compromise – a "culture of listening" – that Frye advanced and that Erickson was to present at Osaka. The Museum of Anthropology (1974-76) (Figure 15.3) carries this argument further. Marching the great totems along a geographical path from those of the gentle south to those of a fiercer north, Erickson draws a conscious parallel with High European art, equating this transit with that from Michelangelo to Hieronymus Bosch and rejecting out of hand any concept of the primitive or other. Indeed, this was a time when

Figure 15.3 Erickson's Museum of Anthropology, 1974-76, funded on Trudeau's initiative to honour the centenary of British Columbia's admission to the Confederation, looks north toward the territory of the Haida and beyond. Erickson cast the building as a portrait of the peoples, settlements, and landscapes of the Pacific Coast. The re-creation of a Native shoreline setting pays homage to the conversation between humankind, climate, and nature, which Erickson believes creates a civil society, while the totems in the great hall testify to the role art plays in forging a communal sensibility and in reconciling communities to the power of nature – detailed and distinct in the softer environment of the south, bolder and more abstract as they move north. | Photograph in Nicholas Olsberg and Ricardo L. Castro, *Arthur Erickson: Critical Works* (Vancouver: Douglas and McIntyre, 2006), 42.

Canadian intellectuals in many fields seem, like Erickson, to have awakened to the qualities of "a broad world," to have forsaken condescension, and to have anticipated the postcolonial attempt to fuse cultures and disregard the layers of ranking value that had been assigned to them. This was not an academic or philosophical position. It was as clear a statement of the values of a possible Canada as was the law that denied citizenship to anyone who accepted a European title.

Thus Erickson's rhetorical programs far transcend any sentimental Canadianness. They willfully eschew the pieties of wood and stone, post and beam, and discretion toward nature that marked the work of those gentle

Regionalists whose approach could never transcend the domestic scale. And they never adopt the rough mannerism and too obvious celebration of the rawness of nature that briefly infected new-style National Romantics, like Raymond Affleck and Desbarats. While they were celebrating the arrival of the Centennial by making the heavy cross-beamed streets of Montreal's Place Bonaventure and the whimsical naturalism that can be found in the coarse-hewn stone walls of the Dorval Hilton, Erickson was locating a national cultural centre in universality and within a great catholic tradition. This was not an advocacy of the neutral, the colourless, or the universal. On the contrary, it was grounded in a private specificity, a body of recollection that embraced a reading of Sufic, Moghul, and Japanese traditions, drew on reminiscences of Greece and Egypt, and took its earliest cues from the transcendental cosmologies of Lawren Harris. Erickson leaps forward from these widespread "memories of space" to argue first for their synchronicity and then for their pliability, the notion that archetypes and derivations are neither to be imitated nor borrowed but, by dwelling on their systemics and avoiding their stylistics, transfigured into a language that is absolutely specific to the moments and locations – the inherent and distinct culture – in which they are made to operate. We are at a juncture here somewhere between Frye's Great Code, McLuhan's complicated tracing of archetype into cliché, and the universal echoes of wonder – from the manmade resonance of the labyrinth to the singing of the spheres – that inhabit the work of a great product of Erickson's Simon Fraser, the composer R. Murray Schafer.

This readiness to express a national identity first through various or contrary universal references and then through their possible reconciliation is faithful to a long tradition of its own. Architecture has nearly always sought after a grander and nobler rhetoric by drawing on its own great and persistently circulated high traditions and by effecting their fusion. This is how the Doric moved across the Mediterranean, how the Rogerian hegemony represented itself to Sicily, why princes of Germany sent surveyors to measure Santa Maria delle Fiore, why Nicodemus Tessin the younger was sent to Paris and the Ticinesi brought to Petersburg. This is also why students the world over at the turn of the nineteenth century were at the École des Beaux-Arts and why republican America looked to republican Athens for a symbolic language in which to build its institutions. Flurries of localization – the Folk Movement in an emerging Hungary, north-European National Romanticism, the Porfirian fusion of Aztec and Andalusian sources in a newly assertive Mexico, the wood and glass moments of the Scandinavian New Humanists – span a mere hundred years. Even in that century, either they borrowed a non-native language – as the American

Arts and Crafts drew on the Japanese house and the Hungarian nationalists on vernaculars from Finland or India – or they quickly fell subservient to the inherent internationalism of the Palladian Swedish Grace or the equally Palladian English neo-Georgian.

It is impossible not to observe, among the pragmatic procedures and conditions that made Erickson's public buildings happen, processes that are also reflective of a national condition. The design process at Simon Fraser, for example, was a set of collaborative engagements in which five different teams of architects were asked to acquiesce in the strict constraints and planning system imposed by the winners of the competition, the master-planning team of Erickson-Massey. Erickson and Geoffrey Massey took for themselves the design of all the interstitial space – the essential anatomy of the campus – and specified all the elements of a design language and a vocabulary of materials and scales, which the other firms were compelled to follow, for its components. In its confidence in the power of infrastructure to govern the whole, this strategy looks almost like a satire of the civil manners and hegemonic practices of Canadian government. The mix between apparent consensus and underlying command that characterized it is an emblem of Canada's oddly courteous approach to democracy, of that passion for solid infrastructures like the railways – the "grand trunks" that are supposed to have made the country – and of the love for rigorous terms of reference that has invariably infected its governing elite and its practice of government. The potency of these forces is apparent in the speed with which the vast Simon Fraser campus was realized. A mere four years spanned the time from competition to occupancy.

It is in this spirit that Erickson's new universities, in forceful contrast to the precious cloister of Ron Thom's Massey College – which was reaching completion just as the Simon Fraser design developed – resisted any reminiscences of a national style or the scent of intimate, ancient privilege that went with it. Instead, they suggested the choreography of a mass society in which none could hide knowledge behind the shield of disciplines or dignities and where all would be accorded, through grand communicating spaces, the great privilege of civil conversation. In their noble intents and in the complex play between authority and consent that made them happen, they remind one of nothing so much as the work of the Modernists at Chandigarh or Ahmedabad. In the same way, these are structures that display the mix of cajoling, provision, and demand and the tight web between layers of government, finance, and industry that characterized Jawaharlal Nehru's patronage of architecture. And their rhetorical purpose and result seem similar: to promote both a modern look for essentially new and slightly neutral nations and a national architecture not by way of identifiable local references but through adopting as national the forward-looking universal. From the first murmurings of Centennial dreams until the representation of Canada on Pennsylvania Avenue, a period that coincided almost precisely with the dominance of Pearson and Trudeau, Erickson was to Ottawa what Le Corbusier or Louis Kahn were to New Delhi – the chosen architectural prophet of a new democracy.

Indeed, in the decade from the mid-1960s to the mid-1970s, Erickson's public projects seem blessed with good fortune, both in the speed with which they were executed and in the sometimes extravagant freedoms accorded the architect in their programming and conception, landscape, and finishing. There were good reasons for this good luck. One had been evident early in Erickson's career: in his contribution to studies for the redevelopment of Vancouver in 1958, he was able to propose converting the whole crest of the city's West End into a manmade mountain range of dwellings and services, simply because one man owned so much of it. For Canada's urban landholdings, after a century of railway takings and wilderness grants, were still on a frontier scale, and still in the cards were the sort of projects that had made the Belgravias and Cadogan Gardens of nineteenth-century London – and the Shaughnessy villages and British properties of Vancouver a little later. A more subtle reason was the extraordinary consolidation of capital. The number of significant banking and insurance companies in Canada could still be counted on the fingers of two hands, and the great mining, steel, and lumber concerns on one. Ultimately, however, it was the power of the government that had the most impact. It was at once intimate and magisterial, its purse and policy were marked by an extraordinary amount of discretion, and its ability to persuade the tight web of land and money to join it in a grand endeavour was extraordinary. It was, for example, Trudeau's personal decision to fund the Museum of Anthropology, ostensibly as Canada's monument to the centenary of British Columbia's membership in the Confederation. The collegiality – and aesthetic respect – that marked his relations with Erickson came more openly into play when their friend Guy Desbarats, now in the prime minister's service, exerted pressure on Toronto's business community to award Erickson the design of Roy Thomson Hall. And this collegiality rose to the level of scandal when Trudeau and Desbarats overrode the selection process to give Erickson the Chancery in Washington.

Other ambitious schemes depended on a local network of association. Almost immediately after the provincial election of August 1972, the socialist lawyer John Laxton, Erickson's friend and client, persuaded British Columbia's first New Democratic Party government to make a courthouse in the "three blocks" that Erickson and Massey had earlier redesigned as a massive, towering, concrete set of platforms and bridged blocks that would restructure the downtown core. This was to be the New Democrats' major gesture of reassurance to a Vancouver business community terrified of its social agenda. It was probably Erickson himself who then proposed laying on its back the great government tower of which he and Massey had first dreamed. This was embraced by government as a way of contrasting social-democratic discretion with Social Credit grandiosity. But it was astonishing that Erickson could persuade the New Democrats to let him stretch that horizontal notion into a great manmade topography of park and walkways that would extend from one shore of the peninsula to another. Only the wonderful innocence of the new government could have tolerated the amazing ambition of the project, its defiance of economic logic, its extraordinary sense of innovation, and its spiralling costs. That so much of this grand scheme to steal the centre of a city survived – to make the wandering wilderness we now see (Figure 15.4) – is a tribute to the matrix of intimacy and command that, like presidential projects for Paris, allowed for work at almost unrivalled scale, extravagance, and speed.

This was the complex of massively concentrated financial and governmental forces that had built the largest of all Mies van der Rohe's projects; that erected the tallest building in the world on the spurious grounds that Toronto's topography impeded communication signals; and that found itself by the late 1970s so overcapitalized that it could discern no profitable new ways to invest in the cityscape of Canada. These financial forces then moved their sense of scale – their Olympia and York and Cadillac-Fairview thinking – to the redevelopment of places like London's derelict docklands and to Los Angeles's forlorn downtown. Erickson moved with them. But once outside the cozy Canadian code of getting things through, stymied by the contraction of the 1980s, unfamiliar with massive compromise or massive delay, and impeded by the debates and disputes of contentious community democracies, they all ran aground. For Erickson had learned to make architecture in more imperious circumstances, where his intellectual force and dignity could carry the day. Nothing in Canada had taught him how to work through the welter of competing agencies and interests or to navigate a world of compromise and revision – as at California Plaza (1979-93). Nor, having refocused his practice on US soil, was he prepared for the competitive salesmanship of American design. Of the legion tried, few public buildings were realized. They were weakened by compromise, and the practice was broken by the strain.

But there is more to politics than the mechanisms that make projects happen. From the first murmurs of Centennial fever right through the 1980s,

Canada wanted to build itself into nationhood. The irony is that in serving Erickson so well during these years, this largely imperious governmental system, with its gentle brand of governance by apparent consensus and actual command, genuinely and quite consciously also served the most generous democratic and aesthetic ideals. These ideals Erickson advanced by consistently cladding them in a complex symbolic language and a sternly lyrical aesthetic costume.

His national pavilion for Expo '67, carefully called "Man in His Community," bathed a common space with dappled light in a way that suggested humankind drawn into conversation on the middle ground a civil mind could carve between the ineffable above and the tangible below. At Osaka '70, he showed the world a Canada that was not a determinate but a reflective presence, a place where the miracles of exchange that make a civil life draw strength not from dominant structures but from the space between them. In his first scheme for the Bank of Canada (1969), he opened for the passerby narrow peepholes into the most impenetrable arm of government. Even the final version hosts a glorious glass atrium for all to use. At Robson Square, for which design began in 1973, the three great civilizing forces are put in their rightful place – a justice that can be seen to be done, a government that sits quietly beneath its people, and a house of culture anchored in memory and fixed to the street – all set within an interlocking spine of gardens among which to gather and wander. The Museum of Anthropology (1974-76) takes Native arts and graces them with the same respect for sequence we afford to European traditions while simultaneously reinvesting them with the remote and godlike presence they were made to serve. Roy Thomson Hall, begun in 1976, had – until the disastrous recent decision to give it "warmth" – surrendered all ceremony, decoration, and colour to focus on a single monochrome shell in which the purpose of the hall – its music – would be relied upon to bring a palette into play. A more explicit iconology informs the Canadian Embassy of 1983-89. Here, one moves through the hollow,

Figure 15.4 *(opposite page)* Vancouver's Robson Square, 1973-78, was the first major initiative of British Columbia's first New Democratic government. Erickson inverted the logic of an existing monumental high-rise civic-centre scheme in which only the lobby would have offered public space, laying it on its back, so that a skyscraper becomes a walkable, penetrable topography. The massing and circulation plan again present Erickson's symbolic philosophy of civilization. The glazed great hall and hanging gardens of the law courts display the administration of justice to a passerby. From this mountain of the law, supported by the nearly invisible offices of civil administration, flows the regulated landscape of a peaceable society – something that only the conspicuous rule of law and unintrusive government can guarantee. Pathways wander at leisure through a garden city that encourages both solitude and congregation, privacy and celebration, toward a gallery of the arts that only such a social geography – and one congruent with the natural environment – can produce. | Photograph in Nicholas Olsberg and Ricardo L. Castro, *Arthur Erickson: Critical Works* (Vancouver: Douglas and McIntyre, 2006), 159.

Figure 15.5 In his two universities – Simon Fraser (1963), shown above, and Lethbridge (1968) – Erickson set out to assert the idea that knowledge was the foundation of a decent civil order, making both campuses read like beacons for the cities they served and organizing progress through them as a movement toward light, or enlightenment. At the same time, he tried to undermine both academic hierarchies and disciplinary segregation through permeability and dispersal, forcing movement and interaction by scattering offices among classrooms in one scheme and doing without dividing walls almost entirely in the other. This reflected his belief in a nation forged by creative mixing in which individuals were respected but not the conventional boundaries between them. | Photograph in Nicholas Olsberg and Ricardo L. Castro, *Arthur Erickson: Critical Works* (Vancouver: Douglas and McIntyre, 2006), 88.

uncapped columns that point out the fragile, imperial ambitions of its host to the integrity of the Native peoples and resources (i.e., water, minerals, vegetation, and human dispute) that generate its prosperity. But its real Canadianness lies in its less ironic gestures – the embassy eschews a ceremonial entrance, it has a vast public plaza, and it closes itself off from the grand parade of Pennsylvania Avenue, preferring, instead, to open out onto the skateboarders in the quite unceremonial park across the street. What matters most about Erickson's work surely resides in such projects, all of them grand symbolic prompts toward the ideas that might make a liberal national civilization.

All of the public work is marked by an absolute defiance of the anxiety of influence – an anxiety that is so common among small nations with international aspirations, where everyone is afraid of being seen as a practitioner of other people's ideas. Erickson's central theoretical position is that the architect should neither copy nor stand apart from other cultures but should, instead, draw them inside his own imagination to help find a path expressing a culture, time, and circumstance of his own. This is an extraordinarily inclusive and antichauvinistic model for how to build for a national community of peoples. It is a complex and essentially political idea closely related to Charles Taylor's models for a workable national culture. It is quite firmly in line with what Canadians since Pearson have generally thought their country might become. And it recasts the idea of Canada as an indefinite or generic culture in the quite new and noble light of a place enlightened by the variety of what lies beyond it and by an openness – symbolized in the open spaces of Simon Fraser (Figure 15.5) – to drawing that variousness in.

There is in this quality a sort of productive neutrality that becomes for Erickson not a negative or a colourless force but the spur toward a quite distinctive lyric language. As he negotiates the boundaries of neutral ground – the decisive lines between humans and nature, the universal and the specific, the public and the intimate, the reasoned and the instinctive, remote cultures and near ones, past examples and present needs – he draws out the richness of tension and the eloquence of equilibrium that lie between them all. In this discovery that a certain poetry can be wrought from the uncertain balance required by an instinct for tolerance and breadth, that the apparently vanilla platitudes of decency and civility can generate the force of art, Erickson becomes not just a "great Canadian architect" but a great Canadian.

NOTES

For a fuller discussion of Erickson's career, reference to critical writings on his work, and a comprehensive bibliography, see Nicholas Olsberg and Ricardo L. Castro, *Arthur Erickson: Critical Works* (Vancouver: Douglas and McIntyre, 2006). This chapter has a different purpose but draws from the same sources.

1 Mr. Young's recent descent into pious platitudes will undoubtedly result in a swift repatriation.

16

A Question of Identity

MICHAEL McMORDIE

The quest for a Canadian architecture that somehow embodies a Canadian identity seems misguided. National architectures are no longer relevant or even possible; their very conception was made obsolete by modern building technologies and global communications, as well as by the increasingly problematic role of nation-states in the international order. Calgary, where this is written, seems to exemplify this state of affairs more clearly than older cities with built traditions that reach back to Confederation and before.

Despite a few survivals from the late nineteenth century, including the grid plan of the central city, Calgary is clearly a product of the post–Second World War period. Its buildings, from downtown offices to suburban houses and shopping malls, embody the anonymous modernity that made it the ideal urban setting for the Superman films: a generic, North American, twentieth-century city.[1] Current economic success underscores and exacerbates this characterless anonymity: unlike earlier cities, Calgary has no visible symbols of local resources and production, foundries and factories, wharves and canneries. Instead it houses the geologists and engineers, accountants and lawyers who manage the exploitation of resources from the North Sea to the Sudan, East Asia to Oklahoma. The speculative office tower with repetitive floor-plates and uniform cladding designed to facilitate the leasing of generic office space gives appropriate expression to their activities, interchangeable, placeless, and lacking any distinctive physical identity.

City planners and urban designers now struggle to find something local and specific to uncover or create in this urban matrix. The diverse population from many distinctive cultures supports a remarkable range of restaurants and shops, but only a few surviving older buildings and Chinatown, with its roots in the railway construction of the late nineteenth century, offer a contrast to bland uniformity. The "creative city" movement has a toehold, and the city has formulated a cultural policy, but this also seems generic. It expresses a discontent widely shared with other similar cities across the continent. However welcome the urban amenities that may follow from implementation, especially more support for the arts and better public places to walk, visit, meet, and talk, the question of identity remains, as it does for architects and planners across the country.

However dated it may seem, this issue of identity refuses to disappear. Reviewing a 1998 exhibition in London of the work of sixteen Canadian architects, Jeremy Melvin raised questions central to this discussion. He wrote of some of the work that it did little "to advance the notion of a Canadian architecture." About some of the other work, he asked "what price national identity?" "It would be unfair," he concluded, "to infer that young Canadian architects have little more to offer than clichés and anomalies in addressing their vast country and its identity. At least, I hope so."[2] It's not as obvious as it might seem what Melvin expected when he asked for work "to advance the notion of Canadian architecture" and looked for, but did not find, some sort of "national identity." Nonetheless, questions like this continue to surface.[3] They deserve serious examination.

A number of related issues need to be considered. These, as the review makes clear, include, first, the place: Canada, its vast geography and its history. Then there is the nation, considered culturally and politically. Different cultural groups, notably but not only the French, British, and Aboriginal peoples, continue to grapple with differences and the need for accommodation and reconciliation through the political process. Identity, close to the centre of all this, requires analysis (or, rather, the diverse identities in play, not just national but also personal, ethnic, and professional). Finally, there is architecture: Melvin doesn't use the word "style," but it seems that he is looking for a consistent and identifiable set of common characteristics in the buildings he examines that might be called a national architectural style. Is this a reasonable expectation?

These issues of place, nation, identity, and architecture are far from uniquely Canadian. The anxiety about their conjunction may be. The peculiarly Canadian flavour of this anxiety follows from our unique geography and our special history. This is a northern country, bilingual and multicultural, with its population concentrated close to the southern border with its much more powerful and assertive neighbour. It depends economically on international trade, especially in its natural resources and predominantly with the United States. Here, some familiar but important features of this Canadian experience are reviewed and Melvin's questions addressed.

PLACE

"The vastness of nature and the puniness of man" are seen as distinctive qualities of Canadian experience. Brian Carter and Annette Lecuyer, writing more recently in the *Architectural Review,* make the point that "Canada has become increasingly urban, with 78 percent of its population now living in cities,"[4] despite the popular image of a country of individuals confronting the wilderness. There remains the deeply ingrained sense of an existential predicament – discussed, for instance, in Margaret Atwood's *Survival.*[5]

These qualities of the place have played a significant role in many of the arts. Atwood reviews their place in Canadian literature, and they have been important for much painting, from the Group of Seven to Emily Carr to Toni Onley. In music, R. Murray Schafer pursued wilderness as a theme and setting most imaginatively, and Alan Bell has also found themes in particular experiences of place. Glen Gould's "The Idea of North" is another striking example.[6] In building, utilitarian structures and construction have most clearly captured some of these qualities, from the most rudimentary log buildings to country grain elevators to engineering structures like hydroelectric power dams (the building to which Melvin refers as addressing the issue of vastness and puniness is LeMoyne Lapointe Magne's observation structure overlooking the La Forge dam, part of Hydro-Québec's La Grande complex near James Bay). Most of these don't usually count as architecture, although architects have used, for instance, the grain elevator form for such diverse projects as exhibition structures and light-rail transit stations. In any case, they appear to be important images in most Canadians' mental landscapes.

As these examples suggest, diversity is as characteristic of Canadian places and their expression as it is of its peoples. For this reason, regional approaches are rather easier to identify than is a national architectural style. Percy Nobbs and his McGill University associates early in the twentieth century produced designs based on the seventeenth- and eighteenth-century buildings of New France, and even the cylindrical stone structure at the garden of Ernest Cormier's Montreal house reflects this sense of a regional tradition.[7] Perhaps the most persuasive movement with clearly regional characteristics through this period was the largely residential (mostly single-family) buildings associated with the Pacific Northwest, spanning the US-Canadian border from the states of Washington and Oregon to south-western British Columbia. Although clearly not uniquely Canadian, it did produce a good deal of high-quality work by such architects as Arthur Erickson, Ron Thom, and others. These were sensitive, thoughtful, and creative responses to the characteristics of the region: a generally benign but rainy climate, a variety of difficult but beautiful building sites, and the availability of excellent building timber.

Similarly, Brian MacKay-Lyons has championed an East Coast regionalism, responsive to the climate and the sites inspired by the characteristic buildings of the Atlantic Coast, from houses to fishing sheds.[8] Other examples can be found from across the country of architects looking to local and regional forms and traditions for appropriate design. Such regional design is important and true to significant strands of the modern project, if quite at odds with others. National themes are quite another matter.

NATIONS AND IDENTITY

Canadian independence was marked and symbolized by the patriation of the Constitution under Pierre Elliott Trudeau in 1982. The country had already gained international recognition for its efforts through the United Nations to establish a more secure international order. Also under Trudeau, the complexity of Canadian society was recognized by an explicit commitment to multicultural policies. In effect, a redefinition of nation was under way. Canada was internationalist in outlook and, unlike the United States, ready to accept the superior jurisdiction of international institutions like the World Criminal Court, whose founding it promoted. Further, it was not dominated by one ethnic group and one language and set of traditions but explicitly and deliberately recognized and celebrated the diversity of the cultural groups composing it. Although from many points of view this all seemed admirable, it greatly complicated any attempt to assert a clear national identity.

In recent years, national identity has become the subject of heated debate. In the United Kingdom the devolution of limited powers to Scotland and

Figure 16.1 Library of Parliament, Ottawa, architects Thomas Fuller and Chilion Jones, 1859-76. | McMordie Collection, Canadian Architectural Archives, University of Calgary.

Ireland has provoked debate about "English" identity and the proper use of "British" rather than "English" (still often taken to be synonymous). The idea of an explicitly multicultural nation continues to be a problem for such countries: the myth of a unitary national identity still prevails despite a multi-ethnic population. As with costume, buildings often identify religious or ethnic communities and when distinctive in form or style can be the target of destructive opposition. The turmoil continues despite the actual complexity and variability of the idea of identity.

We use "identity" to refer, variously, to personal identity,[9] the identity of a community or group within a nation, and "national identity." None of these is simple or unchanging, despite the apparent stability of the word and idea. Amartya Sen, for instance, makes clear the multiple identities he can properly claim.[10] Further, some of these component identities may change through time. One becomes a spouse, a parent, a lawyer, and so on, joining or leaving significant categories or groups as one does, entering in on new experiences that bear directly on the understanding and representation of oneself: one's identity.

Among other groups asserting distinct identities are ethnic communities, with practices and traditions they wish to maintain and enjoy. The values attached to recognizing and respecting these have led to a national policy. Although much debated, and dissented from by some, multiculturalism has also been advanced as a distinctive feature of the Canadian polity, to be contrasted with the US "melting pot."

Both individual identities and those of many groups and, especially, ethnic communities find architectural expression. Private dwellings may be significant examples, with as much variety as there are owners who wish to express themselves in this way. Ethnic examples include such distinguished works as Ray Moriyama's 1963 Japanese Canadian Cultural Centre (now renovated by Moriyama for the Noor Cultural Centre) and Bruno Freschi's 1985 Ismaili Jamatkhana and Centre in Burnaby. Both are thoroughly modern in conception and execution yet express evolving ethnic traditions.

National identity similarly can have no unchanging essence but must evolve. As Stanley Stein and I have argued elsewhere,[11] Canadian identity is like a yarn spun from many different individual fibres, none of which continues through its whole length but all of which contribute to its substance, strength, and colour. It is dialogic, negotiated, and dynamic.[12] Whereas in the case of ethnic or religious traditions architecture can carry forward essential elements of the tradition – forms and symbols or functional arrangements needed to serve rituals and other distinctive activities – no equivalent national requirements exist. What is there in the national identity for architecture to express?

Figure 16.2 West block, Parliament Buildings, Ottawa, architects Stent and Laver, 1859-75, addition by Thomas Scott and the Department of Public Works, 1875-78. | McMordie Collection, Canadian Architectural Archives, University of Calgary.

ARCHITECTURE: STYLE

Architectural expression and style are inseparable. Style is the characteristic way of executing a work of art that distinguishes it from otherwise similar work with respect to its creator, its period, or its place of origin. Because of the long dominance of historical reference over architectural design, at least from the Renaissance to the early twentieth century, and the attempt to break free from this, style for Modernists became identified with the historic styles and thus an anathema. Architecture in Canada has followed this progression, from Victorian and Edwardian preoccupation with design in a variety of historic modes to the rise in the late 1930s of Modernist, "styleless," or perhaps International Style design. As the latter suggests, none of this was in fact without "style," but by the 1950s explicit reference to the forms and decoration of earlier periods had been abandoned.[13]

Between confederation and the Second World War, there had been various stylistic experiments. The federal government had used versions of Second Empire as a kind of national style for a number of buildings in Ottawa. Even earlier, Victorian Gothic had been chosen for the Parliament Buildings in Ottawa because that seemed to make an appropriate link with the Westminster Parliament and the British origins of parliamentary democracy (Figures 16.1 and 16.2). For the Château Frontenac, Bruce Price found inspiration in the French Loire Châteaux. Together with Second Empire, and a dash of the Scottish Baronial, variants on these themes appeared in hotels across the country (Figure 16.3).[14] After the First World War, the impact of European thinking and the work of US pioneers like Frank Lloyd Wright made various approaches to Modernism more and more influential. Important transitional work was carried out by Canadian architects like Ernest Cormier and John Lyle. John Lyle's 1929 Bank of Nova Scotia in Calgary adopts motifs from agriculture, ranching, and the oil industry, all as a way of connecting this building to the surrounding region. These details were set within a *Moderne* classical facade. As Modernism advanced, its rejection of all referential detail made Lyle's solution no longer acceptable.

The post–Second World War triumph of Modernism in Canada made this the prevailing approach. It was ostensibly based on a rational and universal approach to design. The possibility of national identifiers disappeared completely from Canadian architecture, and regional references were to be limited to appropriately functional responses to local climates and other geographical factors (such as the availability of exceptional building timber in British Columbia).

Figure 16.3 Banff Springs Hotel, Banff, architects W.S. Painter and J.W. Orrock, 1911-14, 1925-28. | McMordie Collection, Canadian Architectural Archives, University of Calgary.

Figure 16.4 Pratt House, West Vancouver, architect C.E. Pratt, c. 1946. | McMordie Collection, Canadian Architectural Archives, University of Calgary.

These references did result for the US Northwest and for southwest British Columbia in something like a regional style of open-plan, usually one-storey, often post-and-beam houses with plentiful glass and luxuriant planting (Figures 16.4 and 16.5).[15]

There was a brief phase in the 1960s when some of the first atrium-centred commercial buildings, Royal Bank Plaza and the Eaton Centre in Toronto, for instance, received international attention. A large, multistorey interior space around which the rest of the building could be organized was briefly seen as a uniquely appropriate response to the northern climate (Figures 16.6 and 16.7).[16] Canadians could not claim priority in the development of these buildings. Some of the grandest were built elsewhere – for instance, John Portman's hotels in the United States.

Among the best, certainly the most prominent, buildings of this period were works by non-Canadians: I.M. Pei, Mies van der Rohe, Viljo Revell, as well as the multinational but US-based Moshe Safdie. These were widely reviewed in the international press as significant additions to Canadian architecture. The

Figure 16.5 Woodward/Trier-Pevecz House, North Vancouver, architect R.J. Thom, late 1950s. | McMordie Collection, Canadian Architectural Archives, University of Calgary.

Figure 16.6 Eaton Centre, Toronto, architects Zeidler Partnership with Bregmann and Hamann, 1973-81. | McMordie Collection, Canadian Architectural Archives, University of Calgary.

Figure 16.7 Atria North, North York, architects Thom Partnership, 1978. | McMordie Collection, Canadian Architectural Archives, University of Calgary.

Figure 16.8 Mississauga City Hall, Mississauga, architects Jones and Kirkland, 1982-86. | Image courtesy of the City of Mississauga.

dual openness of Canadian Modernism seems evident: it was open to diverse international sources for design and designers, and the absence of cultural identifiers from Modern design made it seem more accommodating to Canada's complex social fabric.[17]

Some ventures were more closely identified with architectural style. The work of Percy Nobbs and others has already been mentioned. After the Second World War, this interest in something like a regional style appears with Peter Rose's Quebec houses and even more explicitly in George Baird's instructions as professional advisor for the Mississauga City Hall competition, which set out regional character as a desirable goal. The winning submission by the firm Jones and Kirkland fulfilled these with a variety of references in the building form and siting to the architecture of the surrounding region, both older and contemporary (for instance, suburban tract houses) (Figure 16.8). All of these were regionalist. More recently still, Fred Valentine of the firm Culham Pedersen Valentine in Calgary has pursued regional forms and other regional references

Figure 16.9 Administration Building, Lester B. Pearson International Airport, Toronto, architects John B. Parkin Associates, 1958-64, demolished 1997. | Panda Architectural Photography Collection, Canadian Architectural Archives, University of Calgary.

in the buildings at Canada Olympic Park and the Rozsa Centre at the University of Calgary.[18] Similarly, the firm Saucier and Perrotte has been identified by George Admczyk as having "carved out a uniquely creative path in the cultural world of Canadian architecture ... nourished by the simple beauty of Canada's landscapes ... inspired by towns and villages, human signs, occupied dwellings and incandescent landscapes," and "their works are shaped by an embraced modernism."[19]

Valentine's work from the beginning of his career with John B. Parkin in Toronto in the 1960s has also been clearly Modern in intent and execution. There has also been the resurgent Modernism of a younger generation of architects, which, combined with the more general concern for environmental issues and "green" building, has produced many more buildings functionally responsive to local geography. There is not yet in any of this recent work any appearance of an identifiable and consistent style, nor is this surprising. In keeping with Modernist rationalism, the buildings present technical solutions to technical problems; their expressive language is international (Figure 16.9). There is in none of this any discernible move toward the expression of Canadian identity, no hint of a national style.

A COMPARISON

A not very close, but still instructive, parallel can be drawn between Canada after 2000 and Britain after 1800.[20] Britain as it emerged from the Napoleonic Wars experienced rapid economic and social development and the vast extension of its international influence and power. As well, it was a period of extreme social and economic dislocation and stress. It was soon to enter the Victorian period, when creativity in architecture, advances in technology, and economic success all combined to produce a series of remarkable works.

Throughout most of this period, national identity was taken for granted. Identification with the global empire subsumed the wide variety of local and historic divisions even within Great Britain. More recently, the question of national identity has stimulated lively debate.[21] Decline in international standing and the devolution of powers to Scotland and Wales in different degrees has been one stimulus; this has raised issues of national identity for the residual, although largest and dominant, English segment of the United Kingdom. Even more unsettling have been the problems associated with the assimilation of the various ethnic and religious groups: Jamaicans, Pakistanis, those with African roots, and many others. Together, these make modern Britain and particularly England very much a multicultural society, putting "English" identity in question.

Canada in the twenty-first century also has a reduced international presence. This has diminished from a peak in the 1960s, when our contribution to the Allied war effort in the Second World War and our leading presence in postwar international bodies like the United Nations gave the country a significant (but perhaps illusory) international importance. Since then, internal issues and economic buffeting have reduced the Canadian role. It has also been diluted by an increase in the number of middle-size players internationally, with the end of the Soviet Union and the emergence of a number of European countries as international actors both through and along with the European Community. A combination of internal and external factors have been contributors, including reduced leadership from the federal government in the face of provincial demands for exclusive jurisdiction and, in recent years, a lack of interest from any level of government or any powerful sector of society in cultural issues. Instead, security, the military, and related matters like intelligence, immigration, and border control, along with the need to grapple with a variety of crises, from

SARS to BSE to softwood lumber, have dominated public discourse and political attention. Diversion of public attention from creative cultural action by public bodies has left national cultural institutions like the Canadian Broadcasting Corporation compromised and marginal. With respect to problematic national identities and their expression, Canada and Britain now have a good deal in common.

THE NATIONAL IDENTITY: CANADIAN CITIES

National identity on the Canadian model does not lend itself to simple representation or to clear and iconic expression.[22] This model, as mentioned, is "dialogic, negotiated, and dynamic." Such qualities apply less easily to individual buildings than to cities. It may be that the expression of national identity in built form can now best be pursued in the design, planning, development, and governance of Canadian cities. The result would not be iconic forms as much as harmonious political and social entities that offered the best possible opportunities for richly satisfying lives in environmentally responsive settings.[23] The best Canadian precedents suggest that a federal role would be important to provide leadership, conduct research, negotiate standards, and support demonstration projects, as it has in the past. One example of such a project was Vancouver's Granville Island.

Perhaps the proposed move of the National Portrait Gallery away from Ottawa could be a similar venture. At one point it seemed destined for Calgary, to be incorporated into the downtown EnCana development (designed by Foster and Partners of London, associated with the Zeidler Partnership). Proposals have now been invited from a number of centres, Calgary included.

For Calgary, the presence of such a national institution would help it to move beyond its old "Stampede City" identity. Any attempt to abandon the distinctive but limited cattle-and-ranching image (celebrated each July during the Stampede with hay bales strewn about the downtown, banks and offices festooned with rough-cut timber siding lashed over doors and counters) underscores the architectural problem. No longer is there a local, autochthonous source (Figure 16.10). Architectural style is international; architectural prestige comes from designs by Norman Foster, Frank Gehry, Zaha Hadid, and others who work globally, wherever their home base. They may, or may not, endeavour to respect any local tradition they can identify, but their work is valued as evidence of the global reach and importance of the community, not its local roots and distinctive history. The work of such celebrity designers may carry us past the anonymity of the post–Second World War "modern" city. It fails to support

Figure 16.10 Downtown Calgary and the Bow River from the west, January 2008. | Photograph by author.

a distinctive local and regional identity. Is this the new model for architecture and nations in the twenty-first century?

CONCLUSION

National identity itself has become a complex and difficult issue for advanced multicultural societies, which is to say for most of the greater part of the Western world. Potential sources of architectural form and expression have ramified, become diverse and confusing. The Enlightenment roots from which Modernism drew inspiration have suffered from post-Modernist dismissal. A romantic attachment to place has lost conviction, as places seem more and more globally homogenized, their distinctive characteristics obscured by the forms and fashions of the international cultural economy.

And yet ... Canada is a distinct and distinguished nation by reason of geography, history, governance, policies, culture, and presence in the world. Moreover, these contexts come together to create a strong, if complex, national identity. Its expression in architecture – the art most closely and intimately concerned with the expression of ways of life – seems a worthwhile challenge.

NOTES

1 Wikipedia, "Superman (film)," http://en.wikipedia.org/wiki/Superman_(1978_film).

2 Jeremy Melvin, "Canadian clichés and anomalies," *Architects' Journal*, 11 June 1998, 65.

3 Introducing the presentation of a number of recent Canadian projects in the October 2004 issue of the *Architectural Review*, Brian Carter and Annette Lecuyer refer to "Canadian identities" in a subheading, but the only specific identity mentioned is "the distinctive identity of Quebec." This seems not to be expressed in the architecture but rather in the buildings' context, associations, or contents. See Brian Carter and Annette Lecuyer, "Comment: Unfurling the Outskirts," *Architectural Review* 216, 1292 (October 2004): 48.

4 Ibid., 46

5 Margaret Atwood, *Survival* (Toronto: House of Anansi, 1972).

6 Glen Gould, "The Idea of North" (excerpt), http://archives.cbc.ca/arts_entertainment/music/clips/1709.

7 The conically roofed stone cylinder stands in stark and effective contrast to the uncompromisingly Modern north face of the house itself.

8 See Brian MacKay-Lyons, *MacKay-Lyons: Selected Projects 1986-1997*, ed. Brian Carter (Halifax: Tuns, 1998).

9 Our identity, our authentic identity, arises essentially out of a relational process. We do not create ourselves out of nothing. In the end, the person we become presupposes a social framework, a culture, and a world. Donald Davidson calls the process "triangulation," which refers to the conditions necessary for understanding ourselves, our peers, and the world we live in. Triangulation has a logical as well as normative aspect. Logically, as Davidson points out, "the ultimate source of both objectivity and communication is the triangle that, by relating the speaker, the interpreter and the world, determines the contents of thought and speech." This is a dialogical process: "our selves are dialogical all the way down ... there is no private core on which to build." This relational process is not a passive one. See Richard Rorty, "Universality and Truth," in *Rorty and his Critics*, ed. R.B. Brandom (Oxford: Blackwell 2000), 15 (for the Davidson quotation), 16.

On issues of multiculturalism and identity in Canada, see Michael McMordie, Thomas Harper, and Stanley M. Stein, "Telling Stories," unpublished conference paper, Association of European Schools of Planning (AESOP), Vienna, July 2005; Amy Gutmann, ed., *Multiculturalism: Examining the Politics of Recognition* (Princeton, NJ: Princeton University Press, 1994); Rhoda Howard-Hassmann, "Canadian as an Ethnic Category: Implications for Multiculturalism and National Unity," *Canadian Public Policy* 25, 4 (1999): 523-37; Will Kymlicka, *Finding Our Way: Rethinking Ethnocultural Relations in Canada* (Don Mills, ON: Oxford University Press, 1994); Will Kymlicka, *Multicultural Citizenship* (New York: Oxford University Press, 1995); Will Kymlicka, ed., *The Rights of Minority Cultures* (New York: Oxford University Press, 1995); Charles Taylor, *The Sources of Self: The Making of the Modern Identity* (Cambridge, UK: Cambridge University Press, 1989); Charles Taylor, *The Malaise of Modernity* (Toronto: House of Anansi, 1991), also published as *The Ethics of Authenticity* (Cambridge, MA: Harvard University Press, 1991); Charles Taylor, "The Politics of Recognition," in *Multiculturalism*, ed. Gutmann, 25-73; and James Tully, *Strange Multiplicities: Constitutionalism in an Age of Diversity* (Cambridge, UK: Cambridge University Press, 1995).

10 "I can be, at the same time, an Asian, an Indian citizen, a Bengali with Bangladeshi ancestry, an American or British resident, a man, a feminist, a heterosexual, an economist, a dabbler in philosophy, an author, a Sanskritist, a strong believer in secularism and democracy, a defender of gay and lesbian rights, with a nonreligious lifestyle, from a Hindu background, a non-Brahmin, and a non-believer in an afterlife (and also, in case the question is asked, a non-believer in a 'before-life' as well." See Amartya Sen, *Identity and Violence* (New York: Norton, 2006), 19. Kwame Anthony Appiah discusses the formation of identity in *The Ethics of Identity* (Princeton, NJ: Princeton University Press, 2005), 20, passim. See also Bernard Williams, "Identity and Identities," in *Philosophy as a Humanistic Discipline*, 57-64 (Princeton, NJ: Princeton University Press, 2006).

11 Thus there can be no essence to national identity since an essentialist conception of identity presupposes universal conceptions of such identity. The contrary view can be represented in the metaphor elaborated below, in which identity is viewed as a collection of fibres spun together into a substantial and continuing entity: a thread or perhaps a cord of yarn passing through and connecting particular contexts. As Stanley Stein and I have noted, "just as individual autonomy and culture are not at odds, multicultural and national identity are not at odds in a pluralistic liberal society ... Contrary to the search for an essential Canadian identity, a national identity can naturally arise through an analogous dialogical relationship that is found in the formation of individual identity. It is an open dialogue between the various cultures in Canada, including the dominant culture, which can generate and is generating a conception of national identity." See Stanley M. Stein and Michael McMordie, "A Thread of Many Fibres," unpublished conference paper, Russian Association for Canadian Studies: Sixth International Canadian Studies Conference, Saint Petersburg, June 2001.

12 A highly relevant discussion of basic issues can be found in Bernard Williams, "Pluralism, Community and Left Wittgensteinianism," in *In the Beginning Was the Deed: Realism and Moralism in Political Argument*, 29-39 (Princeton, NJ: Princeton University Press, 2005). "What is at issue at the present time is precisely the integrity of states, and questions of what kind of state can reasonably claim a political identity" (38).

13 For one example of this architectural trajectory, see Michael McMordie, "From Somewhere to Everywhere to Nowhere: The Bank of Montreal as a Case of Vanishing Identity," in *Challenging Frontiers*, ed. Lorry Felske and Beverly Rasporich, 231-48 (Calgary: University of Calgary Press, 2004).

14 See Harold Kalman, *The Railway Hotels and the Development of the Château Style in Canada*, Maltwood Museum Studies in Canadian Architectural History, No. 1 (Victoria: University of Victoria, 1968); and the further discussion in Harold Kalman, *A Concise History of Canadian Architecture* (Toronto: Oxford University Press, 2000), esp. 370-77. A highly pertinent discussion can be found in Rhodri Windsor Liscombe, "Nationalism or Cultural Imperialism? The Château Style in Canada," *Architectural History* 36 (1993): 127-44.

15 See the discussion in Douglas Shadbolt, *Ron Thom* (Vancouver and Toronto: Douglas and McIntyre, 1995), 20-22.

16 "Canada's adaptation of the idea of the atrium to virtually all building types"; see "Next Month the *Architectural Review* Looks at Canada," *Architectural Review* 147, 998 (April 1980): 261. See also Peter Collymore, "New Atria of Canada," *Architectural Review*, special issue on Canada, 167, 999 (May 1980): 273.

17 I'm grateful to Rhodri Windsor Liscombe for these observations. They deserve more extensive discussion than I can give them here.

18 See Frederick Valentine, *L.F. Valentine: Career Works, 1963-2005* (Calgary: Stantec Architecture, 2006). Culham Pedersen Valentine is now part of Stantec, a multidisciplinary international design firm.

19 George Adamczyk, "Paysage et sensation," in *Saucier and Perrotte Architectes, 1995-2002*, ed. Brian Carter (Halifax: Tuns, 2004), 135.

20 Tony Judt, reflecting on the broader social and economic conditions that provoked Karl Marx, wrote recently that "the world appears to be entering upon a new cycle, one with which our nineteenth century forebears were familiar but of which we in the West have no recent experience. In the coming

years ... we are likely to hear more, not less, about inequality, injustice, unfairness, and exploitation – at home but especially abroad." See Tony Judt, "Goodbye to all that?" *New York Review,* 21 September 2006, 92.

21 See, for instance, discussion of these issues in the *Times Literary Supplement,* much of it summarized in Norman Davies, "The Decomposing of Britain," *Times Literary Supplement* (London), 6 October 2000.

22 Carter and Lecuyer note that the "idea of a Canadian architecture is a tenuous one," but they still argue for its "unique position." See Brian Carter and Annette Lecuyer, "Canada," *Architectural Review* 193, 1155 (May 1993): 6.

23 Magali Sarfatti Larson suggests that any public discourse about architecture beyond utility "must address the question of how architecture exists in cities ... asking what kinds of architectural objects should be built, in what kinds of cities, and for whose comfort and delight, are crucial (if not the most crucial) *theoretical* questions architects can ask for themselves." See Magali Sarfatti Larson, "Patronage and Power," in *Reflections on Architectural Practices in the Nineties,* ed. William S. Saunders (New York: Princeton Architectural Press, 1996), 140, original emphasis.

17

Memory, the Architecture of First Nations, and the Problem with History

DANIEL M. MILLETTE

When it comes to the history of the architecture of Canada's First Nations, there is a wide gap between what we know and what remains to be understood.[1] Virtually no body of work directly or comprehensively dealing with the subject has been assembled. And in spite of at times impeccable descriptive accounts by anthropologists,[2] archaeologists,[3] ethnographers,[4] early explorers,[5] and missionary-priests,[6] architectural historians have almost entirely neglected the subject. There are a few exceptions, such as brief mentions in Harold Kalman's work and the outlines in Keith Thor Carlson's edited *A Stó:ló Coast Salish Historical Atlas*.[7] The former, however, is highly generalized, without mentioning, for example, the architectural historical material related to western Canada's First Nations, and the latter deals specifically with the architectures of only a few of the hundreds of First Nations in Canada. In time, the assembly of a more comprehensive body of work on the subject will undoubtedly prove that it is vast, diverse, and conducive to cultural understanding, social comprehension, and insight into architectural complexity.[8]

The difficulty with the history of First Nations architecture is that the research focus has thus far been overly bounded to theory – postmodern and postcolonial – in spite of very little primary material on which to base the same theoretical work. The architectural history of the First Nations of Canada cannot be readily explained; nor can it be assumed to be homogeneous. The geography and topography alone, not to mention the cultural diversity, are such that the resulting architectures vary much more than those of the Euro-Canadian vernacular. Yet the difficulty for architectural historians, in terms of understanding Aboriginal architectural design, lies beyond these complexities; it lies in the very nature of colonizing and "missionizing." These processes include components that specifically aimed at erasing, altering, and reinventing Aboriginal collective memories, including architectural know-how. Simply put, the architecture of most First Nations in Canada has been forgotten and is therefore extremely difficult to study in a historical sense. This brings me to the main purpose of the present work.

This chapter proposes an avenue of primary research that has not yet been addressed. Here, I explore two things: first, in a general sense, the ways Aboriginal architectures were, and to some extent continue to be, deleted from the collective architectural memory; and, second, the ways that the same architectures are being relocated within the same collective memory, archaeologically, ethnographically, and more important, through a lived, quotidian, and persisting onsite and local knowledge. During the colonial era, traditional Aboriginal architectures were gradually forgotten, replaced by Western practices and then, more recently, through a process of active "remembering," reproduced. This process included the initial obliteration of ways of life, the subsequent forgetting of the same ways, and then the conscious effort at collectively remembering the ways, albeit within a set of present-day realities. It is my contention that by studying the re-emergence of "traditional" architectures, it is possible to retrace hints of what has for the most part been assumed to have disappeared. I turn to the Coast Salish example, although I believe the same processes apply throughout Canada.

There are three parts to this chapter. First, I discuss the architecture and subsequent loss of architectural collective memory within West Coast Aboriginal culture. I describe, broadly, the architecture of the Coast Salish (one of the main areas of architectural history that has been omitted from the literature), while exploring the processes through which memory has been erased.[9] I use the Tsawwassen nation to make my point. Second, I discuss the notions of memory, history, and heritage and the way these can be altered through time. Third, I outline very generally the way the obliterated architectural memories are being regained within Coast Salish culture, again using the Tsawwassen as an example.

ARCHITECTURAL MEMORY: THE TSAWWASSEN PEOPLE

When in 1792 Captain George Vancouver carried out his explorations along the coast of what is now north-western Washington State and south-western British Columbia, he noted a structure that he said housed some six hundred Dwanish people.[10] The building had a single-pitched, shed-style roof and extended to a length of about 365 metres.[11] Along the more prominent elevation making up the main facade were large columns, some 6 metres high and 8 metres apart. In what must have been a spectacular cross-section, beams of 19 metres extended from the front posts to lower ones at the rear. This was the longhouse at North Bay in Washington State, and although it is large by any standard, it turns out that there were others of considerable size both on the banks of the Fraser River and along the shores of the Washington and British Columbia mainland coasts.[12]

In both areas, shed-roofed and pitched-roofed longhouses were built as post-and-beam assemblies, with smaller lateral spandrels between the beams for roofing and between the posts for partitioning. Wide planks of cedar were used as sheathing, overlapping horizontally. The planks were held into place with cedar ties. And along the roof, the same type of cedar plank was fixed, tightly, with stones used to keep them in place. Some villages had longhouses with gable roofs; others had mansard roofs.[13] Inside, there were partitions delimiting family or clan spaces, as well as fire pits, placed at specific locations. During the summer, when people moved up the Fraser River, they often took the planks with them, presumably to be utilized in conjunction with longhouse frames left during previous visits.[14] Artist Paul Kane travelled extensively in the area during the 1840s, sketching and painting scenes of Aboriginal day-to-day life. Significant is that, from his work, we know that contrary to what can be portrayed in museums and popular drawings, these structures were decorated only sparsely on their exterior faces. The intent was in fact to make the buildings as inconspicuous as possible; they were consequently sited and adorned with this in mind. At Tsawwassen, the architectural traditions were undoubtedly very similar.

Details of Tsawwassen's traditional longhouse(s) persist in at least two fields: first, ethnographically derived descriptions and concluding depictions by ethnographers and anthropologists; and, second, the archaeological record. Here, I limit myself to the interviews and conclusions of one anthropologist in particular, Homer Barnett, who worked intensely with the Tsawwassen people during the early and mid-1900s, and to the archaeological investigations along a set of transects bisecting a portion of Tsawwassen lands carried out during the 1980s.

According to Barnett, the longhouses at Tsawwassen had the same basic characteristics as those of other Coast Salish peoples, including the Musqueam, located north of the Tsawwassen village.[15] These were shed-roofed buildings, sloped toward the rear, with four main posts, the back ones being lower than the front ones. Large beams spanned from front to back; the beams were approximately 20 to 22 metres long. There may have been additional posts at intermediate distances between the front and the back, depending on the span and beam strength. Poles extended from beam to beam and from post to post; cedar planks covered the entire outer surfaces (roof and walls), and inside there were partitions.[16] As elsewhere, there was little or no decoration.[17]

Still, within Barnett's notes and according to interviews carried out in the 1930s with Chief Joe, a Tsawwassen,[18] the longhouse occupied by Chief Joe in the 1860s was split into two spaces measuring some 55 metres and some 95 metres in length. This was a large structure, and the recollections of Chief Joe reflect the general descriptions of the region's structures by Peter Nabokov and Robert Easton, as well as evidence found during the course of archaeological excavations in Tsawwassen during the 1980s.[19] Without a doubt, longhouses persisted at Tsawwassen; when interviewed, today's Elders have similar, albeit fragmented, recollections of their features.[20] The recollections are quite sparse, and it is by reviewing the principal historical events at Tsawwassen that we begin to understand why there are only a few memories of the longhouse.

When the Europeans arrived in the late eighteenth century, they would have quickly made contact with the Tsawwassen people; their village site was at a strategic place located at the base of English Bluff, at one extremity of a path that led from a major canoe landing to Boundary Bay. We know that trade was rapidly established, with the Hudson's Bay Company eventually actively exchanging beaver pelts with individuals living at English Bluff. Later, in the 1850s, Catholic missionary-priests were busily making their rounds from one Native settlement to another, baptizing newborns, adults, and Elders desiring to participate in the faith. We have Tsawwassen baptismal records from as early as the 1860s, when Catholic priest Léon Fouquet visited the Tsawwassen community.[21] And we also have the latter's notes telling of the "savages that were once again practicing their dancing and rituals and therefore had to be chastised and confessed."[22] The priest was making it a priority to rename individuals (through baptism), while banning traditional practices (through religious indoctrination). At the same time, James Douglas was negotiating treaties with Aboriginal peoples on Vancouver Island, many of whom were related to Tsawwassen people and therefore inextricably linked in terms of traditional practices. Douglas's efforts resulted in fourteen treaties that altered Aboriginal ways of life and that are still significant for these communities. Early on, then, through contact with the Catholic clergy and less directly through trade contacts and via the Douglas treaties on Vancouver Island, traditional ways began to be set aside for new ways. With increasing contact and the introduction of new economic, religious, and cultural ways, acculturation began to take place, with the resulting erosion of collective memory.[23]

At almost the same time in the 1860s, Joseph Trutch, Indian lands commissioner, made it legally impossible for Native people to pre-empt Crown land. This is significant in the sense that although the Tsawwassen community lived within its village site, the same community accessed – and indeed possessed – a series of traditional sites, some a considerable distance from the village itself. In a letter to the lands commissioner, Father Fouquet requested that lands be set aside for the Tsawwassen people, fearing that these would be pre-empted by European settlers.[24] In fact, due to pre-emption, key traditional sites were taken away from the Aboriginal community,[25] further erasing the community's collective memory.

A little later, the Canadian government started making laws and policies that radically altered cultural practices. First, the Indian Act of 1876 began controlling all aspects of traditional life. These came to include, in 1884, traditional practices such as the potlatch and, in part, the use of traditional longhouses for potlatches. Later, the residential school policies of the 1880s saw the Tsawwassen children taken and sent to the schools, further alienating the population from its cultural ways and memorial activities. The latter was in many ways connected to "missionizing" by the Catholic Church, creating a generation of children who ultimately "forgot" traditional ways. At the same time, and throughout the late nineteenth century, a policy of establishing reserves and relocating Aboriginal populations was put into place, resulting in the obliteration of First Nations collective memory. Slowly, the longhouse of Chief Joe fell into disuse and eventually ruin as the Tsawwassen population moved some 1,000 metres north along the coast. The earlier mentioned archaeological excavations confirmed Chief Joe's settlement account, although very little mention of it was made during the rest of the twentieth century. Thus the longhouses were gradually forgotten as families established themselves in conventional homes.

ON MEMORY, HISTORY, AND HERITAGE

"Memory" is a term I use recognizing that it is subject to differing views and that there are different ways of defining it, especially when referring to "collective memory" and "cultural memory." Quite obviously, "memory" is closely linked to any discussion of the history of architecture. The term can be problematic in these memory-obsessed times, and there are a few things that require clarification. There are different collective architectural memories: the collective architectural memory of the builders of the day, the collective architectural memory of the interpreters of architecture, be it yesterday's chroniclers or today's historians, and the collective architectural memory of today's readers.

What I am most concerned with here is, on the one hand, the collective architectural memory of a people and, on the other hand, the collective architectural memory of historians. In a First Nations context, I am talking about what might best be understood as "orally passed-down histories"; this collective architectural memory is generally accepted by the collective yet not necessarily textually documented or organized along a linear or temporal continuum. It is a memory that involves legends, stories and architectural accounts, and building traditions, among many other types of knowledge, passed down through generations. And when I refer to the collective architectural memory of historians, I am talking about "history" – the organization and reorganization of past events rationalized generally along a temporal continuum, usually presented as the "official" version of some social or cultural entity, and largely purported to be objective and authoritative. "History" can also be generally accepted by the collective (although not always), and by virtue of its textualization or formalization through mechanisms such as related monument building, it represents the past and thus realigns the collective memory. When we refer to "memory," then, we have to realize that the term is somewhat contentious and that its definition is shifting.

As knowledge is passed down – orally or textually – there is opportunity to alter information. And here, the gaps that exist between visual depictions and textual descriptions afford the opportunity to activate the imagination. On the one hand, generalized descriptions become compelling and immediate because the reader can imaginatively fill in what is missing; the reader participates in imaginative constructions, combining personal familiarity and cumulated and learned histories with the ideals presented in the descriptions. But on the other hand, as soon as more detail is provided, which initially liberates the imagination, the same detail becomes etched along a new imaginary track and is bound to a particular rendition. Inevitably, more recent and detailed renditions force the reader's interpretation to *fit* new memorial renditions.[26]

The act of remembering can certainly be seen as an activity that is individual and socially constructed. Maurice Halbwachs, in his various studies, has made this abundantly clear, writing "that the mind reconstructs its memories under the pressure of society."[27] Memorializing and remembering can also be social activities, and within this set of social activities, memory becomes objectified through, for example, the rebuilding of a longhouse. This means that the scripted "historical" narrative, in this case of a longhouse's architecture, becomes etched into the individual and collective memory with devices that traditionally occur "in real life." And here, what I mean is that an Elder's oral history-telling, for example, is an event that normally happens and that is therefore more readily memorialized and eventually recollected by the listener.

Another important thought that Halbwachs has passed on is that tradition ends where history begins. This is closely related to Pierre Nora's notion that as soon as history, as a discipline, establishes itself as narrator of the past, traditions (and therefore memories) begin correspondingly to disappear.[28] Thus "documented" descriptions of Aboriginal architecture are not without their transformative aspects, and they are, I contend, one way of presenting a past and in turn, if desired, reassigning a history's meaning and thereby reshaping the collective memory.

There is a very close relationship between the employment of a "thing" or a "narrative" to cue memory and the connecting of the present to the past. Interestingly, however, these things eventually take on a history of their own. This is why many stories told within ethnographic (or other) historical descriptions can come to have meanings that are completely detached from their initial purposes; along the way, the collective somehow forgets – or perhaps is re-instructed regarding – the meaning of certain examples, and this is the specific moment when the collective memory can be realigned. Key here is that whether we acknowledge it or not, and whether it be intentional or not, collective memory is neither history nor heritage but what we choose as a group to recall and what trusted individuals claim it to be.

Related to history, memory, and imagination is the notion of "heritage." The rapid acceleration of commemorative activity during recent decades has been well documented.[29] Both the phenomenon and its documentation are closely linked to the fields of architectural history. Although the latter was initially concerned with buildings and preservation, it has recently been expanded to include the protection and interpretation of traditional environments, landscapes, ways of being, artistic practices, and so on. It is thus inextricably linked to First Nations architecture and leads to the important question for architectural historians of what happens when Native traditions, traditional environments, landscapes, ways of being, and artistic practices are stymied? Well, for one thing, a void is created within the collective memory. And this is where the collective memory is most vulnerable to realignment.

It is clear, then, that at specific points the collective memory can be altered, either willingly or at times less willingly and either in a sudden and violent way or in a subtle and gentle way. When sudden change occurs in society, the opportunity to fill memorial voids emerges. Colonizing and missionizing create enormous voids, as does the sudden emancipation of a culture.

RECONSTRUCTING ARCHITECTURAL MEMORY

When in 1998 the people of Tsawwassen decided to build a new longhouse, they wanted more than a place where cultural ways could be practised. They wanted a building that, on the one hand, would have features in keeping with ancient mores and, on the other hand, would take into account contemporary realities; large gatherings with outsiders, modern facilities, new building materials, construction techniques, and fire precautions all had to be taken into account. In other words, the building would have to accommodate large traditional fire pits and a modern food preparation area and also have to take into account present-day building realities. It was primarily through interviews with Elders and other cultural advisors, and secondarily through advice from building trades, that a design solution was arrived at. There are no formal construction drawings for this building; verbal instruction was thus key.

"Tsawwassen" translates as "land facing the sea." It should be of no surprise that the site chosen to build the new longhouse is along the shore. The original site was rendered completely unusable when the major highway leading to a ferry causeway was built atop its ruins.[30] Thus the area selected is relatively prominent, not as inconspicuous as its traditional precedents. On the appointed construction start-up day, an Elder from the broader Coast Salish community was invited to give general direction on the orientation and size of the longhouse. No conventional lot plan was prepared. Of fundamental importance is that in most Aboriginal communities, members, especially Elders, possess architectural design knowledge that is still in use, outlining a vernacular traditional architecture that remains undocumented.[31] This is the case with Coast Salish communities, including Tsawwassen.

Figure 17.1 The Tsawwassen First Nation Longhouse. | Photograph by author.

The space resulting from the generalized design is delineated by two frames (Figure 17.1).[32] One is a traditional post-and-beam structure that generally reflects the above description of a longhouse, although we are not talking about a shed-roofed structure. And the second is a contemporary stud-wall system that encloses, for the most part, the former. The first frame pierces the second and reaches upward to form a pitched roof 12 metres in height. It is supported by large posts, some 70 centimetres in diameter, linked together at the top by beams, about 22 metres across. The bays resulting from the post-and-beam assemblies are linked, laterally, with beams, also about 50 centimetres in width. Smaller cross-members are installed throughout. The eight posts – four on each side – define the main, unobstructed space inside. The roof assembly is made up of an A-frame of 50-centimetre beams tied together with smaller cross-members. These roof "trusses" are part of the traditional frame and operate independently of the outer frame.

The outer frame uses standard studs of 2 inches by 6 inches, which are just over 5 metres in height and anchored to a plate directly onto a concrete footing. The top of this stud wall supports the secondary section of the roof (Figure 17.2). With the exception of the latter roof section being tied to the post-and-beam structure, the outer frame works independently of the inner one. The whole makes for an impressive set of dimensions: 45 by 22 metres in overall

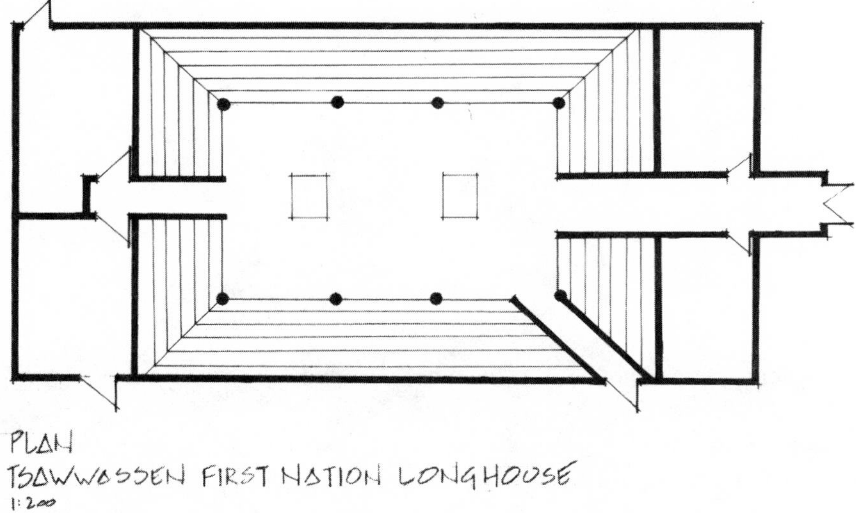

Figure 17.2 The Tsawwassen First Nation Longhouse – Plan. | Drawing by author.

surface, excluding the main entrance niche, with a roof extending to, as mentioned, some 12 metres in height. The result is the juxtapositioning and amalgamation of two techniques.

When we consider the exterior wall and roof sheathing of the building, the mix becomes more complex. The post-and-beam structure is covered with plywood sheathing and asphalt shingles, and the stud-wall frame is covered with traditional cedar planks, cut from logs specifically brought to the site for this purpose. We thus have the traditional component covered by a contemporary material and the contemporary component covered by a traditional material.[33] The combination of roofing and wall sheathing provides an exterior that appears as a single, relatively well-unified, and cohesive structure. There are few openings, the whole is solemn, and with the exception of two decorative posts installed on each side of the main entrance, there are no decorative features.

Moving inside, we find a plan that is well articulated (Figure 17.3). Key here is that the discrete disposition of the traditional frame's posts governs the spatial delimitation. Two very different spaces result. The first one corresponds to the traditional frame; the second is aligned with the more modern frame. The first one has a beaten-earth floor; the second has a concrete floor. There is thus a central, open space surrounded by a peripheral, more confining space. There

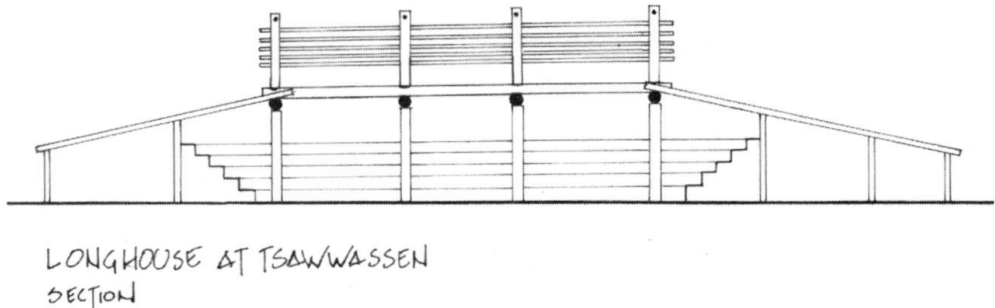

Figure 17.3 The Tsawwassen First Nation Longhouse – Section. | Drawing by author.

are secondary areas, of course; these accommodate food, guest-dancer, and washroom requirements. One door, to the southeast, pierces the secondary space; it is there to allow for the provision of firewood. Within the traditional space, there are two fire pits, located just below the large roof outlets. The pits are slightly depressed within the earth floor. No concrete slab or substructure lies beneath and all of the traditional cultural activities take place within this central area.

From a cross-section, we can better see the second space, which is filled with ascending benches for guests (Figure 17.3). Although the presence of guests in traditional longhouses is not a new phenomenon, the celebrations now undertaken as "spectator events" in a contemporary sense are a more recently highlighted cultural facet; the bleachers accommodate this new need. The permanent benches limit circulation, and once one is seated, it is difficult to move about without being observed; leaving becomes a conspicuous move. Thus, although the new spectator element has become part of the design, it is the traditional element that governs: a spectator cannot override the performance and presence of a traditional dancer.

CONCLUSION

First Nations in what is now Canada have a set of rich architectural traditions. These vary according to geographical regions, cultural settings, and internal ways. Traditional knowledge precepts persist within individual communities, and although new, contemporary needs have become architectural realities, they are fused to traditional mores and know-how. The longhouse at Tsawwassen exemplifies the conjoining of traditional ways to contemporary needs. It is an architecture that remains overlooked. The design amalgamates traditional and contemporary materials and methods that in turn accommodate traditional and modern realities. It juxtaposes two moments, produces two spaces, and in turn generates a new architectural form.

We have assumed that through a complex process of colonizing, missionizing, and re-educating, the architectural collective memory of First Nations has been obliterated. However, through very close examination of present-day building practices, we find valuable traces of precontact architectural design. This traditional knowledge, however, has persisted within local communities where individuals possess knowledge, direct actions, and provide design expertise that is directly linked to traditional activity and past, precontact architectures.

What remains to be pursued is the combined analysis of present-day traditional architecture and archaeological, ethnographical records. It is through an interdisciplinary approach that a clearer body of traditional architectural know-how will be assembled.

NOTES

1 By "First Nations architecture," I mean the architecture within which traditional ways were, or are, practised. This chapter does not include discussion of the present trend of community- or architect-designed, purpose-built spaces related to First Nations culture.

2 See, for example, Wayne Suttles, ed., *Coast Salish Essays* (Seattle: University of Washington Press, 1987).

3 See, for example, Arcas Consulting Archaeologists, *Archaeological Investigations at Tsawwassen, B.C.*, vol. 1 (Victoria: Ministry of Transportation and Highways, 1991).

4 See, for instance, Franz Boas, ed., *General Anthropology* (Boston: Heath, 1938); and Roy L. Carlson, *Indian Art Traditions of the Northwest Coast* (Burnaby, BC: Simon Fraser University Press), 1984.

5 One explorer who wrote detailed accounts is John Work. See T.C. Elliot, ed., *Journal of John Work, November and December 1824* (Washington, DC: Washington Historical Quarterly, 1912).

6 One priest travelling during early colonial times was the Oblate Father Léon Fouquet. See Missionnaires Oblats de Marie Immaculée, *Missions de la Congrégation des Missionnaires Oblats de Marie Immaculée*, vol. 12 (Paris: Typographie A. Hennuyer, 1874).

7 Harold Kalman, *A Concise History of Canadian Architecture* (Don Mills, ON, and London: Oxford University Press, 2000), 1-23; Keith Thor Carlson, ed., *A Stó:lō Coast Salish Historical Atlas* (Vancouver/Seattle: Douglas and McIntyre/University of Washington Press, 2001).

8 I here omit the literature that focuses on present-day architectural design on First Nations reserves.

9 The literature on Coast Salish architecture is sparse. For a summary, see Carlson, ed., *Stó:lō Coast Salish,* Plate 13.

10 See Randy Bouchard and Dorothy Kennedy, "Tsawwassen Ethnography and Ethnohistory," in *Archaeological Investigations at Tsawwassen, B.C.*, vol. 1, ed. Arcas Consulting Archaeologists, 151-53 (Victoria: Ministry of Transportation and Highways, 1991); Homer Barnett, *Tsawwassen Field Notes,* University of British Columbia, Main Library, Special Collections, folder 1, box 1, book 8, 1935-36.

11 See Wayne Suttles, "The Shed-Roof House," in *A Time of Gathering,* ed. R.K. Wright, 212-22 (Seattle: University of Washington Press, 1991). More generally, see also Peter Nabokov and Robert Easton, *Native American Architecture* (Oxford: Oxford University Press, 1989), 234-35.

12 Other early descriptions exist. See, for example, Geoffrey Simmins, ed., *Documents in Canadian Architecture* (Peterborough, ON: Broadview, 1992), 1-5.

13 Some longhouses were partly excavated.

14 This may in part explain why some travellers thought villages looked abandoned.

15 Homer Barnett, *The Coast Salish of British Columbia*, University of Oregon Monographs – Studies in Anthropology, No. 4 (Portland: University of Oregon Press, 1955), 36, 53-55.

16 A version of this description can also be found in Bouchard and Kennedy, "Tsawwassen Ethnography and Ethnohistory."

17 Suttles, "Shed-Roof House," makes similar remarks related to the shed-roofed longhouse.

18 Barnett, *Tsawwassen Field Notes.*

19 Bouchard and Kennedy, "Tsawwassen Ethnography and Ethnohistory"; Nabokov and Easton, *Native American Architecture.*

20 Daniel M. Millette, ed., *Traditional Use Study of the Tsawwassen First Nation* (Victoria: Tsawwassen First Nation and British Columbia Ministry of Forests, 1998); Daniel M. Millette, *Traditional Use in the Vicinity of Certain Crown Land Parcels in the Lower Mainland of British Columbia: History, Archaeology and Ethnography* (Vancouver: Vancouver Port Authority, 2001).

21 Father L. Fouquet, letter to the Lands and Works Department, New Westminster, 15 August 1865, British Columbia Public Archives, document B1328.

22 See Missionnaires Oblats de Marie Immaculée, *Missions de la Congrégation.*

23 On acculturation in Aboriginal communities of the region, see Margaret Blackman, "Creativity in Acculturation: Art, Architecture and Ceremony from the Northwest Coast," *Ethnohistory* 23, 4 (1976): 387-413.

24 Father Fouquet wrote, "I beg to introduce to you the bearer of This, the Missionnaires Oblats de Marie Immaculée, chief of the Tchwassen village. He and His people are very anxious to see their reservation staked out by the government." Father L. Fouquet, letter to the Lands and Works Department, New Westminster, 15 August 1865, British Columbia Public Archives, document B1328.

25 Daniel M. Millette, *Cultural Resources Heritage Study of the Tsawwassen First Nation* (Victoria: Tsawwassen First Nation and British Columbia Ministry of Forests, 1998).

26 This means that a structure such as a longhouse becomes altered as it is described, depending on the listener's (or reader's) perspective and experience; as cultural context is altered, so too is its architecture.

27 Maurice Halbwachs, *On Collective Memory*, ed. and trans. Lewis A. Coser (Chicago: University of Chicago Press, 1995), 51.

28 Pierre Nora, *Lieux de Mémoire*, 3 vols. (Paris: Gallimard, 1984-92).

29 John R. Gillis, ed., *Commemorations: The Politics of National Identity* (Princeton, NJ: Princeton University Press, 1994).

30 I refer to Highway 17 leading to the British Columbia Ferries causeway at Tsawwassen Beach, British Columbia.

31 On vernacular traditional architectural knowledge, see Peter Nabokov and Robert Easton, *Native American Architecture* (Oxford: Oxford University Press, 1989).

32 Portions of the following description were previously included as part of an earlier article. See Daniel M. Millette, "Re-building Memories: On the Reconstruction of a 'Traditional' Longhouse at Tsawwassen," in *Journal of the Society for the Study of Architecture in Canada* 27, 4 (2002): 45-50.

33 I here acknowledge that the exterior planking is installed vertically; traditional building tenets call for the horizontal placement of planks.

Conclusion
Future Writing on Canadian Architectural History

RHODRI WINDSOR LISCOMBE

This anthology grew out of a lecture series held by St. John's College at the University of British Columbia exploring the cultural politics of Canadian architecture. The series had been stimulated by three major factors. First, the inherent interest of architectural practice and discourse in both colonial and confederated Canada, as underscored by Harold Kalman, yet also the relatively low profile of Canadian architectural history, especially in the academic literature. Second, that the vigour and range of critical theory enabled closer study of both the broader themes and more situated aspects of the development of architectural culture in the Canadas: its several registers of community no less than the confederated nation. Third, that a sequence of focused studies of particular episodes or features from this development would contribute to understandings of architecture's role in the formation of collectivities from the local to the national scale, especially if such a process encompassed intention and impact. Consequently, all of the chapters in the anthology interrogate the multiple agency either achieved by or ascribed to architecture, including building, urban planning, and, latterly, the broader practice and discourse of design.

Architecture in this volume is as noted defined broadly, well beyond the confines of style, technique, or type, and is understood to fulfil a broad swathe of requirements, aspirations, or tasks – ones that have variously contributed to the Canadian national fabric. Taken together, the contributions herein further link architectural design and planning to the ways that desired future built environments are first imagined and then specified; they demonstrate how buildings are central yet also peripheral to the formation of communal association – especially in the building-up of national consciousness – through the articulation of shared emblematic affiliation and their underlying material systems or networks of influence; they lay out how architects contribute to marking individual and institutional status or policy while also often unintentionally rendering visible disparities of social order and wealth; they reveal how architecture might be preoccupied with matters of aesthetic but nonetheless operates to make place and thereby meaning at the mundane level of social activity; they reconfirm the extent to which architectural design both reflects and moulds the larger social condition while forming the visual scenery for unifying significant ceremony and quotidian ritual; and they acknowledge the interstices between levels of design expectation, execution, and enterprise.

Although comprehensive in thematic and temporal scope, this collection cannot, by its very nature, be complete. For example, there is no chapter on drill halls and related buildings erected for the Militia. The architectural iconography of drill halls, generally neo-Gothic or Château-Baronial, has been recounted and related to the confederating activity of the federal Departments of Militia and Defence and of Public Works in a 1989 report compiled by Jacqueline Ardell for the Historic Sites and Monuments Board of Canada that builds on Desmond Morton's *A Military History of Canada* (published from 1999).[1] But the deeper, and wider, implications of their construction have been less investigated, including their conflicted impact upon community identity. This building type was particularly significant during coinciding decades of the consolidation of the early Confederation and zenith of British imperialist allegiance in Canada, from the 1880s through to 1914. Sir John A. MacDonald placed his chief political ally, Sir George-Étienne Cartier, in charge of the Militia during his first federal administration. The local regiments of the volunteer Militia operated on a number of socio-economic levels beyond territorial defence or regulation, much as their architectural facilities represented national and imperial power, signified expanding settlement patterns, and figured regional and municipal status, but also, through symbolic articulation, exposed the actual diversity even then of Canadian polity and society. Thus the chapters on other building types in this anthology, it is to be hoped, demonstrate the value of regarding matters of context as well as of reception and affect.

Indeed, a major legacy of this anthology could be an extension of its guiding analytical principles: a catholic concept of both architecture and architectural history; that each can legitimately relate the so-called commonplace to the aesthetically or politically distinguished; that the suburb or utilitarian commission is less a mundane cul-de-sac of market forces involving design and construction than a specialized screen of the panoply of the conceptual-to-technical and social-to-economic processes also operating in more conventionally defined architecture; that architecture, in particular, forms an essential part of the fabric of public activity; that certain building types at certain places and times – notably in Canada, churches, railway infrastructure, or grain silos – assume remarkable importance for the constitution of local community as well as national identity; and lastly that architectural history benefits by an alliance of theoretical hypothesis, disciplinary inclusivity, archival research, and formal analysis.

Particular allusion is made to the range of analytic approaches associated with postmodern critique as especially defined in spatial theory: the questioning of essentialist (or meta) narratives, the repositioning of viewpoint away from hegemonic centres either material or cultural, the relational perspective on all forms of production, the positioning of so-called high culture in the broader sphere of usual social practice, and the recognition of supposedly marginal factors or agents. Aspects of this analytic expansion of more traditional architectural history together with greater attention to the specificities of design have been influential, particularly since receiving commendation from Annmarie Adams and Martin Bressani in their article "Canada: The Edge Condition"; and the study of the specificities of design can be traced through the articles successively published in *Architecture Canada,* the journal of the Society for the Study of Architecture in Canada.[2]

This concluding discussion therefore seeks to indicate how the chapters extend the critical compass of writing the history of architecture and open lines of new inquiry on Canadian design culture. Overall, they move between those interpretative parameters marked out by the more recent discourses of materiality and visuality exemplified by such studies as Daniel Miller, *Materiality* (2005), Anthony Woodiwiss, *Visual in Social Theory* (2001), and with greater attention to architecture, *Rethinking Architectural Historiography* (2006), edited by Dana Arnold, Elvan Ergut, and Belgin Turan Özkaya.[3] They inhabit a more sociological than aesthetic space of inquiry and more investigative than historical space of analysis. In not reifying architecture, or for that matter nation, they come at building design in a manner comparable with the active social presence of other material-mechanical objects investigated by Bruno Latour in *Aramis, or The Love of Technology* (1996) or, with respect to architectural environments, by Annmarie Adams and Sally McMurry in *Exploring Everyday Landscapes* (1997) and, to the broader social environment, by Elsa Lam in "A Fertile Wilderness: The Canadian Pacific Railway's Ready-made Farms, 1908-1914" (2010).[4]

Those chapters in this anthology concerned more directly with design form or plan, notably by Thomas and Vattay, use aesthetic and historical factors to present arguments about larger political and social ordering. Similarly, Carr and Windover use architectural style and decoration to define the lineaments of contemporary professional and popular attitudes and preferences – dynamic, rather than static, negotiations of local and international flows of design economy. The political dimension of societal values, including the mediation of changing ethnic relations, appears in Hanks's chapter on federal institutional commissions at Ottawa and in Marcus's on federal town planning in the Canadian Arctic. The societal aspect of elitist architecture enables Magrill to reconstruct attempts to enhance the profile of Toronto literally and metaphorically, while revealing its discrepant social order. Morisset traces the influence of architecture on populist cultural production through her rehabilitation of the Quebec bungalow. The visual, as in the imaginary representations of preferred actual or future built environments, predominates for Grignon, while material qualities are shown by Legault to have been a primary attribute of the popularity of Brutalism in Canada. McGrail links the absence of both visual and material distinction with the extreme utility of consumer economy during the erection of big-box stores as well as with resurgent Marxist analysis of capitalism. The individuated instead of communal model of recent urban development conveyed in my chapter obviously encompasses sociological discourse.

Historiographical analyses weave in and out of the critical fabric of the anthology. The three chapters forming the final part present fresh versions of conventional, liberal-humanist history. Olsberg introduces a literary dimension to the assessment of how architectural reputation is formed over time: the history of Arthur Erickson (whose death in 2009 justifies a more interpretive review than academic summation of his design career). To some extent McMordie's reconsideration of the critical relevance of identity invokes the paraphernalia of historical composition: why the social subject seeks a supposedly objective record of its temporal and material context. Millette, as noted already, influenced by Pierre Nora's theorization of memory, proposes a new type of history that embraces communal memory, storytelling, and traditional knowledge. The shifting record of architectural and cultural analysis alike form the scaffolding of the chapters, especially in Parts 2 through 4. For instance, Thomas reviews prior interpretation of intended meaning in the architecture of the Confederation Parliament; Carr and Windover address earlier readings of major civic buildings and of the stylistic features with which these were preoccupied; Morisset and Marcus engage with the definition of Modernism; Legault studies the promotion, especially in Canada, of Brutalism; and Hanks brings in the literature on museum history as well as the institution's role in the constitution of nationhood. In attending to specific inflexions or resonances, the contributors yet avoid the exaggeration of determining systems of capital, ideology, or privilege challenged by a leading Canadian scholar, Ian Hacking in *The Social Construction of What?* (1998).[5]

The trace of Marxist and poststructural discourses is stronger in the first and last parts. Loach clearly demonstrates deep appreciation of the postcolonial critique and of the analyses of the imprint of text on structure pioneered by Michel Foucault – since taken up by such contemporary architectural historian-theorists as Anthony Vidler. But Loach is careful to contextualize the Jesuit *Relations* and to indicate their colonial legacy without either reifying the Jesuit mission or denigrating Aboriginal society. Grignon, Hanks, and Marcus are equally sophisticated in their respective reference to postcolonial sensibility and policy. Grignon carries back postmodern theories of the spatial constitution of power, and its contestation, in his analysis of the public domain. Theories of public space and culture, especially associated with Pierre Bourdieu, Henri Lefebvre, or Ali Madaupour inform Windover's and Carr's approaches, as well as my chapter's argument, which is further framed by the critical literatures of advertising, media, lifestyle, and consumerism. Carr and Windover neatly draw in identity politics and the more expansive arena of cultural studies deployed by Morisset. The equally complex and critical realm of the everyday as set out by Jean Baudrillard and Michel de Certeau is particularly germane to McGrail. But this realm intersects with the commerce of taste found by Magrill, adapting Bourdieu's idea of *habitus,* to be at work even in church architecture.

Magrill's essay is the most evident demonstration of the application of a specific methodology, the case study. Vattay also mobilizes this method but builds in typological and urbanist analyses. Neither, deliberately, engages as closely as the other contributors with what some would differentiate as high theory, which is a strong force within spatial theory and particularly associated with deeper and more abstract diagnoses of cultural practice. This searching into normative process is evident in Grignon's reviewing of the 1688 representation of Quebec City and, for another example, in Carr's unstitching of speculative development at Edwardian Vancouver. It is necessarily foregrounded in my identification of a genus of architectural commerce that threatens the kind of authentic practice enjoined by such magisterial theorists of culture as Walter Benjamin and Martin Heidegger. Some imprint of reception theory is generally apparent in Vattay's attention to users and in the acknowledgment of wider public assessment by Olsberg and McMordie. However, the most comprehensive deployment of critical theory occurs in Cavell's excavation of McLuhan's thinking about the fast-approaching megalopolitan global social order – neither here nor there.

Besides illustrating the multiple, and in this sense multidisciplinary, strategies for understanding the role and work of architecture in Canada, what might this anthology contribute to future critical framing? First and foremost, the anthology reiterates the need of recovering Aboriginal practice – especially of enlarging the respect for and information on indigenous building practice. Second, the anthology indicates that connections between architecture and the creative arts in Canada, including their association with official and public cultural ethos, merit the kind of exploration undertaken with respect to the visual and theatrical fields respectively by Leslie Dawn in *National Vision, National Blindness* (2006) and by Sherrill Grace and Albert-Reiner Glaap in *Performing National Identities* (2003).[6] Third, and by extension, the anthology highlights the value of filling in a partial lacuna in this collection, most notably renewed study of construction traditions and technologies across Canada. This filling-in should extend the start made in 1967 by Thomas Ritchie in *Canada Builds* but also bring in further analyses of Aboriginal and vernacular practice plus the commercial and socio-cultural dimension.[7] Fourth, patterns of settlement and urban development deserve both more multidisciplinary and more specific study. Research of the evolving and distinctive character of Canadian town planning and urban development would contribute to the discourses of Canadian polity and culture, as well as to renewing the heritage debate. Fifth, the interdisciplinary methodology within the anthology – exemplified by Windover's interweaving of biographical, iconographic, historical, and theoretical analytics – legitimates a more inclusive framing of buildings as markers/condensers of socio-cultural activity. Sixth, the anthology shows that the commercial armature of architectural aesthetic and practice clearly afford powerful lenses for re-examining the Canadian built environment. Seventh, further study of the design professions, including their sociology, would be invaluable, notwithstanding Kelly Crossman's *Architecture in Transition* (1987), Geoffrey Simmins's *Ontario Association of Architects* (1989) or *Documents in Canadian Architecture* (1991), and Annmarie Adams and Peta Tancred's *Designing Women* (2000).[8] A corollary is a comprehensive account – well beyond my study in *The New Spirit* (1997) – of architectural training and media in Canada that brings a Canadian context to the examination of modes of architectural discourse in *This Is Not Architecture* (2001), edited by Kester Rattenbury.[9] Eighth, and as each chapter acknowledges, architecture needs to be understood in terms of reception no less than inception and, indeed, as a process of making and being made by its users at particular moments and over time.

Finally, it is to be hoped that this anthology will reinforce attention to Canadian architectural patrimony and demonstrate its significance for the international discourse and practice of design.

NOTES

1 Desmond Morton, *Military History of Canada*, 5th ed. (Toronto: McClelland and Stewart, 2007). The wider socio-political context is examined by James Wood in *Militia Myths: Ideas of the Canadian Citizen Soldier, 1896-1921* (Vancouver: UBC Press, 2010).

2 Annmarie Adams and Martin Bressani, "Canada: The Edge Condition," *Journal of the Society of Architectural Historians* 62, 1 (March 2003): 75-83.

3 Daniel Miller, *Materiality* (Durham, NC: Duke University Press, 2005); Anthony Woodiwiss, *Visual in Social Theory* (London: Athlone, 2001); Dana Arnold, Elvan Ergut, and Belgin Turan Özkaya, eds., *Rethinking Architectural Historiography* (London: Routledge, 2006).

4 Bruno Latour, *Aramis, or The Love of Technology* (Cambridge, MA: Harvard University Press, 1996); Annmarie Adams and Sally McMurry, *Exploring Everyday Landscapes* (Knoxville: University of Tennessee Press, 1997); Elsa Lam, "A Fertile Wilderness: The Canadian Pacific Railway's Ready-made Farms, 1908-1914," *Architecture Canada* 35, 1 (2010): 3-16.

5 Ian Hacking, *The Social Construction of What?* (Cambridge, MA: Harvard University Press, 1998).

6 Leslie Dawn, *National Vision, National Blindness: Canadian Art and Identities in the 1920s* (Vancouver: UBC Press, 2006); Sherrill Grace and Albert-Reiner Glaap, *Performing National Identities: International Perspectives on Canadian Theatre* (Vancouver: Talon, 2003).

7 Thomas Ritchie, *Canada Builds, 1867-1967* (Toronto: University of Toronto Press, 1967).

8 Kelly Crossman, *Architecture in Transition: From Art to Practice, 1885-1906* (Montreal and Kingston: McGill-Queen's University Press, 1987); Geoffrey Simmins, *Ontario Association of Architects: A Centennial History, 1889-1989* (Toronto: Ontario Association of Architects, 1989), and *Documents in Canadian Architecture* (Peterborough, ON: Braodview, 1991); Annmarie Adams and Peta Tancred, *Designing Women: Gender and the Architectural Profession* (Toronto: University of Toronto Press, 2000).

9 Rhodri Windsor Liscombe, *The New Spirit: Modern Architecture in Vancouver, 1938-1963* (Montreal: Canadain Centre for Architecture, 1997); Kester Rattenbury, ed., *This Is Not Architecture: Media Constructions* (London: Routledge, 2001).

Contributors

Geoffrey Carr holds a doctorate from the University of British Columbia, where he lectures on North American architecture and art produced in the Modern and post-Modern periods. His doctoral research examines the largely overlooked architectural history of the Indian residential school system in Canada as well as the problems pertaining to the preservation and commemoration of these contentious places. In addition, he is interested in issues related to memorialization, heritage preservation, state apology, and discourses of social reconciliation.

Richard Cavell is the author of *McLuhan in Space: A Cultural Geography* (2002), the first book to articulate the spatial turn in media studies and McLuhan's foundational role within it. Professor Cavell is also editor of *Love, Hate, and Fear in Canada's Cold War* (2004), co-editor (with Peter Dickinson) of *Sexing the Maple: A Canadian Sourcebook* (2006), co-editor (with Imre Szeman) of the special double issue of the *Review of Education, Pedagogy, and Cultural Studies* (2007) on "Cultural Studies in Canada," creator of the website http://spectersofmcluhan.net, and he has published more than seventy chapters, articles, and reviews. His current research project examines the biopolitics of English domestic architecture.

Marc Grignon completed a doctorate in architecture at the Massachusetts Institute of Technology in 1991. He has taught the history of architecture in the Art History Program at Université Laval in Quebec City since 1991. His research and his teaching are driven by theories of fiction applied to the study of architecture. His book *"Loing du Soleil": Architectural Practice in Quebec City during the French Regime* (1997) focuses on the relation between clients and builders at the end of the seventeenth century and examines the determining role of urban images in the design of important buildings. More recently, theories of fiction have led him to examine architectural decor in Canadian and in French architecture of the nineteenth century. An example of this research is Martin Bressani and Marc Grignon, "Henri Labrouste and the Lure of the Real: Romanticism, Rationalism and the Bibliothèque Sainte-Geneviève," *Art History* 28, 5 (2005): 712-51.

Laura Hourston Hanks is an associate professor in the Department of Architecture and Built Environment at the University of Nottingham, where she is course director for the Masters of Architecture in Theory and Design and co-ordinates Year 5 of the Diploma in Architecture Program. She studied architecture at the University of Liverpool and gained her doctorate in architectural history and theory from the University of Edinburgh in 2002. Her research interests include contemporary museum and exhibition design and the expression of identities through architectural form. Notable among her publications are *Museum Builders II* (2004) and papers in *Architectural Design* (2003) and *Architectural Research Quarterly* (2010). In 2010 she collaboratively convened the international interdisciplinary conference, "Narrative Space," and is a co-editor of the resulting book, *Museum Making: Narratives, Architectures, Exhibitions* (2011).

Réjean Legault studied architecture at the Université de Montréal and holds a doctorate in architecture from the Massachusetts Institute of Technology. In 1996 he developed the Canadian Centre for Architecture's Visiting Scholars Program and set up the institution's Study Centre, which he directed until 2000. Since then he has been a professor at the École de design of the Université du Québec à Montréal, where he teaches the history and theory of modern architecture. His research, lectures, and publications focus on the historiography of modern architecture, on the relationship between materials and architectural modernity, and on tectonics and building cultures. His publications include *Anxious Modernisms: Experimentation in Postwar Architectural Culture* (co-edited with Sarah Williams Goldhagen, 2000) and numerous articles in journals, books of essays, and exhibition catalogues.

Judi Loach trained in architecture at the Architectural Association, London; worked in archtectural journalism, publishing, and exhibitions; and then took her doctorate in architectural history at the University of Cambridge, specializing in seventeenth-century provincial France but also researching twentieth-century France, notably certain aspects of Le Corbusier. She ran architectural history and theory in the Oxford School of Architecture, Oxford Brookes University, before transferring to the Welsh School of Architecture, Cardiff University, where she was later appointed director of the Researcher and Graduate School in Humanities. She has published widely on seventeenth- and twentieth-century French culture, including on early-modern Jesuit culture, and for nearly the past decade she has been the sole editor of *Architectural History.*

Barry Magrill is a postdoctoral fellow at the University of Victoria, where he is conducting a socio-economic study of contemporary mosque architecture in Canada in the Department of History in Art. He was the 2010 recipient of the Phyllis Lambert Prize for writing in architecture, awarded for his doctoral dissertation, "A 'Commerce of Taste' in Pattern Books of Anglican Church Architecture in Canada, 1867-1914," completed at the University of British Columbia. He publishes and lectures on the architecture of North America and medieval architectural sculpture. As a practising artist, he has exhibited widely in Toronto and now focuses on arts administration by serving as president of the Richmond Art Gallery, vice-president of the Society for the Study of Architecture in Canada, and treasurer of the Universities Arts Association of Canada.

Alan Marcus is Head of Department and Reader in Film and Visual Culture at the University of Aberdeen. He studied industrial design and cinematography at the University of Illinois and received a master's in polar studies and a doctorate in cultural history from Cambridge University. His publications on architectural form and urban representations include *Visualizing the City* (2007), and guest-edited special issues of *The History of Photography* (2006), *The Journal of Architecture* (2006), and *Film Studies* (2007). Research on northern environments has involved fieldwork in four Inuit communities in the Canadian Arctic, from which followed articles in *Polar Record* and *Visual Anthropology* and two books, *Out in the Cold* (1992) and *Relocating Eden* (1995). Films he has made include *People of the Four Winds* (1988), a study of cultural change in a Sami community in northern Sweden, and four films for the In Time of Place (2006-10) project. His research on Erskine's architecture formed the focus of a visiting fellowship in 2010 at the Centre for Research in the Arts, Social Sciences and Humanities at Cambridge University.

Justin McGrail is Chair of Visual Art in the Department of Art and Design at Vancouver Island University, where he teaches courses in art history and theory. He attended McGill University, graduating with a bachelor's degree in history in 1991 and a master's degree in art history in 1995. He completed a doctorate in architectural history in 2009 at the University of Victoria; his dissertation is entitled "Value Space: An Architectural Geography of New Retail Formats on Southern Vancouver Island." His research interests concern everyday buildings and urban life in Canada, along with the historical production and consumption of modernity.

Michael McMordie studied architecture at the University of Toronto, graduating with a bachelor's degree in architecture in 1962. After admission to the profession in 1965 as a member of the Ontario Association of Architects, he began doctoral studies as a British Council scholar at the University of Edinburgh. He joined the Edinburgh Department of Architecture in 1966 and taught there until moving to the Faculty of Environmental Design at the University of Calgary in 1974. In Calgary he served in a variety of roles, as director of the Architecture Program from 1979 to 1982 and as dean of the Faculty of General Studies (now incorporated into the Faculty of Arts) from 1990 to 1998. From 1999 until his retirement in 2005, he directed the Interdisciplinary Graduate Program (formerly Resources and the Environment Program) in the Faculty of Graduate Studies. He was instrumental in the creation in 1974 of the Canadian Architectural Archives.

Daniel M. Millette is an architectural historian, archaeologist, and planner. He teaches history and theory at the University of British Columbia's School of Architecture and Landscape Architecture. His primary focus is on exploring the ways architectural theory and knowledge are produced. His research follows two primary streams. The first is centred in Rome and its colonies, where early planning precedents, monuments, and monument reconstructions are investigated. The second is sited closer to home, where early (and present-day) architectural and planning precedents on Aboriginal lands are studied by meshing together architectural history, archaeology, traditional-use studies, and land-use planning. Land-use plans are developed as case studies, informed by close work with First Nations community members.

Lucie K. Morisset is an architectural and urban historian and a professor in the Department of Urban and Tourism Studies at the Université du Québec à Montréal. She is a member of the university's Institut du patrimoine, associate to the Canada Research Chair on Urban Heritage, and a researcher with Centre interuniversitaire d'études sur les lettres, les arts et les traditions. An extension of her work on the hermeneutics of built landscape and urban representations, her current research focuses on Quebec's patrimonial memory and the history of the province's heritage.

Nicholas Olsberg is a cultural historian, archivist, and curator with a special interest in reading the visible world as a social document. He served sixteen years (1989-2004) with the Canadian Centre for Architecture (CCA) in Montreal. During his tenure there, first as chief curator and then as director, the CCA excited international attention for its exhibitions and publications, its record of public debate and scholarly research, and the widening scope of its collections. He was a visiting fellow in Atlantic history and culture at the Johns Hopkins University and holds an honours degree in modern history from the University of Oxford (1965) and a doctorate in American history from the University of South Carolina (1972). His exhibitions and publications include work on Marcel Breuer, Frank Lloyd Wright, Carlo Scarpa, and Marshall McLuhan, with major recent monographs and exhibitions on the work of Arthur Erickson (Vancouver Art Gallery, 2006) and John Lautner (Hammer Museum, 2008-10). A series of thematic studies and exhibitions on California architecture and a major study of Frank Lloyd Wright are forthcoming.

Christopher Thomas is an associate professor at the University of Victoria, where he teaches the history of art and architecture. Born and raised in Ottawa, he has focused much of his work on federal design in Canada and the United States. He is the author of a number of books and articles on subjects in North American architecture and culture, of which *The Lincoln Memorial and American Life* (2002) is probably the best-known.

Sharon Vattay holds a doctorate from the University of Toronto, where she lectures on the history of architecture. She is currently an associate at Goldsmith, Borgal and Company Architects (GBCA) – a firm specializing in historic restoration and adaptive reuse, with projects across Canada. Her expertise lies in the research, assessment, and management of heritage resources. She has also undertaken archival research for various levels of government for the purposes of publication and education.

Michael Windover holds a doctorate in art history from the University of British Columbia. He has been the recipient of several awards and fellowships, including Canadian Graduate Scholarships at the master's and doctorate levels from the Social Sciences and Humanities Research Council (SSHRC) of Canada. Windover's research explores visual and material culture of modernity, including the incorporation of Art Deco into everyday environments and lifestyles around the world in the interwar years, which is the subject of his dissertation. As a SSHRC postdoctoral fellow at McGill University, he is currently investigating the architectures of radio in Canada, from the intimate spaces of the home to the institutional infrastructure of the Canadian Broadcasting Corporation. Windover's work has been published in the *Journal of the Society for the Study of Architecture in Canada*, *BlackFlash Magazine*, and *Architectural History*.

Rhodri Windsor Liscombe is Associate Dean of Graduate Studies at the University of British Columbia. Former chair of the Interdisciplinary Graduate Studies Program and head of the Department of Art History, Visual Art and Theory, his major publications include *William Wilkins, 1778-1839* (1980), revisited in *The Age of Wilkins: The Architecture of Improvement* (with David Watkin, 2000); *Francis Rattenbury and British Columbia: Architecture and Challenge in the Imperial Age* (with A. Barrett, 1983); *"Altogether American": Robert Mills, Architect and Engineer, 1781-1855* (1994); and *The New Spirit: Modern Architecture in Vancouver, 1938-1963* (1997), winner of the Vancouver Book Prize at the Vancouver International Writers' Festival in 1998.

Awarded a J.S. Guggenheim Fellowship in 2000-01, he has served as vice-president and president of the Society for the Study of Architecture in Canada and was local chair of the 2005 Annual Meeting of the Society of Architectural Historians. He is a life member (fellow) of Clare Hall at the University of Cambridge.

Index

Note: "(i)" after a page number indicates an illustration.

Printed and bound in Canada by Friesens
Set in Machine, Meta, and Minion by Artegraphica Design Co. Ltd.
Copy editor: Robert Lewis
Proofreader: Jenna Newman
Indexer: Natalie Boon